DANTE'S BRITISH PUBLIC

Dante's British Public

Readers and Texts, from the Fourteenth Century to the Present

NICK HAVELY

OXFORD

UNIVERSITY PRESS

OXFORD

UNIVERSITY PRESS

Great Clarendon Street, Oxford, OX2 6DP,
United Kingdom

Oxford University Press is a department of the University of Oxford.
It furthers the University's objective of excellence in research, scholarship,
and education by publishing worldwide. Oxford is a registered trade mark of
Oxford University Press in the UK and in certain other countries

© Nick Havely 2014

The moral rights of the author have been asserted

First Edition published in 2014
Impression: 1

Published in the United States of America by Oxford University Press
198 Madison Avenue, New York, NY 10016, United States of America

British Library Cataloguing in Publication Data
Data available

Library of Congress Control Number: 2013956094

ISBN 978–0–19–921244–6

As printed and bound by
CPI Group (UK) Ltd, Croydon, CR0 4YY

For
C.A.P.H.
the better writer

Contents

List of Figures viii
Abbreviations x
Introduction xiii
Acknowledgments xvii

Prologue: A Wandering *Comedy* 1

1. Around Chaucer: Clerics, *Comedy*, and *Monarchy* 8

2. The 'Goodly Maker': Conscripting Dante in Henrician England 33

3. 'The Hungry Sheep': Protestant and Catholic Readings, 1556–1637 50

4. 'Few can understand him': Reputation, Ownership, Reading,
   *c.*1600–*c.*1800 68

5. Expatriate Poetics: Foscolo and the British Public 128

6. Seeing the Seer: Victorian Visions 154

7. Dominions, Possessions, Dispersals: British Dantes Abroad,
   *c.*1820–1882 194

8. Widening Circles, 1320–2013 260

Appendix 1: Chronology, c.1320–2013 284
Appendix 2: New/Old Dantes, c.1600–c.1700 299
Bibliography 305
 Manuscript and Archival Sources 305
 Printed Sources 307
 Electronic Sources 338
Index 339

List of Figures

1. Berlin, Staatsbibliothek MS Hamilton 207, f. 202^r, by permission of Bildarchiv, Preußischer Kulturbesitz, Berlin   2

2. Milan, Biblioteca Ambrosiana MS C 198 Inf, f. 52^r, spheres, orbits, zodiacal signs, © Veneranda Biblioteca Ambrosiana—Milano/De Agostini Picture Library   81

3. Milan, Biblioteca Ambrosiana MS C 198 Inf, f. 58^r, quadrant and zodiac, © Veneranda Biblioteca Ambrosiana—Milano/De Agostini Picture Library   91

4. Milan, Biblioteca Ambrosiana MS C 198 Inf, f. 115^v, sphere of Venus and its epicycle, courtesy of Biblioteca Ambrosiana, © Veneranda Biblioteca Ambrosiana—Milano/De Agostini Picture Library   92

5. From *Opere di Dante Alighieri* (Venice: Zatta, 1757–8), vol. 1, facing p. B b 1, the flight of Geryon, courtesy of All Souls College, Oxford   118

6. Ary Scheffer, *Paolo and Francesca* (1835), © by kind permission of the Trustees of the Wallace Collection, London   163

7. William Dyce, *Francesca da Rimini* (1837), courtesy of the National Gallery of Scotland, Edinburgh   167

8. John Flaxman, 'The Lovers Surprised' (Paolo and Francesca), engraved by Tommaso Piroli, from *Compositions by John Flaxman, R.A., from the Divine poem of Dante Alighieri* (1807), copy in the George Smith Special Collection, University of York   169

9. Detail from William Dyce, *Francesca da Rimini* (1837), courtesy of the National Gallery of Scotland, Edinburgh   170

10. Anon., copy of Dyce's *Francesca da Rimini* (probably dating between 1837 and 1882), in private collection, Italy, courtesy of the owner   174

11. William Dyce, *Dante and Beatrice* (1840s?), courtesy of Aberdeen Art Gallery and Museums   175

12. Berlin, Kupferstichkabinett, MS Hamilton 201, Botticelli, illustration for *Paradiso* 2, by permission of Bildarchiv, Preußischer Kulturbesitz, Berlin   176

13. Edinburgh, NLS MS 2168, f. 2, courtesy of the Society of Antiquaries of Scotland   215

14. Edinburgh, NLS MS 2168, f. 5, courtesy of the Society of Antiquaries of Scotland   219

15. Edinburgh, NLS MS 2171, f. 68, courtesy of the Society of Antiquaries of Scotland   224

16. Edinburgh, NLS MS 2170, f. 21, courtesy of the Society of Antiquaries of Scotland   225

17. Edinburgh, NLS MS 2168, f. 61, courtesy of the Society of Antiquaries of Scotland   227

18. Edinburgh, NLS MS 2168, f. 22, courtesy of the Society of Antiquaries of Scotland 228

19. Edinburgh, NLS MS 2172, f. 47, courtesy of the Society of Antiquaries of Scotland 229

20. Edinburgh, NLS MS 2169, f. 94, courtesy of the Society of Antiquaries of Scotland 230

21. Edinburgh, NLS MS 2170, f. 116, courtesy of the Society of Antiquaries of Scotland 233

22. Edinburgh, NLS MS 2171, f. 92, courtesy of the Society of Antiquaries of Scotland 234

23. Edinburgh, NLS MS 2172, f. 66, courtesy of the Society of Antiquaries of Scotland 235

24. Oxford, Bodleian Eng. misc. d. 639, f. 193[r], Seymour Kirkup, 'Lucifero', by permission of the Bodleian Library, Oxford 237

25. Steve Bell, cartoon, *Guardian*, 9 April 2013, courtesy of Belltoons 282

Abbreviations

BL   British Library, London

BLJ   *Byron: Letters and Journals*, ed. L. A. Marchand (13 vols., London: Murray, 1973–94)

BMS   *Illuminated Manuscripts of the Divine Comedy*, ed. P. Brieger, M. Meiss, and C. S. Singleton (2 vols., New York and London: Routledge & Kegan Paul)

BnF   Bibliothèque nationale de France, Paris

CCR   *Calendar of the Close Rolls preserved in the Public Record Office: Henry VI* (6 vols., London: Public Record Office, 1933–47)

CHIL   *Cambridge History of Italian Literature*, ed. P. Brand and L. Pertile (Cambridge: Cambridge University Press, 1996)

CPR   *Calendar of Patent Rolls preserved in the Public Record Office: Henry VI* (6 vols., Norwich: Norfolk Chronicle Co. for HMSO, 1901–10)

CSPV   *Calendar of State Papers and Manuscripts, relating to English Affairs, existing in the archives and collections of Venice, and in other libraries of northern Italy*, ed. R. Brown *et al.* (38 vols. in 40, London: Longman Green, 1864–1947)

DBI   *Dizionario biografico degli italiani*, ed. A. M. Ghisalberti *et al.* (78 vols. to date, Rome: Istituto della enciclopedia italiana, 1960–)

DDJb   *Deutsches Dante-Jahrbuch*

DE   *The Dante Encyclopedia*, ed. R. Lansing (New York and London: Garland, 2000)

DEL   P. Toynbee, *Dante in English Literature, from Chaucer to Cary (c. 1380–1844)* (2 vols., London: Methuen, 1909)

ED   *Enciclopedia dantesca*, dir. U. Bosco, ed. G. Petrocchi (6 vols., Rome: Istituto della enciclopedia italiana, 1970–8)

EN 9.1   *Edizione nazionale delle opere di Ugo Foscolo, volume IX. i Studi su Dante*, ed. G. Da Pozzo (Florence: Le Monnier, 1979)

EN 9.2   *Edizione nazionale delle opere di Ugo Foscolo, volume IX. ii: Studi su Dante*, ed. G. Da Pozzo (Florence: Le Monnier, 1979)

EN 11   *Edizione nazionale delle opere di Ugo Foscolo, volume XI: Saggi di letteratura italiana*, ed. C. Foligno (Florence: Le Monnier, 1958)

Ep. 6   *Edizione nazionale delle opere di Ugo Foscolo XX: Epistolario di Ugo Foscolo tom. VI*, ed. G. Gambarin and F. Tropeano (Florence: Le Monnier, 1966)

Ep. 7   *Edizione nazionale delle opere di Ugo Foscolo XX: Epistolario di Ugo Foscolo tom. VII*, ed. M. Scotti (Florence: Le Monnier, 1970)

Ep. 8   *Edizione nazionale delle opere di Ugo Foscolo XX: Epistolario di Ugo Foscolo tom. VIII*, ed. M. Scotti (Florence: Le Monnier, 1974)

Ep. 9   *Edizione nazionale delle opere di Ugo Foscolo XX: Epistolario di Ugo Foscolo tom. IX*, ed. M. Scotti (Florence: Le Monnier, 1994)

GD 2   *The Gladstone Diaries*, Volume II. *1833–1839*, ed. M. R. D. Foot (Oxford: Clarendon Press, 1968)

GD 3   *The Gladstone Diaries*, Volume III. *1840–1847*, ed. M. R. D. Foot and H. C. G. Matthew (Oxford: Clarendon Press, 1974)

GD 5   *The Gladstone Diaries, Introduction to Volumes V and VI. 1855–1868*, ed.
           H. C. G. Matthew (Oxford: Clarendon Press, 1978)
GD 10   *The Gladstone Diaries: With Cabinet Minutes and Prime-Ministerial Corres-*
           pondence, Volume X. *January 1881–June 1883*, ed. H. C. G. Matthew
           (Oxford: Clarendon Press, 1990)
GSLI   *Giornale storico della letteratura italiana*
HCA   Highland Council Archive, Inverness
JBBRAS   *Journal of the Bombay Branch of the Royal Asiatic Society*
JEH   *Journal of Ecclesiastical History*
MLR   *Modern Language Review*
NAS   National Archives of Scotland, Edinburgh
NLS   National Library of Scotland, Edinburgh
ODNB   *Oxford Dictionary of National Biography*, ed. H. C. G. Matthew (60 vols.,
           Oxford: Oxford University Press, 2004; and online)
PMLA   *Publications of the Modern Language Association*
QBSAL   *Quarterly Bulletin of South African Libraries*
RES   *Review of English Studies*
RVF   Petrarch, *Rerum vulgarium fragmenta*, in *Francesco Petrarca: Canzoniere*, ed.
           G. Contini and D. Ponchiroli (Turin: Einaudi, 1964)
TNA   The National Archive, Kew, London

Introduction

Dialogues with Dante on the part of such authors as Chaucer, Milton, Shelley, both Eliots, Joyce, Heaney, and others have been the subject of a number of important monographs, but the big voices will be heard only intermittently here.[1] This account of the British public for Dante's work reckons with but does not centre upon the individual responses of major writers in English. It seeks, rather, to investigate some of the conditions—intellectual, religious, political, bibliographic, textual—under which such responses took shape. Through selected examples and case-studies, it records and places in context some of the wider conversations about and appropriations of Dante that developed—with varying degrees of information and understanding—across more than six centuries, as access to his work extended and diversified. Hence this book's main title uses the term 'public', rather than 'readers'.[2]

Readers and owners of books (the latter being not always identical with the former), however, form a substantial part of that public, as the subtitle acknowledges. Circulation of texts and reading practices served to shape and sustain the wider conversations about Dante, and evidence about such activities will be a substantial feature of this book's case-studies. The texts that provided access to Dante's work over this period are of many kinds: they include not only manuscripts, printed editions, and complete translations, but also, for example, polemical writing, encyclopedias, historical works, and (at a later stage) anthologies, critical discussions, and introductory guides. The forms in which opinions about and appropriations of Dante appear are likewise highly diverse, and some of them—such as journals, letters, and annotations—offer significant evidence about reading practices. A number of individual readers and ways of reading will be addressed here—from the fourteenth-century Benedictine Adam Easton's argument with Dante's *Monarchia* to William Gladstone's close and repeated interrogations of the *Commedia*, and beyond.

An author's public is not, however, wholly made up of diligent, informed, and attentive readers like Gladstone.[3] It can also include those whose treatment of the text is markedly prejudiced—like some of the Protestant conscriptors of Dante who will be encountered here—as well as those whose knowledge of it may be partial, oblique, or even non-existent. Fragmentary acquaintance with Dante's work and peripheral awareness of his reputation is, as this book will argue at several points (especially in Chapter 4), often a significant feature of the poet's presence over this

---

[1] Thus the authors named above will be mostly off-stage, and Shakespeare is not in the theatre at all. On Dante as absence or 'analogue' in Shakespeare, see *DEL* 1. xxiv, and Kirkpatrick 1995: 299–302 and 309–10.

[2] On the idea of a 'literary public', see e.g. Randall 2008: esp. 242–3 and n. 67.

[3] On kinds of reader, see Iser 1980: 27–30.

period. Even indirect knowledge of the text can result in some apt appropriation—such as Steve Bell's recent graphic parallel (based solely on the Gustave Doré illustrations) between Dante's Farinata and the late Baroness Thatcher.[4]

Dante's potential public also becomes a subject of interest particularly to those addressing a widening audience later in the period. Thus, for example, Maria Rossetti's successful introduction to Dante of 1871 (Rossetti 1884) asked how the poet's work might be made 'a topic of conversation' for 'the many'; the *Times* in 1882 raised questions about whether any of the newly educated 'millions' might ever be able to see 'a MS. copy of "Dante" illustrated by the pencil of SANDRO BOTTICELLI'; and the most recent translator of the *Commedia* has admitted to 'hoping that a small proportion of Dan Brown's audience . . . might want to check up on the poem'.[5]

As a way of describing many of the activities of such a diverse public over this long span of time, the term 'conversation' has been and will continue to be used here, perhaps with excessive frequency. The resonance of Osip Mandelstam's quirky and vividly materialist 'Conversation about Dante' of 1933 is partly responsible for this.[6] So also, however, are the views of the Regency grandee Thomas Grenville, about Dante's role 'in the conversation of this country', and those of the late Victorian, Maria Rossetti, considering the poet's possible future 'in cultivated society . . . as a topic of conversation'.[7] I cannot think of a better term to convey the expansive interaction between various voices and the networks of contacts that are of interest here.[8]

In order to explore and reconstruct some of the relevant conversations and contexts, a substantial range of archival evidence will be investigated—especially that concerning collectors, owners, and readers of Dante manuscripts and early printed editions—and a considerable amount of previously unpublished material from a wide range of journals, letters, annotations, and inventories is thus included. Different media and genres must also be reckoned with: due prominence is given to the roles of collectors, readers, and writers of various kinds, but account is also taken (especially from the nineteenth century on) of the appropriation of Dante's work in, for example, illustration and performance.

The culture of that 'British public', too, should not be narrowly circumscribed. The initial scope and title of this book was 'Dante in the English-speaking World'; and although it has not been possible within the constraints of a single volume to do justice to even a limited range of other anglophone cultures—let alone the variety of

---

[4] See Fig. 25, below. The artist acknowledges that 'my knowledge of Dante is limited to Doré's illustrations as I've never actually read the "Inferno"' (Steve Bell, personal communication).

[5] See below, pp. 260, 283, and 298.

[6] Mandelstam 1991. On Dante's 'resonance' in Mandelstam's own text, see Dimock 2001: 179.

[7] See below, pp. 146, 262, and 267.

[8] The term implies a more dynamic form of response than 'reception'. The latter term will also be used here (see Jauss 1982), whilst acknowledging that there are 'several problems with Jauss'[s] approach that have direct bearing on later "readers" of Dante'—e.g., overemphasis on 'the conformity of reading practices within designated periods' and 'direct contact between reader and text', and 'underestimating the legacy of tradition' (Gilson 2005: 7 and nn. 19–20); see also Ginsberg 2002: 5–6.

'global' Dantes—their importance is to some extent acknowledged here, for instance, in the accounts of Mountstuart Elphinstone in India and George Grey in South Africa (Chapter 7).[9] Throughout, the role of Anglo-Italian cultural contacts and intermediaries in shaping the public understanding of Dante in Britain will be given prominence—from clerics and merchants 'around Chaucer', through itinerant scholars, collectors, and tourists in the early modern period, to the exiles and expatriates of the nineteenth and twentieth centuries.

Thus the Prologue to this book carries the title of 'A Wandering *Comedy*' and explores the contexts and history of the first surviving manuscript of the *Commedia* (Berlin Hamilton 207) that is known to have reached Britain, where it was the object of a transaction between Italian merchants in mid-fifteenth-century London. It was probably re-exported to Italy soon after, but its origins, purchasers, its return to Britain, and eventual migration to Germany as part of the Hamilton collection form part of a narrative about manuscripts as 'cultural possessions' that will be taken up again later on.[10]

Meanwhile, the book's first chapter, which traces a century-long itinerary 'Around Chaucer', relates the activities of four clerics—two Italian Franciscans and two English Benedictines—in disseminating ideas about Dante and acting as intermediaries between Italy and England during the late fourteenth and early fifteenth centuries. The next two chapters (Chapters 2 and 3) outline the earlier and later stages in the formation of the British 'Protestant' Dante', focusing upon the perception of Dante's status as one of the 'crowns of Florence' in the late fifteenth and early sixteenth centuries, his potential for recruitment as a 'writer against Rome', and the polemics and debates relating to his conscription as 'proto-Protestant' in the later sixteenth and early seventeenth centuries. Chapter 4 then relates the gradual and complex process by which, over the course of two centuries, public understanding of Dante began to extend from the 'few' to the (relatively) 'many'. It thus presents some new evidence about allusions to Dante, identifies the presence of his work in some major seventeenth- and eighteenth-century collections, and reviews some of the activities and publications which reflected and sustained the poet's 'rehabilitation' among the late eighteenth-century reading public.

Resources for and reflections of the British 'reading nation's' growing cult of Dante in the early nineteenth century are the wider subject of Chapter 5.[11] Contributions to this cult on the part of the Italian exile Ugo Foscolo, resident in London during the last decade of his life, are assessed here, along with the influence of other Italian and British expatriate writers, critics, and editors. Visualization of and close engagement with Dante and his work intensify in the middle of the

---

[9] Also in some of the examples in the Chronology (Appendix 1). On the 'globalization of Dante', see Dimock 2001: 181; her long list of languages into which the *Commedia* has been translated (n. 18) should also include Afrikaans; see Cullinan and Watson 2005: 14, 33–6, and 94. For American (United States) Dantes, key works are La Piana 1948, Giamatti 1983, Verduin 1996, Looney 2011, and Dupont 2012. Yet more widely, see also Branca and Caccia 1965, and Esposito 1992.

[10] In the final section of Chapter 7.

[11] For the term 'reading nation', see St Clair 2004.

century, at a time when the poet is being authoritatively identified as the 'central man of all the world'.[12] Three case-studies in Chapter 6 thus illustrate how this 'Seer' was being scrutinized: through the eyes of an actor (Frances Kemble), a painter (William Dyce), and a scholar politician (William Gladstone). Through the century, British material ownership of the poet as a cultural possession took a variety of forms and underwent several significant changes. Three main examples are investigated in Chapter 7: the acquisition and donation of manuscripts as a feature of the imperial enterprise (Elphinstone in India, Grey in South Africa); the activities of Anglo-Florentine collectors and scholars (Isabella Macleod, Francis Brooke, Lord Vernon, Seymour Kirkup); the sale of the Hamilton collection of manuscripts (including the Botticelli illustrations in MS Hamilton 201) to Germany in 1882 and the accompanying concerns about Dante's status as part of a national heritage. Finally, the chapter about 'Widening Circles' brings some aspects of the story up to the present, illustrating ways in which the poet's work has been seen (from the fourteenth century onwards) as accessible to 'the many'. Whilst acknowledging the important work that has been and continues to be done on the responses of the major modernist and post-modern writers, it deals primarily with some of the means by which Dante has reached a yet wider British public over the past century, particularly through translation, illustration, fiction, and various forms of performance.

Chronologically and geographically, the scope of the project has proved challenging, and (as the subsequent acknowledgements and footnotes will indicate) it has depended on earlier and more expert scholars, together with the support of a wide community of researchers, not only in Britain and Italy, but also in (for example) Australia, India, South Africa, and the United States. It has also exploited the patience of archivists and librarians from Milan to Mumbai, and from Cambridge to Cape Town. A colleague at Harvard once likened the conduct of these enquiries to the shambling persistence of the late Peter Falk's detective Lieutenant Columbo; whilst one at York (more sinisterly) compared it with the patient arachnid vigilance of an Elizabethan spymaster.

Five key works have throughout inspired and directed the lines of investigation: three monumental surveys, by Paget Toynbee, Marcella Roddewig, and Michael Caesar (which together identified most of the suspects to be hauled in for questioning); and two ground-breaking critical studies of Dante reception by Steve Ellis and Alison Milbank.[13] The work that follows does not aspire to be *sesto tra cotanto senno* ('sixth among so much wisdom'),[14] since it would be hard to match, let alone challenge, the prominence of such scholarly landmarks. It takes those landmarks, instead, as departure points from which to explore and map some more of the 'cultural hinterland'.[15]

[12] Ruskin 1851: 2. 342; 3. 158.
[13] *DEL*; Roddewig 1984; Caesar 1989; Ellis 1983; Milbank 1998.
[14] *Inferno* 4. 102; R. M. Durling's translation in Dante 1996: 75.
[15] The last phrase is used in an exemplary study of Petrarch in Protestant England, Usher 2005: 187 and 195.

Acknowledgments

Thanks are due in the first place to Andrew McNeillie, then Senior Commissioning editor at OUP, for a conversation at a bus-stop in 2005. This led to a contract for the book, and in 2006 the Leverhulme Trust awarded a Fellowship, which enabled much of the primary research for the project to be completed.

As the Introduction and many of the notes to the subsequent chapters indicate, a large number of students, friends, and colleagues have heard, discussed, read, and commented upon parts of this book. For thirty years of conversations about the *Commedia* and its reception, I am much indebted to undergraduates and post-graduates who followed courses on Dante at the University of York. For invitations to give papers on the subject, for discussion, and for all sorts of assistance with the project over several decades, I am grateful to (amongst others) Guyda Armstrong, Aida Audeh, John Barnes, Caroline Barron, Piero Boitani, James Bolton, Paolo Borsa, Helen Bradley, Trev Broughton, Mike Caesar, Caron Cioffi, Lilla Crisafulli, Christian Dupont, Patsy Erskine-Hill, Godfrey Evans, Cristina Figueredo, Anne Hudson, Daniel Karlin, Chris Kleinhenz, Christoph Lehner, Ilaria Mallozzi, Martin McLaughlin, Paola Nasti, Philip Norcross, Christopher Norton, Anna Pegoretti, Alessandra Petrina, Claudia Rossignoli, David Rundle, Corinna Salvadori, Bill Sherman, James Simpson, Wayne Storey, Chris Taylor, Aroon Tikekar, Jonathan Usher, Daniel Wakelin, David Wallace, Tim Webb, and Jocelyn Wogan-Browne.

Those who have further endured the trial of the written word by generously commenting on drafts and chapters include: Aliette Boshier, Will Bowers, Andrea Campana, Kenneth Clarke, Godfrey Evans, Olga Ferguson, Stefano Gattei, Peter Hainsworth, Barbara Hardy, Mike Jones, Dennis Looney, James Robinson, Diego Saglia, Helen Smailes, Jeremy Tambling, and Vidya Vencatesan. A complete draft was read by Cicely Palser Havely, whose editing has enabled the book to say what it has to say more clearly and in better order.

Throughout, the research has been aided and enhanced by a number of librarians and archivists across the world. Especial thanks are thus due to: Rachel Bond and Penny Hatfield (Eton College Library), Monica Del Rio (Archivio di Stato, Venice), Melanie Geustyn (National Library of South Africa), Christine Hiskey (Holkham Hall Archives), Susan L'Engle (Vatican Film Library, St Louis University), Peter Mennie (Highland Council Archive, Inverness), Caroline Pilgermann (Zentralarchiv der Staatlichen Museen zu Berlin), Mridula Ramanna, Mangala Sirdeshpande, and Usha Thakkar (Asiatic Society, Mumbai), Suzanne Reynolds (Holkham Hall Library), Julianne Simpson (John Rylands Library, Manchester), Joanna Soden (Royal Scottish Academy, Edinburgh), Chris Taylor (National Library of Scotland, Edinburgh), and (constantly) the staff at the Taylorian Institution, Oxford.

Permission to reproduce privately owned archival material at the Highland Council Archive, Inverness (from the Macleod of Cadboll Papers), has kindly been granted by the Trustees of the Torquil Macleod Estate. The author and publishers would also like to thank the institutions and individuals mentioned in the List of Figures for permission to reproduce works in their collections. We are particularly grateful to the Society of Antiquaries of Scotland for their generous permission to reproduce the images in Figures 13–23 free of charge; to Philip Norcross for help in locating an early copy of William Dyce's *Francesca da Rimini*; and to Roberto Donnini for permission to reproduce it. A further debt of gratitude is owed to the Leavis Fund and the Department of English and Related Literature at the University of York for a grant towards the cost of obtaining images and permissions.

Completion of the whole process has been facilitated by the patience and skill of staff at Oxford University Press, especially Jacqueline Baker, Suzanne Downie, Rachel Platt, and Rebecca Stubbs; whilst the expertise of Jeff New as copy-editor has been invaluable, and the reader should be especially grateful—as the author is—for the vigilance of Deborah Renshaw, as proofreader, in spotting numerous missing cross-references and bibliography entries. The work of indexing has (for the third time in as many years) been undertaken by Dr James Robinson (Leverhulme Early Career Fellow at Durham University), to whom I am also much indebted for many informative conversations about Dante's British public.

Prologue: A Wandering *Comedy*

An unprepossessing manuscript of Dante's *Commedia* in the Berlin Staatsbibliothek, MS Hamilton 207, bears the marks of its travels. Bound simply in parchment, its 200 or so paper folios are towards the end increasingly ragged and stained. It is amongst the smallest of the *Commedia* manuscripts—measuring a mere 30 by 27 centimetres—a portable item for a reader on the move.[1] Its date is generally agreed to be the early fifteenth century.[2] The text is written in a single scribal hand and is probably Tuscan. A few annotations, in hands dating from the fifteenth to the sixteenth centuries, identify notable names; for the first three cantos of the *Inferno*, a variant version of the vernacular Selmi Glosses (produced in Florence or Siena before 1337) appears in the margin; and vernacular rubrics preface each canto of the *Paradiso*. On the final page a Latin colophon gives the date and place of Dante's death and prays for his soul.[3] On the face of it, then, this is an ordinary Tuscan *Commedia*, of a kind that circulated among mercantile readers of the time—one of the many paper copies of the poem that came in the course of the fifteenth century to outnumber the more expensive parchment manuscripts by more than two to one.[4]

What makes the manuscript less ordinary is that—some fifty years after Chaucer's appropriations of Dante—it is the first copy of the *Commedia* to locate itself at a place and a time in Britain.[5] Two-and-a-half lines in the vernacular follow the Latin colophon at the foot of its final page (Fig. 1).

In a mercantile hand, the inscription records exactly where and when this text of the *Commedia* was sold: on 1 August 1451 in London. It is difficult to read, since the water damage and staining that affects part of the manuscript is at its worst in the final outer leaves, and a number of scholars from 1887 onwards have partially deciphered the text.[6] With the help of ultra-violet light, however, it is now possible to propose a fuller reconstruction.

'I bought this book in London' (*Questo libro chonpr'i[o] i[n] londra*) is clearly how the note begins, and the following word might be either *istando*, or possibly

---

[1] On the sizes of *Commedia* manuscripts, see Boschi Rotiroti 2004: 29–32.

[2] Roddewig 1984: 11 (no. 19) dates the watermark of the paper 1416–18, but it could be a little earlier, possibly 1411–13; see Piccard 1980: nos. 464 and 474.

[3] Berlin, Staatsbibliothek MS Hamilton 207, f. 202ʳ: *Explicit paradisus & Chomedia Dantis Alagerii d[e] Florentia: Qui decessit in ciuitate Rauenne i[n] An[n]o d[omi]nice i[n]carnationis mcccxxi die s[anc]te crucis de mense septembris. Anima eius requiescant* [sic] *i[n] pace Am[en] deo gr[aci]as.*

[4] Miglio 2001: 298. On the production of *Commedia* manuscripts in the fifteenth century, see also Bertelli 2007: 39–76.

[5] On Chaucer and Dante, see below, pp. 4–5, 8–9, 31, 261–2.

[6] For partial readings, see Biadene 1887: 328; Wiese 1929: 47; and Roddewig 1984: 11.

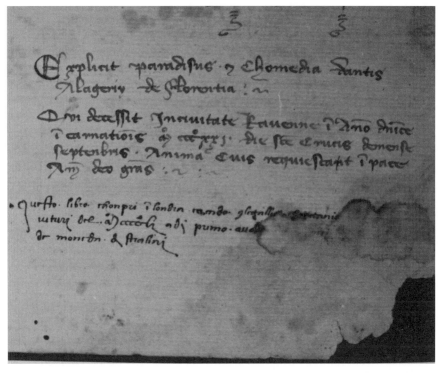

Fig. 1. Berlin, Staatsbibliothek MS Hamilton 207, f. 202^r, by permission of Bildarchiv, Preußischer Kulturbesitz, Berlin

c'andò (he came). The next is the common abbreviation for *con* ('with'). At the very edge of the water stain we can (though with some difficulty) read *le gallee* ('the galleys'). With the assistance of UV light on the worst part of the water stain, a name and a possible sum of money then swim into view.[7] The name is 'Miss[er] Benideto', which, with the more legible word at the start of the next line, gives the full title of this galley captain: *miss[er] benideto uituri*. In the second line of the note, following *auosto* ('August') is a group of possibly fifteen characters, of which several look like numerals. These are much more difficult to read, but it is likely that they represent '£1. 10*s*. 4*d*. sterling'.[8] The owner's entire note thus reads:

Questo libro chonpr'i[o] i[n] londra c'andò con le gallee chapitanio mi[sser] benideto uituri del mccccli a dì primo auosto [di unum £ x s iv d] de moneda d[i] stralini.

I bought this book in London, when Captain Messer Benedetto Vituri was there with the galleys on the first day of August in the year 1451 for £1. 10*s*. 4*d*. in sterling currency.

---

[7] I am grateful to the staff of the Handschriftenabteilung at the Staatsbibliothek, Berlin, for allowing the page to be inspected by this means.

[8] Assistance with the notation here was given by Prof. James Bolton of Queen Mary's University of London, Prof. Linne Mooney, University of York, and Dr Francesco Guidi-Bruscoli.

The note thus seems to record a transaction between two Italians. Who, then, might have imported this *Commedia* into England and sold it on that early August day in 1451? It might have been 'chapitanio Misser Benedetto Vit[t]uri' or one of his fellow merchants—since this would be the most obvious reason for the buyer's note to mention the arrival of 'the galleys'.[9]

Venetian galleys had been active in the trade with Flanders and England since the early fourteenth century, and continued to make regular voyages on this route during the first half of the fifteenth.[10] Groups or 'nations' of Italians were subject to consular control in London by the early fifteenth century, and by 1409 there was a Venetian vice-consul who, together with twelve merchants, constituted the presidency of the London factory.[11] Venetian vessels also called in at Southampton, and, according to English customs records, one 'Benedictus Victorio' brought cargo there in a carrack twice in 1437–8, presumably on his way to and from Flanders.[12]

During the year in question (1451), a decree of the Venetian senate was issued on 11 March 'for fitting out three galleys for the Flanders and London voyage'.[13] This fleet was almost certainly 'the galleys' which the note in Hamilton 207 refers to, since an account of customs duty payable at Venice on its cargo names the same commander:

Enforcing payment of the duty of one per cent on merchandise brought from England by the galleys commanded by Ser Benetto Victuri, to be consigned to the masters of the Arsenal, according to the Act of 20th December.[14]

Capitan[eus] vir nobilis / S[er] Benedictus Victuri (as the original document describes him) is thus the *capitanio* who was present in London 'with the galleys' on 1 August 1451. Ser Benetto (as the title and the epithet *nobilis* indicate) was no ordinary seadog: he was descended from a family that was listed among patrician notables in the fourteenth century and continued to produce high-level administrators and military leaders on into the sixteenth.[15] A senate decree of 12 August 1451 acknowledges a significant role that he played on its behalf through negotiating with the Duke of Burgundy in Flanders, 'on our affairs and those of our merchants', during the voyage that had brought him to London.[16]

---

[9] See Ruddock 1951: 19 and Spufford 2002: 396–8.

[10] Lane 1973: 337–52 and map 9; see also Fryde 1983: 320–4. The Venetian trade involved the export of items such as cloth, skins, block tin, and lead, and the import of luxury goods, such as spices, silk, jewellery, carpets, etc.; see Bradley 1992: 103–4, 143, and 186. It had been affected by recession at the time of the galley voyage in 1451 (see Nightingale 1995: 470–1) but would recover later in the century (Sutton 2005: 232).

[11] Ruddock 1951: 133–6.

[12] London TNA E122/209/1, ff. 22ᵛ, 26ʳ, 56ᵛ, and 58ᵛ. I am grateful to Dr Helen Bradley of the London Record Society for providing these references.

[13] *CSPV* 1. 74–5. The original document is in Venice, Archivio di Stato, Senato Deliberazioni Mar, registro 4, ff. 37ᵛ–40ʳ; it names the commanders (*patroni*) of the three galleys, but not the *capitanio* in charge of the whole fleet.

[14] *CSPV* I. 76; original in Venice, Archivio di Stato, Senato Deliberazioni Mar, registro 4, f. 117ʳ (3 May 1452).

[15] See Chojnacki 1973: 73; Mallett and Hale 1984: 296; and Queller 1986: 179.

[16] Venice, Archivio di Stato, Senato Deliberazioni Mar, registro 4, f. 82ᵛ: *mandato n[ost]ro fuerit ad Illu. d[omin]um ducem Burgundie/pro aptantis cau[s]is [?] n[ost]ris et mercatorum n[ost]ror[um] in illis partibus* [not in *CSPV* 1].

The Venetian records thus indicate a plausible means of transport for this migrant *Commedia* and a possible vendor, but the buyer remains anonymous, despite the trouble he took to record his purchase. He is likely to have belonged to one or other of the Italian mercantile communities in England or Flanders; for example, the Florentine Medici Bank had branches in Bruges and (from 1446 to 1478) in London.[17] Members of this class were already cultivators of Dante's poem during the fourteenth century, whilst in inventories of fifteenth-century merchants' libraries the *Commedia* figures with the second-highest frequency after the Gospels, and much more often than the *Decameron*.[18] Such merchants were 'readers with pens in their hands', and, like the later family bibles, copies of the *Commedia* became sites to record births, marriages, deaths, current events, recipes, and even (as here) recent purchases.[19] There is also some evidence of copies like this one accompanying and even being produced by members of the notarial and merchant class in the course of long-distance travels.[20] The evidence about the importation, acquisition, and annotation of this *Commedia* in London in 1451 thus contributes something further to the knowledge about Italian mercantile readings of Dante—a subject on which 'much work remains to be done'.[21]

Selling the *Commedia* in this form, at this time, and at this distance from its origin is not only of interest with regard to the poem's Italian circulation. It also has significance for the presence and reception of Dante in late medieval Britain. The sale in London demonstrates one specific means—merchant shipping—by which further copies of Italian texts (vernacular and Latin) could have reached England from Italy during the second and third quarters of the fifteenth century.[22] It also raises the possibility that books of this sort could have arrived by similar means even earlier—for example, through merchants from Italian towns such as Lucca, who had been trading in London around Chaucer's time.[23] Moreover, although the sale of this particular *Commedia* was clearly a deal done between Italians abroad, it took place at a time when some British readers had already become interested in the poem. As the following chapter will show, around Chaucer's late fourteenth-century appropriation of *the grete poete of Ytaille* in dream poems, the *Troilus*, and the *Canterbury Tales*, such interest was particularly evident in clerical circles, and the Latin translation of and commentary on the *Commedia* (1416–17) by Giovanni Bertoldi da Serravalle, with the support of an Italian cardinal and two

[17] On the Medici in London, see Holmes 1996.
[18] Bec 1983: 103–4. On merchant readers of Dante, see also Branca 1965, and Gilson 2005: 8.
[19] Miglio 2001: 311 (*lettori con la penna in mano*) and 317–19.
[20] This seems to have been the case with a manuscript similar to Hamilton 207: Florence, Laurenziana 4024, which was copied by a cloth-merchant of Prato in 1418–19, in the course of a journey to the far south of Italy (Otranto); see Roddewig 1984: 51 (no. 116) and Miglio 2001: 312.
[21] Gilson 2005: 241, n. 26.
[22] On another possible source, book-purchases by British 'academic tourists' in Italy around this time, see Rundle 2013: 545–6.
[23] See Childs 1983: 67, 69, 71, 78; and Nightingale 1995: esp. 83, 85, 93–4, 182, 223, 225–6, and 279. Copies of one of Dante's key texts—Brunetto Latini's *Livres dou Tresor*—were circulating in England from early in the fourteenth century; see Reynolds 1982: 22–3 and n. 17, Holloway 1987: 15–17, and Galloway 2011: 76–8 and 111–14. On Italian merchants and their languages, see Guidi-Bruscoli 2014.

English bishops, must have arrived in Britain—along with whatever text(s) Chaucer used—considerably earlier than Hamilton 207.[24] The vernacular *Commedia* that was sold on 1 August 1451 probably did not remain in Britain long, yet its presence prompts some questions about the nature of Anglo-Italian cultural contacts in London around that time.

The Paston Letters offer one glimpse of such contacts a few years after that sale. Around 1458 a London civil servant, Henry Windsor, writes to John Paston I about their mutual friend William Worcester, an accountant, physician, writer on chivalry, and avid bibliophile:

Item [also], sir, I mey sey to you that Wiliam [Worcester] hath goon to scole to a Lumbard called Karoll Giles, to lern and to be red in poetré or els in Frensh, for he hath byn with the same Karoll euery dey ii tymes or iii, and hath bought diuerse bokes of hym, for the which, as I suppose, he hath put hymself in daunger [debt] to the same Karoll. I made a mocion to William to haue knoen part of his busines, and he answered and said that he wold be as glad and as feyn of a good boke of Frensh or of poetré as my Maister Fastolf wold be to purchace a faire manoir; and therby I vnderstand he list not to be commynd [spoken to, admonished] in such matiers.[25]

The nature of the shared reading in *poetré* and in *Frensh* and the extravagant book-buying remains tantalizingly unspecific, although it seems that Boccaccio's *De casibus virorum illustrium* was among the texts on which William Worcester spent all that money.[26] 'Karoll Giles', the *Lumbard* who provided this service was actually Carlo Gigli, a merchant descended from a family who were among the leading members of the governing class in Lucca.[27] The Giglis' wealth, like that of other prominent Lucchese families, was founded on the silk trade, and they were socially and geographically mobile.[28] Carlo himself was born in Bruges around 1400, and was the eldest of six brothers, two others of whom seem also to have had connections with London. He is known to have been in London by 1452, where he had documented dealings with English merchants and gentry in that year and in 1454–5, and letters of denization were issued for him, his wife, and his heirs in March 1460.[29] Documents—including letters from him about the

---

[24] See below, p. 17.

[25] Dated 'Probably 1458, 27 August'; see Davis 2004: 174–5 (no. 574).

[26] Oxford, Magdalen College, MS lat. 198; cited by Wakelin 2007: 94. On Worcester's range of reading, see Wakelin 2007: 93–108.

[27] On the identification, see Hughes 1992: 132 and nn. 122–3. For Gigli's ancestry and the status of his family in Lucca, see Meek 1978: 190; Bratchel 1995: 94, 106, and 240 (n. 212); and Clough 2003: 124 and n. 10.

[28] On the Lucca silk trade, see Bratchel 1995: 132–44 and 157–66; and on the Lucchesi as merchants in late medieval London, see Nightingale 1995: esp. 225–6 and 279, and Sutton 2005: 40–1, 228–9, and 301. For Carlo Gigli's career and travels, see Bianchi, 1988: 71–6, Bradley 1992: 290–1, and Clough 2003: 124–8.

[29] *CCR 1447–54*, 347–8 (11 July 1452); *CCR 1454–61*, 30 and 61 (7 Nov. 1454 and 25 Nov. 1455); and *CPR 1452–61*, 579 (1 Mar. 1460). One of Carlo's brothers, Ser Nicolao (referred to as 'Nicholas Gyles, merchant of Luke/Lucca'), was granted an exemption from subsidies in return for supplying 'divers cloths of silk and gold' to the King's Great Wardrobe (*CPR 1446–52*, 375 (22 May 1450)), and he is also recorded as selling silver and gilt plate to a leading member of the Grocers' Company, Stephen Brown, in the same week as Benetto Vitturi's arrival in London (*CCR 1447–54*, 284 (3 Aug. 1451); see also Nightingale 1995: 437, 442–3, and 465).

English civil war[30]—continue to place him in London up until 1465, when his will bequeaths his books in England and Italy to his eldest son, Giovanni.

Johanni filio meo primogenito lego ac dono libros omnes . . . quos in italia . . . ad usum suum ac studium emptos[,] ceteros quoque omnes humanitatis libros quos tumque in anglia teneo seu tenere solebam latine prescriptos, quorum ego delectabar . . .

To my first-born son Giovanni, I give and bequeath all the books that were bought in Italy for his use and study, as well as all the books to do with the *studium humanitatis* and written in Latin, which I have thus owned and enjoyed in England . . . [31]

Around 1467 Carlo left for Bruges, where his family had been trading earlier in the century, and where he himself died.[32] His son, Giovanni (born in 1434), would in the 1480s become papal collector in England, archdeacon of London, and canon of Lincoln, also acting as Henry VII's envoy to Rome and ending up as bishop of Worcester.[33]

Thus, although Italians in London were few in number at this time and based in a small number of wards in the City, their communities were by no means isolated or culturally inactive. Some could and did collect books, develop literary interests, and make contacts that went socially, geographically, and intellectually well beyond their enclaves. Carlo Gigli is known to have had dealings with the upper echelons of Venetian society and the Roman curia, including the humanist pope Pius II, to whom he addressed one of his letters about the English wars.[34] During the early 1450s his son Giovanni is said to have studied at Oxford (where he could have benefited from Duke Humfrey's donations), and he also seems to have made use of those books his father left him, since he was also a humanist writer of some reputation who played some part in 'promoting the revival of English literary culture after the conclusion of the Wars of the Roses'.[35] With their Tuscan, mercantile, and literary connections, then, Carlo Gigli and his family look like the sort of people who would have been interested in the kind of deal which brought books of high status to fifteenth-century London.

Evidence about the sale of a vernacular *Commedia* by and to an Italian in London around the time when Giovanni and his father were in the city (and when William Worcester was buying foreign books from Carlo Gigli) may thus be of relevance not only to the reception of Dante in the fifteenth century, but also to the forms and levels of contact between England and Italy. Insofar as Dante was being read at all in England in the late fifteenth and early sixteenth centuries, he is most likely

---

[30] For Gigli's letter to Pius II about events in England from April to July 1460, see Bianchi 1988: 110–22. On three other letters of February 1461 (to Michele Arnolfini in Bruges), see Clough 2003: 126 and nn. 24 and 27.

[31] Will of Carlo Gigli, registered 12 July 1465, London, London Metropolitan Archive, MS 9171/5/, f. 376Aᵛ. I am grateful to Dr Helen Bradley for this reference.

[32] Clough 2003:127–8 and n. 33.

[33] Clough 2003: 128–40. See also Weiss 1947; *DBI*, s.v. 'Gigli, Giovanni', and *ODNB*, s.v. 'Gigli, Giovanni (1434–1498), papal official, diplomat, and bishop of Worcester'.

[34] Bianchi 1988: 110–22.

[35] See Weiss 1947: 384, Carlson 1988: 284–5, *ODNB*, s.v. 'Gigli, Giovanni (1434–1498), papal official, diplomat, and bishop of Worcester' [last paragraph], and Wyatt 2005: 54.

to have been read in Latin; and the appearance of a vernacular *Commedia* at this time looks like a rather rare migrant. Moreover, the export of such texts by those travelling away from a source of cultural activity is considerably less frequent than imports by those visiting such a source—like, for example, William Gray, Chancellor of Oxford, studying and collecting books in Florence and Rome during the 1440s—or John Tiptoft, Earl of Worcester, in Padua and Ferrara in the late 1450s.[36] Nonetheless, the Italian deal done in London on 1 August 1451, as outlined here, creates some wider cultural reverberations in the international reception of the *Commedia*, suggesting a conversation about the poem that may have gone some way beyond the question of its price.

The preliminary account of this particular *Commedia* prompts a number of questions about manuscripts and editions of Dante's works, and their collectors, owners, and readers, which will be addressed at a number of points in this book. How did they come to be in the collections and locations where they are recorded? Why were their owners interested in acquiring them? What do the acquisitions suggest about the knowledge and reading of Dante's work? How does the British public for that work relate to ownership and readership elsewhere in the world?

Some time after 1451 MS Hamilton 207—as it would eventually become—presumably travelled back to Italy with its Tuscan purchaser or his heirs, returning to Britain in the early nineteenth century as an item in the major aristocratic collection from which it takes its name, and migrating once more, to become part of the *Preußischer Kulturbesitz*, in 1882.[37] The wanderings of this *Commedia* can thus be related to issues that will be investigated over some six more centuries in the chapters that follow. The nature of a British reading public for Dante before and around the time of Chaucer will be explored in Chapter 1; the manuscript's probable absence from Britain extends over a period in which he is thought to have been little known (Chapters 2–4); its return coincides with what has been seen as a 'rehabilitation' or 'cult' of Dante in the nineteenth century (Chapters 5–6); and its final journey to Berlin at the end of that century forms part of a diffusion of 'British Dantes', reflecting the movement of the *Commedia* from private, limited ownership to wider public use (Chapters 7–8).

---

[36] Dr David Rundle (personal communication); and Rundle 2013: 545–6. See also Childs 1983: 83.

[37] On the Hamilton Collection, its development and dispersal, see below, pp. 243–59.

1

Around Chaucer: Clerics, *Comedy*, and *Monarchy*

Most of Chaucer's clerics have contacts with Italy or with Italian literature. The Pardoner has roamed as far as the papal curia, now re-established at Rome.[1] The Clerk not only appropriates Petrarch's (and Boccaccio's) work in his *Tale*, but also claims to have made direct acquaintance with the late *lauriat poete* at Padua.[2] Chaucer's Monk reports on the latest mayhem in Milan and goes on immediately to retail a tabloid version of an older story from Pisa: a terrifying and heart-rending *tragedye* of *Hugelino*, whose attributed source is 'the grete poete of Ytaille | That highte Dant'.[3] Invocations to the Virgin Mary by the Prioress and the Second Nun both draw upon St Bernard's appeal at the beginning of the last canto of the *Paradiso*.[4] Friar Hubert implies an infernal public for Dante, through a vagrant devil's tribute to the poet's expertise on Hell.[5] The Wife of Bath—a clerk in all but name—actually translates a whole *terzina* from the *Purgatorio* on the subject of true nobility.[6] Her exploitation of the 'wise poete of Florence', among other 'auctoritees' from 'scoles of clergye', attracts the patronizing attention of clerical professionals such as the Friar.[7]

Over the past few decades much work has been done on Chaucer's reading of and response to Dante: on how the English poet might have accessed the Italian texts; on the cultural and political impact of his journeys to Italy; on the presence of Italian mercantile communities in late fourteenth-century London; and to some extent on responses to Dante on the part of contemporaries, such as Gower and the *Gawain*-poet.[8] More recently, attention has been turning to Chaucer's dealings

---

[1] (Following its return from Avignon *c.*1378.) Chaucer *General Prologue*, line 671 (in *The Riverside Chaucer*, ed. L. D. Benson (3rd edn., Oxford: Oxford University Press, 2008); all subsequent line references are from this edition, unless otherwise indicated).

[2] Chaucer *Clerk's Prologue*, 26–38.

[3] Chaucer, *Monk's Tale*, 2399–462.

[4] Chaucer, *Prologue of the Prioress's Tale*, 474–80, and *Second Nun's Prologue*, 36–56, both appropriating lines and phrases from *Paradiso* 33. 1–21.

[5] Chaucer, *Friar's Tale*, 1515–20.

[6] Chaucer, *Wife of Bath's Tale*, 1125–30, translating *Purgatorio* 7. 121–3. The Wife's arguments about nobility also parallel some of those in the *Convivio* 4 (see e.g. the discussion in Schless 1984: 183–94 and Minnis 2005), but the *Convivio* was much less widely disseminated than the *Commedia*: it survives in only 46 manuscripts (some of them fragmentary) and is mentioned in only a handful of fourteenth-century sources (see Dante 1995*a*: lxxx–lxxxi).

[7] *Friar's Prologue*, 1276–30.

[8] See e.g. Boitani 1983; Schless 1984; Wallace 1985; Taylor 1989; Bradley 1992; Wallace 1997; Edwards 2002; Ginsberg 2002; Havely 2005. For a review of the scholarship, see Clarke 2011b. On

with Italian textuality, to the 'materiality of the book' as part of his complex encounter with *trecento* culture, as well as (once again) to his activities as translator and inheritor of Italian authors.[9]

This chapter explores the hinterland of that encounter by investigating the role of some learned and highly mobile clerical readers around the time of Chaucer in accessing, publicizing, and debating Dante's work at an early stage of his reception in Britain—from the middle of the fourteenth century to the middle of the fifteenth. Traces here are intermittent and difficult to assess. Even in Chaucer, the presence of the 'grete poete of Ytaille' has been described as necessarily 'a Dante of fragments'.[10] And (to change the vehicle of the metaphor) investigating even a part of Dante's complex itinerary around Chaucer recalls the poet of *Paradiso*'s warning to those small vessels seeking to follow in his wake across deep and uncharted waters:

> non vi mettete in pelago, ché forse,
> perdendo me, rimarreste smarriti.
>
> Do not set out into the deep, lest perhaps you lose me and remain adrift.[11]

The clerics who are of interest here originate from a wide range of European locations: Sicily, Rimini, St Albans, and Norwich; and their itineraries include an equally wide range of places, including Cambridge, Konstanz, Pavia, Siena, and Avignon. There was, by Chaucer's time, a long-standing and increasing two-way traffic of clergy, students, and academics between England and Italy.[12] Destinations included, for example, the *studia* of Padua and Bologna, Oxford and Cambridge; whilst ecclesiastical business led to Italy or, earlier in Chaucer's time, to that place which, like the House of Fame, stood 'in middes of the way': the papal court at Avignon, whose culture, as we shall see, mediated Dante's reputation and work on a number of occasions through the fourteenth century and beyond.

Amongst the clerics 'around Chaucer' there are some readers and writers of particular interest here: two Italian Franciscans who promoted the *Commedia* and had contacts with England; and two English Benedictines who visited Italy and show awareness of several aspects of Dante's work. It is not claimed that any of these four clerics actually knew Chaucer—although at least one of them must have heard of him. Instead, the aim is to outline some of the ways in which their approaches to Dante may relate to and differ from those of the English poet. When exploring this area of cultural interaction—the trafficking and circulation of texts— it is easy to overstate the function of individual agency. Thus, whilst attention will be given to these writers' specific dealings with Dante—to such activities as quotation, allusion, commentary, translation, and political debate—it is essential

---

Gower and Dante, see Watt 1999: 389–91 and 403–8.; and for further discussion of the *Gawain*-poet and the *Commedia*, see Shoaf 1995: 190–7, and Putter 1996: 4–6 and 188–9.

[9] See Clarke 2007 and 2011a (esp. 5–6 and 163), and Rossiter 2010.

[10] Ginsberg 2002: 30.

[11] *Paradiso* 2. 5–6. All quotations from the *Commedia*, unless otherwise indicated, are from the edition by A. M. Chiavacci Leonardi (Dante 1997).

[12] See Parks 1954: part 3 and Childs 1983: 77–82.

to relate these activities to the wider cultural issues in which Dante's work and reputation are implicated: the circulation of and access to texts; fourteenth-century writers' negotiation of the 'new vernacular author';[13] and the relationship between Latinity and vernacularity. Thus, this chapter does not deal directly with 'what Dante meant to Chaucer' but with how a wider public of learned readers and writers around the English poet's time and place read and wrote about his daunting precursor.

THE MYSTERY OF FRIAR ROGER: TRANSLATING THE '*POETA VULGARIS*'

The first of these scenes from late medieval clerical life involves a Franciscan friar. Dante's vernacular enterprise in the *Commedia* has on a number of occasions been compared to the work of the mendicant orders, so it is not surprising to find the friars involved in the reception of the poem and in the use and abuse of the poet's work at an early stage in its afterlife.[14] One such reading is the extensive commentary on the *Inferno* completed between 1328 and 1333 by the Carmelite, Guido da Pisa, who is described as 'one of the most important of the earliest students of the poem' and who appears to have been citing Dante as early as 1318.[15] A very different response was the attack on Dante and his *Monarchia* by the Dominican, Guido Vernani of Rimini, some time between 1327 and 1334. Vernani's *De reprobatione monarchiae* is associated with the condemnation of the treatise by the papal legate to Emilia Romagna in 1328 or 1329 and with other evidence of hostility to Dante among the early *trecento* Dominicans.[16]

For the Franciscans, the *Commedia*, with its exaltation of their founder and of evangelical poverty, provided congenial reading from soon after the time of its composition, and there is some evidence of its conscription by radical elements, such as the *fraticelli* in mid-fourteenth-century Florence. In 1361 an apocalyptic poem by one Fra' Giovanni of Florence (probably a *fraticello*) presents St Francis and Joachim of Fiore as witnesses to the travails of St Peter's 'ship' (the Church), and then has them allude to Dante by describing how 'modern pharisees' are drinking the blood of the Church (as in *Paradiso* 27. 58–9).[17] The same friar may have been the author of another Joachimist apocalyptic poem which describes *pellegrina Italia* by echoing Beatrice's words about humanity as a starving child (*Par.* 30. 141); this again foresees shipwreck in the sea of 'greed' (*cupidigia*) and ends with an exact quotation of the prophetic last line from *Paradiso* 27: 'and the true

---

[13] See Minnis and Scott, with Wallace 1991: 439–58.

[14] Connections between Dante's enterprise and that of the friars are noted by Hawkins 1999: 28–30 and Havely 2004*a*: 186–7.

[15] See Kelly 1989: 19.

[16] See below, pp. 27–8. Vernani's treatise was probably begun in 1327 and circulated in 1329; see *DE* 855, also Matteini 1958:27–43 and Cassell 2004: 44–9.

[17] Compare *Inferno* 27. 85 (*nuovi farisei*) and Paradiso 27. 58–9 (the blood of the Church).

fruits will then appear after the blossoms'.[18] For some more orthodox Franciscans, too, the *Commedia*—with its promotion of St Francis and evangelical poverty, and its ways of staging Christian history and dogma—provided congenial reading, and the poem was also amongst the vernacular texts that they continued to use in preaching through the fourteenth century and on into the period of the Observants and San Bernardino.[19] A notable product of such interest in Dante was a Latin translation of and commentary on the *Commedia* which will feature later in this chapter, but in Italy there is other evidence also of a Franciscan reception of Dante well before this.

An early—perhaps very early—example is the citation and discussion of passages from the *Commedia* in a cycle of Lent sermons for students and clerics, the *Quadragesimale de scolis* or *scolarum* by the Sicilian Franciscan, Rogerius de Platea or de Heraclea (*c.*1304–83). Rogerius was a prominent member of the Franciscan Order and was Provincial of the Order and bishop of several dioceses from about 1336 to 1383.[20] According to several of the manuscripts, he obtained his baccalaureate at the University of Naples and was subsequently active on behalf of the Inquisition in Calabria. From 1336 to 1345 he served as Sicilian Provincial for the Franciscan Order; in 1360 he was created bishop of Bosa on the west coast of Sardinia and in 1363 he was translated back to his Sicilian homeland, to the see of Mazara near Trapani, where he remained for the last twenty years of his life.[21]

Friar Roger's sermons exist in various forms in seven manuscripts. In two of the four manuscripts containing the full cycle of fifty-six Lenten sermons a range of passages from all three parts of the *Commedia* are quoted, but not all, even of these full versions, contain equal amounts of quotation from the poem.[22] Such quotations occur mostly in sermons concerned with specific sins, such as avarice, and in those designed to promote penitence and unworldliness.

One of the most striking features of this Franciscan reading is its sustained interest in Dante's role as visionary and authoritative poet. In the sermon on the epistle for the third Sunday in Lent (Ephesians 5: 1, *Estote imitatores Dei*), Friar Roger refers to St Paul's journey to Paradise (2 Cor. 12: 2–4) and notes that similar uncertainties about the corporal or incorporeal nature of the vision are also expressed by Dante in the *Paradiso*, which he then quotes (with a southern Italian accent):

---

[18] *Paradiso* 27. 148 (*e vero frutto verrà dopo il fiore*). See Reeves 1969: 214–17 and Havely 2004*a*: 181–2.

[19] See Moorman 1968: 478 and Casciani 2006.

[20] Allusions to Dante in one of the manuscripts of his sermons (Assisi, Sacro Convento MS 492) was first annotated in 1949, and at that time relatively little was known about Rogerius; see Palumbo 1966. More recent studies of 'Rogerius de Platea [modern Piazza Armerina]' aka 'Rogerius de Eraclea [modern Gela]' are: Roccaro 1987; Roccaro 1992: 1–36; Cenci 1995; and Romano 2008.

[21] Palumbo 1966: 465–7.

[22] All fifty-six sermons are in four of the manuscripts: Assisi, Sacro Convento MS 492; Florence, Laurenziana plut. 24 cod. 5; Nürnberg, Stadtbibliothek MS lat. theol. Cent. IV, 3; and Berlin Staatsbibliothek MS Magdeb. Domkirche 231. For lists and descriptions of the known manuscripts, see Cenci 1995: 279–90 and Romano 2008: 172–3. There are thirteen passages from the *Commedia* in the Assisi MS, but only six in the full Florentine version, and only two in the Nürnberg and Berlin texts.

raptus fuit usque ad [terciu]m celum et audivit archana verba quae non licet homini loqui.
Quod configurans poeta uulgaris ait/

> Sy yo era supra di me quel che creasti
> nouelamente, amor ch'el ciel gouerni,
> tu 'l say ke col tua lume mi leuasti

[St Paul] was taken up to the third heaven and heard mysterious words which it not given to
humans to tell about. In imitation of this, the vernacular poet says: 'Whether I transcended
myself by being there in spirit, you will know, Love that rules the heavens, since you drew
me upwards with your light.'[23]

Several folios later he then launches into an ambitious mythographic account of
Dante's journey through learning (*scientia*) to wisdom (*sapientia*) through the first
two *cantiche* of the *Commedia*, with the final stage being signalled through the
invocation to the god Apollo at the beginning of the *Paradiso*:

Sed duo erant Dii sub quorum nomine poetae coronabantur, scilicet Bachus et Apollo.
Bachus enim solummodo Deus scientiae vocabatur seu dicebatur; Apollo vero dicebatur
Deus Sapientiae. Unde sic fiebat quod qui laureandi erant in scientia sola coronabantur sub
nomine Bachi et illi qui in Sapientia laureabantur sub nomine Apollis et illi qui in utraque
sub nomine utriusque. Unde poeta vulgaris tractavit de poesis Inferni et Purgatorii sub dictu
Bachi, quasi dicat quod ratio naturalis seu moralis potest illa dictare quia ulterius tractaturus
erat de Paradiso ubi sunt illa quae ratio naturalis nescit dictare, hinc est quod ipse dixit:

> A buono Apollo allu oltimu lavoro
> fammi de lu tuo lavor si fatto vaso
> comme dumandi da lo amato alloro
> infine a quell'uno jogo di Parnaso
> mi fu ma or con ambedue
> mo opo intrare nelle ringa rimaso.

... there were two Gods under whose names poets were crowned, that is, Bacchus and
Apollo. Bacchus in fact was referred to or named only as the God of Knowledge; whilst
Apollo was called the God of Wisdom. Hence it so happened that those who were to be
made laureate for knowledge alone were crowned under the name of Bacchus, those for
wisdom under the name of Apollo, and those for both under the name of both. Hence the
vernacular poet deals with Hell and Purgatory in his poems under the command of Bacchus,
as if to say that natural and moral reason sufficed to deal with those things, whilst the final
matter to be dealt with was Paradise where there are things that natural reason cannot
convey, hence he says:

'Good Apollo, for this last task, make me the kind of vessel worthy of your beloved laurel.
Till now, one of the peaks of Parnassus gave me enough, but now I need to call upon both as
I face the final challenge.'[24]

Here, the Franciscan friar also approaches the *poeta vulgaris* as an authoritative
figure, but he seems to be on the verge of validating theology through poetry, in a
way that might have made some of his clerical contemporaries (particularly

[23] *Quadragesimale de scolis/scolarum*, in Assisi Comunale MS 492, f. 62v (partly transcribed by
Palumbo 1965: 470), quoting *Paradiso* 1.73–5 in an unknown southern Italian version.
[24] *Quadragesimale*, f. 69ᵛ–70ʳ, transcribed by Palumbo 1966: 472.

Dominican ones) uncomfortable and might well have been viewed sceptically by Chaucer.[25] The appeal for Apollo's guidance in the last stage of the *Commedia* is a passage that Chaucer turns to and reshapes at the beginning of the 'lytel laste boke' of *The House of Fame*, and he acknowledges Dante's poetic authority whilst qualifying his own position in relation to it.[26]

These passages, and the other appropriations of the *Commedia* in Friar Roger's sermons, have been known, at least to Franciscan scholars, for the last half-century. Their dating, as we shall see, is uncertain, but they provide important evidence about the early dissemination of Dante's work in southern Italy. They show that the preacher must have had access to all three parts of the *Commedia*, or at least to an anthology that included excerpts from them. Copies of the *Inferno* were certainly present in Sicily by about 1370, whilst a vernacular commentary on part of St Matthew's Gospel (*Sposizione del Vangelo della Passione secondo Matteo*), dated 1372, contains a number of Dantean images and expressions—and it has been suggested that the latter may be a late work by Friar Roger himself.[27]

In mid-career, this Franciscan preacher and commentator on Dante may have travelled as far as England and the University of Cambridge. During the fourteenth century Cambridge had been gaining status among European universities, especially for its faculty of theology, due partly to the presence of its Franciscan community, which had become well established by 1267 and by the middle of the next century numbered some sixty friars.[28] In the Bull *Redemptor noster* (issued in 1336) Pope Benedict XII had set out a number of new Constitutions for the Franciscans. Its ninth section, *De studiis*, amongst other things, provides for the Minster General of the Franciscans and the General Chapter of the Order to present a non-English friar from 'north or south of the Alps' every third year to lecture on the *Sentences* in order to obtain the master's degree at Paris, Oxford, and Cambridge (the three universities with theological faculties at that time).[29] There is some evidence of Italian friars being selected to lecture at Oxford under this scheme during the mid-to-late fourteenth century, although the dates are not always precise, and some of those selected did not appear.[30] For Cambridge, however, there is a list of seventy-three *magistri fratrum minorum* ('Franciscan masters') attached to Thomas of Eccleston's *Chronicle*.[31] At number seventy in this list, and

---

[25] On Chaucer's implied attitude to Dante as *poeta theologus* or as 'scribe of God' in the *House of Fame*, see Ellis 1988 and Taylor 1989: 39–49.

[26] Chaucer, *House of Fame* 1091–100.

[27] See Resta 1967: 414 on the *Inferno* listed in an inventory of Federico IV in 1367. Another (clearly in a southern Italian dialect) formed part of the estate of the Franciscan archbishop of Palermo, Matteo della Porta who died in 1377; see Monfrin 1961: 229 and n. 2, and Williman 1980: 264, no. 98 (see below, p. 29). On the St Matthew commentary, see Resta 1967: 419, Bruni 1980: 226–7, and Rotolo 1981: 541–2 and n. 121.

[28] See Moorman 1952: 78–9.

[29] Benedict XII, *Redemptor Noster*, ed. M. Bihl, in *Archivum Franciscanum Historicum*, 30 (1937), 309–90 and 346.

[30] See Little 1938: 205–9; and Moorman 1947: 295.

[31] In Little 1951: 58–61.

probably present at Cambridge during 1351–2, is one *frater Rogerius de Cicilia*.[32] It seems likely that, although there were several friars of this name, this Rogerius was the author of the *Quadragesimale*.[33] A papal decree of 1367, awarding a *magisterium* at the University of Paris to *dilectus filius Rogerius de Heraclia, ordinis fratrum Minorum professor*, mentions that this Sicilian friar had already studied and lectured on the *Sentences* (as provided for in Benedict XII's Bull of 1336) *in diversis studiis*.[34]

How, then, might the friar's mid-century lecturing on Peter Lombard's *Sentences* at Cambridge relate to his cycle of sermons which quote the *Commedia*? One proposed date for that cycle is a few years earlier than 1336, soon after Friar Roger's graduation from the University of Naples and shortly before he became Provincial Minister for the order in Sicily. This quite early dating in his long career (which lasted until 1383) would give the *Quadragesimale* considerable interest as a response to the *Commedia* not much more than a decade after the poem's completion; and it would mean that 'Rogerius de Cicilia' would have been on record as a reader of and commentator upon Dante well before his arrival to lecture at Cambridge in 1351.

Other dates, however, have been proposed. It has also been shown that four of the manuscripts refer to the death of Richard Fitzralph at Avignon in 1360, and that they also mention the teaching of the Franciscan Giovanni della Marca from 1350 onwards—which would suggest a much later date of composition.[35] On the other hand, the *Quadragesimale* evolved over a period, in at least two and possibly three redactions, and whatever the dates of composition or compositions, it would still be possible to envisage the Sicilian friar as having read Dante at some point before his forties, when he went to Cambridge.[36] Of course, lecturing on Peter Lombard's *Sentences* is a rather different exercise from reading and interpreting, let alone enthusing about or promoting the *Commedia*—for which we have only the Italian material in the *Quadragesimale* and the uncertainty about the date of that text. But, given his willingness to share Dantean material with the scholarly audience of his sermons, it seems likely that 'Rogerius de Cicilia' would also have been ready to discuss this prominent vernacular poet with Franciscan colleagues at home and perhaps also abroad.

Not much seems to be known in detail about the academic and intellectual culture of Cambridge Franciscans in the years immediately after the plague of 1348, let alone whether they would have been interested in the work of the new Italian *poeta theologus*.[37] But the probable location of the Sicilian friar in mid-fourteenth-century Cambridge has at least two wider possible implications. It

---

[32] See Moorman 1947: 293–5.   [33] Palumbo 1966: 466; Roccaro 1992: 28 and n. 32.
[34] Decree of 1367, quoted in Cenci 1995: 294.   [35] Cenci 1995: 272–5.
[36] On the two or three possible redactions, see Cenci 1995: 292, and on the issue of dating the *Quadragesimale*, see Romano 2008: 173–4 (concluding that the question 'cannot be resolved at present').
[37] See Moorman 1952: ch. 6; and Cobban 1975: ch. 2, and (on the theology faculty) Cobban 1988: 224–31.

indicates an early channel of communication and a context for interest in Dante's work in England, perhaps among Franciscans or other cultured clerics some thirty years before Chaucer's reference to Dante alongside Virgil and Claudian and his subsequent allusions to the *Commedia* in *The House of Fame*.[38] Secondly, it reflects a clerical investment in a commented and Latinized Dante that will continue beyond Chaucer into pre-humanist England, through the work of a later and more well-known Franciscan who had both Dantean interests and more ascertainable English connections.

'RUSTIC LATIN': SERRAVALLE'S *COMMEDIA*

At the Council of Konstanz between January 1416 and January 1417, Giovanni Bertoldi da Serravalle, who was then bishop of Fermo near Rimini, completed a Latin translation of and commentary on Dante's *Commedia*, which now survives, unlike its original, in very few manuscripts.[39] The Council itself, ending the schism in the Papacy and debating reform in the Church, was an international affair, and so was Serravalle's project.[40] Two English bishops and an Italian cardinal were, according to him, involved in 'enjoining and encouraging' the work, which was completed quite rapidly, taking less than five months over the translation and less than twelve for the commentary. Their role is acknowledged several times in the text, for example, at the end of the translation:

Explicit translatio libri dantis edita a re[ver]endo patre et d[omi]no fr[at]re johanne de s[er]aualle Arriminensis dioces[is] Ep[isc]opo et principe firmano de ordine mi[n]ore assumpto. Principiata de me[n]se januarii Anno d[om]ini m[illesim]° ccccxvi° et completa de me[n]se maii euisd[em] anni in ciuitate Constanciensis . . . Que translatio fuit [com] pilata & f[ac]ta ad instantia . . . Domini Amedei . . . Cardinalis de Saluciis . . . Nycolay de Bubwych . . . et d[om]ini Roberti hal[u]m
. . . qui ambo sunt de Regno Anglie in quo suas sedes habent . . .

here ends the translation of the Book of Dante, produced by the reverend father and lord, Brother Giovanni da Serravalle of the diocese of Rimini, bishop of Fermo and member of the Franciscan Order. It was begun in the month of January AD 1416 and completed in the month of May of the same year in the city of Konstanz. This translation was compiled and produced at the instigation of Lord Amedeo . . . Cardinal of Saluzzo . . . ; Nicholas

[38] Chaucer, *House of Fame*, 445–50, 499–508, 523–8, 530–44, and 1091–109.
[39] On Serravalle's life, see *DBI* s.v. 'Bertoldi, Giovanni (Giovanni da Serravalle)'; and on his translation of the *Commedia*, see esp. Lombardi 1987 and Wallace 1999. The three surviving manuscripts of his translation and commentary are: Vatican, BAV MS Capponiano 1; London BL MS Egerton 2629; and an incomplete text at Eger (Hungary), Bishop's Library, containing the translation and the commentary on *Inferno* (see Vaisz 1883).
[40] See the chapter on Konstanz (ch. 82) in *Europe: A Literary History 1348–1418*, ed. D. Wallace (Oxford: Oxford University Press, forthcoming). On other forms of literary production at the Council, see Hobbins 2009: 193–7; and on the subsequent dissemination of texts from Konstanz to collections in Germany, Poland, Sweden, France, and elsewhere in Europe, see Lehmann 1959: esp. 256–69.

Bubwith ... and Lord Robert Hallum, both from the realm of England where they hold their sees.[41]

Serravalle's translation of the *Commedia* might initially be seen as a humanistic project, giving the text, through Latin, the linguistic identity and status that some *trecento* critics thought it ought to have had *ab initio*. In his prologue, however, Serravalle insists on the 'rough and inept' way in which his 'rustic' Latin prose renders the 'sweetness and beauty' of Dante's verse, and acknowledges that 'in such a short time I do not think it would be possible to accomplish a fitting translation, following high rhetorical standards' (*non puto fore possibile in tam parvo tempore ... fieri translationem decentem in bona rhetorica et laudabile*).[42] What Serravalle presents here to his colleagues, therefore, is not a humanistic Latinization of the *Commedia*, but a rough-and-ready 'window onto a vernacular text for non-Italian clerics',[43] and especially for his two named English associates: Nicholas Bubwith, bishop of Bath and Wells, and Robert Hallum, bishop of Salisbury.

Unlike his earlier Franciscan colleague Friar Roger, Serravalle thus tells us something specific about his English contacts and a potential British readership for his translation. He not only mentions the two English bishops; he also indicates how he might previously have got to know them. In his commentary on *Inferno* 20 he mentions that he had himself actually been to England:

Prope Sibiliam, forte per centum leucas, est mons Giubelcar, iuxta quem montem mare Oceanum per angustum spatium septem leucarum fluit et vadit, et ingreditur mare Mediterraneum; et ego iam transivi per illud angustum spatium, quando redibam de regno Anglie ad partes Ytalie per mare ...

Around 100 leagues from Seville is the mountain of Gibraltar past which the Ocean flows for seven leagues through a narrow strait to enter the Mediterranean; and I once travelled through that narrow strait when I was returning by sea from the realm of England to the land of Italy.[44]

During his busy career as lector, preacher, bishop, and diplomat in places including Ferrara, Pavia, Florence, Rome, and Perugia,[45] one of the few times when he could have taken such a journey would have been around 1398, the year in which he also visited the Holy Land and the eastern Mediterranean.[46] This is not to suggest that his voyage to England in the late 1390s might have brought him into contact with the—then rather elderly—author of the *Canterbury Tales*. But by that time Serravalle was already a well-informed reader of the *Commedia*, having benefited directly from Benvenuto da Imola's exposition of the text whilst at the Franciscan

---

[41] Serravalle, *Liber Dantis* in Vatican, BAV MS Cappon. 1, f. 474ᵛ. The same names occur in the *incipit*, the dedication, and the *conclusio* to Serravalle's commentary; see Serravalle 1891: 3, 5, and 1215.

[42] The 'Dedicatio', in Serravalle 1891: 5–6. On Serravalle's attitude and procedure as translator (with examples), see Wallace 1999: 13–16 and 19–20 (with n. 32).

[43] Wallace 1999: 23—although it needs to be noted that the translation and commentary are also dedicated to an Italian cardinal, Amedeo di Saluzzo (see below, pp. 31–2 with n. 131).

[44] Commentary on *Inferno* 20. 124–6, in Serravalle 1891: 259.

[45] Lombardi 1987: 101–3.   [46] Ibid. 102, and Serravalle 1891: xvi–xvii.

convent in Ferrara from 1379 to 1383.[47] It is possible, therefore, that if his acquaintance with his English fellow clerics, Bubwith and Hallum, began in 1398, so might the dialogue on Dante that was later to yield the text produced at such speed during the Council of Konstanz.

Serravalle's translation of and commentary on the *Commedia* had a significant English afterlife in and beyond the fifteenth century. Of the two English bishops who encouraged the production of the text, the more intellectually dominant was Robert Hallum of Salisbury, but he can have had little time to read Serravalle's work, let alone bring it back to England, since he died at Konstanz in September 1417.[48] It is likely, on the other hand, that his colleague Nicholas Bubwith, bishop of Bath and Wells, who was the principal English envoy at the Council, did bring a copy home. This was probably the text that the antiquary John Leland saw in Wells Cathedral Library some time in the 1530s, and described (slightly inaccurately) as *Dantes tra[ns]latus in carmen Latinum.*[49] That manuscript no longer exists, but there were others in British libraries in the fifteenth century, although they too have since disappeared. At some point between 1417 and 1444 the uncle of Henry VI, Duke Humfrey of Gloucester, acquired at least one copy (from whatever source) for his collection at Greenwich Palace. Duke Humfrey's use of books seems largely to have been for self-promotion rather than self-improvement; nonetheless, his collection would eventually be of some considerable benefit to the world of learning.[50] His third donation of books to the University of Oxford in February 1444 comprised 135 manuscripts, two of which (nos. 117 and 120) are books of or about Dante:

Item **commentaria Dantis** secundo folio *et tormentabunt* [. . .]
Item **librum** [*sic*] **Dantis** secundo folio *a te* [or *ate?*][51]

The first of these two items, from the evidence of the contemporary catalogue, was clearly Serravalle's commentary. The phrase *et tormenta* (very close to the phrase which the catalogue gives as the start of folio 2 of the Oxford volume) occurs in the second preamble to the commentary, near the beginning of folio 2 in both the Vatican and the Egerton manuscripts; furthermore, Leland's later account explicitly identifies Serravalle as the author of the 'Commentarii . . . super opera Dantis Aligerii' that was still in the library in the early sixteenth century.[52]

---

[47] Lombardi 1987: 101. On the influence of Benvenuto's commentary on Serravalle's, see Barbi 1934: 79–98.

[48] On Hallum, see *ODNB*, s v 'Hallum [Hallam], Robert (d. 1417), bishop of Salisbury'.

[49] See *ODNB*, s.v., 'Bubwith, Nicholas (*c.*1355–1424), administrator and bishop of Bath and Wells'. Leland's listing of the Serravalle manscript at Wells is in Leland 1715: 3. 155 (no. 4 on the list).

[50] On Humfrey and his books, see Vickers 1907: 426–38; Weiss 1967: 40–53 and 64–7; Petrina 2004: ch. 4; and Wakelin 2007: 25–31.

[51] Catalogue of Books donated to the University of Oxford by Duke Humfrey of Gloucester, Indenture dated 25 February 1443/4, in Oxford, Bodleian Library University of Oxford Archives, MS Registrum F, f. 68ᵛ. See also *DEL* 1. 20–2, and Sammut 1980: 82–3 (nos. 117 and 120).

[52] Leland 1715: 3. 58. On the subsequent dispersal of Duke Humfrey's manuscripts at Oxford, see Rundle 2004: 115.

The second of Duke Humfrey's Dantes is more problematic: the *librum Dantis* with *a te* or *ate* occurring as the first word on its second folio. This has been read as two separate words, as *Inferno* 1. 91: '*A te* convien tenere altro viaggio' ('You must take another way', Virgil's advice to Dante), which would thus indicate 'the... existence in England of a copy of the "Divina Commedia" in the original at this date—the earliest copy on record'.[53] The evidence for Humfrey's ownership of an Italian *Commedia* is, however, by no means conclusive. The manuscript of the Oxford list of books has a little space between the *a* and the *te*, but on close inspection it appears that the letters are linked, which makes it possible that the Latin morpheme *-ate* is being referred to. Two of the three extant manuscripts of Serravalle's *Liber Dantis* (Vatican and Egerton) begin with the commentary, but the third (Eger) starts with the translation. If the latter ordering (translation then commentary) was that of the Oxford *librum Dantis*, then the Latin *-ate* ending would have occurred numerous times in the prologue and summaries which precede that translation. Furthermore, the Oxford cataloguer's rendering of the title as *librum* [rather than *liber*] *Dantis* could have derived from a misreading of the manuscript's colophon, which in this case would have been the *explicit* to the commentary. Hence, the second of these *libri Dantis* could have been a complete version of Serravalle's text, comprising the translation followed by the commentary. Moreover, Duke Humfrey's donation includes no vernacular texts—which would make it yet more likely that both the Dantes he gave to Oxford in 1444 were Serravalle's Latin work.[54]

Neither the Oxford nor the Wells copy of Serravalle's Dante has survived, yet their early importation certainly indicates the availability of the *Commedia* to a wider British public beyond Chaucer.[55] Serravalle's Latin prose translation and commentary offered a convenient annotated version of the poem for a new educated class of reader: for clerics such as Bubwith, Hallum, and their circles, and for those students and scholars who might later have had access to Duke Humfrey's books. The complex European itineraries of this Latin *Commedia* will be returned to later in this chapter; meanwhile, we should take account of a prominent English cleric (and associate of Duke Humfrey) who knew and referred to both Serravalle's and Dante's work.

'NOTABLE COMEDIES': DANTE AT ST ALBANS

The Benedictine monk John Whethamstede was a prominent figure on the English religious and intellectual scene during the early and mid-fifteenth century. Born in

---

[53] P. Toynbee, letter to the *Times Literary Supplement* (22 Apr. 1920), p. 256, col. 2.

[54] The four texts by Boccaccio and the seven by Petrarch all (as far as they are identifiable) appear to be in Latin; see *DEL* 1. 21–2. As Weiss (1967: 65) points out, it is very unlikely that Humfrey could have read the *Commedia* in Italian, 'considering that he had [Boccaccio's] *Corbaccio* translated into Latin [BL MS Lat. Misc. d. 34] and owned the *Decameron* in French [Paris BNF Fr. no. 12421]'.

[55] The origins of the manuscript that is now in the British Library (MS Egerton 2629) are uncertain: it may have arrived in Britain only around the beginning of the nineteenth century and could be the copy donated by Philip II to the Escorial Library some time before 1576 (see Roddewig 1984: 38 and 397).

Hertfordshire around 1392/3, he entered St Albans Abbey some time between 1405 and 1408. He became Prior of Students at the Benedictine house of Gloucester College in Oxford around 1414 and incepted in theology about 1417. He served as Abbot of St Albans twice: first from 1420 to 1440 and then from 1451 until his death in 1465.[56] He is known to have founded libraries both there and at Gloucester College; and he was recognized in his own time as 'an eminent churchman, diplomat, preacher, letter writer and encyclopaedist, a munificent builder at St Albans and Oxford, a magnate, a patron and benefactor'.[57] His leading role as churchman and diplomat led him to undertake a long journey to Italy during 1423–4, in order to attend the Councils at Pavia and subsequently Siena; and more will be said later about the effects of clerical conference-going in Italy and elsewhere during this period.[58]

Prominent visitors to St Albans in the abbot's time included Henry VI and his uncle, Humfrey of Gloucester, well known for his book-collecting, literary patronage, and cultivation of Italian humanists.[59] Whethamstede's own patronage extended to 'scribes, scholars, composers, poets, goldsmiths, painters and glaziers', and he contributed significantly to the expansion of the monastic library at St Albans.[60] He also acted as patron to another Benedictine monk and member of Duke Humfrey's circle, the poet John Lydgate, whom he commissioned to write the *Liff and Passion of Seynt Alboon* during his first tenure as abbot in 1439.[61]

Characterized as 'one of the last of the English medieval polymaths', Whethamstede was a prominent figure in the 'monastic renaissance at St Albans' and in the development of fifteenth-century English classicism; he was almost as prolific in his literary output as his fellow Benedictine Lydgate, and as historiographer, anthologizer, and encyclopedist he was 'working within well-defined genres of monastic literature'.[62] His output comprises nearly fifty texts, of which several are ambitious encyclopedic projects, and three of them provide specific examples of how this abbot of St Albans read and referred to Dante.

The abbot's own name, deriving from his birthplace, Wheathampstead, was Latinized as *Frumentarius* ('Corny'), and he continues the cereal punning when giving titles to his works: to one of his main historiographical projects, the *Granarium*; to his collection of quotations, the *Pabularium* ('fodder') *poetarum*; and in that of his classical dictionary, the *Palearium* ('chaff-store') *poetarum*. Several of these contain references to Dante, as we shall see, but the *Palearium* also provides evidence both of Whethamstede's actual reading of passages in the *Commedia* and of the form in which he accessed the text.

---

[56] Weiss 1967: 30–8, and *ODNB*, s.v. 'Whethamstede [Bostock], John (*c.*1392–1465), scholar and abbot of St Albans'. On his life and work, see also Gransden 1974–82: 2. 371–86; Carlson 1999; and Alakas 2009: ch. 2

[57] Howlett 1975: 6.   [58] See below, p. 22.

[59] On Duke Humfrey, see above, p. 17.

[60] Howlett 1975: 6, and Howlett's contribution to Sharpe 1996: 542–4 and 563–83.

[61] Howlett 1975: 249.

[62] Weiss 1967: 38; Clark 2004: 234–7; and (as quoted last) Alakas 2009: 73.

The *Palearium poetarum* is found in a handsomely illuminated manuscript of 140 parchment folios and 692 entries dealing with a wide range of mostly classical persons, places, and things.[63] It is said to have been 'obviously modelled on Boccaccio's *De Genealogiis Deorum*';[64] yet, although Whethamstede does cite the latter throughout (alongside classical sources such as Ovid, Virgil, and Statius), he is not engaging in a Boccaccio-like project of mythographical interpretation, still less a defence of poetry.[65] Instead, he aims to provide a detailed guide to literary references and sources, which is organized alphabetically, cross-referenced, and linked to places in the books or chapters of the texts.[66]

Whethamstede's frequent, precise, and accurate references to Boccaccio's *De Genealogiis* in the *Palearium*—at least ninety of them—are, however, indicative of his appetite for the works of Italian writers in Latin. The various manuscripts of his *Granarium* indicate that he also knew Latin works by Petrarch, Salutati, and Bruni.[67] In the *Palearium* he devotes a complete entry to Paolo da Perugia, librarian of Robert of Naples, who is often cited by Boccaccio in the *Genealogiae*.[68] His article on *Sacra* (rites) shows that he knew a work on Roman politics which he attributes to 'Andrea Fflorentino', Andrea Fiocchi.[69] Two articles here also make several quite precise references to Dante.[70]

The first are in an article about names (*Nomen*), where Whethamstede has added a footnote about Roman practice in his own hand:

Vero quare omnes romani pro maiori parte sunt binomii. Vide in commento Johannis Ariminensis super Comediam Dantis capitulo sexto bene citra medium.

Indeed, therefore, all the Roman names are generally in two parts. See the commentary by John of Rimini on the *Comedy* of Dante, the sixth canto [of *Paradiso*] well before the middle.[71]

Whethamstede here makes two further specific references: to *Paradiso* 6 and Justinian's speech about famous Romans (especially lines 46–7); and to the source in which he read about the subject—Giovanni Bertoldi da Serravalle, who describes himself as *Arriminensis* in the colophons to his translation of and commentary on the *Commedia*.[72]

The second appearance of Dante in the *Palearium* also involves a passage in the *Paradiso* and occurs in another of Whethamstede's autograph additions. The article

---

[63] BL Add. MS 26764.

[64] Weiss 1967: 36, n. 14. Weiss's view of Whethamstede's intentions here (as elsewhere) seems to reflect an 'attempt to cast the abbot as either an early humanist or a failed humanist'; see Alakas 2009: 48–50.

[65] Although he does refer to Boccaccio's 'commendation' of poetry in Books 14 and 15 of the *Genealogie* in the course of his article on *Poeta* (BL Add. MS 26764, f. 99ʳ).

[66] Thus citing references 'well before' or 'well after the middle', 'near the end', or 'throughout'.

[67] Weiss 1967: 36, nn. 7–11.

[68] BL Add. MS 26764, f. 88ʳ, on *Paulus perusinus* (see the frequent references in Boccaccio's *Genealogiae*, e.g. 1. 14 and 15. 6).

[69] BL Add. MS 26764, f. 111ᵛ.

[70] These were first noticed by Weiss 1936: 358 and 359, n. 6.

[71] BL Add. MS 26764, unpaginated slip attached to f. 79.

[72] On Serravalle, see above, pp. 15–18.

on *Rhipheus* begins as an account of a mountain in Thrace, but the abbot then adds a note on a minor yet important character in the *Commedia* at the foot of the page:

Troiano qui tantam pietatem exercuit et iustitiam quod iuxta opinionem Dantis suis meruit virtutibus perpetuam salvationem. Vide in eodem Dante comedia tercia capitulo vicesimo. Vide eciam de eodem in Virgilio in secundo Eneidorum.

A Trojan who practised such loyalty and righteousness that in the view of Dante he deserved eternal salvation for his virtues. See the third [part of the] Comedy of Dante, the twentieth canto; also, on this same man, Virgil in the second [book of] the Aeneid.

This second note shows Whethamstede beginning to address a problematic feature of Dante's soteriology: the redemption of the noble pagan Rifeo in the sixth heaven of Paradise.[73] The allusion to Book 2 of the *Aeneid* in this context also suggests that, like many other readers of *Paradiso* 20, he may have been perplexed to see a character from Virgil's poem in Heaven, whilst its author is condemned to Hell. Elsewhere in the *Palearium* there are articles on such potentially Dantean topics as the rivers of Hell; on Geryon, the three-bodied monster; Glaucus, 'the poor fisherman who became a sea-god' (as Whethamstede summarizes it); and Marsyas, the satyr drawn out of his body by Apollo; but these prompt references to Roman authors, not to Dante, nor to Serravalle's translation or commentary.[74] Nonetheless, the *Palearium*'s actual allusions to the *Commedia* can be seen to reflect several significant aspects of the reception of the poem in northern Europe: first, how important Latin would be as a vehicle; and secondly, how quickly Serravalle's Latin translation and its commentary went into circulation in England and provided 'fodder' at least for a clerical and monastic readership. Whethamstede might perhaps have been using one of the copies of Serravalle's work that Duke Humfrey would donate to Oxford University, but it is also possible that other manuscripts of the translation were to hand.[75]

Whethamstede, however, knew very well that Dante's *Commedia* was composed in Italian, not Latin. In a brief compendium of poets' lives, which may have been intended to form one of the sheaves in his great *Granarium* project, he includes Dante, along with Petrarch and Boccaccio:

Dantes de aldigeriis poeta florentinus tres de Paradiso videlicet P[ur]gatorio & inferno [f. 160ᵛ] in suo vulgari eloquio scripsit notabiles comedias//

Dante Alighieri the Florentine poet wrote in his vernacular speech three remarkable comedies, namely on Paradise, Purgatorio, and Inferno.[76]

---

[73] BL Add. MS 26764, f. 110v; cf. *Paradiso* 20. 67–72. The problem of justice for the 'noble pagans' is articulated in the previous canto, *Paradiso* 19. 67–90.

[74] BL Add. MS 26764, ff. 47ᵛ, 50ᵛ, 51ʳ, and 68ʳ. The folio (51ʳ) carrying the article on Glaucus has a lower section excised; might that perhaps have contained another of the abbot's Dantean notes?

[75] On Duke Humfrey's donation, and on the copy that remained at Wells until the sixteenth century, see above, pp. 17–18.

[76] *Vitarum quorundam poetarum compendium*, in BL Cotton Titus D XX, f. 160 ʳ⁻ᵛ. I am much indebted to David Rundle of the University of Essex for identifying this source.

The 'three crowns of Florence' are the only moderns to be included in this compendium of chiefly Roman writers (along with a few token Greeks). In the case of Petrarch and Boccaccio, Whethamstede is concerned solely with their Latin works, which were those mainly circulated in northern Europe. Petrarch is identified mainly as the author of 'the excellent work on the Punic war which he called the *Africa*'; whilst the long account of Boccaccio is devoted almost entirely (and as might be expected) to a summary of the fifteen books of his 'most excellent work on the genealogies of the gods'.[77] Dante, on the other hand, stands out amongst all this Latinity as one who wrote his 'remarkable comedies' *in suo vulgari eloquio*. Use of the Serravalle translation of the *Commedia* did not, it seems, blind Whethamstede to the fact that he was dealing with a pre-eminently vernacular poet. Moreover, this account is of some interest as an early (perhaps the earliest) English representation of Dante as one of the 'three crowns of Florence', a triumvirate that was to provide a model for the formation of an English vernacular canon later in the fifteenth and the early sixteenth centuries.[78]

Whethamstede's active role as churchman and diplomat led him to undertake a long journey to Italy during 1423–4, in order to attend the Council at Pavia and subsequently Siena, and to defend his monastery's interests at the papal curia.[79] In the course of this journey he had the opportunity to encounter Italian intellectuals, lament the quality of his own Latin, and explore some of his 'literary assumptions'.[80] Yet his interests were not only in poetry and mythography, but also in the ecclesiastical politics of his time. He was well informed about conciliarism in general, and was clearly interested in controversies about papal power.[81]

Ecclesiastical politics provide a context for further direct reference to Dante in another of Whethamstede's works. A small, plain manuscript at Cambridge is Whethamstede's commonplace book, written mostly in his own hand,[82] and its second half contains—along with a considerable amount of verse, epitaphs, and recipes—two major articles on 'Pope' and 'Nation'.[83] These articles are thought to be the only surviving fragments of one of the abbot's other encyclopedic works, the *Manipularium doctorum*. The entry on 'Papacy' covers twenty pages, and addresses issues such as the title and authority of the pope and the vexed question of the Papacy's temporal power and possessions.[84]

It is in the context of 'temporalities' and the nature of the Pope's entitlement to them that Whethamstede cites a group of sources, beginning with Dante:

Iuxta quartos cum quibus concorda[n]t Dans de monarchia mundi Thomas de potestati papali et Alvarus de planctu ecclesie Marsilius de ecclesiastica potestate ac alii multi.

---

[77] It does, however, mention that Boccaccio wrote 'things worthy of note about his own time' (*no-[ta]bilia te[m]pore suo*), which could refer to Boccaccio's *De casibus*, a version of which Whethamstede's colleague Lydgate translated.

[78] See below, pp. 36–7.   [79] On this eventful journey, see Riley 1870–1: 1. 129–82.

[80] Riley 1870–1: 1. 136–8; on his letter to a learned Venetian and its views on rhetoric and reading, see Alakas 2009: 68–72.

[81] See Harvey 1985.   [82] Cambridge, Gonville and Caius College MS 230/116.

[83] See Howlett 1975: 152–3.

[84] Cambridge, Gonville and Caius College MS 230/116, ff. 142ʳ–f. 151ᵛ.

Concurring with those holding the fourth viewpoint [on papal possessions] are Dante [in] Of World Monarchy, Thomas [prob. John of Paris], On [Royal and] Papal Power, Alvaro [Pelayo], On the Lamentation of the Church, Marsilius [of Padua] On Ecclesiastical Power [i.e. *Defensor pacis*], and many others.[85]

The reference to Dante's *Monarchia* here has been seen as 'the first English allusion to this text', and one that thus 'opens interesting possibilities on other manuscripts either [Duke] Humphrey or Whethamstede might have possessed'.[86] But what kind of reference is this, and what kind of reading on the abbot's part might it imply? A cursory scanning of the article might suggest that Whethamstede was aware of Dante's condemnation of the Donation of Constantine in Book 3 of the *Monarchia*, and of his assertion there that the Church, by virtue of its apostolic foundation, is 'utterly unsuited to receiving temporal things'.[87] Indeed, a couple of pages before citing *Dans de monarchia mundi*, Whethamstede has summarized the views of those who claimed that no one could pretend to be a true pontiff,

si presumat temporales divitias in usum p[ro]prium possidere. Et adducu[n]t isti pro ipsis ex scriptura sacra auto[rita]tes plures ut puta *Nolite thesaurizare &c* M[t.] 6° *nolite possidere aurum &c* M[t.] 10°

if he presumes to possess temporal riches for his own use. And in support of their case, they cite many authoritative passages from the holy scriptures, for example: *Lay not up for yourselves treasures etc.* (Matthew 6: 19); *Do not possess gold* (Matthew 10: 9).[88]

The argument that possession of temporal wealth negates the pope's apostolic authority thus parallels Dante's case, and one of the scriptural passages it draws upon (Matthew 10: 9) is actually cited for the same purpose in *Monarchia* 3.10. But Whethamstede attributes this argument to the Waldensians and their followers, not to Dante. Conversely, he lists the Dante of the *Monarchia* amongst those who considered the pope *entitled* to hold temporal possessions, thus imputing to him 'a moderate view of papal power, giving pope and king separate spheres and not deriving the one from the other'.[89] The idea of the separation of temporal and spiritual powers is indeed consistent with Dante's views in Book 3 of the *Monarchia*, but the 'moderate' view that Whethamstede attributes to him on papal property is certainly not.[90]

Where and how might Whethamstede have obtained his rather confused information about the *Monarchia*? Dissemination of Dante's political treatise was very limited in the fourteenth and fifteenth centuries, and only about twenty manuscripts survive today.[91] And although it has been established that Duke Humfrey

---

[85] Cambridge, Gonville and Caius College MS 230/116, f. 145[v].
[86] Petrina 2004: 352.   [87] Dante, *Monarchia* 3.10.14.
[88] Cambridge, Gonville and Caius College MS 230/116, f. 144[r].
[89] Harvey 1985: 117–18.
[90] Harvey 1985: 118. As Harvey points out here: 'at most [Dante] would allow the pope to receive property as a guardian and does not approve wholeheartedly of property owning by the church'. On the argument about property and the authority of the papacy in *Monarchia* 3, see Havely 2004a: 155–7.
[91] See Kay 1998: xxxiii–xxxv. The fourteenth-century manuscripts of the *Monarchia* all date from the second half of the century and may 'show signs of having been regarded as dangerous (hidden amongst other kinds of writing; made anonymous)' (Caesar 1989: 3). For accounts of the manuscripts, see Dante 1995c, and Shaw 2011.

owned and donated copies of Serravalle's *Commedia* and that Whethamstede read the text in this version, there is no evidence of a manuscript of the *Monarchia* having been either in Humfrey's library or in the abbot's collection at St Albans. It seems likely that Whethamstede knew the *Monarchia* at second hand, and that the source for his references both to Dante and to Marsilius of Padua (whose views on papal property he similarly misrepresents) is the attack on both writers by another English Benedictine whose work he knew: the theologian and papal polemicist Adam Easton, who composed a work in which Dante is cited a number of times at Avignon, probably in the 1370s.[92] The first English reading of Dante's *Monarchia* thus involves an earlier cleric who was a contemporary, not of the Abbot of St Albans, but of the poet of the *Canterbury Tales*. It also leads to Avignon as a context for that reading, and as a possible location for the wider transmission of Dante's work.

EASTON'S *MONARCHIA*

Adam Easton (born around 1330 in Norfolk) entered the Benedictine order at the Cathedral Priory in Norwich probably around 1348, made a distinguished academic debut at Oxford in the 1350s, and was highly regarded by his monastic colleagues.[93] Subsequently, however, from about 1368/9 onwards, he was to spend most of his career at the papal curia, initially in Avignon, where he was in the household of the English cardinal Simon Langham until the latter's death in 1376, and acted as a proctor for the English Benedictines.[94] With the Papacy's return to Rome and the election of an Italian pope, Urban VI, in 1378, he relocated to Italy and remained there through the beginning of the schism and through very turbulent times—including imprisonment from 1385 to (probably) 1387 at the hands of the paranoid pope.[95] His last years were spent as 'a venerable man of learning' at the curia of Boniface IX, and his tomb in the church of Santa Cecilia in Trastevere gives the date of his death as September 1397.[96]

Easton's main interests, activities, and influence seem to have been scholarly rather than actively political, but his most substantial surviving work, the *Defensorium ecclesiastice potestatis*, is a polemical text which was probably presented to Urban VI soon after his election in 1378 and gave Easton the status of 'a leading pro-papalist at the outbreak of the Schism'.[97] The *Defensorium* attracted interest

[92] Harvey 1985 (118 with n. 74 and 120 with n. 89) identifies Easton as the likely source for Whethamstede's references to Dante's *Monarchia* and Marsilius's *Defensor pacis*. Whethamstede's library at St Albans contained copies of the work in which Easton cites Dante (the *Defensorium ecclesiastice potestatis*, as discussed below), and he compiled a *tabula* (index) for it; see Bale 1990: 5 and 516, and Sharpe 1996: 567 (no. 18) and 579 (no. 53).

[93] On his early career, see Pantin 1955: 175–7; and *ODNB*, s.v. 'Easton, Adam (*c.*1330–1397), Benedictine monk, scholar, and ecclesiastic'.

[94] MacFarlane 1955: 14–15.   [95] Harvey 1999: 196–202.

[96] MacFarlane 1955: 32–3. Harvey (1999: 211 and n. 187, citing K. Eubel, *Hierarchia catholica medii aevi*, 1 (Münster, 1898), 24) gives the date as 15 August 1398.

[97] Harvey 1999: 213. For earlier accounts of the *Defensorium*, see Grabmann 1931; Pantin 1936 and 1955: 178–80; and MacFarlane 1955.

during the debates about papal authority in the middle of the following century, and its three surviving manuscripts date from that time.[98] The work takes the form of a dialogue between a King (*Rex*) and a Bishop (*Episcopus*), disputing ecclesiastical rights to both temporal and spiritual dominion, and, as the summary of its planned fifth book indicates, one of its main aims is to assert the primacy of the pope's authority as 'the true monarch of the kingdoms of this world'.[99] It is a substantial work (366 folios in the Vatican manuscript) and it eventually secured Easton the main prize of his career: elevation to the cardinalate in 1381. Had its full programme, as laid out in the prologue, been realized it would have been even more substantial: Easton planned six books, one of which would have been devoted entirely to refuting Marsilius of Padua's *Defensor pacis*. In the existing text of the *Defensorium* Marsilius is not much of a presence, but especially in the second half of the work Easton identifies and engages closely with several other adversaries to papal power. One of these is Wyclif, and it has been shown how Easton makes use of *De civili dominio* from the middle of the *Defensorium* onwards.[100] Another was Dante, whose *Monarchia* is cited a number of times in the last third of the existing work.[101]

Book 3 of the *Monarchia* forms the keystone of Dante's thinking on the Papacy—declaring its unsuitedness to be more than a guardian of *temporalia* and denying its claim that the authority of the Empire was dependent on that of the Church. Easton accurately quotes and closely interrogates Dante's text (sometimes at considerable length) on no less than eight occasions, beginning with an exchange, initiated by the King, on the means by which the monarchy (*officium regis*) was instituted in Israel. The Bishop's initial response cites *Dans in suo libello de monarchia mundi* among a number of authorities who deal in various ways with the question:

Episcopus: Dans in suo libello de monarchia mundi in tercio libro eius disputat questionum. Jacobus etiam de Viterbo . . . in libro suo de regimine christiano . . . Quaedam etiam glosa Decretalium . . . tenet quod temporalis jurisdictio & spiritualis sunt penitus disperate & inmediate utraque etiam a Deo, sicut etiam tenet iste Dans—clamans quod contrarie opinionatis solum excita ambicione ducti talem sententiam determinant & figurant.

Bishop: Dante in his little book Of World Monarchy debates this question [on the institution of kingship]; so does James of Viterbo . . . in his book Of Christian Government . . . A certain gloss on the Decretals [?] . . . holds that temporal and spiritual jurisdiction are entirely distinct and that both of them derive immediately from God. This Dante also maintains the same, claiming that those of the contrary opinion are led solely by the promptings of ambition to reach and articulate such a conclusion.[102]

---

[98] These are: Vatican, BAV MS Vat. lat. 4116; Seville, Biblioteca Columbina MS 57-1-7, and Madrid, National Library 738 (see Harvey 1999: 235–6). I have consulted only the Vatican copy.

[99] *Defensorium* in Vatican, BAV MS Vat. lat. 4116, f. 3ᵛ.

[100] MacFarlane 1955: 146; and Harvey 1999: 228.

[101] The first account of Easton's references to Dante's *Monarchia* (as far as I am aware) is in Grabmann 1931: 575; see also the passages from Part 4 of the *Defensorium* transcribed in Macfarlane 1955: 2. 104–5, 138, 142, 228–9.

[102] *Defensorium* in BAV Vat. lat. 4116, f. 293ʳ. Cf. Dante, *Monarchia* 2. 10. 3, 3. 3. 8 (on his opponents), and 3. 16. 1 (on the different jurisdictions).

Drawing upon Easton's avowed 'twenty years of studying the Book of Kings' (including, it seems, the Hebrew text),[103] the Bishop then focuses on the role of the Jewish priesthood, especially Samuel as the vicar of God anointing Saul (1 Sam. 10). The book that the Bishop has cited subsequently provides material for the King, who uses exactly the same terms and simile as Dante's in his response:

Rex: Ista fundamenta opinionis tue Dans in suo libro de monarchia mundi soluit leuiter& refellit, nam dicit quod Samuel non fuit vicarius dei . . . sed Samuel fuit solum dei nuncius uel legatus & solum fecit non ut vicarius sed ut nuncius mandatum domini sibi dictum, & sic quemadmodum malleus operatur in sola uirtute fabri, sic nuncius in eius arbitrio qui hunc misit . . .

King: Dante in his book Of World Monarchy easily deals with and rebuts this basic point in your argument, for he says that Samuel was not God's deputy whose jurisdiction was conferred with legal right and authority (for such a person may act against someone whom his lord does not know), but he was only God's messenger or legate and acted not as a deputy but only as a messenger does when given a message from his lord. And exactly as a hammer strikes only through the strength of the smith, so [does] the messenger [act], following the authority of the one who sent him.[104]

The royal and episcopal debate about Samuel's authority and that of priesthood over kingship continues to rage during the rest of the *Defensorium*, and it invokes, quotes, and disputes Book 3 of the *Monarchia* on a number of further occasions. On one of them the Bishop accuses *Magister Dans* of having misunderstood the Gospel, and the last reference to Dante, near the very end of the whole work, seeks to refute his views on the invalidity of the 'Donation of Constantine'.[105] In most of these citations Easton uses exactly the same name and title that is found in Whethamstede's article on the Papacy in the Cambridge manuscript: *Dans in libro suo de monarchia mundi*. The wider and English implications of Easton's encounter with Dante will be considered later in this chapter, but first we need to take into account the context of his reading and writing in papal Avignon.

DANTE AT AVIGNON

Easton's *Defensorium* was the product of his residence in Avignon, and its appropriation of the *Monarchia* can be seen as one reflection of that papal city's role in the fourteenth-century reception and transmission of Dante. Avignon's literary culture and its intermediary role call for some attention here, as they have a bearing upon several of these clerical readers around Chaucer's time.

Dante's own representations of the Papacy's removal from Rome and of the actions of the two Avignon popes of his lifetime (Clement V and John XXII) had

---

    103 *Defensorium* in BAV Vat. lat. 4116, f. 2ʳ; see also Grabmann 1931: 579; and Harvey 1999: 192.
    104 *Defensorium* in BAV Vat. lat. 4116, f. 294ʳ.
    105 *Defensorium* in BAV Vat. lat. 4116, ff. 325ʳ and 360ʳ.

been unremittingly hostile.[106] It seems that the hostility was mutual: as early as 1320 the first reference to Dante in the Avignon records implicates his name in an alleged Italian plot to poison the second of these popes, John XXII.[107] Towards the end of that decade John XXII's legate in the Romagna, Bertrand du Poujet, condemned and burnt the text of the *Monarchia*—and the pro-papal Dominican Guido Vernani anticipated Adam Easton by attacking it in writing.[108]

Dante's politics and the *Monarchia* also continued to command some significant attention in and around Avignon about the middle of the century. There is evidence at this time of a convergence of interest in the subject—perhaps even some kind of dialogue—between Boccaccio, Petrarch, and at least one other Italian writer, all of whom were engaged in various dealings with the Papacy. In May to June 1354 Boccaccio made the first of his two visits to Avignon—heading a diplomatic delegation from the Florentine Signoria to reassure Innocent VI of the city's loyalty to the Papacy, at a time when renewal of the Holy Roman Empire's involvement in Italian affairs looked imminent.[109] Whilst thus acting in a pro-papal capacity, Boccaccio in the early 1350s was also working on a text that was leading him to take a close look at the earlier Avignon Papacy's treatment of Dante. This text, the first redaction of his *Trattatello in laude di Dante*, is the main source for the Papacy's posthumous campaign against Dante and the *Monarchia*:

Questo libro [*Monarchia*] più anni dopo la morte dell'autore fu dannato da messer Beltrando cardinale del Poggetto e legato di papa nelle parti di Lombardia, sedente Giovanni papa XXII [. . .] il detto cardinale, non essendo chi a ciò s'opponesse, avuto il soprascritto libro, quello in pubblico, sì come cose eretiche contenente, dannò al fuoco. E il simigliante si sforzava di fare dell'ossa dell'auttore a etterna infamia e confusion della sua memoria, se a ciò non si fu opposto uno valoroso e nobile cavaliere fiorentino . . .

This book (*Monarchia*) several years after the death of its author was condemned by Cardinal Bertrand du Poujet, legate of the pope in northern Italy during the pontificate of John XXII . . . The said cardinal, there being no one to oppose him on the matter, got hold of that book and, treating it as a heretical document, publicly consigned it to the flames. And he would have sought to do the same to the bones of its author, to the everlasting shame and destruction of his memory, had he not been prevented from doing so by a courageous and noble Florentine knight . . . [110]

Around this time, too, Petrarch's awareness of Boccaccio's Dante project and a rereading of the *Commedia*—perhaps in a copy that Boccaccio had presented to him around 1351–2—may have served to intensify his sense of Rome and Italy's

---

[106] On Dante and Avignon, see Vasina 1982, and the poet's letter to the Italian cardinals at Avignon (Dante 1966: 121–47).

[107] See Eubel 1897, Michel 1909, and Arnold 2008: 1–9.

[108] On Vernani, see also above, p. 10 with n. 16.

[109] V. Branca, in Boccaccio 1965: 96–7 (of the *profilo biografico*, separately paginated).

[110] Boccaccio 1974: redazione I, paragraphs 196–7.

claim upon his and the Papacy's attention.[111] Having met Boccaccio at Padua in the spring of 1351, he may have been reminded of the papal condemnation of Dante and his idea of Rome, which Boccaccio was about to describe at length in the first redaction of the *Trattatello*. Indeed, writing from Milan a few years later (in the autumn of 1357), Petrarch would describe the book-burning papal legate Bertrand du Poujet himself as a 'bandit' (*predo*) rather than an apostolic emissary, and as one who resembled not St Peter but Hannibal—thus identifying the censor of the *Monarchia* with the greatest enemy ever faced by Rome.[112]

Also around the middle of the century, Petrarch, in the earliest group of the *Sine nomine* letters, was engaging in a more polemical critique of the 'western Babylon' and the pretensions of Avignon's tower-building 'Nimrod' (Clement VI). The second and third of these letters express his support for the short-lived revolution staged in 1347 by the 'tribune' of Rome, Cola di Rienzo, and his concern that Cola should show what could be done for and by 'the Roman people and the whole of Italy'. The fourth of the *Sine nomine* letters dates from the autumn of 1352, when Cola was a prisoner at Avignon; it is addressed to 'the most unconquerable and world-leading people [of Rome]' and is comparable, to some extent, with Book 2 of Dante's *Monarchia* as an investigation of Rome's right to rule.[113] The subject of this letter of Petrarch's was himself a writer on Dante.[114] It may have been during his time as prisoner of the emperor in Bohemia before being transferred (in June 1352) to the custody of Clement VI in Avignon that Cola di Rienzo composed his *Commentarium in Monarchiam Dantis*, which introduces Dante to a wider audience as writer of the *Commedia* and addresses contentious issues about the Papacy's temporal wealth and power.[115]

Dante's political position in relation to the Papacy was thus a very live issue for several significant Italian authors who had had dealings with Avignon in the 1350s, and it is not surprising, therefore, that the *Monarchia* continued to be a text for an English Avignon writer to reckon with later in the century. The accuracy of Easton's quotations indicates that he must have had access to a copy of Dante's text during his years at Avignon in the 1370s.[116] The English Benedictine's knowledge of the *Monarchia* has long been known to historians, but it does not seem to have attracted much attention from Dante scholars. It does not seem to be included in standard accounts of the *Monarchia*'s medieval reception; a recent and

[111] The *Commedia* presented to Petrarch is Vatican MS lat 3199; see Farinelli 1908: 1. 141; Billanovich 1947: 147–8, 161, 163; Mombello 1971: 89; Roddewig 1984: 270–1 (no. 632); and Pulsoni 1993. It contains a note (f. 4ʳ, commenting on *Inferno* 2. 24–7) and some markings which may reflect Petrarch's interest in the *Commedia*'s concerns about Rome, the Papacy, and the Church; see Pulsoni 1993: 157–60 and 198–200.
[112] *Sine nomine* 17, in Petrarca 1974: 182.
[113] Petrarca 1974: 42; my translation; compare Dante, *Convivio* 4.4.8.
[114] See Falconieri 2002: 171–2.
[115] For example, Cola refers his readers to what Dante 'writes in the text of his *Commedia* against the corruption of Church leaders' (*in libro Comedie sue contra Pastorum pravitates expressit*), Ricci 1965: 699.
[116] On the likelihood that the *Monarchia* 'was well known in Avignon', see also Harvey 1999: 226 and n. 163.

very thorough survey of early 'assaults' upon Dante's text does not refer to it; whilst the introduction to a new parallel-text edition simply states that 'before the *editio princeps* of 1559, the *Monarchia* attracted hardly any interest outside of Italy'.[117] We may perhaps have to make at least one exception for the culture of the Avignon curia.

Although there is no mention of the *Monarchia* in the existing Avignon library catalogues nor in the surviving details of Easton's collection, there is some textual evidence to associate both it and Dante's *Commedia* with the papal city. As we have seen, at least one earlier Avignon cardinal (Du Poujet) knew enough about Dante's book to want to burn it;[118] and later in the century one of the few surviving manuscripts of the *Monarchia* suggests a possible connection by following its text of the treatise with Avignon-related material.[119] It may also be significant, from several points of view, that during 1377, the year in which Adam Easton was completing his dialogue with Dante and other anti-papal writers—a southern Italian text of the *Inferno* was being acquired at Avignon. This was not a regular purchase for the papal library and does not appear in the catalogues; instead it was obtained under the terms of the *ius spolii*—a provision instituted in 1316, entitling the pope to the moveable goods of certain deceased clerics. The cleric in question here was a Franciscan, Matteo Porta, who had been archbishop of Palermo since 1367, and among the hundred books in his library appear texts by Ovid, Virgil, and Lucan—together with a paper copy of the *Inferno* with what appear to be southern Italian features:

Item liber de Dantis in papiro, qui incipit 'Nel mezo camin di nostra vita', et finit 'Et quindi simu a vidir li stilli'.

Also a book of Dante, written on paper and beginning: 'In the middle of the way through life' and ending 'And so we emerged to look upon the stars'.[120]

DANTE, EASTON, AND CHAUCER

At the time when that manuscript of the *Inferno* reached Avignon, Adam Easton was relocating from there to Rome. Easton's *Defensorium*, as this chapter has shown, provided a channel by which some specific knowledge of another Dantean text (the *Monarchia*) reached English readers. Easton also possibly anticipated Chaucer as the first English writer to refer to Dante by name. His polemical Latin treatise constitutes a very different context from that of Chaucer's dream-poem, *The House of Fame* (late 1370s/early 1380s) since the English Benedictine

---

[117] Cassell 2004; and Kay 1998: xxxiii.
[118] On Du Poujet and the condemnation of *Monarchia*, see above, pp. 10 and 27–8.
[119] BL Add. 6891, dated to the third quarter of the fourteenth century. On ff. 18–20 a later hand has added a copy of a letter of Clement VI (dated 15 September 1349, from Avignon) to the Archbishop of Salzburg about the forthcoming Jubilee of 1350. On this manuscript and the Avignon material, see Quaglioni 2011 and Shaw 2011: 225-6.
[120] Williman 1980: 264 (no. 98). On other manuscripts of Dante later associated with Avignon, see below, p. 31 and n. 129. On Matteo, see above, p. 13, n. 27.

was taking issue with Dante, not as an authority on the afterlife or literary model, but as a commentator on contemporary and contentious political issues. Moreover, the *Defensorium*'s known English reader, John Whethamstede, seems to have misunderstood or deliberately distorted Easton's account of what *Dans de monarchia mundi* had to say about papal possessions.[121] Yet the two Benedictines were senior and influential figures on the British and international ecclesiastical scene in the late fourteenth and early fifteenth centuries, and the nexus of references in their works, from Easton's *Defensorium* to Whethamstede's *Manipularium doctorum*, implies a continuing clerical conversation about Dante.

The *Defensorium* is not likely to have reached England until a few years after Chaucer's death, but during the 1370s and 1380s the English poet could well have known about the career and interests of this prominent English cleric in Avignon and Rome.[122] Easton and Chaucer were both in Italy during the dramatic events leading to the Great Schism in the late summer of 1378. Easton was then in Rome for Urban VI's election and probably presented the *Defensorium* to him shortly afterwards; whilst Chaucer was on a mission to confer 'on matters concerning the conduct of our war' with Hawkwood and Bernabò Visconti at Milan.[123] The upheaval in papal politics—which Easton witnessed and of which he was eventually a victim—occurred during Chaucer's second Italian visit, and it has been argued that this may underlie the reference to 'Linian' along with Petrarch in the prologue to the *Clerk's Tale*, since the jurist Giovanni da Legnano was then writing on behalf of the Roman pope Urban VI to whom England would also declare allegiance.[124] Easton also knew *Linianus*: he refers to him respectfully several times in the *Defensorium* and both are said to have served as advisers to the pope about the canonization of Bridget of Sweden around 1378–80.[125]

An even closer possible connection between Easton and Chaucer has also been envisaged, and it is one that might have had consequences for the poet's work in the early 1380s. It has been argued that Chaucer's life of St Cecilia in his *Second Nun's Tale* could have been written for the monks of Easton's former house, the Cathedral Priory at Norwich, and as a way of exercising some influence with the English cardinal on behalf of the English Crown.[126] The *Second Nun's Tale* concludes with the burial of the martyred protagonist in the church from which Easton took his name as cardinal and in which he himself would eventually be buried: Santa Cecilia in Trastevere.[127] In the context of contemporary ecclesiastical politics, it has also

---

[121] See above, p. 23. For evidence about the presence of Easton's *Defensorium* in the library at St Albans, and for Whethamstede's reference to it in his *Granarium* (BL Cotton Nero C VI, f. 35ᵛ), see Harvey 1985: 118, n. 74; also above, p. 24, n. 92.

[122] Easton's books arrived at Norwich in 1407; on their subsequent dispersal, see below, p. 32 and n. 134.

[123] On Easton at Rome in 1378, see Harvey 1985: 197–8. MacFarlane (1955: 15 and 147) dates Easton's presentation of the *Defensorium* a little later (*c.*1379–80). On Chaucer's mission to Milan, *pur ascunes busoignes touchantes lexploit de nostre guerre*, see Crow and Olson 1966: 54.

[124] McCall 1965: 484–9.

[125] MacFarlane 1955: 171; Harvey 1999: 199–200 and 229–30.

[126] Giffin 1956: 29–48.   [127] Giffin 1956: 38–40.

been suggested that Chaucer's choice and treatment of material in the *Tale* could echo concerns about the Great Schism itself.[128]

Indeed, the authoritative and subsequently mutilated figure of Cecilia could be seen as in part an image of the suffering and enduring Church. The name of the early pope who presides over the burial of the saint is reiterated by Chaucer with some frequency in the *Tale* and is the same as that of the Roman pope supported by Easton and his countrymen: Urban. And, to stretch speculation a little further: if the *Second Nun's Tale*, or word of it had reached the cardinal of Norwich and of Santa Cecilia at Rome, he would also have been struck by both the Dantean and the Marian features of its prologue. To an English Benedictine writer who had earlier entered into detailed argument with *magister Dans* and was in the 1380s himself engaged in texts relating to the cult of the Virgin, Chaucer's rewriting of the invocation to Mary from the last canto of the *Paradiso* would probably have been of some interest.

AVIGNON, KONSTANZ, AND BRITISH READERS

In the early fifteenth century Dante's circuitous route towards a British readership also involved texts, readers, and writers associated with Avignon. During the closing years of the Avignon anti-Papacy two manuscripts of and a commentary on Dante's *Commedia* are mentioned in its records. A catalogue produced for the last Avignon pope, Benedict XIII, in 1407 lists a manuscript of 'Dante' (presumably the *Commedia*) and describes it simply as *in vulgari ytalico*. Later (around 1417), among a much shorter list of books 'to be bought (*emendi*) for the Benedict's library in Spain, is 'Dante translated from Tuscan into Latin'—*reductus de lingua florentina ad latinam*—and this may, as we shall see, be a copy of a very recent translation of the *Commedia*: the one that had been completed at Konstanz by Giovanni Bertoldi da Serravalle.[129]

Evidence about other responses to Dante in earlier Avignon culture, as we have seen, is tantalizingly fragmentary.[130] Yet one of the three senior clerics mentioned as supporters of Serravalle's project was an Avignon cardinal, Amedeo di Saluzzo (*c.*1361–1419), who had been a leading advocate for Petrarch at the papal city in the 1380s and 1390s.[131] In associating himself with two English bishops as an instigator of Serravalle's translation, the (Piedmontese) Italian Amedeo was

[128] Hirsh 1977: 129–33.

[129] See Faucon 1886: 2. 140 (item 935); and Jullien de Pommerol and Monfrin 1991: 1. 221 (item 405) and 2.767 (item 322).

[130] See above, p. 29; also Mombello 1971: 88–9, and Roddewig 1984: 282–3 (no. 660).

[131] Amedeo is mentioned alongside the English bishops in Serravalle's dedications and conclusions; see Serravalle 1891: 3, 5, and 1215. On his career, see: Serravalle 1891: xx–xxi; Chacón 1630: 1010; Berton 1857: 1499; Jarry 1873: 446–50; and the online *Cardinals of the Holy Roman Church*, at <http://www2.fiu.edu/~mirandas/bios1383a.htm#Saluzzo>. For his role in Avignon culture, see: Coville 1934:178; Simone 1961: 26; Sottili 1966; Ornato 1969: 161; and Cecchetti 1996: 56, 59, 73.

continuing to promote Italian writing and engaging in an Anglo-Italian conversation about Dante.

Serravalle's translation of the *Commedia* was probably brought to Britain by one of those English bishops—Nicholas Bubwith of Bath and Wells—soon after the end of the Council of Konstanz.[132] Ten years earlier, the late Cardinal Adam Easton's library had been delivered to his former monastery at Norwich in six barrels.[133] Only nine of its nearly 300 volumes can now be identified, and there is no evidence that works by Dante were among them, but—with its quotations from *Dans de monarchia mundi*—it does seem to have reached Norwich in 1407 and later to have been copied and provided with an index (*tabula*) at the library of another Benedictine house, St Albans, by a clerical reader, John Whethamstede, who, as we have seen, would continue to cite *Dans de Monarchia Mundi*, as well as the vernacular author of the *notabiles comedias* that had been commented upon by those two Italian friars.[134]

The work of these clerical writers, moving around Europe and around the time of Chaucer, thus shows that Dante was a name to be reckoned with in the actual and possible dialogues between England and Italy at that time. Such a reckoning involved, as we have seen with the two Italian Franciscans, recognizing and promoting, glossing, and even translating the *Commedia* and its vernacular author—activities that were occurring contemporaneously among other classes (merchants and aristocrats) and in other speech-communities (such as France, Castile, and Catalonia).[135] English clerical reception at this time also—in the cases of the two English Benedictines, Easton and Whethamstede—reflects an emphasis in several ways on Dante's Latinity and the Latinizing of Dante to which the culture of Avignon contributed.

In the case of the *Monarchia* (as cited by Easton and then by Whethamstede) there is a response to Dante as both eminent Latin author and political voice, but Whethamstede, in preparing his article on 'Poets', also recognized that 'the Florentine poet wrote in his vernacular speech three remarkable comedies'. Dante's status as vernacular poet would be acknowledged in fifteenth-century Britain, and not only by that Tuscan merchant who bought a copy of the *Commedia* in London on 1 August 1451. It would also be evident 'around Chaucer' through the multiplication of manuscripts and (later in the century) printed editions in which Chaucer had named and appropriated 'the wise poete of Florence' and 'the grete poete of Ytaille'.[136] Claims about the status of the vernacular 'maker', issues of religious politics, and Latinity too, will continue to affect British responses to Dante in the early sixteenth century.

---

[132] See above, p. 17.

[133] In 1407; *CCR Henry IV vol. 3 (1405–9)*, p. 299.

[134] On Whethamstede's acquisition of and index for the *Defensorium*, see above, p. 24 and n. 92. On Easton's library and its further dispersal, see Harvey 1999: 222–4.

[135] See Friederich 1950: 14–45 and 58–62; more recently, *DE* 259 and 279–83.

[136] See Appendix 1 (Chronology, for 1477, *c.*1483, and 1532).

2

The 'Goodly Maker': Conscripting Dante in Henrician England

Around 1513 to 1515 an English scholar, John Pennant, was in Italy, enrolled at the University of Perugia.[1] It was probably then that he acquired a book which he would present to a prominent courtier, Henry Parker, tenth Baron Morley, in 1520: the earliest known copy of the *Commedia* to have been inscribed by a British reader.[2] Shortly before Pennant's gift to Morley, an Eton schoolmaster had placed Dante's name at the head of a list of 'goodly makers of feyned narrations'.[3] A few years later, at a difficult time for Henry VIII's government in the mid-1530s, one of the king's propagandists cited Dante on the subject of popular discontent, describing him as 'that good Italian poet'.[4] And in the 1540s Dante's name would be conscripted both to bolster the prestige of Henrician culture and to help legitimize the Reformation.[5]

Reception of Dante in England during the first half of the sixteenth century has received relatively little attention so far, although much work has recently been done on the 'cultural revolution' of the time and the ways in which its medieval past was then being mapped and read.[6] This chapter will therefore focus on three main areas of enquiry: the circulation of Dantean texts in the period; the perception of the poet's status, especially in relation to England as 'empire'; and his potential for recruitment as a 'proto-Protestant' writer.[7] Within the wider context of early Tudor culture, it will also be concerned with two of the myths that have been identified in the argument about literary tradition at this time: 'myths of empire and myths about the continuity of Protestant thought'.[8]

---

[1] On Pennant, see below, p. 41 with n. 56.

[2] The 1493 Venice edition of the *Commedia* with Cristoforo Landino's commentary, now in the John Rylands Library, Manchester. On Pennant's inscription and his conversation with Morley about Dante, see below, pp. 41–2.

[3] Horman 1519; see below, pp. 36–7.

[4] Morison 1536; see below, pp. 37–8.

[5] By Morley (1543) and Bale (*c*.1545); see below, pp. 40, 42, and 47.

[6] For example: Ross 1991; Gordon 1996; Simpson 2002; Walker 2005; McMullan and Matthews 2007.

[7] It thus includes material from an earlier article on the subject: Havely 2010.

[8] Ross 1991: 61.

EARLY TUDOR DANTES

What were the means by which English readers in the first half of the sixteenth century could have accessed Dante's text? Firm evidence about circulation of the *Commedia*—not to mention other Dantean works—in England is still quite sparse at this time, as it is during the previous two centuries. As we have seen, in the later fourteenth century Chaucer and his less well-known contemporary Adam Easton probably had access to manuscripts, but we do not know what kind of manuscripts they were and can only guess at how these English readers obtained them;[9] whilst the earliest documented evidence about an original manuscript of the *Commedia* coming to England is a note in the 'book bought in London' by an Italian in 1451.[10]

With the advent of the first printed editions of the *Commedia* in the 1470s and the growing importation of books from Italy in the early Tudor period, the likelihood of Dante's work arriving by this means increases.[11] Scholarly travellers, such as the English students who frequented the University of Padua in the 1520s, could quite easily have obtained the *Commedia* in any one of the sixteen editions that had been printed at Venice; and by the end of Henry VIII's reign twenty-nine editions of the *Commedia* and three of the *Convivio* had been published by presses in Italy.[12]

Readers in Henrician England also had access to Dante by other means, including the *Commedia* in other languages. Since early in the previous century English readers of Latin would have been able to find the poem in the prose translation with commentary which had been completed by Giovanni Bertoldi da Serravalle at the Council of Konstanz.[13] The presence of Serravalle's Dante at Oxford and at the cathedral library in Wells was recorded by Henry VIII's self-styled 'antiquary' John Leland during his topographical and literary itineraries through England and Wales from 1533 to 1542. Leland noted in some detail the origin and associations of Oxford's copy of the *Commentarii Joannis de Serauala ... Latine scripti, super opera Dantis Aligerii*, and in the earliest edition of his survey this entry is accompanied by a number of references to Duke Humfrey and his books.[14] Rather more elliptical and enigmatic is Leland's listing of *Dantes tra[ns]latus in carmen* [sic] *Latinum* as the

---

[9] On Chaucer's means of access to Dante see Havely 2005: 313–22, and above, pp. 4 and 8–9.

[10] See above, Prologue, pp. 1–3. On the 'large but diminishing Italian mercantile community' in early Tudor London, comprising Genoese, Florentines, Lucchesi, and representatives of Venetian companies, see Bratchel 1978 and 1980. On other groups of Italian expatriates in early Tudor England, see Trapp 1999: 303–5; Mumford 1971; and Wyatt 2005: 47–64.

[11] See Ruddock 1951: 75 (on books traded by Venetian galleys in 1488 and 1495). Venice appears to have dominated the market, providing 32 per cent of all books imported to England and Scotland in the 1490s, but its share diminished rapidly in the early sixteenth century; see Lane Ford 1999: 184–5 (with fig. 8.1) and 190.

[12] On the English at Padua, see Woolfson 1998; for the Venetian and other editions of the *Commedia*, see Richardson 1995: 255–8.

[13] On Serravalle's translation and commentary, see above, pp. 15–18.

[14] Leland 1715: 3. 58.

fourth among forty-seven items at the cathedral library in Wells, Somerset, and this item was also probably Serravalle's version.[15] Amid the upheaval of the Henrician and Edwardian Reformations, the dissolution of the monasteries, and the dispersal of libraries, both the Wells and Oxford texts were in a precarious position and have since disappeared.

At the time when Leland's laborious itineraries were reaching their conclusion, evidence emerges about another translation of Dante that had been owned by a devout Catholic reader even closer to the court of Henry VIII. In the 1542–3 inventory of the 'goods of Westminster Palace', one of the items listed is 'Dantis workes in the Castilian tonge'.[16] This Castilian Dante was once thought to be a manuscript of the early fifteenth-century prose translation of the *Commedia* by Enrique Villena, but it was probably the printed translation of the *Inferno* by Pedro Fernández de Villegas *de lengua toscana en verso castellano* (Burgos, 1515), which was dedicated to Juana de Aragon, was owned by Henry VIII's first wife, Catherine of Aragon, and is now in the British Library.[17] Villegas's verse *Inferno* would thus have been among the twenty-one books (including two Petrarch texts) which came into Henry's possession after her death in 1536, and which reflect both the queen's concern to keep up her Spanish connections and the range of her pious and studious interests later in life.[18]

Other ways in which Dante's name and text reached British readers at this time are more fragmentary, but they too have connections with the Henrician court. During the previous century, along with circulation of Serravalle's Latin *Commedia*, allusions to and even some translation of Dante would have been disseminated through manuscripts (and later printing) of Chaucer. Following the first printings of Chaucer's work by Caxton, Pynson, and De Worde in the last three decades of the fifteenth century (and the Pynson reprints of 1526), Chaucer finds prominence for a court readership in 1532 through the edition produced by Henry VIII's Clerk of the Kitchen, William Thynne.[19] Thynne's edition included a new text of the poem in which Chaucer introduced and named Dante to readers of English for the first time: *The House of Fame*.[20] Along with this went the allusions to the *Commedia* in several of Chaucer's other short poems and the *Troilus*, as well as his citing of 'the grete poete of Ytaille' and/or the paraphrasing of passages from his work in texts such as the *Monk's*, *Wife of Bath's*, and *Friar's Tales*.[21]

Chaucer also has some bearing upon the second main subject of this chapter's investigation: that of Dante's status as vernacular and canonical poet before and

[15] Leland 1715: 3. 155.   [16] London, TNA E.315/160 no. 222.
[17] *DEL* 1.32 and (for the later identification) Carley 2004:120–1.
[18] Carley 2004: 120–1. Amongst the potentially consolatory items in the queen's collection, there is another Castilian translation, that of Petrarch's *De remediis utriusque fortunae* (Saragossa, 1518).
[19] See Boswell 1999: 1–2 and 11–12.
[20] Thynne's text of *The House of Fame* is considered to have some independent textual authority and is cited in modern editions of the poem alongside the three fifteenth-century manuscript witnesses and Caxton's 1483(?) print.
[21] See Boswell 1999: 1–2, 4, 7, and 10. Comparable references, including the description of Chaucer as 'Daunte in englisshe' would also have been found in two early printed editions of Lydgate's *Fall of Princes* (1494 and 1527); see Boswell 1999: 5 and 10.

during the Henrician Reformation. Since the late fourteenth century Dante had been regularly acknowledged as one of the 'three crowns of Florence' (along with Petrarch and Boccaccio): the triumvirate features in the Italian humanists' canon from the beginning of the fifteenth century onwards, and its pre-eminence seems to have been acknowledged in England shortly afterwards, when Abbot Whetham-stede names all three Italians as the only vernacular writers among his compendium of poets.[22] Not long after Whethamstede, a parallel English vernacular triumvirate was beginning to emerge, comprising Chaucer, Gower, and Lydgate. This canon-ical formation is evident in Caxton's printing of English authors during the 1480s, and it is clearly articulated by writers such as Ashby, Dunbar, Hawes, and Skelton in the decades between 1470 and the beginning of the sixteenth century.[23] Not surprisingly, then, a convergence between the English and Italian triumvirates begins to take place, and evidence for it can be found early in Henry VIII's reign.

Foreshadowings of such a parallel emerge in Skelton's *Garlande or Chaplet of Laurell*, begun in 1495 and printed in 1523. Here, in an encounter with a host of classical and vernacular poets—including 'Bochas' and 'Petrarke' (ll. 365, 379)—the laureate 'Skelton' finds himself singled out by the 'Englysshe poetis thre' (Gower, Chaucer, Lydgate), who greet him in turn with 'godely chere' and accompany him to the pavilion of Pallas Athene (ll. 386–448).[24] Dante's shadowy presence in this encounter—despite his absence from the Italian list—is implied by the marked similarity between Skelton's scenario and the Florentine pilgrim's meeting with his five pagan predecessors in Limbo.[25]

A more explicit link between the Italian and English triumvirates was made in 1519, when the schoolmaster, grammarian, and fellow of Eton College, William Horman, published his *Vulgaria uiri doctissimi*, a guide to writing Latin by means of the translation of English sentences on a wide range of topics, from religion and government to architecture and household management.[26] Horman's work is divided into thirty-seven chapters, the eighth of which is on 'training of the mind' (*de cultu animi*). Here, in between sentences about study and generalization and about Aesop and Apuleius as 'maruaylous feynars of morall talys', he includes a list of vernacular authors:

Dantes Patrarcke/Boccasse/Chaucer/Gowar/and Lydgate were goodly makers of feyned narratio[n]s.

Dantes Patrarcha/Boccatius/Chaucerus/Gowarus/et Lidgattus fuerunt egregii logographi.[27]

---

[22] See Thompson and Nagel 1972: 34, 85–6, and 90–1 (for examples from Bruni, Palmieri, and Manetti) and above, pp. 21–2 (for Whethamstede's account of the triumvirate).

[23] Lerer 1999: 729–30; see also Brewer 1978: 6, 81–5 and Simpson 2002: 41, n. 26.

[24] Petrarch may have attained some presence at the Henrician court not only through the interest of poets such as Skelton and Wyatt, but also through musical settings of his work; see Mumford 1971: 60–7.

[25] On the composition of the *Garlande*, see Scattergood 1983: 496. The parallel with the welcoming of Dante into the company of the five pagan poets (*Inferno* 4. 85–105) is noted by King 1982: 44.

[26] London 1519, repr. 1530; see also Boswell 1999: 9 and 11. On Horman's books, see also Birley 1970: 9 and 11 and *ODNB*, s.v. 'Horman, William (1457–1535), schoolmaster and librarian'.

[27] Horman, *Vulgaria* f. 89ᵛ.

This does not, of course, imply knowledge of Dante as more than a name.[28] Yet the act of naming itself carries some significance: the parallel between the 'crowns' of Florence and those of the medieval English vernacular is presented by Horman as something that every schoolboy—or at least every Etonian schoolboy—ought by this time to know.[29]

In the course of the Henrician Reformation views of the English medieval triumvirate would undergo considerable change. The Benedictine monk Lydgate's religious works cease to be published after 1534, and he is 'omitted from a much more restricted version of the pre-Reformation official literary canon', whilst by the early 1540s a Protestantized Chaucer 'had been isolated as the official Tudor representative'.[30] Conversely, the Florentine triumvirate continues to be imprinted for the English reader during the rest of the century and beyond, for instance through Hoby's and Bartholomew Clerke's English and Latin translations of Castiglione's *Libro del Cortegiano*.[31] What, then, were the implications for the perception of Dante during Henry VIII's and Cromwell's 'cultural revolution' of the 1530s and 1540s?

'THAT GOOD ITALYANE POET' AND HIS USES

Dante's authority is deployed alongside that of Chaucer in a text which addresses one of the most dramatic moments in the Henrician Reformation: the 'Pilgrimage of Grace' risings that took place in Lincolnshire and Yorkshire during the autumn of 1536 as a protest against the king's new religious policy.[32] A vigorous governmental response to the rebellion was expressed in a tract called *A Remedy for Sedition*.[33] Its author, Richard Morison, at that time in his late twenties, was making his way in the new order of things, and has been characterized as 'the man who wielded far and away the best propagandist pen in Henrician England'.[34] He had studied at Padua in the early 1530s and would later provide intelligence from Italy for Henry's principal secretary (and later vicegerent in Spirituals), Thomas Cromwell, at a crucial time during the breach with Rome.[35] Recalled to England in May 1536, he became a member of Cromwell's household, and it is from this position at the centre of government that his writings on Henry VIII's supremacy and on obedience to royal authority were delivered. Directing his *Remedy for Sedition* against the northern rebels, Morison opens his argument on

---

[28] A *nominis umbra*, as Wilson (1946: 50) hastens to emphasize.

[29] For later sixteenth-century examples of English triumvirates paralleling the three crowns of Florence, see below, p. 71.

[30] Simpson 2002: 40–1 and 330–1.   [31] *DEL* 1. 48 and Boswell 1999: 23, 42–3.

[32] For a recent account of the 1536 risings, see Bernard 2005: 293–404.

[33] Ed. Berkowitz 1984.

[34] Elton 1972: 199. On Morison's career and writings, see: Berkowitz 1984; Mottram 2005; *ODNB*, s.v., 'Morison, Sir Richard (c.1510–1556), humanist and diplomat'; and, more recently and fully, Sowerby 2010.

[35] Woolfson 1998: 63–72 and 117.

behalf of the powers that be by citing examples 'to shewe the lyghtnes and lewde iudgement of [the] communes', immediately going on to note that

> Dante, that good Italyane poet seyth full truely of them [the commons], It is seldome sene, that the people crie not, *Viua la mia morte, muoia la mia vita*, That is, Let lyue my dethe, lette dye my lyfe, let that go forthe that bryngeth my distruction, lette that be banysshed, that is my welthe and safegarde.[36]

The ultimate source for this is Dante's attack in *Convivio* 1. 11. 54 on the 'blindness' of those Italians who devalue their own vernacular. It is possible that Morison may have known the *Convivio* itself; following its *editio princeps* (Florence, 1490), it had been printed at Venice in 1521 and 1529, and Morison had been in Padua during the following decade. He could also have accessed Dante through Machiavelli's *Discorsi* on Livy, which misattributes the quotation to the *Monarchia* but places it within a more immediately relevant context: a discussion of how 'the populace, deceived by false goods, often seek their own destruction'.[37] As his library list (probably compiled *c.*1550) shows, Morison read widely in Italian authors, including Petrarch, Boccaccio, and the *quattrocento* humanists, and the anti-papal Dante would have been of interest to him.[38]

Morison's appropriation of Dante in the *Remedy for Sedition* has wider cultural and political implications. Following his Dantean/Machiavellian portrayal of the people's perversity, he goes on to note ironically that 'Geffrey Chauser sayeth also somewhat in their prayse' (sig. B 1[r]). He then quotes (not quite accurately) the stanza on the ill-judgement and inconstancy of the populace from Chaucer's *Clerk's Tale*—and it has been suggested that the Petrarchan and Boccaccian antecedents of this text enable Morison to demonstrate further, for a king to whom Thynne's 1532 edition of Chaucer had been dedicated, 'the vitality of the humanist bond between England and Italy'.[39] Morison's deployment of classical as well as vernacular literary authorities, such as Chaucer and Dante, also needs to be seen in terms of his chief polemical purpose in the *Remedy*: to argue for due obedience to the quasi-imperial authority of the king. He thus later on draws a parallel between the (false) offer of pardon which 'our most gracious sovereign lord' was then extending to the rebels and 'the clemency of [Emperor] Augustus'.[40]

Henry VIII's claim to imperial authority formed part of the platform of the 'King's Reformation'. Early in his reign Henry had used the adjective 'imperial' in the naming of royal ships, and had claimed in his treatise against Luther (1521) that Rome had conferred on the English monarchy 'our crown imperial'.[41] As the challenge to papal authority over the king's marriage intensified in the early

---

[36] Morison, *Remedy for Sedition* sig. B 1[r].   [37] Machiavelli, *Discorsi*, bk. 1, ch. 53.
[38] Berkowitz 1984: 66, 74, 147, and 149, n. 13. Sowerby (2006: 43, n. 90) considers it 'possible that [Morison] had read Dante's works'. Dante does not feature in the list of nearly 500 volumes (BL Add. MS 40676) which Sowerby was the first to attribute to Morison; however, Petrarch and Boccaccio are listed here (ff. 113[r] and 114[v]), as is Horman's *Vulgaria* (f. 113[r]).
[39] Berkowitz 1984: 150.   [40] Berkowitz 1984: 126.
[41] Scarisbrick 1997: 270. It was an Italian writer and Latin Secretary to Henry, Andrea della Rena (Ammonio), who had greeted his succession in 1509 with verses identifying him as Octavius and Augustus; see Rundle 1995: 74 and Wyatt 2005: 59–61 and 282, n. 156.

1530s, Henry's supporters publicly asserted his claim to imperial status, which was further buttressed by the iconography of the domed crown on the Great Seal (1532), by the assertion in the 1533 Act of Appeals that 'this Realme of Englond is an Impire', and by recourse to the precedent of Constantine as British king and Roman emperor.[42] Morison's conscription of such medieval authors in the *Remedy* for this 'imperialist' agenda coincides in time and purpose with a British rewriting of Dante's contemporary, Marsilius of Padua. In the 1535 translation of the *Defensor pacis* by William Marshall, a fellow member of Cromwell's intellectual entourage, the Henrician *imperium* is again at issue, and here the legislator is recast as the 'Lutheran godly prince', exercising 'supreme coercive jurisdiction'.[43]

A similar convergence of ideas had taken place slightly earlier in the 1530s, in the preface to Thynne's edition of Chaucer. Here Thynne's collaborator, the king's secretary and treasurer of the chamber Sir Brian Tuke, dedicates the work to 'my most grattious souerayne lorde H[en]ricus the eight', presenting Chaucer as a linguistic and poetic renewal in his own time, as an editorial 'restauracion' for the present, and as 'an ornament of the tonge of this your realme'.[44] Committing the project to the shield of 'royall protection and defence', Tuke then concludes by locating the source of that 'defence' in

the glorious tytell of Defensor of the christen faithe | whiche by your noble progenytour | the great Co[n]stantyne | somtyme kyng of this realme | & emperour of Rome was nexte god and his apostles | chefely maynteyned corroborate | and defended.[45]

A few years after Tuke's preface and Morison's *Remedy*, Henry's claims to imperial authority would once again be linked to Dante and Italian culture, in another work dedicated to the king by Henry Parker, tenth Baron Morley. Morley had more long-standing courtly connections than either Tuke or Morison. He had been brought up in the household of Henry VII's mother, Margaret Beaufort, attended Catherine of Aragon at the Field of the Cloth of Gold in 1520, was linked by his daughter's marriage to the Boleyn family, and counted Thomas Cromwell as a 'singular good friend' in the 1530s, presenting him later in that decade with copies of Machiavelli's *Istorie fiorentine* and *Il principe*.[46] At the same time he cultivated the friendship of Princess Mary, whose restoration of the old religion on her accession to the throne Morley was to greet with an allusion to the *Nunc dimittis*. This 'deeply conservative backwoods peer' survived and prospered through turbulent times by assiduously demonstrating allegiance to the regime in power: he was, for example, party to the convictions for treason of both his son-in-law Viscount

---

[42] See Koebner 1953, Ullmann 1979: 195–203, Scarisbrick 1997: 271–3, and Bernard 2005: 202. For recent discussion of imperial ideas and their expression in this period, see Mottram 2008.

[43] On Marshall's translation, and its rewriting of parts of the text to represent Marsilius's legislator in this light, see Lockwood 1991, esp. 91–3, n. 31, and 109.

[44] Thynne 1532: sig. A iii[r]. On Tuke's collaboration with Thynne in this edition, see Walker 2005: 56–72.

[45] Thynne 1532: sig. A iii[r].

[46] *ODNB*, s.v. 'Parker, Henry, tenth Baron Morley (1480/81–1556), nobleman and translator'.

Rochford (brother of Anne Boleyn) in 1536 and his own daughter, Lady Rochford, in February 1542.[47]

Less than a year after his daughter's execution (for complicity in Catherine Howard's adultery) Morley presented to the king an ornate manuscript of his translation of the first forty-six lives from Boccaccio's *De mulieribus*—a gift which 'may well represent . . . a "public" repudiation . . . of his daughter's actions and an act of submission to Henry'.[48] Empire and its renewal is a theme that runs through the dedicatory preface to this translation: it begins by wishing an 'infynyte of yeres to your imperiall Maieste', and ends by presenting the work 'vnto yo[ur] imperiall dignyte'.[49] In between these points Morley traces the decline and renewal of 'eloquens and goode lernynge' from Cicero, Virgil, and others in 'the greate Augustus days' to their subsequent 'decay' and present revival, which he dates to the reign of one of Henry's fourteenth-century 'imperial' ancestors: ' . . . in the time of the flowre and hono[ur] of prynces, Kynge Edwarde, the thyrde of that name, holdynge by ryghte the septre of thys imperiall realme, as yo[ur] Grace nowe dothe . . . '[50] Instead, however, of associating such a revival of imperial learning and letters with Chaucer (as Tuke might have done), Morley goes on immediately to identify it with the three crowns of Florence, beginning with Dante. Thus he describes how in Edward III's time

there sprang in Italy three excellente clerkes. The fyrst was Dante, for hys great learnynge in hys mother tunge surnamyde dyvyne Dante. Surely, not withoute cause. For it is manyfest that it was true, whiche was grauen on hys tumbe, that hys maternall eloquens touchede so nyghe the prycke that it semyde a myracle of nature. And forbecause that one shuld not thynke I do feyne, I shall sett the wordes in the Italiane tunge, whych is thys:

> Dante alegra son minerua obscura
> De arte & de intelligentia nel cui ingenio.
> Le elegantia mat[er]na aio[n]se al scengo.
> Que se tient pour miracol de natura.[51]

Morley's account of Dante's status within the empire of letters and its history was conditioned by several factors. He was reading Dante to some extent in the context of Boccaccio and Petrarch, about whose work (as this preface shows) he is specific and knowledgeable. Immediately after this description of Dante he acknowledges the wide circulation in Italy of Petrarch's 'sonnetes [and] hys Tryumphes or hys other rhymes', along with a number of Latin works, such as the *Africa* and the widely disseminated *Remedia utriusque fortunae*, a Castilian translation of which had consoled Catherine of Aragon in her later years.[52] Petrarch's *Triumphi* may

---

[47] See Starkey 2000: 20.   [48] See Carley 2000*b*: 43.
[49] Chatsworth, Devonshire Collection MS ff. 1ʳ and 2ʳ; Wright 1943: 1 and 3; also in *DEL* 1.33.
[50] Chatsworth, Devonshire Collection MS f. 2ᵛ; Wright 1943: 2; also in *DEL* 1.34.
[51] Chatsworth, Devonshire Collection MS f. 2ᵛ; Wright 1943: 2; also in *DEL* 1.34. This (garbled) quotation may be translated: 'I am Dante Alighieri, the dark divine source of wisdom and art, in whose work the elegance of the mother tongue so struck home as to be considered a miracle of nature.' See below, n. 54.
[52] See above, p. 35 and n. 18.

have been the first of Morley's own translation projects, composed in the 1520s but not printed until the 1550s. His knowledge of Boccaccio's work includes not only *De mulieribus claris* (which had been printed at Basle and Berne in 1531 and 1539) but also, as the preface here shows, the *Decameron, De casibus*, and the *Genealogiae*.[53] His view of Dante's 'maternall eloquens', moreover, appears to have been transmitted through his reading of Boccaccio, since the 'epitaph' he quotes is not one of those written by Dante's contemporaries but is instead a mangled version of the first quatrain of a sonnet which was once attributed to Boccaccio and was said to have been intended to preface a copy of the *Commedia*.[54]

There is evidence that Morley himself had since 1520 owned an early printed edition of the *Commedia*. The John Rylands Library in Manchester early in the last century acquired a copy of the 1493 Venetian edition, with Landino's commentary and illustrated with woodcuts at the start of each canto.[55] On the recto of the first illustrated page it carries the following inscription:

.1520.

Mag[istr]o D[omin]o meo, Do[mino] Morleyo, Jo. Pennandus dono mittit:⁓
Ideo mentiebar hu[n]c Da[n]ten Petrarcha formosiorem,
quo te in mei ac rer[um] mear[um] desyderium m[a]gis
ince[n]derem:⁓

Vale

Tuus Jo: P:

1520. To my lord and master Lord Morley John Pennant sends this gift.
Therefore, I wrongly claimed this Dante to be more beautiful than Petrarch, for whom, through you, my enthusiasm should have been more greatly inflamed. Greetings from your John Pennant.

The donor of this Dante was probably the John Pennant who studied at Cambridge (1502–3) and in Italy (1513–15) and was canon and prebendary of St Paul's in London from 1524 till his death in 1529.[56] His inscription clearly reflects some kind of conversation between the cleric and the courtier about the relative merits of these two 'crowns of Florence'. It also records Morley's interest in Petrarch, which led him to produce a translation of the *Triumphi* which was 'undertaken for Henry [VIII] some time in the late 1520s or earlier'.[57] Despite Pennant's downplaying of Dante by comparison with Petrarch, his *Commedia* seems to have been treated with considerable respect by its aristocratic recipient, and some time between 1521 and 1533 the king's bookbinder adorned its new covers with stamps of the royal coat of arms, St George's Cross, the Tudor rose, and even the Castilian pomegranate

---

[53] On the early editions of *De mulieribus claris*, see Scarpati 1977: 214.

[54] *DEL* 1.34. The lines are no longer thought to be by Boccaccio.

[55] Dante 1493.

[56] Pennant also served as chamberlain (1515, 1517) and warden (1523–5) of the English Hospice in Rome. I am grateful to Dr Julianne Simpson of the John Rylands Library for a summary of the information about his career. Some details are also in Venn and Venn 1924: 3. 341.

[57] *ODNB*, s.v. 'Parker, Henry, tenth Baron Morley (1480/81–1556), nobleman and translator'. See also Carley 2000*a*: 28–9 and 40–2.

(Catherine of Aragon's badge). So, although this is unlikely to be 'Henry VIII's Own Copy' of the *Commedia*—as a later optimistic book-dealer claimed—it is certainly one that was highly valued by one of his courtiers.[58] When Morley was translating Petrarch's Italian and Boccaccio's Latin, he could thus have sampled some of their predecessor's verse in the original.[59] By the time he wrote in his dedication to *De mulieribus claris* of how in Plantagenet times 'there sprang in Italy three excellente clerkes', he may well have read in his *Commedia*'s preface about Florentines who were 'outstanding (*excellenti*) in learning and eloquence'.[60] And a few years after Morley's English tribute to the poet 'in hys mother tunge surnamyde *dyvyne* Dante', an enterprising Italian publisher would give the *Commedia* the additional title of *Divina*.[61]

Through Morley's acknowledgment of their canonical status, Dante and his two compatriots are thus becoming denizened in Henrician England in a way that reinforces (as Morison had done) the humanistic bond with Italy and occludes the pre-Reformation English tradition. It has been noted that Morley makes no reference to the English tradition here or elsewhere in his work, and his adoption of the humanists' literary stance implies 'that Henry is the new Augustus; that cultivation of literature and imperial power are mutually sustaining; and that the renovation of imperial letters is about to begin in England'.[62]

What is not evident here—even at this late stage of Henry VIII's reign—is any explicit attempt to 'protestantize' Dante, notwithstanding the fact that such an operation had already been performed on the corpus of Chaucer's works that year, through the addition of the virulently anticlerical *Plowman's Tale* (*c.*1532) to the 1542 edition of Thynne's *Workes*.[63] Morley himself was capable of some quite energetic anti-papalism, as had been demonstrated by a commentary on one of the Psalms which he published three or four years before the Boccaccio translation.[64] This tract shares some political and polemical ground with the Boccaccio preface: for instance, its own preface addresses the king as presiding over the renewal of 'this youre Empire mooste triumphant', following its liberation from 'the Babylonicall seate of the Romyshe byshop'.[65] It presents Henry as the ruler anointed to govern

---

[58] The use of this prestigious binding led the dealers who sold this *Commedia* to the John Rylands Library early in the twentieth century (J. & J. Leighton) to claim that Morley 'held it in such high esteem that he deemed it worthy of presentation to his Sovereign who, in his turn thought so highly of it that it was bound by the Royal Binder, John Reynes' (Leighton catalogue, n.d., p. 2030). Reynes's bindings for the king, however, 'tended to be more elaborate and to use gold, and a number of books bound like Morley's are not of royal provenance' (Dr Julianne Simpson, personal comunication).

[59] Morley, or some other sixteenth-century reader, has quoted a line from a 1534 comedy by Pietro Aretino (*La Cortegiana*), about Dante being rightly damned for, as it were, 'frightening the horses' (Morley's copy, title-page). The same hand may have marked four passages of text and commentary from Virgil's discourse on love in *Purgatorio* 17–18 (f. CLXXXI^v–CLXXXIII^r).

[60] Morley's copy, sigs. a iii^v and a iiii^r.

[61] In the edition by Lodovico Dolce, (Venice: Giolito, 1555).

[62] Simpson 2002: 411 and n. 71.

[63] On this 'Chaucerian' work and its polemical contexts, see Jones 2011: 94–102, esp. 100–2.

[64] Morley 1539.

[65] Morley 1539, sig. A. ii^v.

'the Empyre of Englande', and it condemns the Papacy's acceptance of 'temporall possessions' under the Donation of Constantine as a 'fall' from grace.[66] It also interprets Revelation 17 so as to portray the Papacy as a 'dronken strompette, soused in the bloudde of sayntes and martyrs', in a way that is at least consonant with the Dante of *Inferno* 19 and *Paradiso* 27.[67] Yet Morley's religious views were, despite his association with Cromwell, predominantly conservative, and he does not, in the preface nor (to my knowledge) elsewhere, show any sign of extending Dante's role within Henry's imperial heritage by any attempt to enlist the Italian poet in the cause of the English Reformation.

Other British anti-papal writing of the late 1530s does not yet seem to recruit Dante to its cause. The author of the *Remedy for Sedition*, Richard Morison, had, shortly before Morley's exposition, turned his formidable 'propagandist pen' to writing against Rome. In support of Cromwell's policy, Morison published a response to a Catholic polemicist (Cochlaeus) who had opposed Henry's remarriage and his claims to supremacy.[68] His *Apomaxis calumniarum* of 1536–7 has a great deal to say about papal avarice and claims to temporal power, but it draws almost entirely on scriptural, patristic, and occasionally classical authorities, making no use of vernacular writers, except for a brief allusion to Machiavelli.[69] There is no sign here of Morison following up his use of the 'good Italyane poet' as a remedy against domestic sedition by conscripting him as a witness against Rome.

CALLING UPON REFORMATION

It has, however, been suggested that Dante might have been used for anticlerical purposes by English evangelical writers even earlier.[70] In 1528 a couple of lapsed Observant Franciscan friars, who had absconded from the convent at Greenwich in protest against Wolsey's programme of visitations, produced and had printed at Strasbourg a verse satire against Wolsey with the title of *Rede me and be nott wrothe*.[71] One of these friars, William Roy, had earlier in his exile assisted Tyndale, probably as amanuensis, in the preparation of the first English New Testament translated from the Greek, published at Worms in 1526.[72] The other, Jerome Barlowe, joined Roy in Strasbourg, a city whose relatively 'open-minded' religious policy was coming to be dominated by the reformers Martin Bucer and Matthias Zell, and to which a number of religious radicals gravitated in the late

---

[66] Morley 1539, sigs. A iv[v] and A. vii[v].
[67] Morley 1539, sig. C iv[v]. See also sig. B vi[v] where Morley refers to 'Babylon . . . that made al nations dronke with the wyne of her hooryshe fornication'. For other examples of Henrician uses of this image, see below, n. 80.
[68] Morison 1537.
[69] Morison 1537, sig. X 2[v].   [70] *DEL* 1. 25–6.
[71] Roy and Barlowe 1528; the full title is *Rede me and be nott wrothe for I saye no thynge but trothe*.
[72] Schuster 1973: 1068; Brown 1986: 113 and 116. See also *ODNB*, s.v. 'Roy, William (d. in or before 1531), Observant friar and evangelical author'.

1520s.[73] Here, around 1527–8, they composed their 3,000-line diatribe, 'a brefe Dialogue betwene two prestes servauntes', which not only attacks Wolsey himself ('the englisshe Lucifer'), but also bishops, possessioners, and 'worst of all', the Order that they themselves had just abandoned: the friars. Roy and Barlowe portray the friars as 'the devils messengers', 'chickens of the devils broode', 'diligent imageners of lyes', 'antichristes godsones'.[74] The ways in which the mendicants 'imagine lies' and corrupt the Gospel in their preaching are then described at some length:

> Their preachynge is not scripture/
> But fables of their coniecture/
>   And mens ymacinacions.
> They brynge in olde wyves tales/
> Both of Englonde/Fraunce/and Wales/
>   Which they call holy narracions.
> And to theym scripture they apply/
> Pervertynge it most shamfully/
>   After their owne opinions
> Wherwith the people beynge fedde/
> Into manyfolde errours are ledde/
>   And wretched supersticions.[75]

This passage has been seen as 'inspired by a similar denunciation by Dante in the *Paradiso* of the follies and false doctrine of the preachers of his day', and as possibly 'an imitation or reminiscence of *Par.* xxix. 94–6, 106–8'.[76] The parallels with Beatrice's attack on vain preachers are close, if not entirely conclusive. The passage perhaps echoes some of her accusations about distorting the Scriptures ('la divina Scrittura ... è torta'); about the preachers' production of inventions and fables ('invenzioni ... favole ... ciance'); and about the way in which they 'feed' these to their ignorant audience ('pecorelle ... pasciute di vento') (*Par.* 29. 90, 95, 104, 110, and 106–7).[77]

Roy's and Barlowe's invective also shares some other characteristics with Dante's. For instance, they vividly describe the corpulent Cardinal Wolsey ('a great carle ... and a fatt'), riding in procession 'with worldly pompe incredible' on a mule, preceded and followed by servants and sheltered by a canopy.[78] Their portrait might well recall how Dante's Peter Damian, in the *Paradiso*, vividly (though much more concisely) describes 'modern pastors' swathed in their mantles and propped up on their palfreys.[79] *Rede me*'s recurrent images of the clergy and Papacy drinking 'the bloudde of povre simple soules' or 'soules innocent' (ll. 1256–7, 1567, 3025–6) also have something of a Dantean ring, although—as with

---

[73] See *ODNB*, s.v. 'Barlowe, Jerome (*fl.* 1528–1529), Franciscan friar and writer'. On Strasbourg culture at this time, see MacCulloch 2004: 179–89 and McGrath 1999: 95–6 and 230–1.
[74] Roy and Barlowe 1992: ll. 2993, 1331, 1716–20.
[75] Roy and Barlowe 1992: ll. 1750–61.   [76] *DEL* 1. 26, n. 1.
[77] On the persistence of this last trope in anti-Catholic polemic, see below, pp. 58–67.
[78] Roy and Barlowe 1992: ll. 1094–1132.   [79] *Paradiso* 21. 130–5.

Morley's use of the same idea in his *Exposition*—the image here may derive directly from Revelation 17: 6.[80] The Dantean parallels are thus not wholly conclusive, nor are they reinforced by further allusions to the *Commedia* elsewhere in *Rede me*.

Several features of Roy's and Barlowe's cultural context, however, might strengthen the case for their having some degree of awareness of Dante as precedent. Their Order, the Observant Franciscans, whose first house in England had been founded at Greenwich in 1482, had strong continental connections, and prominent early members of the Order in Italy, such as San Bernardino and Giacomo della Marca, were readers and promoters of Dante.[81] The English Observants—following a general decree about the importance of study in the mid-fifteenth century—would have established their own schools, and although their book catalogues have not survived the Dissolution, there is some documentary evidence of expenditure on and donations to their libraries.[82] During the reign of Henry VIII their ranks included a number of Oxbridge scholars, and they had connections with court humanist circles around Catherine of Aragon.[83] Roy—about whose life and work we know rather more than that of his co-author Barlowe—does not seem to have been in the top rank of his Order's scholars.[84] Yet he was known to have had a flair for languages, including Greek and very likely German, and his collaboration with Barlowe on *Rede me* shows familiarity with long-standing Franciscan traditions.[85] For instance, when describing how Observants exploit the beliefs of the gullible about Purgatory, *Rede me* cites a text about the life of St Francis—Bartholomew of Pisa's late fourteenth-century *Liber de conformitate*—a work which may itself have been influenced by Dante.[86]

Despite Wolsey's efforts to destroy all the thousand copies printed at Strasbourg, *Rede me* survived to reach some readers in Henrician England, and Thomas More was sufficiently concerned to mention it in his *Dialogue Concerning Heresies*.[87] Around 1528–32 *Rede me* appears to have been among the small number of 'evangelically inclined books . . . imported into England [which] had a disproportionate and dramatic effect on the culture that received them', since it is listed in the proclamation against heretical books issued on 22 June 1530 and 3 December 1531.[88] Moreover, it was also reprinted as Henry's reign was drawing to a close in 1546, possibly in London (although the colophon gives the place of publication as 'Wesell').[89] The 1546 edition announces a shift in emphasis, whereby 'the

---

[80] Morley 1539: sig. C iv^v. It had been also applied to the Papacy by an English Lollard on trial in 1489; see Cross 1999: 31. In Simon Fish's anti-monastic *A Supplicacyon for the beggers* (Antwerp[?]: Grapheus[?], 1529), the characterization of the pope as *bloudesupper* and England as *kingdome of the bloudsuppers* seems to have a similar biblical source (ff. 3^v, 4^r, and 5^v). I am grateful to Prof. Greg Walker for drawing my attention to Fish's use of the term.

[81] See above, p. 11 wlth n. 19.   [82] Brown 1986: 90–1.   [83] Brown 1986: 75 and 97.

[84] Clebsch 1964: 229.   [85] Schuster 1973.

[86] Roy and Barlowe 1992: l. 2247. On Bartholomew, see Havely 2004a: 96.

[87] More 1981: 291–2. More also noted with satisfaction at the start of his *Confutacyon of Tyndall's Answere* (1532) that Roy had 'made a mete ende at laste and was burned in Portugale' (ed. Schuster 1973: 8). On Roy's end (1531?), see also Clebsch 1964: 239, citing later evidence from Foxe.

[88] Walker 2005: 47 and 49. For the proscription of *Rede me* at St Paul's Cross on 3 December 1531, among 'some thirty heretical books', see also Schuster 1981: 1251.

[89] Roy and Barlowe 1546; see also Roy and Barlowe 1992: 39.

Byshoppes speake in the Cardinall'; it also addresses itself to 'Papistes' in general, and edits the text to take account of the changed political situation. However, despite its emendations and occasional misreadings of the 1528 text, it reproduces the quasi-Dantean passage on Observant preachers in full and exact form, and it thus brings to an evangelical readership at the end of the Henrician era a possible allusion to the writer whom Morison had described as 'that good Italyane poet'.[90]

It may well have been the London printer of the 1546 edition of *Rede me* (Richard Jugge) who, about two years later, published what is probably the first English text to recruit Dante explicitly as a witness against the Papacy. The lengthy title of this work is worth quoting in full:

> THE IMAGE
>
> OF BOTHE CHURCHES
>
> after the moste wonderfull and heauen-
> ly Reuelacion of Sainct John the Euan
> gelist, contayning a very frutefull expo
> sicion or paraphrase vpon the same,
> Wherin it is conferred with the
> other scripturs, and most auc-
> torized historyes. Compy-
> led by John Bale an
> exile also in this life
> for the faythfull
> testimonye of
> Jesu.

This work is a product of the last few years of Henry VIII's reign, when—following the promulgation of the Six Articles in 1539 and the execution of Thomas Cromwell in the following year—the king's religious policy was taking a conservative turn. John Bale was a former Carmelite friar who became a protégé of Cromwell, surviving his master's fall and two periods of subsequent exile: one in this period (1540–7) and the other under the Marian persecutions of 1553–8.[91] Bale has been described as 'the most influential English Protestant author of his time', with a range of work that serves 'to chart the evolution of English Protestant thought throughout the mid-century (*c.* 1536–63)'.[92] His *The Image of Bothe Churches* was probably composed around the middle of the 1540s and is of key importance, not only for its articulation of the contrast between the 'true' Church of the Gospel and the 'false' Church led by the papal Antichrist, but also because it is 'the first commentary upon the whole of Revelation that was printed in the English language', and one which 'furnishes a historical paradigm that underlies most if not all of [Bale's] other works'.[93]

---

[90] Roy and Barlowe 1546: sig. D 8ᵛ.

[91] See *ODNB*, s.v. 'Bale, John (1495–1563), bishop of Ossory, evangelical polemicist, and historian', and King 1993: 27–35.

[92] King 1982: 56–7.   [93] King 1993: 31.

The third and final part of *The Image of Bothe Churches* opens with a commentary on chapter 18 of Revelation, specifically on the 'voice from heauen' which denounces 'Babylon' and calls God's people to 'come away from hyr . . . that ye be not partakers in her synnes'.[94] This leads Bale to interpret the biblical passage as a call to 'Haue no more to doe with that whorish churche. Forsake hir false religion and defiled Sacramentes. Refuse her wanton ceremonies, detest hir superstycyon, leaue hir beggerly baggage'.[95] To this end he cites examples of major saintly figures (Jerome, Peter Damian, Celestine V) who abandoned their rank in the Church, and then adds:

Besydes the wholsome and monishmentes ['admonishmentes' in the 1570 edition] of the scrypture hath manye godlye men geuen warnings of these matters, both in the primatyue churche, and in euery age sens. Manye notabile doctours and fathers, sens the popes fyrst rayse [i.e. 'elevation, ascent to power'], hath in theyr famouse wryttynges called upon the churches reformacion.[96]

Bale then embarks on a list of fifty-one such 'notabile doctours', which includes writers such as Peter Damian (once more), Bernard of Clairvaux, Joachim of Fiore, William of Saint-Amour, Ubertino of Casale, Marsilius of Padua, John Wyclif, John Hus, Lorenzo Valla, and Girolamo Savonarola.[97] Between Wyclif and Hus and Lorenzo Valla (debunker of the Donation of Constantine) we find the name of 'Franciscus Petrarcha', and immediately before that 'Dantes Aligerius'.[98]

Bale's naming of Dante as one of those who have 'geuen warnings' and 'called upon the churches reformacion' has a number of significant implications. It draws upon the kind of bibliographic work that his more conservative colleague, John Leland, had done in mapping the medieval past in the light of Henry VIII's imperial present. Indeed, Leland had very shortly beforehand celebrated Thomas Wyatt in an elegy as 'an Englishman equal to the Italians' and had cited Dante and Petrarch for that purpose.[99] Bale's formation of a literary canon would, later in this spell of exile, lead him to extend Leland's scholarly work in his 1549 edition of the latter's *Laboryouse Journey & Serche*, and there to conscript British writers from Bede to Wyclif and Chaucer as further witnesses against papal claims to supremacy.[100]

Bale's list of witnesses in the apocalyptic scheme of *The Image of Bothe Churches* provides a model for the later succession of sixteenth-century polemicists who, like him, sought to establish Protestant legitimacy through historical precedent rather than (as Tyndale had done) through appeal to royal authority.[101] A number of such polemicists, like John Foxe (Bale's companion in his second exile), would later use passages from the *Commedia* and *Monarchia* to conscript Dante as 'an Italian writer

---

[94] Bale 1548: sig. Aa 7ᵛ, citing Rev. 18: 4–7.   [95] Bale 1548: sig. Aa 8ʳ.
[96] Bale 1548: sig. Aa 8ᵛ.   [97] Bale 1548: sigs. Aa 8ᵛ–Bb 1ʳ.
[98] Bale 1548: sig. Bb 1ʳ.   [99] Leland 1542: sig. A iiiᵛ. See also *DEL* 1. 30–1 and 155.
[100] Bale 1549; see also King 1993: 33. On Bale's view of Wyclif as 'the "morning star" of the Reformation' and his project for the 'apocalyptic periodization of history', see Ross 1991: 68–9, and Heal 2006: 108.
[101] Ryrie 1996: 1. 85.

against the Pope'. *The Image of Bothe Churches* thus not only anticipates Foxe's references to Dante in the 1570 edition of the *Ecclesiasticall History*, but also pre-dates by about twenty years what has (until now) been claimed as the first citation of Dante in the role of writer against Rome: Bishop Robert Horne's *Answeare . . . to . . . Iohn Fekenham* (1566).[102] Bale himself, at the end of his second period of exile in the 1550s, would become more specific about Dante's role in relation to the Papacy when, in his massive survey of British and other writers, the *Scriptorum illustrium maioris Brytannie . . . Catalogus*, he mentions that

Dantes Aligerus, . . . poeta Florentinus, opusculum scripsit de Monarchia. In quo fuit eius opinio, quod Imperiu[m] ab ecclesia minime dependeret.

Dante Alighieri, . . . Florentine poet, wrote a little book *De monarchia*. In which it was his opinion that the Empire should not at all be dependent on the Church.[103]

The 1557–9 edition of Bale's *Catalogus* was published at Basel by Johannes Oporinus (Johann Herbst), who in 1559 would also publish the *editio princeps* of the *Monarchia* itself.[104] Bale would have been aware of this Protestant project, and references elsewhere in the *Catalogus* suggest that he knew how Dante's views on the Papacy in that text had been treated by a much earlier English writer: the Benedictine, Adam Easton.[105]

Bale shared an interest in Dante as 'witness' with another major Protestant polemicist of the mid-sixteenth century, Matija Vlačić, better known as Matthias Flacius (1520–75). Flacius was born in Venetian Istria, but most of his career was as a follower of Luther in various German cities and universities, and another work of Protestant historiography in which he played a leading part was the *Magdeburg Centuries* of 1559–74.[106] His own *Catalogus testium veritatis qui ante nostram aetatem reclamarunt Papae* ('Testament of witnesses for the truth who before our age spoke out against the Papacy') was printed by Oporinus in 1556, the year before Bale's *Catalogus*. The references to Dante in his work would be enlarged and reprinted several times during the later sixteenth and early seventeenth centuries; and they would have a far-reaching influence on English Protestant polemic.[107]

Flacius's role as reader of Dante and Protestant historiographer serves as conclusion here and as an introduction to the next chapter. Born in 1520, he was considerably younger than Bale, and his historical and literary perspective appears at several points to have been influenced by the older writer.[108] Both Bale's and

---

[102] Boswell 1999: xvi and 27. On Horne, see below, p. 52.
[103] Bale 1557–9: 1. 377.   [104] See below, p. 53.
[105] Bale 1557–9: 1. 516–17; on Easton and the *Monarchia*, see above, pp. 24–6. For Bale's earlier notes on Easton (and the listing of copies of the *Defensorium*), see also Bale 1990: 4–6.
[106] On Flacius's life and work, see Preger 1859–61 and Frank 1990: 11–25; also Olson 2002: 83–93 and MacCulloch 2004: 349–52 and 490. His work on the *Magdeburg Centuries* is discussed in Mentzel-Reuters and Hartmann 2008, and on his later influence among English Protestant writers, see below, p. 55 and 59–62.
[107] Further editions of his *Catalogus* continued to appear, e.g. at Strasbourg in 1562, Lyon, 1597, and Geneva, 1608. On Flacius and Dante, see Köhler 1867 and Frank 1990: esp. 171–2 and n. 435.
[108] King 1982: 60, 69. On Flacius's use of Bale as a source, see also Frank 1990: 105, 211, 218, and 222–3.

Flacius's *Catalogi* clearly share an interest in the anti-papal potential of the *Monarchia*; indeed, Flacius's description of how Dante there disputes the pope's supremacy over the emperor ('probauit Papam no[n] esse super Imperatorem') is echoed by Bale in the passage cited from the *Scriptorum illustrium . . . Catalogus* above.[109] Flacius's early education was in the Venice of Aldus Manutius;[110] he thus had ample opportunity to acquire a first-hand knowledge of Italian and Dante, which he seems to have put to use by actually translating passages from the *Commedia* into Latin for the second (Strasbourg, 1562) edition of the *Catalogus testium veritatis*.[111] Finally, his anticlerical use of the *Commedia* and pro-imperial use of the *Monarchia* show how the mid-century Protestant historian and polemicist would draw together several leading strands of early Reformation thought in his appropriation of the medieval Catholic poet. One of these strands had, as we have seen, been spun by English writers of and around the Henrician Reformation, and it would be woven into the fabric of the Protestant Dante in Britain during the later sixteenth century and beyond.

[109] Compare Flacius 1556: 868.   [110] Preger 1859–61: 1. 14, Olson 2002: 84.

[111] For further discussion of Flacius's specific references to and translations from Dante, see below, pp. 51–2 and 59 with nn. 56–7.

3

'The Hungry Sheep': Protestant and Catholic Readings, 1556–1637

Conscription of Dante as a witness against Rome continues apace among the Protestant writers of the later sixteenth and early seventeenth centuries, and Catholic resistance to this reading likewise gathers force. The poet's arguments about papal authority and temporalities in Book 3 of the *Monarchia*—and their official Catholic reception in the period—play a large part in qualifying him to be written into the scheme of Protestant history. His portrayals of the Papacy and the clergy in the *Commedia*—some of them, too, subject to censorship—provide part of the stockpile of medieval apocalyptic and 'anticlerical' ammunition that was drawn upon by Protestant polemicists. Increasingly, however, the basis of such 'anticlericism' is challenged by Catholic adversaries, and in the process a closer reading of passages from the *Commedia* enters into the debate.[1] One such passage is the description of preachers feeding their 'flock' with 'wind' (*Par.* 29. 103–8). As images of priestly authority and discourse and of the demands of religious readers and listeners, Dante's false shepherds and hungry sheep attract attention (and translation) throughout the period, from Flacius to Milton.[2]

'A BOOKE AGAINST THE POPE'

Dante's *Monarchia* is a key text in the Protestant construction of Dante's identity as—in the words of the English Reformation's chief martyrologist—'an Italian writer against the Pope'.[3] Its treatment—particularly in its third and final book—of the relationship and potential conflicts between ecclesiastical and secular power and with the bases of papal authority had early on drawn official opposition and condemnation. Shortly after Dante's death in 1321, and in the midst of the conflict between John XXII and the Holy Roman Emperor Ludwig of Bavaria, the *Monarchia*'s relevance to the dispute was acknowledged by two attacks from within the Church. One response soon came from Avignon, through the papal legate in

---

[1] On Catholic and Protestant religious controversies in the Elizabethan and Jacobean periods, see Milward 1977 and 1978, and Heal 2006.

[2] The following chapter thus attempts to clarify the arguments of two rather rambling earlier essays: Havely 2003 and 2004*b*.

[3] The phrase appears in a shouldernote in Foxe 1570: 485.

Italy who, in the late 1320s, ordered it and its author's remains to be burnt.[4] Around the same time, an apologist for the Papacy argued that it would indeed be a good thing for the world to have a single ruler, as Dante had argued in Book 1, but unfortunately 'the spirit of faction [had] darkened his foolish mind and he was unable to discover the true monarch', namely 'the supreme pontiff of the Christians, the vicar-general of Jesus Christ'.[5] Such adverse judgements affected the circulation of Dante's treatise, but they did not prevent it from continuing to be read and commented upon in the fourteenth century and even translated during the fifteenth.[6] They also sharpened an interest in Dante from various points of view: from orthodox monastic writers such as Adam Easton and John Whethamstede, to early Protestant polemicists, such as those mentioned at the end of the last chapter: John Bale and his younger contemporary, Matthias Flacius.[7]

　　Flacius's *Catalogus testium veritatis* ('Catalogue of witnesses to the truth') appeared first at Basel in 1556 and presented an account of writers who, according to the title-page, 'before our age spoke out against the Papacy'.[8] 'Dantes Florentinus' appears in the book's initial list of these: in the 1556 edition he is subsequently referred to in three passages, and the first of his works to be mentioned is the *Monarchia*:

Dantes Florentinus floruit ante annos 250. Fuit uir pius & doctus, ut multi scriptores, & praesertim ipsius scripta testantur. Scripsit librum, quem appellauit Monarchiam. In eo probauit Papam no[n] esse supra Imperatorem, nec habere aliqod ius in Imperium, ob eam [que] rem à quibusdam haereseos est damnatus. Scripsit et vulgari Italico sermone non pauca, in quibus multa reprehendit in Papa, eiusq[ue] religione.

Dante of Florence flourished 250 years ago. He was a devout and learned man, as many authors and above all his own writings bear witness. He wrote a work called *Monarchia*. In this, he proved the Pope not to be superior to the Emperor, nor to have any jurisdiction over the Empire, and because of that he was by certain persons convicted of heresy. He also wrote not a few passages in the Italian vernacular where he inveighs against the pope and his religion.[9]

Earlier, the *Catalogus* had mentioned papal conflicts with emperors, such as Frederick II, Henry of Luxemburg, and Ludwig of Bavaria, and, when discussing Ludwig's dispute with John XXII, Flacius had twice enlisted Dante among the 'learned men' and 'friends' of the emperor—once again with the *Monarchia* in mind, since he immediately goes on to reproduce at length Ludwig's defence against the pope's 'calumnies'.[10] Dante had been dead for several years before that particular imperial and papal quarrel erupted, and Flacius's enlistment of the poet as a participant is probably based upon a misreading (or at least a judicious

　　[4] See above, p. 10 and 27–8.　　[5] Vernani (above, pp. 10 and 27); see Caesar 1989: 110–14.
　　[6] Marsilio Ficino translated the *Monarchia* into Tuscan in 1467–8. For an edition, see Shaw 1974–5, and for an English version of Ficino's preface, see Caesar 1989: 217–18.
　　[7] On Easton and Whethamstede, see above, pp. 23–4, and on Bale and Flacius, see above, pp. 48–9. Having studied in Venice, Basel, and Tübingen, Flacius was active as leader of the conservative Lutheran faction around the middle of the century at Wittenberg, Magdeburg, and Jena.
　　[8] An enlarged edition was published at Strasbourg in 1562.
　　[9] Flacius 1556: 868.　　[10] Flacius 1556: 815, 819, and 820–31.

stretching) of Boccaccio's account of the *Monarchia*'s afterlife as a contentious text in the mid-fourteenth century.[11]

What made the *Monarchia* yet more useful for Protestant writers of the mid-sixteenth century was that it was by then appearing in the official indexes of prohibited books. This fact was highlighted by the appearance in 1560 of an edition of the most recent (1559) Index, together with annotations by the Italian Protestant convert, Pier Paolo Vergerio.[12] Vergerio was himself a good catch for the Protestants: he had been papal nuncio in Germany and bishop of Capodistria, before being subjected to a protracted heresy trial and fleeing from Italy to Switzerland and Germany in 1549.[13] His annotations about Dante in the 1560 volume cover about four pages and focus almost entirely upon the *Monarchia* (mentioning only briefly that the poet 'wrote much in Italian'). Once again, perhaps following Flacius, he links Dante with Ludwig of Bavaria; and he finds a parallel between Ludwig's dispute with John XXII and the contemporary quarrel between Ferdinand I and Paul IV over the pope's right to authorize the election of an emperor.[14] For the Protestant proponents of 'magisterial reformation', with their emphasis on the role of secular powers, the *Monarchia*'s assertions about the limitations of papal power were obviously attractive, since such claims could be and were also advanced on behalf of other rulers beside the emperor.

Hence also in England, a few years before Pius V formally revoked Elizabeth I's authority through the Bull *Regnans in Excelsis* of 1570, several Protestant apologists were citing Dante to their Catholic adversaries in defence of 'the Q[ueene's] maiestie's Lawfull and due authoritie' and against 'the Tyrannie of the *Bisshoppes* of Rome and their Barbarous Persianlike Pride'. The two apologists thus quoted were Robert Horne, bishop of Winchester, writing in 1566, and John Jewel, bishop of Salisbury, writing in 1567.[15] Both had been among the Protestant dissidents who had sought exile in Germany and Switzerland during Mary Tudor's reign. They were also both familiar with the work of Flacius and Vergerio; indeed Jewel cites both in his *Defence of the Apologie of the Churche of England*.[16] Of the two, Horne is slightly earlier in his citation of Dante, but Jewel, whose *Defence* was reprinted four times in the sixteenth and seventeenth centuries, appears to have been the more influential.

Even more influential in the British Protestant conscription of Dante during this politically and polemically turbulent period is the martyrologist John Foxe.[17] Like Horne and Jewel, Foxe had been an exile on the Continent during the Marian persecutions. Whilst at Basel (from November 1555 to October 1559), he was

---

[11] Flacius's contemporary, Johann Herold, in the biography of the poet appended to his German translation of the *Monarchia* (1559), extended Dante's life till 1341 for the purpose (it seems) of linking him with Ludwig of Bavaria; see Friederich 1950: 348–9.

[12] See Vergerius 1560: ff. 18ʳ–19ᵛ. Excerpts are translated by Caesar 1989: 274–5.

[13] On Vergerio and the context of Italian religious dissent, see Friederich 1950: 348; Grimm 1973: 228–9; Cochrane 1988: 141–3; and Caesar 1989: 273–6. He also addressed two pamphlets to Edward VI in 1550 (Wyatt 2005: 84–5).

[14] Vergerius 1560: f. 18ᵛ; translated by Caesar 1989: 274.

[15] Horne 1566: f. 130ʳ; and Jewel 1567: 457.   [16] Jewel 1567: 43–4.

[17] See *ODNB*, s.v., 'Foxe, John (1516/17–1587), martyrologist'.

befriended by the elderly John Bale, then working on his major bibliographical project, the *Scriptorum illustrium Maioris Brytannie* (1557–9), in which Dante's ideas about papal authority in the *Monarchia* are mentioned.[18] Foxe was employed as a proofreader by the printer Oporinus (Johann Herbst), who during those four years published Flacius's *Catalogus* and the first ever printed edition of Dante's *Monarchia*, and he was thus probably involved in the production of both these titles.[19] He certainly reflects Flacius's views on Dante in the enlarged 1570 edition of his *Ecclesiasticall History*, where he follows the *Catalogus* closely in linking Dante to Ludwig of Bavaria, and quite literally in asserting that Dante (presumably in *Monarchia*, though Foxe doesn't say so) 'proueth the pope not to be aboue the Emperour, nor to haue any right or iurisdiction in the empyre'.[20] Foxe also refers in the same passage to a text (the *Chronica Iordanis*) that was published in the same volume as the 1559 Basel *Monarchia*; and in his initial list of 'the Authors alleged in this Booke' he includes both 'Dantes Italicus' and 'Illyricus', the name by which Flacius is generally known.[21]

Hence, by 1570 Dante has become written into the English Protestant scheme of history as 'an Italian writer against the Pope'—as he had been in Flacius's *Catalogus* and would continue to be in later Protestant polemic. Within the broad historical framework adopted by Flacius, Foxe, and their followers, 'Dantes Florentinus' forms part of a procession of proto-Protestants 'invoked by . . . reformers to support the thesis of a long-established anti-papal tradition'.[22] There he joins the band of medieval apocalyptic and polemical writers, such as Joachim of Fiore, William of Saint-Amour, Marsilius of Padua, William of Ockham, John of Rupescissa, and Wyclif—as well as writers such as Petrarch, Boccaccio, Chaucer, and Langland.[23]

'THE WHOORE OF BABYLON'

An attractive feature of Dante for northern European Reformers is that he is not just a 'writer against Popes' but is also an Italian and a writer whose work addresses the whole structure of Catholic doctrine. He thus provides useful material for breeding the virus that Protestant polemicists sought to implant within Rome's ideological system. Awareness of this procedure is quite explicit in the discourse of a number of the English Protestant texts that conscript Dante. For instance, Bishop Jewel, directly confronting his Catholic adversary (Thomas Harding) in 1567, turns against him '*Petrarcha, Dantes,* and a great number of other youre owne

---

[18] On Bale and Dante, see above, pp. 46–9. On his years in Basel, see: *ODNB*, s.v. 'Bale, John (1495–1563), bishop of Ossory, evangelical polemicist and historian'; and King 1993: 34–5.
[19] See Toynbee 1921: 109–10.   [20] Foxe 1570: 485.
[21] Foxe 1570: sig. 1ᵛ.   [22] Caesar 1989: 273.
[23] For some examples, see Boswell 1999: 40–1, 63, 64, 132–3, and 187.

Doctours'.[24] In 1610 John White, a prominent opponent of the Jesuits, names Dante resoundingly among those by whom 'the present religion of the Romane Church was observed and resisted in all ages', and having linked him with the usual fourteenth-century suspects (Marsilius, Ockham, Wyclif, and others), he seeks to clinch the argument by claiming that: 'in the Popes owne Librarie are bookes both Latin and Greeke written against his Primacie'.[25] Dante thus comes to participate in the polemical trope by which an opposing ideology is made to condemn itself out of its own mouth.

English Protestant polemicists illustrate several specific anti-Catholic themes from Dante's work, such as the identification of Rome and the Papacy with Babylon, the Antichrist, and the 'woman drunken with the blood of saints' (Revelation 17): these, as they knew, had precedents in the *Commedia* and in earlier apocalyptic exegesis.[26] Even the titles of some of their works suggest the kind of resources and discourse to be drawn upon—for instance: *De Turcopapismo*; *Mysterium Iniquitatis seu Historia Papatus*; or *Antichrist the pope of Rome, Or the pope of Rome is Antichrist. Proved in two treatises.*[27] Within this apocalyptic context, references to Dante often go together with those to Petrarch. Already in the 1540s John Bale had named 'Franciscus Petrarcha' immediately after 'Dantes Aligherius' in his list of 'notabile doctours' who 'called upon the churches reformacion'.[28] Petrarch has been shown to be a source for other sixteenth-century English Protestant polemicists, who drew specifically upon his sonnets denouncing the corruption of Avignon (especially *RVF* 137 and 138) and the invective of his eighteenth and nineteenth *Sine nomine* letters.[29] Jewel and Foxe, for example, once again follow Flacius's lead in citing Petrarch as well as Dante on the papal curia as 'the Whoore of Babylon', and towards the end of the century one of the most prolific and energetic of the English writers against Rome, Matthew Sutcliffe, quotes the Avignon sonnets and the *Sine nomine* letters at some length in the original, as witness to the 'Church of Rome' being a 'school of error' and 'temple of heresy'.[30]

Throughout the period Dante, as 'Italian writer against the Pope', is thus linked or (as Foxe puts it) 'adioyned' quite closely with Petrarch. In addition to citing

---

[24] Jewel 1567: 721 (also in Boswell 1999: 28). Earlier Jewel has referred to Nicholas of Lyra as 'one of your owne late Doctours' (243).

[25] White 1610: 386. This work went through four editions between 1608 and 1616; see *ODNB*, s.v. 'White, John (1570–1615), Church of England clergyman and polemicist'.

[26] For instance Flacius in the 1556 edition of the *Catalogus* cites Petrus Iohannis Olivi as one of his 'witnesses' (Flacius 1556: 872–3).

[27] These are the titles of works by, respectively: Matthew Sutcliffe (1599*b*); Philippe de Mornay (published in Latin and French in 1611 and translated by Sampson Lennard as *The mysterie of iniquitie* in 1612); and Thomas Beard (1625). On the widespread trope of Catholic Rome as Whore/Babylon and the pope as Antichrist, see Shell 1999: 24–33, and on the Protestant polemicists' approach to apocalyptic history, see Heal 2006: 111–12.

[28] See above, p. 47.

[29] See Usher 2005: 191 and 193.

[30] Flacius 1556: 871–2, Jewel 1567: 460 (Boswell 1999: 28); Foxe 1570: 486 (Boswell 1999: 42); Sutcliffe 1592: 53. For a further direct quotation from Petrarch by Sutcliffe, see Usher 2005: 192 (citing *RVF* 137).

Petrarch, Jewel also asserts that '*Dantes* an *Italian Poete* by expresse woordes calleth Rome the Whore of Babylon', and specifically cites canto 32 of *Purgatorio*, where the vision of the giant and the prostitute on the chariot of the Church can be thus construed; and Foxe less precisely refers to the same idea in 'the canticle of purgatory'.[31] Both are directly influenced by the extended summary of the episode in *Purgatorio* 32 that had appeared in the second (1562) edition of Flacius's *Catalogus*.[32] Other, more explicitly anti-papal passages from the *Commedia* come to be quoted and even translated in subsequent English Protestant polemic. These include the attack on Nicholas III and other avaricious popes in *Inferno* 19; and, with increasing frequency, the passage in the *Paradiso* where the corruption of the Papacy is envisaged as the transformation of the shepherd into a wolf.[33] The second of these (*Par.* 9. 126–42) had already been quoted and translated by Flacius in the second edition of the *Catalogus*.

From the mid-sixteenth century onwards, therefore, the *Commedia*'s anticlerical and anti-papal imagery reinforces that of Protestant polemic. The citing and translating of passages in relation to this theme (the Papacy as Whore, Babylon, Antichrist, ravening wolf) show that some of the polemicists are reading (or quite closely *mis*reading) parts of the poem's text. Thus, while Dante in Reformation England was often, like Petrarch, a name rather than a text,[34] he is becoming more than a mere name to conjure with.

'NEUER . . . ANY IOTE OF PROTESTANT RELIGION': CATHOLIC READINGS

On the other side of the main religious divide, Catholic writers were, in the second half of the century, beginning to contest this Protestant conscription of Dante. Some of the Protestant polemicists who drew upon the *Monarchia* and the *Commedia* were directly engaged in dispute with specific Catholic opponents, and an early example of such an exchange dates from the 1560s. In citing the *Monarchia* to support Elizabeth I's authority against that of the pope, Bishop Horne was answering the objections to the Oath of Supremacy that had been raised by the former abbot of Westminster, John Fekenham; and the following year he received a response from another Catholic exile who was to become prominent in the expatriate culture of Douai and Louvain. From Louvain in 1567 the punningly titled *Counterblast to M[aster] Hornes vayne blaste against M[aster]*

---

[31] Jewel 1567: 460 (also Boswell 1999: 28); Foxe 1570: 485 (Boswell 1999: 41).

[32] Flacius 1562: 507: 'In cantione 32. purgatorii non obscurè ostendit Papam esse meretrice Babylonyam.'

[33] For references to Nicholas III and *Inferno* 19, see Boswell 1999: 135, 163, 183, and 202. For allusions to the pope as wolf in *Paradiso* 9. 132, see e.g.: Flacius 1556: 868; Foxe 1570: 485; Boswell 1999: 69 (citing Humphrey 1584: 347, but not attributing to *Par.* 9); De Mornay (tr. S. Lennard) 1612: 444–5; and Boswell 1999: 199–202.

[34] Cf. Usher 2005: 189.

Fekenham was issued by Thomas Stapleton.[35] In the course of answering Horne's points about the rights of the emperor as secular ruler and arguing that Ludwig of Bavaria was 'no lawfull Emperour, but an usurper', Stapleton here gives short shrift to the authorities (including Dante) that Horne has enlisted in support of his case: for him, Dante is just one among a motley crew of poets and heretics, and his contemptuous shouldernote here reinforces the point: 'M[aster] Horne proueth his new primacie [i.e. that of the emperor] by poets'.[36] Stapleton's dismissive tactic was followed by some other Catholic polemicists. One apologist of the early seventeenth century described Dante as a talented poet but ignorant theologian who should have stuck to his main trade and not strayed into contentious areas of doctrine.[37] In a work published posthumously (in 1600) Stapleton himself continued to belittle the poet as one of a number of childish rebels, vainly hurling themselves against the solid rock of the Roman Church, 'all of whose insults, wrath and rage this Rock of Rome has easily shrugged off, destroyed and dashed to pieces'.[38]

A more sophisticated response from Rome was to challenge the Protestants' conscription of Dante and their whole attempt to construct the Reformation out of Catholic anticlerical writing.[39] During the later sixteenth century a major polemical voice in this respect, as in others, was the eminent controversialist Robert Bellarmine; and his approach to Dante is largely shared by a fellow Jesuit, the missionary to England and rector of the English College in Rome, Robert Persons.[40] In his *Treatise of Three Conversions of England from Paganisme to Christian Religion* (1603), Persons undertakes a comprehensive critique of Foxe's scheme of ecclesiastical history—of 'the visible succession (forsooth) which Iohn Fox hath deuised to sett downe for the proofe of his new Church'.[41] Like Stapleton (to some extent), he dismisses a large number of Foxe's fourteenth- and fifteenth-century witnesses to Protestantism as 'paltry heretiks' or 'a rabblement of Sectaryes'.[42] Unlike Stapleton, however, Persons argues forcefully against what he describes as the 'conioyninge' of writers like Dante and Petrarch with this 'company', since, he says, they: 'neuer held any iote of protestant religion in the world. And yet are brought in here by Iohn Fox, as men of his Church and beleefe.'[43] Although he does not cite or quote

---

[35] On Stapleton's life and work, see O'Connell 1964: 26–52, 56–61, and 154–210, and *ODNB*, s.v., 'Stapleton, Thomas (1535–1598), Roman Catholic theologian'.

[36] Stapleton 1567: 334ʳ. His shouldernote about mere 'poets' is omitted in the transcription of the passage by Boswell 1999: 29–30.

[37] Schulckenius 1613: 64.

[38] *Quorum omnium insolentiam, furorem, rabiem, inuicta haec Romana Petra, veluti rupes solidissima facilè decussie, labefactauit, fregit* (Stapleton 1600: 1. 27–8).

[39] Compare the cautionary remarks about Boccaccio and 'medieval anti-clericalism' in Ó Cuilleanáin 1984: 255–6.

[40] On Bellarmine's approach to Dante and its post-Tridentine context, see Friederich 1950: 82–3; and Caesar 1989: 34–7. For a more detailed account of how, in the appendix to vol. 1 of *Disputationes...de Controversiis Christianae Fidei* (1581–93), Bellarmine rebutted the Protestant interpretations of passages in the *Commedia*, see Looney 2011: 28–9 with nn. 18–19. On Persons, his career and his vision of a restored English Catholic Church, see Bossy 1976: 21–4, Aveling 1976: 57–9 and 67–8, and *ODNB*, s.v. 'Persons [Parsons], Robert (1546–1610), Jesuit'.

[41] Persons 1603: 516. [42] Persons 1603: 353 and 514. [43] Persons 1603: 538–9.

any of the *Commedia*'s critical passages about the Papacy or the Church, Persons seems to be taking them into account (along with Petrarch's anti-Avignon invective) when he goes on to claim that for Foxe to build a 'visible succession' out of this kind of criticism 'is as good an argument, as if a man would proue, that *Saint Paule* was not of the faith, or religion of the *Corinthians*, for that he reprehended them sharply, for fornication among them'.[44] Persons shows some further signs of having actually read Dante a few years later when, during an argument about Papacy and Empire posthumously published in 1612, he corrects a Protestant opponent about the identity of Pier delle Vigne (chancellor to the emperor Frederick II and a prominent figure in *Inferno* 13). He here twice cites not only Dante himself but also the commentaries on the *Commedia* by Landino and Vellutello, which had first been printed together in 1564.[45]

Further evidence of close reading of Dante by English Catholics in response to Protestant claims about him continues to be found in the early decades of the seventeenth century. One of Persons's fellow Jesuits, 'John Clare', prefect of studies at the English Colleges in Rome and Louvain, is named as the author of *The Converted Jew*, a series of dialogues about Catholicism and Protestantism 'betweene Micheas a learned jew, and others, touching divers points of religion controuerted betweene the Catholicks and Protestants'.[46] In the second of these dialogues, the 'learned Jew' Micheas (who by this point shows signs of turning into a Bellarminian Jesuit) continues Persons's attack on Foxe's 'visible' Protestant succession by arguing that even Wyclif 'cannot be truly claymed for a Protestant . . . in that (besides he was a Catholicke Priest, and no Church of the Protestants, then known to him) he still retayned many Catholicke Opinions'.[47] The 'Appendix' to these dialogues is designed as a reply to the Protestant theologian and biblical scholar George Abbot's treatise on 'papistry', which amongst other things had described the *Monarchia* as 'a book against the Pope'.[48] In his appendix, 'John Clare' reviews a number of Abbot's alleged proto-Protestant witnesses (including, at some length, Chaucer).[49] With regard to Dante and Petrarch, 'Clare' inherits something of Stapleton's prejudice—rebuking Abbot for relying on 'the testimonies euen of Poets (*as Chaucer, Dantes, Petrarch*)'—but he does do something to substantiate his general claim that 'what the foresaide Poets did Satyrically wryte, was written only against some disorders in the Church of Rome, and against the presumed faults of some particular Popes; but neuer against their supreme dignity in the Church of Christ'.[50] Unlike his Protestant adversary, 'John Clare' goes

[44] Persons 1603: 539. Compare the debate about Boccaccio's portrayals of the clergy in the *Decameron* during the late sixteenth and seventeenth centuries, described in Ó Cuilleanáin 1984: 17–25.

[45] Persons 1612: 500 and 503 (in Boswell 1999: 146). Landino and Vellutello are referred to twice here: in shouldernotes *m* and *n* on p. 500; and in the text on p. 503.

[46] 'Clare' 1630. The dialogues appeared two years after Clare's death, and are not thought to be by him; see *ODNB*, s.v. 'Clare, John (*c.*1579–1628), Jesuit).

[47] 'Clare' 1630: 49.

[48] The appendix is in 'Clare' 1630: 121–53. For Abbot's reference to Dante's *Monarchia*, in his *Reasons which Doctour Hill hath Brought for Upholding Papistry, Unmasked*, see Boswell 1999: 123–4.

[49] 'Clare' 1630: 140.   [50] 'Clare' 1630: 144.

directly to the *Commedia*, quoting several passages from the *Inferno* and the *Paradiso* and even translating one of them (the praise of St Peter as *gran viro* in *Paradiso* 24. 34–6). Such interpretations—especially his account of the portrayals of the popes in *Inferno* 19 and 27—may be somewhat slanted and decontextualized; but what we have here is, nonetheless, a *reading* rather than a mere naming—thus beginning to shift the grounds of the debate from the generalities of the 'true Church' and the 'visible succession' to actual engagement with Dante's text.

FEEDING THE FLOCK WITH WIND

A text from the *Commedia* that receives close attention from Protestant writers throughout this period is one that, appropriately, involves preaching. At a late stage in the ascent through Paradise, Dante's Beatrice engages in a violent tirade of about forty lines, denouncing human error and vanity, especially the vanity of certain earthly preachers. The tone of her diatribe has been described as one of 'unexpected harshness' that seems, at least initially, 'out of tone with paradise'.[51] Such harshness is typified by the vivid metaphor through which Beatrice represents the effects that vain preachers have upon their impressionable hearers:

> 'Non ha Fiorenza tanti Lapi e Bindi
> quante sì fatte favole per anno
> in pergamo si gridan quinci e quindi:
> sì che le pecorelle, che non sanno,
> tornan del pasco pasciute di vento,
> e non le scusa non veder lo danno.'

'Even the names of Lapo and Bindo aren't so common in Florence as are these tales that are bawled out year by year from pulpits everywhere. Thus the poor, unwary flock come back from those fields fed with wind, but can't be excused for not seeing what's wrong.'[52]

Dante's metaphor of feeding the flock with wind has a number of biblical and traditional parallels,[53] but the concise way in which it combines the notions of intellectual futility and commercialized corruption was to attract attention from commentators on the *Commedia* during the fourteenth and fifteenth centuries. In the notes to his Latin version of Dante's poem (1416–17), the Franciscan Giovanni da Serravalle explained how the metaphor conveys the effect of 'useless words' on 'simple people', concluding 'Et bona metaphora est' ('And it's a good metaphor'); whilst Cristoforo Landino, in the prologue to his influential commentary (first

---

[51] Payton 1995: 435.
[52] *Paradiso* 29. 103–8.
[53] Ezekiel calls the delinquent 'shepherds of Israel' to account and accuses them of having gorged themselves but failed to feed the flock (Ezek. 34: 1–31); Hosea uses the term *pascit ventum* ('feeds upon wind') to describe a futile strategy (Hosea 12: 1–2). In the New Testament, both true and false shepherds are prominent—most notably in John 10: 11–16 and 21: 15–17, but also in Acts 20: 28, 1 Corinthians 9: 7 and 1 Peter 5: 2.

published at Florence in 1481), cites the same passage as one of his five examples, showing how Dante 'is highly agile in his figurative language' ('È molto pronto nelle translazione').[54]

'Feeding the flock with wind' also reflects concerns about the conduct of preaching that were expressed with increasing urgency during the Reformation period. Again, Matthias Flacius may be the first Protestant writer to draw specifically on *Dantes Florentinus* for this purpose, (although William Roy and Jerome Barlowe perhaps alluded to the same passage much earlier).[55] In the 1556 edition of his *Catalogus testium veritatis*, immediately after he has identified Dante as eminent writer and summarized the argument about papal power in the *Monarchia*, Flacius goes on to paraphrase Beatrice's lines about preaching in the *Paradiso*:

Queritur alicubi prolixe, intermissam esse verbi Dei praedicationem, & pro ea praedicari a monachis vanissimas fabulas, eorumque nugis fidem haberi: atque ita oues Christi non vero pabulo Evangelii, sed vento pasci . . .

In one place he laments at length that the preaching of the word of God had been allowed to lapse and instead vain fables are being preached by the friars, and that trust is being placed in their frivolities: and thus the sheep of God are being fed not with the true fodder of the Gospel, but with wind . . .[56]

In a later edition of the *Catalogus*, published at Strasbourg in 1562, Flacius becomes much more specific, quoting and translating sixty-six lines of anti-papal and anticlerical material from the *Paradiso*, including this particular passage from Beatrice's diatribe in canto 29:

> Non habet Florentia tot Lapos, totque Bindos
> Quot huiusmodi fabulae per annum
> E suggestu hic & illic declamitantur,
> Ita oviculae quae hoc ignorant,
> Redeunt e pascuis pastae vento,
> Nec eas excusat sui ignorantia damni.[57]

Flacius's repeated references to Dante's metaphor of 'feeding the flock with wind' subsequently caught the attention of a number of English Protestants, from Foxe onwards, who then made use of it to attack a particular form of 'Popish abuse'—namely, vain preaching. Use of the Dantean trope, quoted and retranslated into

---

[54] For Serravalle's comments, see Serravalle 1891: 1163. For Landino's, in the *proemio* to his commentary on the *Commedia*, see Landino 1974: 150–1.

[55] On Flacius, see above, pp. 48–9 and 51–2. On Roy's and Barlowe's *Rede me and be nott wrothe*, see above, pp. 43–6.

[56] Flacius 1556: 868.

[57] Flacius 1562: 506, closely translating the Italian of *Paradiso* 29. 103–8, as above, p. 58. This later enlarged edition of Flacius's *Catalogus* contains a further reference to Dante, under the discussion of the Donation of Constantine (p. 490), and the section on 'Dantes' is itself substantially expanded (pp. 505–7). The passages translated here are from *Paradiso* 9, 18, and 29; they are followed by comments on *Purgatorio* 32 which assert that Dante identified the Papacy with the Whore of Babylon and the Antichrist (p. 507). Foxe and other English Protestant polemicists probably drew much of their material on Dante from this edition. Further editions of Flacius's *Catalogus* appeared in 1597 (Lyon) and 1608 (Geneva).

English by Foxe and his followers, can, moreover, be seen in the context of a larger debate about this aspect of the Church's mission.

The 'godly preaching ministry' became a watchword for many Protestant writers on pastoral duties during this period.[58] Their concern could be reinforced with the biblical imagery of shepherds, sheepdogs, and hirelings (John 10 and 21)—as it was, for instance, in the polemical eclogues of Spenser's *Shepheardes Calendar* (1579).[59] In the 1570s the 'View of Popish Abuses' that was appended to the Puritan *Admonition to Parliament* (1572) drew upon the imagery of John 21 in order to put the case for the 'office of preaching'. Here, the protestors argue that their ceremonialist adversaries have turned this office into a mere 'office of reading', and their satirical portrayal of the consequences converges at several points with the terms and imagery of Beatrice's diatribe in *Paradiso* 29:

Christ said go preach, they in mockery give them the Bible and authority to preach, and yet suffer them not, except they have new licences. So that they make the chiefest part preaching, but an accessory that is as a thing without which their office may and doth consist . . . [T]hey are enjoined to feed God's lambs, and yet with these, such are admitted and accepted, as are only bare readers that are able to say service and minister a sacrament. And that this is not the feeding that Christ spake of, the scriptures are plain. Reading is not feeding, but it is as evil as playing upon a stage, and worse too . . . These are empty feeders, dark eyes, ill workmen to hasten in the Lord's harvest . . . evil dividers of the word.[60]

The meaning of the injunction to 'feed my sheep/lambs' in John 21 (and the subsequent recurrence of the metaphor in Acts 20: 28 and 1 Peter 5: 2) had been hotly contested between the more orthodox English Protestants and their Catholic opponents in the 1560s, as part of a larger argument about authority and rule in the Church.[61] Both this debate and that about proper preaching thus provide part of the wider context for the first appearance of the Dantean trope in English Protestant polemic, in the third and longest reference to Dante in the 1570 edition of John Foxe's *Ecclesiasticall History*.

In his initial list of 'names of the Authors alleged in this Booke', Foxe includes both 'Dantes Italicus' and Flacius, as 'Illyricus'. He mentions Dante as one of the writers alive during the reign of Edward I, and he follows Flacius's erroneous claim that Dante was an active supporter of Ludwig of Bavaria in his quarrel with Pope John XXII.[62] In his fourth and longest reference to Dante, Foxe draws upon Flacius

---

[58] Collinson 1989: 185–220.

[59] Notably those for May and September.

[60] From 'A View of Popish Abuses yet Remaining in the English Church' (1572), reprinted in Cressy and Ferrell 1996: 84.

[61] The debate about 'spiritual jurisdiction', following the Elizabethan Act of Supremacy and its Oath, involved on the one side Robert Horne, bishop of Winchester, and on the other the Catholics John Feckenham (formerly abbot of Westminster) and Thomas Stapleton (in exile at Douay). On their dispute about the meaning of 'feeding the flock' in the biblical texts, see O'Connell 1964: 192–3 (with nn. 16–18).

[62] Foxe 1570: 440, sig. P4ᵛ, and 485, sig. T3ʳ.

for most of his material: for Dante's views on the authority of the emperor and the Donation of Constantine; for the *Paradiso*'s satirical portrayal of preaching and the Papacy; and for *Purgatorio*'s representation of the Pope as Whore of Babylon and Antichrist:

Dantes an Italian writer a Florentine [shouldernote: 'Dantes an Italian writer against the Pope'], lyued in the tyme of Ludovicus themperour ... and tooke his part with Marsilius Patauinus agaynst three sortes of men, which he said were enemies to the truth ... [Pope, religious orders, canon lawyers] ... Certayne of his writinges be extant abroade, wherein he proueth the pope not to be aboue the Emperour, nor to haue any right or iurisdiction in the empyre. He refuteth the Donation of Constantine to be a forged and a fayned thing, as which neither dyd stand with any law or ryght [shouldernote: 'Donation of Constantine a thyng forged']. He complayneth moreouer verye muche, the preaching of God's word to be omitted: and in stede therof, the vayne fables of Monkes and Friers to bee preached and beleued of the people: and so the stock of Christ to be fed not with the foode of the Gospel, but with winde. The Pope saith he, of a pastor is made a woolfe, to wast the church of Christ, and to procure with his Clergye not the word of god to be preached, but his own decrees. In his canticle of purgatory, he declareth the Pope to be the whore of Babilon. [shouldernote: 'The pope the whore of Babylon'] And to her ministers, to some he applieth ii. hornes: to some .iiii. As to the patriarches, whom he noteth to be the tower of the said whoore Babilonicall. *Ex libris Dantis Italice.*

Hereunto may be added the saying out of the boke of Iornandus imprinted, with the foresayd Dantes: that forsomuch as Antichrist commeth not before the distruction of the Empire, therefore such as go about to have the empire extinct, are foreru[n]ners and messe[n]gers in so doing of Anti-christ. Therefore let the Romains (saith he) & theire Bishops beware, lest their sinnes and wickednes so deserving by the iust iudgment of God, the pristehode be taken from them ... [63]

Foxe's version of the 'feeding with wind' trope here is dependent not on Flacius's direct translation of the lines from *Paradiso* but on the paraphrase that had first appeared in the account of Dante in the 1556 edition of the *Catalogus*.[64] It is worth quoting the passage at length, however, since the later part of it shows clearly that Foxe must have had access to the 1562 edition, with its sixty-six lines of translation from the *Paradiso*. Thus, from 'In his canticle of purgatory' onward, Foxe's comments on Dante's Whore of Babylon and the Antichrist are translated closely from Flacius's account of these in the later (Strasbourg) text of the *Catalogus*.[65] Even his version of the name of the chronicler whose work on the Holy Roman Empire had appeared alongside the first print of Dante's *De Monarchia* in 1559 ('Iornandus' for 'Iordanes') follows that in Flacius.[66]

This was the form and context in which Dante's 'good metaphor' from *Paradiso* 29 was first appropriated in Protestant England, and it continued to be recycled in polemical writing long after 1570. Foxe's own version reappeared in subsequent editions of the *Ecclesiasticall History*; and it was itself lifted word for word in an

---

[63] Foxe 1570: 485–6, sig. T3ʳ⁻ᵛ.   [64] Flacius 1556: 868.   [65] Flacius 1562: 507B.
[66] On Foxe's involvement in the production of the earlier edition of Flacius's *Catalogus*, see above, p. 53. His notes on Iordanes and 'Antichrist' are omitted in the above quotation.

English version of a French Protestant text: Simon de Voyon's *Testimonie of the True Church of God*, translated in 1585 by William Phiston.[67] Also in the 1580s, Foxe's friend, the contentious president of Magdalen Laurence Humphrey, made use of the trope in an anti-Catholic tract, *Jesuitismi pars secunda: Puritanopapismi*.[68] As the title of Humphrey's work implies, he was active in polemic against the Jesuits—notably Edmund Campion, whose work had been circulating in Oxford shortly before his capture and execution in 1581. Against Campion's claims for the apostolic authority of Rome, Humphrey cites both Dante and Petrarch as adversaries of the curia and then proceeds to cite first the *Monarchia*, then *Paradiso* 29:

Praetereo etia[m] illustres Ro. Curiae adversarios, Dantem Florentinu[m] [shouldernote: '*In Monarchia. Dantes*'], & Franciscu[m] Petrarcha[m], quorum ille firmissima[m] papatus Arcem demolitur, contenditque papale[m] potestatem non esse Imperatoria maiorem aut superiore[m]: conqueritur oves Christi non pabulo sed vento pasci [shouldernote: '*In c[antione] 29*'], ex Euangelio fieri clypeu[m] & hasta[m], nunc iocis & facetiis ad praedicandu[m] iri, & modo bene rideatur, intumescere cucullam: Papam denique ex pastore LUPUM evasisse [shouldernote: '*Illyr. in Test. Verit.*']

I shall also pass over briefly those two noble adversaries of the Roman curia, Dante the Florentine and Francis Petrarch, of whom the former cast down the stout fortress of the Papacy and asserted that the powers of the Papacy were no greater or higher than those of the Empire. He [Dante] laments that Christ's sheep are being fed not with proper food but with wind, that the Gospel is to be used as a shield and weapon, that preaching is nowadays done though jokes and humour, and that the preacher's hood puffs up with pride only when laughter is aroused. Moreover [he claims that] the pope has turned from a shepherd into a WOLF.'[69]

Humphrey's version of the Dantean trope itself ('oves Christi non pabulo sed vento pasci') reproduces Flacius's paraphrase which had first appeared in the 1556 edition of the *Catalogus*. Like Foxe, however, Humphrey also makes use of the 1562 edition. His subsequent quotations from *Paradiso* 29 (from 'ex Evangelio' to 'intumescere cucullam') are taken almost word for word from Flacius's Latin translation in the Strasbourg text. Unlike Foxe, he acknowledges his secondary source—Flacius—as 'Illyr[icus] in Test[ium] Verit[atis]', in a shouldernote.

What kind of 'reading' of Dante's text does this represent? Did any of the English purveyors and recyclers of the trope ever go back to the original text? There is no evidence (as far as I know) to suggest that Foxe knew any Italian; and, as we have seen, his account of Dante is largely dependent upon Flacius. On the other hand, Humphrey had something of a reputation as a linguist, and, had he been so inclined, he might have been able to consult one or other of the editions of the *Commedia* in the original that are known to have been in Oxford around

---

[67] The relevant excerpt from Phiston's version (London: Henry Middleton for Thomas Charde) is in Boswell 1999: 72.

[68] Humphrey 1584.　　　[69] Humphrey 1584: 346–7.

this time.[70] He and other English polemicists who cite Italian authors as witnesses against Rome might also have been introduced to their work by Italian reformists, several of whom had found refuge in England since the time of Edward VI.[71]

By the turn of the century the citing of the trope from *Paradiso* 29 reflects the direct attention that English controversialists—both Protestant and Catholic—are beginning to pay to Dante's text. We thus find not only canto and verse being cited in shouldernotes, but phrases from the *Commedia* being cited in the original—for instance, in the work of Matthew Sutcliffe. Sutcliffe was immensely active in the field of anti-Catholic polemic, founding and endowing a college at Chelsea for this purpose, and was himself a prolific writer against Rome.[72] Possibly the first of his references to Dante is in a Latin treatise on the Papacy, dedicated to Archbishop Whitgift and explicitly directed against the leading Jesuit controversialist, Robert Bellarmine.[73] Here Sutcliffe disputes Bellarmine's interpretation of *pasce oves meas* in John 21; and he goes on to contest the Jesuit's claims about the apostolic authority of *praecepta prelatorum*, using Dante's denunciation of preachers in *Paradiso* 29 for support:

Respondet Bellar[minus] [. . .] *ut servemus praecepta prelatorum secundum illud Christi: 'qui vos audit, me audit'.* Sed fallere conatur imperitum lectorem. Non enim voluit nos simpliciter audire quaecunque illi docent; multas enim saepe docent tales praelati fabulas & nugas, ut asserit Dantes poeta Italus . . .

Bellarmine answers that *we should obey the precepts of prelates according to that precept of Christ: 'He who hearkens to you hearkens to me.'* Yet he seeks to delude the unwary reader. He [Christ] certainly did not intend us blindly to follow whatever they teach us. For such prelates often teach us a lot of fables and foolishness, as the Italian poet Dante claims.[74]

The next reference to Dante, in Book 5, also invokes the same passage from *Paradiso* 29, but here Sutcliffe uses the trope in a more apocalyptic context as one of the 'signs and prodigies of the Antichrist': 'Dantes Florentinus suo etiam tempore significat monachos huiusmodi fabulis populum pascere solitos' ('Dante the Florentine, even in his time, shows such monks to be adept at feeding folk with fables').[75] He then goes on to quote the relevant five lines (*Par.* 29. 103–7) in the original Italian. He also cites and summarizes Dante's trope at least four more times in works where he is concerned with Catholic preachers' alleged use of 'fabulous martyrologies and lying legendes' and with their casting over their

---

[70] At least five copies of the *Commedia* were in the Bodleian by 1605; see below, p. 98. On Humphrey, see *ODNB*, s.v. 'Humphrey, Laurence (1525x7–1589), college head'.

[71] See Wyatt 2005: 84–99. One of the later refugees, Alessandro Citolini (who was in London from around 1566 to 1582), is known to have published comments on Dante's language (Wyatt 2005: 206–7 and 326, nn. 10–12).

[72] On Sutcliffe's career, see *ODNB*, s.v. 'Sutcliffe, Matthew (1549/50–1629), dean of Exeter'. On his more 'nuanced' approach to the use/abuse of Langland and Chaucer by a Protestant opponent, see Jones 2011: 150–1.

[73] Sutcliffe 1599*a*. An earlier 'reference' to Dante in Sutcliffe's *De catholica, orthodoxa, et vera Christi ecclesia* (London: Reg. Typog., 1592) is listed in Boswell 1999: 90, but this is based on a mistranslation (of the participle *dantes*).

[74] Sutcliffe 1599*a*: 334.   [75] Sutcliffe 1599*a*: 477.

audience a 'dark and mistie cloud of ignorance'.[76] Much of this is predictable, as the common currency of anti-Catholic propaganda. But once again the move to the direct use of the original text is a significant development in the reception of Dante and in the debate about his status as 'writer against the pope'.

As has been shown, a Catholic response to the Protestant conscription of Dante—*The Converted Jew* of 1630—participated in this development by engaging directly with passages from the *Inferno* and the *Paradiso*, and translating one of them.[77] Four years later Simon Birckbek, vicar of Gilling in Yorkshire, went yet further in *The protestants evidence, taken out of good records* (1634).[78] In his 'evidence' Birckbek proceeds century by century through the usual succession of 'worthy *Guides* of *God's* Church', and pays close attention to some of his 'good records' by translating both from two of Petrarch's sonnets and at some length from three cantos of *Paradiso* and one of the *Inferno*—thus outdoing his Catholic predecessor ('Clare') in quantity at least.[79] Birckbek also (once again) paraphrases the 'feeding with wind' trope in *Paradiso* 29. 106–7, along with other material from the *cantica* that he subsequently goes on to quote and translate:

Dante in his Poeme of Paradise, written in Italian, complaines that the Pope of a shepheard was become a wolf, & diverted Christs sheep out of the true way; that the Gospell was forsaken, the writings of the Fathers neglected, and the Decretals onely studied [*Paradiso* 9. 127–35]. That in times past warre was made upon the Church by the sword, but now by a famine and dearth of the Word, which was allotted for the food of the soul, & not wont to be denied to any that desired it [*Paradiso* 18. 127–9]; that men applauded themselves in their owne conceites, but the Gospel was silenced; that the pore sheepe were fed with the puffes of winde, and were pined and consumed away.[80]

Birckbek's version—like his references to the other passages in *Paradiso*—is substantially indebted to the account of this *cantica* in Sampson Lennard's 1612 English translation of Philippe De Mornay's *Mysterium Iniquitatis* (published in 1611).[81] There is, however, no reason to suppose that the subsequent versions of the four passages from the *Commedia* are not his own, although he could well have used Flacius's Latin translations in the 1562 *Catalogus* for assistance.[82] He cites Dante's text in the original with relatively few errors; his summary of *Paradiso's* critique of the Church is reasonably accurate; and the fourteen couplets of his translation from *Paradiso* 29 display a kind of rude and rollicking energy, as he contrasts Dante's godly apostles with contemporary preachers:

---

[76] See Sutcliffe 1599*b*: 29 and 84–5 (excerpts in Boswell 1999: 150–1); and Sutcliffe 1600: 1. 43, and part 2. 8 (excerpts in Boswell 1999: 114).
[77] See above, p. 57–8.
[78] On Birckbek's career and publications, see *ODNB*, s.v. 'Birckbek, Simon (1583/4–1656), Church of England clergyman and religious controversialist'.
[79] Boswell 1999: 198–203. On Birckbek and Petrarch, see also Usher 2005: 193 and 196.
[80] Birckbek 1634: 57 (Boswell 1999: 200).
[81] De Mornay 1612: 444.
[82] Birckbek refers to his own 'Catalogue of Witnesses' as a *Catalogus Testium Veritatis*, thus echoing Flacius's title; see Boswell 1999: 199.

Christ sayd not to th'Apostles, goe
And preach vaine toyes the world unto:
But he did give them a true ground,
Which onely did in their eares sound.
So providing for to fight
And to kindle faith's true light,
Out of the Gospel they did bring
Their sheild and speares t'affect the thing.
Now the way of preaching, is with toyes
To stuffe a sermon; and herein joy's
Their teachers; if the people doe but smile
At their conceits, the Frier i'th'meane while
Huffes up his Cowle, and is much admir'd
For that's his aime; there's nothing else requir'd:
But in this hood there is a nest
Of birds, which could the vulgar see,
They might spie pardons, and the rest,
How worthy of their trust they bee.[83]

'Toyes to stuffe a sermon' (lines 1–2) vigorously reflects this Protestant vicar's concern with proper preaching, and 'Huffes up his Cowle' concisely renders the metaphor of vanity as wind (*gonfia il cappuccio*).

Birckbek's lusty rendering of *Paradiso*'s attack on vain preachers appeared only three years before John Milton's appropriation of Beatrice's invective during St Peter's outburst in 'Lycidas' (1637):

how well could I have spar'd for thee young swaine
anough of such as for thire bellies sake
creepe, and intrude, and clime into the fold
of other care they little reckining make
then how to scramble at the shearers feast
and shove away the worthy bidden guest
blind mouths! that scarce themselves know how to hold
a sheephooke, or have learn't ought else the least
that to the faithfull heardsman's art belongs!
what recks it them? what need they? they are sped;
and when they list, thire leane and flashie songs
grate on thire scrannel pipes of wretched straw,
the hungrie sheep looke up and are not fed,
but swolne with wind, and the rank mist they draw,
rot inwardly, and foule contagion spred . . .[84]

Milton's 'radical' invective in this poem of the late 1630s has, as we have seen, a long polemical tradition behind it.[85] 'Lycidas' makes the shepherds who feed their

---

[83] Birckbek 1634: 59; also Boswell 1999: 201–2. Boswell's reprint of the passage makes Birckbek's Italian look rather worse, since it introduces three more mistakes in its transcription of the original.

[84] 'Lycidas', ll. 113–27 (spellings as in Trinity College Cambridge MS).

[85] On Milton's radicalism at this time, see Lewalski 1998.

flocks on wind not Catholic friars but the Laudian priesthood—the kind of clergy whom their opponents accused of attending more to ceremonial, 'reading' or superficial sermons than to proper 'godly preaching'. The poem's discourse thus converges with that of earlier nonconformists who had insisted that 'reading is not feeding' and denounced the ceremonialist priesthood as 'empty feeders'—and those who (like George Gifford's 'Zelotes') had denounced the kind of preacher who merely dispenses 'a smooth tale' or 'some rotten allegory', letting 'the people come out of the church blowing [i.e. boasting], that they were fed full as ticks, when they go home with empty bellies'.[86] In 'Lycidas' the metaphor of feeding upon wind is developed obliquely, suggestively, and even punningly: the 'hungrie sheep' are not only 'swolne with wind' but also with 'mist'—a word that in his time could carry not only its modern meaning (as a metaphor of obfuscation), but also that of 'things mystical' or even 'mystification'.[87] There are, to be sure, tensions and uncertainties in the ideological stance of Milton's invective here. Its mouthpiece (St Peter) shakes '*mitred* locks' before embarking on his stern speech (l. 112), and it has been questioned 'whether this passage supports the prelatists' view that the apostles' ruling power derives to bishops, or the Presbyterian view that such power pertained only to the apostles'.[88] The way in which Milton shifts the application of the 'feeding with wind' trope from its traditional anti-Catholic slant (as in Flacius, Foxe, and other Protestant controversialists) to concern with pastoral care within the English Church suggests an inclination towards the latter view. His appropriation of Dante here reinforces the sense of 'Lycidas' as a poem harbouring 'an intensity of both intertextual self-consciousness and sharp political criticism'.[89]

How deliberate was Milton's reorientation of the Dantean trope? By this time (shortly before his journey to Italy) Milton's Commonplace Book shows that he was reading Dante's *Commedia* in Italian and could have first encountered Beatrice's attack on vain preachers in its original context.[90] In *Paradiso* 29 this portrayal of earthly corruption contrasts with a subject which (as has recently been shown) also informs 'Lycidas': the nature and role of the orders of angels.[91]

Milton was, however, also reading (amongst much else) Foxe's *Ecclesiasticall History*, the seventh printing of which had appeared in 1632.[92] He would have been well aware of how frequently other Protestant controversialists since Foxe had conscripted Dante, and of the various and frequent ways in which they had

[86] See 'A View of Popish Abuses yet Remaining in the English Church' (1572), reprinted in Cressy and Ferrell 1996: 84 and 103.

[87] *OED* 'mist *sb*²', which is etymologically different from 'mist' in the sense of 'vapour' (*sb*²). Milton later uses 'in mist', with ironic reference to theological glossing (*Paradise Lost* 5. 435–6).

[88] Lewalski 1998: 58.   [89] Raymond 2008: 140.

[90] The Commonplace Book can be found in Milton 1953–73: 1. 344–513 For the entry referring to Daniello's 1568 edition of the *Commedia* (dating from between 1635 and 1638) see p. 418 and n. 1). For the Dante items only, see also *DEL* 1. 121–2.

[91] On Catholic and Protestant 'angel theology' see Raymond 2008: 142–5.

[92] On Milton's knowledge of the *Ecclesiasticall History* (probably in the seventh edition), see Boswell 1975: 105 (item 617). Milton refers to Foxe in a number of later polemical works, including *Of Reformation* (Milton 1953–73: 1. 544 f.) and *Areopagitica* (Milton 1953–73: 2. 502 and 548).

exploited the trope of feeding the flock with wind. He was himself alert (as the 1630s entries in his Commonplace Book show) to the ways in which Dante could be recruited as a writer against Rome.[93] *Paradiso* 29. 106–7 is thus in no way a simple source for St Peter's invective in 'Lycidas' 125–7; by the 1630s it has become part of a wider and increasingly complex controversial context. Dante and Foxe have come to coexist un-peacefully in the 'dread voice' that breaks into Milton's pastoral elegy.

Like many of his compatriots in the medieval and early modern periods, Milton actually travelled to the source of much of his reading: Italy. Like other British intellectuals of his time—such as Thomas Hobbes, William Harvey, John Evelyn, and Andrew Marvell (and others, who will feature in the next chapter)—he engaged with the culture of cities, such as Florence, Rome, Naples, and Venice.[94] Unlike most (except for Kenelm Digby), he also attended and corresponded with literary societies and academies.[95] At Florence, for example, he became acquainted with the secretary of the Crusca, Benedetto Buonmattei, who had lectured exhaustively on the first half of Dante's *Commedia* over the previous five years.[96] At Venice he would accumulate more Italian books to add to the range of authors (including Dante) that had been listed in his Commonplace Book.[97]

Milton's dialogue with Dante would continue to inform his polemical writing after his return from Italy in 1639. Shortly before the Civil War he would extend it by translating a *terzina* from the *Inferno* (alongside passages from Petrarch and Ariosto) as part of his ongoing argument against prelacy.[98] His rendering of Dante's lines about the 'Donation of Constantine' into 'English blank verse' would be quoted approvingly by a writer against 'Popery' during the Protectorate.[99] His wider dialogue with the *Commedia* in *Paradise Lost* would venture beyond what his British contemporaries could attempt in prose or rhyme.[100] Whilst his early appropriations of passages from the *Commedia* can be related to the polemical strategies of the writers who have been the subject of this chapter, his encounters with Italian culture also give him significant affinities with the British travellers, collectors, translators, and readers who will appear in the next.

---

[93] For the polemical references to Dante dating from the 1630s in the Commonplace Book, see the entries under: *Avaritia* (Milton 1953–73: 1. p. 366 and n. 1); *De Usurâ* (1. p. 418 and n. 1); and *Rex* (1. pp. 438–9 and n. 4).

[94] Stoye 1989: 87, 98, 119, 121, 138–9, 216, and 351, n. 27. On his itinerary, see Arthos 1968: xi–xii.

[95] Stoye 1989: 155–7. For Kenelm Digby's association with the Accademia dei Filomati at Siena, probably in the 1620s, see below, pp. 102–3.

[96] On Buonmattei (1581–1647), Dante, and Milton, see Samuel 1966: 34 and 38–43; also Caesar 1989: 39–40 and 323–5. For a general review of the effects of Milton's 'Italian experience', see Griffin in Di Cesare 1991: 19–27, and Lewalski 2000: ch. 4.

[97] See above, p. 66 and n. 90; and Lewalski 2000: 106 with n. 80.

[98] *Inferno* 19. 115–17, in *Of Reformation* (1641); see Milton 1968: 283.

[99] Henry Stubbe(s) 1659: 174–5; see Appendix 2, below. The significance of this reference to Milton's use of blank verse for translating Dante's *terza rima* is discussed by von Maltzahn 2008: 407.

[100] See Samuel 1966: 69–268 and Wallace 2007: 287–9.

4

'Few can understand him': Reputation, Ownership, Reading, *c*.1600–*c*.1800

VOLP[ONE]. The *Poet*,
As old in time, as *Plato*, and as knowing,
Say's that your highest female grace is *Silence*.

LAD[Y POLITIC]. Which o' your *Poets*? *Petrarch*? or *Tasso* or *Dante*?
Guerrini? *Ariosto*? *Aretine*?
Cieco di Hadria? I haue read them all.
[. . .]
Dante is hard, and fewe can vnderstand him.
But for a desperate wit, there's *Aretine*;
Onely, his *pictures* are a little obscene—
You marke mee not?

VOLP[ONE]. Alasse, my mind's perturb'd.[1]

Lady Politic Would-Be—here inflicting her literary preferences upon the supposedly bed-ridden Volpone—thus appears as an *inglese italianata*, laying claim to authority on a range of authors—including the 'hard' Dante. Actual readers and writers whom Jonson knew—and some he loved to hate—also had close connections with Italy. John Marston, whose verbal extravagances Jonson had savaged in *Poetaster* (1601), was of Italian descent and used Italian in dedicating *The Malcontent* (*c*.1603–4) to his recent assailant.[2] From 1605 and into the 1620s Jonson collaborated, not always harmoniously, on court masques with Inigo Jones, who had spent long and productive periods in Italy.[3] William Drummond of Hawthornden, whom Jonson would visit in Scotland during 1618–19, was 'deeply immersed in Italian literature' and had acquired a copy of Dante's *Commedia* in London.[4] John Florio—to whom, as 'louing Father & worthy Freind . . . The ayde of his Muses', Johnson presented a copy of the 1607 quarto of *Volpone*—was not only of Italian

---

[1] Jonson 1607: sig. G2ʳ (Act 3, scene 2).
[2] Marston's mother Maria (d. 1621) was 'daughter of Andrew Guarsi; possibly a descendant of Katherine of Aragon's Italian physician, Balthasar Guarsi' (*ODNB*, s.v. 'Marston, John (*bap.* 1576, *d.* 1634), poet and playwright'). See also Kirkpatrick 1995: 269–73.
[3] On Jones's six-year residence in Italy around 1600 and his visits to Venice, Vicenza, Rome, and Naples in 1613–14, see *ODNB*, s.v. 'Jones, Inigo (1573–1652), architect and theatre designer' and Stoye 1989: 88, 105, 338 n.44, and pl. 6.
[4] Jack 1986: 13–21. On Drummond's edition, see *DEL* 1. x and 113, and below, p. 90.

descent and a producer of guides to Italian for the British public; he was also the source of the phrase Lady Pol parrots, about Dante's difficulty.[5]

'Fewe can vnderstand him.' How pertinent would Lady Pol's claim have been to the British public's awareness of and attitude towards Dante around Jonson's time? Does it have any bearing upon the views of this 'Gran-Master of the *Italian* tongue' in the reading, writing, and collecting culture of the seventeenth and eighteenth centuries?[6] The chapter that follows here may share something of Lady Pol's prolixity, but it is necessarily a long one—not only because it aims to address these questions (and related ones) over a span of some 200 years, but also because it seeks to trace various continuities in the assessment of Dante's reputation, in the access to and collection of his texts, and in the quotation, appropriation, and translation of his writing. While the eventual emergence of complete translations of the *Commedia* in the late eighteenth and early nineteenth centuries, and the Romantic engagement with Dante as a 'modern' writer may seem to signal a rapid and dramatic revaluation and 'rehabilitation', it can also be shown to have its roots in more extended conversations and in slower and subtler processes of accumulation.

A CENTURY WITHOUT DANTE?

[L]iterary historians are universally agreed that if the seventeenth century is analogous to any season in Dante's reputation, it is mid-winter [. . .] if it does indeed represent a low point in the appreciation of the poet, it is at the bottom of a graph that has been making its way downwards for a long time, and will take a long time to swing upwards again.[7]

On the face of it, the evidence for this cooling of interest is compelling. Only four new editions of the *Commedia* were published in the whole century (most of them within the first three decades)—as against the thirty or so that were put out between 1500 and 1600.[8] Recognition of 'the divine spirit of the architectonic poet'[9] on the part of the Calabrian Dominican friar Tommaso Campanella (1568–1639) seems to stand out 'in marked contrast to Dante's denigration at the hands of most of the readers and writers of the seventeenth century, which has been called 'the century without Dante'.[10]

Yet the climatic metaphor and the emphasis on denigration have been exaggerated, and it has also been acknowledged that 'the period is neither entirely silent nor

---

[5] For Florio's original phrase, see *DEL* 1. 86. Jonson's inscription in Florio's copy of the 1607 *Volpone* (now in the British Library, at C.12.e.17) is on the verso of the eighth front flyleaf, opposite the title-page. On Florio, see esp. Wyatt 2005: part 2.

[6] For this description of Dante (by the translator, James Howell), see below, p. 74 and n. 48.

[7] Caesar 1989: 36.

[8] Caesar 1989: See also Parker 1993: 133–57 (listing thirty-six sixteenth-century editions) and Richardson 1995: 255–7 (listing twenty-six and acknowledging five others).

[9] Campanella's *Poetica* (1596), trans. in Caesar 1989: 304.

[10] Girardi 2003: 107, citing Firpo 1969: 31.

entirely uniform in its judgment of Dante'.[11] Despite his 'hardness' for readers such as Jonson's Lady Pol and writers such as Francesco Guarino—despite his antiquity and some signs of continuing disapproval in some quarters among the Catholic hierarchy[12]—Dante still carried weight as a linguistic precedent, a 'famous' author, a 'writer against the pope', and a source of memorable sayings for both his European and his British seventeenth-century publics.

The frequency and diversity of that public's views should indeed not be under-estimated. Two major surveys have amassed around 200 pages of references to Dante and his work from English texts of the period.[13] A search of material for this chapter in the *Early English Books Online* database has yielded thirty or so further citations that are not found in previous collections.[14] These examples derive from British writing on a variety of subjects, ranging from language and literary culture to history, politics, religion, science, and the visual arts, and they will be used (along with previously identified sources) to investigate how Dante was presented to the reading public over the course of the seventeenth century.

For those engaged in learning Italian grammar and vocabulary—and for those interested in the history of the vernacular—Dante was there at the source. Recent studies investigating the processes of learning Italian in early modern Britain have underlined the effect of language-teaching and of the manuals published in six-teenth- and seventeenth-century London.[15] Amongst the latter are several which explicitly invoke Dante amongst authors whose work is to be drawn upon or aspired to. In the middle of the sixteenth century William Thomas had made use of several Italian grammarians in his *Principal Rules of the Italian Grammer, with a Dictionarie for the better understanding of Boccace, Petrarca, and Dante* (London, 1550), and following their example he had given close attention to some of the *Commedia*'s usages.[16] Around the turn of the century John Florio, in the 'Epistle dedicatorie' to his 1598 *Worlde of Wordes*—one of the texts in Lady Pol's capacious handbag—proclaims the value of his dictionary for the understanding of 'hard' authors such as Petrarch, Boccaccio, and Dante and access to 'strange bookes... and... fantasticall subjects as be written in the Italian toong'.[17] Over a dozen words are ascribed to Dante in Florio's dictionary itself (although two of these are not in

---

[11] Caesar 1989: 36.

[12] For the placing of *Monarchia* on the Index and the official expurgation of the *Commedia* (in 1581 and 1614), see above, p. 52; also Toynbee 1921: 111–12.

[13] *DEL* 1. 101–83; Boswell 1999: 112–214 (for 1600 to 1640).

[14] Accessed at: <http://eebo.chadwyck.com> up to 02/11/12. For the basic results, see Appendix 2, below.

[15] Pizzoli 2004, Lawrence 2005, and Wyatt 2005. See also Simonini 1952, esp. 11–41 and 110–14.

[16] Alberto Accarisi's *Vocabolario, Grammatica et Orthographia de la lingua volgare* of 1543 had offered to provide 'explanations' (*ispositioni*) of many passages in Dante, Petrarch, and Boccaccio. For examples of Thomas's references to the *Commedia*, see *DEL* 1. 39–40; on his career and other works, see Griffith 1966: 281–4; Lawrence 2005: 3–4 and n. 8; Wyatt 2005: 70–2 and 211–12; and Woolfson 2009: 410–12. As Wyatt notes, Thomas's grammar and dictionary were republished three times (1560, 1562, and 1567).

[17] Excerpts in *DEL* 1. 86 and Wyatt 2005: 227.

the poet's works).[18] Florio had also cited Dantean usage at least twice much earlier, in his 1578 'induction' to Italian (*Florio his firste Fruites*); whilst later, in the expanded *Queen Anna's New World of Words* (1611), he refers to four editions of/commentaries on the *Commedia* and draws on Landino's interpretation of the names of Dante's devils in canto 21 of the *Inferno*.[19] Compared, of course, to the burgeoning lexicographical range of Florio's work (74,000 entries in the 1611 dictionary), this level of recourse to the *Commedia* seems rather meagre.[20] Yet, like other grammarians and writers on language in this period, Florio keeps Dante in view as a name and authority, even if his text is not always fully 'understood' or accurately reproduced.[21]

As name and authority, Dante clearly continues to feature for readers of English critical, historical, and political texts throughout the seventeenth century. As we have seen, his canonical status within the Florentine triumvirate had earlier in the sixteenth century been mediated through, for example, Leland's epigrams, Thynne's Chaucer, and Hoby's Castiglione.[22] That position continues to be emphasized, for instance in Sidney's account of the three writers who had made 'the Italian language ... aspire to be a Treasure-house of Science'.[23] Such canonization served the cause of the home vernacular: Sidney compares '*Dante, Boccace, and Petrarch*' with 'our English ... *Gower* and *Chaucer*'.[24]

Frequently reprinted works, such as Sidney's *Apologie*, helped to make Dante's own name 'flourish in the Printer's shoppes' and to keep it current among a wider seventeenth-century British readership.[25] Throughout the period Dante is recognized not only as 'famous' but also as a bearer of fame, and of infamy. Sidney, as is well known, appears to be the first English writer to portray Dante as the devotee of Beatrice.[26] During the century after him hitherto unidentified citations in this chapter will include references to others who are (as one writer puts it) 'celebrated by the Poet *Dante*' in the *Commedia*: Peter Damian (*Paradiso* 21), Farinata degli Uberti (*Inferno* 10), Pier della Vigna (*Inferno* 13), and the House of

---

[18] *DEL* 1. 86 lists the mysterious word *Alheppe* (*aleppe*, Plutus in *Inf.* 7. 1; glossed even more mysteriously by Florio as: '*Alehebbe*, he had wings'), and *giuggiola* (not in Dante). Wyatt (2005: 229 and n. 121) adds 11 more (10 of these following a note in in the Wesleyan University Library copy), viz.: *ita* (cp., perhaps, Dante's Lombard and Lucchese form *issa* in *Inf.* 23. 7 and *Purg.* 24. 55); *accismare*; *appulcrare*; *attuiare*; *inculare*; *lulla*; *lurco*; *piorno*; *roffia*; *rubecchio*; and *turgere*. Of these, *inculare* does not seem to be used in the *Commedia*; all the other words are.

[19] Boswell 1999: 57 refers to Florio's citation of Dantean forms of numerical adjectives (*ambodue* [*sic*] and *amendue* in *Florio his firste Fruites*, f. 122ʳ); Dante is also cited as a source earlier, on f. 118ʳ.

[20] On the increasing volume of entries, see Wyatt 2005: 228.

[21] A comparable contemporary example is the Oxford scholar John Sanford, whose *Grammer, or Introduction to the Italian Tongue* (1605) cites Dante four times (not always accurately), and uses Adam's words about the nature of language (*Par.* 26. 130–2) as its epigraph (verso of title-page); see *DEL* 1. 107–8.

[22] See above, pp. 35, 37 (with n. 31), and 47 (with n. 99).

[23] *An Apologie for Poetrie* (1595) sig. B2v, excerpted in *DEL* 1. 70–1 and Boswell 1999: 96–7.

[24] See above, p. 36 with n. 23 and pp. 40 and 42.

[25] *An Apologie* was first printed (several times) in 1595; it appeared frequently alongside *The Countesse of Pembrokes Arcadia* (reprinted sixteen times between 1598 and 1638); see Boswell 1999: 97. Leland's earlier epigrams and eulogies mentioning Dante also seem to have had a fair amount of currency during the seventeenth century; see *DEL* 1. 147, 155, 172, 179.

[26] Toynbee emphasizes this twice, in *DEL* 1. 69 and 71 n. 1.

Este (*Purgatorio* 8).[27] The same list also features names of souls for whom the *Commedia* bore the fruit of infamy: Michael Scot (*Inferno* 20), Charles of Valois (*Purgatorio* 20), and Philip the Fair of France (*Paradiso* 19).[28]

Other familiar targets of Dantean invective also, of course, included corrupt popes and abuses of the institutional Catholic Church, and amid the controversies and conflicts of seventeenth-century Britain the political and ecclesiological arguments of Dante's *Monarchia* continued to be visited.[29] The poet's conscription begun by British Protestant writers in the sixteenth century extended throughout the next.[30] That doughty polemicist and adversary of Robert Persons, Matthew Sutcliffe (1550?–1629), for instance, invoked Dante as a witness against Rome around the turn of the century,[31] and he returned to the fray in the last decade of his life, to insist once again that

the friers of his [Dante's] time wrested scriptures and little regarded them [...] they desired their owne glorie, and preached their owne inuentions, hiding the Gospell in silence [. . .] they tel fables, and feede ignorant and simple people with wind.[32]

As in earlier anti-fraternal assaults, Sutcliffe then calls upon ten lines from *Paradiso* 29 (89–90, 94–6, and 103–7) to prove his point, in a section of this work that is headed 'The miserable estate of Papists under the Popes tyrannie'. In *Of Reformation* (1641) Milton cited and translated Dante's arguments;[33] and in the 1680s and 1690s Dante still continues to feature as a writer against Rome. He is thus listed again amongst those witnesses (notably Petrarch and Marsilius of Padua) who have condemned 'the abuses of the *Court* of Rome', the 'Rapine, Debauchery and Excess of those Popes, and particularly of *Clement* the Fifth and *John* the Twenty-second', and the 'Insolency of the Bishops of *Rome*, in challenging to themselves the Right of the Empire'.[34] In 1692 Bishop Gilbert Burnet (a supporter of the 1688 'Glorious Revolution') aligns the medieval poet with 'the Authors of this Age in any way inclining to reformation', who are now subject to Catholic censorship: 'set to School to learn the *Roman* language, and agree with the *Trent* faith'. Claims of this sort thus helped to propel the anti-papal Dante into the period of the 'Whig supremacy'.[35]

---

[27] See: *Estates, Empires & Principalities* (1615); *A German Diet* (1653); *History of Naples* (1654); *History of the House of Este* (1681)—all in Appendix 2, below.

[28] See: *The History of Magick* (1657); *History of France* (1683); *Considerations about the Raising of Coin* (1696), in Appendix 2, below.

[29] See below, pp. 98–9, 101 and 108, and the translations of Grotius (1655) and Campanella (1660), in Appendix 2, below.

[30] See Chapters 2 and 3, above.

[31] On Sutcliffe's earlier work, see above pp. 54 and 63–4.

[32] *The Blessings on Mount Gerizzim* (1625), p. 105; see Appendix 2, below. The same text was reprinted in 1629 under the title of *A true Relation of Englands happinesse, under the Raigne of Queene Elizabeth and the miserable estate of Papists under the Popes Tyranny.*

[33] See above, p. 67 and n. 98.

[34] See: *An Historical Defence of the Reformation* (1683); *Bishop OVERALLs Convocation Book* (composed 1606; printed 1690); *The Life of Henry Chichele* (Latin version 1617; English translation 1699), in Appendix 2, below.

[35] Burnet, *The Life of William Bedell, D.D.* (1692), in Appendix 2, below. On Dante and Whig ideology and aesthetics, see Yates 1951: 99 and Milbank 1998: 8–29 and 121.

How 'rough' or 'refined' was Dante perceived to be by those seventeenth-century critics and readers, who looked beyond the name to parts of the text? There are certainly further citations—especially from the Restoration period—suggesting that some readers (like Florio and Lady Pol) still considered him difficult and obscure. Others echo Francesco Guarino's unease about Dante's rough-hewn, unpolished 'sculpture' (1620) or Emanuele Tesauro's concerns about his 'difficult', 'old-fashioned and plebeian' vocabulary', along with 'the rust and imperfections of . . . early speech' (1654).[36] Madeleine de Scudéry (1607–1701), reflected such views in her ten-volume novel *Clélie: histoire romaine* (1654–61), when one of her characters embarks on a prophetic account of Italian literary culture. An English translation of this popular romance appeared in 1678 (under her brother's name), and would have helped to confirm the reputation of the *Commedia*'s author as 'a man, who shall choose a very difficult Subject to treat of in Verse, and express himself so obscurely, that he shall scarce be understood by those of his own age'.[37] Such assertions did not pass without challenge in mid-seventeenth-century Britain. An Oxford cleric, poet, and editor, Barten Holyday (1593–1661), also included '*Dante*'s Three Themes' of Hell, Purgatory, and Paradise among the thousand couplets of his *Survey of the World in Ten Books* (1661).[38] In the commentary to his later edition of Juvenal (1673), Holyday also engaged in a lively comparison between censurers of style and diction in ancient Rome and a more recent Italian 'Hypercritick' who had deplored Dante's lack of 'elegant words'.[39]

Similar concerns are reflected in English translations of French texts during the last quarter of the century, thus relaying neoclassical strictures upon Dante's failures to meet certain critical standards. It has long been known that René Rapin's *Réflexions sur la poètique d'Aristote* (1674) targeted the *Commedia*'s lack of modesty and its obscurity—allegations that were rapidly reproduced in Thomas Rymer's translation of the same year.[40] It is also worth noting that an earlier work by Rapin, his *Observations sur les poèmes d'Homère et de Virgile* (1669), contained criticism of the *Commedia*'s failure to observe proper 'unity of action'; and that this stricture, too, made its way three years later into an English version by the Welsh translator, John Davies of Kidwelly.[41] Here an unnamed Italian apologist who had argued for the *Commedia*'s achievement of epic unity through 'the action of one single person'

---

[36] Caesar 1989: 37 with n. 66 and 327.

[37] *Clelia, an Excellent New Romance* (1678), in Appendix 2, below.

[38] *DEL* 1. 680. See also *ODNB*, s.v. 'Holyday [Holiday], Barten (1593–1661), Church of England clergyman and poet'.

[39] *Decimus Junius Juvenalis and Aulus Persius Flaccus Translated and Illustrated* (1673), in Appendix 2, below. The 'Hypercritick' in question was Lodovico Nogarola who had censured the *trecento* Tuscan writers at the end of an epistle attached to *Ocellus Lucanus philosophus De universi natura* (Venice: Gryphius, 1559), 61.

[40] *DEL* 1. 161–3; see also Caesar 1989: 328–30.

[41] *Observations on the Poems of Homer and Virgil* (1672), in Appendix 2, below. On Davies's work and career, see *ODNB*, s.v. 'Davies, John (1625–1693), translator'. He also translated Gabriel Naudé's *Apologie pour tous les grands personages faussement soupçonnez de magie* (1625, 1652) as *The History of Magick* (1657), which cites Dante several times; and he transmitted two further references to the *Commedia* in his translation of David Blondel's *Des Sibylles* (1649), as *A Treatise of the Sibyls* (1671); see Appendix 2, below.

is answered by Rapin's assertion: 'That the Epick Poem ought to present the perfect Idea of a great Captain and General of an Army, and not of a Knight-Errant, who most commonly is but a phantasm and a Romantick Palladine . . .'[42] Rapin's status as 'Judicious Critick' of Dante and other 'Moderns' is reinforced by another French treatise on epic, René Le Bossu's *Traité du poème épique* (1675). The English translation of this (by 'W. J.', 1695) reproduces Rapin's argument (in his *Réflexions*) that not only Dante but also Petrarch and Boccaccio 'deserve not the very name of Heroick Poets'.[43]

Yet a number of the considered and influential critical views of Dante and his work being articulated in Britain during this period are far from dismissive or denigratory. As a recent discussion of debates about the Italian vernacular during the previous century has indicated, 'Dante's status for *la questione della lingua* was a vexed one'. [44] The idea of the 'refinement' of the vernacular was gathering force in Britain in the seventeenth century, and a number of writers on language in the period emphasize (as Sidney had in the *Apologie*) how important was the role of the older authors such as Dante, Petrarch, Boccaccio, and Chaucer in preparing their vernacular to become 'a Treasure-house of Science'.[45]

Amongst notable linguists around the middle of the century is another Welsh translator, James Howell.[46] During a turbulent career, spanning the Civil War, Commonwealth, and Restoration, Howell travelled widely in Europe (including Italy) as businessman and would-be spy, and later in his life he produced a multilingual dictionary—the *Lexicon Tetraglotton* of 1659—in the preface to which he speaks of how Latin, the romance languages, and English became 'refined'—in the case of Italian, at the hands of '*Dante, Petrarca* with *Boccace* his [Petrarch's] scholler and *Ariosto*'.[47] Earlier in the 1650s—perhaps to strengthen his credentials as foreign observer with the new regime—he had published a series of imaginary 'Elaborat Orations' about characteristics of various nations of Europe. Here he not only describes Dante, Petrarch, and Boccaccio as 'a triumvirate, who were Gran-Masters [*sic*] of the *Italian* tongue' but also refers specifically to one of the 'souls known to fame' in the *Commedia*: 'Who hath not heard of *Farinata Uberti*, celebrated by *Dante*?'[48]

---

[42] *Observations on the Poems of Homer and Virgil* (1672), pp. 89–90, in Appendix 2, below.

[43] *Monsieur Bossu's Treatise of the Epick Poem* (1695), in Appendix 2, below. For the source of Rapin's assertion, see *DEL* 1. 163 (Rymer's version) and Caesar 1989: 330 (modern translation).

[44] Wyatt 2005: 206. On some sixteenth-century Italian views (Bembo, Della Casa, *et al.*), see Havely 2003: 129–3 with n. 3, and for a valuable account of the debate about the 'living language' (and the *trecento* writers' place in it), see Faithfull 1953: esp. 279, 284, 286, 288–9.

[45] On early modern views of the English vernacular, see Jones 1953, esp. 214–92, and Blank 2006.

[46] On his political and literary career, see *ODNB*, s.v. 'Howell, James (1594?–1666), historian and political writer'. The role and linguistic contexts of Welsh Italianists and translators in the early modern period would be worth further investigation. On William Thomas and John Davies of Kidwelly, see above, pp. 70 and 73 (with n. 41); and on Thomas Salusbury, see below, p. 77 (with n. 59).

[47] See *DEL* 1. 151–2. On Howell's descriptions of his travels in Italy, the Low Countries, and Spain, see Stoye 1989: 75, 103, 137, 181, 266–7.

[48] *A German Diet: or The Balance of Europe . . . Made fit for the Meridian of ENGLAND By* James Howell *Esq.* (1653); see Appendix 2, below.

In the later decades of the century, too, a number of positive critical judgements and references stress Dante's contribution to vernacular 'refinement' rather than his 'roughness' or irregularity. In his lines prefaced to the Earl of Roscommon's *Essay on Translated Verse* (1684), Dryden's tribute to the Italian *trecento* as 'a silver, not a golden age'—encompassing amongst other things the 'fair barbarity' of Petrarch's verse—is elegantly backhanded, but it significantly allots a key role in this medieval 'restoration' to 'Dante's polished page' (ll. 19–23). In the prose preface to his opera *Albion and Albanius* the following year Dryden would return to the subject of Italian's 'beautiful barbarism', arguing that it had 'in a manner been refined and purified from the Gothic ever since the time of Dante'; and the preface to his *Fables* (1700) reiterates the view 'that Dante had begun to file their language, at least in verse, before the time of Boccace'.[49] Such views, of course, reflect historical commonplaces going back at least to sixteenth-century English and Italian criticism, but their restatement in this measured and prestigious form gives a significant degree of wider currency to Dante around the turn of the century, at a time when his works were frequently appearing in British readers' personal collections.[50]

Views like Dryden's perhaps form part of a British reaction to the strictures of critics such as Rapin, yet neoclassical disapproval of Dante was by no means uniform, even in French writing of the time. Dryden's recognition of Dante's linguistic role can be seen in the context of a scholarly treatment of the subject in the Abbé Claude Fleury's *Traité du choix et de la méthode des études* (1686). In chapter 9 of the *Traité* Fleury turns to the relationship between Latin and the vernacular in the thirteenth century, comparing writers of French at that time rather unfavourably with their contemporaries in Italy. The English translation of the *Traité* published in 1695 presents his comparison thus:

It seems to me that they [French writers in the 'ordinary Tongue'] ought to have applied the Art of Grammar to this Language, chusing the most proper Words, and the most natural Phrases, fixing the inflexions, and giving Rules for *Construction* and *Orthography*. The *Italians* did so; and about the end of the same Age, there were some *Florentines* who Studied to Write well in their Vulgar Tongue; as *Brunetto Latini, John Villani*, and the Poet *Dante*.[51]

Translation in this period continues to foster awareness of Dante in several ways. Out of the many seventeenth-century English versions of (for example) French historical and critical works—from D'Avity's *Estates, Empires & Principalities* (translated 1615), through Naudé's *History of Magick* (1657) and Blondel's *Treatise of the Sibyls* (1657), to Rapin's *Observations* (1672), Claude's *Historical Defence of Reformation* (1688), and Fleury's *History of Studies* (1695)—a variety of attitudes emerge.[52] These range, as we have seen, from denigration through neutral information to celebration

---

[49] Excerpts in *DEL* 1. 171–2.

[50] Dryden's *The Art of Painting* (1695)—a translation of Charles-Alphonse Dufresnoy's 1668 poem *De arte graphica*—contained notes ('by another Hand') in which Giotto is said to have 'flourish'd in the time of the famous *Dante* and *Petrarch*'; see Appendix 2, below. On Dante in libraries around the turn of the century, see below, pp. 99–105.

[51] *The History, Choice and Method of Studies by Monsieur Fleury* (1695), 35.

[52] For all of these, see Appendix 2, below.

of the 'famous poet', and they include a substantial amount of specific referencing, quotation, and even passages of direct further translation. John Davies of Kidwelly's various literary projects brought him into contact with Dante's work and reputation on several different occasions from the mid-century onwards,[53] and his 1657 version of Gabriel Naudé's portrayal of '*Michael* the Scot' in *The History of Magick* not only cites the description of *Michele Scotto* as sorcerer in the fourth ditch of *Inferno*'s eighth circle (*Inf.* 20. 115–17), but also accompanies the Italian text with a lively English verse rendering:

> -------- See you that trifling fellow there?
> 'Twas *Michael the Scot,* who knew his part
> In all the roguing cheats of Magick Art.[54]

Throughout the century, Dante is also being kept before the British public through reference or quotation in translations of more familiar Italian authors. Many modern critics see Ariosto's reading of Dante as oblique and possibly subversive, yet when Sir John Harington, the English translator of *Orlando Furioso in English heroical verse*, discusses poetic influence in his 1591 preface, he invokes the author of the *Commedia* as 'that excellent Italian Poet *Dant*'—going on to cite and even (on one occasion) to translate from the *Inferno* in his commentary on Ariosto's poem.[55] Harington's *dantismi* in his Ariosto were reprinted in two further early seventeenth-century editions (1607 and 1634) as well as in the mid- and later eighteenth century. Versions of several texts by Ariosto's great Florentine contemporary Machiavelli produced by English translators in the sixteenth and seventeenth centuries would have publicized Dantean texts and contexts even more extensively and sustainedly.[56] In the *Discorsi* Machiavelli appears to have had difficulty in telling his *Monarchia* from his *Convivio*, but his misattributed quotation from the latter and his version of Dante's dictum about *umana probitate* (*Purg.* 7. 121–3) had been printed in John Wolfe's Italian text of the *Discorsi* (London, 1584), and were subsequently available in translations that went through at least seven editions between 1636 and 1695.[57]

Evidence of attention to passages from Dante's original text, as well as their subsequent transmission to a British audience, can be found in translations from a number of other Italian writers. How much close reading this really represents is

[53] See above, p. 73 and n. 41.

[54] *The History of Magick* (1657), 233. Here, as in a number of other cases, the tendency is to translate Dante's *terzine* into couplets.

[55] Harington quotes and translates the first three lines of the *Inferno* in his 'Allegorie of the Fourth Booke' and he cites (rather less favourably) Dante's 'wolfe, pined with famine' by comparison with Ariosto's symbolic *bestia* in *Orlando Furioso* 26, st. 31–3. For these passages and an excerpt from Harington's prefatory 'Apologie of Poetrie', see *DEL* 1. 83–4 and Boswell 1999: 85–6.

[56] On Machiavelli in England, see esp. Wyatt 2005: 187–91 and Petrina 2009; for the references to Dante in sixteenth- and seventeenth-century editions and translations of the *Istorie fiorentini* and the *Discorsi*, see *DEL* 1. 92–3, 132–3, 166–8 and Boswell 1999: 77, 94–6, 209–10.

[57] Wyatt 2005: 187 and fig. 12. On Morison's earlier reference to Dante's *Convivio*, perhaps via Machiavelli, see above, p. 38. Seventeenth-century translations of the *Discorsi* are by Dacres (1636, 1663, 1674) and Henry Neville (1675, 1680, 1694, 1695).

uncertain, but—since the best way to get to know a work is to translate it—the process could well have been a productive one for some of the more intellectually able translators of the time. Examples would include not only some of those mentioned so far—such as Harington, Davies, and Howell—but also a couple of less well-known figures from the middle of the century.

In 1645 the Jesuit historian and moralist Daniello Bartoli (1608–85)—described by De Sanctis as 'the Marino of Baroque prose'[58]—published a treatise on the disorders of learning, *Dell'huomo di lettere difeso ed emendato*, in the course of which he quoted several passages from the *Commedia* to reflect in an oblique way upon his main targets and concerns. Thus, the simile of sheep emerging from the fold that describes the timid souls in Ante-Purgatory (*Purg.* 3. 79–84) here applies to those who blindly follow tradition; whilst the poet's exhortation in *Inferno* 9 to look behind the 'veil of the strange verses' (61–3) is ingeniously presented as a potential pornographers' charter; and Dante's portrayal of himself as a cautious fledgling stork, raising then lowering its wings (*Purg.* 25. 10–15), is offered as a warning against premature intellectual ventures. Bartoli's challenging text was 'English'd' by an ambitious and well-travelled translator, Thomas Salusbury—once again, of Welsh origin—and it appeared as *The Learned Man Defended and Reform'd* in 1660.[59] Salusbury translates all three of Bartoli's Dantean passages into workman-like couplets. He misreads the scenario of the stork simile (and thus its relevance to Bartoli's argument), but his version of the pastoral simile from *Purgatorio* 3. 79–84 is attentive to the details of Dante's image of the timid souls:

> As silly sheep, when two or three more bold
> And venturous than others leave the fold,
> The rest, affraid, dejecting eyes and head,
> Without inquiry follow those that led:
> And if one stay, the rest in heaps, bestride
> Him, not knowing why, and simply there abide.[60]

A better-known contemporary of Salusbury who also encountered and Englished Dante as part of a mid-seventeenth-century translation project was the poet and classicist Thomas Stanley. Stanley's acquaintance with Italian was wide-ranging: he had been tutored as a child by the son of Edward Fairfax (translator of Tasso), and both Tasso and Guarini are cited as sources for several of his *Poems* of 1651.[61] His major undertaking during the Commonwealth was a monumental *History of Philosophy, in Eight Parts* and in four folio volumes, which appeared between 1655 and 1662. The second of these (1656) includes an account of Plato, and

---

[58] *CHIL* 315

[59] See Appendix 2, below. For the little that is known about Salusbury (including his connections with Italy and Galilean science and his lost biography of Galileo), see Zeitlin 1959 and the online Archimedes Project article on 'Thomas Salusbury' at <http://archimedes2.mpiwg-berlin.mpg.de>. On Welsh translators in this period, see also above, p. 74 and n. 46.

[60] Cf. e.g. Henry Boyd's prolix and confused rendering over eight lines, in his complete *Commedia* a century-and-a-half later; Dante 1802: 81 (st. XVI–XVII).

[61] On Stanley's life and work, see *ODNB*, s.v. 'Stanley, Thomas (1625–78), poet and classical scholar'.

for this purpose Stanley includes a translation of Pico della Mirandola's 'Platonick discourse' on love (1486), a commentary on a *canzone* by Girolamo Benivieni.[62] Addressing the concept of the Platonic 'idea' in relation to human craftsmanship and divine creation, Pico here cites two lines from *il nostro poeta Dante* in the third *canzone* of the *Convivio*.[63] These are concisely translated by Stanley as:

> None any work can frame,
> Unless himself become the same.

It is not clear whether Stanley knew that he was translating from the *Convivio* (Pico does not identify the source, nor does Stanley's version), but several references to 'the Poet *Dant* his banquets' had been made in Barker's 1568 translation of Gelli's *Capricci del bottaio*; Donne had owned a copy of the 1531 edition; and Milton's Commonplace Book had referred to 'Dante the Florentine's excellent treatment of true nobility' in 'canzon. 4'.[64] It seems quite likely, then, that Stanley, an accomplished and scholarly student of Italian and of Platonism, would have had some acquaintance with the *Convivio*, which itself had contributed significantly to the medieval Neoplatonic tradition and invokes the name of Plato no less than fifteen times.[65]

Suggesting such knowledge, of course, calls for caution. This account of seventeenth-century responses is not intended to give the impression that the British reading public was at that time twitching with incipient Dantemania. Indeed, a translator of the period quotes and translates Dante's own warning against: 'Treating of shadows, as substantial things'.[66] Yet the range of evidence presented here (including the new examples) seems to confirm that—even during this 'wintry' season—dissemination of ideas about Dante's reputation and work was continuing to take various forms in Britain, as it did in Italy. It indicates that access to his writing was available through an increasingly large number of popular and scholarly works (especially translations), even if such engagement was often of an indirect and fragmentary kind. It suggests that—whether 'rough' or 'refined'—Dante remains in this period a 'good' (even 'excellent') old author and a famous giver of fame. It also shows that the *Commedia*, and occasionally other Dantean texts, are increasingly quoted and translated for illustrative, proverbial, and ideological purposes, both Catholic and Protestant. A paradoxical feature of appropriation

---

[62] Stanley's version of 'A Platonick Discourse upon Love, written in Italian by John Picus Mirandola, in Explication of a Sonnet [*sic*] by Hieronymo Benivieni' had earlier appeared as a section in the 1651 London edition of his *Poems* (with separate title-page but continuous pagination, pp. 213–60).

[63] *Conv.* 4. canzone 'Le dolci rime', ll. 52–3: 'poi chi pinge figura, | se non può esser lei, non la può porre.'

[64] On Barker's translation of Gelli, see *DEL* 1. 42, 45 and Boswell 1999: 32, 35; and on Barker's travels in Italy, see Woolfson 2009: 407 and n. 9. On Donne's *Convivio* (now in the Bodleian, Oxford), see Wilson 1946: 51; for the reference in Milton's Commonplace Book (f. 191), see *DEL* 1. 122.

[65] Durling in *DE* ('Plato') cites *Conv.* 2.4 and 13; 3.5, 9 and 14; 4.6, 15, 21, and 24. On Platonism in Dante, see also Havely 2007*a*: 79–81.

[66] 'J.L. Gent', quoting and translating *Purg.* 21. 136 ('trattando l'ombre come cosa salda') in Lionardo di Capua's preface to *The Uncertainty of the Art of Physick* (1684); see Appendix 2, below.

from the latter point of view is that—whilst, as previous chapters have shown, certain anticlerical passages in the *Commedia* were fuel for writing against Rome—conversely, the fact that a third of Dante's poem is devoted to a 'Popish superstition' (Purgatory) might have worked against more extensive translation for a predominantly Protestant reading public.[67]

As for the material resources available to this reading public in the seventeenth century, there is also, as will be seen, a significant amount of evidence to suggest that texts of the *Commedia* formed part of British trade in and collections of Italian books. Milton's sustained reading of Dante may have been unusual, but there were others in the period who, like him, owned copies of the *Commedia* and whose ownership may also have extended to readership.[68] For the history of that group of owners, collectors, and possible readers, we return to the beginning of the century and to the first known British owner of an Italian manuscript of the *Commedia*.

SEGET'S *COMEDY*: A SCOTS SCHOLAR, GALILEO, AND DANTE, *c.*1600

British names were, as we have seen, inscribed in several printed texts of Dante acquired during the sixteenth century. That of Henry Parker, Lord Morley, appears in a 1493 edition of the *Commedia* presented in 1520, along with that of a donor who may have acquired it in Italy a few years earlier.[69] The name of another eminent British translator of Italian attaches to a later printed text (also acquired in Italy) in the middle of the century. During the last week of July 1550 Thomas Hoby, the future translator of Castiglione's *Libro del cortegiano*, was in Venice and there acquired a copy of the 1544 quarto edition of the *Commedia* with commentary by Alessandro Vellutello; hence the volume (now in the library of his former college) bears the name of 'Thomaso Hoby Inglese', with '1550' above and 'In Vineggia' below.[70] Hoby was at the time fresh from Cambridge, in his late teens and on his way to becoming (in Ascham's and Florio's phrase) an *inglese italianato*; thus, 'something of the playfulness and role-playing element of the *Cortegiano* is perhaps captured in the way [he] chose to inscribe his name in his copy of Dante's *Divina Commedia*'.[71]

---

[67] On Protestant appropriations and translations from the *Commedia* in the seventeenth century, see above, pp. 64–7 and 72.

[68] On Milton's reading and appropriation of Dante, see above, pp. 65–7; also Samuel 1966 and Wallace 2007: 286–9. For John Donne's discussion of Dante in a letter (possibly to Sir Henry Wotton), see Wilson 1946: 58; and on Donne's *Second Anniversary* (1611–12) in relation to the *Paradiso*, see Frontain 2003.

[69] See above, pp. 41–2.

[70] In the course of his continental tour, Hoby left Siena on 19 July. In his *Travels* (ed. Powell 1902: 61–2) he describes his route to Venice but gives no date for his arrival or departure; however, since he was in Augsburg by 5 August, he must have been in Venice during the final week of July. His copy of the *Commedia* (Venice: Marcolini, 1544) is now in the Library of St John's College, Cambridge, and images of it can be accessed at the website of the library's Special Collections, at: <http://www.joh.cam.ac.uk/library/special_collections/early_books/pix/provenance/hoby/hoby.htm>.

[71] Woolfson 2009: 414.

About fifty years later another scholarly British traveller in Italy entered his name and nation—this time in Latin and at the beginning of a much older Dante text. On the front flyleaf of the manuscript of the *Commedia* now at the Biblioteca Ambrosiana in Milan (MS C 198 inf) this owner/reader has written: 'Thomae Segeti Scoti', and the same hand has signed the same name (omitting 'Scoti') on the reverse of the page. This text seems to have been copied in the late fourteenth century or the very early fifteenth.[72] Despite its relatively late date, it 'counts as one of the best of the known manuscripts of the poem'.[73] Written on parchment in an elegant gothic book-hand, it has elaborate ornamentation on the opening page of each *cantica*.[74] It also contains extensive marginal glosses in Latin and a substantial number of diagrams (geographical, cosmological, and astronomical) accompanying and following the text, such as the chart of spheres, orbits, and zodiacal signs that follows its text of the *Inferno* (Fig. 2). The extent and significance of these diagrams will be considered later on; meanwhile, to return to the beginning of the manuscript, a note by the Ambrosiana's librarian in 1609 (beneath the signature on the verso of the flyleaf), confirms that it was owned at one point by a scholarly Briton in northern Italy, the Scot, Thomas Seget.[75]

Seget's immediate family were probably from Seton near Edinburgh.[76] It may have been his father or uncle, 'Thomas Segatus', who received his MA from the newly founded University of Edinburgh in August 1588, and then matriculated in 1589 at Leyden, where the great humanist editor and historian Justus Lipsius was lecturing.[77] The fullest documentation concerning the Seget who owned the *Commedia* manuscript follows an encounter with Lipsius, after the Dutch scholar had moved to the Catholic culture of Louvain in the early 1590s. The young Seget then went to study with him there, receiving from his master a testimonial describing him as one who 'even from early youth has . . . been my pupil or auditor' and acknowledging the Scot's 'acute and excellent genius', 'the ardour of his application to study', and 'his progress in every department of elegant and useful learning'.[78] Since the middle of the sixteenth century the 'album of friends' (*album amicorum*) had become increasingly popular as a form of social networking; and as the collection of names in Seget's album shows, Lipsius's support enabled the young scholar to acquire further learned and influential acquaintances during his subsequent travels through Germany and on to Italy in the autumn of 1597.[79]

---

[72] The Ambrosiana catalogue dates the MS '1391–1410', thus also Rossi 1990: p. ix. An earlier date (between 1355 and 1383) is suggested by Roddewig 1984: 180 (no. 430).

[73] Roddewig 1984: 179.   [74] ff. 1ʳ, 53ʳ, and 105ʳ.

[75] For the text of the librarian's note, see below, p. 87.

[76] Rosen 1949*a*: 93.   [77] Rosen 1949*a*: 94 and n. 5.

[78] Irving 1804: 113; original text in Banfi 1938: 3, n. 1. For accounts of Seget's life and interests, see also Favaro 1911, Purves 1940, Odložilík 1966 (still the most thorough account), and McInally 2012: 90–4.

[79] On the development of the *album amicorum*, see Kellas Johnstone 1924: 1 and more recently Schlueter 2011. For details of Seget's album (now BAV MS Lat. 9385), see Banfi 1938 and Odložilík 1966: 5–13; an edition by Dr Stefano Gattei has recently appeared in *Nuncius* 28 (2013), with an account of his life and transcriptions of his letters.

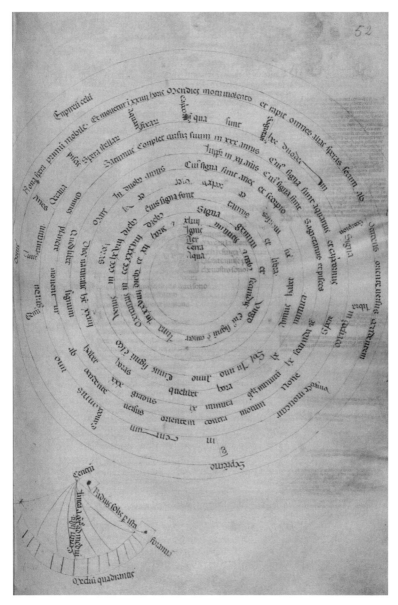

Fig. 2. Milan, Biblioteca Ambrosiana MS C 198 Inf, f. 52ʳ, spheres, orbits, zodiacal signs, Ⓒ Veneranda Biblioteca Ambrosiana—Milano/De Agostini Picture Library

Lipsius's testimonial was addressed to the Paduan scholar and bibliophile Gian Vincenzo Pinelli (1535–1601), in whose household Seget was resident from late 1597.[80] Seget remained in and around Padua for several years, during which period he is documented as matriculating in jurisprudence at the university (1 June 1598) and acting as *consigliere della Nazione Scozzese* (identified as such in August 1602).[81] He made several visits to Venice from Padua in 1599, and in August of that year he met Galileo at the home of the glassmaker and poet Girolamo Magagnati. On that occasion Galileo (identifying himself as professor of mathematics at Padua, where he may already have met Seget) contributed to the *album amicorum* as 'a sign of esteem and friendship'.[82] The purpose of Seget's journeys to Venice and his travels elsewhere in northern Italy is uncertain, but they eventually led him into trouble.

On 22 October 1603 the Venetian Council of Ten ordered his arrest on an unspecified charge and in December 1604 sentenced him to confinement 'in one of our strong prisons for a period of three years', followed by twenty years' banishment from Venetian territories.[83] To make matters worse, he was then falsely accused of libel, being eventually acquitted and released only in September 1605, thanks to several intercessions by James VI and I's new ambassador in Venice, Sir Henry Wotton, whose plea to the Doge and the Collegio Secreta on 11 August 1605 eloquently outlined the young scholar's predicament and seems to have had its due effect.[84]

Having finally been acquitted on 28 September 1605, Seget did indeed go some distance away from Venice, into central Germany, where for several years he seems to have concentrated on the safer activity of writing eulogies and verse on classical subjects: two epitaphs to mark the death of Lipsius, five poems to accompany the biography of his Paduan host and mentor Gian Vincenzo Pinelli, and a slim collection of verse entitled *Thomae Segheti Meletemata Ypogeia*, published at Hanau near Frankfurt in 1607.[85] He then travelled north

---

[80] A letter from Lipsius on 28 December the following year congratulates his pupil on his 'reception into the house of the great Pinelli'; see Banfi 1938: 15 with n. 1 for the text. On the date of Lipsius's letter, see Rosen 1949*b*: 63–7.

[81] See Padua Archivio antico dell' Università di Padova, MS M.U.L.J. 30 (for 1598), f. 143ᵛ (no. 17), and MS A.V.L. 15 (for 1602), f.109ᵛ. I am grateful to Dr Francesco Piovan of the Archivio for assistance in locating these references. On other foreign students in Padua during the early modern period, see Woolfson 1998.

[82] *Hoc . . . observantie et amicitie . . . signum*; Vatican, BAV, MS Lat. 9385, f. 79ʳ, cited in Odložilík 1966: 10, n. 29.

[83] On the possible nature of the first offence described by Wotton as an *errore giovanile* (it may possibly have involved an unauthorized visit to a nunnery in the company of Pietro Pellegrini, secretary of the Council of Ten), see Favaro 1911: 629–30 and, for the initial proceedings against Seget, 640–2. On Seget's poem addressed to Pellegrini, see also below, p. 86 (on poem 25).

[84] Venice, Collegio—*Esposizioni Principi*, filze, pezzo 15, in Favaro 1911: 649; translated in Brown 1900: 10. 267.

[85] By September 1606 he was in Frankfurt; see Odložilík 1966: 19 and n. 67, citing a letter in Zürich, Zentralbibliothek, Msc. S 159, no. 62. The two epitaphs for Lipsius represent Seget's early mentor as heroic restorer of Rome's literary heritage and appeared in *Iusti Lipsi Sapientiae et Litterarum antistitis Fama Postuma* (Antwerp: Plantin-Moret, 1607), 66–7. On *Meletemata Ypogeia*, see below, p. 86 and n. 108. For this period in Seget's travels, see Odložilík 1966: 18–22.

to Hamburg in 1609, before heading south again for an important appointment in Bohemia.[86]

It was Seget's friendship with Galileo, whom he had met several times during his years in Italy, that led him to undertake perhaps his most historically and scientifically important mission. In April 1610 he was in Prague, where on behalf of the Tuscan ambassador Giuliano de' Medici he delivered a copy of Galileo's work on the mountains of the moon and the four satellites of Jupiter (*Sidereus nuncius*) to the Imperial Astronomer, Johannes Kepler.[87] In a letter to Giuliano de' Medici prefacing his *Dissertatio cum Nuncio siderio* later that year, Kepler mentioned Seget's role in delivering Galileo's work, and in the main text he also speaks of 'our Thomas Seget' as 'a man of manifold learning' (*multiplici vir eruditione*).[88] Seget remained in Prague for some time, and he is referred to as a colleague several times in Kepler's *Narratio* on the moons of Jupiter, for example in this entry for 5 September:

Die 5. Septembris mane, vnus clarus satelles Iouis ad orientem, tertia parte instrumenti; nulli praeterea coelo clarissimo, sed iam multum albicanti, ob auroram et lumen Lunae. Vidit et THOMAS SEGETHUS Britannus, vir iam celebrium virorum libris et litteris notus...

The 5th of September, early in the morning: a bright moon of Jupiter to the east, with the third part of the instrument; moreover the sky not at all clear, but already lightened by dawn and the brightness of the Moon. Seen also by THOMAS SEGET, a Briton and a man already noted among famous men of learning and letters...[89]

Seget's detailed observations of the 'Medicean stars' on 6 and 9 September 1610 are also recorded by Kepler; and there are further references to him in the correspondence of both Kepler and Galileo.[90] Seget himself corresponded with Galileo, late in 1610, when he was still in Prague, mentioning a number of Latin poems he had attached to Kepler's work on the moons of Jupiter.[91] The seventh of these celebrates Galileo's city, Florence, for having given the name of its rulers to 'newly discovered stars'. The sixth, addressed to Galileo himself, conveys the writer's sense of sharing in the glamour of the occasion:

Keplerus, Galilaeae, tuus tua sidera vidit:
Tanto quis dubitet credere teste tibi?
Si quid in hoc, et nos Mediceïa vidimus astra,
Vultava marmoreum fert ubi flava iugum.
Vicisti, Galilaee! Fremant licet Orcus et umbrae,
Iuppiter illum, istas opprimet orta dies.

[86] Odložilík 1966: 23–8.
[87] On *Sidereus nuncius* and its impact, see Frova and Marenzana 2011: 153–82.
[88] See Von Dyck and Caspar 1941: 4. 285 and 306.
[89] Von Dyck and Caspar 1941: 4. 320.
[90] Von Dyck and Caspar 1941: 4. 321–2, and Caspar 1954: 16. 341–2; also Favaro 1900: 10. 428, and 1901: 11. 12 and 43.
[91] Favaro 1900: 10. 454.

Your Kepler, Galileo, has seen your stars; so who now can hesitate to believe you? Thus we as well have seen the Medicean moons, here where the tawny Vltava strikes the marble bridge. You have conquered, Galileo! Let Orcus and his shades, Jupiter himself, grumble; against them all the rising day prevails.[92]

It was soon after sharing and celebrating this moment of scientific history that Seget set off on his travels again, his departure from Prague for Poland early in 1611 being noted in a letter from Giuliano de' Medici to Galileo on 7 February.[93] His interests in new thinking extended to religion as well as science, and led him to visit the Socinian (non-trinitarian) communities of the Polish Brethren, first at Lublin and then at Raków in southern Poland.[94] Nor were his literary ventures neglected. At Cracow in the New Year of 1611 he had published a couple of 'Idylls' in a pamphlet dedicated to his travelling companion and guide David Riches (*Riquius*). Later in the following year he met the poet and humanist Szymon Szymonowicz, several of whose Latin odes he had earlier managed to get published during his time at and near Frankfurt.[95]

Meanwhile—adding a fourth string to his intellectual bow—Seget seems also to have been drawn into the world of politics. He had earlier developed close contacts with the Polish court, and in 1612 he accompanied a Polish mission back to Prague.[96] At Prague (where he had at least one highly placed friend at the Imperial court) he seems to have been considering some form of further diplomatic employment, and early in October 1613 he communicated with James VI and I through James's ambassador, Sir Stephen Lesieur, noting that he had now spent sixteen years

cum animo optimis disciplinis excolendo, moribusque hominum et rerumpublicarum institutis noscendis, exteras gentes perlustrandas . . .

eagerly absorbing the highest forms of learning, becoming acquainted with human behaviour and the structure of states, widely surveying foreign nations . . .[97]

The letter—which mentions Seget's travels in 'Belgium, Italy, Germany, Denmark, Bohemia', his recent experiences in Poland and Lithuania, along with his mission to Prague and his indebtedness to both Lesieur and Wotton—is clearly designed with employment in mind. However, its author still did not return to Britain, and within two years he was back in Germany, perhaps re-establishing contacts with Kepler again at Regensburg—then entering academia once more and registering as a student at the nearby University of Altdorf (another centre of radical Protestantism) in March 1614.[98]

---

[92] Favaro 1900: 455.   [93] See Favaro 1901: 11. 43.

[94] The visit (13–19 July 1612) was recorded by the Socinian theologian Valentinus Smalcius, who described Seget as *nobilissimus vir . . . veritatis divinae . . . amplius investigandae causa*; see the *Supplementa* in Zeltner 1729: 1196.

[95] *Thomae Segheti Idyllia duo* (1611). Seget's role in publishing Szymonowicz's work would be acknowledged in the preface to a later edition by Joachim Morsius, *Simonus Simonidae Poematia Aurea cum antiquitate comparanda* (1619), sig.3ʳ. The Morsius edition also contains two letters from Szymonowicz to Seget, dated 10 December 1612 and 13 June 1613 (pp. 49–50).

[96] Odložilík 1966: 29–31.   [97] London, TNA, SP 80/3 f. 43ʳ.

[98] Odložilík 1966: 33 and n. 108. Later that year (7 October 1614) Seget was in Frankfurt again, where he signed the *album amicorum* of a fellow Scot, Thomas Cumming; see Kellas Johnstone 1924: 41.

From this point, and for the last thirteen years of his life, evidence about Seget's life and studies is much sparser. He still seems to have harboured some ambitions for employment at or for the British court. At Magdeburg early in 1622 he published a pamphlet exonerating himself 'from serious calumny'—namely, the charge of having celebrated the assassination of Henry IV of France back in 1610 when he was in Prague.[99] The immediate purpose of the pamphlet seems fairly clear: it was dedicated to James VI and I, and Seget sent copies to both James and his heir, Prince Charles.[100] The copy sent to the king is now at St John's College, Cambridge, and is prefaced by a long handwritten letter (flyleaf 1^r–2^v, dated from Hamburg in March 1622), in which Seget draws attention to the purpose of his 'vindication', and looks forward to appearing before James and offering his services to king and country:

Cis paucos menses ipse me Tibi, Deo annuente, sistam, coram obiecta (si opus erit) diluturus, et qualescumque studiorum itinerumque meorum fructus post tot annorum absentiam Tibi patriaeque dicturus.

Within a few months, I shall myself (God willing) appear in your presence to resolve (if need be) any questions put to me and, after so many years of absence, to dedicate to you and my country any fruits of my studies and travels.[101]

The last phrase ('studiorum itinerumque meorum fructus') replicates one which Seget had used in his application to James nine years earlier and suggests he may have been keeping records on the subject.[102] Later that same year (26 September 1622)—and perhaps as a result—James's Latin Secretary, Thomas Reid, wrote to Seget in friendly terms, exonerating him from the charge of 'Spagnolisme', claiming 'to be compted one of your partie', and asking to be remembered 'to all good friends'.[103] Seget does not seem to have exploited this opening, and within two years he had moved from war-torn Germany to Holland. Returning yet again to academia, he then appears in the records of the University of Leyden, where on 20 September 1625 he enrolled as a very mature student to read law, not much more than two years before his death in December 1627.[104]

Even judging by the standards of the time—and the frequency of the *peregrinatio academica* for British students—Thomas Seget seems to have been a widely wandering scholar and one with several eminent acquaintances. The motives for some of those wider wanderings, especially in the last fifteen years of his life, are not entirely clear, and it is tempting to apply to him a recent description of a near-contemporary Scots scholar and Latinist, Thomas Dempster, who died in Bologna

[99] Seget 1622. For Seget's account of his situation when in Prague and his protestations of loyalty, see esp. slgs A 2 i^{r-v}, A 3 iv^v, and A 3 vi^r.

[100] The two copies are now at Cambridge, St John's MS S.10 (sent to James I), and the British Library C.190.a. 30 (sent to Prince Charles); see also Birrell 1994: 413–14.

[101] St John's Cambridge MS S.10, flyleaf I^v.

[102] The letter of October 1613, in London, TNA SP 80/3, f. 43^v: *simulque me et studiorum itinerumque meorum qualescumque fructus M[aiesta]ti V[ostr]ae consecrare.*

[103] Reid's *Letterbook* in BL Add MS 38597 ff. 71^v–72^r. On Reid, see also *ODNB*, s.v. 'Reid, Thomas (d. 1624)', and McInally 2012: 90–1.

[104] On the records for these final years of Seget's life, see Odložilík 1966: 36–8 and esp. nn. 122–3.

in 1625 and who is said to have gone 'from place to place all over Europe with a mobility that can only be called suspicious'.[105] Seget's connections with the world of humanist scholarship and science and with courtiers and diplomats (along with the evidence of his later publications) suggest that he might have been, or aimed to be, involved in some form of intelligence-gathering.[106]

Writings by and about Seget thus include letters preserved in the documents of the British court as well as in the collections of distinguished correspondents, such as Galileo, Kepler, and Lipsius. Evidence of the extent of his early contacts is in the Vatican *album amicorum* (BAV, MS Lat. 9385), which contains the signatures and greetings of over a hundred friends of various nationalities—Scots, Italians, Germans, Netherlanders, Poles, and some English—and charts his initial European itinerary over the course of three years (September 1597 to December 1600) from Louvain, via Frankfurt and Augsburg, and on to Padua and Venice.[107]

Humanistic ambitions as a writer of Latin verse and student of the classics are reflected in Seget's collection of twenty-nine poems, which was originally published at Hanau near Frankfurt in 1607 and subsequently reprinted in volume 2 of the *Delitiae poetarum Scotorum*, ten years after the Scots scholar's death.[108] The collection contains two poems relating to Seget's own recent experiences and concerns: the opening *Carmen* is a morale-building defiance of Fortune; and poem 24 is an appeal to God on behalf of an innocent falsely accused. *Meletemata Ypogeia* ('Underground Examples'? 'Hidden Gems'?) also includes dramatic snap-shots of a number of famous Romans and their adversaries, together with several other heroic figures (Polyxena, Ajax, Sophonisba) at the moment of their deaths.[109] Of its last five items, four are addressed to eminent Venetians, amongst them a eulogy of Leonardo Mocenigo, a member of the Council of Ten who had taken an interest in his case (poem 26), and a more complex address to the Secretary of the Council, who may also have been implicated in the original offence for which Seget was imprisoned (poem 25).[110] The final poem (29) appropriately keeps James VI and I in view as a potential patron by paraphrasing the prefatory sonnet to *Basilikon doron*, and can thus be seen as a preliminary to those later addresses to the king in 1613 and 1622.[111]

---

[105] Morét, 2000: 251. See also Irving 1804: 1. 107–8; the article on Dempster and his troubled career in *ODNB*, s.v. 'Dempster, Thomas (1579–1625), writer'; and McInally 2012: 88–90.

[106] A comparable suggestion (based on similar evidence) is made about a contemporary of Seget: the expatriate actor Francis Segar, who was based in Kassel around this time; see Schlueter 2011: 156–8.

[107] See above, p. 80 and n. 79. Banfi (1938: 8–10) lists 124 names; more details are in Favaro 1911: 623–5 and Odložilík 1966: nn. 5, 10, 13, 15, 20, 21–2, 25, 27, 30–42.

[108] *Meletemata Ypogeia* (1607), a rare item: there is a copy in the Augsburg Stadtbibliothek (Odložilík 1966: 21 and n. 72) and one at Trinity College, Cambridge (Lower Library G.10.151 [4]). The twenty-nine poems were published after Seget's death (and without his elaborate glosses) in an anthology of Scots Latin poetry: *Delitiae Poetarum Scotorum huius aevi Illustrium* (Johnston 1637: 2. 490–504). Translation of some of these poems (not Seget's) is the subject of a current research project, led by Dr Steven Reid at the University of Glasgow.

[109] Johnston 1637: 2. 490–504, nos. 2–15, 16–17, and 20–3. I am grateful to Prof. Timothy Webb for discussion of how Seget's rather obscure title might be translated.

[110] See above, n. 83.   [111] See above, pp. 84–5 (with nn. 97 and 101).

Seget may also have hoped to increase his appeal to the British court through a later and more extensive published work in prose. This was an account of the eleven principalities of Italy, *De principatibus Italiae: tractatus varij*, which, according to the title-page, he had translated from Italian, and which was first published by Elzevir at Leyden in 1628. The author's aim of strengthening his now somewhat diminishing credentials as an Italy-watcher is reflected in his dedication to a British Italophile and diplomat and in his reference at the close of this to the prospect of royal patronage.[112] Although the work was a considerable success (going into a second edition in 1631), Seget himself was unable either to pursue this ambition any further or even to complete the whole of the project. His contribution amounted only to the first fifty pages or so, whilst the remaining 300 were completed by 'one of the principal collaborators of the Elzevirs, Jan de Laet'.[113]

Seget's life, travels, contacts, and works thus cover a striking range within the world of seventeenth-century European culture. Early in the nineteenth century David Irving's *Lives of the Scotish Poets* described him as 'a scholar of no common proficiency', and his humanistic and scientific milieu has been the subject of discussion by a number of European scholars over the past century.[114] His acquisition of texts has, however, received little attention, although the catalogue that mentions his ownership of several Ambrosiana manuscripts (including the *Commedia*) had been published in 1933.[115]

That catalogue, and a note in Ambrosiana MS C 198 inf. itself, provide some information about Seget's acquisition of this *Commedia*. On the verso of the Ambrosiana manuscript's flyleaf the first librarian of the collection, Antonio Olgiati, notes its provenance in some detail:

Codex hic diligentissime conscriptus et notis antiquioribus illustratus primum fuit Thoma[e] Segeti, mox Vincentii Pinelli v[iri]. cl[arissimi]. a cuius heredibus tota eiusdem biblioteca Neapoli empta fuit, iussa Ill[ustrissi]mi Federici Borrhomaei Ambrosiana[e] biblioth[ec]a[e] fundatoris.

Olgiatus scripsit anno 1609.

This manuscript, carefully written and remarkable for its ancient glosses, first belonged to Thomas Seget and soon after to Vincenzo Pinelli, a most distinguished man. His [Pinelli's] whole library was bought from his heirs at Naples by order of the most illustrious Federico Borromeo, founder of the Ambrosiana Library.

Written by (Antonio) Olgiati 1609.[116]

---

[112] The dedication (dated November 1627) is to Sir Dudley Carleton, Charles I's ambassador to the Low Countries, who had himself earlier acted as James I's ambassador to Venice (Seget 1628: 3 and 6). On Carleton's studies at Padua, see Woolfson 1998: 139 and 269.

[113] Odložilík 1966: 38 and n. 126. See also Seget 1628: 55, dated 'Idibus Decemb, Anni 1627'.

[114] See Irving 1804: 1. 113, and above, nn. 78–9.

[115] Purves (NLS MS 15879, f. 13) mentions the work that is crucial from this point of view (Rivolta 1933), although he does not appear to have known of Seget's possession of the manuscript. Since then the question of Seget's ownership has been addressed briefly by Roddewig (1984: p. lxxxvii with n. 105, and 180A) and by Rossi 1990: pp. xlvi–xlix.

[116] Milan, Biblioteca Ambrosiana MS C 198 inf: note on verso of paper flyleaf. On Olgiati, see Rivolta 1933: pp. lxxix–lxxx, n. 3.

The change of ownership that Olgiati mentions brings us back to Padua and the household of Gian Vincenzo Pinelli, which Seget frequented from 1597 to the year of Pinelli's death in 1601.[117] Pinelli had been in Padua since 1558, and his wide circle of learned acquaintances included not only Lipsius and Galileo but also, for example, Torquato Tasso, the Venetian theologian and reformer Paolo Sarpi, and the scholarly cardinals Roberto Bellarmino and Federico Borromeo (founder of the Ambrosiana).[118] His library has been described as 'the most important in sixteenth-century Italy . . . for the sheer number of volumes acquired . . . passion for collecting and . . . fidelity to the goal of constructing a great tool for research'.[119] His tastes were wide-ranging in both classical and vernacular literature, and he is said to have been fluent not only in Latin and Greek but also in Hebrew, French, Provençal, and Spanish. As his friendship with Tasso suggests, Pinelli also showed considerable interest in the literature of the Italian *volgare*. This enthusiasm is reflected in his acquisition of works by Dante—not only Seget's *Commedia* manuscript, but also one of the *Vita nuova* (now Ambrosiana MS F n. 399 R, ff. 229ʳ–252ʳ), along with a letter said to be from Dante to Guido da Polenta—and works on the history and features of the vernacular.[120] Part of this interest seems to have been transmitted to Pinelli's Scottish guest, Seget, who, along with the *Commedia*, is also known to have possessed at least two other vernacular manuscripts now in the Ambrosiana. One of these is a finely illustrated fifteenth-century text of Ovid's *Heroides*, 'translated . . . into the Italian language' (MS I 69 sup.). The other is a fifteenth-century copy on paper of Boccaccio's *Decameron* (MS C 225 inf.); the parchment flyleaf at the front of this volume (before the numbered contents pages) once again has Seget's name in his hand ('Thomae Segeti Scoti'), and he has also added below: 'Decameron del Boccacio [*sic*]'.[121]

When, how, and why did this Scots Latinist acquire a share of such important vernacular Italian manuscripts, and what might have interested him in the presentation of Dante in this particular form? We can date Seget's possession of the *Commedia* to within about three years, between his arrival in Padua in late 1597 and the death of Pinelli, who by that time owned the manuscript (August 1601). How Seget as an 'impoverished twenty year old' (*un ventenne squattrinato*) could have had the means to acquire this *Commedia* has been questioned; and there is some evidence that the purchase could have formed part of the dealings between Pinelli and the Venetian aristocrat and book collector Alvise Mocenigo (1532–98), who is known to have possessed a 'Dante with glosses in Latin'.[122] As a major centre of the book trade Venice was a prime source of works for Pinelli's library, and

---

[117] For accounts of Pinelli's household, collections, and contacts, see: Gualdo 1607: esp. 25–6; Favaro 1911: 619–22 and the 'notizie biografiche' in Rivolta 1933: pp. ii–xxxii.

[118] See Rivolta 1933: pp. xxi–iii and (on Tasso) xxv–viii.

[119] Nuovo 2007: 39. For the dramatic story of the collection's fortunes after Pinelli's death, see Nuovo 2007: 42–3 and Hobson 1971: 215–33.

[120] Rivolta 1933: 177 and 229.   [121] Rivolta 1933: 26 and 213–14.

[122] Rossi 1990: p. xlvii, citing Braggion 1980/81: 54–7. For evidence about dealings between Mocenigo and the Roman bibliophile Fulvio Orsini that mention a Latin-glossed Dante, see Nolhac 1887: 109, n. 1.

it is known that 'when he was not well enough to travel to Venice . . . his erudite friends kept him informed of newly arrived books and bought on his behalf'; hence this could have been one reason for his Scottish guest's journeys there during the last years of the Paduan patron's life.[123] Seget's temporary ownership (or borrowing?) of the *Commedia* and the other manuscripts could thus have been a kind of reward for services rendered. It may also be significant that during his imprisonment at Venice his visitors included several who were associated with the Venetian book trade.[124]

The Dante manuscript may have held particular attractions for the Scottish scholar. Its marginal diagrams and sketches may provide a clue to his motives for possessing and putting his name to it, especially if we view them through the glass of Milton's 'Tuscan artist', Galileo. It was probably through Pinelli that Seget had become acquainted with Galileo, whose work he would later help to disseminate and whose friendship is documented in the *album amicorum* during the time when and in the place where Seget is likely to have acquired the *Commedia* manuscript.[125] A few years before taking up his post in Padua (1592) Galileo had delivered two lectures on *il nostro Dante* to the Florentine Accademia, and here, amongst other things, he calculated the precise dimensions of the divisions of the *Inferno*, the height of some of its inhabitants, such as Lucifer and the Giants, and the size of the mouth of Hell. Amongst his conclusions about the 'shape, location, and size of Dante's underworld' is the following exact measurement:

> troveremo che il vano dell'Inferno occupa qualcosa meno di una delle 14 parti di tutto l'aggregato: dico quando bene tal vano si estendessi sino alle superficie della terra, il che non fa; anzi rimane la sboccatura coperta da una grandissima volta della terra, nel cui colmo è Ierusalem, ed è grossa quanto è l'ottava parte del semidiametro, che sono miglia 405 15/22.

> we find that the opening of Hell occupies something less than a fourteenth part of the entire aggregate, even if, I say, this opening really extends up to the earth's surface, which it does not. Indeed, the opening remains covered by a very great vault of earth, at whose peak lies Jerusalem, and which is as deep as one-eighth of the radius, amounting to 405 and 15/22 miles.[126]

Galileo's interest in the details of Dante's cosmography was shared by the fourteenth-century scribe of the Ambrosiana *Commedia*. It is very likely that members of Galileo's intellectual circle, such as Seget and Pinelli, would have had their attention caught by the prominent images of celestial spheres, star signs, solstices, and epicycles that appear in the Ambrosian manuscript. Two full-page charts of the Ptolemaic universe, with details of zodiac signs and planetary orbits, are strategically

---

[123] Nuovo 200/: 44. Nuovo also points out here (and in n. 14) that Pinelli had dealings with a variety of Venetian booksellers, some of whose letters to him survive in the Ambrosiana (S 105 sup.).

[124] These included (on 4 June 1605) the Sienese bookseller and publisher Giovanni Battista Ciotti, and (on 13 December 1604 and again on 3 September 1605) Giacomo Castelvetro, who was working for Ciotti in Venice from 1599 to 1611. For the documents relating to these visits, see Favaro 1911: 642 (doc. IV), 647 (doc. X), and 650 (doc. XVI). On Ciotti, see *DBI* (s.v. 'Ciotti'); also Rhodes 1987: 225–39, and (for Ciotti's earlier dealings in books for another Scottish scholar, William Fowler) Petrina 2009: 79–80. On Castelvetro, see *DBI* (s.v. 'Castelvetro, Giacomo') and Wyatt, 2005: 192–3.

[125] See Favaro 1911: 633–6.

[126] Ed. in Chiari 1970: 51; trans. in Caesar 1989: 303.

placed for reference immediately before the *Purgatorio* and immediately after the *Paradiso* (Fig. 2).[127] Marginal diagrams illustrate terms such as *quadrante* and *zodiaco* in *Purgatorio* 4. 42 and 64 (Fig. 3).[128] The orbit and epicycle of Venus are prominently displayed at the start of *Paradiso* 8 (Fig. 4); and the gloss on Saturn's position in the sign of Leo (*Par.* 21. 13–15) directs the reader to a chart further down the margin ('vide figura[m] celi sic designata ut hic').[129] As well as clarifying various physical features and images in the *Commedia*—from the topography of Umbria to the geometry of triangles[130]—the illustrative programme of the Ambrosiana manuscript thus seems particularly designed to clarify the poem's references to astronomy. This degree of attention to the movements of Dante's *alte rote* is very likely to have been noticed by an adventurous young reader who would not only study Galileo's *Siderius nuncius* but would also work for a considerable period with another leading astronomer, Kepler, when the latter was in the process of formulating the laws of planetary motion.[131]

Seget is not the first British bibliophile who is known to have possessed a copy of the *Commedia*. John Pennant in 1520 is the first known and named British owner of a printed text; and Thomas Hoby, like Seget, obtained his copy in Italy.[132] He is, however, the first British reader whose ownership of a manuscript (as opposed to a printed edition) of the *Commedia* in Italian can be firmly documented, and he is amongst the earliest Scots readers known to have possessed any copy of the poem.[133] Very soon after Seget's dealings with the Ambrosiana manuscript, a better-known Scots poet, William Drummond of Hawthornden, bought a copy of Lodovico Dolce's duodecimo edition of the *Commedia* (Venice: Giolito, 1555) at London in 1610, and his autographed copy is now in the National Library of Scotland at Edinburgh.[134]

Ownership of a text does not, of course, mean familiarity with it. Moreover, contemporary Scots readers and translators of Italian, such as William Fowler (another visitor to Padua) and John Stewart of Baldynneis, were rather more interested in Petrarch, Machiavelli, and Ariosto than they were in the *Commedia*.[135]

[127] Milan, Ambrosiana MS C 198 INF, ff. 52ʳ and 155ᵛ.

[128] Also the *quattro cerchi* and *tre croci* of *Par.* 1. 39; and *dal centro al cerchio* and *giunture di quadranti in tondo* in *Par.* 14. 1, 102; Milan, Ambrosiana MS C 198 INF, ff. 58ʳ, 105ᵛ, 124ʳ, 125ʳ.

[129] Milan, Ambrosiana MS C 198 INF, ff. 115ᵛ and 135ʳ.

[130] Milan, Ambrosiana MS C 198 INF, ff. 120ʳ and 129ʳ (illustrating *Par.* 11. 61 and 17.15).

[131] On Kepler's three laws of planetary motion (the first two of which he had already formulated by the time of Seget's visit in 1610), see Crombie 1969: 187–92.

[132] See above, pp. 41–2 and 79 with n. 70.

[133] Although, some twenty years before this, the first items to reach the infant James VI's library from his mother's collection in 1573 included a copy of 'Dante en Italien'; see Warner 1893: pp. xvi–xx and xxxi. James VI was later taught Italian in 1591–4 by Giacomo Castelvetro; see Purves 1940: pp. cxii–cxiv and Wyatt 2005:192.

[134] This copy has a nineteenth-century note on the first recto after the flyleaf: '1865 D[uke]. of Grafton's sale £1.5.0 Belonged to Drummond of Hawthornden. See his autograph on the title page. This is the first edition bearing the title of Divina commedia', a claim that seems to be borne out by the autograph *Gu. Drumond* at the top of the title page and an Italianate note at the foot of the title-page in the same hand: *Londra 1610*. On Drummond's other Italian books (including Petrarch, Boccaccio, Ariosto, Tasso, and Machiavelli—as well as Florio's 1598 *Worlde of Wordes*), see Lievsay 1969: 40–2.

[135] See e.g. Purves 1940; Jack 1972: 54–144, and 1986: 1–21; Heddle 2008; Petrina 2009.

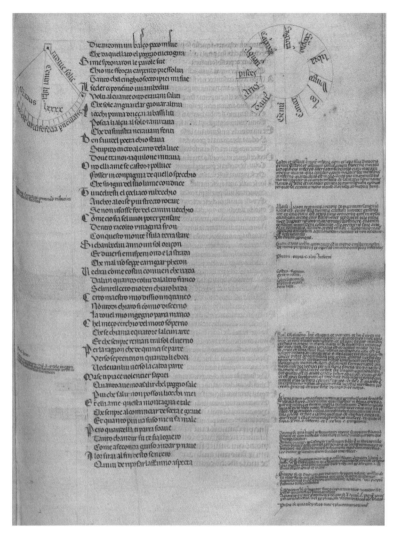

Fig. 3. Milan, Biblioteca Ambrosiana MS C 198 Inf, f. 58ʳ, quadrant and zodiac, © Veneranda Biblioteca Ambrosiana—Milano/De Agostini Picture Library

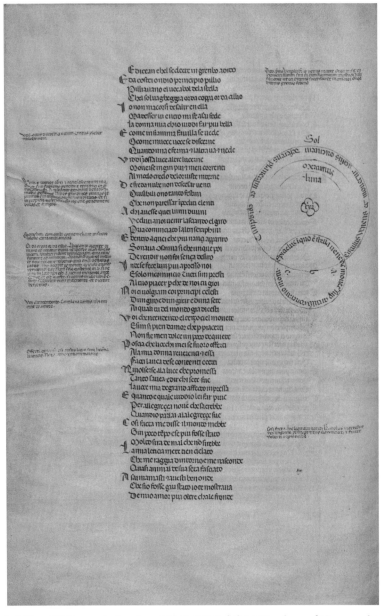

Fig. 4. Milan, Biblioteca Ambrosiana MS C 198 Inf, f. 115ᵛ, sphere of Venus and its epicycle, courtesy of Biblioteca Ambrosiana, © Veneranda Biblioteca Ambrosiana—Milano/De Agostini Picture Library

For them, Dante still seems to remain a 'perhaps' among their continental authors.[136] Yet the evidence and context for Seget's ownership of the Ambrosiana *Commedia* have suggested some further reasons why and how interest in *il nostro Dante* (as Galileo called him) might have been communicated to itinerant and Italianate British scholars.[137]

Religious controversy may also, once again, form part of the context for this encounter with the *Commedia*. Dante was at this time, and well into the seventeenth century, still being conscripted for the Reformation by many Protestant readers and polemicists, a number of whom, like Milton, were well versed in Italian culture and texts.[138] As part of the Counter Reformation response to such polemic, the *Commedia* at least was being reclaimed for Catholicism by Jesuits such as the English exile Robert Persons and by Pinelli's friend (and Galileo's later judge) Cardinal Bellarmine.[139] It is very likely, then, that Seget's interest in Dante may owe something to his contrasting experiences of the Protestant ethos of late sixteenth-century Scotland and the Catholic cultures of Italy and central Europe— and to his participation in debate about religion in communities such as the Polish Brethren at Raków and theologians at the University of Altdorf.[140]

Seget's ownership of the Ambrosiana Dante, short-lived as it was, thus raises a number of important cultural issues. There is not much further evidence about his knowledge of Dante, although he did (as we have seen) own at least two other medieval vernacular Italian works, and he seems to have been familiar enough with the *Commedia* to supply a missing line in the Ambrosiana text of the *Paradiso*.[141] His attention, as I have suggested, may have been directed primarily to passages where the poem's cosmology could be compared to Padua's 'new learning', which would eventually yield some scientific results that he himself would have a hand in disseminating. His encounter with Dante, like much of his vagrant and various career, thus takes place at a number of cultural interfaces: between literature and science; between Reformation and Counter Reformation; between Renaissance Italy and the new Kingdom of England and Scotland; and (not least) between *latinitas* and the *volgare*. The story of and around Seget's dealings with the Ambrosiana manuscript also contributes materially to the evidence about the presence of the *Commedia* in British book collections during the seventeenth century—a presence that has further implications for Dante's later British public.

---

[136] For tentative suggestions about Stewart's possible knowledge of and appropriation of Dante, see: McDiarmid and Stewart, 1948: 12–18 (esp. pp. 17–18); and McDiarmid 1950: 52–63 (esp. 62: 'perhaps Dante'). I am grateful to Dr Katherine McClune of Oxford University for references to both these articles.

[137] On Kenelm Digby's public reference to Dante whilst in Italy soon after Seget, see below, pp. 102–3.

[138] See above, pp. 64–7.   [139] See above, pp. 55–8.

[140] See above, p. 84 and n. 94.

[141] On f. 115ʳ the missing line ('In [*sic*] far l'huom sufficiente a rileuarsi', *Par.* 7. 116) is written in what appears to be Seget's own hand. See also Rossi 1990: p. xlvi and n. 4.

LADY POL'S HANDBAG: COLLECTIONS
AND CATALOGUES, *c.1600–c.1700*

Lady Politic Would-Be's canon of Italian poets—including the obdurate Dante—was probably being imagined by Ben Jonson at the very time when Thomas Seget was imprisoned in Volpone's city. During his confinement, the Scottish scholar continued, as we have seen, to have literary visitors (Castelvetro, Ciotti), whose conversation was probably more congenial than Lady Pol's. His eventual rescuer, Sir Henry Wotton—friend of Donne, Bacon, and Milton, collector of artworks and books, and writer on architecture—was himself (to quote the words he used when pleading for Seget) 'litterato et nutrito tra le buone arti'.[142] The British ambassador's more prominent career may also have contributed in some measure to the presence of Dante's work in British collections and catalogues of the seventeenth century.

Like Seget, Wotton was an accomplished classicist and modern linguist, fluent in French and German as well as Italian. Beginning with his continental tour in 1591, he visited Italy several times—becoming especially familiar with the Grand Duke's court in Florence—before taking up the first of his three appointments as James I's ambassador to Venice (1604–10). His talents do not, however, seem to have been matched by results. In a diplomatic career beset by unforced errors, Wotton's achievement in gaining Seget's release from prison was one of his few real successes, and later, following the less-than-brilliant conclusion to his final diplomatic mission (1623), he 'turned away from Venetian politics to indulge his deep admiration for Italian art', publishing his *Elements of Architecture* in 1624 and collecting Italian paintings, some of which ended up in Charles I's collection.[143] Over the last fifteen years of his life (1624–39) his main role was an academic one, that of provost at Eton College, where some evidence of his literary and antiquarian interests is still to be found.

Two years before his death Wotton's will bequeathed 'to the Library at Eaton College all my Manuscripts not before disposed'.[144] Despite the absence of an inventory or inscriptions linking them with Wotton, it has been suggested that 'probably nearly all the Italian manuscripts came from him and certainly most of them did'.[145] Items thus 'probably' owned by Wotton include a substantial number of classical Latin texts, for example, the earliest (tenth-century) manuscript of Ovid's *Heroides* and a late fifteenth-century copy of Cicero's *De officiis*.[146] Amongst them, however, are also two Dantean items.

One of these (Eton College MS 115) is a fifteenth-century paper copy of the vernacular commentary on the *Inferno* and *Purgatorio* by Iacopo della Lana.[147] This

---

[142] 'Learned and bred in the arts', Favaro 1911: 649, trans. in Brown 1900: 267; see above, p. 82 and n. 84. On Wotton's career, see Smith 1907 and *ODNB* s.v. 'Wotton, Sir Henry (1568–1639)'. On Donne's letter about Dante which may have been addressed to Wotton, see above, p. 79, n. 68.

[143] *ODNB* 7. On Wotton's artistic (and scientific) interests while in Italy, see Stoye 1989: 98–100.

[144] Smith 1907: 1. 218.   [145] Birley 1970: 26.   [146] Birley 1970: 26–7.

[147] Lana's was the earliest complete vernacular commentary on the *Commedia*, composed between 1324 and 1328; see *DE* (s.v. 'Iacopo della Lana').

was one of three manuscripts presently in the collection that were owned by Cardinal Giovanni Delfino, who died in Venice in 1622, and it suggests that Wotton—like Hoby, Seget, Fowler, and Milton—was taking advantage of the trade in books and manuscripts there, shortly before the end of his last residency in the city.[148] The other Dante manuscript (Eton College MS 112) is a mid-fourteenth-century copy on vellum of the whole *Commedia*.[149] Like four others in the Florentine 'Cento' group, it carries the Alighieri coat of arms (f. 1ʳ); and an attached note suggests that 'the MS. no doubt was given by Wotton'.[150] Both these items are known to have been in the Eton collection before the end of the seventeenth century, since they are listed in the *Catalogi manuscriptorum Hiberniae et Angliae* that was initiated by the Oxford scholar Edward Bernard in the mid-1690s.[151] Like the 'Comedie di Dante D'Algieri [*sic*], *viz.* Inferno, Purgatorio, Cielo'—which appeared (in between two missals) amongst 200 or so codices at Westminster—the Eton Dante manuscripts formed part of a collection which is primarily of classical and patristic texts.[152] Their acquisition by Sir Henry Wotton reflected not only an antiquarian aim of collecting medieval manuscripts but also an informed interest in Italian language and culture and a desire to sample both text and commentary.

Manuscripts of Dante continued to accumulate in British collections in the later seventeenth and early eighteenth centuries, and their significance for their owners and those who might have had access to them will need to be considered further. But even clearly written codices like Seget's and Wotton's were obviously not as legible or (in many cases) as portable as the printed editions of the *Commedia*—such as the Aldine octavos and the smaller-format Venetian and Paduan texts—that were being produced in the sixteenth and early seventeenth centuries.[153] The increasing description and acquisition of such editions is symptomatic of an interest among some quarters of the British reading public throughout the seventeenth century.

Such an interest on Wotton's part is reflected in the 'List of Italian Authors Selected and Censured by Sir Hen. Wotton' (*c.*1628–30) which mentions '*Il Dante col Commentario di Landino*, in fol[io]', a printed text which presumably he possessed or had used—and comments that it is 'Worthy the studying'.[154] The list of thirty-six items (nearly all with the format of their editions indicated) may

---

[148] On the Venetian book trade, see above, pp. 34, nn. 11–12, and 88–9. The name 'Jo. Delphini' appears on the flyleaf (f. iii), and a librarian's note (by M. R. James) concludes, 'No doubt given by Wotton'. See also Ker 1977: 725–6.

[149] As a note by M. R. James on its inside cover points out, the script is similar to that of a manuscript of the 'officina del Cento' group that was copied by Francesco di Ser Nardo in 1337. On the origins, grouping, and script of the 'Cento' manuscripts, see Boschi Rotiroti 2004: 77–88, and *DE* 198–9.

[150] James's note. For full descriptions of Eton 112, see Ker 1977: 724–5 and Roddewig 1984: 38–9 (no. 84).

[151] The catalogue was published very shortly after Bernard's death, in 1697. On his career and interests, see *ODNB* (s.v. 'Bernard, Edward 1638–1697').

[152] On the Westminster codices, see Bernard 1697: 2.2. 27–9, and for the *Commedia* manuscript, see 28A, item 1162.72.

[153] See Richardson 1995: 255–7.   [154] Smith 1907: 2. 484–6.

seem initially a rather eccentric selection. Neither Petrarch nor Ariosto feature at all; Tasso is represented only by his (admittedly important) pastoral drama *Aminta*; and Dante's *Commedia* (at no. 14) follows the 'eloquently vain' sermons of an early fifteenth-century Franciscan. On closer scrutiny, however, it seems that Wotton's aim is an ambitious one: to sample a wide chronological, geographical, and generic range of Italian texts, as a means of introducing the reader to the country's religious, architectural, scientific, and literary culture.[155] Dante with Landino's commentary (the one referred to by, amongst others, Sidney in the *Apologie*) may thus have several reasons—historical, linguistic, religious—for inclusion in this rough guide for potential students, readers, and travellers.

Those who travelled to Italy—like Pennant around 1513–15, Hoby in 1550, Fowler in 1593, and Milton in 1638–9—could purchase books there, especially in Venice, and ship them back to Britain.[156] As their catalogues show, several British booksellers in this period also imported Italian texts. The earliest of these, Henry Fetherstone's *Catalogus librorum in diversis locis Italiae emptorum, anno 1628*, contains—at the end of its list of theological, medical, mathematical, and legal items and works in Hebrew, Chaldean, Arabic, Greek, Latin, and Spanish—a quite substantial collection (well over 130 titles) of 'Libri Itallici [*sic*]', many of which are very recently published editions.[157] Poets in this section include several contemporaries such as Guarini (d. 1612) and Giambattista Marino (d. 1625); there is also an octavo edition of Ariosto's *Orlando furioso* published the same year (1628) in Venice; a quarto *Decameron* (Venice, 1612); and three volumes of Petrarch.[158] Amongst these, readers might have encountered an indirect presence of Dante: as a character (along with Beatrice) in Petrarch's *Triumphus Cupidinis* (4. 28–31); and as a source for proverbial wisdom in the last item of Fetherstone's catalogue: 'Ia [*sic*] Ciuil Conuersatione del Sig. Guazzo 8. [octavo] 1621.'[159] Stefano Guazzo's *La civil conversatione* (1574) rivalled Castiglione's earlier *Libro del cortegiano* as a guide to courtly conduct, and by this time had been translated into English and other languages. Several of its quotations, from the *Inferno* (illustrating the danger of incredible truths) and the *Paradiso* (on encouraging natural talents), along with lines from elsewhere in the *Commedia*, had been given verse renderings in George

---

[155] An interesting example linguistically is No. 21: '*The Annotations of [Leonardo] Salviati* upon the Decameron of Boccaccio, With one of his Novelle told in 13 several languages of Italy'. Palladio's *Quattro libri dell'architettura* and Galileo's *Discorso . . . intorno alle cose che stanno in su l'acqua o che in quella si muovono* also feature in the list (Nos. 34 and 36).

[156] On Hoby and Fowler, see above, pp. 79 and 89–90. On Milton's travels and purchases in Italy, see Stoye 1989: 121, 123, 155–7; and the essays in Di Cesare 1991.

[157] Fetherstone 1628: 42–6. On other features of the catalogue, see Rhodes 1966: 131–3. A large number of the items among Fetherstone's 'Libri Itallici' are, of course, in Latin; but in the light of the (selective) examples cited here, the claim that 'not a single book among those listed . . . *is* in Italian' (Lievsay 1969: 44) seems odd.

[158] See Fetherstone 1628: 44 (Guarini, *Il pastor fido* and Ariosto, *Orlando furioso*); 45 (Boccaccio, *Decameron*, Petrarch *De gli uonimi* [*sic*] *famosii* [presumably an Italian translation] and *Triumphi* [illustrated fol., Venice 1488], and five works by Marino, including what could be a first edition of his main narrative poem. *L'Adone* ['Poema fol. 1623']); and 46 ('Il Petrarcha' [perhaps the *Rime sparse*, in a 12° edition, Venice 1612]).

[159] Fetherstone 1628: 46.

Pettie's 1581 translation of Guazzo's work.[160] And whoever bought the 1621 copy of *La civil conversatione* in Fetherstone's catalogue would have been able to sample Dante's lines about 'quel ver c'ha faccia di menzogna' (*Inferno* 16) and the 're . . . da sermone' (*Paradiso* 8)—along with a number of others—in the original.

Fetherstone's successors continued to import substantial quantities of books from Italy. In a catalogue of 1647 his former apprentice George Thomason advertised nearly 2,000 books that had been acquired there—amongst them a two-volume folio collection of *Petrarchae opera omnia* and several more Boccaccio works (two copies of the *Genealogia* and one of *De montium*) alongside the *Decameron*.[161] Another of Fetherstone's former employees, Robert Martin, was even more active in importing books from Italy, and his advertised stock included several editions of Dante. Martin published five catalogues between 1633 and 1650, and those of 1633, 1635, and 1640 all advertise editions of the *Commedia*: the1529 Venice folio with Landino's commentary (in 1633, 1635, and 1640); the 1568 Venice quarto with Daniello's (in 1633); and a minuscule (24°) Venice edition (in 1635 and 1640).[162] To this it should be added that the 1639 list— described as 'the most important of Martin's catalogues' and one that represents 'the whole of typographical Italy'—also includes among its 'Libri Italici' the 1529 folio and the more recent (and much more portable) 1629 24° editions of the *Commedia*.[163] These both appear in a list which includes works by Boccaccio and Petrarch, as well as more recent authors such as Ariosto, Tasso, and Guarini.[164] Furthermore, a single copy of 'Dante la Divina Commedia 24[o]' (presumably the Venice 1629 edition) appears in Martin's fifth and final catalogue (1650), again alongside a number of Dante's successors.[165] Several of these *Commedia* entries— like many other items in Martin's five catalogues—may represent identical (and slow-to-shift) copies, but they still show Dante maintaining a position, together with other Italian authors, in the mid-seventeenth-century British book market.

---

[160] On Pettie's translation (including those of *Inf.* 16. 124–6 and *Par.* 8. 142–8), see *DEL* 1. 66–8 and Boswell 1999: 60–3. On translation of passages from Dante in a variety of this period's texts, see above, pp. 76–8.

[161] On Thomason, see *ODNB* (s.v. 'Thomason George (*c.* 1602–1666)') and Rhodes 1966: 135–8. His *Catalogus librorum diuersis Italiae locis emptorum Anno Dom. 1647* includes the titles mentioned on p. 24 and (in a list of about 300 'Libri Italici') pp. 37 and 40. Also on sale are three more Petrarchs (pp. 39 and 40) and works by Guicciardini, Guarini, and Tasso (pp. 37 and 41). Several of the titles (e.g. the quarto *Decameron* and 'il Petrarca 12[o]') could perhaps have been items from Fetherstone's stock.

[162] See Boswell 1999: 197, 208, 214. On Martin's catalogues, see also Rhodes 1966: 133–5 (the most thorough survey) and Lievsay 1969: 43–8.

[163] Martin 1639: 49. The two editions are respectively: by Jacob da Borgofranco for Lucantonio Giunte with Landino's commentary (Venice, 1529) and the miniature plain text 'con gli Argomenti & Allegorie per ogni Canto' and tables of 'hard words' and 'notable topics', published by Nicola Misserini (Venice, 1629).

[164] Martin 1639: 45 (Ariosto), 46 (Boccaccio), 52–3 (works on Tasso), 55 (Petrarch), 57 and 59 (Tasso), 62 (Guarini). The headings of this catalogue are somewhat similar to those used by Fetherstone in 1628, but among Martin's additions are a substantial list of 'Comedie & Tragedie Italici' (pp. 58–63, also a feature of his 1635 catalogue) and sections of Latin, Italian, and Hebrew manuscripts (again, as in 1635).

[165] Martin 1650: 39, again among a substantial section of 'Libri Italici', pp. 36–44. On this list and that of 1640, where Martin's 'standards of cataloguing have decidedly fallen off', see Rhodes 1966: 135.

During the first half of the century too, Dante's presence is evident in the catalogues of a newly refounded library dedicated 'to the publique use of Students' by Sir Thomas Bodley at Oxford.[166] Amongst the 2,000 books acquired by Bodley as its initial stock, there were, according to the handwritten catalogue of 1602–3, two copies of the *Commedia* and one of the *Monarchia*.[167] The Daniello *Commedia* was presented by the soldier and former page of Sir Philip Sidney, Sir Henry Danvers, and it reflects Bodley's ability—as he put it a few years earlier—to 'stirre up other mens benevolence, to helpe to furnish [the library] with bookes'.[168] Bodley himself had, in his previous career as a diplomat, mastered Italian, and he bought from London booksellers who were making purchases on the Continent and in Italy.[169] As part of such donations and purchases, three more copies of the *Commedia* (with the commentaries of Landino and Velutello) had been added to the catalogue by 1605.[170]

The author of the 1605 catalogue, and of two others up to 1620, was Bodley's first librarian, Thomas James, who, as well as being a 'bibliographical pioneer', was also noted for his anti-Catholicism.[171] Early in his career (1598), and shortly before being selected as keeper for Bodley's planned library, James had translated work by the Italian humanist and Bible translator Antonio Brucioli; he edited two of Wyclif's anti-fraternal treatises (1608); and he published works with titles such as *A Treatise of the Corruption of Scripture* (London, 1611) and *The Jesuits Downefall* (Oxford, 1612), seeking to show that Catholic theologians had deliberately falsified the texts of the Church Fathers.[172] As with a number of Protestant writers during this period and earlier, James's interest in Dante and other 'witnesses against Rome' was sharpened by such writers' exposure to censorship or prohibition in the various Catholic Indices.[173] In a polemical work of 1625 he lists 'Dantes' along with Ariosto, Petrarch, Valla, *et al.* as 'Authors [who] with their seuerall bookes, are

---

[166] Bodley 1647: 15; see also *ODNB* (s.v. 'Bodley, Sir Thomas (1545–1613)').

[167] These were the quarto *Commedia* with Daniello's commentary (Venice, 1568); the second Aldine *Commedia* (1515); and a folio *Monarchia* (probably the Basle edition of 1566); see *DEL* 1. 103.

[168] In a letter of 1598 to the vice-chancellor of the university; see Wheeler 1927: 4. Gifts of books and money for books up to 1603 were published under the names of the donors in an elegantly printed ninety-page book: *Munificentissimis atque optimis . . . dedicauit* (London: Barker, 1604), which records the sources of all the newly acquired Dante volumes, including Danvers's Daniello and an earlier Landino edition (Venice, 1484) presented by an Oxfordshire dignitary, Sir Michael Dormer (pp. 44 and 73). According to this source, both Danvers and Dormer also donated other Italian books, including copies of the *Decameron* (both in the Venice 1522 edition).

[169] One of these was John Bill, who was employed by the firm of John Norton and was on his travels in France, Germany, Spain, and Italy between 1602 and 1604; see *ODNB*, s.v. 'Norton, John (1556/7–1612), bookseller'.

[170] See *DEL* 1. 104, Boswell 1999: 126–7. This catalogue also includes items by Petrarch (pp. 111, 368, 622), Boccaccio (p. 291), Ariosto (p. 183), and Tasso (p. 634), amongst many other Italian authors; for further examples, see Lievsay 1969: 35–7.

[171] See *ODNB*, s.v. 'James, Thomas (1572/3–1629), librarian and religious controversialist'. For Dante texts in his 1620 Bodleian catalogue, see *DEL* 1. 104, Boswell 1999: 169–70, and for other Italian items in it, see Lievsay 1969: 37–40.

[172] James's 1598 publication was a translation of the *nuovo commento* on *La cantica di Salomo* which Brucioli had translated *dalla ebraica verità in lingua Toscana* (Venice, 1536).

[173] See above, pp. 52, 70 (n. 12), and 72 with n. 35.

rescued out of the Papists hands, and restored by me'.[174] Precisely what this process of 'restoration' entailed is not entirely clear, but one example of the recovery that James is congratulating himself upon here would be the acquisition of several important editions of the *Monarchia*, which were published in Switzerland and Germany and appear, along with various editions of the *Commedia*, in the Bodleian catalogues for 1602–3 and 1620.[175] A yet more ideological context may account for the presence of a copy of 'Dant. *Aligherius*. De necessitate Monarchiae' in the catalogue of the (then) Presbyterian Sion College in London, compiled by John Spencer in 1650.[176] In this catalogue—whose preface acknowledges James's work in demonstrating the 'use and utility' of a library—Dante's *Monarchia* appears in a collection which is primarily theological and includes a number of Protestant polemical works, such as texts by William Prynne and Matthew Sutcliffe.[177]

James and Bodley both used the word 'public' of the library they had collaborated in founding, and the editions of the *Commedia* and *Monarchia* listed in James's catalogues were thus now available to a wider university readership.[178] With a number of such editions in place by 1620 and with the librarian's concern to rescue them 'out of the Papists hands' and continue conscripting for the Protestant cause, seventeenth-century Oxford seems to recognize to some degree that—as Sir Henry Wotton was very soon to acknowledge—Dante might well be 'worthy the studying'.[179] Yet owners of such works in private collections of the time may well have had rather different interests and agenda.

One important private collection was built up in the course of the century by the Digby family. The 'Bibliotheca Digbeiana', which was auctioned at London in 1680, consisted of books that had been owned by two Catholic aristocrats: Sir Kenelm Digby (d. 1665) and his kinsman George Digby, second earl of Bristol (d. 1677).[180] The catalogue for the sale describes the books as 'published in various languages, and ones which, following that most learned man, Kenelm Digby, the lately deceased and most illustrious George, earl of Bristol, came to own'.[181] Its

---

[174] See *An explanation or enlarging of the ten articles in the supplication of doctor James, lately exhibited to the clergy of England* (1625), 7–9, quoted in Boswell 1999: 185.

[175] See *DEL* 1.103–4; and Boswell 1999: 170. The rare 1610 Offenbach edition of *Monarchia*, to which both Toynbee and Boswell refer, is not listed under 'Dante' in the current Bodleian catalogue. There are, however, two copies now under the heading of 'Engelbertus' (Engelbert of Admont), in which the *Monarchia* is bound together with the *Tractatum de ortu et fine Romani imperii*; one of these is the copy to which James refers and which (after some 400 years) still carries the same shelfmark.

[176] *Catalogus universalis librorum omnium in bibliotheca Collegii Sionii* (London, 1650), 6; see *DEL* 1. 141.

[177] On Sutcliffe and Dante, see above, pp. 63–4 and 72. The Sion catalogue also features an English version of Sarpi's history of the Council of Trent; and under Petrarch's name, a work that could be one of his anti-papal letters; *Catalogus universalis librorum omnium in bibliotheca Collegii Sionii*, e.g., pp. 138–9 and 144.

[178] Bodley 1647: 15 and James's *Humble supplication* of 1607, in which he describes himself as 'keeper of the publike librarie at Oxford'.

[179] On Wotton's list of Italian authors, see above, pp. 95–6.

[180] See *ODNB*, s.v. 'Digby, Sir Kenelm (1603–1665), natural philosopher and courtier', and 'Digby, George, second earl of Bristol (1612–1677)'.

[181] *Biblioteca Digbeiana sive Catalogus Librorum In variis Linguis Editorum, Quos post Kenelmum Digbeium eruditiss[imum] Virum possedit Illustrissimus Georgius Comes Bristol. nuper defunctus*; see Appendix 2, below.

title-page also mentions the addition of another (unnamed) 'Bibliotheca non minus Copiosa, & Elegans'—so the items on sale may not all have been part of the Digby libraries. It seems likely, however, that of the numerous and varied items in this 135-page catalogue, some of the 'Libri Italici' in folio, quarto, octavo, and duo-decimo (pp. 69–79) and some of the manuscripts (pp. 132–5) were those acquired by Kenelm Digby during his visits to Italy much earlier in the century, or, perhaps, inherited from his Oxford tutor, the Catholic sympathizer and associate of Thomas Bodley, Thomas Allen.[182]

Whatever its origins, the 1680 sale catalogue is of considerable interest for its quantity of 'Libri Italici'.[183] Reflecting a continuing interest in learning the language, these include over a dozen Italian dictionaries and grammars (pp. 72, 76, and 78). There are also works by Boccaccio (not only the *Decameron* in quarto and duodecimo, but also other texts such as the *Fiammetta* and *Filocolo*); twelve editions of Petrarch in various formats; two of Ariosto's *Orlando furioso* (one of them the 1634 folio edition of Harington's translation); two of Machiavelli; eight of Tasso (including six of the *Gerusalemme liberata*); and three of Guarini's *Il pastor fido*, one in an undated quarto pamphlet 'Englished by Esq. *Fanshaw*'.[184]

The Digby catalogue also records six Dantean items: five printed texts and one in manuscript.[185] One of the additionally interesting features of the copy of the catalogue now in the British Library is that prices have been entered by hand alongside most of the lots.[186] Thus, among the 'Libri Italici in Folio' the 1564 Venice edition of 'Dante, con l'Expositione di Ch. Landino & di A. Vellutello' attracted the relatively high price (among items in this section) of 10 shillings.[187] Of those in quarto, the [Venice] 1544 'Comedia di Dante con l'Espositione di Aless [andro] Vellutello'—one of the editions listed in the Bodleian catalogues from 1605 onwards—fetched 3s. 2d.[188] More unusually, a miscellaneous group of three octavo items, priced together at 1s. 8d., includes 'L'Amoroso Convivio di Dante [Venice] 1531', the edition that was also owned by Donne.[189]

---

[182] On Digby's residences in Italy (1620–2 and 1645–8), his book collecting, his friendship with Allen, and his major donation of manuscripts to the Bodleian in 1634 (which included 200 of Allen's manuscripts), see *ODNB*, s.v. 'Digby, Sir Kenelm (1603–1665)'; also Gabrieli 1957 and Macray 1883.

[183] For the 'Libri Italici' of the 1680 catalogue, Gabrieli 1957 counted 404 Italian works from the fourteenth to the sixteenth century (pp. 23–4 and n. 3).

[184] For examples, see *Biblioteca Digbeiana*, pp. 70 (nos. 16 and 18), 73 (nos. 132–3 and 135–42), 74 (nos. 148 and 151), 78 (nos. 2–7 and 11–12), 79 (nos. 24, 26–7, 31), 82 (no. 108), and 105 (no. 6). On Kenelm Digby's reading and marking of passages in Boccaccio, see Gabrieli 1957: 25 with n. 2, and 107 with n. 4.

[185] *Biblioteca Digbeiana*, pp. 69 (no. 21), 73 (nos. 130–1), 77 (nos. 116–17), 133 (no. 26).

[186] On examples of 'early catalogues in which contemporaries who attended the sale noted the prices of the books sold in the margins', see Lawler 1898: p. xxi.

[187] *Biblioteca Digbeiana*, p. 69 (no. 21); by comparison, the Venice 1545 folio of Castiglione's *Il cortegiano* (no. 12) sold at 5s.

[188] *Biblioteca Digbeiana*, p. 73 (no. 130); by comparison, the Pavia 1594 and Venice 1628 quartos of Tasso's *Gierusalemme liberata* (nos 132–3) are valued at respectively 1s. 11d. and 1s. 2d. Higher prices are placed on books that may have been illustrated, such as those on travel, geography, and architecture.

[189] *Biblioteca Digbeiana*, p. 77 (no. 116); for Donne's edition, see above, p. 78, n. 64. The other items in this lot are Pietro Bembo's dialogues of *c.*1497–1502, *Gli Asolani*, and an Italian translation of Appian of Alexandria, *Della Guerra Rom[ana]* (1538).

Amongst the six Dantean texts in the *Biblioteca Digbeiana*, there are three more unusual items. A 1602 edition of one of several defences of Dante by the Bolognese physician and poet, Girolamo Zoppio (d. 1591) appears immediately after the Vellutello *Commedia*.[190] Among the octavo editions of Petrarch and Boccaccio and following the lot that includes the *Convivio*, is the '[Trattatello] del Sito, Forma, & Misure dello Inferno di Dante [Florence, 1544]', which is by another defender of Dante, Pier Francesco Giambullari (1495–1555), a founder member of the Florentine Accademia, to which he also presented lectures (*Lezzioni*) on the *Commedia* (1551).[191] Giambullari's *Trattatello* was illustrated with lively woodcut diagrams, many occupying a full page, showing the location, shape, and main divisions of Dante's Hell; it thus occupies a significant place in the tradition of works illustrating the structure of the *Inferno*.[192]

Finally, in the relatively small category (sixty-nine lots) of 'Manuscripti Diversis Voluminibus' at the end of the whole Digby catalogue, there is a manuscript of a text deriving from the Florentine culture of the 1460s: 'Monarchia di Dante Alighieri tradotta da Marsilio Ficino di Lingua Latina in Lingua Toscana.'[193] It seems very likely that Ficino's Platonizing of Dante in the preface to his translation of the *Monarchia* would have chimed with Kenelm Digby's interests and ideas.[194] For example, the claim in Digby's *Observations* on Browne's *Religio Medici* that 'it is Love only that can give us *Heaven* upon Earth' is part of a Neoplatonic argument and is followed by a reference to and quotation of Dante as 'the *Thuscan Virgil*', although in fact, as has been noted, the passage Digby cites 'does not occur in Dante's works'.[195] A number of the items in this section (particularly those on astrology, chemistry, and medicine) seem to have come both from his collection and that of his kinsman George Digby.[196]

Whether or not Kenelm owned all six of the Dante texts in the catalogue, it is evident that several of them represent a quite substantial range of texts, critical writing, illustration, and early translation of his work. They may also reflect signs of an interest in Dante that is evident in some of Digby's writing. For instance, in the *Memoirs* his own romanticized persona ('Theagenes') finds himself called to encourage his crew in the face of imminent danger on a voyage in the far eastern

---

[190] *Biblioteca Digbeiana*, p. 73 (no. 131). This is *Riprove delle Particelle poetiche sopra Dante disputate dal Sig. I. Zoppio, bolognese* (Siena: Bonetti, 1602); it could perhaps be the copy that is now in the John Rylands Library, Manchester (Bullock Coll. 369). On the Dante criticism by Zoppio and the Sienese Bellisario Bulgarini (1539–*c*.1619), see also Caesar 1989: 32–4, 37, and 292–3.

[191] On Giambullari and his circle in the Accademia, see Caesar 1989: 250.

[192] See e.g. the diagrams on pp. 18, 21, 40, 59, 76, 79, 107, and 148 of Giambullari's treatise.

[193] *Biblioteca Digbeiana*, p. 133 (no. 26), in the same lot as a treatise 'de Numero Atomorum totius Universi' (possibly the text published at Rome in 1518), priced together at 5*s*. Ficino's translation of *Monarchia* exists in only six manuscripts (five of which are in Italian and French collections), and the Digby copy could perhaps be the early sixteenth-century paper manuscript subsequently owned by the Victorian collector R. Monckton Milnes and auctioned at Christie's on 29 June 1994.

[194] On Ficino's translation of the *Monarchia*, see Shaw 1974–5 and Gilson 2005: 142–5.

[195] *DEL* 1. 134, n. 2.

[196] Astrology (a shared interest of both Digbys) is the subject of nos. 29, 46–7, 52, 57; there are two documents (nos. 5–6) relating to the first earl of Bristol (George Digby's father); excerpts from the Church Fathers selected 'per G. Digby' (no. 23), perhaps compiled when he was converting to Catholicism in 1659; and (no. 63) Sir Kenelm's 'Translation of *Virgil*'s Eclogues into French, &c (when he was a Youth)' (priced at 10*d*.).

Mediterranean, and delivers 'an oration to them, such a one as the shortness of the time permitted, calling to their minds their past victories that they had gloriously obtained together, and how they had been absolute lords of the sea in all places where yet they came'[197]—a brief 'oration' which perhaps owes something in its form, content, and context to the *orazion picciola* with which Dante's Ulysses had inspired his crew at the other end of the Mediterranean.[198]

A more explicit allusion—to Dante's *Paradiso*—occurs in the first of three 'orations' which Digby himself delivered (in Italian) to the Sienese 'Accademia de' Filomati', probably during his residence in Italy in the early 1620s.[199] Here, the precocious Digby (he would have been about 18 at the time) sets out to expound 'the Ancients' abstruse manner of writing, through which may yet be discovered some of their deepest mysteries, as embodied in their texts'.[200] In the course of exploring some of his interests in cabbalism and cosmology, he then turns to the ascent to God as the centre-point of the universe, noting that:

cosi anchora dicono i sauj che noi non possiamo salire per gl'istessi gradi, per tutti i mondi, ed arrivare all' istesso mondo Archetypo creatore e prima cagione di tutti gli altri, e dal quale procedono tutti le cose, secondo che dice il vostro Poeta,

-----------------------da quel punto
depende il cielo e tutta la natura:

as the learned people still say, we cannot ascend by the same degrees through all the spheres to reach that archetypal creative sphere which gives rise to all the others and from which everything takes its motion, as your Poet says,

------------------------------------- upon that point
revolve the heavens and the whole of nature:[201]

The quotation is from the initial stages of Beatrice's extensive account of the orders of angels that takes place as she and Dante arrive in the ninth and final sphere of Paradise, the Primum Mobile, in *Paradiso* 28. 41–2. Its presence here reflects several continuing features of Digby's thinking and reading, such as his interest in the angelic orders and in the potential Neoplatonism of 'the *Thuscan Virgil*' (i.e. Dante).[202] It reflects specific acquaintance with a late stage in the *Commedia*,

[197] Digby 1827: 317.

[198] *Inferno* 26. 112–22. On Digby's interests in Italian authors including Dante, see also Gabrieli 1957: 24 and 47.

[199] BL Add. MS 41846, ff. 118ʳ–123ʳ; see also Gabrieli 1957: 28–36. This is one of several such orations in the same ms.; the last ('before my departure') is on ff. 140ʳ–141ᵛ. These could perhaps date from Digby's later residence in Italy (his political mission to Rome in 1645–8), but Gabrieli (pp. 27–31) argues that they relate more plausibly to the contacts he established around Siena in 1621–3. They must have been delivered before 1654, which was when the Filomati were absorbed into the Intronati; see <http://www.accademiaintronati.it/storia.html>.

[200] *De' secreti modi di scrivere degli antichi; ove si discorre anchora d'alcuni de' loro mysteri più alti nelle loro scritture contenuti*; BL Add. MS 41846, ff. 118ʳ, also in Gabrieli 1957: 33, where it is presented as an example of the speaker's 'bombastic style' (*frasario ampolloso*).

[201] BL Add. MS 41846, f. 119ᵛ (not noted by Gabrieli 1957).

[202] Evident in a long letter to a French cleric at the start of Add. MS 41846 and the comments on Browne's *Religio Medici* (above, p. 101 with n. 195).

and its concern with progression towards God perhaps relates to his later references to Dante.[203] Furthermore, the introduction to the lines of the *Paradiso* in the Siena *orazione* acknowledges, through its form and capitalization, the pre-eminence of the author as *il vostro Poeta* ('your Poet').[204] Conversely, Petrarch—whom Digby mentions by name several times in this collection of papers (once as 'my Melancho-like fri[e]nd')—is referred to in this oration as only '*one* of your poets', when Digby quotes him later on the subject of literary fame.[205]

Dantean interests seem to be evident in two other late seventeenth-century catalogues of books formerly owned by (as one such list puts it) 'EMINENT and LEARNED MEN Deceased'. The earlier of these, produced for an auction later in the same year as that of the 'Bibliotheca Digbeiana' (1680), advertised the libraries of two unnamed 'eminent and learned' collectors, and amongst a relatively small group of Italian, French, and Spanish books in folio (seventeen items) there is the Venice 1596 edition of Dante's *Commedia* with the commentaries of Landino and Vellutello.[206] In this group there are also signs of those collectors' interest in papal (and anti-papal) politics: Paolo Sarpi's history of the Council of Trent (published under a pseudonym in London in 1619), and a copy of Philippe de Mornay's *Le Mystère d'Iniquité ou l'histoire de la papauté* (1611)—the latter being a work which discusses and quotes Dante's views on the Papacy at some length.[207]

One or other of these book-owners may perhaps have been clerics, and towards the end of the century (1697) the collection of a named Anglican clergyman, 'the Reverend and Learned Dr Scattergood', came on the market. Anthony Scattergood was a biblical scholar who had been chaplain of Trinity Cambridge, canon of Lincoln, and a prebendary of Lichfield. His collection included a substantial number (fifty-nine) of 'Libri Italici' in folio, quarto, and octavo, together with '*Diverse other* English *and* Italian *Tracts, both in Verse and Prose; together with betwixt Fourscore and an Hundred* Italian *Plays*'.[208] One of the two folio volumes

---

[203] For example, when Digby elsewhere in this collection of papers compares his absence from and hoped-for reunion with his late wife to the state of 'soules in Purgatory'; BL Add. MS 41846, f. 62[r].

[204] BL Add. MS 41846, f. 119[v].

[205] BL Add. MS 41846, f. 53[v] (Petrarch as Digby's friend). The line from *Triumphus fame* 1.9, about literary fame raising the writer from the tomb and restoring him to life (*trae l'uom del sepolcro e 'n vita il serba*), is cited *secondo il detto d'un vostro poeta* (ibid., f. 122[v]); see Petrarca 1996: 354.

[206] *A Catalogue of two Choice and Considerable Libraries of Books* (Nov. 1680), 15; see Appendix 2, below. Among the quarto volumes to be sold are also editions of Ariosto, Tasso, Petrarch, and Boccaccio (nos. 14–18). The octavo volumes include two editions of Boccaccio's *Filocolo* (nos. 59–60), Tasso's *Aminta* in French and Italian (no. 78), and Guazzo's *Civil conversatione* (no. 61; for its citation of Dante, see above, pp. 96–7). The 'learned men' specified may not have been two specific collectors, since there seems to have been a practice among auctioneers 'of selling the "deadheads" of their own stocks under the disguise of selections from the libraries of learned persons recently deceased' (Lawler 1898: 149).

[207] *A Catalogue of two Choice and Considerable Libraries of Books*, 15 (nos. 9 and 13); on Sion College books, see above, p. 99, and on Paolo Sarpi, see above, p. 88. De Mornay's work was also translated into English in 1612; for its references to Dante, see Boswell 1999: 144–5 and above, pp. 54–5 (nn. 27 and 33). A copy was also owned by Sir Edward Coke; see below, p. 108 with n. 244.

[208] *A Catalogue of the Library Of the Reverend and Learned Dr Scattergood* (July 1697), 56–7; see Appendix 2, below; also *ODNB*, s.v. 'Scattergood, Anthony (bap. 1611, d. 1687), Church of England clergyman'.

was the 1529 Venice *Commedia* with (again) Landino's commentary, an edition that had featured in three of Robert Martin's catalogues earlier in the century.[209] Among the thirty-seven Italian 'Quartos' there are copies of Boccaccio, Castiglione, Sannazzaro, Ariosto, Petrarch, Guarini, and Marino;[210] and they are joined in this section of the catalogue by a 'Dante con Nuove Ispositioni', which was probably the 16° edition of the *Commedia* published by Guillaume Rouillé at Lyon in 1551.[211] Dr Scattergood's interests in Italy's religious culture and politics (as well as literature and drama) are also reflected by the presence of three works by the Venetian Paolo Sarpi amongst his 'Libri Italici'.[212]

A more eminent and better-known book-collecting cleric around the end of the seventeenth century was Bishop John Moore.[213] According to a contemporary bibliographer in 1714, Moore's library was 'universally and most justly reputed the best furnish'd of any (within the Queen's Dominions) that this Age has seen in the Hands of any private Clergyman'.[214] Its 30,000 books and 1,800 manuscripts were sold to George I after the bishop's death and then in 1715 presented to the University of Cambridge, where (as the Royal Library) it formed the core of the modern collection.[215] It would be surprising if such a large library by this time did not contain some Dante texts, but Moore's manuscripts notably also included three parchment copies of the *Commedia* which are now at Cambridge.[216] There is little documentation of their provenance, but it seems likely that one (and perhaps all three) came, like a number of the Greek manuscripts, from the collection of the bibliophile and numismatist Jean-Baptiste Haultin (1580–1640), who had been active in cataloguing the French Royal Library earlier in the century.[217] Moore's particular interests seems to have included medicine, law, and the accumulation of early printed books, many of which were obtained when he was bishop of Norwich (1691–1707) and are already described in Edward Bernard's account of the Moore collection in 1697.[218] Bernard's account of Moore's 674 manuscripts and 201 incunables at that stage of the collection's development includes two early Boccaccio editions (*De casibus* and a 1470 *Decameron*) and a very early printed Petrarch

---

[209] *A Catalogue of the Library Of... Dr Scattergood*, 56. On Martin's catalogues, see above, p. 97.

[210] *A Catalogue of the Library Of... Dr Scattergood*, 57, nos. 20, 24, 26–31, 33–5.

[211] *A Catalogue of the Library Of... Dr Scattergood*, 57, no. 32; also in this section is a work on the Tuscan dialect by Pier Francesco Giambullari, one of Dante's sixteenth-century advocates (see above, p. 101 with nn. 191–2).

[212] See above, pp. 88 and 103. There are quarto editions of Sarpi's *Historia del Concilio Tridentino* and *Dell'inqisizione* (p. 56, nos. 7 and 20).

[213] See *ODNB* s.v. 'John Moore (1646–1714), bishop of Ely' and Ringrose 1998: 79–87.

[214] W. Nicholson, *The English historical library* (2nd edn., London 1714), p. xii, cited in Ringrose 1998: 86.

[215] See Fletcher 1902: 125–9 and Ringrose 1998: 78 and 87–9.

[216] These are: CUL MSS Gg. 3.6, of the early 15th century; Mm. 2.3 (a and b), both of the late 14th century. For full descriptions, see Barlow 1864: 66–9; Moore 1889: 538–41; Roddewig 1984: 27–8 (nos. 57–9) and the notes by M. R. James at CUL. Gg. 3.6 has Latin glosses (abridged from Benvenuto da Imola), together with *capitoli* (verse-summaries) by Iacopo di Dante and Bosone da Gubbio, and three sonnets by Pietro di Dante; Mm. 2.3 b has the vernacular commentary by Jacopo della Lana.

[217] See Roddewig 1984: 27–8 and Ringrose 1998: 87.

[218] Ringrose 1998: 80–2. On Bernard, see above, p. 95 with n. 151.

(Venice 1488), with commentary on the vernacular poems by Niccolo Peranzone.[219] There is little, however, about Moore's life and career to suggest any specific motive for acquiring Italian texts. Like many of those who acquired Dante texts, especially in the following century, he is mainly of importance here as an energetic, compulsive (and perhaps ruthless) collector, who had scholarly contacts and whose monumental library luckily stayed together in the public domain.[220]

Dante's work thus took a variety of forms in collections and catalogues by the turn of the seventeenth and the eighteenth centuries, as it did in the perceptions of writers and the reading public. Manuscripts, like those of Seget, Wotton, the Digbys, and Moore, were beginning to be acquired, as were—on a much larger scale—early printed editions. Some of the manuscripts and many of the printed texts of the *Commedia* would have communicated a strong visual impression of Dante's otherworlds, through illuminated title-pages, diagrams, and the woodcut illustrations frequently found in editions with the Landino and Vellutello commentaries.[221] Access to the texts was also beginning to extend through their presence in the libraries at Oxford and Cambridge, and (as we have seen) through language-learning, citation, and translation of Dantean passages and other forms of appropriation in a wide range of popular and scholarly works—from anti-papal clerics such as Simon Birckbek and Matthew Sutcliffe, through professional translators such as John Davies and Thomas Salusbury, to erudite gentry such as Kenelm Digby and Thomas Stanley. Ownership, however, seems still to have been the privilege of relatively few, and especially of those who, in the eighteenth century, would regard their libraries as (in the words of a major collector) 'one of the greatest ornaments to a gentleman'.

'ORNAMENTS TO A GENTLEMAN': THE HOLKHAM HALL MANUSCRIPTS

> During my voiage round Italy I have bought several of the most valuable authors that have write [*sic*] in Italian or about the country, the reason that I incroach so far on your kindness to me & venter to put my guardians to that risk is, that if I miss'd the occasion of buying books while I am travelling, I should not be able to find the best of them, & it's impossible to buy them to my mind unless I myself am present, & certainly one of the greatest ornaments to a gentleman or his family is a fine library.[222]

---

[219] See Bernard 1697: 2.2: 361–4, and esp. 374, 381, 383.

[220] The antiquary Richard Gough claimed that Moore extorted books from the clergy in his diocese under the pretext 'Quid illiterati cum libris?' ('What are the unlettered doing with books?', *British Topography* (London, 1714), p. xii, cited in Ringrose 1998: 86), but the *ODNB* entry on Moore notes that 'this was a frequent allegation made against book-collecting bishops of the period'.

[221] e.g. Florence 1481, Venice 1544 and 1564. For examples, see Nassar 1994: 30, 35, 37, 48, 51, 56, 62, 76, 80, 86, 91, 106, etc. See also the illustrations in Giambullari (above, p. 101 n. 192).

[222] Thomas Coke to Sir John Newton, 3 Jan. 1715, cited in Mortlock 2006: 36 and 2007: 139. Further excerpts are in James 1929: 189–90. The original is in Holkham Hall Archives F/G2/2, ff. 463–4 (reference provided by the Archivist, Christine Hiskey).

This confession of bibliomania formed part of a letter home, written at the beginning of 1715, the year in which Bishop Moore's collection, with its Dante manuscripts, entered the University Library at Cambridge. Its aristocratic author—then on tour at Turin—was the seventeen-year-old Thomas Coke (1697–1759), who in 1718 would take control of the family estates at Holkham in Norfolk, would later begin to build a vast Palladian mansion, and eventually acquire the earldom of Leicester. Before that he would also become owner of the largest number of Dante manuscripts that are still to be found in a British private collection. The acquisition, organization, and perception of the Holkham collection will provide a major point of reference for British reception of Dante during much of this century and on into the next.

All but one of the Dante manuscripts acquired by Thomas Coke are still in the library at Holkham Hall. Those remaining in the collection include five texts of the *Commedia*. The earliest (MS 513) is of the second half of the fourteenth century, on parchment, with some painted initials; another, of the early fifteenth century (MS 515, also parchment), was owned by the humanist pope Aeneas Sylvius Piccolomini (Pius II), whose arms appear in the opening initial of the *Inferno*, and has Latin glosses to the first ten cantos of the poem.[223] The other three (MSS 516–18) are all on paper; the first (early fifteenth century) has some lively penwork decoration; the second (later fifteenth century) contains the summaries (*capitoli*) of Iacopo di Dante and Bosone da Gubbio; the third is dated 1474 and signed by its Florentine scribe, Marbettino di Tuccio Manetti.[224] A much rarer item is an early fifteenth-century parchment manuscript (MS 530) of the *Convivio* which is one of only forty-six surviving witnesses and is also signed by a Florentine scribe.[225] The Holkham *Convivio* was the subject of interest to one of the leading Dante scholars of the late nineteenth and early twentieth centuries, Edward Moore of Oxford, who was able to borrow it in 1901 for temporary deposit in the Bodleian.[226]

There have been more permanent migrations of books and manuscripts from the Holkham collection to the Bodleian over the past century, and amongst these was what the former's librarian calls 'a remarkable illustrated version of Dante's *Divina Commedia*'.[227] In 1981 this *Commedia* (then MS 514) was offered to the British Treasury, along with six other manuscripts, in part payment of capital transfer tax and was subsequently assigned to the Bodleian, where it is now

---

[223] I am much indebted to Dr Suzanne Reynolds, Curator of Manuscripts at Holkham Hall, for guidance and information about the collection and its Dantean items.

[224] Descriptions of all the *Commedia* manuscripts still at Holkham (and references to previous scholarship) are in De Ricci 1932: 45–6 and Roddewig 1984: 151–4 (nos. 363 and 365–8).

[225] Ser Antonio di Maria Francisci Nini (d. 1461) copied it 'probably early in his career—he is far better known as a humanistic scribe, so this is an interesting example of him using a Gothic script' (private communication from Dr Reynolds).

[226] Holkham Hall Archives, uncatalogued item: 'E. Moore and P. Toynbee: correspondence with Holkham Hall 1901–1924' (letters to the librarians, A. Napier and C. W. James).

[227] Mortlock 2006: 126. Earlier, in 1952, 492 printed books were sold to the Bodleian (Mortlock 2006: 11 and 125), including all of Sir Edward Coke's Italian books (see below, pp. 107–9); and 112 of the Greek manuscripts went to the Bodleian in 1954.

Ms Holkham misc. 48.[228] It dates from the second half (possibly the third quarter) of the fourteenth century and it is one of the very few *trecento* manuscripts of the *Commedia* to provide a complete canto-by-canto programme of illustrations.[229] Descriptions of the miniatures in the nineteenth century speak of 'a very rude and singular style, yet not wholly without merit', and of 'illustrations . . . roughly done in the style of the early Siena school'.[230] A recent and more nuanced view argues that the images of Holkham misc. 48 constitute 'a unified visual narrative sequence' and are distinctive in approach to gesture, colour, and use of inscriptions— concluding that the illustrations, 'albeit crudely executed, do justice to the *visibile parlare* that Dante describes in *Purgatorio*', and that through them the manuscript has 'created a commentary of its own'.[231] Whatever view one takes of the Holkham Dante's visual impact, the manuscript has certainly become much more publicly visible in its Oxford setting. As the cover of the present volume shows, it has (at the time of writing) literally hit the streets—or at least the hoardings of the New Bodleian site in Broad Street—and all of its images are viewable online.[232]

The history of this manuscript's ownership, its acquisition in Italy around 1717, and its place and its possible accessibility among the 'ornaments' of a great eighteenth-century library will be considered shortly. But for its context at Holkham we have to look back to the books acquired by the founder of the family's fortunes: the lawyer, politician, and chief justice, Sir Edward Coke (1552–1634). Sir Edward is said to have 'lived his life on the cusp between the international aspirations of Renaissance learning—extensive in its breadth, Latin in its ancestry—and the insular, assertive traditions of the English common law'.[233] His substantial library (1,237 items) was catalogued under his supervision shortly before his death.[234] Religious works account for about a quarter of its total—and there are, as might be expected, a large number of legal texts—but it is striking that about a third of the whole collection consists of books in modern foreign languages: French, Spanish, and particularly Italian.[235] Many of the Italian titles, which include six copies of various works by Boccaccio and four editions of Petrarch, were acquired from the collection of Elizabeth I's lord chancellor, Sir Christopher Hatton (d. 1591),

---

[228] Mortlock 2006: 126–7; the remaining three Greek manuscripts were also included. On the family's decision to maintain the estate by selling works of art rather than land, see Sager 2002: 441–2.

[229] Except where pages have been lost—as between *Purg.* 25 and 31 and *Par.* 9–15, 18–19, 21–2, and 24–32. The illustrations (148 in all) are listed in BMS 1. 252–7. The fullest discussion of them to date is as yet unpublished (Figueredo 2004), but see also briefer accounts in: BMS 1.252; Hassall 1970: 26 and pls. 77–84 and 1983: 83–6; De la Mare 1982: 333–4 and 1985: 131. Figueredo (2004: 5–6 and n. 26) points out that very few of the extant *trecento Commedia* manuscripts are fully illustrated. The manuscript as a whole is described by Roddewig 1984: 151–2 (no. 364).

[230] William Roscoe and Frederic Madden, unpublished catalogue at Holkham Hall (1816–28) 7. 479; Barlow 1867: 388b. C. W. James's view of the illustrations (in the pamphlet produced for the exhibition of the Dante manuscripts and books for the 'Dante Sexcentenary' of 1921 at Norwich Public Library) is more positive: 'The pictures may not be specimens of the highest art of their time, but they are inexhaustibly interesting' (pp. 4–5).

[231] Figueredo 2004: 6–7, 14, 30, 44, 68.

[232] At: <http://www.bodley.ox.ac.uk/dept/scwmss/wmss/medieval/mss/holkham/misc/048.a.htm>.

[233] *ODNB*, s.v. 'Coke, Sir Edward (1552–1634)'.

[234] Hassall 1950*a*: pp. xi–xii.   [235] Hassall 1950*a*: pp. xix–xx.

through Coke's marriage (in 1598) to the widow of Hatton's heir.[236] But Sir Edward's list of over a dozen 'Italian books of Philologie and Grammar' and his ownership of John Florio's and William Thomas's dictionaries suggests an interest in accessing Italian authors in the original.[237] Moreover, in a section headed 'Poetry', standard authors, such as 'Homer in Englishe', 'Virgil . . . with two Commentaries', and 'Chaucer in fol[io]' are accompanied by the 'Poet Dantes Workes'.[238]

Other items in Sir Edward's collection suggest some possible contexts for his ownership of this poet's works. If Coke read his French translation of Guazzo's *Civill conversacion* and his Italian copy of 'Galatheo di Mons: della Casa', he would have encountered significantly different views about Dante's poetic language, together with copious illustrations of passages from the *Commedia*.[239] Religious controversy may also be relevant to his ownership of the poet's works. Sir Edward had, like Matthew Sutcliffe and other British Protestants, engaged in argument with the Jesuit Robert Persons, a number of whose works appear in Coke's catalogue under the heading of 'Popishe Books'.[240] Amongst the latter is a text referred to as 'Parsons against Barlowe in 4°', which must be the posthumously published 1612 polemic (with a much longer title) where Persons had shown detailed knowledge of the *Commedia* and several of its commentaries.[241] Persons had denounced the *conioyninge* of Dante to Protestant polemic;[242] however, that was precisely what one of Sir Edward's other authors, the French Huguenot leader Philippe de Mornay (1549–1623), had continued to do.[243] Coke also seems to have been given 'by the author' a first edition of De Mornay's *Le Mystère d'Iniquité ou l'histoire de la papauté* (1611; English translation 1612), and cites anti-papal passages from the *Monarchia* as well as the *Commedia*.[244] It seems likely, then, that

[236] On the Hatton books at Holkham, see Hassall 1950*b*. For Boccaccio (the *Decameron*, the *Genealogia*, and, more unusually, the *Teseida* and an Italian version of *De claris mulieribus*), and the four Petrarchs, see Hassall 1950*a*: 53, 70, 83, 89, 94.

[237] Hassall 1950*a*: 63–4 and 71–2 (nos. 883 and 891). On Thomas and Florio, see above, pp. 69 (with n. 5) and 70–1.

[238] Hassall 1950*a*: 69 (no. 860), suggesting that this could be either Venice 1568 (with Daniello's commentary) or Venice 1578 (with Landino's and Vellutello's).

[239] Hassall 1950*a*: 86 (no.1082) and 93 (no. 1167). On Guazzo, see above, pp. 96–7; on Della Casa and Dante's unmannerly diction, see Caesar 1989: 267–70. Like Guazzo, Della Casa had also been translated into English in the sixteenth century (1576). For the latter's quotations from Dante see *DEL* 1. 59–62 and Boswell 1999: 49–56 and 152; these include 'the first specimen of the Italian text of Dante printed in England' (*DEL* 1. 61, n. 1).

[240] The section (Hassall 1950*a*: 17–20) includes over forty titles. According to Mortlock (2006: 25), Coke owned 'seven pieces' by Persons.

[241] Hassall 1950*a*: p. xix and n. 51; 18 (no. 245). On Persons and his references to Dante in *Discussion of the Answere of M. William Barlow* (posthumously published in 1612), see above, p. 57 and n. 45.

[242] See above, p. 56.

[243] De Mornay's work features in a number of the 'Divinitie Books' in the collection; Hassall 1950*a*: 4, 12, 15, 20 (nos. 46, 166, 209, 274).

[244] Mortlock 2006: 19. On De Mornay, see above, pp. 54 and 64. His 1611 text of *Le Mystère d'Iniquité* was published at Saumur in both Latin and French, and the Dantean passages are translated in both (pp. 436–7 of the Latin and pp. 419–20 of the French).

'Dantes Workes' and references to them could have served several purposes at this early stage in the formation of the Holkham collection.[245]

The precedent of collecting Italian books on a vast variety of subjects (including works by and referring to Dante) had thus been set within Thomas Coke's family; yet the cultural and intellectual context within which he would add to the collection in the early eighteenth century was different in a variety of ways. The young Thomas Coke's 1715 letter about book-buying in Italy (quoted at the opening of this section) refers to acquiring 'the most valuable authors' and achieving the 'ornament to a gentleman' of 'a fine library'. It reflects the cultural programme and conventions of the Grand Tour, which by the later seventeenth century had become 'part of the ordinary education and experience of the educated classes'.[246] More specifically, it conveys the traveller's sense of the purposes and scope of his 'voiage round Italy', for by the beginning of 1715 Coke had already visited a number of Italian cities, including Florence, Venice, Naples, and Rome, where he had become acquainted with the artist and subsequent architect of Holkham Hall, William Kent, who advised him on purchases of paintings there and acted as his agent.[247]

Thomas Coke's letter from Turin also reflects the influence of his travelling companion: the Cambridge don Dr Thomas Hobart. Hobart, who was Fellow in Medicine at Christ's from 1699 until his death in 1728, is noted in the college records chiefly for his absences abroad as private tutor.[248] When introduced to Thomas Coke's guardians in 1712, he had recently returned from accompanying another youthful aristocrat to Rome the previous year.[249] It would be chiefly under his guidance that Coke made his manuscript purchases at Padua, Venice, and elsewhere.[250] Hobart may well have embarked on this particular tour with 'a general plan for acquisitions' and the 'aim … to create a scholar's, as opposed to a collector's library'; and by the time his pupil left him in Paris and returned to England in May 1718, their initial purchase of manuscripts had risen to over 400 items, along with a number of early printed books.[251] The range of the collection was considerable too. By 1718 it had already acquired about forty Greek manuscripts, and it would also come to include large numbers of Latin classics, patristic and theological texts and Renaissance prose writers.[252]

Out of the 700 or so manuscripts that eventually comprised Thomas Coke's collection, the texts in Italian were a substantial component, amounting to over 140 items (slightly more numerous than those in Greek).[253] Along with his seven

---

[245] On the fortunes of Coke's library in the later seventeenth century, see James 1922: 220–1.

[246] Stoye 1989: 138.

[247] James 1929: 185–8; Connor Bulman 2003: 29; Mortlock 2006: 140 and 144.

[248] For the scant evidence about Hobart's background and activities, see James 1929: 176–7, Rook 1969: 119, and Gialluca and Reynolds 2009: 13–15.

[249] On Hobart's earlier tour, with Edward Hyde, Viscount Cornbury (1691–1713), see Connor Bulman 2003: 28–9 and n. 10.

[250] James 1922: 221–6   [251] Mortlock 2006: 36–7; James 1922: 222.

[252] James 1922: 224, 225, and 226–7.

[253] 'Italian Authors' are listed in the handlist of 1932 (based on the unpublished Roscoe–Madden catalogue of 1816–28) as nos. 513–657 (De Ricci 1932: 45–55).

Dante codices, Coke also owned two fifteenth-century Petrarch manuscripts (*Rime sparse* and *Trionfi*) and an illuminated parchment copy of Boccaccio's *Decameron* written for Teofilo Calcagnini, a member of Borso d'Este's court at Ferrara some time before 1467.[254] Some of the Holkham Italian manuscripts—such as this *Decameron* and the Piccolomini *Commedia* (MS 515)—have indications of previous ownership. The *Decameron* may perhaps have been bought from the Observant Franciscan convent at Reggio nell'Emilia, to which it belonged in the seventeenth century, and another of the *Commedia* manuscripts (MS 518) has the library stamp of the Florentine Ricasoli family, from whom Coke is likely to have acquired it.[255]

According to the account book for the tour, Coke spent substantial amounts on manuscript purchases during his time in Italy, with the largest single sum being paid at Padua on 10–11 June 1717: 4,779 livres for thirty to forty items from the nearby monastery of San Giovanni in Viridario.[256] But whilst it is possible to identify several of the main locations of Coke's Italian purchases, the precise provenance of many items is undocumented. It has been suggested that the illustrated *Commedia* (Bodley MS Holkham misc. 48) could possibly have been 'one of the manuscripts that he [Coke] bought in Naples from the collection of Giuseppe Valletta (d. 1714)'.[257] Valletta's library of around 10,000 titles was well known both in Italy and elsewhere.[258] Like other foreign visitors (such as Bishop Burnet earlier), Coke and Hobart may possibly have met its owner very shortly before his death, in the course of their few months' stay at Naples in the first half of 1714, and a number of the Holkham collection's Italian manuscripts are definitely ascribed to this source.[259] Whether Holkham misc. 48 (or any of the other five Holkham *Commedia* manuscripts) was also part of that purchase is uncertain. In 1716—two years after his death and before the main sale of his library in 1726—it was said that Valletta had owned two *Commedia* manuscripts, and one of these is described as *in cartap[ecora]* ('parchment') and *figurato* ('illustrated').[260] However, since the latter is also said to have *note latine marginali* ('marginal Latin glosses'), it cannot be identified with Holkham misc. 48, which has no such glosses. Stretching the meaning of these terms a little, they might be made to apply to Holkham MS 515, the *Commedia* owned by Pius II, which is on parchment, has some

[254] De Ricci 1932: 46–7 (nos. 519–20 and 531). On the *Decameron* manuscript (now Bodley MS Holkham misc. 49), see esp. De la Mare 1982: 334–5.

[255] De la Mare 1982: 335. MS 518 may be one of those being disposed by the Ricasoli family in the early eighteenth century: 'some now appear among the Harley MSS at the BL' (Dr S. Reynolds, personal communication).

[256] James 1922: 222–3 and 1929: 204; Hassall 1959: 251; Mortlock 2006: 44; Gialluca and Reynolds 2009: 14–15.

[257] De la Mare 1982: 334; see also Roddewig 1984: 152.

[258] Comparato 1970: 98–105.

[259] On Burnet's visit to Naples in 1685, as part of Valletta's encounter with 'the Protestant world' and a stimulus to his interest in England, see Comparato 1970: 115–17. Hobart was in Naples at some point before 1709 (*DBI*, s.v. 'Ferrari, Domenico Antonio'). For his arrival there with Thomas Coke early in 1714, see James 1929: 186, and for the suggestion that they may have met Valletta, see Mortlock 2006: 40.

[260] The descriptions come from the *Giornale de' Letterati d'Italia: Tomo ventesimoquarto; Anno MDCCXV* (Venice, 1716), 85, under *codici italiani* (pp. 82–95).

striking illumination, and has marginal Latin glosses for the first ten cantos of the *Inferno*.[261] It remains possible that another Valletta *Commedia*—referred to in the 1716 *Giornale* simply as 'un' altro testo in foglio della stessa Commedia' ('another text in folio of that same *Commedia*')—could be Holkham misc. 48, or perhaps one of the other manuscripts of the poem now at Holkam.[262]

Another possible provenance for Holkham misc. 48 has emerged recently through the discovery of letters from a Florentine bibliophile Anton Francesco Marmi (1665–1736), the disciple of Antonio Magliabechi and, after Magliabechi's death in 1714, the custodian of his library. One of these was written on 20 April 1717 when Coke and Hobart were in Florence, and it mentions that they were then acquiring the 'Ariosto del Porro' and 'un bellissimo Dante'.[263] Of the Dantes that went to Holkham, the latter epithet would most appropriately apply to Holkham misc. 48.

On the other hand, 'un bellissimo Dante' could just as well apply to another profusely illustrated *Commedia* manuscript that Coke's tutor, Thomas Hobart, may by then have bought for himself.[264] Hobart's own *Commedia* (now New York, Pierpont Morgan Library MS M 676) is worth some attention, since it not only reflects the tutor's and pupil's common acquisitive enterprise, but also shows what kinds of visual experience of the text they could have shared. The Pierpont Morgan copy is said to be of the late fourteenth century (perhaps written and illustrated in Naples around 1380–5); its illustrations are less comprehensive and show more signs of wear than those of Holkham misc. 48, but they convey the movement of souls and pilgrims more dynamically, and are in some cases more expressive in their rendering of gesture.[265] It has a good chronological claim to be the *Dante* to which Marmi referred in April 1717, since it seems to have been acquired by Hobart from the Ferrarese priest and poet Girolamo Baruffaldi (1675–1755), who notes clearly in the manuscript itself that it had been given to him at Ferrara on 7 January 1702.[266] During the later part of their tour, in the autumn of 1716, Hobart and Coke had been in that region, travelling between towns on the north-eastern side of the Apennines, before returning to Rome and on to Florence the next spring.[267]

---

[261] See above, p. 106; also Roddewig 1984: 152 (no. 365).

[262] *Giornale de' Letterati d'Italia: Tomo ventesimoquarto; Anno MDCCXV* (Venice, 1716), 85. However, if Valletta's ms had been Holkham misc. 48, some reference to its impressive programme of illustrations would likely have been made.

[263] 'Letter to Alessandro Capponi [bibliophile and antiquarian at Rome], dated 20 April 1717 (Vatican City, BAV, MS Capponiani 271), probably referring to *Orlando Furioso di M. Ludouico Ariosto nuouamente adornato di figure di rame da Girolamo Porro Padouano* (Venice: Francesco de Franceschi, 1584). A copy of this text is at Holkham (BN 166) and has an armorial binding datable to 1744–1759 by Jean Robiquet' (note in Dr S. Reynolds's forthcoming catalogue of the Holkham manuscripts, vol. 1). On Coke's four periods of residence in Florence and Tuscany between December 1713 and May 1717, see Gialluca and Reynolds 2009: 31–3.

[264] Reynolds, catalogue of Holkham manuscripts, vol. 1 (forthcoming).

[265] These features can easily be compared through adjacent examples from both manuscripts (Holkham misc. 48 and Morgan M 676) in BMS 2. 247b–c, 365a–d, 418a–b, 437a–b, 484b–c, 489a–b, 493b–c.

[266] Pierpont Morgan Library MS M 676, f. 1ʳ, also on the back paper flyleaf. See also Roddewig 1984: 215.

[267] James 1929: 202–3.

The *Commedia* manuscript from Ferrara purchased by Hobart might well have been one of the acquisitions in the course of that busy itinerary. In addition to this *Commedia*, Hobart bought a number of other manuscripts for his own collection—amongst them an illustrated French translation of Boccaccio's *De mulieribus claris*—and he is known to have purchased material for the Holkham library on a return visit to Italy (and Florence) in 1719.[268] His continuing partnership with his pupil beyond the end of their five-year tour is one example of Thomas Coke's close associations with experts who could have unlocked the significance of the vast quantity of texts he was so rapidly acquiring.

Another example of such collaboration (and possible conversation) involves a scholar who was himself an Italian: Domenico Antonio Ferrari (*c.*1685–1744). In the early years of the century Ferrari, as a young lawyer in Naples, seems to have become acquainted with Thomas Hobart, who assisted him in his relocation to England (via Geneva), where in 1709 he formally abjured Catholicism and, as doctor of law, was incorporated at Cambridge University (1710).[269] Ferrari's association with Thomas Coke was initially as tutor during the first year of the Grand Tour and subsequently as librarian, helping to organize and extend Coke's collection in its initial London location: Thanet House in Bloomsbury.[270] His obituary in 1744 describes him as a 'Fellow of the Royal Society, as well as Member of several learned foreign Academies', and records that 'he left a valuable Library to the Earl [i.e. Coke]'.[271] Ferrari's interests seem to have been in Italian reformist and humanist writers such as Bernardino Ochino, Pier Paolo Vergerio, and Giordano Bruno, rather than in Italian poetry, but his presence and activities during the formation of Coke's collection provided an obvious point of access to its Italian content.[272] As custodian of the Dante manuscripts over several decades, he would very likely have recalled the use that Vergerio and other religious dissenters had made of the *Monarchia* and *Commedia*.[273]

Also among Coke's domestic circle—although more intermittently—was a bibliophile whose library was one of the major collections of the early eighteenth century and 'equalled and probably surpassed Thomas Coke's'.[274] Dr Richard Mead, one of the leading court physicians of the time, attended also Coke's family

---

[268] Hobart's Boccaccio was a Parisian manuscript of *c.*1450–75, *De cleres et nobles femmes*, now New York Public Library MS Spencer 033. In 1719 he bought on Coke's behalf the unique autograph manuscript of Thomas Dempster's work on the Etruscans (*De Etruria regali*, now Holkham MS 809; see Hassall 1959: 253 with n. 12, and Gialluca and Reynolds 2009). For other Hobart items in the Holkham Library, see De Ricci 1932: 44 (nos. 503–5) and (for further discussion of him and his collection), the forthcoming vol. 1 of the catalogue of Holkham manuscripts by Dr Suzanne Reynolds. His own manuscripts were sold at auction in 1730 (see James 1922: 222), and his *Commedia* was purchased for the Pierpont Morgan Library from Quaritch (London) in March 1923.

[269] *DBI*, s.v. 'Ferrari, Domenico Antonio' and Vinay 1965: 598–601 and 603.

[270] James 1929: 182–3; Hassall 1959: 254; Mortlock 2007: 67 and 140–6.

[271] *Gentleman's Magazine*, 14 (1744), 282 (21 May); this was also the month in which Coke acquired the earldom of Leicester. For the fifteenth-century manuscript left to Coke, see De Ricci 1932: 44 (no. 500). Ferrari also left books to his Cambridge college (St John's); see Vinay 1965: 597 and n. 2.

[272] Vinay 1965: 612–14.   [273] On Vergerio and Dante, see above, p. 52 with nn. 12–13.

[274] Mortlock 2006: 76.

in the 1720s, and seems on one occasion at least to have added provision of books to that of his medical services.[275] Mead had travelled extensively in Italy in the mid-1690s, and it was probably there that he acquired some or all of his seven early editions of the *Commedia* (including the *editio princeps* of 1472 and the Aldine Bembo edition of 1502).[276]

There were thus around Thomas Coke a number of professional figures who, for various reasons, would have been interested in his collection of Italian books and authors. The extent of Coke's own attention to such books remains uncertain, but—although a keen pursuer of various blood-sports—he was no mere trophy hunter. His broader interests and education in music, theatre, and especially the visual arts are well attested, as was his earlier study of the classics, modern languages, and mathematics.[277] A Norfolk neighbour's recollection of 'reading the Ancient Authors' with Coke after a day's hunting may seem a little idealized, but this neighbour (Edward Spelman) was himself a 'formidable' classical scholar and translator whose work was admired by Gibbon.[278]

Other scholars seem to have had access to Coke's collection at an early stage. In May 1721, while major items were still arriving, the pioneer Anglo-Saxonist and palaeographer Humphrey Wanley—who had much earlier collaborated on Edward Bernard's bibliographic *Catalogus* of 1697 and was now librarian for another major private collector, Edward Harley—mentions a visit 'to Mr Coke of Norfolk who shewed me part of his MSS. with much humanity for above 3 hours together, and will send to me to see the rest, as soon as he can have Leasure'.[279] The manuscripts in question were Greek texts, including ones from the Venetian Giustiniani family for which Wanley's employer had been a rival bidder, but it seems that the competition between the Coke and Harley collections extended in smaller measure to Dante texts, since the Harleian manuscripts also included five copies of the *Commedia*.[280]

Competition and a predilection for the classics are certainly features of Coke's accumulation of manuscripts and books. His manuscripts remained (until the early

---

[275] According to Hassall (1959: 253), the Holkham accounts show that 'books were sometimes obtained through Dr Mead'. For a further example, see Mortlock 2007: 88.

[276] On Mead's travels to Turin, Florence, Padua, Rome, and Naples and on the composition of his library (sold after his death in 1754), see *ODNB*, s.v. 'Mead, Richard (1673–1754)'. For further details of his Dante editions, which also included the 1490 *editio princeps* of the *Convivio*, see *DEL* 1. 276.

[277] On music and theatre, see Mortlock 2007: 131–8; and for the significance to Coke's art collecting and 'moral education' of the six history paintings he commissioned in Rome in 1714, see Connor Bulman 2003: 27 and 29–30. For Hobart's view of his pupil's studies on tour in 1713, see James 1929: 182.

[278] Hassall 1959: 253 and n. 11. On Spelman and his 1742 translation of Xenophon (*The Expedition of Cyrus*) whose dedication contains this reminiscence, see *ODNB*, s.v. 'Spelman [formerly Yallop], Edward (d.1767), writer and translator'.

[279] BL MS Lansdowne 771 (1721, 18 May), cited by James 1922: 225; see also Mortlock 2006: 77. On Wanley's career as 'one of the greatest palaeographers and librarians of his age', see *ODNB*, s.v. 'Wanley, Humphrey (1672–1726), Old English scholar and librarian'. On Bernard's *Catalogus*, see above, p. 95 with n. 151.

[280] James 1922: 224–5. On Edward Harley's *Commedia* manuscripts (bought by parliament in 1753 and subsequently acquired by the British Museum), and his early printed editions of Dante, see *DEL* 1. 243 and 255.

nineteenth century) unbound in the tower rooms of Holkham House—which might suggest either that 'he believed their value lay in their research potential' (he certainly loaned a number of them to classical scholars), or that his own preference was 'for the printed word, in finely bound editions ranged in the splendour of his "Grand Library"'.[281] However, his credentials as an Italianist and antiquarian were certainly recognized by his election as an early member of a society, several of whose members would have significant interests in Dante: the Society of Dilettanti.[282]

DANTE AND THE DILETTANTI

The term *dilettante* and the activities of the Society of Dilettanti in the mid-eighteenth century cover a wide range.[283] The intermediate status of the dilettanti has recently been emphasized as that of neither 'professionals nor amateurs'—as neither 'precursors of the modern scientist' nor 'insignificant collectors of curiosities'.[284] Their interests in the antiquities of the eastern Mediterranean developed initially as an offshoot of the Grand Tour, but the publications resulting from a mid-century expedition to Greece, Asia Minor, Syria, and Egypt in 1750–1, funded by a member of the Society (James Dawkins), are of importance to the history of British classical archaeology.[285]

Prominent amongst the mid-century Dilettanti was a figure whose early archaeological and architectural studies during the eight years of his Grand Tour (1746–54) would combine with a developing interest in Dante and the history of Italian poetry. James Caulfeild, first earl of Charlemont, was elected to the Society in 1756, a few years after his brief expedition of 1749–50 to Asia Minor, Alexandria, and Greece.[286] Very little of Charlemont's writing on either his eastern Mediterranean travels or his Italian studies was published during his lifetime, but both his antiquarian and literary interests were sustained in later years, alongside his better-known activities in the cause of Irish constitutional reform.[287] Both are also reflected in papers he read to the Royal Irish Academy, which he helped to found in 1785, and his commitment to the study of Dante is also reflected in his correspondence and in his manuscript essay, which has been recognized as an important Whig attempt at the turn of the century 'to claim the Italian Catholic Dante for a northern Protestant canon'.[288]

---

[281] Mortlock 2006: 80. 'Italian Literature' (along with 'Classics') was a subject heading in the arrangement of the printed books in the library.

[282] Hassall (1959: 253) claims that 'Coke was the most conspicuous of the young Italophile aristocrats who founded the Society of Dilettanti in 1733', but the records seem to indicate that he and his young son were elected in 1740–1 (Cust and Colvin 1898: 20).

[283] For some definitions, from 'collector' to 'serious students of the fine arts who were not practicing artists', and the relationship of *dilettante* to *virtuoso*, see Kelly 2009: 8–12.

[284] Kelly 2009: 11.   [285] Kelly 2009: 125.

[286] Kelly 2009: 114–15; see also the list in Cust and Colvin 1898; and *ODNB*, s.v. 'Caulfeild, James, first earl of Charlemont (1728–1799), politician'.

[287] For his travel writing, see Stanford and Finopoulos 1984.

[288] For Charlemont's various articles on classical and Italian topics in the *Transactions of the Royal Irish Academy* (between 1786 and 1797), see Kelly 2009: 295 (n. 25), and *DEL* 1. 433–6. On his participation in the debate about Dante during his travels in northern Italy in 1754, and on his later

A yet more influential Whig politician, member of the Dilettanti, and Italophile of the later eighteenth century was Charles James Fox (1749–1806). Following his uncompleted studies at Oxford, Fox's two-year continental tour (September 1766 to August 1768) took him to a number of Italian cities, including Florence, and during his travels he is described as 'devouring Dante and Ariosto'.[289] It may well have been his enthusiasm for Italy (to be further fostered by the Holland House circle early in the following century) that ensured his election to the Society of Dilettanti in 1769, and his name is linked to the ownership of several *Commedia* manuscripts, not all of which are now identifiable.[290] Several of his comments about Dante in his later correspondence go somewhat beyond the usual banalities, and perhaps imply a link between the 'obscurity' of the medieval poet's allusions and the British reader's ignorance—even then being dissipated—'of that part of [medieval] history to which he [Dante] refers'.[291]

Among other members of the Society in the later years of the eighteenth century and the first decade of the nineteenth were a number who played a yet more active part in the acquisition and (in some cases) promotion of Dante. These included translators such as the 'Della Cruscan' William Parsons, whose 'free' and rather wordy version of 'The Story of Francesca' (*Inferno* 5) appeared in the *Florence Miscellany* in 1785, and Charles Burney, whose lost prose translation of the whole *Inferno* is said to have been completed in 1761.[292] More typically, there were also members who played a leading role as investors in Dante, through patronage and the collection of books and manuscripts. Amongst the former was the banker Thomas Hope (1769–1831), who commissioned one of the most influential programmes of illustrations of the *Commedia*: John Flaxman's 110 drawings, which were first published privately at Rome in 1793.[293]

Amongst the Dilettanti there were also avid and competitive collectors, such as the socialite and politician Anthony Storer, who became a member of the Society in 1781, and whose bequest of nearly 2,800 books to Eton College Library include thirty-four incunabula, 388 quartos of English plays ('along with the first three

---

studies, see Talbot 2012: 308–9 and 313–19 (p. 319 is quoted here); and for an edition of his *History of Italian Poetry from Dante to Metastasio*, see Talbot 2000.

[289] *ODNB*, s.v. 'Fox, Charles James (1749–1806), politician', notes that along with his other reading in the classics, Spanish, French, and Italian, Fox 'had a particular liking for the work of Dante, Boccaccio and Ariosto'. See also *DEL* 1. 609.

[290] See Roddewig 1984: p. lxxxvii and nos. 51, 409, 507. On the subsequent ownership of one of the manuscripts, see *DEL* 2. 587.

[291] For his comments on Dante in letters and memoranda of 1802–3, see *DEL* 1. 610–11.

[292] Parsons's translation of *Inferno* 5 was reprinted in London in 1787 (*A Poetical Tour in the Years 1784, 1785 and 1786*), 201–7, along with several other poems making serious and facetious allusions to Dante (pp. 54 and 102). On Parsons, the Della Cruscans, and the *Florence Miscellany*, see McGann 1996: esp. 90–2, and Saglia 2007: 18–27; the group is also the subject of ongoing research by Ilaria Mallozzi (Royal Holloway University of London). On Burney's *Inferno*, see *DEL* 1.323 and Tinkler-Villani 1989: 74.

[293] See *ODNB*, s.v. 'Hope, Thomas (1769–1831), art collector and connoisseur'; on his patronage of Flaxman, see Bindman 1979: 23 and 98–9.

Folios of Shakespeare'), and some 450 sixteenth-century Italian books.[294] One of Storer's incunables was the *Commedia* printed at Venice in 1477 (with the Lana commentary and Boccaccio's life of Dante) by Wendelin of Speier. His ten later editions of the *Commedia* comprise a virtual publishing history of the poem in the sixteenth century. Beginning with Bembo's Aldine *Terze rime di Dante* (1502), they include the rare and much-sought-after Florentine octavo edition of 1506, published by Filippo Giunta (with Manetti's dialogue on the 'place, shape and dimensions of Dante's hell').[295] Storer also acquired the Venetian editions of 1512, 1515, 1569, and 1578, along with two mid-century Lyon editions (1547 and 1551) and the text edited at the end of the century by members of the Accademia della Crusca (Florence, 1595). Along with these, he owned several other Dantean works: the *Convivio* (Venice, 1529) and the *Vita nova di Dante Alighieri. Con xv canzoni del medesimo. E la vita di esso Dante scritta da Giovanni Boccaccio* (Florence, 1576). Yet more unusually, he had two editions of a substantial anthology of other poems by Dante and his contemporaries: *Sonetti e canzoni di diversi autori toscani in dieci libri raccolte* (Florence 1527 and Venice 1532).[296] Sixteenth-century criticism of Dante is represented in the collection by Giovan Battista Gelli's earlier *lezioni* to the Florentine Academy: his commentaries on parts of the *Paradiso* (in 1541) and the *Purgatorio* (in 1543 and 1551).[297]

Several examples of contemporary responses to Dante—and the change in taste that they signal—are also evident in Storer's library. He owned the very slim volume of *Poems* (1773) by Byron's guardian, Frederick Howard, fifth earl of Carlisle, which included his 'Translation from Dante, Canto xxxiii', one of the more well-known—and subsequently anthologized—eighteenth-century versions of the Ugolino story (*Inf.* 33. 1–75).[298] And what may have been his latest acquisition with Dantean associations was an even slimmer pamphlet containing Carlisle's 1790 poem 'To Sir Joshua Reynolds on his Late Resignation of the President's Chair of the Royal Academy'.[299] This is a rather tortuous tribute to the painter, whose influential portrait of *Count Hugolino and his Children in the Dungeon* (exhibited at the Royal Academy in 1773) may have inspired Carlisle's own Dante translation in the same year; and in it the poet is moved to see the hand

[294] See *ODNB*, s.v. 'Storer, Anthony Morris (1746–99), politician and collector'; and on his bequest to Eton, Birley 1970: 47–55.
[295] On both of these editions, see Richardson 1995: 255.
[296] As well as lyrics by Dante, this also included poems by Cino da Pistoia, Guido Cavalcanti, Dante da Maiano, and Guittone d'Arezzo, along with *diversi canzoni e sonetti senza nome d'autore*. I am grateful to Dr Rachel Bond of Eton College Library for providing the detailed records of these items.
[297] *Tutte le lettioni di Giovanbattista Gelli, fatta da lui nella Accademia Fiorentina* (Florence, 1551); this also includes his lectures on Petrarch. On Gelli and his later Dante criticism, see Caesar 1989: 259–66 and above, p. 78 with n. 64.
[298] Eton College Library Cg. 2.4.02. On versions of Ugolino in this period (including those of Richardson, Gray, and Carlisle), see Yates 1951, Tinkler-Villani 1989: 59–76, Roe 1998, and Braida 2004: 10–13. For Carlisle's version, see *DEL* 1. 334–6 and for discussion Tinkler-Villani 1989: 66–8. Perhaps it was his guardian's genteel and unambiguous conclusion—with Ugolino succumbing simply to 'pale hunger'—that would prompt Byron's insistence that Dante's line (*Inf.* 33. 75) refers instead to cannibalism (*DEL* 2. 387–8).
[299] Eton College Library Cg. 2H.2A; see *DEL* 1. 336–7.

of both 'Nature' and 'Learning/Science' helping to render palatable Reynolds's image of 'famish'd Ugolino's woe'.[300]

Dantean items in Storer's library thus run from the late fifteenth century to the late eighteenth, and—whether or not he actually opened the fine (mostly eighteenth-century) bindings of his editions—this avid Dilettante certainly seems to have aimed at comprehensiveness. One apparent omission from his rich and crowded shelves, however, was a more recent edition of the *Commedia* which several other eighteenth-century collectors regarded as a highly desirable item. The second collected edition of Dante's work was published by Antonio Zatta at Venice in five quarto volumes between 1757 and 1758.[301] Its text of the *Commedia* was accompanied by the commentaries of G. A. Volpi (1726–7) and the Jesuit P. Venturi (1732), and was illustrated with 106 copper engravings by various artists, with full-page illustrations—such as the tumultuous descent of Geryon (Fig. 5)—placed at the beginning of the relevant canto.[302] It also included a *Vita di Dante* by the Florentine Giuseppe Pelli (1729–1808) which has been described as 'the most important [Dantean] biographical contribution of the century'.[303] In 1787–8 the Dante scholar Lord Charlemont was still trying (without much success) to obtain the de luxe large-paper version of Zatta's edition.[304]

A few years earlier another copy of that same lavishly illustrated edition had also failed to reach its British purchaser, having formed part of a shipment conveying the products and programme of the late eighteenth-century Grand Tour that was lost on its way to England. On 7 January 1779 the 300-ton armed merchant ship, the *Westmorland*, bound from Livorno to London, was captured by two French frigates off the Spanish coast and taken to Malaga.[305] Its cargo, valued at £100,000, consisted primarily of items which had been collected by a number of British aristocrats during their travels and were eventually purchased by the Spanish Crown, to be transferred in 1783 to the Real Academia de Bellas Artes de San Fernando in Madrid. Amongst the nearly 400 books captured in what came to be known as the 'English Prize' were the five volumes of Zatta's *Opere di Dante* in their temporary red-and-white Dutch paper binding.[306] The deprived British owner of this Dante was Frederick Ponsonby, Viscount Duncannon (1758–1844), who had been in Italy from November 1777 until 1778, when he returned to England.[307]

---

[300] On Reynolds's 'Hugolino', and its reception, see *DEL* 1.342–3, Yates 1951: 106–7, Tinkler-Villani 1989: 56, Roe 1998: 23–4, Braida 2004: 21–3. For the wider context of Reynolds's 'subject pictures', see Postle 1995.

[301] The first had been published (in five octavo volumes) at Venice a few years earlier, in 1739–41; see Caesar 1989: 44 and Tissoni 1993: 71–2.

[302] On Volpi and Venturi, see Caesar 1989: 80–1 (n. 77) and 356–7.

[303] Caesar 1989: 44. See also *DBI*, s.v. 'Giuseppe Bencivenni Pelli'.

[304] Passages from Charlemont's correspondence on this with Edmond Malone are in *DEL* 1.434.

[305] Sánchez-Jáuregui and Wilcox 2012: 11–13 and 38–40.

[306] Sánchez-Jáuregui and Wilcox 2012: 13, 144, 146 (fig. 105). The cargo included, amongst other things, twenty-three crates of marble statuary and twenty-two crates of prints, portraits, and books. The latter ran to 378 titles—ranging from Piranesi prints and literary classics to dictionaries and travel guides.

[307] Sánchez-Jáuregui and Wilcox 2012: 23–4 and 230; see also *ODNB*, s.v. 'Ponsonby, Frederick, third earl of Bessborough (1758–1844), politician and landowner'.

Fig. 5. From *Opere di Dante Alighieri* (Venice: Zatta, 1757–8), vol. 1, facing p. B b 1, the flight of Geryon, courtesy of All Souls College, Oxford

As the son and heir of the second earl of Bessborough—who had travelled to the eastern Mediterranean in 1736–8 and become a founder member of the Society of Dilettanti—Duncannon was following in his father's footsteps.[308] In the crate of items that had been on its way to him in the *Westmorland*, the Dante edition was accompanied by a large number of architectural drawings and views, more than a hundred musical scores, and a quantity of painted fans.[309] The traveller's interest in trying to learn the language is reflected in the presence of a contemporary Italian text, which he had probably purchased before setting off on the tour.[310] Duncannon may have acquired the Zatta Dante at a late stage of his Italian journey when he was in Venice, and if so, would have had little time to read it before it was crated up with his other acquisitions; yet his choice of this classic Italian text in this form carries some significance for the developments in literary taste during the late 1770s.

A more direct indication of such developments emerges from the correspondence of another young aristocrat and art collector, Philip Yorke (subsequently third earl of Hardwicke, 1757–1834). Duncannon's purchases in Italy took place at almost exactly the same time as Yorke was travelling rapidly through Milan, Pavia, Genoa, Lucca, Livorno, and Pisa in the early autumn of 1778.[311] By 25 September Yorke had arrived in Florence and was writing to his uncle and guardian about his immediate plans to pay homage 'this morning' to that supreme object of Dilettante devotion, the *Venus de' Medici*, and to 'make several more visits'.[312] On the same page of this letter, he also declares his intention to

employ myself whilst we are here in learning Italian of the best master in Italy, the Abbé Polori who has just translated [William] Robertson's History of America. We begin Dante tomorrow, which is rather a bold undertaking but I shall seldom perhaps meet with so good a person to read it with & to explain its difficulties.

A fortnight or so later (12 October) Yorke reports more visits to Venuses and other works of art, as well as progress through the *Commedia*:

I have been reading the Inferno of Dante & have just finished it today: the number of Allusions to stories well known at that time & the words he often uses which are now altogether out of use or merely poetical render it difficult: there are many fine passages and a great deal of imagination but in order to judge of it thoroughly I must give it a second reading.[313]

---

[308] Kelly 2009: pp. xii, 104 and 176.

[309] Sánchez-Jáuregui and Wilcox 2012: 230–7.

[310] The *Commedie scelte di Carlo Goldoni* (1777), which was the first edition of Goldoni's plays in the original to be published in London; Sánchez-Jáuregui and Wilcox 2012: 252.

[311] BL Add. MS 35378 (Hardwicke Papers, vol. 30), ff. 239ʳ–240ʳ. discussed by Sweet 2007: 857 and n. 101. On Yorke's range of interests and activities in Italy, see Black 2003: 44, 91, 110, 175, 189, 191. His father, the lawyer Charles Yorke (1722–70), had composed (*c*.1745) a much-anthologized poem about 'Great Dante's image': the 'Ode to the Hon. Miss Yorke, on her copying a Portrait of Dante by Clovio'; see *DEL* 1. 243–5.

[312] BL Add. MS 35378, f. 241ʳ. On the descriptions and iconography of this Venus, see Kelly 2009: 29–30, 42 (and fig. 27), 57 (and fig. 46), 62 (and fig. 47), 79 (and fig. 52), and 119.

[313] BL Add. MS 35378, ff. 244ʳ–246ʳ and 247ʳ–250ʳ.

This second letter exists in two forms: a fair copy and in the version that was actually sent to Yorke's uncle. It reflects the diligence with which the keen young traveller has learnt his lessons on Dante, and it seems, moreover, designed to reassure his guardian that the *giro d'Italia* is proving good value for money; hence the writer quickly moves on to a request for a 'Letter of Credit for about 300l to finish the year'.[314] Yorke's comments on the *Inferno* (presumably influenced by the Abbé Polori's views) also reflect to some extent how in the later eighteenth century the 'received wisdoms are gradually integrated with other, newer, concerns which play their part in the massive "rehabilitation" of Dante'.[315]

Conflict in Europe meant that neither Yorke nor Duncannon were able to bring their books or other collectables home, but acquisitions of Dante for the major private libraries had long been a symptom of how 'the British nobility became simultaneously seized by a violent desire to collect incunabula'.[316] It is well known that early in the eighteenth century the great collections, such as those of Robert and Edward Harley and Charles Spencer, third earl of Sunderland, were already accumulating, along with manuscripts, early editions of the *Commedia* and other texts such as the *Convivio*, *De vulgari eloquentia*, and the *Vita nuova*.[317] During the second half of the century and beyond, the Zatta illustrated edition of 1757–8 seems to have joined manuscripts and early editions as a Dantean object of desire. Its acquisition and reception deserves some further attention as reflecting and perhaps stimulating a closer interest in Dante and the *Commedia* around the turn of the century.[318] Its value is also evident from its presence—together with a much earlier illustrated *Commedia* (Venice, 1544)—in a greatly admired late eighteenth-century library, that of Thomas Stanley (1749–1818). When the 'Bibliotheca Stanleiana' came up for sale in 1813, the large paper (quarto) edition of the Zatta *Opere*, 'with 212 plates in different coloured inks'—the one that Charlemont had been pursuing in the late 1780s—fetched the then very substantial price of £37 16s.[319] A few years later, in 1824, the author of *Bibliomania*, Thomas Frognall Dibdin, would list the Zatta volumes among the most 'desirable' editions of the *Commedia*.[320]

The relationship between Dante's value for private collectors and the extension of public understanding of his work will be further explored in the chapters that follow. But there are some further eighteenth-century indicators of widening access to Dante that should be identified before moving on to the experiences and

---

[314] BL Add. MS 35378, ff. 244ʳ–246ʳ and 247ʳ–250ʳ.

[315] Caesar 1989: 43.   [316] De Ricci 1930: 33.

[317] For details of the Sunderland and Harley holdings of Dante texts, see *DEL* 1. 185–6, 243, and 320. On the Harleian manuscripts, see also above, p. 113.

[318] The illustrations can be sampled in Nassar 1994: 82, 138, 240, and 280 (for *Inf.* 4, 8, 20, and 24), or, better, in the digitized copy of the Zatta edition that is currently accessible online, through the Bodleian Library's SOLO catalogue.

[319] See *DEL* 2. 136–7. By comparison, the Venice 1544 *Commedia* went for only £2 15s. and the Lyon 1571 edition for £1 15s. Stanley's Dante collection also included copies of Balthazar Grangier's French translation of the *Commedia* (1597) and the Jesuit Carlo d'Aquino's expurgated Latin version (Naples, 1728; on these translators, see Friederich 1950: 85–6 and 96).

[320] In an article for the *Library Companion*, quoted in *DEL* 2.79–80.

attitudes of what has been called 'the reading nation in the Romantic period'.[321]
When considering the various 'received wisdoms' and the 'newer concerns which
play their part in the . . . "rehabilitation" of Dante' from the 1780s on, and what the
Romantic reception of his work might derive from developments in the eighteenth
century, we should take into account some hitherto unnoticed material in translations, educational writing, and anthologies that both reflected and served to shape
such received wisdoms, concerns, and attitudes. [322]

'EMERGING FROM BARBARITY': TRANSLATIONS
AND ANTHOLOGIES

Translations of cantos, *cantiche*, and the whole *Commedia* over the course of the
eighteenth century—from Jonathan Richardson the Elder to Henry Boyd—have
rightly been given attention as attempts—for various reasons and with varying
degrees of success—to 'find the diction and the forms to render both Dante's world
and the response to it as poetry' and 'to adapt English models to the original
text'.[323] But, as we have seen, selective verse quotation and translation for illustrative, didactic, and ideological purposes have already been increasingly evident over
the previous two centuries. It is important to attend to the literary forms and
cultural contexts from which those quotations and translations emerge—as two
very different examples of translation and paraphrase from early in the century may
serve to illustrate.

The first is an anthologized piece which first appeared in *The Museum: Or the
Literary and Historical Register* in 1746 as 'The Three First Stanzas of the 24th
Canto of Dante's *Inferna* [*sic*] made into Song. In Imitation of the Earl of Surrey's
Stile'. This twenty-four line 'song' (in four stanzas) turns Dante's eighteen-line
pastoral simile conveying his anxiety and relief about Virgil's changing mood into a
kind of bloated sonnet about the lover's responses to his 'Fair One' as she moves
from 'Disdain' to 'smile[s]'. It first appeared (perhaps rightly) in 'anonymous' form
and has thus been reprinted in several modern anthologies.[324] It has been compared
with later examples of 'the fondness for turning excerpts from the *Commedia* into
self-contained lyrics', and seen as anticipating 'the enthusiasm for the poet's
brilliance with analogies which is a marked feature of his later popularity'.[325]

However, the infernal 'song' is not, in fact, anonymous, at least not in its
appearance in a 1782 anthology, which corrects the misprint in its title and adds

---

[321] St Clair 2004 (title).
[322] On some of these developments, see Caesar 1989: 43 and Braida 2004: 10.
[323] Tinkler-Villani 1989: 58 and 77. Aliette Boshier at the Scuola Normale Superiore di Pisa is
currently engaged in doctoral research on Jonathan Richardson and the reception of the Ugolino
episode in eighteenth-century England; her thesis aims to shed new light on Richardson's contribution
to the development of knowledge about Dante at the time.
[324] *DEL* 1.246; Griffths and Reynolds 2005: 53–4.
[325] Griffths and Reynolds 2005: 53.

beneath: 'BY MR. SPENCE.'[326] As that anthology's index makes clear, the reference is to Joseph Spence (1699–1768), Professor of Poetry at Oxford, who conversed about Dante in Florence in 1732–3, quoting in his *Anecdotes* the opinion of the physician and antiquary Dr Antonio Cocchi that the poet 'is very singular and very beautiful in his similies'—a comment that could well have had some influence on Spence's choice of a passage to translate.[327] The Italian travels that led to this conversation about Dante also suggest a wider cultural context for the translation, since Spence was then accompanying, and would continue to be associated with, a founder member of the Society of Dilettanti.[328] His assumption in his 'Song' that the eighteen lines of Dante's simile constitute 'three stanzas' is potentially significant: although its rhyme-scheme is different, his treatment, with its leisurely pace and Spenserian diction, could have set a precedent for the amplificatory six-line stanza that Henry Boyd would use for his translation of the *Inferno* in 1785.[329]

Ten years or so earlier than Spence's version of the lines from the *Inferno*, an English prose paraphrase of a passage from the *Commedia* had performed a very different function, and one that also carries other implications for the reception of Dante up to and beyond the end of the eighteenth century. In 1731 a translation of a work on *The Authority of Holy Scripture* by the Italian non-trinitarian reformer Fausto Socino (1539–1604) had appeared in London. It concludes its whole argument by quoting in Italian (and paraphrasing over a few pages) Dante's response during his examination on Faith by St Peter (*Par.* 24. 88–111)— a response which presents the 'old and new' scriptures as 'divine speech', affirmed through the acts of the Apostles.[330] This use of Dante as himself an 'Authority'— the word used in the index to a subsequent edition of the translation—may initially seem surprising.[331] Indeed, the 'Advertisement' itself raises the question of whether it is appropriate to end 'so serious and important an Undertaking with Verses out of a Poem', then answers its own objection with a number of examples of how 'Quotations out of Poets have been used by most Authors to adorn and illustrate their Writings'.[332] The Socinian text's quotation and discussion thus reflect how the poet continues to be appropriated by British nonconformists.[333] It may also

---

[326] *A Select Collection of Poems, with Notes Biographical and Historical*, vol. 8 (London: Nichols, 1782), 24.

[327] *DEL* 1. 219. On Cocchi, see also Kelly 2009: 17.

[328] He was accompanying Charles Sackville, earl of Middlesex, and their tour included Venice and Rome as well as Florence; see Kelly 2009: 14–19.

[329] On sources for Boyd's stanza form, see also Tinkler-Villani 1989: 130. In addition to its appearance in 1782, Spence's translation had been published (without attribution) in *The Fugitive Miscellany* (London, 1775), vol. 2, pp. 98–9.

[330] *An Argument for the Authority of Holy Scripture: from the Latin of Socinus. After the Steinfurt* [1611] *Copy. To which is prefix'd a short account of his life* (London: Meadows *et al.*, 1731), pp. 159–65. The original work had been printed as *De Auctoritate sacrae Scripturae* in 1588 and 1611.

[331] The translation was reprinted the following year as *A Demonstration of the Truth of the Christian Religion* (London, 1732), and the added reference to Dante as 'Authority' is on p. 159.

[332] *An Argument*, sig. A3 1[r–v].

[333] The reference to the dire state of St Peter's 'vineyard' (*Par.* 24. 111) provides a suitably anti-papal note to end the quotation; *An Argument*, p. 161.

provide a precedent for the successors to the Socinians: the Unitarians, whose interest in Dante, as we shall see, forms a significant element in his reception during the nineteenth century.[334]

Translations in periodicals and anthologies such as *the Literary and Historical Register* and the *Florence Miscellany*, together with accounts of Dante for the readers of journals such as the *European Magazine and London Review* and the *Italian Magazine* around the turn of the century anticipate the critical attention to Dante and other Italian writers that will later be provided by major authors in better-known titles such as the *Quarterly* and *Edinburgh Reviews*.[335] Less familiar but equally striking are the various images of Dante projected by some of this period's widely circulated educational works.

A conduct guide, *Beauties of History or, Pictures of Virtue and Vice drawn from Real Life; Designed for the Instruction and Entertainment of Youth*, by L. M. Stretch, vicar of Twyford and Ouselbury, went through ten editions between 1770 and 1798.[336] Its lessons are mostly drawn from Greek and Roman antiquity (although 'Lord Clive at the Siege of Arcot' features under 'Courage'). Dante, however, does not provide a very good role model for the Revd Stretch and his readers. The Petrarchan story about Dante, the jester, and Cangrande (from *Rerum memorandarum libri* 2) is here discussed at some length as one of the main cautionary examples under 'Politeness', as a warning to those who take pleasure in 'speaking their minds': 'Dante probably gratified his own vanity, as much as he mortified that of others; it was the petulant reproach of resentment and pride, which is always retorted with rage and not the still voice of reason, that is heard with complacency and reverence . . .'[337] Another clerical popularizer, the Revd John Seally ('Member of the Roman Academy'), adopted a more straightforwardly informative approach. In *The Lady's Encyclopedia or a Concise Analysis of the Belles Lettres the Fine Arts and the Sciences*, Dante leads the group of 'Italian Poets', followed by Petrarch, Ariosto, and Tasso.[338] The poet's exile is again viewed quite critically as the consequence of 'misplaced ambition', but his status is made clear for the novice reader, not only by his position in this section of the work but also through the acknowledgement of his 'lively and fertile imagination' and the assurance that his *Commedia* is 'an epic poem, replete with every characteristic of genuine poetry'.[339]

It has been argued that around 1800 the appeal of Italian 'was limited almost entirely to the scholar, the traveller, the musician, the artist and the better educated

---

[334] See below, pp. 148 and 271, n. 67.

[335] Articles on Dante's life and work from the 1783 and 1784 and numbers of the *European Magazine* are excerpted in *DEL* 1. 394–5, see also no. 41 (1802) 453, and esp. no. 66 (1814), where a 'review' of the *Commedia* extends over several issues (pp. 104–6, 197–8, 315–16); for excerpts see *DEL* 2. 201–4. The first issue of the *Italian Magazine* (1795, reprinted as *Italian Tracts* in 1796) carried essays on Petrarch, Ariosto, Tasso, and Dante (see esp. pp. 17–21).

[336] Quotations are from the tenth edition (1798).

[337] Stretch 1798: 313. This Dantean anecdote had been reproduced in English since 1540 (*DEL* 1. 31); it also features in Desmaizeaux's 1735 translation of Bayle's *Dictionnaire historique* (*DEL* 1. 228), which Stretch may perhaps have used.

[338] Seally 1788.   [339] Seally 1788: 1. 284.

young lady'.[340] Women readers like those of Seally's *Encyclopedia* feature frequently as dedicatees of and subscribers to works on Italian writers and on Dante; for example, of about 170 names of those who ordered copies of Boyd's *Inferno* in 1785, around twenty are female, and the proportion is much higher in the case of subscribers to some anthologies of Italian literature.[341] Such anthologies, along with an increasing number of linguistic and literary guides, provided a growing readership with resources for the study both of Italian and of Dante. There is also some evidence that already in the second half of the eighteenth century some introductions to the language were designed for a yet wider public: not only 'for persons of literary education . . . but for those also of the meanest capacity, who do not understand any other language but the English'.[342] For example, Arthur Masson's *Rudiments of the Italian Language*, published at Edinburgh in 1771, included 'a select collection in prose and verse, from some of the best Italian authors', and its preface encouragingly suggests the suitability of the older authors for the student of modern Italian: 'No language in Europe, during the space of five hundred years, hath undergone fewer changes. The language of Dante and Petrarca is still spoken and understood in Italy.'[343] Other guides, such as Antonio Curioni's *Istoria dei Poeti italiani ad uso dei Principianti nella Lingua Italiana* of 1788, gave more extensive attention to Dante. In his six-page essay on Dante, Curioni invites the British reader (including his dedicatees, 'Madama Carlotta e Madama Anna Villiers') to entertain comparisons with Milton and the poet Edward Young. His view of the *Commedia* as 'un Poema nazionale . . . contenendo tutto ciò che la Nazione aveva di più grande in genere di conoscenze' ('a national poem, reflecting all the best of what the Nation had achieved in the branches of knowledge') begins to indicate the kind of political reasons for reading Dante that would appeal to the liberal-minded expatriates of the Romantic period.[344]

A convenient resource that would have been available to such early nineteenth-century readers was the dual-language anthology of 1798 which announced itself on its first title-page as *I fiori del Parnasso italiano ovvero una raccolta di rime estratta dall'opere de' più celebri Poeti Italiani*, and on its second as *Extracts from the Works of the Most Celebrated Italian Poets, with Translations by Admired English Authors*. This

---

[340] Brand 1957: 40, thus setting rather wide 'limits'. On the study of Italian in England at the turn of the century, see Brand 1957: 36–45, and more recently Pizzoli 2004: 50–6.

[341] For Boyd's list of subscribers, see Dante 1785: 1. pp. vii–viii. Of the seventy subscribers to Nardini's six-volume *Saggi di prose e poesie* (London, 1796–8), around forty were women, as were two-thirds of the 148 subscribers to the 1798 *Fiori del Parnasso italiano* (see below, next paragraph).

[342] Preface to the third edition (1777–8) of Francesco Sastres's *Introduction to Italian Grammar*, published in London, and sold in Dublin, Bath, and Bristol; quoted in Pizzoli 2004: 64–5 and 405. See Pizzoli's comments on other Italian and Italianist linguists of the later eighteenth century, such as Johnson's friend (and defender of Dante), Giuseppe Baretti (pp. 50–4). On Baretti, see also *DEL* 1. 256–74 and Concolato 1993; Baretti's *Italian Library: Containing an Account of the Lives and Works of the Most Valuable Authors of Italy* (London: Millar, 1757) contained three short excerpts from the *Commedia*; see Spaggiari 2005: 28 and n. 2.

[343] *Rudiments of the Italian Language*, p. vii, quoted in Pizzoli 2004: 196, n. 36. On the teaching of the Italian classical canon, see also ibid. 85–8 and on Masson (whose work was reprinted in London in 1771 and 1791), see ibid. 405.

[344] Curioni 1788: 13 and 16.

was published anonymously in London, and included within a single volume of just under 300 pages a collection of excerpts and lyrics from popular Italian poets in the original, with following translations. The 'Advertisement' makes clear that it was aiming quite confidently at a wider market:

Private gratification was originally the only motive, and the pleasing and improving employment of many leisure hours was hitherto the only view of the collector.

The prevailing taste for Italian of late years has excited in many persons a wish to be more acquainted with the works of the Italian Poets: and the study of that elegant language, being now made a branch of polite education, will render that wish still more universal.[345]

The collection focused mostly upon Petrarch, Ariosto, Tasso, Guarini, and the ubiquitous Metastasio, but it also included five passages from Dante's *Inferno*, amongst them a short excerpt from the episode of Paolo and Francesca (*Inf.* 5. 119–41) and the whole of Ugolino's story (*Inf.* 32. 125–33. 90).[346] The 'Admired English Authors' whose translations were used were William Hayley, the patron of Blake, who had published versions of the first three cantos of the *Inferno* in 1782, and Henry Boyd, whose *Inferno* had appeared in 1785 and would soon be followed by the first complete English *Commedia* to be published.[347] The anthology offered a conveniently portable dual-language selection to, for example, literary travellers to Italy, such as the British expatriates in the second decade of the next century.

A yet more extensive resource newly available to British readers around the turn of the century is the six-volume *Saggi di prose e poesie de' più celebri scrittori d'ogni secolo*, which was produced by the poet, printer, and editor Leonardo Nardini and published in London between 1796 and 1798. Like Curioni's guide and several others of these decades, Nardini's hefty collection reflects erudite traditions of Italian literary scholarship in the period.[348] His final volume is devoted entirely to writers of the thirteenth and early fourteenth centuries, including poems by Guido delle Colonne, Brunetto Latini, Guido Guinizzelli, Cecco Angiolieri, and Guido Cavalcanti. Over eighty pages of this volume are devoted to Dante, including complete cantos and substantial passages from all three *cantiche* of the *Commedia* (totalling over 2,000 lines)—together with three of his *canzoni*, three sonnets, and a *ballata*. Nardini's anthology in some ways points backwards to the selective, 'diamonds in a dunghill' view of medieval authors; for instance, it cites Saverio Bettinelli's view of the poet as 'attempting to emerge from barbarity'.[349] However, along with more well-known anthologies and editions around the turn of the century, such as the texts published by Thomas Mathias—recently described as

---

[345] Anon. [*I fiori del Parnasso italiano*] 1798: pp. v–vi; see also *DEL* 1. 570.
[346] Anon. [*I fiori del Parnasso italiano*] 1798: 36–9 and 184–95, with Boyd's translation. The other episodes are *Inf.* 3. 1–30 and 81–120 with Hayley's and Boyd's versions (ibid. 30–3 and 96–9) and *Inf.* 24.1–15 with Boyd's version (ibid. 48–9).
[347] On Hayley, see *DEL* 1. 359–70, Tinkler-Villani 1989: ch. 5, and Griffiths and Reynolds 2005: 56–62. For Boyd, see Tinkler-Villani 1989: ch. 8, and Griffiths and Reynolds 2005: 66–73.
[348] For discussion of the 'literary-historical work of Muratori, Crescimbeni, Quadrio, Tiraboschi', *et al.*, see Caesar 1989: 43–4.
[349] Nardini 1796–8: 5. p. vi. On Bettinelli, see also Caesar 1989: 377–83, Tissoni 1993: 73–87, and Capaci 2008: 159–76.

'the English author most active in popularizing Italian poetry' at this time—the *Saggi di prose e poesie* provided substantial samples of Dante's work in the original for an increasingly interested British public.[350]

Nardini's contacts also included several of those who were prominent in collecting, publishing, and promoting Dante in the early years of the nineteenth century, including Lorenzo da Ponte (poet, librettist, book-dealer, professor of Italian), who was in London in 1793–8 and again from 1800 to 1804.[351] He also seems to have had access to at least one high-level private book collection. Volume 6 of his *Saggi di prose e poesie* (containing the work of Dante and his contemporaries) is prefaced by a verse *epistola* addressed to Earl Spencer's librarian, Tommaso de Ocheda, which not only exalts Dante in Dantean terms as *signor del triplice poema* ('master of the threefold poem'), but also has a note indicating that Nardini made use of the early editions of the *Commedia* in Spencer's collection, with a view to publishing his own text *con note* ('with notes') by subscription in 1799.[352]

The increased opportunities for dealers in Italian books at this time (and their increasing prices) were noted by Lorenzo Da Ponte in his account of his early years in London. Da Ponte's own 'Catalogue of Italian Books' for 1800 lists at least ten editions of the *Commedia*, at prices from 16*s*. 6*d*. to 12 guineas, and ranging in date from 1481 to 1784.[353] According to a letter of December 1802, he himself contemplated producing an edition of the *Commedia* from his own press—one that would be slightly expurgated, so that

i maestri di lingua ed i lor allievi non di troverebbero imbarazzati e confusi al suono d'una *trombetta* assai sporca de' demoni di Dante . . .

the teachers of the [Italian] language and their pupils should not find themselves embarrassed and confused by the sound of a very filthy 'trumpet' blown by Dante's demons . . . '[354]

Neither Da Ponte's nor Nardini's complete British Dante editions—both planned around the turn of the century—seem to have materialized, but their other activities in publishing and the book trade at this time clearly reflect a growing level of interest, as did the appearance, in the same year as Da Ponte's letter, of

---

[350] Also available were the fifty-six volumes of Andrea Rubbi's *Parnaso italiano ovvero Raccolta de' Poeti classici italiani* were published at Venice between 1784 and 1791; they included the three parts of Dante's *Commedia* (vols. 3–5, published in 1784) and were used by, amongst others, Leigh Hunt in the following century. On Mathias's editorial and critical work, e.g. several selections of Italian lyric poetry, including Dante (London 1802, 1808, 1819), see *DEL* 1. 556–64, and Spaggiari 2005: 32 and n. 14. For a contemporary view of his status as linguist and critic, see Da Ponte 1918: 251–2.

[351] On Da Ponte's respect for Nardini, see Da Ponte 1918: 1. 254. On their book-dealing and publishing partnership, see ibid. 1. 250, 260–1, 269, and 2. 168–9 and Zagonel 1995: 195.

[352] Nardini 1796–8: 6. v and vi, n. 1. His aim to produce what would have been the first complete *Commedia* to be printed in Britain remained unfulfilled. On Earl Spencer's collection and contacts, see below, pp. 141–2, and on Ocheda, see also Lister 1989: 69.

[353] On the trade in Italian books at this time, see Da Ponte 1918: 1. 249–51. The page (p. 16) of his *Catalogo di libri italiani di L. Da Ponte, No. 5, Pall Mall: Novembre 1800*, listing the Dante editions, is reproduced in Zagonel 1995: pl. 68. His copy of the 1481 illustrated *Commedia* is also listed on this page of the catalogue.

[354] Letter to Giambattista Casti, whose *Gli animali parlanti* Da Ponte would publish in 1803; printed in Zagonel 1995: 194–7. His allusion in this passage is to the demon who 'makes a trumpet of his arse' as a signal to his followers, in *Inf.* 21. 138–9.

Henry Boyd's English version of the whole *Commedia*.[355] Within a few years, one of Nardini's compatriots and colleagues in the London book trade would produce and publish the first annotated edition of the *Commedia* in the original to be designed for the British public.[356]

Italian expatriates in London thus helped to accelerate a process of acquisition and familiarization that, since the sixteenth century, had been gradually shaped by generations of British collectors, polemicists, translators, and educators. Their further contributions to the production and promotion of Dante for a wider readership will be the subject of the following chapter. A significant number of their readers—as subscriber lists and dedications continue to indicate—were women, whose interest suggests (*pace* Lady Pol) that, whilst Dante might have remained 'hard', more were ready to make the effort to understand him.

[355] Dante 1802.

[356] On Romualdo Zotti and his edition of 1808–9, see below, pp. 137–9. Nardini collaborated with Zotti on the second edition of his *Opere scelte dell'abate Pietro Metastasio* (1806) and on the second and subsequent editions of his anthology of eighteenth-century Italian drama, *Teatro italiano* (1800–8).

5

Expatriate Poetics: Foscolo
and the British Public

AN EXILE'S DANTE

On Friday, 4 December 1818, John Cam Hobhouse—friend of and commentator on Byron—had a busy day. As his diary records:

Foscolo called in the morning and told me he was going to get some money by selling his goods[;] this I thought just. I called on Henry [Hobhouse's brother] and my father—poor Harry is ill of the gravel—he does not sail therefore for India tomorrow as he intended ... I went then to Ludgate Hill Paternoster Row and saw Rees of Longman's house—he would not engage for Foscolo at all and told me the world was sick of Dante.[1]

The Italian poet and critic Ugo Foscolo (1778–1827) had been in London for over two years when this entry was written, and he had already published two important articles on Dante in a leading British journal. This account of his 'expatriate poetics' begins by considering his self-presentation as exile, and the ways in which his poetic (and exiled) predecessor contributed to that image. It then focuses upon some of the cultural and material contexts of his work in presenting Dante to a new public, giving attention to the production of texts (translations, editions of, and commentaries on the *Commedia*) for the British market early in the nineteenth century. Finally, it will consider the role and interests of those who sought to promote the project and were in one way or another influenced by it. It thus seeks to relate Foscolo's writing in exile to what William St Clair has called the British 'reading nation in the Romantic period',[2] and to consider what kind of appetite that public still had for the kind of Dante that the Italian expatriate could provide.

Foscolo had arrived in England, by way of Switzerland and Germany, in September 1816.[3] Hobhouse's first encounter with him took place a year or so

---

[1] BL Add. MS 56540, f. 21ʳ; most of the passage is also in Vincent 1949: 56. For the Hobhouse Diaries up to 1824, see also the online edition at: <http://petercochran.wordpress.com/hobhouses-diary>.

[2] St Clair 2004 (title).

[3] On his years of exile, see Viglione 1910, Wicks 1937: ch. 4, Vincent 1953, Scotti 1972, Cambon 1980, Lindon 1987, Terzoli 2000: ch. 7, Nicoletti 2006: ch. 10, Luzzi 2008: 71–6, and Isabella 2009 (*passim*). His views of English writers have been recently investigated by Parmegiani 2011, and his role in the literary culture of London from 1816 to 1824 currently forms part of research by Will Bowers (University College, London), to whom I am grateful for discussion of this chapter. On Italian exiles in Britain generally during this period, see Wicks 1937, Brand 1957: ch. 2, Brand 1971, Isabella 2009, and Verdecchia 2010: 11–173.

later, and a few months before that fruitless approach to 'Rees of Longman's house'. On 23 March 1818 a dinner at the house of the elderly Whig bibliophile Roger Wilbraham was attended by London luminaries, such as the scientist Sir Humphrey Davy, the classicist Payne Knight, the historian Francis Cohen, and the book collector Richard Heber.[4] It was here—whilst 'a great deal of Italian [was] talked'— that Hobhouse had met Foscolo, describing him shortly afterwards as

very like his picture before J[acopo] Ortis[,] a lively taking [i.e. charming] man—he is about to publish on Dante and I [f. 7ᵛ] offered him a *puff* in the notes to Child Harold. [H]e made one fine observation—that in the age of Dante every man of genius did something to distinguish himself. [F]ame acquired any way was the great object. [Fo]r this reason Dante puts Francesca da Rimini the daughter of his master Guido da Polento [*sic*] in hell & also his instructor. il sodomita to whom chinò il capo. [F]ame was the great object & it was no comparative disgrace so as Dante made these two persons known [*sic*] . . . [5]

Hobhouse's dispatch from the dinner-table identifies some significant features of Foscolo and his milieu. The Italian exile already had a substantial reputation in Britain as a poet and especially as the author of a famous epistolary novel, *Ultime lettere di Jacopo Ortis* ('The Last Letters of Jacopo Ortis'), which Hobhouse had read soon after its publication in Zürich; hence the reference in this passage to Foscolo's youthful portrait, which had recently appeared opposite the title-page of the novel's 1817 London edition.[6] Their encounter in March 1818 led directly to an ill-fated collaboration on an essay about contemporary Italian literature that would be appended to Canto 4 of Byron's *Child Harold*.[7] The diary entry also reflects the role of British Italophiles—many associated with the Holland House circle—who were helping to support the exile during his eleven increasingly difficult years in London, from 1816 until his death in 1827.[8]

Yet more significantly, Hobhouse's diary records Foscolo's initiation of a conversation about a key theme in Dante's *Commedia* (fame) and about specific figures and episodes in the *Inferno* (Francesca da Rimini and Brunetto Latini). It also mentions his (perhaps rather condescending) offer to promote ('puff') the first of Foscolo's two articles on Dante for the *Edinburgh Review*—an article which, within

---

[4] On Wilbraham, see Vincent 1953: 19–20 and 225 n. Both Wilbraham and Heber were collectors of early Dante texts. Wilbraham owned copies of the 1478 Milan edition of the *Commedia* and the 1481 Florence edition with 20 engravings after Botticelli; the latter was purchased by Earl Spencer between 1807 and 1815 and is now in the John Rylands Library at Manchester (Spencer No. 17280; see Hind 1938–48: 1. 106–7 and n. 1, and Keller 2000: 332 and n. 39). Heber's huge collection was based on Greek, Latin, and English texts, with a secondary interest in French and Italian (Hunt 1996: 89–91); at his death in 1833 he had 'upwards of 70' copies of various works by Dante, including six manuscripts of the *Commedia*, a wide range of its earliest printed editions, and the *editiones principes* of both the *Convivio* and *De vulgari eloquentia* (*DEL* 2. 300 and 587).

[5] Hobhouse Diaries BL Add. MS 47235, f. 7ʳ–ᵛ.

[6] On the Zürich edition, Hobhouse Diaries BL Add. MS 56538, f. 17ᵛ (22 Nov. 1816) and f. 21ᵛ (28 Nov. 1816). The 1817 London edition was published by John Murray.

[7] For accounts of this troubled partnership, see Vincent 1949: 1–37; also Havely 2002, and Crisafulli 2002.

[8] On the Holland House circle and its politics, see Sanders 1908: 255–63; Vincent 1953: 23–32; and Crisafulli 2003: 269–75.

a month of this meeting, would reach many thousands of British readers.[9] It thus marks an early stage in the promotion of his medieval compatriot that was to become one of the main achievements of the Italian exile's final decade in Britain.[10]

Like a number of expatriates—from Lord Byron to Giuseppe Mazzini and beyond—Foscolo imagined the exiled Dante as an alter ego. As Maurizio Isabella argues, for Italian political exiles of the nineteenth century Dante's experience 'provided legitimacy for their own condition, dignity to their status, and consolation for their sense of defeat and alienation, thus boosting their patriotic beliefs with the example of a noble forerunner'.[11] Whilst on the run, as a wounded soldier of the Italian National Guard in 1799, Foscolo—combining his interest in Sterne and Dante—had himself taken the name of 'Lorenzo Alighieri'.[12] A few years later, in his best-known poem *Dei Sepolcri* (1806), Dante appears as 'il Ghibellin fuggiasco' ('the fugitive Ghibelline', l. 174).[13] The phrase heralded the development of Foscolo's own anticlerical 'Neo-Ghibelline' stance, which was would help to win him the sympathies of the Whig Holland House circle during his own exile.[14]

During his exile in Switzerland (1815–16) Foscolo had added to the Zürich edition of *Ultime lettere di Jacopo Ortis* a passage which has the protagonist lament his own loss of his homeland in words that derive directly from Dante's Francesca: 'piango la patria mia, "Che mi fu tolta, *e il modo ancor m'offende*"' ('I bewail my homeland, "Which was taken from me in a way that wounds me still"').[15] What Dante's Francesca had lamented was not the loss of *patria* but of her *bella persona*, her own 'fair form', yet the two concepts are closely linked for Foscolo and his hero Ortis: loss of land and personal identity are the main deprivations addressed by the novel.[16] Allusions to Dante are frequent in *Ortis*, and a number of them reflect on the protagonist's dispossession by alluding to moments in the *Commedia*.[17] Thus, the vagrant Ortis alludes to Cacciaguida's evocations of *patria* and exile in *Paradiso* 16 and 17; to the traveller's homesickness in *Purgatorio* 8. 1–6; and the loss of homeland inflicted on the Florentine Guelfs at Montaperti (*Inferno* 10).[18] Near the end of the novel and its protagonist's life, Ortis visits and addresses *padre* Dante's tomb at Ravenna, finding moral and physical courage by meditating upon 'l'alto animo tuo, e il tuo amore, e l'ingrata tua patria, e l'esilio, e la povertà, e la tua mente divina . . .' ('your noble spirit, your love, your ungrateful country, your exile and poverty, your godlike mind . . .')[19] Even before the author of *Ortis* reached London

---

[9] On the circulation and readership of the *Edinburgh Review*, see below, p. 135 with n. 48.

[10] On Foscolo's Dante criticism, see: Marzot 1969: 58–67; O'Neill 1985; Lindon 2000*a*: 150–7; Braida 2004: 77–87, Palumbo 2004, Havely 2011*b*, and Luzzi 2012.

[11] Isabella 2006: 498.   [12] Terzoli 2000: 180.

[13] On Foscolo's early allusions to Dante, see Cambon 1980: 16, 88–94 and 338, O'Neill 1985: 9–10, and Palumbo 2004: 396–9.

[14] See Crisafulli 2003 273–9 and Braida 2004: 77–8; on Foscolo and English Protestant and Nonconformist culture, see below, pp. 147–9.

[15] *Inf.* 5. 102, quoted in Foscolo 1991: 47.

[16] O'Grady 2003: 229 sees an allusion here to the ceding of the Venetian Republic to Austria in October 1797.

[17] Cambon 1980: 88–94.   [18] See Foscolo 1991: 15, 58, 75, 125.

[19] Foscolo 1991: 163.

in 1816, this passage and other Dantean allusions in the novel would have been known to British readers through its 1814 English translation (*The Letters of Ortis to Lorenzo*).[20]

At the beginning of October 1816, very soon after his arrival in Britain, Foscolo was invoking and identifying with Dante in letters to both Italian and British contacts. Writing to his friend the Brescian physician and editor Francesco Aglietti, who himself had links with the Holland House circle, he evokes past Italian friendships and conviviality by conflating verses from the *Purgatorio* and *Paradiso* to produce a macaronic Dantean line: 'E la dolcezza ancor dentro mi stilla' ('Its sweetness is infused upon me still').[21] Later on, in the same letter—whilst citing Virgil and his own *Dei Sepolcri* to convey the extent of his wanderings—Foscolo also describes his recent travels through Germany by means of an unflattering reference to the 'Tedeschi lurchi' ('gross Germans') of *Inferno* 17. 21.[22] On the same day (2 October 1816), he wrote his first brief letter to the central figure of the Holland House circle, Henry Richard Vassall Fox, third Baron Holland, who was to become one of his most loyal supporters. This ends with the exile adapting and applying to himself the words with which Beatrice introduces Dante to Virgil (*Inf.* 2. 61):

En attendant, Mylord, daignez me regarder aujourd'hui et demain, et après demain, et tant que je vivrai *Come amico riconoscente e rispettoso e leale* 'AMICO TUO, E NON DELLA VENTURA'——Dante—*ecc.*

Meanwhile, my lord, I beg to remain, today, tomorrow, thereafter and as long as I may live, your obliged and respectful friend 'YOUR FRIEND, BUT NOT FORTUNE'S'—Dante—*etc.*[23]

Eighteen months later, in March 1818, Foscolo wrote Lord Holland a longer letter in which both the agenda and the self-presentation have Dantean inflections. Here—during the month of the dinner party at which he talked about Dante to Hobhouse—he begins by complimenting Lord Holland on the latter's recent publication: a privately circulated dialogue between various historical figures on education and literary patronage.[24] He then deftly moves on to promotion of his own plans, whilst acknowledging the patronage of those members of the Holland House circle—Sir James Mackintosh, John Allen, Samuel Rogers—who were then helping him to initiate his British critical work on Dante in the *Edinburgh Review*. More deviously, he then presents his larger Dantean project, underlining the difficulties—and by implication, the expense—of getting his work translated by quoting Parini's lines to Alfieri about mighty thoughts being obscurely expressed:

Puisque mon travail des *Lettres* sur l'Angleterre est reussi inutile pour l'impossibilité de les traduire vîte en Anglais, j'ai continué à ecrire sur Dante en Français; et pour m'exprimer *à la maniere de Dante*:

---

[20] The relevant excerpts from the English version are in *DEL* 2.160.
[21] *Ep.* 7: 24–6. As Mario Scotti notes there, the pilgrim's response to the song of Casella (*Purg.* 2. 114) is combined with Dante's memory of his final vision (*Par.* 33.62–3).
[22] *Ep.* 7: 29.   [23] *Ep.* 7: 29.   [24] *Ep.* 7: 306–10.

Dove il pensier tuona
Non risponde la voce amica e franca.

Since my work on the *Letters Written from England* has come to nothing, it having proved impossible to translate them swiftly into English, I have continued to write about Dante in French; and—to put it as Dante might have done: 'where the thought is thunderous, the words do not sound easy and plain.'[25]

Significantly for Foscolo's self-image, he turns Parini's question, prefaced by *perchè* ('why?'), into a statement and presents these lines as if they were Dante's—or at least permits his reader to think they might be. His recourse to a programme of critical writing on Dante at this early point in his English career was thus not only a means of practical survival; it can also be seen as part of the expatriate writer's project to reinvent his poetic and political identity.

The political and potentially nationalist dimensions of Foscolo's reading of Dante would be echoed by a number of contemporary and later writers, English and Italian. His doomed hero's visit to *padre* Dante's tomb towards the end of *Ultime lettere di Jacopo Ortis* reinforces the sense of Italian 'collective memory' that he had earlier expressed in *Dei Sepolcri*.[26] Both texts probably influenced Byron's *Prophecy of Dante* (composed in 1819), which invokes 'Padre Alighier' in its preface before resurrecting him into 'this frail world', and concludes by foretelling a time when 'those who will not hear' shall be made to 'own the Prophet in his tomb'.[27] Later in the development of the Italian Risorgimento, Giuseppe Mazzini would continue to conscript the prophet for the cause and would assert, in an early article for British readers, that Foscolo 'recognised in Dante . . . the poet of the religion, the prophet of the nationality, of Italy'.[28]

Among Foscolo's London supporters in 1818, Hobhouse—though 'battered' by the problems stemming from his ill-fated collaboration with the exiled poet—seems to have retained respect for Foscolo's judgement on several immediate political issues, and was even planning yet another joint project with him, on a 'history of the Revolutions of Italy'.[29] By the time of Hobhouse's approach to Longman, Foscolo had already produced two major articles for the *Edinburgh Review* (April and September 1818).[30] His project would soon yield further significant results, in

[25] *Ep.* 7: 310, quoting from the sestet of Parini's sonnet to Alfieri ('Tanta già di coturni, altero ingegno', composed in 1783). On Foscolo's continuing problems with translation and his use of French as an intermediary between Italian and English, see Havely 2011*b*: 61–4.

[26] See above, p. 130. On the *Sepolcri* and the 'cult of the nation', see Lyttelton 1993: 75.

[27] On the *Prophecy*, see also Ellis 1983: 58–62.

[28] *Westminster Review* (Oct. 1837), excerpted in *DEL* 2.623–4. On Mazzini, Dante, and nationalism, see also Milbank 1998: 83–99, Jossa 2012: 38–41, and Looney 2012: 288–91. Mazzini would also famously declare, nearer to the 'year of revolutions' (1848), that 'the secret of Dante is a thing which concerns the present time' (*Foreign Quarterly Review* (Apr. 1844), excerpted in Caesar 1989: 555).

[29] See Hobhouse's Diary in BL Add. 5640, ff. 5ʳ, 7ʳ, and 15ᵛ (on the Revolutions project); also 15ᵛ and 84ʳ⁻ᵛ (on Foscolo's advice and opinions about British politics and policy). Hobhouse was also at this time attempting to get elected as a radical MP.

[30] On the production and impact of the *Edinburgh Review* articles on Dante (vols. 29 (no. 58), 453–74, and 30 (no. 60), 317–51), see Corrigan 1971 and Havely 2011*b*; also below, pp. 135–6.

the form of 'A Parallel between Dante and Petrarch', which was published in English as one of Foscolo's *Essays on Petrarch* (1823), and in which the exile makes a particularly striking 'attempt to identify his own life with that of Dante'.[31] Promotion of Dante would also form part of Foscolo's plan to present Italian classics to a British audience, for example, through the twelve public 'Lectures on Italian Literature' of 1823 and through his proposed edition of 'major Italian poems' including the *Commedia*—a plan which would remain uncompleted at his death in 1827.

A 'WORLD SICK OF DANTE'?: FOSCOLO'S *COMMEDIA* AND THE BRITISH PUBLIC

The idea of a public 'appetite' for Foscolo's critical work on Dante recalls the discouraging response of the publisher at Longman.[32] That publisher, Owen Rees (1770–1837), came from a Welsh clerical background and, following some years in the book trade in Bristol, had been taken into partnership by Thomas Norton Longman, the head of the London house.[33] Longman was the biggest publisher of the Romantic period: it had half a share in the *Edinburgh Review*, which would publish several of Foscolo's articles on Dante, and it was regarded by the poet Thomas Moore (a close friend of Owen Rees) as the 'establishment publisher'.[34] Rees himself had that same year (1818) reported to a parliamentary committee about the publishing trade and its costs, so he was speaking from a position of some authority within the literary and commercial world.[35]

Longman's pre-eminent status as a publisher was recognized not only by Hobhouse but also by several of Foscolo's British advisers. As early as October 1816 Lord Holland had provided the newly arrived exile with a letter for Longman, urging their consideration of Foscolo's 'high and merited literary reputation' and politely suggesting that they might provide 'the best advice and assistance in giving his works to the English publick'.[36] Later in the month, however, another devoted supporter of the newly arrived exile, the poet and translator William Stewart Rose, would note regretfully:

mi dispiace . . . che il libraijo, al quale v'indirizzava il Lord Holland, abbia trattato freddo; chè m'immagino che sarà stato uno di quelli che non vorrebbero nemmeno giuocare uno scudo. Ma voi non dite nulla di *Murray* pel quale io vi avea data una lettera.

---

[31] Ciccarelli 2001*b*: 129, discussing the 1821 Italian version. On the circulation of the *Essays on Petrarch*, see below, pp. 146–7.

[32] See above, p. 128.

[33] His father had been a dissenting minister, and his elder brother, Thomas, was a Unitarian minister and writer on theological history; see *ODNB*, s.v. 'Rees, Thomas (1777–1864)', and Owen Rees's obituary in *The Times*, 12 Sept. 1837.

[34] St Clair 2004: 159, 188, and 573.

[35] St Clair 2004: 168–9 and (for data Rees provided to parliament) 506.

[36] *Ep.* 7: 54.

I'm sorry that the publisher Lord Holland sent you to was so negative in his response; I suspect he may have been the sort who's unwilling to put a penny of his money at risk. You don't, though, say anything about Murray, for whom I gave you a letter.[37]

John Murray (for whom Rose provided this introduction) was, as Lord Holland had told Foscolo, 'Le *Publisher* le plus à la mode et certainement le plus entreprenant'.[38] As well as bringing out Byron's work, the *Quarterly Review*, and many other major titles, Murray would become one of Foscolo's publishers and would even (up until April 1824) seek subscribers for him.[39] The prestige of Longman, on the other hand, is reflected by the fact that Foscolo himself continued to hope that he might publish with them in some form. Hence, late in 1822, he would write a long letter in English to another member of the Holland House circle, John Allen, about his plan for a periodical to be called the *Quarterly Review of Foreign Literature*, claiming that Murray is 'about to propose it to Messrs Longman and Co.' and expressing preference for Longman as 'great capitalists'.[40] In the end it was neither Longman nor Murray who would sign up Foscolo's Dante and manage to publish the first part of it, but an ambitious newcomer (who will appear on this scene in due course).[41]

Meanwhile, there is some further evidence from Foscolo's letters about the scale of the project that Hobhouse was trying to persuade 'Rees of Longman's house' to 'engage for' in December 1818. During the course of his letter to Lord Holland of March that year (in which he had identified himself with Dante),[42] Foscolo had already been envisaging an ambitious development of his *Edinburgh Review* articles, the first of which was then due to be published:

l'on pourra en faire un volume de *300* pages a peu près, dans les quelles avec boucoup [*sic*] de methode et assez de nouveauté j'ai traité de l'histoire politique, religieuse, litteraire etc.: de son tems [*sic*], et qui ont influé sur son Genie et son Poeme.

they could be turned into a book of around 300 pages in which I have very methodically and with considerable originality discussed the political, religious, and literary history of his [Dante's] times insofar as they have influenced his genius and his poem.[43]

The change of tenses, from the conditional to the historic in the course of one sentence, reads almost as if the writer had already completed those 300 pages on Dante. A further expansion of the project is outlined very soon afterwards, in one of Foscolo's optimistic letters to his long-suffering Italian friend and supporter Quirina Mocenni Magiotti on 15 May 1818. Here he confidently announces

mio progetto di pubblicare illustrate da me alcuni classici italiani; con le loro vite e la storia del loro secolo, in guisa che tutto il gran numero di studiosi della nostra letteratura abbia in trentasei volume non solo il testo, la critica, e la vita de nostri maggiori scrittori, ma anche le cause politiche da cui derivarono i mutamenti nella storia della letteratura.

---

[37] *Ep.* 7: 55.   [38] *Ep.* 7: 54.   [39] See below, pp. 136, 144, and 145–6.
[40] *Ep.* 9: 152–4.   [41] William Pickering; see below, pp. 141, 149, and 152.
[42] See above, pp. 131–2.   [43] *Ep.* 7: 310.

my plan of publishing certain Italian classics and my commentary on them, along with the lives [of the authors] and the history of their times, so that the numerous students of our literature may have before them not only the text, criticism, and biographies of our major writers, but also the political factors on which developments in the history of that literature have depended.[44]

With—he anticipates—two thousand subscribers vying to invest in this venture, Foscolo then blithely goes on to predict that within four or five years he will be 'free as air and comfortably off'.[45]

Such confidence, in hindsight, sounds optimistic, but at the time the admiration and encouragement that Foscolo was receiving from readers of the *Edinburgh Review* articles and from the editors themselves might well have made more ambitious work on Dante for a British public appear very practicable. In November 1818, soon after the publication of his second article, the doyen of Whig Italophiles and bibliophiles, Roger Wilbraham—at whose dinner-table Foscolo and Hobhouse had first met earlier in the year—wrote to express his appreciation for the exile's 'magisterial discussion' of Dante.[46] Wilbraham's letter also emphasizes one of the most important and influential features of the *Edinburgh Review* articles: their insistence on historicizing Dante within the Italian society of the Middle Ages:

La parte historica spiega ed illustra chiaramente vari passaggi del Poeta, ed i vostri commenti sostenuti come sono, dai vostri ragionamenti sottili, schiariscono ogni difficoltà.

The historical sections clearly explain and contextualize various passages in the Poet's work, and your comments, supported as they are by subtle argumentation, resolve all the difficulties.[47]

Wilbraham's compliments in Italian on articles that had been written in a form of French and translated into English reflect the continuing complexity of Foscolo's communication with his readers, yet that communication was, nonetheless, now reaching a substantial audience. With a sale that year of 12,000 copies, his *Edinburgh Review* articles would, according to the estimates of the time, have reached some 50,000 readers.[48] His presentation of Dante in that form—along with Samuel Rogers's accompanying promotion of H. F. Cary's 1814 translation of the *Commedia*—would have reached a vastly greater British public than the hundred or so who attended Coleridge's two lectures on the subject in February 1818 and March 1819.[49]

Over the following years the impact of the *Edinburgh Review* articles continued to be felt in Britain and abroad. They soon appeared in a Milan journal, *Il Raccoglitore* (January 1819), and in the same month Quirina Mocenni Maggiotti reported intense interest in Foscolo's critical work—especially on Dante—among

---

[44] *Ep.* 7: 322.   [45] 'liberissimo e agiato', *Ep.* 7: 322.
[46] 'un trattato da Maestro', *Ep.* 7: 428 (4 Nov. 1818).   [47] *Ep.* 7: 428.
[48] St Clair 2004: 266 (on reading 'multipliers') and 573 (circulation of the *Edinburgh Review*).
[49] On Coleridge's lectures, see: *DEL* 1. 620–6 and 633; Caesar 1989: 439–47; and Braida 2004: 67–77. On Coleridge's earlier reading of Dante, see Pite 1994: 68–71 and Zuccato 1996. On the relationship between the roles of Cary, Coleridge, Foscolo, and Rogers in promoting Dante at this time, see Milbank 1998: 17 (with n. 38, on Coleridge's audience) and Braida 2004: 69.

northern Italian journals.[50] In March 1819 Foscolo wrote to the dilettante and bibliophile Robert Finch, whom he had met in Switzerland three years earlier and who had now settled in Italy, shortly to encounter the Shelleys in Rome.[51] Presumably in response to Finch's enquiry, he here acknowledges that the two Dante articles are his own, whilst taking the opportunity to publicize his work on other Italian poets (such as Ariosto and Pulci) in the forthcoming edition of the *Quarterly Review* (April 1819). At home, Francis Jeffrey, editor of the *Edinburgh Review*, remained keenly interested in Foscolo's larger critical project, and on 3 June he wrote to propose a further 'literary contribution such as you have already furnished us with on the subject of Dante'.[52] All this suggests that there was indeed a continuing demand for Dante among the British reading public, and that Owen Rees's diagnosis might have been based on his firm's habitual caution rather than an unprejudiced reading of the market.

British readership for Dante at this time needs to be seen in the context of its exposure to a multiplicity of Italian cultural media and of language-learning, in which exiles like Foscolo played a major part. It also needs to be related to the demand for a range of *classici italiani*, including authors such as Ariosto, Tasso, and later Goldoni and Metastasio—who were more widely read and in some cases more accessible. The prospectuses for Foscolo's editorial programme took account of some of these other interests. The one published by John Murray shows him proposing an edition of Italian classics that would include 'Dante's Poem . . . 3 volumes', and a two-volume 'History of Italian Poetry in the Age of Dante'. It also includes works by Petrarch (two volumes), Ariosto (five), and Tasso (one), together with a further four volumes on the 'History of Italian Poetry' in their respective ages.[53] The whole collection would thus run to eighteen volumes, at a total cost of nearly £38, and would require to be 'encouraged by Three Hundred Subscribers'.[54] The series of 'Italian Classic Poetry' texts that Foscolo eventually contracted to edit was planned to include a yet more ambitious twenty volumes, of which the *Commedia* comprised the first four, followed by Petrarch, Boiardo, Ariosto (now in six volumes), and Tasso (now in three).[55] It is clear from such evidence that— although Dante was for British readers not yet the canonical 'central man of all the world' (as he would become for Ruskin in the middle of the century)—he was by the early 1820s very much part of the Italian-reading public's programme.

Significant changes of taste, as has often been pointed out, had by now accompanied and helped to generate the production and publication of texts of and works on Dante in Britain.[56] Along with the poet's increasing presence in late eighteenth-

---

[50] *Ep.* 8: 11 (letter to Foscolo on 18 Jan. 1819). Another Italian friend (Giuseppe Bottelli) wrote in similar terms a year or so later (*Ep.* 8: 174).

[51] *Ep.* 8: 31. See also *ODNB*, s.v. 'Finch, Robert (1783–1830), antiquary and connoisseur of the arts' (also described there as a 'pretentious ass').

[52] *Ep.* 8: 57.   [53] *EN* 9.1: 665.   [54] *EN* 9.1: 665–6.

[55] *EN* 9.1: 668–9. This was to be the edition for which Foscolo would contract with William Pickering (see below, pp. 141–4 and 148–9). For its 'competent number of Subscribers' it would be rather cheaper than the one proposed by Murray, costing between £12 and £18 in total.

[56] See e.g. Brand 1957: 49–71; Caesar 1989: 43–7; Pite 1994:1–27; and above, pp. 116 and 120–7.

and early nineteenth-century anthologies, translations of the whole *Commedia* into English were by now widely available in print. Henry Boyd's first complete translation had been moderately well received; and that of H. F. Cary—following its promotion by Foscolo, Samuel Rogers, and Coleridge—quickly appeared in a new, corrected, and more imposing edition.[57] Readers of the Romantic period could, moreover, visualize the *Commedia* and its author not only through rare and expensive Italian editions, but also through the reproduction of more readily available illustrations, such as those by Flaxman and Fuseli, or through the images of Dante that appeared, for example, as frontispieces to Boyd's and Cary's trans-lations and to editions of the *Commedia* published in London.[58] Frequent and prominent poetic appropriations—such as Leigh Hunt's amplification of Dante's and Boccaccio's Francesca in *The Story of Rimini* (1816) and Byron's epigraphs from, allusions to, and ventriloquizations of Dante, in poems up to about 1820— were also enabling the *Commedia* and its poet to gain wider currency.[59] The relationship of Foscolo's Dante commentary to such early nineteenth-century views and readings of the poet and the poem—including those of British expatriates in Italy—will be considered later; meanwhile, some account should be taken of the context of, and competition with, his critical and editorial project among the British public closer to home.

COMPETING *COMEDIES*: EDITIONS FOR BRITISH READERS, 1808–1823

By the time of Foscolo's 1818 *Edinburgh Review* articles on Dante, British readers had been making much use of eighteenth-century and earlier editions of the *Commedia*—such as those of Venturi, Zatta, and Rubbi—which had appeared in Italy.[60] For at least ten years they had also been able to obtain both annotated and plain-text copies of the poem that had actually been published in London. One of these was produced by an expatriate printer and teacher of Italian, Romualdo Zotti, whom Lorenzo Da Ponte had met in London in 1801 and later described as 'a man of much merit in the field of literature'.[61]

---

[57] On Boyd's and Cary's versions and their reception, see: *DEL* 1. 410–22 and 465–502; De Sua 1964: chs. 1–2; Cunningham 1965: 14–22; Tinkler-Villani 1989: chs. 8–9; Crisafulli 2003; and Braida 2004: ch. 2.

[58] On the artistic rediscovery of Dante around the turn of the century, see Bindman *et al.* 2007: 23–31, and Salvadori 2005. For the frontispiece portraits of Dante in Boyd's translation (Stothard) and Cary's (Toffanelli), see Ellis 1983: 52 (with pls. 1 and 2) and Bindman 2007: 44 and 78. The Toffanelli portrait (admired by Carlyle) was also used as frontispiece to the London editions of the *Commedia* published by Zotti (Dante 1808*a*) and Pickering (Dante 1822–3), see below, pp. 138–9 and 141.

[59] On Hunt's *Story of Rimini*, see Edgecombe 1994: ch. 2, Havely 2007*b*: 100–2, and Webb 2011*a*. On Byron and Dante, see: Beaty 1960; Ellis 1983: ch. 2; Pite 1994: ch. 6; MacMillan 2005: 19–25; and O'Neill 2011:17–19 and 26–7.

[60] On Zatta, for example, see above, p. 117.

[61] 'Uomo di molto merito nelle lettere', Da Ponte 1918: 1. 252; although Da Ponte then speaks of him in parenthesis as 'no longer a friend of mine or of the truth' (alluding to Dante, *Par.* 17. 118). On Da Ponte, see also above, p. 126.

Zotti's *Commedia* comprised the first three volumes of a four-volume edition of Dante's works with commentary which he published in 1808–9.[62] Its editor, as one of Foscolo's friends would remind him, had been forced during his residence in England to teach Italian for a living, and amongst his publications the *Grammaire françoise et italienne* seems to have been highly popular, going through six editions by 1818.[63] Zotti also produced successful editions of other Italian authors, for example: Tasso (1806); Petrarch (1811); Metastasio (Foscolo's *bête noire*) in six volumes (1813); and Ariosto (1814). His Dante edition was competitively priced by comparison with English poetic texts published in the first decade of the century, selling at £1. 11*s.* 6*d* for the three unbound duodecimo volumes of the *Commedia*, or two guineas for the 'complete' works.[64]

Zotti's experience as a teacher in a girls' school may well have helped him to understand the requirements of the British reader: the three volumes of his 1808 *Commedia* are each dedicated to an English lady.[65] In his preface to the first volume he emphasizes his aim of giving clear linguistic guidance and 'very concise' (*brevissime*) historical and mythological information, and is quite precise about the level of the readership he is addressing:

Ho supposto che il Lettore non sia uno dei più gran Letterati, e che insieme non sia uno di quegli uomini privi di ogni coltura che non hanno mai quasi udito a parlare di Dante.

I have assumed that the Reader is not among the great *literati*, but at the same time is not one of those wholly uncultured persons who have never, as it were, heard tell of Dante.[66]

With such readers in mind, Zotti also makes reference in his notes to the recent English translations of the *Commedia* by Boyd (1802) and 'Mr Carry' (i.e. Cary), whose version of the *Inferno* had appeared in 1805–6.[67] His awareness of the English readership is evident not only from his style of glossing difficult words in Dante's text, but also from his allusions to those who had cultivated that readership around the turn of the century. In his preface to the fourth volume, published in 1809, he pays tribute to the work of 'luminaries of the present age who have contributed much to the increasing presence of Tuscan literature in these northern regions', singling out two familiar British Italophiles of the early nineteenth century: William Roscoe (author of popular works on Lorenzo de' Medici and Leo X) and Thomas Mathias, prolific editor of Italian lyric poetry, whose own poem Zotti quotes for its celebration of Italian influence on British culture:

---

[62] On the edition and the sources of its commentary, see Tissoni 1993: 102–3.

[63] W. S. Rose's letter of early 1824 sought to dissuade Foscolo from following Zotti's example as language-teacher (*Ep.* 9: 478 and n. 1)

[64] Cf. the table of prices for octavo editions of poems by Scott, Byron, Wordsworth, *et al.* in St Clair 2004: 194.

[65] *Inferno* is dedicated to Augusta Fane, countess of Lonsdale (wife of William Lowther, the literary patron who assisted Wordsworth in 1818); *Purgatorio* to the countess of Dartmouth; *Paradiso* to Mrs Pilkington.

[66] Dante 1808*a*: 1. iv.

[67] For example, he mentions both translators in his note on line 42 of *Inf.* 1 (pp. 5–6).

Talch' esulti goioso, e non indarno
Oda il Tamigi l'armonia dell'Arno.

So that the Thames may rejoice and listen not in vain to the music of the Arno.[68]

More practically, Zotti made extensive and often unscrupulous use of previous Italian editors of the *Commedia*, such as Venturi and Lombardi.[69] Yet he also kept up to date with later British discussion of Dante: thus, when he republished this edition in 1819 (shortly before his death), he took issue in a footnote with Foscolo's scepticism about the 'alleged' sources for Dante's vision in the second *Edinburgh Review* article, referring to the author of the article as 'this recent and ill-informed journalist' (*il nuovo e mal informato redattore*).[70]

Foscolo himself included a brief reference to Zotti's Dante in his draft 'serie delle edizioni' for his own edition of the *Commedia*.[71] However, he made no reference there to another three-volume text published in the same year as Zotti's by Lorenzo Da Ponte's brother Paolo, and edited by G. B. Boschini. Boschini's edition is in a rather more portable format (11×7 cm, 16°) than Zotti's: it provides a plain text, with a portrait of Dante based on Raphael as frontispiece; it is accompanied only by short prose summaries (*argomenti*) for each canto and is prefaced by a very brief 'Vita di Dante'. Again, it is dedicated to aristocratic ladies (of the Percy family) as 'distinguished devotees and supporters of Italian writing'.[72] Not much is known about the editor's career: he is probably the 'Boschini' whom Lorenzo Da Ponte listed among the 'learned and cultivated Italians' whom he met in London at the beginning of the century;[73] and, like Zotti, he also edited several other Italian authors for publication in London (Guarini in 1809, Tasso in 1813, Alfieri in 1815). With regard to the British and expatriate reception of Dante at this time, it is also worth noting that both these initial London editions of the *Commedia* (Zotti's and Boschini's) were owned by Foscolo's *carissimo amico* Robert Finch who, during his residence in Italy, was also a reader of the *Edinburgh Review* articles on Dante.[74]

More authoritative and influential than either Zotti's or Boschini's editions, however, was a *Commedia* of which Foscolo made mention in his first *Edinburgh Review* article: that of Niccolò Giosafatte Biagioli, which was then being published in Paris.[75] More is known about Biagioli than about Boschini or Zotti. His early life

---

[68] Dante 1809: v–vi. This is the fourth volume of Zotti's 'works of Dante', containing the lyric poems (pp. 211–43) and a long dissertation on the *Commedia* (pp. 1–210) by the French critic J. B. Mérian, on whom see Caesar 1989: 82 n. 87. On Mathias, Italian, and Dante, see above, pp. 125–6 and n. 350; his friendship with Da Ponte is recorded in the latter's memoirs (Da Ponte 1918: 251–4 and 1929: 285–9). On Roscoe, see below, pp. 142–3 and nn. 95–102.

[69] See Tissoni 1993: 103.

[70] Dante 1819: xix n. Foscolo had corresponded with Zotti, mostly involving a dispute about the edition of *Ortis* which Zotti had published in 1811; see *Ep.* 7: 31 (with n. 3), 173, and 185–8.

[71] *EN* 9.2: 293.

[72] 'Fautrici e prottettrici egregie delle italiche lettere', in Dante 1808*b*, following the title-page.

[73] Da Ponte 1918: 1. 254.

[74] On Finch, see above, p. 136. Like other books in his collection, the Zotti and Boschini editions of the *Commedia* were bequeathed to the University of Oxford and are now in the Taylorian Institution; see Craster 1952: 283.

[75] Dante 1818–19.

had been eventful: he had been first a monk, subsequently a Jacobin radical, was sentenced to death for elopement in 1798, and became a supporter of the short-lived Roman republic in 1799. Following the Austrian suppression of the republic that year he became an exile in Paris, where he remained most of the time until his death in 1830. Thanks to some influential patronage he became teacher of Italian at the court of the Duchesse de Berry and a kind of court poet to Napoleon, writing Italian odes and *canzoni* on events in the emperor's career. His publications included works on Italian grammar and vocabulary, an important French–Italian and Italian–French Dictionary (published posthumously and frequently reprinted), and translations and editions of Italian writers, including (in 1821) Petrarch.[76]

At the time of writing his first *Edinburgh Review* article, Foscolo had only the first eight canti of Biagioli's *Inferno* to hand, and he uses them chiefly as a departure point for a critique of 'commentators on Dante', noting 'the very little service which they have done to the poet or the reader', whilst acknowledging (somewhat condescendingly) that Biagioli, 'if he has improved . . . has not fundamentally changed the plan of his predecessors'.[77] Foscolo had first met Biagioli in Paris in 1804; he continued to correspond with him in 1818, advising him to send copies of the *Inferno* edition to Murray in London, and later (in 1820) received a copy for himself.[78] Biagioli's own earlier hopes that Foscolo might help to secure British publicity for his edition were not without some foundation. As the list of subscribers attached to the third volume of his *Commedia* indicates, he already had orders from a number of British readers (male and female), as well as from some Italian teachers of language in London. Among the latter was Romualdo Zotti— described as 'Professeur des Belles Lettres à Londres'—who was issuing the second edition of his own annotated *Commedia* at the time and was presumably keeping a careful eye on the competition.[79] Biagioli's commentary is at times intemperate in tone—as when he accuses a previous editor, Lombardi (1791), of 'horribly distorting and assassinating' several of Dante's verses in *Inferno* 5.[80] His edition was, however, reprinted a number of times in nineteenth-century Italy; its interpretations have been described as a step forward in the progress of 'spiegar Dante con Dante' ('explaining Dante through Dante');[81] and it would also continue to be used by a number of nineteenth-century British readers.[82]

Biagioli's *Commedia* would later be described in Foscolo's draft notes for his edition as 'lucid and correct'.[83] Foscolo's regard for his fellow exile and editor continued to be evident in March 1827, when, only few months before his death,

---

[76] *DBI*, s.v. 'Biagioli, Niccolò Giosafatte'; also (more briefly) Tissoni 1993: 98–102.
[77] Foscolo 1818*a*: 454.   [78] *Ep*. 7: 301–4 and 8: 174–5.
[79] Dante 1818–19: vol. 3, pp. 571–83.
[80] Dante 1818–19: vol. 1, pp. 92–3, commenting on *Inf*. 5. 84 and 86.
[81] *DBI*, s.v. 'Biagioli, Niccolò Giosafatte', p. 10.
[82] Including Tennyson, who described it as his 'favourite Dante'; see Straub 2009: 147–8 (n. 17). This copy—mentioned also by Milbank 1998: 267 (n. 88)—is now in the Tennyson Research Archive at Lincoln. On Frances Kemble's acquaintance with Biagioli himself, as well as his edition, see below, pp. 156–7.
[83] 'Edizione nitida, e corretta', *EN* 9.2: 296.

he poignantly expresses hope for his own Dante project: 'Pur s'io non morrò, l'edizione un dì o l'altro uscirà com'io avevala disegnata' ('If I don't die first, that edition will, one day or other, come out as I had imagined it').[84] It would be a grim (and redundant) task to rehearse yet again the story of Foscolo's dealings with the publisher who eventually in May 1824 contracted with him to produce the *Poemi maggiori italiani illustrati da Ugo Foscolo*, beginning with an edition of Dante: an edition that would not (as published in his lifetime) reach beyond the 400 pages of its introductory *Discorso sul testo*.[85] The fraught relationship between the dynamic young entrepreneur William Pickering and the debt-burdened expatriate poet has already been well described and amply documented in English and Italian sources.[86] It is, however, worth adding one other, little-known item to the list of competing *Comedies* that preceded Foscolo's final and monumental fragment.

William Pickering had himself already offered Dante to British readers even before he signed that contract with Foscolo. He had worked for Longman and other publishers; he had set up in business on his own by 1820 (at the age of no more than 24); and by 1822 he had launched a series of 'MINIATURE CLASSICS with Portraits finely engraved'.[87] The Miniature Classics were produced in tiny volumes (measuring 9×5.25 cm, 48°), that were nonetheless finely designed, legibly printed in 'diamond type', and (a further innovation) presented in cloth-binding. The series included Latin authors (Horace, Virgil, Terence, Cicero), as well as Italians: Petrarch, Tasso, and in 1822–3 (the year before Pickering signed the contract with Foscolo), a two-volume plain-text edition of Dante's *Commedia*. Pickering dedicated this edition and the whole collection to Earl Spencer, and a title-page in the first Dante volume thus reads:

All' illustrissimo ed onoratissimo Signor[,] il Signor Giorgio Giovanni CONTE SPENCER delle arti liberali fautore benigno questo minutissima edizione dell'opera divina di Dante suo divotissimo servo G[uglielmo].P[ickering]. umilmente dedica.

To the most illustrious and honourable Lord George John, Earl Spencer, generous patron of the liberal arts, this minuscule edition of the divine work of Dante is humbly dedicated by his most devoted servant, William Pickering.[88]

The second Earl Spencer was one of the great bibliophiles of the period, and Pickering's edition of Dante must have seemed particularly 'minuscule' to one whose library by this time included three of the earliest printed editions of the *Commedia*, together with the 1481 Landino edition in folio, with twenty of the

---

[84] Letter to Biagioli, 16 Mar. 1827, quoted in *EN* 9.1: LXIV, n. 4.

[85] Foscolo 1825. On Mazzini's completion of the project, see below, pp. 152–3.

[86] e.g. by Viglione 1910, Wicks 1937, Vincent 1953, Da Pozzo 1979 (*EN* 9.1: XLV–LXV), and Lindon 1987: 100 and n. 36, 104–5 and n. 61, 119, and 122–4.

[87] On Pickering's origins and early career, see Keynes 1969: 9–12 and *ODNB*, s.v. 'Pickering, William (1796–1854)'.

[88] Dante 1822–3, second title-page. On Spencer's patronage of the whole series, see the list of titles at the end of vol. 2 (following p. 374). He was also believed to have been Pickering's father; see Keynes 1969: 9 and Lindon 1987: 100, n. 36.

engravings after Botticelli.[89] Da Ponte mentions Spencer as an important customer for Italian books in 1801; his colleague (and previous anthologizer of the *Commedia*) Leonardo Nardini already knew of the earl's library in the 1790s and had envisaged making use of it for work on a complete edition.[90] In 1817 Foscolo himself had already presented Spencer with a 'small volume'—his translation of speeches commemorating a leading Whig politician who had died in Italy.[91] The favour seems to have been returned, with a set of Shakespeare being presented by Spencer to Foscolo in February of the following year.[92] Here, as in other cases, there are connections between Foscolo and the British bibliophiles, whose libraries, like Spencer's, were by now important and (for some, at least, of the Regency literati) accessible sources of material on Dante.

FOSCOLO'S DANTE: FRIENDS, CONNECTIONS, INFLUENCES

Of these great aristocratic collections, perhaps the greatest from the Dantean point of view was, as the previous chapter has shown, the library of the Coke family, earls of Leicester, at Holkham Hall.[93] As far as we know, Foscolo never visited this collection, although his protégé Antonio Panizzi, who had arrived in England in 1823, certainly did.[94] One of Foscolo's most loyal Italophile friends had close connections with the Coke family and their manuscripts. This friend and supporter was the Liverpool banker, reformer, botanist, bibliophile, and literary historian William Roscoe.[95] Amongst his many literary, social, and educational activities, Roscoe was also engaged at points throughout the period of Foscolo's residence in London with the process of binding and then cataloguing the Holkham manuscript collection.[96] In the latter task he eventually employed a

[89] On the Spencer collection in general (most of which is now in the John Rylands Library at Manchester), see: Dibdin 1814–15; Fletcher 1902: 308–13; De Ricci 1930: 71–7; and Lister 1989. On its Dante items, including the 1481 *Commedia*, see: Dibdin 1814–15: 4. 97–116; *DEL* 2: 79–80; Hind 1938–48: 1. 106–7 and n. 1; Speight 1961–2; and above, p. 129, n. 4.

[90] On Nardini's work on Dante, see above, pp. 125–6.

[91] In June 1817; see *Ep.* 7: 182–3. The dead expatriate was Francis Horner (1778–1817), a parliamentarian and co-founder of the *Edinburgh Review*, who was himself a student of Dante whilst in Italy during the last few months of his life; see his notes and letters on Dante in *DEL* 2. 239–41; also Sanders 1908: 263–4 and Vincent 1953: 43–5.

[92] *Ep.* 8: 467.

[93] See above, pp. 105–14.

[94] For Panizzi's career and contacts, see: Fagan 1880*a*; Vincent 1953: 203–4; Brand 1957: 29–34; Brooks 1931; Miller 1967; Esposito 1982; Anceschi 2002; Spaggiari 2005: 32–9, and *ODNB*, s.v. 'Panizzi, Sir Anthony (1797–1879), librarian'. See also below, pp. 143–4, 151–2, and 179. Panizzi's knowledge of the Holkham manuscripts is evident from a letter he wrote to Foscolo from Liverpool in February 1826, excerpted in Fagan 1880*a*: 65–6.

[95] On Roscoe, see Roscoe 1833, and *ODNB*, s.v. 'Roscoe, William (1753–1831), historian and patron of the arts'. In his translation of the *ballata* 'Io mi son pargoletta' (1820, published 1833), he is 'one of the first English translators to show an interest in Dante's lyric poems' (*DEL* 1.533; Griffiths and Reynolds 2005: 74–5).

[96] Roscoe's attention to the Holkham collection, including its 'MSS of Dante', had been drawn by his friend, the Norwich botanist Dr James Edward Smith, in September 1812; see *DEL* 1. 503–4 and

professional manuscript expert, the irascible Frederic Madden; and he also received some assistance from Panizzi, whom, on Foscolo's recommendation, he had earlier helped to find work as a language teacher in Liverpool.[97]

Foscolo and Roscoe had earlier clashed about the merits of Homer versus Virgil in London, but they were certainly on very good terms when they met during Foscolo's visit to Liverpool in June 1822, and two years later Roscoe made several offers of help towards the Dante project.[98] In May 1824, very shortly after the contract for the *Poemi maggiori italiani* had been signed with Pickering, he wrote to Foscolo expressing willingness 'to become a subscriber to your great work of Dante'.[99] Not much more than a month later a mutual friend, Jonathan Hatfield (with whom Foscolo had stayed when he visited Liverpool, and from whom he had borrowed money), wrote to offer a yet more material form of assistance: 'Our venerable friend Mr Roscoe before he left town, enquired particularly after you, and desired me to tell you that if an old edition [*sic*] of Dante (1379) now in his possession, w.^d be of any use to you in your researches, it is much at your service . . .'[100] This 'edition' was in fact a Ferrarese paper manuscript of the *Commedia*;[101] it was one of the two codices which Foscolo actually consulted and referred to, both in the 1825 *Discorso* and in his variants for the *Inferno* edition.[102]

Over the three years of work for the Pickering series and beyond, Foscolo continued to benefit from the direct assistance and support of various friends. A generous young Polish diplomat, Xavier de Labensky, who was taking Italian lessons with him in 1824, immediately signed up for the whole eighteen volumes of Murray's non-existent and never-to-be-published Italian classics at the full cost of 36 guineas—somewhat, it seems, to Foscolo's embarrassment.[103] Amongst fellow exiles, too, advice and support were forthcoming: an eloquent letter of the same year from the Piedmontese revolutionary, Count Santorre Santa Rosa, acknowledges Foscolo's commitment to the 'new edition of our four great Authors', whilst

---

Wade Martins 2009: 158. The correspondence between Roscoe and Thomas William Coke (1754–1842) began immediately afterwards, and continued until 1830. Roscoe's letters to Coke are in the Holkham Archives, F/TWC 5. He initiated the whole project in December 1815; the binding of the manuscripts was completed by Jones of Liverpool (except for the Dante manuscripts) and paid for by early 1823; and the cataloguing of the collection seems to have occupied him at intervals from 1821 to 1827. See also Roscoe 1833: 2. 79–98 and Wade Martins 2009: 159–62.

[97] Roscoe entrusted the catalogue to Madden in February 1826, and it was completed by September 1828 (Holkham Archives, F/TWC 5, ff. 190^r and 219^r). He seems to have regarded Holkham's 'Six MS. copies of Dante' as a special item, since they were not dispatched until the whole project (including the eight-volume catalogue) had been completed. His reliance upon 'the assistance of Sig.^r Panizzi' for advice about manuscript material relating to Boccaccio is mentioned in a letter of August 1825 (F/TWC 5, f. 176^v). On Roscoe and Panizzi, see also Roscoe 1833: 2. 406–8, and (on Panizzi's early career in Liverpool) see Lindon 1987: 48–9.

[98] See Vincent 1953: 20. On Foscolo's visits to Manchester (prompting him to quote from Dante's condemnation of Florence in *Inf.* 16. 73–4) and to Roscoe at Liverpool, see *Ep.* 9: 69–71 and Vincent 1953: 150–2.

[99] *Ep.* 9: 400.   [100] *Ep.* 9: 409.

[101] Now BL Egerton 2567; for description of the 'Codex Roscoe', see Roddewig 1984: 164 (no. 394).

[102] *EN* 9.1: LXXIII and 552; and 9.2: XXXII.   [103] *Ep.* 9: 479–82 (five letters).

implying regret for his abandonment of plans to join the independence struggle in Greece.[104] A new arrival (and future British Museum librarian), Antonio Panizzi, offered both enthusiasm and material assistance with the Oxford *Commedia* manuscripts (the Canonici collection, recently purchased by the Bodleian), which Foscolo acknowledged would be 'of the greatest usefulness'.[105] Amongst his English friends, one of the most loyal was the banker and aspiring poet Hudson Gurney, who bailed the poet out in 1824 (by paying off £150 worth of his debts) and continued to support him financially to the last. It was to Gurney that the first volume of the projected Dante edition, the *Discorso sul testo* of 1825, was dedicated.[106]

Gurney had also been witness to a public event which not only brought Foscolo's supporters together but was potentially productive for the readership of his work on Italian literature and on Dante. This was the series of 'Lectures on Italian Literature' which Foscolo delivered in May and June 1823. The twelve lectures were put on with the support and advice of the lecturer's aristocratic friends Lord and Lady Dacre.[107] The subscribers to the lectures (not all of whom may have attended) paid the quite substantial sum of £5. 5s. for the whole course of twelve—more than twice the amount that had been paid by the audience for Coleridge's fourteen lectures (including those on Dante) in 1818.[108] The prospectus for the series was issued by John Murray, who presumably saw them as publicity for the proposed edition of Italian poets.

Foscolo's fourth lecture, 'On the life, the poem and the age of Dante', took place on 15 May 1823 and left his patron Gurney somewhat mystified: 'Thurs. May 15. 1823. Foscolo's lecture. Dante and his age—a strange account of the extreme rusticity of Italy at the commencement of that era.'[109] Part of the 'strangeness' of the experience may have been due to the lectures being delivered in Italian, a fact that was noted with a degree of amusement by some British reporters: 'Mr Foscolo's Italian Lectures are to be the fashion . . . A total ignorance of the language in which they are to be delivered is not the slightest objection to a subscriber.'[110] However, at least two of the senior subscribers—Roger Wilbraham and William Stewart Rose—would probably have had no difficulty in

---

[104] *Ep.* 9: 406–8. Santa Rosa (then teaching Italian in Nottingham) would be killed in action in Greece the following year; see Vincent 1953: 169.

[105] Foscolo, letter to Panizzi on 2 March 1826, in Fagan 1880*b*: 34–5.

[106] See Vincent 1953: 186, 194, 197, 205 (on Gurney's support for Foscolo during his final years), and on Gurney's career and interests *ODNB*, s.v. 'Gurney, Hudson (1775–1864), antiquary and banker'.

[107] On the organization and programme of the lectures, see Vincent 1953: 156–8 and *EN* 11. xxi–xxv.

[108] Vincent 1953: 156 and St Clair 2004: 514.

[109] Gurney's Diary for 15 May 1823, quoted in Vincent 1938: 104. Foscolo's notes for this lecture are in *EN* 11: 160–7. Later, in 1824, he also made Dante the main subject of an article (designed for the *European Review*) on the 'third period' of Italian literature; see *EN* 11: 137–69.

[110] Vincent 1953:157 citing *John Bull* on 11 May 1823. A much later article on 'Foscolo and English Hospitality' in *Fraser's Magazine* for April 1845 (vol. 31, no. 184) recalls half the audience 'appearing to take an interest in what they did not understand' (p. 405).

following Foscolo's argument, since they had, since very early in his exile, been corresponding with him in Italian.[111]

Other subscribers to the 1823 lectures included a number of those directly involved in Foscolo's long Dante project.[112] Hobhouse, who had initially sought to interest Longman, was amongst them; so also was Henry Hallam, the Whig historian whose work on medieval Europe Foscolo had cited in the second *Edinburgh Review* article, and with whom he had discussed his 'intended edition of the Italian poets, chiefly Dante', in the spring of the previous year.[113] Another member of the audience was Payne Knight (1750–1824), the classicist whom Foscolo had met at that dinner with Wilbraham, Hobhouse, and others in March 1818 and to whom he would respectfully refer in his *Discorso* on Dante's text, when discussing editing, philology, and the *indagine delle date* ('investigation of dates').[114]

Two other important subscribers to the 'lectures on Italian Literature' also provided perceptive encouragement. One of the exile's most long-standing English supporters, William Stewart Rose, has already been mentioned as an early adviser about publishers for Foscolo's Dante.[115] Rose was about to start issuing his own translation of Ariosto's *Orlando furioso* (between 1823 and 1831), and he would write to Foscolo at some point in 1824 urging him to concentrate not on earning money by teaching (as Zotti had) but on getting subscribers for his edition of Italian poetry:

e se, a questo effetto vorreste eseguire l'antico mio progetto di pubblicar Dante ossia altra opera classica Italiana *by subscription*, siate sicuro che io farei ogni mio sforzo di secondarlo quando voi conveniste della cosa.

and if, to this end, you should wish to put into effect that earlier idea of mine, to publish Dante or other classic Italian authors by subscription, you may be sure that I would do everything in my power to give you the assistance that is required.[116]

This must have been the advice that, as Foscolo said in a letter to Lord Dacre of April that year, 'caused a *prospectus* to be printed [the one issued by Murray] with some hope that the undertaking would prove of some present and future advantage to me, and of some utility to the Italian scholars in England'.[117] In this context it seems likely that an unaddressed and currently unattributed letter in English, dated 24 March 1824 (and headed 'Di Hants' in the *Edizione nazionale*), is actually a testimonial from Rose himself (who lived in 'Hants'/Hampshire), and that it was intended for Foscolo to use in his dealings with Murray, who is specifically mentioned as the prospective publisher. Rose here suggests that Foscolo might produce a 'faithful, easy, intelligible . . . Italian paraphrase' on a facing page to

---

[111] See the letters from them in e.g. *Ep.* 7: 21–2 and 428.

[112] Vincent 1953: 157 and 238 (n. on line 21) cites Murray's list of subscribers in two of the Labronica MSS: (50, f. 64 and 20, f. A2).

[113] Foscolo, letter to Murray 29 March 1822, *Ep.* 9: 50.

[114] See above, p. 129 and *EN* 9.1: 195. Foscolo subsequently describes Knight as a 'man of powerful intelligence' (*uomo di forte intelletto*, ibid. 197).

[115] See above, pp. 133–4.   [116] *Ep.* 9: 478.

[117] 17 Apr. 1824, *Ep.* 9: 378.

Dante's original, and concludes by referring back to May 1823 and claiming that 'the numerous and elegant assembly which attended his [Foscolo's] lectures last spring make him secure of every encouragement which is to be obtained from an ample subscription'.[118] However, the capacity of the wider British public to digest Dante, in whatever form, remained in question. Another distinguished member of that 'numerous and elegant assembly' that gathered to hear Foscolo in May 1823 was the diplomat, Whig MP, and bibliophile the Hon. Thomas Grenville—a figure of some prominence on the political and cultural scene, although he had retired from parliament in 1818 to spend time 'in the company of his friends and his books'.[119] In a letter of February 1818 to Quirina Mocenni Magiotti, Foscolo had described Grenville as an 'excellent man' (*ottimo uomo*) who one day might enable him to travel to Florence under British protection.[120] He had presented Grenville with a copy of Homer, as well as of his own *Ortis* (in the 1817 London edition), and he had received in return copies of Spenser and Pope.[121] By the time he attended Foscolo's lectures in 1823, Grenville was not only on good terms with the lecturer; he was also the owner of a major private library which by then also (like Earl Spencer's) included the Florence 1481 edition of the *Commedia* with nineteen of the Botticellian engravings.[122] He would also come to possess among his vast collection other early texts of Dante, including two of the 1472 editions of the *Commedia* and the *editio princeps* of the *Convivio*.[123] He was, moreover, no mere collector, and his comment, two years earlier, on receiving one of the limited de luxe copies of Foscolo's *Essays on Petrarch* (printed by Samuel and Richard Bentley in March 1821) had offered some thoughtful observations about the audience Foscolo was aiming to address:

The names of Petrarch and of Dante are familiar enough in the conversation of this country, but I doubt whether that familiar use extends itself to their works, and therefore I rejoice to see a powerful temptation offered to the publick in the Commentaries of one so well qualified to recommend and to explain the merits of those great authors.[124]

The measured tones of the Whig grandee, whose 20,000 books would eventually (thanks to his friendship with Panizzi) be bequeathed to the British Museum, pose a key question concerning the British public's 'familiarity' with and 'conversation' about the great names of medieval Italian literature at this time.[125] Were the latter—as Foscolo himself said of ancient authors at the beginning of the *Discorso*— 'more reverenced than understood'?[126]

By the early 1820s, when Grenville made his remarks, it could be argued that British public understanding of Dante had already been very much advanced. Anthologies, critical writing (including Foscolo's own), translations with commentaries (such as those of Boyd and Cary), and annotated editions (such as those of

[118] *Ep.* 9: 368 (in Labronica MS 45, f. 305).
[119] See *ODNB*, s.v. 'Grenville, Thomas (1755–1846), politician and book-collector'.
[120] *Ep.* 7: 290–1.   [121] Vincent 1953: 52; *Ep.* 7:152–3 (17 May 1817).
[122] Clarke's *Repertorium Bibliographicum* of 1819, cited in *DEL* 2: 300.
[123] *DEL* 2. 665.   [124] Thomas Grenville to Foscolo, 24 May 1821, *Ep.* 8: 283.
[125] *DEL* 2. 665.   [126] 'Anzi ammirati che intesi', *EN* 9.1: 176.

Zotti and Biagioli) had for several decades been providing introductions and interpretation of the *Commedia*, and even some of Dante's other works, for the Italianist and non-Italianist reader. By 1820 selective translations, epigraphs, allusions, and appropriations, were featuring frequently in the works of well-known authors such as Byron and the Shelleys.[127]

Several of Foscolo's women readers and correspondents indicate that—despite Grenville's scepticism—a familiarity with Petrarch and Dante did indeed 'extend to their works'. Barbarina Wilmot, Lady Dacre, provided translations for his *Essays on Petrarch* (1823), which are dedicated to her, and is well known to have been one of his most perceptive advisers from 1818 onwards.[128] So is Maria Graham, who received the proof sheets of the *Essays on Petrarch* in 1821, but who had much earlier become familiar with 'the Inferno of Dante' and 'well-acquainted with Ariosto'.[129] A less well-known figure, who nonetheless conversed perceptively with Foscolo on the subject, was a Miss G. Pigou, who was reading the *Commedia* in the summer and autumn of 1817 and looking forward keenly to Foscolo's account of it in the *Edinburgh Review*.[130] A year later she was returning books she had borrowed from him, including a copy of (presumably) the *Commedia*; and her comments throughout convey a response that is more direct than that of his more exalted readers.[131]

Foscolo's critical work was itself influenced by some features of British public opinion. One example is the emergence—especially in the *Discorso*—of a 'Protestant' Dante.[132] Convergence between his anticlerical, 'Neo-Ghibelline' stance and the views of his British Whig friends and supporters had been apparent already in Foscolo's 1818 *Edinburgh Review* articles, especially the second.[133] The view of Dante as 'reformer' of the Church is yet more fully and frequently articulated in the 1825 *Discorso sul testo* and the manuscripts associated with the editing of the

---

[127] On Byron and Dante, see above, pp. 130, 132 (with n. 27), and 137 (with n. 59). On Percy Shelley and Dante, see: Webb 1976: 276–336; Ellis 1983: ch. 1; Pite 1994: ch. 5; Braida 2004: ch. 4.

[128] On their correspondence and conversations, see Vincent 1953: 77–81 and Havely 2011*b*: 63; also *ODNB*, s.v. 'Brand [*née* Ogle], Barbarina, Lady Dacre (1768–1854), poet and playwright'.

[129] Dante was studied 'with great care' as part of her reading programme over the winter of 1806–7; see her 'Reminiscences' (early 1840s) in Bodley MS. Eng. C. 2731, f. 111^v. On her career, see *ODNB*, s.v. 'Callcott [*née* 'Dundas *other married name* Graham], Maria, Lady Callcott (1785–1842), traveller and author'.

[130] 'Mi metterò a studiare Dante colla speranza del vostro articolo' ('I shall set myself to study Dante in expectation of your article'; *Ep.* 7: 214–15, 17 Aug. 1817). Miss Pigou was apparently associated with the circle of Samuel Rogers (Vincent 1953: 68). Foscolo also sent her a draft of the first *Edinburgh Review* article (*Ep.* 7: 212), and intended to dedicate a work on the study of Italian in England to her (Viglione 1910: 163). Her later letters of 1817 are in *Ep.* 7: 220–3 and 227–8.

[131] A summary of her letter of 4 Aug. 1818 is in *Ep.* 7: 497.

[132] On Foscolo's experience of English Protestant and Nonconformist society helping 'to shape [his] view of Dante as a religious reformer', see Lindon 2000*a*: 156 (and n. 48), citing Marzot 1969: 66. See also Lindon's comments on how 'the content and character of [Foscolo's] criticism were . . . conditioned by his situation in England' (p. 146).

[133] See Foscolo's reference to 'Protestant writers' quoting Dante's 'authority as one of the Witnesses of the Truth', together with the subsequent attack on the Jesuit commentators in the first article (*Edinburgh Review*, 29, pp. 462–3, repr. in *EN* 9.1: 24–6), and the extended account of the 'religious state of Italy' in Dante's time in the second article (*Edinburgh Review*, 30, pp. 321–9; in *EN* 9.1: 70–88). On Foscolo and the Holland House Whigs, see also above, p. 129 and n. 8.

Commedia.[134] In an autograph draft of an address 'To the Reader' which was intended to be prefaced to his edition, Foscolo describes some of the material he has (or will have) been forced to omit from Pickering's edition:

E alla Cantica terza era da premettersi un discorso su lo stato della Chiesa d'allora, della quale Dante si professa riformatore per diritto della sua Missione Apostolica esposta nel Discorso sul Testo. Osservando come la religione fosse sentita e praticata a quei giorni; quanto riuscisse utile o dannosa all'Italia; quanto e perché Dante volesse rivocarla a' suoi primi istituti, avrei forse indotto taluni a percorrere d'allora in qua colla loro memoria i vantaggi che la loro misera patria derivò dalla Chiesa.

And the third canticle (i.e. *Paradiso*) was meant to be prefaced by an account of the prevailing conditions in the Church, of which Dante proclaimed himself to be a reformer by virtue of his apostolic mission, as described in the *Discorso sul testo*. By showing how religion was understood and practised at that time; the extent to which it was beneficial or harmful to Italy; how and why Dante meant to recall it to its primal form—I should perhaps have persuaded some people to consider over time what advantages their wretched nation has gained from the Church.[135]

The passage, with its ironic final phrase, certainly echoes the views of Dante's portrayal of and reception by the Church and the Papacy that are expressed throughout the published *Discorso*.[136] Foscolo's 'Protestantizing' tendency is reflected in his reading of certain passages in Dante's text, such as the identification of the Wolf of *Inferno* 1 not only with avarice but also with Rome, and the association of her adversary the Greyhound (VELTRO) with Luther (LVTERO).[137] And as section CXXI of the *Discorso* shows, Foscolo was aware of the 'usefulness' to Protestantism not only of such passages in the *Commedia*, but also of the ideas about Church and State in Book 3 of the *Monarchia*.

Foscolo's inclination towards what has been called a 'heretical-sectarian' reading of Dante continues to distress some contemporary critics, leading at least one of them to dismiss the whole *Discorso* as a 'formless rigmarole' (*informe sproloquio*) prompted by 'rancorous malice' (*astioso livore*).[138] A more nuanced and productive approach to the context and cultural history of Foscolo's 'Protestant' Dante has been taken in some recent research, suggesting that the *Dante riformatore* of his *Discorso* draws not only upon the heritage of Foxe and that of Locke's 'liberty of conscience', but also reflects Foscolo's links with British nonconformists and Unitarians such as Samuel Rogers and Edgar Taylor, whom Foscolo mentions in the *Discorso* as 'a man deeply versed in French literature and the Romance

---

[134] For excerpts from the *Discorso* in English (particularly its political reading of the *Commedia* and its emphasis on the 'centrality . . . of Dante's own experience'), see Caesar 1989: 483–9.

[135] 'Prefazione alla Divina Commedia manoscritta', in Varallo, ms foscoliani 6, ff. 9–10, ed. in *EN* 9.1: 704–5. This was eventually printed in Mazzini's edition (Dante 1842–3: 1: xxi–xxx), see below, p. 152.

[136] See e.g. sections III–IV, XLIII–XLIV, LVI, LXXXVIII, CXI, CXIV–CXVIII, CLXXXI–CLXXXII, and CLXXXV–CLXXXVI of the *Discorso*.

[137] *EN* 9.1: 474, 502, 513. On the Protestant ancestry of this anagram, see Friederich 1950: 83.

[138] See the provocative but perfunctory account of Foscolo in ch. 9 of Tissoni 1993: 104–10, esp. pp. 106 and 108.

languages'.[139] Taylor was among the exile's supporters during the last year of his life in London, and it was to him that Foscolo wrote about his project late in 1826.[140] The letter expresses concerns about Pickering's handling of the edition, which Foscolo plans to preface with

una lunga lettera agl'Italiani sulla mia vita pubblica, e sulle mie opinioni relative alla presente condizione e alle future speranze d'Italia. E poi non mi occuperò più di politica.

a long letter to Italians on the subject of my life in public and my views concerning the present state of and future hopes for Italy. And then I shall have nothing further to do with politics.[141]

Another Italian expatriate was also adopting a politicized stance in his Dante criticism at this time. Foscolo's fellow exile Gabriele Rossetti published his *Comento analitico* on the *Commedia* shortly after Foscolo's *Discorso*, in 1826–7, and it, too, attracted Whig and radical sympathizers and subscribers.[142]

Other kinds of connection and interaction between Foscolo's appropriations of Dante and those of British expatriates in Italy deserve more investigation— particularly those involving the circle of Byron and the Shelleys. For example, Foscolo knew of another ambitious and eventually uncompleted Dante project that had recently been launched by a member of this circle, John Taaffe.[143] Taaffe's *Comment on the Divine Comedy of Dante Alighieri* was the first free-standing English commentary on the poem to be published, although in this form it covered only the first twelve cantos of the *Inferno*.[144] It had been recommended to publishers (and to Foscolo) by both Byron and Shelley, and John Murray issued the first and only volume in 1822.[145] It took a savaging from Cary, whose translation Taaffe had criticised, but received more moderate reviews in British and Italian journals, and several modern critics, from Toynbee onwards, have recognized its value and importance, especially as an influence upon the second generation of British

[139] *EN* 9.1., 353, note b. On Rogers's Presbyterian background, see *ODNB*, s.v. 'Rogers, Samuel, poet (1763–1855)', and on Taylor (who was also publishing on Dante in 1825), see *DEL* 2. 439–41, Lindon 1987: 91–112, and *ODNB*, s.v. 'Taylor, Edgar (1793–1839), lawyer and author'. For important discussion of the Nonconformist contexts, I am much indebted to a paper on 'Foscolo e l'influsso del dantismo inglese', given by Dr Andrea Campana of the University of Bologna at the conference on *Foscolo critico* at Gargnano del Garda on 25 September 2012; see also Campana 2014.

[140] Taylor subsequently helped Foscolo to negotiate new terms for the completion of the *Commedia* edition with Pickering early in 1827; see Lindon 1987: 67.

[141] Letter from Foscolo to Taylor on 5 Sept. 1826, in Foscolo (1850–), 8 (*Epistolario* 3), no. 652, p. 216.

[142] See Milbank 1998: 121 and nn. 16–17. On Rossetti's commentary, see *DEL* 1. 491–3, 629–30; and on his later work on Dante and 'the Antipapal Spirit', see *DEL* 2. 446 and Caesar 1989: 501–15. See also Tissoni 1993: 111–13, who notes the convergence between Rossetti's radicalism and the 'favourable Anglo-Saxon environment' (my translation, p. 112).

[143] On Taaffe's background and role in Byron's and Shelley's Pisan circle, see Cline 1952: 14–25 and (on his *Comment*) 31–3, 56–8, 68–9, 148–9, 161, 164.

[144] Substantial annotation had also accompanied the translations of Boyd (1802) and Cary (1814 onwards). The 1814 edition of Cary's translation carried over 150 pages of notes (see Dante 1994: xxx).

[145] See e.g. Byron's letter to Murray from Pisa on 22 Jan. 1822, suggesting Foscolo as an adviser about Taaffe's Dante project (*BLJ* 9. 90).

Romantics.[146] Murray failed to send Foscolo a copy of Taaffe's *Comment*, as had been intended;[147] nonetheless, the *Discorso sul testo* takes account of it early on. In section XX, without naming Taaffe, Foscolo pays tribute to the labours of this 'most learned Englishman' (*dottissimo Inglese*), recognizing the value of his archival and historical work in Italy, whilst taking issue with some of his conclusions and regretting Taaffe's 'prolixity'—perhaps unfairly, in view of his own work's comparable length.[148]

The extent of actual (direct or indirect) conversations about Dante between the Italian exile in London and the British expatriate Romantics in Italy also deserves some attention. It seems very likely that, for example, Byron and the Shelleys would have had access to Foscolo's 1818 articles in the *Edinburgh Review*, and they clearly knew texts such as *Dei Sepolcri* and *Ultime lettere di Jacopo Ortis*, along with the freight of Dantean allusions that they carried.[149] Conversely, Foscolo knew Byron's work well, and his assessment of it has been described as 'among the most detailed and explicit writing on a British author to emerge from [his] . . . letters'.[150] Byron's uneasy relationship at a distance from his Italian contemporary is vividly documented in his letters, which show him to have known that Foscolo was one of the 'back shop synod' of critics at Murray's who had found his *Prophecy of Dante* (1819) 'very grand' but had 'not so much admired' his translation of 'Fanny of Rimini' (*Inferno* 5, also completed in 1819).[151]

It has recently come to light that, not long after his judgements on Byron, Foscolo also advised Murray about another important—and Dantean—work by a leading member of the Byron–Shelley 'circle'. In the summer of 1822 Mary Shelley's father, William Godwin, was attempting to interest publishers in her recently completed historical novel *Valperga*, set in fourteenth-century Tuscany.[152] Early in August that year Godwin approached Murray, who then sought Foscolo's advice.[153] Foscolo responded to Murray promptly but rather

---

[146] See esp.: *DEL* 2. 340–8; Ellis 1983: 30, 51, and 252 n. 22 (concurring with Taaffe's critique of Cary); Caesar 1989: 83 n. 91; and Pite 1994: 46–8 (on the influence of the *Comment*) and 55 n. 41 (on Taaffe's praise of Flaxman's illustrations).

[147] See Braida 2004: 90 and Cline 1952: 213–22.

[148] *EN* 9.1: 204–6. Foscolo had earlier given attention to Taaffe's comments on Dante's *Vita nuova* in his essay on the 'third period' of Italian literature, describing the *letterato inglese* in similar terms; see *EN* 11: 139–40.

[149] See e.g. Byron's letter to Murray of 1819 (below, n. 151). Mary Shelley was reading *Ortis* late in 1821; see Sunstein 1989: 205.

[150] Parmegiani 2011: 128.

[151] On the relationship in general, see Vincent 1949: 1–3 and more recently Parmegiani 2011: 122–8. Foscolo also features in some of the letters between Murray and Byron: e.g. 19 Mar. 1819 (Murray quoting Foscolo on the need for Byron to spend time on a 'Subject worthy of you'), and Byron's predictably tart response from Venice on 6 April 1819: 'why does not *he* [Foscolo] do something more than the letters of Ortis—and a tragedy—and pamphlets . . . ?' (*BLJ* 6. 105). Byron's view of Foscolo was usually more respectful; see e.g. letters of 1820 in *BLJ* 7. 54, 194–5, 201, 205, 238. On Foscolo's judgement of Byron's Dantean poems, see Murray's letter of April 1820 and Byron's reference to Murray's 'synod' in a letter of May 1820 (to Thomas Moore).

[152] See Shelley 1996: xii–xiii and xvii, n. 16. The novel was eventually published in February 1823, not by Murray but by Whittaker (p. xiii).

[153] He received the manuscript of *Castruccio* (then the novel's title) on 8 August; *Ep.* 7: 79.

cautiously, since he was basing his report mainly on the first of *Valperga*'s three books and did not know who the novelist was—although he rightly guessed he was reading 'a she-Author'.[154] In hedging his judgement, he also freely acknowledged a lack of sympathy with the novel's (historical) genre, with that genre's prime exponent (Walter Scott), and with the kind of 'metaphysical' historians (notably Sismondi) on whose work and ideas Shelley drew.[155]

Foscolo's 'mini-treatise on the historical novel'[156] shows that he had paid quite careful attention to Shelley's treatment of sources in her portrayal of the age of Dante. Although he belittles the range of Shelley's reading in contemporary history and in 'the old Italian chronicles', Foscolo could not have failed to notice her frequent Dantean references and allusions. *Valperga* opens with a Sismondian evocation of a European dawn, heralded by Dante as a 'revolutionary' shaper of language, very much akin to Percy Shelley's simultaneous view of the poet as a 'Lucifer', the 'first awakener of entranced Europe', who 'created a language . . . out of inharmonious barbarisms'.[157] Dante, as poet of 'liberty' and of 'that clash and struggle which awaken the energies of our nature' (another Sismondian concept), is also, at key points in Book I, explicitly identified with the ethos of the novel's optimistic but doomed heroine, Euthanasia.[158] Foscolo (in 1822 at least) did not read more than 'several pages at random' of *Valperga*'s second and third volumes, so he may not have encountered the darker Dante evoked later on by Euthanasia's pessimistic counterpart: the ironically named Beatrice.[159]

What the surviving members of the Shelley and Byron circle—and other English readers—made of the Dante that Foscolo went on to portray in 1825 would be a further chapter in the history of the Italian exile's *fortuna* in Britain. Leigh Hunt, a member of the 'Pisa circle' and author of *The Story of Rimini* (1816), not only owned a copy of the *Discorso* but also annotated it.[160] That copy is now in the Brewer–Leigh Hunt Collection at the University of Iowa, and the extent of Hunt's dialogue there with both Foscolo and Dante remains to be explored.[161]

A more indirect effect of Foscolo's Dante project upon the British public seems to have been mediated through his legacy to the newer, politically minded generation of Italian exiles such as Antonio Panizzi and Giuseppe Mazzini. Panizzi, as we

---

[154] Foscolo to Murray, 11 Aug. 1822, in *Ep.* 7: 80–3. The letter is discussed in detail by Parmegiani 2011: 121–2; it does not yet seem to have been considered by the Shelley scholars who have written on *Valperga*.

[155] Sismondi 1819 deals with Dante in vol. 4, introducing him as the poet 'qui n'a pas cessé d'échauffer et d'inspirer tous les homes de génie de sa nation' (p. 184).

[156] Parmegiani 2011: 121.

[157] Shelley 1997: 7, and compare Shelley, *A Defence of Poetry*, e.g. in *DEL* 2. 207.

[158] Shelley 1997: xxi (on Sismondi and the 'convulsions of civil war'), 109, 144, and 148. On Mary Shelley and Dante, see De Palacio 1969: 46–61, Havely 1999, and Saglia 2012: 196–200.

[159] For Beatrice's references to Dante's Ugolino and the last line of the inscription over Hell's gate in *Inf.* 3. 9, see Shelley 1997: 328 and 330. For the sardonic mercenary Benedetto Pepi's allusions to Dante's attacks on Florentine legislators (*Purg.* 6. 125–6 and 143–7), see Shelley 1997: 69 and 71–2, and Havely 1999: 35–6.

[160] See Burke 1933:105, and Eberle-Sinatra 2005: 134 (and n. 30).

[161] University of Iowa, Brewer-Leigh Hunt Collection 858 D 192 Ffo.

have seen, was a keen and loyal supporter of his mentor's work on Dante: in the *Westminster Review* for January 1827 he hailed the *Discorso* and the projected edition as a 'work...superior to all others' and one which 'entitles [Foscolo] to the gratitude of Italy'.[162] After Foscolo's death he continued his and Pickering's project for the series of 'Italian Classic Poetry' by publishing the Orlando romances by Boiardo and Ariosto in nine volumes (1830–4).[163] No further volumes appeared, however, and it was only after having 'lain for fifteen years in the dust of the English publisher's bookshelves' that Foscolo's Dante papers were bought from Pickering (for £400) by an Italian bookseller, Pietro Rolandi,[164] who then enabled the edition of Dante to be completed by Giuseppe Mazzini.

Mazzini did not put his name to any part of the *Commedia di Dante Allighieri* [sic] *illustrata da Ugo Foscolo* which was published by Rolandi in four volumes.[165] The first two—comprising the *Discorso*, prefaced by Foscolo's address to the reader, and the *Inferno*—came out in 1842; whilst *Purgatorio* and *Paradiso*, with a final volume of chronological, critical, and lexical material, appeared the following year. Readers expecting extensive commentary by Foscolo (or Mazzini) on the poetry of the *Commedia* would probably have been disappointed by this edition, whose text is accompanied for the most part by a limited set of variant readings which become thinner from the *Purgatorio* onwards. Mazzini's ultimate goal, as set out in his preface, was a patriotic one: to imagine an ideal edition of Dante which would serve as a 'monument to the genius of the [Italian] nation' and be prefaced by 'a volume of criticism which will form a kind of ante-room to the temple where Dante will be venerated, and that volume will contain the contributions of Foscolo'.[166] His more immediate aim was to discharge a 'sacred debt for Italians' by providing a monument to Foscolo himself through a corrected edition of the *Discorso* and completion of the exile's 'final work'.[167]

Thus, as the signature to the preface ('UN' ITALIANO') suggests, the dialogue about Dante, Foscolo, and Italy here is in large measure directed towards compatriots and nationalists. Yet Mazzini's own presentation of Dante in his London journalism over the previous few years had shown that such a dialogue was also open to British sympathizers.[168] One of these, as we shall see in the next chapter, was William Ewart Gladstone, who was already reading Dante at this time and who

---

[162] *Westminster Review*, no. XIII, art. VIII, pp. 153–69, excerpted in *DEL* 2. 513–15; see also Lindon 1987: 49–50 (and n. 47) and 66 (and n. 5). He also seems to have been the author of the obituary for Foscolo printed in many London journals in September 1827 (Lindon 1987: 107 and n. 70). On Panizzi, see above pp. 142–3 (with nn. 94 and 97) and below, pp. 179 and 258.

[163] For details of the edition, see Keynes 1969: 50 (s.v. 'Ariosto').

[164] On Rolandi, see Vincent 1961, and Spaggiari 2006.

[165] On this edition and its reception, see *DEL* 2. 173, 623, and 682; also Caesar and Havely 2012: 115–16.

[166] Dante 1842–3: 1. xvi: 'un monumento dell' intelletto nazionale...un volume di critica che sarà quasi vestibolo al tempio ove Dante sarà venerato, e que[ll] volume conterrà pure le cose di Foscolo.'

[167] Dante 1842–3: 1. xi (on the many errors in Pickering's 1825 edition) and xix (on the *Discorso* as 'ultimo suo lavoro' and its publication as 'debito sacro per gl'italiani').

[168] For samples of his views on Dante in articles for the *Westminster Review* and other London journals from 1837 to 1844, see *DEL* 2: 623–7 and Caesar 1989: 552–61. On Wordsworth, Mazzini, and Italian nationalism, see Graver 2011: 33–5.

owned copies of Dantean works by Foscolo, including the 1825 *Discorso*.[169] In 1871, the year that saw the completion of Italian unification, Foscolo would eventually be reburied in the national pantheon of Santa Croce in Florence.[170] Meanwhile, for most of the century, as a sombre engraving on the first page of Mazzini's edition shows, he was still in the cemetery of Old Chiswick Church, *sulle sponde del Tamigi*, 'on the banks of the Thames', the river which, however—as Thomas Mathias had earlier intuited—was now beginning to 'respond to the music of the Arno'.

[169] Gladstone's copy of the *Discorso* (apparently with 'no annotations') is at St Deiniol's Library, as are his copies of Foscolo's *Ortis* (1817 edition), his tragedy *Ricciarda* (1820), and his *Essays on Petrarch* (1823).

[170] Vincent 1953: 208. On the monuments of S. Croce (including Dante's), see O'Connor 2008: 89–90 and 96–7.

6

Seeing the Seer: Victorian Visions

Dante and his work came to be ever more frequently and prominently visualized by artists, writers, and readers during the mid-nineteenth century.[1] Several contributors to that process—such as Carlyle, Browning, the Pre-Raphaelites, Eliot, Ruskin—have been given substantial critical attention.[2] So also has the wider relationship of the Victorian reception of Dante to 'the British nineteenth-century understanding of history, nationalism, aesthetics and gender'.[3] This chapter will take some account of those key figures and issues, but its main purpose will be to focus upon close engagements with Dante on the part of three other Victorian celebrities, in each case presenting some new evidence about how they saw this 'seer'.

FRANCESCA, FRANÇOISE, AND FANNY: FRANCES KEMBLE

> Seer of the triple realm invisible,
> When I behold that miserable twain,
> By Rimini's sudden sword of justice slain,
> Sweep through the howling hurricane of hell—
> Light seems to me to rest upon their gloom,
> More than upon this wretched earth above,
> Falls on the path of many a living love,
> Whose fate may envy their united doom.[4]

The picture in which the 'seer' (Dante) and the lovers of *Inferno* 5 are thus 'beheld' is by a Dutch painter working in Paris, Ary Scheffer (1795–1858). Scheffer worked on the subject at a number of points through his career, from the 1820s to around 1855.[5]

---

[1] For some of the relationships between the visual and the literary evidence, see: Poppi 1994: 82–93; Milbank 1998: chs. 6–8; Pieri 2007; Straub 2009: chs. 2–4; Harrison and Newall 2010: 42–61; and Camilletti 2011: 120–4.

[2] On Carlyle's Dante, see Campbell 2000; on Browning and the Pre-Raphaelites, Ellis 1983: 66–139; on George Eliot, Thompson 1991 and 2003; on Ruskin, Milbank 2011.

[3] See esp. Milbank 1998 (the quotation is from its dustjacket) and more recently the work on the nineteenth-century Beatrice by Camilletti 2005 and Straub 2009.

[4] Frances Anne Kemble, *Poems* (Boston: Ticknor & Fields, 1859), reprinted with the title ON A PICTURE OF PAOLO AND FRANCESCA in *Poems by Frances Anne Kemble* (London: Moxon, 1866).

[5] See Ewals 1980: 11.

The eagerness of 'Dante' to uncover what lay at 'the very root' (*la prima radice*) of Francesca's passion had already been reflected in some of the medieval illustrations of *Inferno* 5.[6] The pilgrim's powerful response to Francesca's story had been dramatized by major eighteenth- and early nineteenth-century artists such as Fuseli, Flaxman, Koch, Ingres, and Blake; and Scheffer's portrayal of the scene came to be his most successful work.[7] Scheffer's version of 1835 followed several experiments in arranging the composition's four figures, and its main effect is to place the woman in the most prominent position (see Fig. 6, on p. 163). Against a dark background, peopled only by the shadowy figures of Dante and Virgil, the light falls on the most dynamic element in the composition: the upward swooping body of Francesca, with Paolo fixed, as if crucified, in her arms. Her dark hair flows along the line of her ascent, giving the only indication of the Second Circle's *bufera infernal*, and the pallor of her flesh-tones recalls the 'pale lips' and 'pale forms' that Keats had described floating in the 'melancholy storm' of Dante's second circle.[8]

The poem responding to this image of Francesca was by the actor and author Frances Anne (Fanny) Kemble (1809–93), and its first half—a kind of sonnet octave—is quoted above. Its second half—reflecting on the significance of Dante's and Scheffer's figures for lovers 'wandering in this world'—will return to view later on. Meanwhile, the forms in which Kemble, from a young age, encountered the *Commedia*, her comments and conversation about her reading, as well as her earlier re-enactments of her namesake Francesca, will take centre-stage.

This post-Romantic reader of Dante was for most of her long life very much in the public eye. Niece of two great Shakespearean actors, John Philip Kemble and Sarah Siddons, and daughter of the actor-manager of Covent Garden, Charles Kemble, Frances Kemble became a celebrity early in life.[9] Whilst not yet 20, her performance as Juliet at her father's theatre in 1829 made her an instant star.[10] During a transatlantic tour in 1832 she met a scion of the Philadelphia gentry whom she married in 1834 and from whom she was eventually divorced in 1848. Her friends included a number of major writers, such as Arthur Hallam, John Sterling, Alfred Tennyson, Anna Jameson, and Elizabeth Barrett.[11] She was herself a prolific writer, producing seven volumes of memoirs, two plays, two novels, two collections of poems, an Italian travel-book, and a *Journal of Residence on a Georgia*

---

[6] e.g. in Florence, Riccardiana 1035, f. 10ᵛ, Paris, BNF cod. ital. 2017, f. 71ᵛ, London, BL Yates Thompson 36, f. 10ʳ; reproduced in BMS 2. 88b, 89c, and 91b.

[7] See Nassar 1994: 92–5 and Poppi 1994: nos. 13, 14, and 16. On Francesca in painting and illustration *c.*1790–1840, see Havely 2007*b*.

[8] Keats, sonnet 'As Hermes once . . .' composed *c.*16 April 1819, first published in *The Indicator* 28 June 1820; see *DEL* 2. 248 and n. 1.

[9] See *ODNB*, s.v. 'Kemble [*married name* Butler], Frances Anne [Fanny] (1809–1893), actress and author'; also Ransome (ed.) 1978, Furnas 1982, and Jenkins 2005.

[10] Jenkins 2005: 203–11.

[11] For example Hallam's letters refer to 'the divine Fanny' (as Juliet), 'a person of genius', whose acting was 'magnificent' as Julia in Sheridan Knowles's *The Hunchback* (written for her); see Kolb (ed.) 1981: 348, 472, 549, 563, 569, 601. On Hallam, see below, pp. 158 with n. 26 and 179–180 with n. 135.

Plantation, not published until 1863 but important as a record of slavery in the South during the 1830s.[12]

Kemble's own memoirs provide much of the initial evidence about her responses to Dante and the forms in which she encountered his work. Her *Record of a Girlhood* was published in 1878 but is based on letters written long before, and makes it possible to construct a context for her early reading. Her mother was French and she received a multilingual education. In 1821–4, from the age of 11 to 14, she attended a school in Paris, where amongst other subjects she learned Latin, some Greek, and a considerable amount of Italian. Her Italian teacher was the exile Niccolo Giosafatte Biagioli, who provided a dramatic encounter with the language and with Dante:

Besides the studies pursued by the whole school under the tuition of Mademoiselle Descuillès, we had special masters from whom we took lessons in special branches of knowledge.

Of these, by far the most interesting to me, both in himself and in the subject of his teachings, was my Italian master, Biagioli.

He was a political exile, of about the same date as his remarkable contemporary, Ugo Foscolo; his high forehead, from which his hair fell back in a long grizzled curtain, his wild, melancholy eyes, and the severe and sad expression of his face, impressed me with some awe and much pity. He was at that time one of the latest of the long tribe of commentators on Dante's 'Divina Commedia.' I do not believe his commentary ranks high among the innumerable similar works on the great Italian poem; but in violence of abuse and scornful contempt of all but his own glosses, he yields to none of his fellow labourers in that vast and tangled poetical, historical, biographical, philosophical, theological and metaphysical jungle. Dante was his spiritual consolation, his intellectual delight, and indeed his daily bread; for out of that tremendous horn-book he taught me to stammer the divine Italian language, and illustrated every lesson from the simplest rule of its syntax to its exceedingly complex and artificially constructed prosody, out of that sublime, grotesque and altogether wonderful poem. My mother has told me that she attributed her incapacity for relishing Milton to the fact of 'Paradise Lost' having been used as a lesson book out of which she was made to learn English—a circumstance which made it for ever 'Paradise *Lost*' to her. I do not know why or how I escaped a similar misfortune in my school study of Dante, but luckily I did so, probably being carried over the steep and stony way with comparative ease by the help of my teacher's vivid enthusiasm. I have forgotten my Italian grammar, rules of syntax and rules of prosody alike, but I read and re-read the 'Divina Commedia' with ever increasing amazement and admiration. Setting aside all its weightier claims to the high place it holds among the finest achievements of the human genius, I know of no poem in any language in which so many single lines and detached passages can be found of equal descriptive force, picturesque beauty, and delightful melody of sound; the latter virtue may lie, perhaps, as much in the instrument itself as in the master hand that touched it,—the Italian tongue, the resonance and vibrating power of which is quite as peculiar as its liquid softness.[13]

Like 'his remarkable contemporary, Ugo Foscolo', Biagioli was one of a number of Italian political exiles who, early in the century, were promoting Dante's work

---

[12] Listed in Jenkins 2005: 480–1.
[13] Kemble 1878: 1. 95–6. Part of this passage is also reprinted in *DEL* 2. 425.

abroad.[14] His edition of the *Commedia* had been published shortly before he taught the adolescent Kemble in the early 1820s and was known to Foscolo.[15] Its list of subscribers included a number of British names, and one of them— 'KEMBLE (J.)'—was probably Fanny's uncle, the Shakespearean actor (and amateur scholar), John Philip Kemble, who had retired from the stage in 1817.[16] Biagioli saw it as part of his task to educate such readers out of their limited fascination with the more sensational episodes in the *Inferno*; thus he begins his commentary on the Francesca episode by remarking that

questo il tanto famoso episodio . . . di cui più che gl'Italiani, sono gli Esteri ammiratori, non già perchè ne sentano meglio di noi le bellezze, ma perchè basta a loro studiar questo e quell'altro d'Ugolino, per conoscere a fondo il Poeta, e gracchiarne poi a lor voglia.

this is that well known episode . . . which is admired more by foreigners than by Italians, not because they appreciate its beauties more keenly than we, but because it is enough for them to study this and the other one of Ugolino, in order to understand the Poet fully and then cackle about him to their hearts' content.[17]

Biagioli's scathing remarks on the inadequacies of foreigners' reading are worth considering in relation to some of the isolated Romantic responses to Francesca and Ugolino, and perhaps to Carlyle's later and not entirely successful attempt to escape 'our general Byronism of taste' by looking beyond the *Inferno*.[18]

Frances Kemble continued to be fascinated by 'that miserable twain', although her reading of the *Commedia* was by no means entirely fixated on her namesake Francesca. Her adolescent encounter with her 'Italian master' and the text he had edited is—as presented in the *Record of a Girlhood*—a highly charged episode and one that itself recalls the scene of fatal reading in *Inferno* 5. She responds to Biagioli's physical appearance with 'some awe and much pity', and is transported through the poem by 'my teacher's vivid enthusiasm'. Noticeable here, too, is the physicality of her response to 'the resonance and vibrating power' of 'the Italian tongue' and 'its liquid softness'. That response owes something to the Romantic perceptions of and interest in the sound of the 'soft, Southern' language.[19] It also demonstrates a performer's instinct for absorbing and reproducing other tongues— an instinct that (as she would also recall) was shared with her sister, the singer Adelaide Kemble:

My sister and myself . . . had remarkable facility in speaking foreign languages with the accent and tune (if I may use the expression) peculiar to each; a faculty which seems to me less the result of early training and habit, than of some particular construction of ear and

---

[14] See above, pp. 137–9.

[15] On Biagioli's edition and commentary of 1818–19 and his acquaintance with Foscolo, see above, pp. 139–40.

[16] See *ODNB*, s.v. 'Kemble, John Philip (1757–1823), actor'. On his literary interests, see Jenkins 2005: 31.

[17] Dante 1818–19: 1. 91, note on *Inf.* 5. 75.

[18] In his 1840 *Lectures on Heroes* ('The Hero as Poet'); see *DEL* 2. 504–5.

[19] On such views of Italian, see esp. Webb 2011*b*.

throat favourable for receiving and repeating these sounds; a musical organization and mimetic faculty; a sort of mocking-bird speciality . . . [20]

Kemble's sensual reading of Dante during her Parisian schooldays combined with a heady mix of romantic medievalism and Byronism. One of her more glamorous teachers—the Mme Descuillès referred to in the passage quoted above—used to read her pupils chivalric French ballads as they embroidered on Saturday mornings.[21] Fanny learned by heart at least two of these, and she also missed Walter Scott's poetry so acutely while in Paris that she wrote out *Marmion* and *The Lay of the Last Minstrel* from memory.[22] An even more powerful stimulus to her imagination was her encounter with the poetry of Byron, the first of whose poems to come her way was the tragic narrative of adulterous and incestuous passion, *Parisina* (published in 1816). Like Byron's other poems of that period (such as the *Corsair* and *The Siege of Corinth*), *Parisina* was influenced by Dante's story of Francesca's transgressive passion.[23] Kemble describes how, enthralled by the poem's evocative opening lines, she took what she calls 'the terrible volume' into the dormitory of Mrs Rowden's academy for girls. However, the panic of a companion on hearing that she had 'a volume of Lord Byron under [her] pillow' caused

such a sympathy of fear that I jumped out of bed and thrust the fatal poems into the bowels of a straw *paillasse* on an empty bed and returned to my own to remain awake nearly all night. My study of Byron went no further then . . . I then read no more of that wonderful poetry which in my after days . . . always affected me like an evil potion taken into my blood.[24]

Her account recalls the interrupted reading of another sweetly pernicious text: Francesca's tale of Lancelot. 'My study of Byron went no further then . . . I read no more' evokes the moment when the 'potion' enters the bloodstream of Dante's literary lovers: 'Quel giorno più non vi legemmo avante' ('All that day we read no further there').[25]

   Byron would continue to inform Frances Kemble's reading of *Inferno* 5, but a much wider reading of Dante is evident from her conversations and contacts at the time when her theatrical career was taking shape. Through her scholarly brother John Mitchell Kemble she became acquainted with several of his Cambridge Italianate friends and fellow members of the 'Apostles' society, notably Alfred Tennyson and Arthur Hallam, both of whom attended the Sunday-evening gatherings at the Kemble household in the late 1820s. Hallam's interest in Dante is well attested, and his admiration for 'the divine Fanny' was intensified by their shared enthusiasm for the *Commedia*.[26]

---

[20] Kemble 1878: 1. 83.   [21] Kemble 1878: 1. 84–8.   [22] Kemble 1878: 1. 90.
[23] On *Parisina* and *Inf.* 5, see Ellis 1983: 39; on Byron and Francesca, see Beaty 1960; also Havely 1995: 107 and nn. 10–11.
[24] Kemble 1878: 1. 93.   [25] *Inf.* 5. 138.
[26] See above, p. 155, n. 11, and Jenkins 2005: 232–42 (esp. 238 and n.). On Hallam's interest in Dante, see: *DEL* 2. 416–24; Milbank 1998: 104–5 and 186; Jenkins 2005: 238: and Straub 2009: 92–7.

Such conversations also involved several men in her life who were less worthy objects of her attention. The first of them was one Augustus Craven, an attractive but feckless army officer and diplomat with whom she formed an intense but short-lived relationship in 1831, shortly after she had established herself as a star of the London stage.[27] Kemble's memoirs recall occasions on which they discussed Dante, along with Italy and Shakespeare.[28] Dante—if not Fanny—was to remain an abiding interest for Craven: during his retirement in Rome during the 1860s 'he was always ready to speak of Dante, of whose life and work he was an accomplished student', preferring 'to take Dante's literal meaning wherever possible, and to avoid the political and, indeed prophetic senses frequently attributed to his words'.[29]

The demise of the relationship with Craven was signalled by a 'long and edifying talk' with Kemble's loyal aunt, Adelaide Decamp, about the difficulty of combining a theatrical career with marriage. This conversation, as it appears in *Record of a Girlhood*, ends with Frances recognizing the intractability of the problem and turning to the *Inferno* for consolation:

So that it seems I have fortune and fame (such as it is)—positive real advantages, which I cannot give with myself, and which I cease to own when I give myself away, which certainly makes my marrying any one or any one marrying me rather a solemn consideration; for I lose everything, and my marryee gains nothing in a worldly point of view—says she—and it's incontrovertible and not pleasant. So I took up Dante, and read about devils boiled in pitch, which refreshed my imagination and cheered my spirits very much . . .[30]

The allusion here is to the episode at the end of the 'Malebranche' cantos (*Inferno* 21–2), where the devils tormenting the damned souls in a river of pitch find themselves stuck in the same *bogliente stagno* ('boiling pool').[31] Dante introduces the vivid and theatrical episode to the reader as a novel 'game' or 'performance' (*nuovo ludo*, 118), and it obviously held a grim appeal for this talented female performer facing the constraints of the nineteenth-century marriage market.

A year afterwards, in August 1832, Frances and her father, the actor-manager Charles Kemble, undertook a transatlantic tour which they hoped would restore the family fortunes. During this trip she met her future husband, the Philadelphia gentleman Pierce Butler, 'the indolent heir to vast plantations in North Carolina and Georgia'.[32] Henry Berkeley, a would-be journalist with aristocratic connections, was in New York when the Kembles arrived in that September, and wrote to Butler about Fanny. Berkeley—who had frequented the Covent Garden theatre when she was performing there—seems to have emerged somewhat the worse from an encounter with her in the New World, complaining that:

---

[27] For accounts of the affair, see Furnas 1982: 75–8 and Jenkins 2005: ch. 22.

[28] For example, a letter to her closest friend, Harriet St Leger, in Kemble 1878: 3. 35.

[29] Bishop 1894: vols. 1, p. 263 and 2, p. 195, where it is also recorded that Craven 'left in MS a careful translation of the "Vita Nuova"'.

[30] Kemble 1878: 3. 75–6. The date of the journal entry given there is 22 July 1831.

[31] *Inf.* 22. 141.   [32] *ODNB*; see pp. 155–6, above.

in conversation she is very free but highly educated and accomplished, rather too much so for my way of thinking...because she puts you out of countenance by cursed apt quotations...from horrible old Writers, and if you shew any French, kills you with Racine, if any Italian, knocks you down with Dante...Rather blue!![33]

Pierce Butler does not seem to have been unduly daunted, since a few days later he visited the Kembles on their arrival in Philadelphia.[34] Soon after that, Kemble's journal for 15 October shows her turning to Dante in the midst of hectic preparations for a performance: 'Went and ordered a dress...Came home, put things out for the theatre, practised an hour, dined at three. After dinner read a canto in Dante: he is my admiration!'[35] She does not identify this 'canto', so there is no way of knowing what relevance it might have had to her situation, nor whether she might have been preparing another kind of performance—something, perhaps, with which to knock down the 'genteel youth' whom she had met two days earlier and whose 'pretty spoken' words would have sharply contrasted with those of the poet she admired.[36] Her marriage to Butler was not a success, and was dissolved in 1848. Kemble continued her career as a sought-after performer in public readings of Shakespeare, dividing her time mostly between Britain and the United States.[37] Many of her subsequent friendships had Italian origins and sometimes Dantean dimensions. Shortly before her final separation from Pierce Butler, she had turned to Italy itself and spent nearly a year in Rome, as the guest of her younger sister Adelaide, who had retired early from the operatic stage following her marriage to the wealthy Edward John Sartoris.[38] The final chapter of the book she wrote about her time there reported on the political scene in the papal city, following the election of the 'liberal' pope, Pius IX.[39] On a later visit to Rome she would meet other Italophiles (and readers of Dante), such as Elizabeth Barrett and Robert Browning.[40] Also in that circle, during the winter of 1853–4, was Adelaide Sartoris's young admirer Frederic Leighton, who at the time was working on the historical painting that would establish his reputation: *Cimabue's Madonna Carried in Procession through the Streets of Florence*—a theatrical scene in which Dante has a walk-on part, with his back to the viewer.[41] Kemble herself played a prominent role

---

[33] Letter of 3 Oct. 1832, in the Historical Society of Pennsylvania, Wister Family Collection, as cited in Jenkins 2005: 359.

[34] Ransome 1978: 75.   [35] Ransome 1978: 75–6.

[36] Ransome 1978: 75 (journal for 13 Oct. 1832).

[37] In 1850 Longfellow (who had already begun his translation of the *Commedia*) was an admiring host at Harvard (Ransome 1978: 218–19). Longfellow had begun translating the *Purgatorio* in 1843 and would complete it in 1853; see La Piana 1948: 97. Ralph Waldo Emerson was also struck by the 'abundance' of her character performance at the same Shakespeare reading (Jenkins 2005: 454).

[38] See *ODNB*, s.v. 'Kemble (*married name* Sartoris), Adelaide (1815–1879), singer and author'.

[39] *A Year of Consolation*, 2 vols. (London: Moxon, 1847). For details of this journey and the comments on Pius IX, see Ransome 1978: 185–95 and Furnas 1982: 288–301.

[40] Ransome 1978: 225–6; Furnas 1982: 366–7. On Barrett and Dante, see Milbank 1998: 63–73; and on Browning and Dante, see Ellis 1983: ch. 3.

[41] On Leighton, his friendship with Adelaide Sartoris (whose head and shoulders he compared with Dante's) and with Frances Kemble, see Ormond 1975: 20–2 and pl. 50, and Furnas 1982: 368. For his *Cimabue's Madonna*, see ibid., ch. 4 and pls 34–5; and on its relevance to Dante's comments on Cimabue and the transience of artistic fame in *Purg.*11. 94–6, see Milbank 1998: 54–5. The painting, which Leighton had begun to work on at Frankfurt in 1851, was 'enthusiastically received at the [Royal] academy exhibition of 1855, with rapturous accounts of it in the newspapers and periodicals'

in this expatriate circle, appearing 'upright and magnificent . . . in stately crimson edged with gold', to upstage Elizabeth Barrett, 'dim in her dusky gown'; and not surprisingly Leighton was keen for her to sit for him—not as Francesca but as Jezebel.[42] Twenty years later her presence remained impressive: following in Hallam's and Leighton's footsteps, it was another stage-struck writer, Henry James, who referred to her as 'the terrific Kemble', having first met her at Rome in the early 1870s.[43]

Two further examples from different points in her career may illustrate how Dante, and particularly Dante's Francesca, is performed in Frances Kemble's own writing. The first is her earliest and most successful play: the historical drama *Francis I.* Begun in 1826 when the author was 16, it centres on Françoise de Foix, Comtesse de Chateaubriand, who is betrothed to a friend of her brother but yields to the passion of the king, then decides that she is thus guilty of adultery and kills herself at the end of Act 4. When it was eventually staged, early in 1832, Charles Greville thought it 'an odd play for a girl of 17 to write', but it was admired by Kemble's Cambridge friends, including Arthur Hallam, and was published that year by John Murray.[44] A striking feature of the play is its exploration of the heroine's guilty conscience, showing signs of Francesca's influence, perhaps mediated through Kemble's reading of Byron. Thus, the poet Clement Marot describes how the reading of the king's love-letter affects the as-yet unfallen Françoise:

> . . . thus
> Stood the fair lady, till her eye was fain
> Begin the scroll again; and then, as though
> That moment comprehension woke in her,
> The blood forsook her cheeks; and straight ashamed
> Of its unnatural desertion, drew
> A crimson veil over her marble brows.[45]

Hesitation, the awakening of comprehension, and its visible physical effects combine as in Francesca's description of the lovers' guilty reading in *Inferno* 5:

> Per più fiate li occhi ci sospinse
> Quella lettura e scoloròcci il viso . . .

All that while what we read made our eyes turn from the text, our colour go and come . . . [46]

Kemble's portrayal of the haunted and subsequently doomed Françoise may also reflect Byron's 'interest . . . in the writhings of the conscience that accepts its own

---

(*ODNB*, s.v. 'Leighton, Frederic, Baron Leighton (1830–1896), painter'). On his later *Dante in Exile* (exhibited 1864), see Ellis 1983: 55–6 and pl. 4.

[42] Annie Thackeray's description of Kemble in Rome, as cited in Furnas 1982: 367.

[43] At the end of a twenty-year friendship, James described her funeral as 'quite like the end of some reign or the fall of some empire' (Ransome 1978: 255).

[44] Kemble 1832. Greville's comment is in his *Memoirs*, ed. H. Reeve (London: Longmans Green, 1888), for 16 March 1832.

[45] Kemble 1832: 56 (Act 3, scene 1).   [46] *Inf.* 5. 130–1.

guiltiness' and in 'the Paolo and Francesca story as "a vision of judgment"'.[47] The 'potion' from the 'terrible volume' tasted in that Parisian dormitory a few years earlier may still be having its effect.

Early in the poem quoted at the start of this chapter, the reference to 'many a living love | whose fate may envy their united doom' (ll. 7–8) also suggests that Dante is being read not only in Scheffer's image (and in the light of Kemble's own experience), but once again through Byron's translations and appropriations. In his 1819–20 translation of *Inferno* 5 the lovers share a 'united doom', through which their 'evil fortune' is 'fufilled'—and in his letter to his half-sister Augusta later that year, Byron writes of Dante's 'unfortunate lovers' that, 'although they suffer—it is at least together'.[48]

In the second half of Kemble's poem, Scheffer's portrayal of Francesca and Paolo then moves Kemble to ponder the fate of living lovers:

> There be, who wandering in this world with heart
> Riveted to some other heart for ever,
> Past power of all eternity to sever,
> The current of this life still drives apart,
> Who, with strained eyes, and outstretched arms, and cry
> Of bitterest longing, come each other nigh,
> To look, to love, and to be swept asunder,
> The breathless greeting of their agony
> Lost in the pitiless world-storm's ceaseless thunder.

The thought and the syntax here seem to be floundering in repetitions. The poem had begun with what might have been a quite lucid octave for a sonnet, but here swells into a circuitous hyper-sestet which perhaps justifies Browning's earlier judgement of Kemble's verse as 'mournfully mediocre'.[49] Even so, its very confusion seems to demonstrate the impact of Scheffer's image and Dante's text upon a High Victorian celebrity.[50]

Around the same time as Kemble was composing her Dantean poem, another figure who would become even more prominent in late Victorian culture was also powerfully affected by the same painting. A version of Scheffer's *Francesca* (Fig. 6) was exhibited at the Pall Mall Gallery, London, in 1854, where George Eliot saw it during a bout of low spirits which 'pictures and Nature' (and proof-reading her translation of Feuerbach) seem to have relieved:

On Monday [15 May 1854] I went to look at the French pictures among which is that unforgettable Francesca di [*sic*] Rimini of Ary Scheffer's. It surpasses one's expectations from

---

[47] Ellis 1983: 40. See also Kemble 1832: 97–8 and 108.

[48] Byron, letter of 17 May 1819, in *BLJ* 6. 129. Kemble would not have read this letter, but would have been aware of Byron's other appropriations of Francesca, including his translation of *Inferno* 5. 97–142, which had been available, for instance, in vol. 12 of the 1832 edition of Byron's *Works*; see also above, p. 158.

[49] Robert Browning to Elizabeth Barrett, 2 Aug. 1846, cited in Jenkins 2005: 453.

[50] Scheffer's version also seems to have influenced Gustave Doré's portrayals of the lovers in his 1861 engravings; see Nassar 1994: 99; other examples in Poppi 1994: 109 (18–19).

Fig. 6. Ary Scheffer, *Paolo and Francesca* (1835), © by kind permission of the Trustees of the Wallace Collection, London

the engraving. I could look at it for hours. There is nothing at the Royal Acad[emy] to affect one in the same way.[51]

The turbulence of Eliot's own personal life at this time (a few weeks before she left for Germany with George Henry Lewes) may perhaps underlie this response, but the Francesca myth and Scheffer's depiction of the episode may also have had some longer-term effects upon her work.

Despite the amount of critical attention that George Eliot's responses to Dante have received, the significance of her visual encounter with 'that unforgettable Francesca' does not yet seem to have been considered. Reading of Dante has been shown to inform Eliot's sense of history, identity, moral realism, and nationality in her mature work, from *Romola* onwards. Of episodes in the *Inferno*, that of Ugolino is alluded to at critical moments late in the action of several novels: initially in *The Mill on the Floss* (1860), then in *Romola* (1863) and *Felix Holt* (1866).[52] With its prologue travelling through an infernal landscape, culminating in an allusion to the Wood of the Suicides in *Inferno* 13, *Felix Holt* also proposes a wider Dantean framework for its portrayal of family, memory, and history. As several readers have recognized, this extends to the central tragic figure of Mrs

---

[51] George Eliot, to Sara Sophia Hennell, 17 May 1854, in Haight 1954: 2. 155. On her reading of Dante around this time, see Thompson 2003: 199.

[52] See Thompson 2003: 199–200 (with n. 4), and 202–3 (with n. 1); and 1991: 561–2.

Transome, who, as a victim of her reading—tormented by memory, and bound by secrecy to her former lover—directly recalls Dante's Francesca.[53] Perhaps prompted by Carlyle's impression of the *Purgatorio* as the 'noble embodiment of a noble thought' and her reading of it in 1862–3, Eliot subsequently draws upon the second part of the *Commedia* to map the progressions of other characters, not only in *Felix Holt* but also in *Middlemarch* (1871–2), and especially in the later stages of *Daniel Deronda* (1876).[54]

It may be significant that in Eliot's last novel the voice of Francesca (mediated through Rossini's setting of her words) is heard only at a redemptive moment, when Deronda rescues his bride-to-be.[55] That episode in *Daniel Deronda* could be seen as a deliberate reversal of the predicament in which Eliot had earlier placed Maggie Tulliver, the heroine of *The Mill on the Floss* (1860). In the third chapter of Book 6 ('The Great Temptation'), Maggie's imagination moves towards a passion that will lead her to be 'borne along by the tide': 'It was not that she thought distinctly of Mr. Stephen Guest . . . it was rather that she felt the half-remote presence of a world of love and beauty and delight, made up of vague mingled images from all the poetry and romance she had ever read . . .' In the previous chapter Stephen has attracted Maggie with his account of a book; here 'poetry and romance' have the effect of 'rousing and exalting' her thoughts, and, as with Francesca, reading foreshadows her eventual 'fall'.[56]

Francesca as problematic reader, 'fallen woman', wronged victim, drama queen, continued to play a part in nineteenth-century British culture in its appropriation of Dante and in what has been called 'the Victorian fate of tragedy'.[57] Throughout the century the light of the stage continued to shine on Frances Kemble's 'miserable twain' in a number of operas and plays.[58] Stephen Phillips's verse drama *Paolo and Francesca: A Tragedy in Four Acts* was published in 1889, and in its much-delayed but highly successful production at the St James's Theatre (1902), the Juliet-like Francesca offered a role that Kemble herself, sixty years or so earlier, might have played.[59] In painting, too, the scenes of passion from *Inferno* 5 that had preoccupied Ingres and Scheffer continued to attract Victorian artists. Around the time when Eliot's *The Mill on the Floss* was published and Gustave Doré's engravings were appearing in Paris and London, Frederic Leighton was working on a dramatic version of Paolo and Francesca (exhibited at the Royal Academy in 1861) that

[53] See Thompson 1991: 554–8 (554 notes Eliot's direct reference to *Inferno* 5) and Milbank 1998: 89–90.

[54] For Carlyle's views on Purgatory, see *DEL* 2. 491 and 504–5. On *Purgatorio* in the later Eliot novels, see Thompson 1991: 559–60; Milbank 1998: 96; Thompson 2003: 203–5 and 215–19.

[55] See the reading of this episode in Milbank 1998: 92.

[56] Comparison with the appropriation of the Francesca episode in *Daniel Deronda* is instructive: Prof. Barbara Hardy notes that 'GE (interestingly) criticises Maggie's romantic susceptibility and not Daniel's' (personal communication).

[57] Milbank 1998: ch. 8. On the variety of nineteenth-century versions of the Francesca episode, see also Havely 2007*b* and below, p. 168 and n. 80.

[58] See Poppi 1994: 39–44 and (on plays) Cooper 2007: 26–8.

[59] See Milbank 1998: 150–1 and Cooper 2007: 32. For Max Beerbohm's view of the play as 'very delicate, very smooth, wholly derivative', see *ODNB*, s.v. 'Phillips, Stephen (1864–1915), poet and playwright'.

shows the draped lovers locked in a swirling embrace, with a volume lying open on the ground.[60] Over about twenty years (*c*.1846–*c*.1867), Dante Gabriel Rossetti produced various studies and versions of the subject, and his treatment of it in the 1855 watercolour triptych was commissioned and much admired by Ruskin.[61] By that time the advent of another major 'Victorian muse', Beatrice, was well under way in painting and literature, and the relationship between these two nineteenth-century Dantean heroines forms part of the next group of Victorian visions.

LOSING GIANCIOTTO: WILLIAM DYCE'S FRANCESCA AND BEATRICE

During a life spanning less than sixty years (1806–64) the Scottish painter William Dyce became a variously eminent Victorian. His personal papers, now in his home city of Aberdeen, reveal a wide range of interests, personal contacts, and achievements, all packed into a relatively short career.[62] As well as being a leading portraitist, landscape artist, and pioneer in the revival of fresco painting, he was active and influential in art education and administration, publishing authoritatively on subjects as diverse as electricity, magnetism, and church music.[63]

Dyce's acquaintances and admirers included the German 'Nazarene' artists, such as Friedrich Overbeck and Peter Cornelius, whose work he came to know during his second visit to Rome in 1827.[64] Through his contacts with, for example, Holman Hunt, Millais, and Ruskin he was influential upon (and influenced by) the British Pre-Raphaelite school.[65] On religion and ecclesiology he corresponded with eminent Catholic and Anglo-Catholic churchmen such as Nicholas Wiseman and John Henry Newman; and in the 1850s he undertook a programme of frescos for Edward Pusey's Church of All Saints, Margaret Street, in London.[66] His most public contribution to Victorian medievalism was his group of Arthurian frescos based on Malory's *Morte d'Arthur* for the Palace of Westminster, on which he worked intermittently during the last fifteen years of his life.[67] And for much of his career he was in correspondence with and receiving patronage from an eminent politician, High Anglican, Italianist, and student of Dante: William Ewart Gladstone, whom Dyce first met in 1828.[68]

---

[60] Ormond 1975: cat. 65 (pl. 87 and p. 153).

[61] Surtees 1971: pls. 87–92 and cat. 75–75E.

[62] The Dyce Papers (typescript material related to his life, correspondence and writings, compiled by his son James Stirling Dyce) are in the archives of the Aberdeen Art Gallery and museums; microfiche copies are in the Archive and Special Collections of the Tate Gallery in London.

[63] See *ODNB*, s.v. 'Dyce, William (1806–64), painter and educationist'.

[64] On Dyce, the Nazarenes, and the question of influence, see Melville 2006: 16–21.

[65] See Pointon 1979: 33, 120–3, and 143–54.

[66] See Melville 2006: 39–40 and 47, and Pointon 1979: 128–36.

[67] On this project, which continued into the 1870s, see Andrews 1964: 81–5. Dyce completed five of the seven planned panels (Melville 2006: 71, under 1864).

[68] On Dyce and Gladstone, see Pointon 1979: 15, 55, 61–3, and 165–6; also below, pp. 177 and 179.

Subjects in Dyce's work are similarly wide-ranging. One of his most famous works, *Pegwell Bay* (1859) reflects High Victorian concerns with geology and astronomy, along with his own scientific interests; and apart from his many paintings on literary, religious, and historical themes, his portraits of women and children are highly regarded.[69] Much of his painting was strongly influenced by the Italian *quattrocento*, and in the autumn of 1845—a few years before he began the programme of frescos at Westminster—he travelled again to Rome and northern Italy, taking copious and detailed notes on the techniques of masters such as Raphael, Pinturicchio, Orcagna, Gozzoli, Ghirlandaio, Perugino, and others.[70] Their influence is evident in a number of his religious subjects—notably at least six versions of the Madonna and Child and a large number of Old and New Testament scenes. Apart from the Bible, his literary sources include Malory (who provided subjects for the Westminster frescos), Shakespeare, and, to a significant degree, Dante.

Dyce's earliest Dantean painting was produced soon after Ary Scheffer's *Francesca* had been exhibited in 1835.[71] In the spring of 1837—just before his departure from Scotland to take up the post of superintendent of the new School of Design in London—he submitted five of his paintings for the annual exhibition of the Royal Scottish Academy at Edinburgh.[72] The most prominent of these—as reflected in its relatively high asking price (£150) and in the artist's own correspondence—is the large oil-on-canvas version of *Francesca da Rimini*, now in the National Gallery of Scotland (Fig. 7).[73] Dyce seems to have been working under some pressure at the time: in February 1837, a month before the exhibition opened, he was writing as follows to the Secretary of the Academy—

Tuesday morning...

Will Thursday morning before eleven do for my pictures[?] I am terribly behind[,] having devoted all my forces to the picture of Francesca da Rimini[.]

　　　Yrs in great haste...[74]

and the hectic circumstances attending the production of the *Francesca* may indeed have something to do with its subsequent troubled history.[75]

A second, undated letter responds to a request for a catalogue entry for the 'Francesca' and follows the plea for time with one for more space: 'I send you a quotation of too great length I fear but I could not explain the matter more shortly ... I find not one in a hundred is acquainted with it ... the picture is pretty

<hr>

[69] e.g. Melville 2006: cat. 8, 10, 14, and 22.
[70] His notes on frescos in Italy are in the Dyce papers (see above, n. 62) 794/821–847/74.
[71] See above, pp. 154–5. For a British version of 1837, see below, n. 118.
[72] See McKay and Rinder 1917: 97A. The other works were two portraits of contemporaries and two character studies, one of them of a figure from Scott's *Guy Mannering* ('Dirk Hatteraik').
[73] The price was the second highest (among over 600 items) in the exhibition. The paintings shown included several of Italian scenes and figures and on literary subjects (e.g. Cervantes and Shakespeare). For details, see *The Exhibition of the Scottish Academy ... MDCCCXXXVII* (Edinburgh: H. & J. Pillans, 1837); Dyce's 'Francesca' is item 49 (p. 7).
[74] Royal Scottish Academy MS collection, 'Letters, Exhibition, Scottish Academy 1837', f. 39.
[75] On the evidence of Dyce's working methods in this case, see below, p. 173 and n. 104.

Fig. 7. William Dyce, *Francesca da Rimini* (1837), courtesy of the National Gallery of Scotland, Edinburgh

large & therefore may be allowed to take up more room in the catalogue.'[76] The result is the following descriptive entry in the 1837 catalogue:

Guido da Polenta engaged his daughter Francesca in marriage to Gianciotto, the eldest son of his enemy, the master of Rimini. Gianciotto, who was hideously deformed, foresaw that if he presented himself in person, he would be rejected by the lady. He resolved, therefore, to marry her by proxy, and sent as his representative his younger brother Paolo, surnamed the Beautiful. Francesca saw Paolo arrive and being deceived by one of her maids imagined she beheld her future husband. That mistake was the commencement of her passion; and it was not until after her arrival at Rimini that she was undeceived (*Boccaccio*). Paolo and she were shortly after assassinated by Gianciotto in a fit of jealousy. The occasion of this (which is the subject of the picture) is thus related by Francesca herself, in the 5th Canto of the Inferno.

> 'One day it chanced for pastime we were reading,
>   How Lancelot to love became a prey,
>   Alone we were—of evil thoughts unheeding.
> Our eyes oft met together as we read;
>   And from our cheeks the colour died away;
>   But at one passage we were vanquished.

[76] RSA MS collection, 'Letters, Exhibition, Scottish Academy 1837', f. 39.

And when we read of him so deep in love,
  Kissing at last the smile so long desired,
  Then he who from my side will ne'er remove,
My lips all trembling kissed ...
[...]
Hell's lowest depth—*Caina* dark and dim
  Awaits our murderer—...'[77]

Dyce's comment that 'not one in a hundred is acquainted with [the story of Francesca and Paolo]' is surprising, given the proliferation of fictional and visual reinventions of the subject at this time.[78] His account of the story follows a number of nineteenth-century versions—such as Leigh Hunt's 1816 *Story of Rimini*—in portraying Francesca as the unwitting victim of deception.[79] To this end, like Hunt and others, he explicitly invokes Boccaccio's novelistic version of the affair in his 1373 commentary on the *Commedia*. Boccaccio's account included minute circumstantial details of the lovers' murder by Francesca's jealous husband Gianciotto—a scene which Dyce was following many recent painters in portraying.[80] The Dantean passage is from two of Francesca's speeches in *Inferno* 5 (ll. 127–36 and 107), and the translation provided for the 1837 catalogue is the version in six-line stanzas (based on *terza rima*) which had been published by I. C. Wright four years earlier.[81] The artist is thus, it seems, employing the latest literary resources to 'acquaint' the viewer with the painting's subject.

In its present form—and its change of form will feature later on—Dyce's *Francesca* is now one of the most important works of British art in the National Gallery of Scotland at Edinburgh. It reflects a number of visual influences and traditions. In one view, it evokes 'the consciously pre-Raphaelesque quality of Ingres's painting' of the same subject (especially the version exhibited at the Paris Salon in 1819), and can be seen as 'almost as precocious as Ingres in admiring and assimilating the styles of the Italian and Northern primitives'.[82] It can be linked to some versions even earlier than Ingres, and it has been noticed that Dyce's 'attenuated, adolescent figure of Paolo, leaning sharply forward, represented in flat, linear silhouette probably owes something to the influence of Flaxman' (Fig. 8).[83]

A particularly striking and sinister feature of Dyce's version in its present form is the reduction of the husband Gianciotto's presence on the scene to a few fingers on

---

[77] *The Exhibition of the Scottish Academy ... MDCCCXXXVII* (Edinburgh: H. & J. Pillans, 1837), p. 7.
[78] I am grateful to Dr Helen Smailes, Senior Curator of British Art at the National Gallery of Scotland, for emphasizing the point and for other comments on this section.
[79] See above, p. 164 (with n. 57) and Milbank 1998: 151. For a lively survey of Francesca's nineteenth-century transition from wronged innocent to *femme fatale* (oddly omitting Dyce in the former category), see Farrell 1999.
[80] See Havely 2007*b*: 96–9. The circumstances of the murder are dwelt upon in the *Esposizioni sopra la Comedia di Dante*; see Boccaccio 1965: 315–17. On the evolution of the story between Dante and Boccaccio, see *DE* 410B. For versions of the scene before Dyce, see below, pp. 169–71.
[81] Wright's version of the *Inferno* was well received when it appeared in 1833, although Matthew Arnold was later to say in his essay 'On Translating Homer' (1861) that it 'had no proper reason for existing'; see Cunningham 1965: 32–6.
[82] Rosenblum 1967: 112.   [83] Pointon 1979: 41.

THE LOVERS SURPRISED.

LA BOCCA MI BACIÓ TUTTO TREMANTÉ.

EAGER TO REALIZE THE STORY'D BLISS.
TREMBLING HE SNATCH'D THE HALF RESENTED KISS.

Inferno Canto 5

Fig. 8. John Flaxman, 'The Lovers Surprised' (Paolo and Francesca), engraved by Tommaso Piroli, from *Compositions by John Flaxman, R.A., from the Divine poem of Dante Alighieri* (1807), copy in the George Smith Special Collection, University of York

the parapet, edging menacingly towards Paolo's turned back. A photograph taken during conservation in 1964 clearly shows these to be four fingers of a left hand. In 1975 further photographs were taken, and one of these shows that higher up on this side, above the castle keep, Dyce had earlier sketched a profile of Gianciotto, staring wildly and clutching at his forehead with the same hand (Fig. 9).

Dyce's preliminary attempt to render the gaze of the observer/murderer within the scene suggests a number of parallels and possible influences. It recalls Flaxman's image (Fig. 8), although what can be seen of Gianciotto's face in Dyce's sketch suggests comparison with the older, grotesque figure of Ingres's 1819 version, or perhaps with an earlier watercolour by the Austrian artist Joseph Anton Koch (1768–1839).[84] Like Ingres, Dyce, the 'Nazarenes', and many other foreign artists, Koch had been working in Rome, and he produced a large number of other drawings and paintings based on the *Commedia* during the early nineteenth century.[85] A watercolour of 1805–10 has been suggested as another of the influences

[84] Condon 1983: 29–30, 70, and pls. 1–17, for Ingres; Poppi 1994: 59, for Koch.
[85] Samples of Koch's *Inferno* illustrations can be seen in Nassar 1994: 39, 53, 175, 207, 215, 225, and 291. On his late frescos for the Dante Room of the Casino Massimo, Rome (1827–9), see also Andrews 1964: 48–9 and pls. 48b and 49a–b.

Fig. 9. Detail from William Dyce, *Francesca da Rimini* (1837), courtesy of the National Gallery of Scotland, Edinburgh

on Dyce's painting—although in a more compressed way, it also includes the castle and a mountainous landscape in the background of the scene.[86] Another feature of Dyce's treatment—the husband's sinister hand on the parapet that separates him from the lovers—might have been suggested by the fingers reaching round the column in the Flaxman engraving, or perhaps by the more explicitly threatening

---

[86] See Melville 2006: 104. For four of Koch's versions of Francesca, see Poppi 1994: 59, 69, and 113 (figs. 39 and 40). The mood and composition of *Italia and Germania* (1815–28) by Dyce's friend the 'Nazarene' Johann Friedrich Overbeck has also been proposed as a 'prototype' (Melville 2006: 21 and fig. 2).

gesture in a version by yet another northern artist, Johann Heinrich Fuseli (1741–1825), who worked in Rome in the 1770s. Fuseli's powerful and influential illustrations of scenes from the *Commedia* included several versions of Francesca.[87] In his vigorous and sardonic watercolour of 1808, for example, the elderly murderer lurking in the shrubbery glowers at the youthful, balletic, and fully lit figures in the foreground as he rests his dagger, for the moment, on the balustrade.[88]

In its present form, Dyce's painting conveys the imminent threat to the lovers only through the disembodied hand on the parapet. Somewhat earlier, Eugène Delacroix's *Paolo and Francesca* watercolour (1824–5) had Gianciotto's demonic profile peering out of the dark folds of a curtain with a single maliciously staring eye.[89] A slightly later version (1840), by the Venetian historical painter Michelangelo Grigoletti, signals the jealous husband's presence simply through the glint of a swordpoint emerging from a dark doorway.[90] The scenario of Dyce's *Francesca* could thus be seen as a further example of what has been called 'figurative litotes' in Romantic artists' rendering of the scene.[91]

However, the *Francesca* that now hangs in the National Gallery of Scotland is not what visitors to the Royal Scottish Academy exhibition in March 1837 actually saw. A review of the event in *The Scotsman* mentions Dyce's painting early on as 'a production which has received much and deserved praise', and speaks well of its finish, colouring, and setting. It is more critical of the characters, finding Francesca 'beautiful and pensive' but lacking any 'passing index of excitement', and objecting to the 'ugliness' of Paolo, whose profile, in this view 'immediately strikes the observer as that of a Scotch lout'.[92] It then adds some concerns about a *third* figure in the scene, commenting that: 'The head of Gianciotto appears too extravagant a mass of blackness and ruffianism.'[93]

Gianciotto's appearance in and disappearance from Dyce's painting comprise a story that reflects both his approach to the composition and the status of his *Francesca* later in the century. Shortly after the artist's death in 1864, the painting was offered for sale to the Royal Scottish Academy, and two of the council members were appointed 'to examine the Picture and report'.[94] A few days later, they made two main observations about the work:

they considered it the most important work that Mr Dyce had executed during the time he practised the art in Scotland; one in which many of the high qualities for which he was distinguished are well brought out, and so a desirable acquisition for the Academy . . . It is

---

[87] See Gizzi (ed.) 1985, and *Henry Fuseli* (London: Tate Gallery, 1975), 23 and 101–4.
[88] For Fuseli's 1808 Francesca and earlier versions (*c.*1776–8 and 1786), see Poppi 1994: 62–4 and 111 (figs. 29–30).
[89] Poppi 1994: 108 (fig. 15).   [90] Poppi 1994: 82–3.
[91] For this term (*litote figurativa*), see Salvadori 2004: 61.
[92] *The Scotsman*, Saturday, 4 March 1837, p. 3, from <http://archive.scotsman.com> accessed 23 March 2007, (available through membership of the online *Scotsman Digital Archive*).
[93] *The Scotsman*, Saturday, 4 March 1837, p. 3.
[94] Royal Scottish Academy *Council Minutes, Jan. 1862–Oct. 1867*, p. 169 (14 Mar. 1864). A previous minute, for 19 February (p. 164) records the Council's 'sorrow and regret' at 'the death of their friend William Dyce' and recognition of his 'position and services to Art and its literature'.

right to state, however, that considerable portions of the picture are cracked,—a figure of Giannotto [*sic*] (about half of which is new) which in the way of alteration was painted in the Exhibition on a portion of the canvass on which another figure of Giannotto had been previously painted is cracked all over . . . [95]

Despite this damage (which appears to have extended to parts of Paolo's 'drapery' and 'portions of the foreground and background'), the Academy considered the painting to be a 'worthy memorial' and worth the asking price of 'two hundred guineas'.[96] It remained in this condition in the Scottish National Gallery until the autumn of 1881, when the repainting of the gallery gave the council the opportunity to examine some of its collection 'for the purpose of ascertaining whether they require treatment of any kind'. At the subsequent RSA council meeting another prominent Victorian artist made a decisive contribution to Dyce's *Francesca* by proposing

that in connexion with the examination of the pictures [temporarily removed from the National Gallery], the large picture by Wm Dyce of Paolo and Francesca da Rimini should be reduced in size by cutting away the objectionable part containing the figure in [the] background[,] this figure not being painted by Dyce . . . [97]

Sir Joseph Noël Paton's radical recommendation was approved at the following meeting, and the surgery was duly carried out early in 1882, at a cost to the Academy of £1. 1*s.* 6*d.*[98]

Paton's part in the story reflects not only his status in the art world of the time— particularly in Scotland[99]—but also his own interest in the subject. Like Dyce, he had been one of the artists competing successfully with designs for the new Houses of Parliament in the 1840s;[100] and by 1881 he had become highly successful as a painter, in the Pre-Raphaelite style, of a wide range of medieval, literary, and religious subjects, including three versions of Francesca. Paton's most well-known version of the subject, *Dante Meditating the Episode of Francesca da Rimini and Paulo Malatesta* (1852), has at its centre, above the pensive poet, the figures of the two lovers borne on the air, against the kind of background—glowing evening sky and long landscape perspective—which features in Dyce's 1837 version.[101] He had also produced two other versions of the story, one of them showing the lovers with Gianciotto looming in the background.[102] When Dyce's *Francesca* was reshaped, Paton may well have been influenced by his own earlier versions, in opting to leave

[95] Royal Scottish Academy *Council Minutes, Jan. 1862–Oct. 1867*, p. 173 (19 Mar. 1864).
[96] Royal Scottish Academy *Council Minutes, Jan. 1862–Oct. 1867*, and *Thirty-Seventh Annual report of the Council of the Scottish Academy* (Edinburgh: Constable, 1864), p. 8.
[97] Royal Scottish Academy *Council Minutes, July 1876–Dec. 1887*, p. 186 (5 Nov. 1881).
[98] Royal Scottish Academy *Council Minutes, Jan. 1862–Oct. 1867*, p. 188 (7 Nov. 1881). The invoice for the work was presented the following January.
[99] Paton had been appointed Queen's Limner for Scotland in 1865.
[100] See *ODNB*, s.v. 'Sir (Joseph) Noël Paton (1821–1901), history painter'.
[101] Harrison and Newall 2010: 45 (cat. 2) and Milbank 1998: 154–5 and pl. 4.
[102] Poppi 1994: 114 (fig. 45) and *The Life and Work of Sir Joseph Noël Paton* (London: The Art Journal, 1895), 120.

the hand on the balustrade as a minimal, though sinister, visual indication of her husband's vengeful presence.

There seems to be no warrant for Paton's claim that the original figure of Gianciotto was 'not painted by Dyce', nor is there any further documentary evidence of his or his fellow academicians' motives for ordering the figure to be excised. The simplest and most likely explanation is that the damage noticed in 1864 was caused by the use of bitumen (commonly employed as a darkening pigment in the early nineteenth century) to emphasize what the *Scotsman* critic called Gianciotto's 'blackness and ruffianism', and that this had continued to cause fissuring and cracking.[103] The problem may have been compounded by Dyce's alterations, especially to this area of the painting. The 1864 report mentions further work being done on the figure of Gianciotto 'in the Exhibition' itself. During conservation in 1975 it was noted that in the remaining painting there were 'many areas of fissuring due to alterations clumsily and broadly painted out'; and it was later reported that the infra-red photographs taken at the time

show that Dyce had tried various positions for the figure of Gianciotto before selecting the eventual pose. Some can in fact be seen with the naked eye. The whole picture is full of pentimenti[,] and Dyce's drastic changes of mind over the left hand portion no doubt contributed to the deterioration in its condition. There is bad cracking of the paint surface even in the part of the left side that was not removed, and it may be that if the figure of Gianciotto was irreparably wrecked, the RSA may have felt it was preferable to salvage and exhibit the rest of the picture than to consign the whole canvas to permanent storage.[104]

What, then, might this figure have looked like in the original 1837 composition? Until recently it was assumed that, as the description in the 2006 exhibition catalogue states, 'there is no visual record'.[105] However, in 2004 a sharp-eyed assistant curator at the Royal Scottish Academy discovered that a small (35 × 27 cm) nineteenth-century copy of the painting (under the title of *Lover's Revenge*) was being sold online.[106] This clearly shows a black-haired figure emerging (from the waist up) from a stairway in the lower left-hand corner, clutching the balustrade with his left hand, holding a dagger in his right, and looking towards the lovers (Fig. 10). The rest of the copy—though crude in its rendering of Dyce's delicate details—corresponds closely to the overall composition of the remaining original. It is very likely, therefore, that this surviving version represents what the viewers at the 1837 exhibition actually saw in its entirety—including what the *Scotsman*'s critic referred to as the 'blackness and ruffianism' of the vengeful (but now lost) Gianciotto.

---

[103] On Dyce's use of bitumen, which caused irreparable damage to his 1835 portrait of his nephew, see Melville 2006: 100 and 104. This may also explain why 'the drapery of the figure of Paolo' was also said in 1864 to be similarly affected (see above, p. 172).
[104] National Gallery of Scotland, letter of 4 Sept. 1981 (from Dr Lindsay Errington, then Assistant Keeper, British Art).
[105] Melville 2006:104.
[106] I am much indebted to Nicola Ireland, formerly of the RSA, for this information and for a copy of the webpage, which enabled me subsequently to trace both the sale and the painting itself (now in private ownership).

Fig. 10. Anon., copy of Dyce's *Francesca da Rimini* (probably dating between 1837 and 1882), in private collection, Italy, courtesy of the owner

Thus the *Francesca* that Dyce completed for its initial exhibition was a rather more explicit version of the scene described as 'The Lovers Surprised and Punished'—a tradition initiated by Fuseli (1786 and 1808), Flaxman (1793), and Koch (1805–10).[107] The Dyce/Paton work in its subsequent form continues—partly by accident, partly by design—to reflect a trend in nineteenth-century art merely to hint at the story's violent end, whilst giving greater prominence to the misfortune or 'moral luck' of the lovers.[108] Its troubled case-history reflects a conversation about this Dantean episode that would continue through the later portrayals of the 'gentle pair' by Pre-Raphaelites and Decadents.[109]

Dyce returned to Dante on at least three other occasions in his career. A minor reflection of the growing Victorian interest in Dante's 'second realm' of the afterlife is the design featuring Leah and Rachel (*Purg.* 27. 97–108) which he submitted as a proposal for the reverse of the Royal Academy's Turner Medal in 1858. It is unsurprising, perhaps, that the Academy 'rejected this solemn and esoteric drawing in favour of the light-hearted and more effective design submitted by [Daniel] Maclise'.[110]

[107] For this term and some examples, see Bindman (ed.) 1979: 160–1.

[108] The term 'moral luck' is defined by Milbank 1998: 153.

[109] Hunt, *The Story of Rimini*, canto 3, line 340. On Francesca and the Decadents, see O'Grady 2003: 234–9. On D. G. Rossetti's numerous versions of Francesca, see above, p. 165 and n. 61.

[110] Pointon 1979: 155–6 and pl. 129.

Fig. 11. William Dyce, *Dante and Beatrice* (1840s?), courtesy of Aberdeen Art Gallery and Museums

More significant for the wider Victorian conversation about Dante's women were Dyce's two portrayals of Beatrice. A possibly quite early version of the subject is the unfinished oil on canvas *Dante and Beatrice*, which has since 1940 been in the Aberdeen Art Gallery (Fig. 11).[111] It shows Beatrice as Dante's guide in

[111] Melville 2006: 178–9 (cat. 51). See also Pointon 1979: 199.

Fig. 12. Berlin, Kupferstichkabinett, MS Hamilton 201, Botticelli, illustration for *Paradiso* 2, by permission of Bildarchiv, Preußischer Kulturbesitz, Berlin

Paradiso, with the two figures soaring hand-in-hand from a blue earthly sky (with clouds) up into a golden beyond. In its composition it bears some quite striking similarities to several of Botticelli's illustrations depicting Dante's ascent through the spheres of Paradise—particularly that for *Paradiso* 2, where Beatrice is pointing upwards (like Dyce's figure) with her right hand, and the poet is following her gaze (Fig. 12).[112] Throughout Dyce's lifetime the manuscript containing the Botticelli illustrations was in the Library of Hamilton Palace in Scotland. A letter to a friend, probably in 1836, mentions some of the highlights of the duke's collection:

There is a most noble assemblage of matters of art at Hamilton. The palace is perfectly crammed full of Pictures many, most indeed[,] of high class. In the portrait gallery which is 125 feet in length, there are 5 or 6 Vandykes & a Reynolds all whole lengths. There is also Rubens's famous 'Daniel in the Den of Lions'. But I must not attempt a description of a collection of pictures, as I [78ʳ] think that of all descriptions is the most stupid.[113]

The style of Dyce's own *Dante and Beatrice* has been aptly described as 'linear', 'flattened', 'reminiscent of fresco cartoon transfers'.[114] Earlier in this letter he mentions the possibility of getting a commission for the duke of Hamilton's project

---

[112] See also the illustrations for *Par.* 3, 5–6, 10, 14, and 30 in Berlin, Kupferstichkabinett MS Hamilton 201. On the Hamilton Collection, see below, pp. 243–6.

[113] Edinburgh, NLS MS 8887, f. 76ʳ–8ᵛ. On the visit, see also Pointon 1979: 38.

[114] Melville 2006: 178.

to have the newest part of his palace 'painted in fresco'.[115] His undated and incomplete oil sketch might perhaps have been connected with that venture. It could thus be seen as the combined product of his encounters with the Botticelli drawings in the Hamilton collection and his study of Italian frescos which continued in the mid-1840s.[116] Dyce's close friend and colleague David Scott, who had travelled with him in Italy in 1832, is known to have likewise acquired skill in fresco painting and also to have exhibited his own version of *Dante and Beatrice* at the Royal Scottish Academy in 1846.[117] Both Scott's version of the subject and Dyce's may therefore have been near-contemporary versions, anticipating (and perhaps influencing) the Pre-Raphaelite 'cult of the *Vita Nuova*' and the multitude of later Victorian pictures on this theme.

Dyce's later *Beatrice* was much more in the public eye. Along with his 1837 *Francesca*, his most famous Dantean subject is the one that provided the poster and catalogue cover image for the exhibition on 'William Dyce and the Pre-Raphaelite Vision' at Aberdeen in 2006. This is the oil-on-panel painting of *Beatrice* subtitled 'Lady with a Coronet of Jasmine', painted for W. E. Gladstone in the summer of 1859, with one of Gladstone's 'Magdalens'—the former prostitute Marian Summerhayes—serving as model.[118] It has been said to show the influence both of the photographic studies on which it was probably based and that of Dyce's own earlier Madonna paintings.[119] Gladstone's project of 'rescuing' 'fallen women' has been given ample attention, but his commissioning and purchase of Dyce's last Dantean painting forms a link to a less sensational interest: his lifelong study of the *Commedia*.

'MR GLADSTONE'S POCKET DANTE'

In the midst of his second ministry (1880–85) William Gladstone wrote to the Florentine Dante scholar Giambattista Giuliani (1818–84) to thank him for an essay written in 1865 on the sixth centenary of the poet's birth.[120] He wrote in Italian:

---

[115] Edinburgh, NLS MS 8887, f. 76ʳ.

[116] On his visit to Italy in 1845, see above, p. 166 and n. 70.

[117] See *ODNB*, s.v. 'Scott, David (1806–1849), painter and poet'. On his fresco of 'a scene in Purgatory' on the wall of his studio in Rome (August 1833), see W. B. Scott, *A Memoir of David Scott RSA* (Edinburgh: A. & C. Black), p. 136. For details of the paintings he exhibited with the *Dante and Beatrice* in 1846, see ibid. 280, and McKay and Rinder 1917: 349A. I have not been able to trace any further details about Scott's version (apart from its asking price of 70 guineas).

[118] On the arrangements concerning Summerhayes, see *GD* 5: lx–lxi and 414–15. A possible comparison here is with Charles West Cope's negotiations to employ as model for his *Francesca* (exhibited, like Dyce's, in 1837) 'a young [Italian] woman I had seen at the large confectioner's shop in Bedford Row'. Her husband agreed in return for a copy of her portrait (Cope 1891: 11–12).

[119] Melville 2006: 180. This *Beatrice* could also be seen as a further 'rescuing' of Francesca, whose features in Dyce's 1837 painting recall his Raphaelesque Madonna of 1827–30.

[120] For the text and context of the letter, see Mazzoni 1996; I am grateful to Dr Marisa Boschi for a reference to this article. The letter is also mentioned in *DEL* 2. 601, and subsequently by Chadwick: 1979: 257 and n. 21 (quoting John Morley's English version), but with the mistaken date of 1883.

10 Downing Street
Whitehall
Dec. 20. 82

Ill[ustrissi]mo Signore

Contuttochè io abbia perduto la pratica della lingua Italiana, nondimeno bisogna che io le renda grazie tante e tante della bontà colla quale ella mi ha mandato suo bel lavoro 'Dante spiegato con Dante'.

Ella si è degnato chiamare quel sommo Poeta un 'solenne maestro' per me. Non sono vite [*sic*] queste parole. La lettura di Dante non è soltanto un piacere, uno sforzo, una lezione: è una disciplina fortissima del cuore, del intelletto, dell'uomo.

Nelle scuola di Dante ho imparato una grandissima parte di quella provicione mentale, sia pure molto meschina, colla quale ho fatto il viaggio della vita umana fino al termine di quasi settanta tre anni.

E vorrei anche stendere la sua bella parola, dicendo che chi serve a Dante, serve all'Italia, al Cristianesimo, al mondo.

Suo servitore
molto rispettoso
Gugl. E. Gladstone

My dear Sir,

Despite being somewhat out of practice with the Italian tongue, it nonetheless behoves me to acknowledge most sincerely your generosity in favouring me with your fine study 'Dante spiegato con Dante' ['Dante interpreted through Dante'].

You have been pleased to speak of that supreme Poet as a 'mighty master' to me; nor are those words vain. The study of Dante is not merely a pleasure, an endeavour, a lesson: it must be counted among the most rigorous of disciplines for the heart, the mind, and the whole person.

Under the tutorship of Dante I have acquired a substantial part of those intellectual resources—scant though they be—that have sustained me on the journey of life for almost seventy-three years.

I should desire also to make further use of your own admirable expression by declaring that one who is dedicated to Dante is also dedicated to the cause of Italy, of Christianity, and of the world.

Your most respectful servant
William E. Gladstone[121]

It was no mere polite or overblown gesture. Gladstone's reading of Dante was, like his other intellectual ventures, a serious and scholarly 'discipline', demanding, as he had argued in an article almost forty years earlier, 'continuous study' and 'the greatest mental effort'.[122] The 'supreme Poet', he had also asserted then, 'was not made for annuals in silk covers. He is not to be the plaything of the butterflies of literature.'[123] His 'tutorship' under Dante had developed—if not quite for those threescore years and ten—then for almost half a century by the time he wrote to Giuliani. Conversations with school-friends such as Arthur Hallam, with the

---

[121] Mazzoni 1996: 314. Mazzoni plausibly suggests that *vite* in the second paragraph is a gallicism (for *vuote*).

[122] Gladstone 1844: 166; see below, pp. 183–5 for discussion of this article.

[123] Gladstone 1844: 179. See also Isba 2006: 110–11 and Windscheffel 2008: 203–4.

German theologian Johann Joseph Ignaz von Döllinger, and with Italian exiles such as Antonio Panizzi and Giacomo Lacaita helped to stimulate and sustain the 'tutorship' over that period.[124] Gladstone's dialogues about Dante also extended to artists of the time. During a visit to Rome in 1839 he saw Koch's Dantean frescos and drawings and compared them (not altogether favourably) with Flaxman's illustrations.[125] He corresponded about Dyce's last Dantean painting: the *Beatrice* of 1859;[126] whilst a few years before he had commissioned an important image of Dante's Francesca from Alexander Munro and had even lent the sculptor some 'Dante criticism' to encourage the project.[127]

Twenty years after his death Gladstone's cult of Dante was still a matter for comment. It has recently been noted that the memoirs of the Turkish poet Abdülhak Hamid Tarhan contain a letter of August 1918 in which he recalls encountering Gladstone whilst at the Ottoman embassy in London:

He knew Latin as well as a Pope. He used to read Dante and Homer all the time, and had an affection for Ancient Greek scholars whom he liked to discuss with our old ambassador Muzuruz Pasha. . . . Moreover, there is no doubt that he knew our holy prophet only from that *Inferno* book by Dante.[128]

Gladstone's *lungo studio* of the poet is evident from his work in print and in manuscript, as well as from the account of his reading in the diaries. His writing on Dante includes early *terza rima* versions of passages from all three *cantiche* of the *Commedia*; a manuscript on the poem;[129] an important review of Lord John Russell's translation of the Francesca episode;[130] and a late article reflecting one of his 'cherished beliefs' about Dante's connection with Oxford.[131] As Gladstone's diaries show, he began reading the *Commedia* during his twenties—in 1834–6, close to the time of his verse translations—and intense periods of study followed at intervals throughout his life. His approach to the *Commedia* was highly methodical: he seems initially to have aimed to cover two cantos a day, combining Dante with a range of other reading, although his pace slowed down at points in the *Paradiso*.[132] The *Inferno* was begun on 16 September 1834, the day after the anniversary of Arthur Hallam's death, and followed the reading of a modern Italian classic (Alessandro Manzoni's *I promessi sposi*) and a key British work on the Florentine Renaissance (William Roscoe's *Life of Lorenzo de' Medici*).[133] Not much more than two weeks

---

[124] See Isba 2006: 14–19, 56, 60 and Jenkins 1995: 16–17, 121, 193, 200.

[125] *GD* 2: 559 and 566 (11 and 15 Jan. 1839).   [126] See above, p. 177 with n. 118.

[127] See Windscheffel 2008: 117. On Munro's *Paolo and Francesca*, completed in 1852, see also Isba 2006: 30–8 and Harrison and Newall 2010: 46.

[128] Quoted in Okay 2012: 344 (with n. 15). Abdülhak Hamid also portrayed Dante as 'that old slandering genius' in a play (*The Procession of Ghosts*), where he is made to recant for his representation of 'the prophet of God' in *Inf*. 28 (ibid. 345–6).

[129] In BL Add. MSS 44731, f. 134 f., probably dating from the 1840s; see Chadwick 1979: 253–4.

[130] Quoted above, p. 178 and discussed further below, pp. 183–5.

[131] Gladstone 1892; see also *DEL* 2: 601 and Isba 2006: 5 and 145. For the translations of *Inf*. 33.1–78, *Purg*. 11.1–21, and *Par*. 3. 70–87, see *DEL* 2. 602–4.

[132] For example, he took two days over three cantos (*Par*. 9–11) on 3–4 March 1836 and on 10 March he notes 'read Paradiso XVI—hard' (*GD* 2: 226–7).

[133] *GD* 2: 128.

later (after finishing the *Inferno*), Gladstone reread a reprint of Arthur Hallam's pamphlet on Gabriele Rossetti's *Disquisizioni sullo spirito antipapale*,[134] with its critical account of Rossetti's reduction of the *Vita nuova* to 'Ghibelline enigmas'. The pamphlet had originally appeared in 1832, and was republished posthumously in the *Remains in Verse and Prose*, which Gladstone had received from its editor, Hallam's father, a few months earlier.[135] Gladstone is thus engaging in a continuing conversation about Dante with a dead school-friend whose interests in Dante he had known about much earlier.[136]

His first reading of the *Purgatorio* in Edinburgh a year later seems to have been more immediately conversational in nature, at least for some of its cantos. John Neilson Gladstone, his elder brother, had accompanied him on his first visit to Italy in 1832. He had arrived in Edinburgh on 3 November 1835, just three days before Gladstone began his reading of the *Purgatorio*, which, on three subsequent occasions, he records as a shared activity 'with J.N.G.'.[137]

'Reading with' forms a significant feature of the nineteenth-century conversation about Dante, and it might have taken one (or more) of several forms: reading aloud, sharing translation, discussion, or a mixture of all three. Here, in 1832, it clearly indicates that Gladstone's experience of the text, like that of several other British readers, was at least in part a social activity.[138] Four years later his diary records a visit from a Welsh Catholic heiress, Apollonia Rio (née Jones), in which 'long conv [ersation]' is accompanied by 'read[ing] Dante'.[139] When in the early stages of marriage and of rereading the *Inferno* at Hawarden in the summer of 1841, his diary reports an encounter with 'Inferno IV–VII: some aloud to C[atherine]'.[140] This reading could thus have entailed a performance of Francesca for the young Mrs Gladstone's benefit. Later still, a second generation seems to have shared in the experience: his daughter Mary's diary records how, during a visit to Rome in the autumn of 1866, she 'Began Dante with Papa after breakfast', before going with him to call on a cardinal at the Vatican, and continuing their study of the text the following day.[141]

Revisiting texts was a frequent feature of Gladstone's reading practice and came to represent 'an event in life'.[142] His diaries record subsequent encounters with

---

[134] *GD* 2: 131 (4 Oct. 1834).

[135] On Hallam's pamphlet and other reactions to Rossetti's ideas, see Milbank 1998:121–2 and 257 (n. 21) and Straub 2009: 96; an excerpt from it is in *DEL* 2: 422–3. On Hallam's *Remains*, see Isba 2006: 15–16.

[136] Isba (2006: 2 and 19) suggests that awareness of Hallam's interest in Dante may go back to their years at Eton in the 1820s.

[137] *GD* 2: 204–7; see esp. the entries for 13, 14, and 17 Nov. Appropriately too, activities at this time also included several ascents of Arthur's Seat, the hill near Holyrood (2: 204–5, 28 and 31 Oct. and 7 Nov,).

[138] For other early nineteenth-century examples, see below, p. 201 and n. 33.

[139] *GD* 2: 328 (13 June 1838).

[140] *GD* 3: 127 (29 July 1841). This phase of rereading appears to have begun the day before and ended around the middle of the *Purgatorio* about a month later (23 Aug.; *GD* 3: 132).

[141] See *Mary Gladstone (Mrs Drew) her Diaries and Letters*, ed. L. Masterman (London: Methuen, 1930), 31 (15 and 16 Oct. 1866).

[142] Windscheffel 2008, citing Gladstone's diary for 20 Jan. 1867.

parts of the *Commedia* in late 1836 and 1841; an extended reading of the whole poem in the late summer and early autumn of 1846; and later rereadings in 1866–7, 1879, and 1887–8.[143] By the 1850s and 1860s he was also acquainted with other Dantean works such as the *Vita nuova*, *De vulgari eloquentia*, and the *Monarchia*.[144] The thirty thousand or so volumes of his library at Hawarden came to include not only numerous editions of the texts and several translations, but also a substantial range of critical work and commentary, including a copy of Foscolo's 1825 *Discorso sul testo* and—with Gladstone's annotations—G. A. Scartazzini's *Dante Alighieri: seine Zeit, sein Leben und seine Werke* (1869).[145]

Substantial annotations have been found in one of Gladstone's texts of the *Commedia* itself: the edition published at Padua in 1822 in five large octavo volumes. This is based on the 1791 edition of Lombardi, but with its apparatus extensively revised and amplified by three more recent editors. Gladstone's markings and comments in this copy have recently been transcribed and discussed, and it has been claimed that, '[f]or serious study Gladstone appears always to have used the same copy of the *Commedia*' and that '[o]nly the Minerva [Padua] edition' now in the Gladstone Collection at St Deiniol's Library 'contains [his] own marginalia and endnotes, written in pencil'.[146] This is not quite true. Gladstone's annotations were not restricted to that bulky copy; he also owned a much more portable, single-volume edition, which contains evidence of a possibly earlier and equally serious study of the *Commedia*.

In Eton College Library a slipcase covered in red morocco is embossed in gold letters with the inscription 'Mʀ· GLADSTONE'S POCKET DANTE'.[147] This contains a small (32°) plain text *Commedia* based on the 1727 Comino edition and published at Venice in 1827, and the notes still kept in the case indicate how it came to be there. On 17 October 1898, six months after Gladstone's death, his younger son Herbert wrote from Hawarden to Lord Rosebery, Gladstone's colleague and successor, to present, on his mother's behalf, 'a little Dante which has been much used by my Father & which she hopes you will like . . . '. The volume was subsequently kept as a Gladstonian relic in a locked bookcase, whose key was 'occasionally entrusted' to Rosebery's son-in-law, Captain Charles Grant. Forty years on Grant's wife commemorated her husband's visit to Eton by presenting the 'little volume' to the Provost, adding that, in the intervening Great War, Dante had also served a purpose: 'It seemed apt that during those dreadful moments of the retreat from Mons—his [Grant's] own copy should have proved such a comfort.'[148] The fact that this 'little volume' is extensively annotated has been remarked upon in

---

[143] *GD* 2: 265–9 (rereading of *Inferno* and *Purgatorio* from 11 Nov. to 8 Dec. 1836) and *GD* 3: 12/–32 (further rereading of *Inferno* and half of *Purgatorio* from 28 July to 23 Aug. 1841), and 565–80 (rereading of the whole *Commedia* from 14 Aug. to 30 Oct. 1846). See also Chadwick 1979: 252–3 and Isba 2006: 56–61.

[144] See *GD* 5: 93 (*Vita nuova* read [with *Paradise Lost* and 'Macaulay'] on 25 Dec. 1855); and *GD* 6:1–2 (*De vulgari eloquentia* read on 2–5 Jan. 1861, and *Monarchia* on 5 Jan.).

[145] Isba 2006: 61 and n. 36. On Gladstone's ownership of Foscolo's *Discorso*, see above, p. 153.

[146] Isba 2006: 20 and n. 33.

[147] Eton College Library, shelfmark Loo. I. 14.

[148] Note from Sybil Grant (Rosebery's daughter) to the Provost of Eton, 22 July 1933.

several exhibition catalogues, but has not so far been considered by those concerned with Gladstone's reading practices.[149] As with his other working copies, the non-verbal annotation (all in pencil) takes the form of frequent lateral lines (single and double), underlinings, and signs of approval (+).[150] Some of the latter apply to verses or passages—such as the tribute to Virgil as Dante's source of language (*Inf.* 1. 79–80), the description of avaricious souls turning their gaze to the ground (*Purg.* 19. 118–20),[151] or Beatrice's warning about taking on the commitment of a vow too lightly (*Par.* 5. 73–5)—and they also mark certain entire cantos.[152]

Glossing of individual words and occasionally lines in this copy also reflects Gladstone's interest in the art of translation. This was an interest that had already resulted in some uneven experiments in *terza rima* versions shortly before this copy of the poem came into his hands.[153] The closeness of his engagement with the language can be demonstrated from his glosses to the first two cantos of the *Inferno*. At points, attention is drawn simply to difficult or archaic forms, such as the demonstrative adjective *esto* (in *Inf.* 2. 93), which is underlined and followed by a footnote referring to Cary's translation ('that'). On a number of other occasions Gladstone can be seen thinking rather harder about meanings and equivalences—sometimes harder than Cary. Thus, for example, at the very outset (*Inf.* 1. 5), when the obstructive dark wood is said to be *forte*—which Cary renders 'robust'—Gladstone (the active woodsman) attempts to convey something of its physicality by proposing 'stiff'. Later in the canto, when Dante's heroic rescuer of Italy is portrayed as immune to avarice (*Inf.* 1. 103), the money he despises is represented through a metonymy—*peltro* ('pewter'). Cary renders this as 'base metals'—whereas Gladstone, attending more closely to the word's linguistic register, asks 'hence pelf?'[154] In the following canto—a crucial one for Dante's sense of direction (or redirection) as poet and pilgrim—the narrator musters the powers of his memory, urging it to display its *nobilitate* (*Inf.* 2. 9.), a term which Cary turns verbosely into 'eminent endowments', whilst Gladstone offers the much more concise and dynamic 'mettle'. A key function of the scenario in *Inferno* 2 is to build up the confidence of Dante's timorous traveller, to the extent that at the end (l. 132) he can himself begin to speak to his guide as a *persona franca*—a figure whom Cary imagines romantically as 'one undaunted', whilst Gladstone more incisively (and perhaps with a politician's ear for a soundbite) makes him a 'freeborn soul'.[155]

Gladstone's energetic dialogue with Dante overflows into the outer pages of this copy. The second flyleaf of his 'pocket Dante' contains a number of notes and jottings ranging across the *Commedia*. These are mostly about passages and

---

[149] It is not mentioned by Chadwick 1979, Isba 2006, or Windscheffel 2008.

[150] On Gladstone's highly consistent 'annotation code', see Windscheffel 2008: 48–9.

[151] A footnote on this page (p. 326 of the edition) aptly compares Milton's description of Mammon in *Paradise Lost* 1. 679–84.

[152] e.g. *Inferno* 1–6 and 33, *Purgatorio* 6, *Paradiso* 15.

[153] For a balanced assessment of the Dante translations of the 1830s, see Davie 1994: 389–400.

[154] 'Pelf' is indeed the translation adopted in the standard modern prose version by R. M. Durling; see Dante 1996: 31 (line 103).

[155] A leading modern verse translation, that of Allen Mandelbaum has 'one who has been freed', which is also accurate but rather more wordy (Dante 1995*b*: 66 (line 132)).

characters from the *Inferno* and the *Purgatorio*, although there are a few references to and comments on lines from the *Paradiso*—notably one that describes Dante as 'a scholar of Aristotle' (on the basis of the allusion to the *Politics* and citizenship in *Par.* 8. 115–20), thus linking the poet firmly with one of Gladstone's other 'four doctors'.[156]

The annotations on this front flyleaf also focus prominently upon an episode which, as we have seen, compelled attention from a number of nineteenth-century readers and appropriators, including Byron, Kemble, and Dyce, and held some especial significances for Gladstone: the story of Francesca's (and Dante's) 'fall' in *Inferno* 5. Thus, interrupting a chronological sequence of references here—and following a note about the dramatic story of Buonconte da Montefeltro's last-minute repentance ('*Pg* 5. 85–129')—are three attempts at a verse translation of the line that introduces the second tercet of Francesca's invocation to love—'Amor, ch'a nullo amato amar perdona':

> I[nferno]. 5. 103
> Love that excuses none from love's return
> Love that dispenses not with love's return
> Love that will have the loved one love again[157]

Despite the consequent disruption of chronology, there is a certain underlying continuity in the reader's and annotator's chain of thought. The speech that immediately follows Buonconte's narrative in *Purgatorio* 5 is that of another woman whose fate was of much concern to nineteenth-century readers: Pia de' Tolomei, whose voice may well have reminded Gladstone of Francesca's.[158] And following the three attempts at rendering the infernal soul's claim about love's power, he returns to the 'Great anxiety of the Spirits to be known to Dante' in the *Purgatorio*—thus continuing to sustain an interest in how (as in the encounter with Francesca) the 'Dante' persona is addressed by souls in the *Commedia*'s afterworlds.[159]

Gladstone's experiments with Francesca's line also recall a more public conversation about *Inferno* 5, and translation, which he may have been conducting around the time at which these notes were made. His first public assertion that Dante's work required serious and scholarly 'discipline', 'continuous study', and 'the greatest mental effort' was in an article of 1844, reviewing 'Lord JOHN RUSSELL's *Translation of the 'Francesca da Rimini,' from the Inferno of Dante, Canto V.* 73–142'.[160] The very titles of the journals the two politicians were writing for

---

[156] The other two, according to Gladstone's first biographer, Morley, were Augustine and Bishop Joseph Butler; see Shannon 1984: 180 (citing Morley).

[157] Eton College Library, Loo. I. 14, flyleaf 2^r.

[158] *Purg.* 5. 130–6. See e.g. Felicia Hemans's 1820 poem about La Pia: 'The Maremma' (excerpts in Griffiths and Reynolds 2005: 164–75) and the perceptive comments by Saglia 2012: 192–5.

[159] Eton College Library, Loo. I. 14, flyleaf 2^r.

[160] Gladstone 1844. At this time, during Peel's ministry (1841–6), Russell was out of office but he would continue (as prime minister in 1846–52 and again in 1865–6) to be one of the leading Whigs with whom Gladstone would have to negotiate politically, although 'they were instinctively quarrelsome with each other' (Jenkins 1995: 158).

that year suggest a difference of intellectual temperament: Russell's translation of the Francesca episode (in heroic couplets) had been published in the *Literary Souvenir*, whilst Gladstone's review appeared in the *English Review or Quarterly Journal of Ecclesiastical and General Literature*.

Gladstone's insistence upon the public significance of 'the stupendous work of Dante' is apparent, as we shall see, in the conclusion to his review. It can also be discerned in the manuscript draft of its opening paragraph.[161] The third sentence comprises a sequence of admonitory conditional clauses running to over ten lines in the printed version—beginning with what may be a sideswipe at Lord John Russell and the readers of the *Literary Souvenir*: 'If we desire to escape from the sickly-scented atmosphere of a highly artificial civilization into larger and freer air . . .'[162] It then addresses the weighty motives and consequences that might attach to a serious study of Dante, before turning to a conclusion which, as a cancelled (and not fully articulated) passage in Gladstone's draft makes clear, is beginning to anticipate claims that he will make at the end of the article:

then, and for these reasons, without taking into view many others of a less comprehensive application [~~we fervently believe that these purposes are to be realized more effectually by the study of Dante than by any other high pursuit~~] let his majestic verse share largely in our daily and our nightly toil.[163]

Part of Gladstone's review was reproduced by Toynbee in 1909, although its authorship was not known at that time.[164] The severity of Gladstone's broader judgements on Russell's rendering, their reflection of his views on scholarship and religion, and the relationship of the review to his own performance as translator of Dante have all been given a fair amount of attention.[165] Toynbee's excerpts, however, omit the core of the article (pp. 167–79), containing Gladstone's detailed critique of the translation, and there has been little discussion of that stage of his argument.[166] Hence, although Russell's rendering has rightly been described as 'an easy target',[167] some of Gladstone's specific objections to it can be seen to reflect the close relationship between his very public review and the intense private interrogation of the text that is evident from his 'pocket Dante'.

Russell's tendency to 'dilute' and 'inflate' the 'compression' and 'concentration' of Dante's language and to deal with difficult expressions simply by ignoring them is highlighted in Gladstone's review, and it does indeed contrast sharply with the hard thinking and concision that, as we have seen, characterize his own annotations and translations in the Eton copy of the *Commedia*.[168] Unlike Russell (and Cary,

---

[161] BL Add. MS 44683, f. 107ʳ–14ᵛ; see *GD* 3: 348, n. 10.

[162] Gladstone 1844: 164.

[163] Gladstone 1844: 165, with the cancelled passage from BL Add. MS 44683, f. 107ʳ in square brackets.

[164] *DEL* 2: 686–9.

[165] See Chadwick 1979: 255–6; Davie 1994; Isba 2006: 109–14; Windscheffel 2008: 203–4.

[166] Davie 1994 is the only one of those mentioned in the previous note to have given this section of Gladstone's text some brief attention (p. 387).

[167] Davie 1994: 387.

[168] Gladstone 1844: 167–8, 169, 172–3; see above, pp. 182–3.

and Byron), Gladstone knows that *terra* (as used by Francesca to describe Ravenna in *Inferno* 5. 97) can mean 'city', as he indicates both in his critique of Russell's diffuse rendering of the whole tercet and in his notes on the word in his own text.[169] More importantly, his insistence at several points in the review on the depth and 'intensity' of the lovers' passion is reflected in his objections to Russell's handling of Francesca's lines about their response to their reading:

> Oft from the book
> We raised our eyes, and each commingling look
> Led to a blush.[170]

He taxes Russell with 'levity' and even 'superciliousness' here (for replacing pallor with what Russell might have called a 'conscious blush'). Then his recognition of the tension and confusion in a difficult phrase describing the lovers' gaze ('gli occhi ci sospinse') leads Gladstone into more complex psychological speculation: 'may not the allusion be to the state of the eyes when vision is intercepted and bewildered by strong emotion . . . and would not the idea of Dante almost require the hardy expression, "*smote* our eyes?"'[171] This response to the moment and the phrase is closely echoed by Gladstone's annotation of the passage in the Eton text, where he partly underlines *sospinse* and then in the margin proposes the same words as are suggested in the Russell review: 'smote & so bewildered'.[172] Another difficult line—which, as we have seen, Gladstone's notes to the Eton copy negotiated in three different ways—is Francesca's earlier assertion about the demands of love: 'Amor, ch'a nullo amato amar perdona' (*Inf.* 5. 103), which Russell had rendered fluently but innocuously as: 'True love by love must ever be repaid.'[173] In the review Gladstone compares different versions again, this time by four published translators: Byron, John Dayman (who in 1843 had produced the first *terza rima* translation of the whole *Inferno*), Cary, and Russell—concluding that 'Of the four, it appears to us that Lord John [Russell]'s is the easiest line, Cary's the best version, and Lord Byron's the worst'. Byron's version does indeed at this point (and others) distort the syntax for the sake of rhyme, but Gladstone's concern here is not simply with ranking skills. As elsewhere in the review and at a number of points in the Eton annotations, his engagement with Dante's text here is agonistic: he describes Francesca's line as 'a severe trial'. Both the 1844 review and the annotations in his pocket *Commedia* thus reflect Gladstone's approach to the 'discipline' and 'effort' of studying the poem.

His studies and annotations of Dante cannot be separated from their political and ideological contexts, or from the development of his ideas over time. The Eton

---

[169] On p. 32 of Eton College Library, Loo. I. 14, he compares *Inf.* 9. 106, presumably a slip for 104, where Dis is described as a *terra*.

[170] Russell's translation of *Inf.* 5. 130–1, cited in Gladstone 1844: 177.

[171] Gladstone 1844: 177. Interestingly, the modern translation by Durling again seems to follow the Gladstonian direction: 'drove our eyes together' (Dante 1996: 93 (ll. 130–1)).

[172] Eton College Library, Loo. I. 14, p. 33.

[173] For Gladstone's own alternative versions, see above, p. 183.

Commedia gives a *terminus a quo* for the date of his notes, in the form of a handwritten inscription:

Robert Phillimore Rome 1839
  to C. G.[174]

The lawyer Robert Joseph Phillimore had met Gladstone first at Oxford, when they were both at Christ Church in the late 1820s, and he would remain one of Gladstone's closest friends.[175] Their shared loyalties to High Anglicanism and their common interests in the governance of the Church are, as we shall see, of some relevance to one of the main topics for annotation in this copy of the *Commedia*.[176] The 'C.G.' to whom Phillimore inscribed it was Gladstone's wife—either as 'Catherine Glynne' (if it was actually presented in Rome) or as 'Catherine Gladstone' (if it was a wedding present).[177] In any case, Gladstone appropriated it at some stage—presumably as a conveniently portable working copy of the poem—and it has been suggested that it accompanied him 'on his European travels in the 1840s'.[178] In the absence of internal evidence it is not possible to date the annotations conclusively, but they could perhaps have been initiated during his rereading of the *Inferno* and half of the *Purgatorio* in the summer of 1841, and they might well have been continued during his rather slower rereading of the whole *Commedia* in the late summer and autumn of 1846.[179]

One feature of Gladstone's procedure in annotating this copy recalls a practice described by one of his supporters, the journalist and editor W. T. Stead: 'At the end of the volume he constructs a kind of index of his own which enables him to refer to those things he wishes to remember in a book.'[180] This was, of course, a practice he shared with many other readers writing with a view to future use of their material, but he was more systematic than most. His 'grouping of topics . . . into separate areas', it has been argued, 'demonstrated particularly strong habits of mind', and this was the kind of index that he created in the endpapers of his 'pocket Dante'.[181] The 'things he wishes to remember' here seem to relate particularly to

---

[174] Eton College Library, Loo. I. 14, recto of fourth flyleaf.

[175] See *ODNB*, s.v. 'Phillimore, Sir Robert Joseph, baronet (1810–1885), lawyer'.

[176] Phillimore was already writing tracts on the ecclesiastical courts in the 1840s, and would later, as Dean of Arches, deal with 'several extremely controversial cases concerning ornaments and ritual, resulting from the Oxford Movement' (*ODNB*).

[177] This might be an additional reason for her to consider it later as a Gladstonian memento to be handed on (see Herbert Gladstone's letter of 1898 above, p. 181).

[178] Catalogue for the exhibition *Mr Gladstone 1898–1998* (Slough: Maple Press, 1998), 22.

[179] See above, p. 181 and n. 143. His reading of the text in 1846 is at the rate of two cantos a day rather than three (as earlier). During the periods of reading the *Commedia* in 1841 and 1846 he was moving from place to place in England and Scotland, so it is likely that he was using a portable edition such as the Eton Dante.

[180] W. T. Stead (1849–1912), *Gladstone 1809–1898: a character sketch with portraits and other illustrations* (London, n.d.), 53–4, quoted by Windscheffel 2008: 48.

[181] Windscheffel 2008: 53 and n. 48, referring to the annotations in Gladstone's five-volume 1822 edition of the *Commedia* in the Gladstone Collection at St Deiniol's Library (transcribed in Isba 2006: 141–3).

one of his main preoccupations in the 1840s: ecclesiastical politics and Roman Catholicism.

The last flyleaf of the Eton volume contains the following carefully organized list of phrases, lines, and passages:

I[nferno] 7. 38. 47. Cherci, papi, cardinali
10. 120 Il Cardinale
11. 8 Pope Anastasius
15. 106 cherci violenti contro natura
19. 31 Pope Nicholas III & seqq to the end
23. 103 Frati Bolognesi hypocrites
27. 70 Bonif[ace]. VIII. ibid 85 + seqq.
29. 41 Chiostra & conversi[.] But cf Pg 15.5f[,] 26.128
33. 118. 134 Frate Alberigo.
P[ur]g[atorio] 19. 97. Adrian V.
– 20. 87 Nel vicario suo Cristo catto
24. 20, 29 clerical golosi
32 The grand Allegory
Par[adiso] 9. 125 & seqq - Virgil [,] Trajan Pg 10[,] Cato Pg 1[,] Statius Pg 21[,]
I[nferno] 12. 104 Tiranni (cf 27.37) Par 8. 73[,] 13.108[,] 19.112
Pg 11. 121

and, written vertically along the left-hand margin of the same page, is a list of references, all to the *Paradiso*:

22. 73 State of the Benedictines
Par 25. 15 Vicars of Xt [;]Par 11.84 Ch[urch] before St Francis
                    124 State of the Dominicans
17. 51 Laddove Cristo &c [;] 18. 121–35
Par 27. S. Peter's speech [lines 19–66][;]   20. 55 Constantin
29. 81 & seqq (& end) [;] 21. 120[,]125[;] 24. 111[182]

These references to and descriptions of passages throughout the three *cantiche* of the *Commedia* make it clear that one of Gladstone's major interests during this reading of the poem was Dante's concern with the Church, and his portrayals of the corruption of the clergy, the religious orders, and the Papacy. This preoccupation is more strongly marked here than it is in the indexes created in the front and back flyleaves of Gladstone's five-volume *Commedia* (at St Deiniol's Library), and it is possible that the latter may derive from a later reading of the text.[183] The St Deiniol's copy's index to the *Inferno* parallels some of the references to popes in the endpapers of the Eton Dante (those in cantos 7, 19, and 27); it also notes the line which may allude to Celestine V's resignation (*Inf.* 3. 60). On the other hand, it does not show any interest (as the 'pocket Dante' does) in other clerics or clerical allusions in this *cantica*.[184] Likewise, in the St Deiniol's copy's notes to the

[182] Eton College Library, Loo. I. 14, recto of last flyleaf.
[183] For transcription of these annotations, see Isba 2006: 141–3.
[184] e.g. in *Inf.* 10, 11, 15, 23, 29, 33.

Purgatorio and *Paradiso* there are only two further specific references to the *Commedia*'s negative portrayal of the Papacy.[185]

Most of the anti-papal passages referred to in the endnotes to the 'pocket Dante' are also marked—and at some points further commented upon—in the text itself. Thus, for example, the first pope to be fully recognized and given a voice in the poem is Nicholas III (*Inferno* 19), the pontiff who is planted upside-down among the simonists in the perforated rock of Malebolge's third ditch. Gladstone marks the whole canto with a cross of approval (+), and amongst his underlinings, vertical emphases, glosses, and translations here, he also writes in large letters: 'NB locale.'[186] In *Inferno* 27. 85 the description of Boniface VIII as 'lo principe d'i novi Farisei' ('prince of the modern Pharisees') is heavily under-scored and marked with double vertical emphases in the margin.[187]

In its first reference to the *Purgatorio*, Gladstone's 'index' to the Eton copy draws attention to an earlier pope (Adrian V), who has to explain how he comes to be grovelling on the ground and turning his back to the heavens, among the souls expiating avarice (*Purg.* 19. 97).[188] In the text, that same pope's later lines (103–5) describing how heavy the mantle of office weighs 'on him who seeks to keep it clean' are marked with an additional double vertical and 'NB'.[189] As might be expected, what Gladstone calls in his index 'The Grand Allegory' of *Purgatorio* 32—in which the chariot of the Griffin undergoes several stages of increasingly grotesque metamorphosis—is heavily glossed in his text and he stresses several times its application to the 'Roman Church' and the 'Transformation of the Church'.[190]

The annotations in both text and index of the 'pocket Dante' also reinforce each other in drawing attention to *Paradiso*'s judgements on the state of the Church. The initial reference to this *cantica* in the index is to 'Par 9. 125 & seqq', a passage which contains some of Dante's most vivid and violent anti-papal language. Here, at the end of *Paradiso* 9, the troubadour poet and bishop of Toulouse, Folchetto of Marseilles, portrays the Pope as neglectful of the Holy Land, and as a 'shepherd transformed into a wolf' through addiction to the Florentine florin.[191] Folchetto represents the Roman curia as more concerned with the niceties of canon law than with the Gospel, the Fathers of the Church, or the origins of Christ's ministry (133–8) and concludes on a more prophetic note, that Rome, which is now merely the 'cemetery' of the Apostles, will soon be purged of this 'adultery' (139–42). In the text of the canto Gladstone heads this whole final passage 'Pope', underlines its last three verses, and immediately poses a question about Dante's prophetic imagining of the relationship between Church and State: 'Victory of the Emperor

---

[185] To the 'Puttana' (harlot in *Purg.* 32), and to 'Decretals' (*Par.* 9. 133); Eton College Library, Loo. I. 14, p. 142. The St Deiniol's copy's second reference to the decretals is, however, a positive one: to the appearance of the author of the *Decretum Gratiani* in the Heaven of the Sun (*Par.* 10. 103 f.).

[186] Eton College Library, Loo. I. 14, p. 113, right margin, against ll. 40–2.

[187] Eton College Library, Loo. I. 14, p. 164.

[188] Eton College Library, Loo. I. 14, last flyleaf, recto.

[189] Eton College Library, Loo. I. 14, p. 326.

[190] Eton College Library, Loo. I. 14, pp. 404–6.   [191] *Par.* 9. 125–32.

predicted?'[192] Not surprisingly, the later Apostolic denunciation of contemporary papal Rome/Avignon—'St Peter's speech' (*Par.* 27. 19–66)—also features among the items indexed, and one of its most ferocious metaphors—the transformation of the saint's graveyard into a 'sewer' (22–7)—is highlighted by heavy underlining and marginal emphases.[193] In the course of his reading of the later cantos of the *Paradiso*, Gladstone's interest in the larger issues of ecclesiastical corruption and reform is signalled not only by the index's reference to '22.73[-8] State of the Benedictines', but also by a translation of the text emphasizing how the Benedictine Rule 'NB/is become waste paper'.[194] When St Peter Damian, a few pages earlier in the text, describes the mission of the Church being poured 'merely from one bad vessel into a worse' ('pur di male in peggio si travasa'),[195] Gladstone writes one of his more discursive notes beneath:

Observe that he [Dante] thinks this rebuke of the degenerate a fit subject to excite joy even in that seventh heaven—App[arentl]y there was also prayer for their punishment acc[ording]. to the Apocalypse[.][196]

The Eton annotations thus display a stronger interest in the *Commedia*'s reformist discourse than those in the St Deiniol's copy. Such interest is certainly not absent from the latter (as we have seen),[197] and its annotations have some other features in common with those of the 'pocket Dante'.[198] But while the St Deiniol's notes concern themselves less with anti-papal and anticlerical passages in the poem, they are also at one significant point more nuanced in their account of Dante's political position. Thus, towards the end of his list of references to the *Paradiso* there, Gladstone adds:

[Dante] an imp[erialist]. not a Ghib[elline].
a R[oman] C[atholic] not a pap[alist][199]

Comparison between the two sets of annotations prompts some further questions about the more polemical slant in Gladstone's 'pocket Dante'. One way of viewing the responses to the *Commedia*'s ecclesiology here is in the context of the Protestant constructions of the poet as a 'witness against Rome' that have already been explored here and elsewhere.[200] Gladstone's interest in the *Commedia*'s anti-papal allegory, metaphor, and rhetoric could indeed owe something to the 'Whig' construction of the poet that had recently been reinforced by Foscolo, whose

---

[192] Eton College Library, Loo. I. 14, p. 468.
[193] Eton College Library, Loo. I. 14, last flyleaf, recto, and p. 572.
[194] Eton College Library, Loo. I. 14, last flyleaf, recto, and p. 545. Dante's original reads: 'rimasa è per danno de le carte' (*Par.* 22. 75).
[195] *Par.* 21. 126.   [196] Eton College Library, Loo. I. 14, p. 540.
[197] See the examples from the St Deiniol's copy's 'indexes', above, p. 187 and n. 184.
[198] Both copies, for example contain groups of references to Italian cities (Florence, Genoa, Pisa, Rome) in the *Commedia*. Gladstone was also interested in the poem's earthly topography (see Isba 2006: 23), a subject that was beginning to be treated exhaustively in such works as Ampère's *Voyage dantesque* (Paris, 1839).
[199] Isba 2006: 143; see also her comments on this note on pp. 22–3 and 90–1.
[200] See above, e.g., pp. 47–9, and 50–3.

Discorso he at some point came to own.[201] It could also have received some stimulus from the debate about another Whig-funded project, Gabriele Rossetti's *Disquisizioni sullo spirito antipapale*, and his rereading of Hallam's critique of Rossetti in the mid-1830s.[202]

However, if the annotations to the Eton Dante are viewed in the context of the 1840s—as their links with the 1844 review of Russell might suggest—they can be seen to reflect in a more complex way upon Gladstone's early intellectual and political development. His commitment to an extreme, even 'theocratic', form of High Anglicanism had been articulated at length during the late 1830s in his first lengthy monograph on *The State in its Relations with the Church*.[203] The following decade has been described as 'the crucial period of his political development'— when the unfavourable reception of that monograph, the practicalities of office in Peel's government, and his protracted personal crisis over whether to support the funding of Catholic education in Ireland all seem to have worked to modify his 'tractarian, tory political predilections'.[204] The complexity of his attitude towards Catholicism during this period is evident from his continuing involvement with the Tractarian movement and his fraught relationships with those who would go over to Rome around the middle of the century: first John Newman, then Henry Manning and James Hope.[205] His conflicted stance is frequently apparent in the diary: for instance, in his perplexed encounters with 'idolatry' in continental Catholicism during his second European tour in autumn 1838,[206] and (on the other hand) his sober account of a lengthy (two-hour) conversation about papal policy and Catholicism in Britain with Monsignor Nicholas Wiseman at Rome early in 1839.[207] A developing complexity of attitude continues to be evident in his annotations to the Eton Dante: they not only show a polemical interest in the *Commedia*'s portrayal of the Papacy and its authority but also engage with wider theological issues, such as 'Necessity', 'Justif[icatio]n', and the 'Honour of Holy Scripture', as well as the role and portrayal in the poem of the 'BVM' ('Blessed Virgin Mary'). All of these concerns are evident in the front flyleaves of the Eton Dante: they relate to Gladstone's careful rereading of the *Paradiso*—perhaps the rereading which occupied most of October 1846—and they are also clearly evident in his annotations to the text itself.[208]

---

[201] Although this copy (now at St Deiniol's) is not annotated; see above, p. 153, n. 169.

[202] See above, p. 180 and Milbank 1998: 121 and n. 16.

[203] Gladstone 1838 (two further editions in 1839; fourth edition in 1841). On the context of Gladstone's early religious views, the extremity of the position implicit in *The State in its Relations with the Church* and the book's reception by political colleagues, see Jenkins 1995: 30–4, 47–9, and 53–4.

[204] Foot and Matthew in *GD* 3: xli. On his period of office under Peel and the 'Maynooth' affair, see Jenkins 1995: 66–71.

[205] On these relationships, see Chadwick 1979: 251–2; Jenkins 1995: 74–7; Isba 2006: 84–5. On the Tractarians and Dante, see Milbank 1998: 166–7.

[206] See e.g. his comments on the 'strange' contrasting treatment of images of the Virgin in southern Germany as 'one of the signs of idolatrous tendency' (*GD* 2: 395, 24 Aug. 1838). On his earlier responses to continental and Italian Catholic culture, see Jenkins 1995: 32–4 and Isba 2006: 47–8.

[207] *GD* 2: 564–6.

[208] Thus, on flyleaf 2ᵛ the group of references to the Virgin points to *Par.* 13. 86, 15. 133, 23. 73 and 88, and (mistakenly) 31. 3; and there is further close attention to her iconography in the

   Close scrutiny of both ecclesiological and theological issues in the later stages of the *Commedia* also informed Gladstone's more discursive approach to the poem in a manuscript essay that is also likely to date from the 1840s.[209] This could well be the essay that he says he 'wrote on Dante' during his rereading of the whole poem in the late summer and early autumn of 1846.[210] It addresses some broad doctrinal issues and begins by spelling out more fully those relating to the Virgin Mary: 'As it is impossible to treat of the great work of Dante without entering into its theology, so it is impossible to discuss with propriety the considerations of its theology until after having considered with due care the place which the Blessed Virgin Mary occupies in the Poem.'[211] More narrowly, it then focuses on the relevance of that portrayal to contemporary Roman Catholic and Anglican religious culture, arguing that there must be a 'line of separation' between Dante's 'sentiments' and 'those that can be consistently entertained by a member of the Reformed Church of England', and deploring 'those excesses which have rendered the practical system of that Church [Rome] most offensive & revolting to us'.[212] By contrast, in the St Deiniol's Library copy of the *Purgatorio* and *Paradiso* the references to, for example, 'Merit', 'Beatrice, mystical or real?', 'Heaven why unintelligible', 'Platonism', and 'Evidence of miracles' seem to indicate a shift in the emphasis of Gladstone's interest away from vexed ecclesiological and doctrinal controversies and towards wider theological and philosophical issues.[213] His annotations in the Eton Dante may represent an earlier, transitional stage in that process. Like the opening of the manuscript essay of the 1840s, they play to some of the partisan ecclesiological interests of 'a member of the Reformed Church of England', but, like the annotations in the St Deiniol's copy, they also engage with larger questions, such as 'Necessity' and 'Justif[icatio]n'.

   The 'pocket Dante' annotations actively demonstrate some of the cultural values advocated by his (probably) contemporaneous writing on the *Commedia*: the manuscript essay and the review of 1844. They reflect the review's insistence upon 'the greatest mental effort to reach [Dante's] level',[214] and their range indicates how Gladstone sustains that 'effort' through all three parts of the *Commedia*. The explicit emphasis on that intensive and wide-ranging approach to the poem in the manuscript essay of the 1840s may well have been influenced by Thomas Carlyle's advocacy of the *Purgatorio* and *Paradiso* in his 1838 *Lectures on the History of Literature* and, at more length in the 1840 lecture on 'The Hero as Poet',[215] but Gladstone here develops Carlyle's argument in a markedly more incisive manner:

annotation to *Par.* 23. 64–90 (p. 550), for instance underlining the phrase 'bel fior ch'io sempre invoco' (l. 88). For 'Necessity' the lines cited are *Par.* 17. 40 and 29. 58; for 'Justif[icatio]n', *Par.* 28. 105; and for 'Honour of Holy Scripture', *Par.* 9. 133, 5. 75, and 29. 88.

   [209] BL Add. MSS 44731, ff. 134ʳ–141ʳ; see also Chadwick 1979: 253–4 and n. 16.
   [210] *GD* 3: 573 (25 Sept. 1846), 'Wrote on Dante. Read Purg. 30, 31'. The watermark on the paper is of 1842.
   [211] BL Add. MSS 44731, f. 134ʳ.   [212] BL Add. MSS 44731, f. 134ʳ.
   [213] Isba 2006: 142–3.   [214] Gladstone 1844: 166.
   [215] See *DEL* 2: 491 and 504–6. On Gladstone's reading of the latter in 1841, see Chadwick 1979: 255; and on his preference for the *Paradiso*, see *DEL* 2. 601.

So far as there can be said to subsist among us a public opinion with respect to the relative merits of the three great divisions of the Poem, it appears that the palm is assigned to the first of them.

To this judgment I am altogether opposed. . . . the Inferno is more perfect in its kind. This kind however is a lower one. The expression of the idea is more adequate to the idea itself. Far less mental effort is required to keep pace with the poet's course of thought and feeling in the Inferno than in the Purgatorio and Paradiso.[216]

As the manuscript essay moves towards a conclusion it evokes Carlyle's 'earnest Dante', but it does so in a way that defines its terms more precisely and perhaps suggests a greater degree of personal involvement:

the one quality which appears in Dante to transcend every other, and in which he appears most conspicuously to transcend all other poets is that of intensity. Intensity may perhaps be defined to be, earnestness impassioned. One of its characteristics when in the superlative degree, is, to be dissatisfied with itself, with its own achievements.[217]

Reading, writing, and conversing about Dante would for the rest of his life remain important activities for Gladstone, and a sense of Dante's political 'secret' as—in Mazzini's phrase—'a thing which concerns the present time' would inform his pronouncements about the poet well beyond the 1840s.[218] His views on politics, Italian nationalism, and Dante's bearing on both diverged considerably from those of Mazzini, but his sympathy for the Risorgimento and 'the hurly-burly of modern Italian aspirations' was beginning to stir in the 1840s, prompted in part by his reading of Carlyle's prophecy that 'The Nation that has a Dante is bound together'.[219] It is a striking coincidence that Mazzini's comment—directed to both a British and an Italian public—was published in the same month (April 1844) as Gladstone's wish (in his review of Russell) 'to see a far higher conception of Dante spread abroad among our countrymen', and his subsequent assertion that 'if they are to advance in their moral health and intellectual vigour, he [Dante] must advance in their estimation'.[220] A distinguished historian has dismissed the latter claim as a 'bizarre phrase' and a mere 'absurdity',[221] but there can be little doubting Gladstone's commitment to Dante's broader cultural and political importance for 'the present time'.[222] At the end of the 1882 letter to the Italian *dantista* he would

---

[216] BL Add. MSS 44731, f. 138[r]. Gladstone's diary note on completing his rereading of the *Paradiso* on 30 October 1846 also reflects that degree of 'mental effort': 'Would that I had really read and digested that astonishing work' (*GD* 3: 580).

[217] BL Add. MSS 44731, f. 141[r]. For Carlyle's views of Dante's 'earnestness', see *DEL* 2: 486 and 505.

[218] Excerpts from Mazzini's article (in the *Foreign and Quarterly Review* 33 (Apr. 1844)) are in Caesar 1989: 553–61 and the phrase quoted is on p. 555.

[219] From 'The Hero as Poet', in *On Heroes and Hero Worship* (1840), cited in Chadwick 1979: 255; see also *DEL* 2. 509, citing pp. 105–6 of the 1873 edition. On Mazzini, Gladstone, and British attitudes towards Italian nationalism, see also O' Connor 1998: 62–87, and Isba 2006: 62–4. Biagini (2000:12) also makes some pertinent points about the relevance of Dante to Gladstone's political engagement with Italian problems from the 1850s on, as well as his wider 'sense of the unity of Europe as a Christian civilization whose international relations ought to be regulated by God's laws'.

[220] Gladstone 1844: 179.

[221] Chadwick 1979: 256. See also the end of Gladstone's letter to Giuliani, above, p. 178.

[222] See above, e.g., pp. 184 (with n. 161) and 190 (with nn. 203–7).

reassert what his own *lungo studio* Dante had taught him: that Dante was of relevance not only to (largely) Protestant Britain, but also 'all'Italia, al Cristianesimo, al mondo'.[223]

In that same year, as we shall see, the 'Grand Old Man' of British politics became involved in a more practical way in a debate about the value of a particular Dantean text as part of the national heritage. Gladstone's contribution to that conversation will form part of the following chapter, which moves from High Victorian visions and readings of Dante to the processes by which texts and illustrations of the poet's work were being acquired, negotiated, and dispersed as cultural possessions over the course of the whole century.

---

[223] See above, p. 178.

7

Dominions, Possessions, Dispersals: British Dantes Abroad, *c.*1820–1882

On 16 April 1818 the British owner of a manuscript of the *Commedia* that he would soon donate to a learned society in Bombay wrote rather apprehensively about 'the great strides we are making towards universal dominion'.[1] The poet whom Ruskin in the middle of the century called 'central man of all the world' had a part to play in that imperial venture. Valuable books, including several texts that might be called 'colonial Dantes', can be found accompanying and signalling the prestige of Empire in several far-flung places, from Bombay to Cape Town. Closer to home, in continental Europe, the continuing British appropriation of Italian culture is reflected by the interest in the collection, illustration, and study of Dante on the part of Anglo-Florentine expatriates. And later in the century the acquisition by the German government of a great manuscript collection whose 'gem' was the Botticelli illustrations of the *Commedia* was seen as a reminder of a new nation's ambitions and an old one's need to protect its cultural possessions.

'SO VALUABLE AND SPLENDID A PRESENT': MOUNTSTUART ELPHINSTONE AND THE MUMBAI MANUSCRIPT OF THE *COMMEDIA*

We begin, early in the century, with some books changing hands in Bombay. At a meeting of what was then the Literary Society of Bombay on 29 February 1820, a donation of about 280 volumes was received from the recently appointed governor of the Bombay Presidency: the Hon. Mountstuart Elphinstone (1779–1859). A manuscript of Dante's *Commedia* was amongst them, and is thus described in the Society's catalogue of the donation, as: 'Dante devina [*sic*] Comedia[.] Magnificent illuminated MS on vellum[,] apparently of the 14th century.'[2] On the same day, the Secretary of the Literary Society of Bombay wrote to thank Elphinstone for the donation:

---

[1] Mountstuart Elphinstone, quoted by Colebrooke 1884: 2. 41.
[2] Mumbai Town Hall, Asiatic Society of Mumbai, 'Minute Book 1804–20', the 'List of [*c.*280] Books presented to the Society by the Hon[oura]ble Mounstuart Elphinstone', 29 Feb. 1820.

I have the honour to acquaint you that I had this day the pleasure of laying before a meeting of the Bombay Literary Society the collection of Books which you forwarded to me for that purpose; and that I am directed to communicate to you the Society's most particular acknowledgment for so valuable and splendid a present.

29 February 1820

I have the honour to be &c
(Sig[ne]d) Vans Kennedy
(Secr[etar]y)[3]

The late fourteenth- or early fifteenth-century illuminated manuscript of Dante's *Commedia* (Mumbai, Town Hall MS 19) that formed a major item in this 'collection of Books' remains one of the most valuable possessions of the present Mumbai Asiatic Society. To construct a context for its presence at Bombay in 1820, it will be necessary to focus upon the donor's career and reading practices, the development of his Italian and Dantean interests, and the possible provenance of his manuscript; whilst its subsequent history up to the present will also be investigated.

Mountstuart Elphinstone, the manuscript's owner in 1820, was one of the leading scholar-administrators of the East India Company. Born in 1779, a younger son in an ancient, aristocratic, and well-connected Scottish family, he did not fully complete his education before launching upon his colonial career. But like a number of the Company's leading figures at this time—such as his compatriots Thomas Munro and John Malcolm—he inherited the culture of the Scottish Enlightenment. Initially he attended school at Edinburgh and lectures in philosophy at the university, followed by several more years of tuition in London.[4] On arriving in Calcutta at the age of only 16, early in 1796, he was soon drawn into the thick of East India Company politics. During the next thirty or so years he played an active and sometimes leading military and diplomatic role, furthering British power and interests in western India and beyond. At the British residencies in Poona and Nagpur (1802–18) he was engaged in supervising and negotiating with the local Maratha rulers. In the middle of this stage of his colonial career (1808) he undertook an intelligence-gathering mission to the Afghan border, and his report formed the basis of his most significant early publication, the *Account of the Kingdom of Caubul* (published in 1815). Returning to India in 1811, he became Resident at Poona, playing a leading role in the negotiations and crises that led to the British annexation of Maratha territories in the Deccan (1817–18). He then governed the Bombay Presidency from 1819 up to his final departure from India in 1827, after which he spent the remaining thirty years of his life in scholarly retirement.[5]

---

[3] Mumbai Town Hall, Asiatic Society of Mumbai, 'Minute Book 1804–20', copy of letter following the list of books donated by Elphinstone.

[4] For an account of his early education, see Colebrooke 1884: 1. 5–6 and 8.

[5] For further accounts of his career, see especially *ODNB*, s.v. 'Elphinstone, Mountstuart (1779–1859), administrator in India'; also Colebrooke 1884, Cotton 1892, Choksey 1971, and Sushma 1981. A major primary source is the collection of his papers (especially the journals) in London, BL MSS Eur F88.

When the Anglican bishop of Calcutta, Reginald Heber, visited Bombay in 1825, he was impressed by the formidable scope of the then Governor's reading:

he has found time not only to cultivate the languages of Hindustan and Persia, but to preserve and extend his acquaintance with the Greek and Latin classics, with the French and Italian, with all the elder and more distinguished English writers, and with the current and popular history of the day, both in poetry, history, politics and political economy.[6]

The range that Heber claims for Elphinstone's reading and study can be confirmed from the account of it in the latter's journals.[7] For obvious professional reasons the young administrator needed to gain some familiarity with two of the major languages used in the subcontinent (Persian being the main medium for diplomacy), but he also made up for his rather brief formal education through acquisition of ancient and modern European texts. His ambitions are already evident from the review of his reading that he conducted on his twenty-second birthday (6 October 1801) at Hyderabad; this includes Arabic, Persian, Greek, Latin, French, German, and Italian texts, and it covers philosophical and historical writing, as well as poetry 'and novels innumerable'.[8] Along with English classics such as Shakespeare, Milton, Dryden, and Johnson, he seems to have kept up with recently published contemporary authors, for example: Scott, whose *Lay of the Last Minstrel* of 1805 he was reading two years later; Byron, 'the poet of causeless & cureless dejection', whom he was sampling in 1816, 1817, and 1820; and Burns, whose 'genius' and 'the spirit & correctness with which he describes Scottish manners' are spoken of warmly in a letter of 1813.[9]

Evidence from the libraries, journals, and reading practices of other British officials in India at the time shows that 'cultivating' literature and languages (to use Heber's word) could serve both for recreation and to develop and maintain the necessary professional skills.[10] It could also support the expatriate's sense of

---

[6] Quoted in Colebrooke 1884: 2. 170.

[7] In BL MSS Eur F88, with some of the material from them printed in Colebrooke 1884.

[8] BL MSS Eur F88/368, p. 102; also in Colebrooke 1884: 1. 31–2, where it is (curiously) described as 'a curious record of the desultory character of his reading'.

[9] On 31 July 1807, his journal records that Scott's 'Lay' 'suits entirely with my love of old language & antient ~~times~~ manners & with my passion for the marvellous' (BL MSS Eur F88/359, p. 28), and in July 1815, during a busy period at Poona, he 'found time' for 'a little reading of *Waverley*' (ibid., F88/370, p. 225), which had been published the previous year; whilst in September 1818 he read *Rob Roy* also the year after publication (F88/363, p. 128). He was reading 'some of Child Harolde[*sic*] with ~~[?]~~ ~~admiration~~ sympathy & delight' in November 1816, and some of Byron's 'last [i.e. recent] poems' in June 1817 (F88/370, pp. 11–12 and 32). He thought canto 4 of *Childe Harold* 'very inferior ... to the previous ones' (Sept. 1818, F88/363, p. 128); and while recovering from an injury at Surat in December 1820 he read cantos 3 and 4 again, along with *Parisina* (1816), *Manfred* (1817), and *Beppo* (1818); see Colebrooke 1884: 2. 118. His praise of Burns, whose Second Edinburgh Edition had appeared in 1792–3, is in a letter to Lady Hood of (probably April) 1813, in Edinburgh, National Archives of Scotland GD 46/17/42.

[10] On book collections in India around this time, see Spear 1963: Appendix B, and Shaw 2009. I am grateful to Graham Shaw (former Head of Asia, Pacific and Africa Collections at the British Library) for guidance and information on this subject. Among the 'effects of the Hon. Mr Justice Hyde, late of Calcutta Deceased' (in 1797) are, as well as a large quantity of legal items, a significant number of English poets of the seventeenth and eighteenth centuries, and books in, from, and about Latin, Portuguese, and Italian, including 'Machiavel's Works' and 'Baretti's Italian Dictionary' (see the

identity in alien and often challenging surroundings, and might even help to preserve sanity. Much later in his career—and at the very time when he was donating the collection which included the Dante manuscript—Elphinstone was also, as his journals show, undergoing a personal crisis. In January 1820, as he begins to emerge from what seems to have been a severe bout of what he called 'the blue devils', he affirms the therapeutic value of study and reading:

[16 January] Attention to one's duties & rational studies will be the cure . . .

[17 January] Exclude all desires of unattainable objects & cultivate reading & other simple pleasures . . . Cultivate taste for reading[,] <u>for hard reading & study</u> . . . This will secure, as far as is possible[,] moderate comfort[.] Fortune may add a little more wealth or a little more estimation[.] Fortune may also shorten the time for which the want of both is to be endured . . . [11]

From an early point in his Indian career Elphinstone's discipline of 'hard reading and study' involved learning languages, including Italian. In this respect the culture of British-ruled Calcutta around the turn of the century would have been influential. He had spent a short time at the newly founded Company College at Fort William, and (like many others of the new generation of adminstrators) came under the influence of Richard Wellesley, governor-general since 1797—himself a bibliophile who had read 'parts of Dante' along with Tasso and Ariosto during his Grand Tour.[12] In Elphinstone's journals the first reference to his own Italian studies occurs during a leisurely journey from Calcutta to Poona in company with his friend Edward Strachey, both of them about to take up political appointments, and both, in their early twenties, enjoying a kind of gap year at the East India Company's expense. In October 1801, a month or so after he and Strachey had reached Hyderabad, Elphinstone reviews his programme of reading so far, and it includes several Italian items: 'I looked into the Italian grammar, read the Preface & 70 or 80 verse [*sic*] of Tasso, one Book of Machiavelli history, a novel & Play of his . . . '[13] Use of the 'Italian Grammar' can be seen as reflecting the vogue for learning Italian that then was at its height among British readers, including a number of those in India.[14] The performative listing of texts and authors is a frequent feature of journals in this period, and it suggests certain preferences and

---

'Bengal Inventories' in BL L/AG/34/27/19, ff. 5[r], 7[r], 10[r], 13[r], 14[r–v], and 15[r]). On Sir James Mackintosh's books, see below, p. 204.

[11] BL MSS Eur F88/363, pp. 241–3.

[12] *DEL* 1.464 (letter of 3 July 1791). Dante remained in Wellesley's memory and conversation: well over forty years later (4 Oct. 1839) he is reported as being able to quote 'above fifty lines' of *Inferno* 33 with a 'pure and classic pronunciation of the Italian' (Stanhope 1888: 169–70). I am grateful to John Riddy for the latter reference and for information about Wellesley.

[13] BL MSS Eur F88/368, p. 102 (6 Oct.).

[14] On the teaching and learning of Italian in Britain and the production of grammars, see above, p. 124 with n. 342. Britons learning Italian in India included Sir James Mackintosh in Bombay (see Mackintosh 1836: 1. 342, for 14 Mar. 1807) and Fanny Parkes in Bengal (see Dalrymple 2003: 36, entry for 18 May 1826). Both refer incidentally to an 'Italian master'.

priorities.[15] As an administrator and diplomat working for an expansionist power, Elphinstone would have found much to interest him in the Florentine histories of the late fifteenth century, such as those of Machiavelli and Guicciardini, whom he also read. The 'seventy or eighty verse[s] of Tasso' may be the first evidence of Elphinstone's reading of Italian poetry. He may well have begun by reading some texts in translation, but by early the following year he was engaging with some quite difficult Italian poetry in the original.

I breakfasted[,] set off at 10 [;] read Ariosto[,] my eyes were sore[,] I was obliged to shut up the door of my palankeen & keep a blind or two open; the time past so quick that I thought the watch wrong[.] I read the 3rd to 4th/5th & part of the 6th book [;] where I am not interested I find it difficult to understand the Italian[,] but in the tale of Genevra [*Orlando furioso*, canto 5] [,] when I get into the spirit of it, I read it as fast as English & understand every word[.] The description of the enchanted island [canto 6] is incomparable . . . [16]

Tasso and Ariosto had been making their mark upon British culture since the sixteenth century. A number of Scottish poets since then had been among their translators and imitators, and they were still much favoured by Scottish readers of Elphinstone's era, from Boswell and Smollett to Scott.[17] Along with the reading of other medieval and Renaissance romances and of classical and modern history, these exotic Italian narratives of conquest and chivalry would have seemed particularly appropriate to the journeys, encounters, and conflicts that the young Scots servant of Empire was experiencing at first hand in India.[18] Medievalism thus seems to converge here with orientalism and with a Romantic sensitivity to history that was shared by many of the East India Company administrators.[19]

Also typical of such readers' mentality is Elphinstone's recourse to Italian poets (along with other Western classics) when he comes to describe the country in which he finds himself. His earliest brief reference to Dante forms part of a description of a wild nightscape in the Northern Ghats early in 1808:

February [?] 2nd [1808?] Mungla Jeeree . . . rose very early[;] I had tea[.] I then went for some time in my palankeen till my oil was exhausted & my bearers declared they could not proceed without light[.] I then got out &/walked on through deep shade now & then chequered by the moon[.] I was beginning to think of Virgil (6th book) & Dante when I overtook the baggage[.] [S]oon after day broke & I found the wood to consist of Bamboos mixed with trees[,] some of which very fine . . . [20]

---

[15] For example the accounts of reading and shared reading in Mary Shelley's journals (see below, p. 201 and n. 33).

[16] BL MSS Eur F88/368, p. 133 (1 Feb. 1802).

[17] See Jack 1972: 57–71, 147, 207–12, 216–19; and Jack 1986: 5–9 and 39–45.

[18] Other medieval works that he read included 'the Romaunt of the Rose' and 'Ritson & Ellis's Romances' in September and October 1817 (BL MSS Eur F88/370, pp. 39–40).

[19] See esp. Leask 1992: 94–5, on Elphinstone, Munro, *et al.* as 'Romantic "orientalists"'; also Metcalfe 1995, on the 'Romantic' administrators' awareness 'of history as an organic expression of a society's character' (p. 25), and on the continuing nineteenth-century 'medievalist vision' of Indian society (pp. 72–80).

[20] BL MSS Eur F88/359, pp. 34–5 (misnumbered as 32–3).

Elphinstone continues to impose the vision of Italian poets upon Indian scenery elsewhere in the journals of this period. His interest in Italy and Italian was developing further at the beginning of the following decade, and a journal entry of October 1811 describes how his 'delighted' response to De Staël's *Corinne ou l'Italie* led him to read some recent Italian drama ('two tragedies & two comedies') and several more general works on Italy, including one by Giuseppe Baretti.[21] An Italian touch was added to his more ambitious description of the Northern Ghats near 'Carli' (Karla) shortly afterwards, in January 1812:

We went by an unusual way & past through a large wood on our ride[.] It was composed of high shady trees with no more underwood than was ornamental[.] There were many creepers of a great size that wound in a ~~great~~ variety of fantastic knots among the large branches of the forest trees[.] The wood was generally shady & dark but here & there were breaks that admitted the sun & allowed of our seeing a piece of water below the woods & some fine views of the surrounding hills[.]

In the centre was a clear spot in which stood a very antient & almost ruined temple which accorded wonderfully with the ~~whole~~ scene[.] The whole was wild & romantic & put me in mind of an enchanted wood in Tasso or Ariosto. We saw & enjoyed much fine scenery about the Ghauts besides the chasm over which I sat for some time[.] It loses its wonderful appearance when one is accustomed to it & a knowledge of the country prevents its exciting a number of pleasing associations which it presents to a person from Europe[.] Still the deep solitude of the valley apparently shut out from all mankind ~~the~~ its silence which is only disturbed by the waving of ~~its woods~~ its branches & the picturesque arrangement of the crags & woods which surround it recall many of the ideas with which one has been delighted & lead one to fancy happy hours that might be spent in this retirement ~~in~~ amidst the fullest enjoyment of all the pleasures of the imagination.[22]

Elphinstone's deletions and rephrasing indicate a considerable degree of deliberation here, and terms like 'wild & romantic', 'chasm', 'deep solitude', 'picturesque arrangement', and 'pleasures of the imagination' seem calculated to make the sensitive 'person from Europe' feel at home.[23] So too does his explicit reference to 'pleasing associations', amongst which are those with wilderness scenes in Italian romances such as *Gerusalemme liberata* and *Orlando furioso*.

Exotic texts of this sort enabled him (as the newly appointed British Resident in Poona) to imagine the landscape across which he travelled and which he was by now helping to bring under British control. A more complex act of viewing an Indian landscape specifically through Dante is described three years later, as Elphinstone approached a key point in his Indian career. During a relatively quiet phase of his residency at Poona, on 19 June 1815, he accompanied several British colleagues on an excursion to mountains of the high Junnar valley. Here he describes how the expedition moved towards the edge of a precipice:

We ascended at the W. end where there is a remarkable chasm[.] From the top we saw a narrower valley than those already mentioned[,] through which ran a river in many windings

---

[21] BL MSS Eur F88/370, pp. 96–7 (11 Oct. 1811); on Baretti, see above, p. 124, n. 342.
[22] BL MSS Eur F88/370, p. 99 (21 Jan. 1812).
[23] Cf. Leask 1992: 95 and n. 68 (citing Ainslie Embree) on the 'Wordsworthianization of India'.

shining in the sun[.] The valley was bounded on the N. and S. by hills[;] the west seemed mountainous but was concealed by clouds. We went for about a mile along the top of the hill, on a slope above the precipice and at length descended a steep place to the bridge[,] which was about 4 or five feet broad & 20 long. Though so broad[,] there was something awful in passing it [,] from the depth of the perpendicular black walls beneath [. . .] While we sat beyond the bridge the clouds rolled up the Northern valley & completely concealed it from sight [. . .] We seemed to be standing on the extremity of the universe[,] & looking into chaos to spy 'the secrets of the hoary deep'—a 'dark illimitable ocean'[.] At Logur many sounds were heard to rise from the valley[,]which was sometime imperfectly seen[,] gleaming with a strange mysterious sunshine through the gloom[.] It put me in mind of Dante standing over the gulf of Malebolge[,] and I almost expected a̶ ̶m̶o̶n̶s̶t̶e̶r̶ the monster Geryon to ascend on his broad pinions[.] Here the effect was heightened by a singular circumstance[:] while all on the Northern side of the ridge was lost in gloom & darkness[,] the Southern valley & all on the right hand of the ridge were clear[,] sunny and serene[.] It looked as if we had been placed between Tartarus and Elysium[.] The fear of losing ourselves in the fog made us now hurry back . . . [24]

'Looking into chaos' here initially prompts an allusion to Milton's Satan at a crucial stage of his mission to Earth in Book 2 of *Paradise Lost*.[25] It continues with an evocation of Dante standing over the gulf of Malebolge at the opening of *Inferno* 17, to witness the ascent of 'the monster Geryon'. Elphinstone—like several of the *Commedia*'s illustrators, including Doré—endows Geryon with the wings ('pinions') that he does not actually carry in Dante's text, thus giving him more of an affinity with Milton's Satan travelling across the abyss.[26] More importantly, the allusion to the *Inferno* points to one of the most alarming liminal moments in the journey through Hell, when Dante and Virgil, at the end of canto 16 and the beginning of canto 17, are perched on the very edge of the great precipice plunging down to Malebolge; and the new monster Geryon emerges as 'a figure . . . that would strike even the firmest heart with wonder'.[27]

   Such an intimation of powers latent in this rugged and, in parts, 'awful' landscape may reflect something of Elphinstone's deeper concerns as British Resident at Poona. His conjuring up of 'the monster Geryon'—along with his allusion to Milton's Ulyssean, empire-building Satan—perhaps echoes some related concerns about his and his countrymen's own political journey in India during this decade. It may even convey the premonition of some further violent confrontation, such as he feared might occur and was actually to face during the final phase of the Maratha Wars, not much more than two years later.[28] 'There is', he was to

[24] BL MSS Eur F88/370, pp. 219–21. On p. 219 Elphinstone draws a rough sketch of the natural bridge and chasm in the middle of the page, in between 'something awful' (where the line partly follows the plunge of the chasm) and 'in passing it'. The passage is also transcribed (with some omissions) by Colebrooke 1884: 1. 282–3.

[25] Milton 1979: 2. 891–2.

[26] Milton's Satan by contrast does 'put[] on swift wings' and deploy 'sail-broad vans' for his flight; *Paradise Lost* 2. 631 and 927.

[27] 'Una figura . . . maravigliosa ad ogne cor sicuro'; see *Inf.* 16. 131–2.

[28] On British awareness of a 'hidden fire' in the Indian political landscape at this time, see Spear 1965: 120.

acknowledge, just after the victorious conclusion of those wars in 1818, 'something alarming in the great strides we are making towards universal dominion.'[29] On the edge of that precipice near Poona, then, Elphinstone's evocation of Dante's fierce, exotic, and powerful Geryon (the vehicle for the pilgrim's subsequent journey deeper into the underworld) expresses some of the contemporary 'anxieties of empire'.

Elphinstone—like many Romantic readers in the early stages of the nineteenth-century cult of Dante—thus deployed some knowledge of the *Inferno* and its monsters. But how, and how well, did he get to know the text? There might, in several senses, have been something romantic about that process. Early in 1813 an adventurous young Scottish aristocrat with the imposing name of Mary Elizabeth Frederica Mackenzie had been travelling around India and came to stay with Elphinstone at Poona. She was otherwise known as Lady Hood, following her marriage to the elderly Vice-Admiral Sir Samuel Hood, and amongst other things she claimed to have been the first woman in India to shoot a tiger.[30] Elphinstone never married, but he has been described as 'a passionate, rather shy and angular man' who 'declared himself fond of "nautching" [partying] with Indian dancing girls and "philandering" with Calcutta society ladies in his youth'.[31] He was still only 33 when his journal records the impression that the slightly younger Lady Hood had made on him during her brief visit to the residency at Poona in 1813:

[12 March]Lady Hood has been here for these three ~~months~~ weeks[.] She knows all my friends intimately & gives their characters candidly[,] a treasure to a person who has been so long abroad[.] She is familiar with the French, Italian & English classics[,] has good taste good sense & spirits & a thorough knowledge of the world, joined to perfect good nature[.] I need scarce say I regret her departure which happened today[.] [. . .]

March 23[r]d I still hear often ~~will~~ from Lady Hood[,] but notwithstanding my constant occupation I find time to regret our readings of Dante & our innumerable digressions[.] I hope I shall be able to go to Bagdad & Persia with her next year[.][32]

Whatever 'digressions' Elphinstone may have anticipated in Baghdad and Persia, 'our readings' in this passage raises some interesting questions about the form of the collaboration. 'Reading with' is a phrase that occurs a number of times in his journals, and it could imply a variety of possible scenarios—from an agreed programme of study to reading aloud, and even (in the case of a foreign author), attempts at translation.[33] It frequently occurs, for example, in Elphinstone's accounts of Greek and Latin studies together with male friends.[34]

---

[29] Letter to Captain Close, 16 Apr. 1818, quoted in Colebrooke 1884: 2. 41.

[30] *ODNB*, s.v. 'Mackenzie, Mary Elizabeth Frederica Stewart-, Lady Hood (1783–1862), chief of clan Mackenzie'.

[31] *ODNB*, s.v. 'Elphinstone, Mountstuart (1779–1859), administrator in India'.

[32] BL MSS Eur F88/370, pp. 140–1.

[33] Cf. e.g. the shared reading of Dante by Mary and Percy Shelley in 1818–19 (Shelley 1987: 1. 246–7, 295–7, and 351); and Gladstone's reading of the *Purgatorio* with his brother in November 1835 (see above, p. 180).

[34] e.g. BL MSS Eur F88/370 p. 146: reading Xenophon with Jenkins (on 3 and 8 Sept. 1813, when they finish book 3 of the *Anabasis*), and pp. 155 (2 June 1814), 159 (2 Oct.) and 164 (24 Oct.). Also p. 211: 'read Virgil with [Captain] Close' (13 June 1815).

More can be inferred about the scope of the shared reading of Dante at Poona from a group of twenty letters that Elphinstone subsequently wrote to Lady Hood during the following year.[35] Explicit references to the *Commedia* appear here, and the letters also make frequent use of Italian phrases and allusions to Dante and other Italian authors. Once again, the *Inferno* is inscribed upon an Indian landscape, as when—shortly after Lady Hood's departure from Poona—Elphinstone regrets his inability to share the 'adventure' of her visit to the rock temples in the Ellora Caves (near Aurangabad):

that emprise is not destined for me & I must content myself with reading your description (if you have compassion enough to write me any) & with figuring to myself mountains higher than the Alps, pierced in all directions with caves such as could not be equalled by a general assembly of all the caverns, grottoes, spelonche, tane [caves, lairs] or in in all the Romantic & Epic poems now extant. In the midst of the whole I figure a rock considerably larger than Tabernicch (which you must remember rhyming to *cricch*) cut out into the figure of a temple larger than that of Diana at Ephesus and more elegant than the Parthenon[,] supported by Elephants large enough to be taken for Mammoths. Among all these wonders I figure you upon an elephant surrounded by chobdars [staff-bearers] celebrating your invincible arms & enlarging on the terrors of your countenance . . . [36]

Elphinstone's whimsical apotheosis of Lady Hood invites her to imagine herself enshrined in a rock higher than the Italian mountain (Monte Tambura in the Apuan Alps) which forms part of an elaborate comparison in canto 32 of the *Inferno* (28–30). Dante's peak here—like the tributary chorus of staff-bearers—could be seen as an embodiment of the writer's own genteel libido; whilst his rather pedantic use of words from *Inferno* 32, such as *Tabernicch* and *cricch*—together with his use of Italian elsewhere in the letters—makes it clear that he and Lady Hood had been reading the *Inferno* in the original back in Poona, and had nearly reached the end.

Writing a few days earlier, Elphinstone refers to the actual book in which he and Lady Hood have, like Dante's Paolo and Francesca—'read no more':

We have had very hot weather even here & today it promises to be hotter than ever[.] There is no hot wind as yet but everything out of doors looks so dismally still that I cannot help figuring the horrors of a tent as equal at least to one of the valleys of Malebolge. I am afraid you will think I have got into the Mysore strain of sentiment & want to have a sick lady to condole with[.] However if you will come back[,] you shall neither have be dozed with laudanum & ether nor with tender speeches[.] [. . .] I enclose an extract of a newspaper which I took out of your papers for a mark to put in my Dante[.][37]

The claustrophobia of the lower *Inferno* not only serves as an image for the oppressive climate, it also seeps into the torpid reverie that follows. The book he mentions ('my Dante') could have been one of the numerous printed editions of the *Commedia* that were being published in Italy and (from 1808) in Britain, but

---

[35] These were kept and bound by Lady Hood and are now in the National Archives of Scotland (NAS) at Edinburgh, GD 46/17/42.

[36] NAS GD 46/17/42, letter of 24 Mar. 1813 (p. 2).

[37] NAS GD 46/17/42, letter of 16 Mar. 1813

the erotic overtones of this letter suggest that the volume has now gained further significance for the reader.[38] 'His Dante' thus not only provided him with a key to the 'mysterious' and 'awful' Indian landscape; it also carried intense personal associations which may have informed his donation of that 'valuable and splendid present' to the Bombay Literary Society at the beginning of his governorship in 1820.[39]

Other questions—and a number of problems—involve the form, provenance, and subsequent history of his donation's major item: the Mumbai manuscript itself.[40] The textual status and affiliations of this *Commedia* have not been given much attention, and there is only one really detailed study of its readings, dating from the later nineteenth century.[41] A modern catalogue of manuscripts places its origin 'probably in the second half of the fourteenth century', on the basis of some of its linguistic usages[42]—although the style of the illuminations might suggest a slightly later date, and its relationship with the other manuscript groups remains uncertain.

The manuscript's provenance, too, is problematic. Who might have owned it before Elphinstone, and how might he have obtained it? I have so far found no evidence of such a purchase in his journals or letters, and it is certain that, for thirty-odd years, between his arrival in India at the age of 16 in 1796 and his departure at the end of his governorship in 1827, he did not return to Britain nor travel in Europe. He could have had some direct dealings with Italians (perhaps Catholic missionaries such as the Capuchins and Carmelites) who are known to have been in western India at the time.[43] It seems more likely, however, that, like other British collectors of his time and earlier, he would have obtained the manuscript from a dealer with contacts on the Continent.[44]

Elphinstone seems to have ordered and received other books through friends, relatives, and agents in Britain and Calcutta. In April 1819, for example, his sister offered to send 'any Book or anything you wish for', whilst acknowledging that a Scottish agent 'sends you what you want in general'.[45] Later that year Elphinstone wrote to his cousin, John Adam, then serving on the Governor-General's Council in Calcutta, rather peremptorily presenting a list of Latin, Greek, English, and

---

[38] On British editions of the time, see above, pp. 137–9.

[39] 'My Dante' is unlikely to be the Mumbai *Commedia* itself, which he probably acquired some time after his books and papers were destroyed in the attack on the British Residency at Poona in 1817 (see below, nn. 45–6).

[40] Now Asiatic Society of Bombay, Town Hall MS 19.

[41] See below, p. 207.   [42] Roddewig 1984: 21 (no. 43).

[43] I have discussed this possibility in an earlier article: Havely 2009: 137–8 and nn. 46–7.

[44] As a consequence of the Napoleonic invasions of Italy in the late 1790s many Italian collectors had sold their manuscripts and works of art, rather than risk losing them outright to French plunderers, and a considerable number of such items thus found their way through agents into British hands; see Brand 1957: 138. One such dealer was the Abbé Luigi Matteo Celotti (*c.*1768–*c.*1846), who operated also in France and England and was involved in the sale of Italian books and manuscripts (including those of Matteo Luigi Canonici) around 1816–21; see Munby 1954: 50.

[45] BL MSS Eur F88/254, no. 63; later, in February 1820, she sent him a bible to replace the one lost 'with all your other Books and valuables when your House was burnt [during the troubles at Poona in 1817]' (F88/255, no. 62).

Italian texts which 'can easily be shipped for Bombay' and therefore making 'no apology for the trouble'.[46] The Italian items were specified as:

Tasso's Gerusalemme Liberata
Ariosto [presumably *Orlando furioso*]
[Boiardo] Orlando Innamorato (if it is to be had) &
[Pulci] Morgante Maggiore.[47]

As well as providing important evidence about book-purchasing, the list gives some indication of the Italian dimension of Elphinstone's literary interests shortly before the time he donated the Dante manuscript to his colleagues at the Bombay Literary Society. The continuing significance of such authors is apparent in one of the inscriptions in the volume of his journal for the months immediately after he had made the donation.[48] Here, a stanza in Italian, exhorting a nobleman to exert himself in climbing to the 'summit of the steep and rugged hill of Virtue' rather than linger in the lowly 'paths of pleasure', is unattributed but in fact comes near the beginning of the speech by the wizard (*mago naturale*) admonishing Rinaldo as he returns to the Holy Land in the later stages of Tasso's *Gerusalemme liberata*.[49] Its relevance to the conqueror of newly acquired territories is obvious enough, but it also further underlines for Elphinstone the value of that programme of 'reading and hard study' that he was prescribing for himself at that time and that was physically embodied in the collection which he had just donated to his colleagues.[50]

There were precedents for this ambitious level of acquisition, which took advantage of the trade supplying individual and institutional libraries in British India. Elphinstone's colleague Sir James Mackintosh, who founded the Bombay Literary Society in 1804, according to the Society's records ordered several large consignments of books from Longman, Hurst, Rees Orme & Brown in London, and amongst the more expensive items in the cargo were the 'Operae de Machiavelli 6 tomes octavo vellum £5. 0s' and the 'Vocabulario [*sic*] de la Crusca 6 tomes in 5 folio vellum £14. 14s'.[51] Many of Mackintosh's own books had accompanied him out to India when he began his duties as Recorder of Bombay in 1804, and when Maria Graham visited him there in May 1809 she described him as possessing 'the finest library that ever doubled the Cape'.[52]

Yet it remains uncertain precisely how Elphinstone would have purchased and paid for his own 'valuable and splendid' collection of around 280 volumes, donated to the Literary Society in 1820—especially some of that collection's rarer items.

---

[46] BL MSS Eur F88/282, letter no. 40 (3 Oct. 1819); presumably he felt that the Company owed him for the property lost when the Residency at Poona was destroyed in October 1817.

[47] BL MSS Eur F88/282, letter no. 40 (3 Oct. 1819).

[48] BL MSS Eur F88/364, the inside cover.

[49] Tasso 1968, canto 17, stanza 61 (ll. 481–8).

[50] See above, pp. 194–5.

[51] Asiatic Society, Bombay, 'Minute Book 1804–20' (for 13 Jan. 1812 and 17 Apr. 1813). The consignments also included poetry, novels, history, journals, and dictionaries in English and French.

[52] Her diary (for 27 May 1809), quoted by Gotch 1937: 136; on her own reading of Dante and her later association with Foscolo's circle, see above, p. 147 with n. 129. On Mackintosh, see also above, p. 131.

The 'List of Books presented to the Society by the Hon[oura]ble Mountstuart Elphinstone' included two other manuscripts, three incunables, and a substantial number of sixteenth- and seventeenth-century texts, many of them in Italian or published in Italy.[53] The only firm evidence about the provenance of the 'magnificent' *Commedia* manuscript itself remains within the volume itself. Pasted onto a flyleaf is an Italian inscription in a late eighteenth- or early nineteenth-century hand:

Magnifico codice membranico della Divina Commedia di Dante Alighieri che gareggia in Conservazione e in bellezza Con quelli esistenti nelle primarie Biblioteche d'Europa e Specialmente Con quello esistente nella Biblioteca Ambrosiana di Milano[,] Col quale si è confrontato[.] La forma dei Caratteri manifestano la sua data che è verso la metà del secolo XIV; Cioè trent'anni DopoDopo La morte di Dante che seguì nel 1321 = in Sua età di anni 56[.] Le miniature in fronte a ciascun Canto [*sic*] fanno allusione al contenuto del Canto medesimo, e Mostra^no la Stile dell'arte d[e]l Secolo XIV: de modo che in tutto rende questo Codice preziosissimo[.] III. C

Magnificent vellum manuscript of Dante Alighieri's *Divine Comedy*, which, in its state of preservation and beauty, rivals those extant in the major libraries of Europe, and especially the one in the Ambrosian Library at Milan, with which it has been compared. The script indicates a date around the middle of the fourteenth century, that is, thirty years after Dante's death, which occurred in 1321, thus when he was aged 56. The miniatures preceding each canto [in fact, each *cantica*] reflect the artistic style of the fourteenth century in a way that combines to make this manuscript very valuable indeed. 300 (francs?)[54]

This reads like a dealer's or a librarian's account. In layout and tone it has affinities with the kind of description that, for example, the early nineteenth-century Florentine bookseller Giovanni Claudio Molini inserted in other manuscripts of the *Commedia* which came on the market around this time.[55] But beyond those possible parallels and the note on the manuscript's flyleaf, there seems to be no further evidence about the transactions which brought this particular colonial possession to Bombay, and questions about precisely how Elphinstone was able

[53] Asiatic Society, Bombay, 'Minute Book 1804–20', 29 Feb. 1820. The other manuscripts listed are '[Domenico] Cavalca, Spec[c]hio della Croce M.S. of the 14th Century' and 'Vita di San Paolo primo Romito MS of the 14th Century', and both are said to have been 'cited by the Crusca Academy'. The three incunables are: Jacopo Passavanti's *Specchio della vera penitenzia* (Florence, 1495, 'wood cut [,] very rare'); *Quadriga Spirituale* (Verona, 1475, 'very rare'); and *Sancti Leonis Opera* (Rome, *c.*1470, 'rare').

[54] Asiatic Society of Bombay, Town Hall MS 19, second flyleaf, verso.

[55] Possibly comparable are Molini's table of contents for MS Hamilton 201, pasted on to the inside of the front cover and dated April 1803 (see Altcappenberg 2000: 22 and fig. 8), and his description (dated 1793) of the Milan Trivulziana 1074 *Commedia* ('Ce beau manuscrit . . . d'une écriture trés lisible'), written on several separate leaves, now kept together with the manuscript; see Roddewig 1984: 186–7 (no. 445). A comparable librarians' description of a *Commedia* text is one found in the British Library MS Egerton 943: here three officials of the Biblioteca di Parma have signed a report (dated 25 June 1815) speaking of the manuscript as 'amongst the most valuable for its antiquity, the importance of its readings, the elegance of its script and the quantity, skill and richness of the miniature that adorn it' (f. 1^r, my tr.). I am grateful to Dr Anna Pegoretti of the University of Warwick for the information about Egerton 943 and for an excerpt from her thesis on it (Università di Pisa, 2006–8).

to purchase his manuscript and exactly when it reached India still remain un-answered.

Information about the manuscript's subsequent status during most of the nineteenth century is also hard to come by. The Literary Society would soon (in 1826) transform itself into the Bombay Branch of the Royal Asiatic Society, and subsequent statements about its library resources in the *Journal* understandably give prominence to Asian rather than European texts. Thus, Elphinstone's donations of Sanskrit manuscripts are mentioned in the Society's catalogue of 1861, but not his gifts of European books.[56] In 1886 his 'present of a number of books in foreign languages' is briefly mentioned in a 'Historical Sketch of the Society',[57] but it is not until the final decade of the century that the *Commedia* manuscript is mentioned again, and a possible explanation for that long silence about it has recently emerged.[58]

In an article of July 1890 a former secretary of the Society, Sir George Birdwood, claimed to have rediscovered the manuscript several decades earlier:

on becoming Secretary to the Bombay Branch of the Royal Asiatic Society [i.e. in 1862], I went up under the roof of the Town Hall, and began kicking my heels among the heaps of rubbish lying all about the place, just on the chance of stumbling on some 'hid treasure,' when presently I struck, 'thud,' against a large vellum quarto. It turned out to be an illuminated MS. of Dante's poems [*sic*], with a miniature of the poet, all painted within thirty years of his death; and certified by the Secretary of the Ambrosian library at Milan [*sic*] to be one of the noblest MSS of Dante extant. There was no record of the volume to be traced anywhere, until after going back for years in the minute books of my predecessors I found that it had been presented to the Society in, if I remember rightly, 1827 [*sic*] by the Hon. Mountstuart Elphinstone . . . [59]

Birdwood is not a very reliable witness, as his errors about the content of the manuscript, the note pasted into it, and the date of its donation all suggest; moreover, the account of stumbling on the 'large vellum quarto' in the dusty attic of the town hall sounds somewhat embroidered. But he seems to have had some positive influence in drawing attention to the significance of the 'hid treasure'. At a meeting of the Society two months after his article's publication, the manu-script was displayed; Birdwood's enquiry about its well-being was reported; and the names of several interested parties are mentioned:

The Hon. Secretary, on laying on the table an illuminated MS copy in parchment of Dante's 'Divina Commedia', said that he had much pleasure in exhibiting the MS to the meeting.

---

[56] *JBBRAS* 21: 97-11.

[57] Tivarekar 1886: 36.

[58] I am much indebted to Dr Michael Franklin of the University of Swansea for references to the manuscript's 'rediscovery' and to the *Times* article of Oct. 1890 (below, n. 70).

[59] Birdwood, Sir George C.M., 'Illustrations from the Records and Relics of the Late Honourable East India Company', *Journal of Indian Art and Industry* 3 (1890), no. 31, p. 42. Birdwood continues to recommend this kind of research: 'It is always well worth looking into Parsee godowns, particularly in out-of-the-way up-country stations, in India, for you are sure to be rewarded for your trouble in one way or another . . .' (ibid.).

The immediate occasion for its exhibition arose from an inquiry made by Sir George Birdwood as to the existence of this MS copy in the Society's Library [. . .] Mr Javerilal said that, in a letter, dated the 22nd August, he had from Sir George Birdwood the learned Doctor asked to let him know if the copy was all right still [. . .] In reply to this inquiry, the speaker said he wrote back to Sir George to say that on receipt of his letter he (Mr Javerilal) examined the MS copy very carefully. It was also shown to the Hon'ble Mr Justice Candy, Mr Macdonell, of Messrs Wallace & Co [. . .] who were probably not aware till then of the existence of this literary curiosity in the Library. They all thought that the MS., which was more than five hundred years old, was preserved in good order and condition [. . .]

Mr Jeevanji Jamshedji Mody then read a paper[:] the Game of Ball Bat among the ancient Persians as described in the Epic of Firdousi.[60]

As the minute indicates, one of those present at this meeting was a recently retired Scots East India merchant and former member of the Bombay Governor's Council, William Robert Macdonell.[61] Six months later Macdonell was to deliver the first and (to date) the only first-hand scholarly account of the manuscript to a meeting of the Society.[62] He was not an academic Italianist—his training at Aberdeen and Oxford was in mathematics—but his physical description of the manuscript is careful and methodical, and he drew upon the 'test passages' in Edward Moore's recently published *Textual Criticism of the Divina Commedia* (1889) to reach his conclusions about the status of the Asiatic Society's manuscript and its lack of affiliation to several other groups or individual witnesses.[63] He therefore under-standably gives no attention to its provenance or recent history, but he begins to acknowledge the implications of its presence in India, when, in conclusion, he suggests 'to our Committee that round this noble M[anu]s[cript] they should gradually form, as opportunity offers, a good working collection of books on Dante's work'.[64] The manuscript's 'rediscovery' and Macdonell's acount of it, however, do seem to have prompted further discussion, and comparisons between the *Commedia* and Persian visions of the afterlife were subsequently published by the Parsi philologist and historian Jivanji Jamshedji Modi (1854–1933). Modi was present as a new member of the Asiatic Society at that meeting of September 1890 when the *Commedia* manuscript was put on the table; indeed, as the minute book shows, he himself was due to read a paper about a Persian medieval poet on that occasion.[65] In February 1892 he read and published the first of several papers comparing the *Commedia*'s vision of the afterlife with, especially, that of an 'Iranian precursor', Ardâi Virâf.[66] He concludes that, although 'there seems to be no direct

---

[60] Asiatic Society of Bombay, 'Minute Book 1865–98', 26 Sept. 1890.

[61] *The Balliol College Register, Second Edition 1833–1933*, ed. I. Elliott (Oxford: Oxford University Press, 1934), 82.

[62] On 5 March 1891; see Macdonell 1891.

[63] Thus 'although not in the very first rank, [it] is one of great excellence and will repay more extended examination . . . The great problem is to discover its relation to the MSS in Europe'. His 'negative conclusions' apply to the 'Vatican' and 'Ashburnham' group and to 'Cambridge O' and Milan Ambrosiana C 198 INF (Macdonell 1891: 8, and Appendices I–IV).

[64] Macdonell 1891: 8, and Appendices I–IV.   [65] See above, n. 60.

[66] Modi 1892 and 1911–12. The broad similarities between the *Inferno*'s punishments and those of the Zoroastrian hell in the *Virâf-nâmeh* had much earlier been noted in a paper by the Society's first

relation' between the texts, '[t]heir different parents may have had a common ancestor', and his subsequent papers on the subject attracted favourable attention among European orientalists.[67] Encouragement from such sources seems to have prompted him to draw some rather bolder parallels in his later articles.[68] Modi does not mention Elphinstone's donation in any of his 'Dante Papers', but—as the Asiatic Society's 'Minute Book' for 1890 shows—he certainly knew of its existence.[69] In their different ways, then, both scholars (Macdonell and Modi) seem to have been impelled by the presence of 'this literary curiosity' to consider more precisely how Dante might be located in relation to the culture of the British Raj.

Elphinstone's Dante was to act not only as an intellectual stimulus; it also acquired the status of a cultural icon. In his letter to the Society, quoted in a *Times* article, Sir George Birdwood had also made some claims about Italian interest in the manuscript, and about its likely monetary value:

AN OLD ILLUMINATED MANUSCRIPT OF THE 'DIVINE COMEDY'
In a letter to the secretary [of the Asiatic Society] [. . .] Sir George Birdwood inquired after the volume, and said:- 'It is worth a lakh of rupees, and I made a regular shrine of it, showing it to all distinguished strangers. Every learned Jesuit that passed through Bombay used to be shown it; and I recollect one of them saying that it was absolutely priceless, and that £10,000 would be given for it at once in Italy.'[70]

Again, Birdwood's tone sounds suspiciously effusive, and his claims may well be inflated. Yet the reported valuation of the manuscript itself—at what would amount to over half a million pounds in today's money—raises some interesting questions about Dante's status in the cultural marketplace of the nineteenth century. It may also have helped to shape one of the most popular stories to be told about the manuscript's twentieth-century history.

It is said that in the 1930s Benito Mussolini offered the Society £1 million (dollars in some versions) for the return of the Dante manuscript to Italy, and that, to his surprise, the offer was refused.[71] Read as the resistance of a—by then somewhat impoverished—learned society to the will of a powerful dictator, this is an exemplary and quite plausible story. It is difficult, however, to find any firm

---

Secretary, William Erskine, in a paper 'On the Sacred Books and Religion of the Parsis', *Transactions of the Literary Society of Bombay* 2 (1820), 352. A later short article, on 'A Persian Forerunner of Dante', discussed and illustrated the parallels between the *Sayru'l-Ibād* by the twelfth-century Sufi poet Sanā'ī and the *Inferno*; see Nicholson 1943.

[67] See Modi 1914: v and 72; he visited Europe in 1912, and his comparative studies were admired by, amongst others, the distinguished scholar of Persian literature (and founder-president of the Manchester Dante Society) Bishop L. C. Casartelli; see Panaino 2008: 174 and nn. 16–20. On Casartelli, see below, p. 268, n. 51.

[68] For example, in a short discussion of 'Azidahâka (Zohâk) of the Avesta and Satan of Dante', Modi 1914: 87–91.

[69] See above, p. 207 and n. 60.   [70] *The Times*, Saturday, 25 Oct. 1890, p. 9.

[71] Versions of the story are in *The Asiatic Society of Bombay 1804–2004: A Guide to its History, Collections & Activities* (Bombay: Asiatic Society, 2002), 26, and, e.g., D. Abram *et al.*, *The Rough Guide to South India* (New York, etc., 2005)—which describes the manuscript (among the Society's 'mouldering tomes') as 'a fourteenth-century first edition [*sic*] of Dante's *Divine Comedy*, said to be worth around $3 million' (p. 128).

evidence to support it. Mussolini was indeed, from early in his career, an avid reader (and declaimer) of Dante.[72] Some of his more imaginative admirers saw his advent to power as a fulfilment of Dantean prophecy, and his regime certainly continued to appropriate the poet as an icon of *italianità*.[73] For example, during the first year of his regime the *New York Times* reported on a new official measure:

Busts of Dante for Embassies
The better to ensure the carrying out of his foreign policy, Mussolini has decided that, from Jan. 1 next, all consular agents and clerks in the service of the Government shall be Italians. He has also ordered that a bust of Dante be placed in each Italian embassy and legation as a symbol of the mother country.[74]

Fascist educational programmes under Giovanni Gentile, from 1923 onwards, sought 'through the sacred poem of Dante to quicken the pulse of the Italian soul', and the regime also supported the redesigning of the *zona dantesca* in Ravenna and the planning of a 'Danteum' in Rome.[75]

Mussolini did indeed re-purchase a *Commedia* manuscript from the United States in the 1930s,[76] and several of the regime's orientalist experts were interested in cultural contacts with India, but it has not been possible to find documentation of any project to repatriate the Mumbai manuscript.[77] Nor do the Asiatic Society's minute books for the 1930s (despite recurrent references to 'financial stringency', 'cuts', and 'retrenchment') record correspondence about or inclination to consider the sale of its valuable *Commedia*.[78]

Nonetheless, the scenario of the dictator's thwarted desire, the cultural and financial value of the manuscript, and the (mistaken) claims that it might be a Dantean 'original' or 'one of the two oldest copies' have continued to quicken pulses in the press and on the web up to the present. A patriotic web-posting of 2006 remarked that:

Mumbai's got something that Mussolini couldn't muscle into his grasp. Tucked away in a locker, away from grimy hands, is a rare 14th century manuscript of Dante Aligieri's [*sic*] Divine Comedy. In the 1930's Mussolini [*sic*] government reportedly made an offer for that

---

[72] Bosworth 2002: 53.

[73] See Scorrano 2001: 93 (on Dante as 'precursor of Fascism'); 94–6, 102–3 (on *Monarchia* and Italy); 106–7 and 112–15 (on Mussolini and Dantean prophecy).

[74] *New York Times* for 29 November 1922 (p. 3), accessed online at <http://query.nytimes.com/search/sitesearch/#/Mussolini> on 11 March 2014.

[75] Albertini 1996: 118–22 and 132–7; and Nicoloso 2008: 95 and 218–19. For a detailed account of Giuseppe Terragni's unbuilt 'Danteum' project (to be sited on the Via dell'Impero, opposite the Basilica of Maxentius and Constantine), see Schumacher 1993. On 'mosaics of scenes from Dante' in surviving early Fascist architecture, see Bosworth 2005: 440.

[76] Venice, Biblioteca Nazionale Marciana MS It. IX 692 (dated 1398–1400) was purchased in the USA by the Italian State for 200,000 lire and presented to the library in 1935 as 'DONO di B. Mussolini'; see Roddewig 1984: 341–2 (no. 796).

[77] On the Fascist government's cultural relations with India, Dr Fabrizio de Donno of RHUL comments: 'Two orientalists in particular fostered these relations and their names are Carlo Formichi and Giuseppe Tucci. If Mussolini at any time requested the MS of the *Commedia* to be repatriated, one of these . . . must have been involved in some way' (personal communication).

[78] References to the Society's financial difficulties are in minutes for November 1931, October 1934, and March and July 1938. I am indebted to Mrs C. A. Havely for this information.

they hoped no one would refuse. Except that the Asiatic Society did and today, Mussolini's must-have is Mumbai's treasure.[79]

Not long after I had given a paper on this subject to the Asiatic Society of Mumbai in February 2008, I was approached by a Calcutta journalist who subsequently published an article on the manuscript (which is now kept in a Mumbai bank):

A riddle wrapped in silk inside a vault

One of the oldest manuscripts of Italian poet Dante Alighieri's 14th century work, *Divine Comedy*, lies in Mumbai's Asiatic Society. But a debate now rages as to whether the document is a copy or not. **Rahul Jayaram** looks for answers . . . [80]

The answers received are intriguing, particularly those that appear to derive from a conversation with a confused visiting scholar:

. . . the document, touted as an 'original' and described by the Asiatic Society as 'priceless,' is being looked at very carefully by a British academic. Professor Nick Harley of the University of York, UK, is not so sure about it being Dante's original. 'I believed so initially, but we can't speak of this manuscript as being "only one of two surviving original documents". "Original" would mean Dante wrote it himself. We don't know about that. But yes, it is one of the two oldest surviving ones,' he says.[81]

The spurious claim (allegedly) repeated by this 'British academic' that the Mumbai *Commedia* is 'one of the two oldest surviving ones' is itself of considerable antiquity. It may ultimately derive from a misreading of that late eighteenth- or early nineteenth-century inscription, in which the manuscript 'in its state of preservation and beauty' was said to rival 'the one in the Ambrosian Library at Milan, with which it has been compared'.[82]

The manuscript's status as a desirable cultural possession is vividly conveyed towards the end of the Calcutta *Telegraph* article:

Other anecdotes and offers to buy the [Mumbai Dante] manuscript run thick and fast. In 2002, former World Bank chief Paul Wolfowitz came with his wife and read aloud from the document for an hour. 'So impressed was he that he asked for Society membership, and how much it would cost to buy the manuscript. We laughed it off,' says Aroon Tikekar, president, Asiatic Society, Mumbai.

Then again, it was rumoured that the government of ex-Italian Prime Minister Silvio Berlusconi was 'interested' in acquiring the document. Renato Ruggiero, Italian foreign minister in 2002, came visiting, compared it favourably to the one in Milan, and sent back a

---

[79] Anonymous posting by 'Mysterindia', 7 May 2006.

[80] *Telegraph*, Calcutta, 8 June 2008, accessed at <http://www.telegraphindia.com/1080608/jsp/7days/story_9381261.jsp>, on 9 June 2008.

[81] *Telegraph*, Calcutta, 8 June 2008. The conversation in question took the form of emails, and most of the beliefs, names, and assertions in this paragraph cannot be securely attributed to 'Harley' or to the paper given at the Asiatic Society in 2008. A more accurate account of the views expressed in the paper and in this chapter has been given by Vikram Doctor in the *Economic Times of India* (1 June 2013), under the heading: 'Divine Comedy indeed: Here's the plot [Dan]Brown's Inferno missed out on'; an online version (in July 2013) is available at: <http://blogs.economictimes.indiatimes.com/onmyplate/entry/divine-comedy-indeed-here-s-the-plot-brown-s-inferno-missed-out-on>.

[82] See above, p. 205 and n. 54.

detailed proposal to the Italian ministry for cultural affairs. 'He asked for a quotation, we said, "no,"' says another senior functionary. When contacted, Italian embassy officials in Delhi refused to comment.

What continues to baffle scholars is how the document came to Mumbai—a puzzle that Harley seeks to crack one day.[83]

Large amounts of money and resistance to offers of it thus continue to play a part in the contemporary fortunes of Elphinstone's 'valuable and splendid present', and so too does an increasing cast of questionable and acquisitive political figures. The 'puzzle' of the Mumbai manuscript's origins yet remains, and it is still possible that 'Harley' (or, more likely, someone else) may one day resolve it.

As a 'literary curiosity' the manuscript has thus accrued some further problematic features. Its history and status in nineteenth- and twentieth-century India have highlighted significant cultural and bibliographical issues and raised some additional questions. But, to return to this investigation's starting point: what significance might that 'valuable present' of 1820 have borne at that particular moment during the extension of British power in India? We know that Elphinstone read Dante along with other classics of the Western canon, but did he expect his successors in India and their subjects to do so?

Unlike later British rulers, Elphinstone saw education in Indian languages rather than the imposition of Western culture (subsequently advocated by Mill and Macaulay) as the key to the subcontinent's future: 'native education' would then construct what he called 'our high road back to Europe'.[84] His reading and acquisition of Italian authors seem unrelated to that programme: he corresponded with several scholarly Indians, but not, it seems, on the subject of Dante.[85] His donation to the Literary Society (which did not admit native members until 1841) was probably intended to be of value chiefly to the European governing class—to provide the kind of resources, linguistic training, and solace that he himself had acquired in reading the Western classics. Yet, as we have seen, its most valuable item, the Dante manuscript, eventually came to acquire an iconic status, reflecting, in and around itself, some of the complex interactions between the cultures of India and Western Europe.

'MORE THAN ITS WEIGHT IN GOLD': SIR GEORGE GREY'S MANUSCRIPTS IN CAPE TOWN

Later in the nineteenth century a comparable case of acquisition and donation would involve another colonial administrator and governor: Sir George Grey (1812–98), who held office in Australia, several times in New Zealand, and

---

[83] *Telegraph*, Calcutta, 8 June 2008.
[84] On Elphinstone's educational policy, see esp.: Ballhatchet 1957: ch. 10; Choksey 1971: ch. 21; and Varma 1981: ch. 8.
[85] On interest in Dante among nineteenth-century Indian (and especially Bengali) writers, see Schildgen 2002: 86 and Schildgen 2012.

(from 1854 to 1861) in South Africa (Cape Colony).[86] Grey's donations of books and manuscripts at several points in his career comprise major collections in the Auckland Public Library and the National Library of South Africa in Cape Town. The nature and acquisition of these collections—unlike those of Elphinstone's present to the Bombay Literary Society—have been thoroughly evaluated in recent times, but it is worth noting again that the collection Grey donated to the Cape Town Library when he left for New Zealand in 1861 included—among over 100 manuscripts and more than 300 early printed books—two manuscripts of the *Commedia*.[87] Both have been described in detail on several occasions (the earliest very shortly after Grey's donation), but a few further features help to indicate their status among the governor's possessions.[88]

One of Grey's Dantes is a *Commedia* of the late fifteenth century (MS Grey 3 c 25). This contains a cutting from an early printed catalogue which may have been produced by the first 'custodian' of the Grey collection.[89] That catalogue compares this 'very clearly-written copy' with a manuscript of Boccaccio's *Fiammetta* 'also in the Library' (now Grey 3 c 9), and makes the striking claim that this *Commedia* 'is probably the most precious of all the manuscripts as yet received. Its readings have been ascertained to be very valuable; and I venture to say that some of the libraries in Europe would gladly give more than its weight in gold for it.'[90] The manuscript, like Grey's other *Commedia*, belongs to the 'Siena' group of texts, and modern textual scholars do not seem to have been quite so impressed; but Dr Bleek seems—like Sir George Birdwood in Bombay at about the same time—keen to promote the idea that the colonial collection possessed an important copy of such a canonical work.[91]

There does not seem to be any evidence about how Grey acquired this Sienese Dante, but his purchase of another *Commedia* is well documented. His vellum-and-paper copy (Grey 4 b 11, with miniatures of Dante at the opening of each *cantica*) had been bought in 1813 by an aristocratic politician and collector, the Marchese Antaldo Antaldi (1770–1847), who described its text as 'not very accurate' (*poco corretta*).[92] It then entered a British manuscript collection (that of John Thomas Payne), and was sold in 1857 at Sotheby's for £52. 10s. to the London dealers Thomas and William Boone, who were Grey's main suppliers.[93] On 28 August 1857 Grey wrote a letter to Messrs Boone from Government House in Cape

[86] On Grey's career, see *ODNB*, s.v. 'Grey, Sir George (1812–1898), colonial governor and premier of New Zealand'; and, amongst several biographies, Rutherford 1961.

[87] For an overview of both collections and their acquisition, see Kerr 2000; for descriptions of the medieval and Renaissance manuscripts at Cape Town, see Steyn 2002; and for evidence about the acquisition of medieval manuscripts in the Cape Town collection, see Casson 1959.

[88] Grieben 1869; Roddewig 1984: 30 (nos. 63–4).

[89] The philologist Dr W. H. I. Bleek (1827–75); see also his 'Inventory of Manuscripts in the Grey Collection' (National Library of S. Africa, Cape Town, MS C 57. 23 [1]). On his association with the collection and Grey, see Spohr 1962: 5–6 and 15–16 and Kerr 2000: 91.

[90] National Library of S. Africa, Cape Town, MS Grey 3 c 25, slip pasted on to first flyleaf.

[91] Compare Birdwood's description of making the Bombay Asiatic Society MS 'a regular shrine' to be displayed to 'distinguished visitors', above, p. 208 and n. 70.

[92] National Library of S. Africa, Cape Town, MS Grey 4 b 11, pastedown. The miniatures are on ff. 1r, 68r, and 134r.

[93] Casson 1959: 27 and Kerr 2000: 97–8.

Town.[94] He begins by acknowledging receipt 'upon the 26th [of] the Latin MS Gospels [now Grey 4 c 15] and the Dante [Grey 4 b 11] which you purchased for me'. He does not say how much more than the £52. 10s. auction price he had to pay for the *Commedia*, but he goes on to mention sums for purchase of other manuscript items in Boone's catalogue (twelfth-century Greek gospels at £70; a thirteenth-century illuminated Latin Bible at £50) and his interest in other types of book, especially English incunables.[95] The letter thus provides some evidence about the relative values of manuscripts at the time—shortly before the steep increase in prices later in the century—and it offers some impression of how Grey's illuminated Antaldi Dante related to his other interests, his purchasing objectives, and his overall 'collection development policy'.[96]

Intellectually, politically, and personally, Grey is a more problematic and less engaging figure than Elphinstone, but unlike the governor of Bombay he left—along with the collections that (as he surely intended) now bear his name—a considerable amount of evidence about his purchases of books and his motives for donating them. His two manuscripts of the *Commedia* have not, to my knowledge, contributed to specific cultural interactions, such as are evident, for example, in the recent collection of work on *Dante in South Africa*.[97] But like Elphinstone, Grey had an interest in a wide variety of languages, a strong sense of an educational mission, and a view about the potential uses of a collection which included the Dante manuscripts.[98] Writing about his donation to a trustee of the South African Library just after his appointment as governor of New Zealand, he made several significant statements about his motives in handing over his possessions:

What I have laid up for myself I can neither use nor enjoy, yet it is selfishly shut up from other men, who might profitably use it and greatly enjoy it . . . I believe South Africa will be a great country, that Cape Town, or its vicinity, will . . . be the chief point of education . . . There can, therefore, be no more fitting or worthy resting place for treasures, which I have accumulated with so much care. I propose, therefore, by degrees, to send my whole Library to the South African Public Library at Cape Town.[99]

Collections in this period—their educational motivations, their use, and their dispersal—will be a continuing concern of this chapter.[100] But, remaining for a while in the mid-century, the focus now turns back to Europe and to a group of scholarly British expatriates who, around the time of Grey's acquisition of his manuscripts, were actively amassing material about the *Commedia* in Dante's own city.

---

[94] Western Cape State Archives, Cape Town, GH 30/11, pp. 292–4. The contents of the letter are also described and excerpted in Kerr 2000: 97–8.

[95] Western Cape State Archives, Cape Town, GH 30/11, pp. 293–4.

[96] Kerr 2000: 98.

[97] Edited by Cullinan and Watson 2005. This collection includes artwork, poetry, prose, and the first canto of an Afrikaans translation of the *Commedia* by Delamaine du Toit (pp. 33–6).

[98] See Kerr 2000: 88–91.

[99] Letter from Government House, Auckland, 21 Oct. 1861, to Mr Justice E. B. Watermeyer at Cape Town; excerpts quoted by Spohr 1962: 6, and Kerr 2000: 91.

[100] Below, pp. 246–59.

'OUR DANTE COLLECTION': MRS MACLEOD
IMAGINES THE DIVINE COMEDY

In the National Library of Scotland at Edinburgh there are five large nineteenth-century volumes bound in black-and-red velvet, described, on the title-page of the first, as *DISEGNI AD ILLUSTRAZIONE DELLA DIVINA COMMEDIA DI DANTE ALIGHIERE* (Fig. 13).[101] They contain a wide range of original material and reproductions: portraits of Dante and his characters; landscapes with Dantean associations; engravings of buildings and monuments; coats of arms for families named in the *Commedia*; copies of earlier illustrations and manuscript pages.[102] According to the documentation at the National Library, these volumes were presented to the Society of Antiquaries of Scotland in January 1885, by Robert Bruce Aeneas Macleod, laird of Cadboll (north of Inverness), who describes them as follows:

A collection of drawings, engravings &c. Archaeological, Topographical and Heraldic illustrative of

Le [*sic*] Divina Commedia di 'Dante Alighieri'

Collected and arranged by 'Miss Elizabeth Macleod of Cadboll', in the years 1842–1848 inclusive. The Heraldic and other illustrations taken from antique works in the Private Library of the late Grand Duke of Tuscany in the Pitti Palace Florence, from the Laurentian & Magliabecchiana Public and other Private Libraries, as also from the walls of Ancient Palaces in various parts of Italy.

Presented to the National Library in the Museum of Antiquities Edinburgh under the care of the Society of Antiquaries of Scotland. By
R.B.A. Macleod
(of Cadboll)
J[a]n[ua]ry 1885[103]

Thus the first name we find associated with this ambitious project of the 1840s is that of an Elizabeth Macleod, who was described very briefly by the official family history in 1889 as still alive and 'residing in Florence, Italy, unmarried'.[104] On the basis of this information, the five large NLS volumes could be thought to represent a lone project undertaken by the laird of Cadboll's Anglo-Florentine relative with some good social connections and perhaps much time on her hands. As will be seen here, Elizabeth Macleod, who died in Florence in 1913,[105] does seem to have contributed to the collection, but she was not the only—or even the main—member of the family to have been involved.

---

[101]　Edinburgh, NLS MSS 2168–72; title as in MS 2168, f. 2.
[102]　I am grateful to Prof. Jonathan Usher of the University of Edinburgh and Dr Chris Taylor of the NLS for drawing my attention to this collection, known to them as 'the Dante Scrapbook'.
[103]　Edinburgh, National Library of Scotland (NLS) MS 2212 (Society of Antiquaries of Scotland papers), f. 70r.
[104]　MacKenzie 1889: 431.
[105]　Morrison 1976: 104.

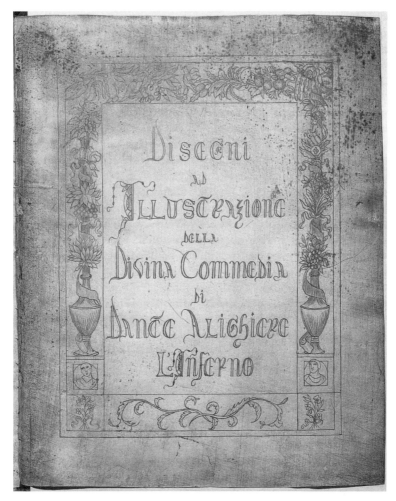

Fig. 13. Edinburgh, NLS MS 2168, f. 2, courtesy of the Society of Antiquaries of Scotland

Amongst the Macleod of Cadboll family papers transferred to the Highland Council Archive at Inverness in the 1990s, there are transcriptions of a large number of letters written by Mrs Isabella Macleod, mostly from Florence between September 1843 and September 1847, and mostly addressed to Captain Francis Brooke (at Pieve S. Stefano in the upper valley of the Tiber), whose connections with several Dante projects will be addressed here.[106] These indicate that the Dante illustration project was conceived and directed not by Elizabeth Macleod but by her

---

[106] Inverness, Highland Council Archive (HCA) D 63/E/2a. The copies appear to have been made early in the last century on a lined notepad. The location of the originals is currently unknown.

mother Isabella (d. 1878), and they record the progress of what Mrs MacLeod calls 'our' or 'my Dante collection'. They also contain a wealth of information about the culture of the *anglo-fiorentini* of the time, together with some lively reportage and commentary on the political situation in Italy in the 1840s as perceived by Britons abroad, reflecting the interests, sympathies, and prejudices of the well-educated Whig gentry.

Born in the 1790s, Isabella Macleod was the daughter of William Cunninghame of Lainshaw, one of the great Glasgow tobacco 'barons' who had made his fortune during the American War of Independence. According to a recent genealogy, she was also descended from Scottish, English, Norwegian, and French royalty.[107] When she married into the Macleods of Cadboll in 1813 she was, therefore, coming from a background of serious money and higher aristocratic connections. Her husband, Roderick IV of Cadboll (1786–1853), served as an MP for several northern Scottish constituencies between 1818 and 1840 and was lord lieutenant of Cromarty from 1833 until his death.[108] His politics appear to have been aligned with the reformist Whigs of that period, although he was not particularly active in parliament.[109]

From the early 1840s Roderick and Isabella Macleod spent considerable periods abroad with their three daughters, first in Paris and then in Tuscany.[110] From 1842 the family must have been in Florence, since this is where various drafts of Roderick's will are dated.[111] British travellers and expatriates in Florence (for example, Robert Browning, Joseph Garrow, John Ruskin, and others) obtained foreign periodicals and books at the Gabinetto Vieusseux (founded by the Swiss businessman and reformer Giovan Pietro Vieusseux in 1820), and Roderick Macleod and Isabella entered their names as subscribers there on five occasions between June 1843 and May 1847.[112] These entries and several of the family letters indicate that during those years they were living in some style, first at the Palazzo Coppini in the Via del Giglio, and then at Casa Vernaccia, the former Palazzo Ferrantini, in the Borgo Pinti. Their aristocratic background gave them an entrée to the higher levels of Florentine society, and Isabella's letters contain a fair amount of gossip about the Italian and expatriate nobility, as well as brisk comments about the Grand Duke of Tuscany's peregrinations around Europe and his uneasy relations with Austria. A characteristically merciless sketch describes the Austrian chargé d'affaires shortly after he had forced the Tuscan government to censor the wording of a new memorial inscription to Alfieri:

I met this Austrian Chargé at the Sloanes—a great fat redhaired sandy German moustache'd bête—very stupid—very puffed up with self- importance, just such a one as you could

---

[107] Morrison 1976: 80.   [108] Morrison 1976: 80.
[109] Thorne 1986: 508–9.   [110] Morrison 1976: 103.
[111] HCA D 63/E/1/1.
[112] See the *Libro dei Soci* of the *Gabinetto Scientifico-Letterario di G. P. Vieusseux*, vol. 3, p. 422; and vol. 4, pp. 83, 93, 124, and 142 (online at <http://www.vieusseux.it>).

suppose capable of this littleness. It is however hoped that he has thereby made himself so offensive to the Tuscan Gov[ernmen]t that his recall will be insisted on.[113]

Isabella MacLeod also records contacts with and views of some important British and American figures on the Florentine cultural scene.[114] The 'Sloanes' who are mentioned as hosts to the objectionable Austrian were probably the family of Francis Sloane who bought and restored the Medicean villa at Careggi in 1848 and financed the neo-Gothic facade of Santa Croce (1857–63). Several of the best known British expatriates—Landor and the Brownings—were not in Florence during the Macleods' main period of residence (1842–c.1847), and there seem to be no references to them in her letters.[115] She did, however, know at least one member of the Trollope family, Thomas Adolphus, elder brother of the novelist, who had been in Florence with his mother (Frances Trollope) since 1843,[116] although her opinion of his abilities was not high. In January 1847, hearing of the imminent appearance of an English journal (the *Tuscan Athenaeum*) under his editorship, she noted tersely: 'There is also an [E]nglish newspaper to be started here, but as T. Trollope is said to be concerned in it, I augur little of its quality.'[117] She admired rather more the abilities of the American sculptor Hiram Powers, who had produced figures for the 'Dante's Hell' waxwork show in Cicinnati and was now an internationally renowned figure on the Florentine art scene.[118]

Her more specialized interests in medieval culture and in Dante were, however, shared by three particular expatriate British scholars. One of these, who features with some frequency in the Macleod correspondence, was George Warren, fifth Baron Vernon (1803–66). Vernon's Dante studies and editions have been described as 'the last of the great whig politico-cultural projects of the regency period',[119] and the relationship between his project and the Macleods' collection will be given closer attention later on.[120] Another member of the circle was an even more well-known (and more eccentric) figure: Seymour Kirkup. Early in his long life Kirkup had been associated with, amongst others, Blake, Shelley, Keats, and Turner; he had lived in Florence since 1824 and would continue to be a prominent presence in the Anglo-Florentine community and in Dante studies until a few years

[113] HCA D 63/E/2a, f. 20 (*c.* Sept. 1844?). The inscription had described Alfieri's contribution to the *regenerazione* of Italy, and, following the Austrian protest, this was replaced by *grandezza*.

[114] On the expatriate scene in Florence around this time, see Artom Treves 1953; Baker 1964: 52–9; and Milbank 1998: 61–2.

[115] The Brownings arrived in Florence in April 1847 and Landor began his second period of residence in 1858.

[116] *ODNB*, s.v. 'Trollope, Thomas Adolphus [Tom] (1810–1892), historian and writer'.

[117] HCA D 63/E/2a, f. 160 (11 Jan. 1847). Isabella MacLeod was well informed about the state of the Italian press and laws governing it: in July of the same year she writes about 'newspapers in Italian & English . . . starting into life all over Tuscany' (ibid., f. 172).

[118] On Powers, see Looney 2011: 16–19 and 63. The Macleods visited his studio in January 1847 (HCA D 63/E/2a, f. 161).

[119] See *ODNB*, s.v. 'Warren [*formerly* Venables-Vernon], George John, fifth Baron Vernon (1803–1866), literary editor'.

[120] Below, pp. 221–2.

before his death.[121] His contribution to the discovery of the Bargello portrait of Dante in 1840 is well known, and Isabella Macleod copied his tracing of it soon afterwards, including it amongst the preliminary images in her collection (Fig. 14), as: 'Ritratto di Dante in Fresca nel Palazzo del Podestà in Firenze copied from a drawing, taken by Mr Kirkup.'[122]

Kirkup and Vernon also knew and consulted a third important expatriate British scholar in the Macleod circle: Captain Francis Brooke (1810–86). Following an early military career, Brooke had in 1836 inherited considerable estates at Ufford in Suffolk and had turned to a life of travel, scholarship, and book collecting.[123] He thus spent much of his time in continental Europe, including eastern Tuscany, and his 'Travel Journals' contain detailed and carefully referenced accounts of Florentine art, architecture, and literature, including Dante. During much of the period when the Macleods were in Florence, he was resident at Pieve Santo Stefano in the upper Val Tiberina, and there and at Ufford he and his family were the main recipients of Isabella Macleod's letters. The letters reflect a developing range of interests during the period from 1843 to 1847, from literature, fine art, and politics to newspapers, gas-lighting, and railways. During the first three years they also make frequent reference to the progress of the project to illustrate Dante. Acquisitions of material for the collection are first mentioned in September 1843:

We have been very fortunate[,] since you went[,] in our Dante collection, having got the Torre della fame, from a drawing of the 16th century when it stood a roofless ruin—A copy of an old drawing of la casa della Pia in Sienna [*sic*] & the Arms copied from the Grave Stone of the Castiglione, which we found at Cercina in one of our explorations of the environs of Florence . . .[124]

This is the first letter in the existing archive, showing that from an early stage the project ('our Dante collection') was to some degree a shared enterprise for the Macleod family, and giving a fair sample of the range of material they were seeking to include.[125] In that collection, prints of buildings are frequently used to illustrate cantos and life-stories—like those (mentioned here) of Ugolino (the Tower of Hunger in *Inferno* 33) and Pia de Tolomei (*Purgatorio* 5)—and the second of the two illustrations of La Pia's house in Siena seems to be identifiable with the 'copy of an old drawing' mentioned in the letter.[126] The Dantean associations of 'the [coat of] Arms' copied from a gravestone at Cercina (near Sesto Fiorentino) are less obvious. The Catellini family, who owned the castle of Castiglione at Cercina, are not major figures in the *Commedia*, but they head the list of ancient Florentine

---

[121] See: Artom Treves 1953: 81–7; *ODNB*, s.v. 'Kirkup, Seymour Stocker (1788–1880), painter and antiquary'; and Lindon 2000*b*. On Kirkup's later Anglo-Florentine contacts, see below, pp. 238–9.

[122] NLS MS 2168, f. 5 (followed by an engraving of the portrait, f. 6). On the discovery of the portrait and its Italian and British contexts and consequences, see: *DEL* 2. 639–42; Holbrook 1921: 73–103; Milbank 1998: 1–4; Smith 2000: 45–9; and O'Connor 2008: 72–3. On Kirkup's later activities, see below, pp. 236–42.

[123] The ten volumes of his 'Travel Journals' are in BL Add. MSS 62142–51.

[124] HCA D 63/E2a, f. 4 (letter of 18 Sept. 1843).

[125] On the main contributors, especially two of the Macleod daughters, see below, p. 223.

[126] NLS MS 2170, f. 19.

Fig. 14. Edinburgh, NLS MS 2168, f. 5, courtesy of the Society of Antiquaries of Scotland

families named by Dante's ancestor Cacciaguida (in *Paradiso* 16. 88), and their heraldry, along with a sketch of their stronghold, occupies two pages in the illustrations.[127]

As a report on progress, this early letter reflects several of the main archaeological and historical interests that prompted the Macleods' 'explorations'. It also seems to indicate, in the first sentence of the paragraph quoted, some degree of collaboration—or at least conversation—on Brooke's part before he left Florence for the Val Tiberina. Their shared interest in, among other things, heraldry associated with the *Commedia* and in other Dantean memorabilia continues to be evident from Isabella MacLeod's later correspondence.[128] For example, in a letter of

[127] NLS MS 2171, ff. 96–7.
[128] Thus late in 1845 sketches of the arms of the Genoese Spinola family (dedicatees of the Chantilly MS of the *Commedia*) and of the Cancellieri of Pistoia (originators of the Black/White Guelph partisanship) were sent to Brooke (as stated in HCA D 63/E2[a], ff. 80 and 89). More dramatically, in an undated letter there is mention of 'above 50 autograph letters from Dante' locked away by the Frescobaldi family (HCA D 63/E/2a, f. 17).

January 1846 she sought a specific contribution from Brooke for her material on *Inferno* 30: 'When idle, pray write a little treatise on your discovery of Fonte Branda, & I shall bind it up in my Dante Illustrations. In my next, I shall send you the size of the paper to write it on.'[129] Brooke's 'discovery' was of the spring near Romena in the Casentino, to which the forger Maestro Adamo alludes in the tenth circle of Malebolge (*Inf.* 30. 78).[130] He also corresponded with and provided some material to Seymour Kirkup and Lord Vernon for what was to become a rival—and much better known—enterprise: Vernon's edition of the *Inferno*, which would later be privately published and would contain an 'Album' of illustrations in its third volume.[131]

Isabella Macleod vividly records, for Brooke's benefit, the activities and the eccentricities of both these fellow Anglo-Florentines and the ways in which they impinged upon her own Dante project. Her letters document the interest that Kirkup and Vernon displayed in the Macleods' material, offering a number of insights into the British expatriates' cult of Dante, their location of his work in Florentine and Tuscan places of memory, and the occasionally competitive nature of their activities. Seymour Kirkup, now in his late fifties, is a frequenter of the Macleod household at Casa Vernaccia and is referred to familiarly as 'old Kirkup' or 'Cricky'.[132] Lord Vernon's whims are treated more warily, and his initial appearance in a letter of August 1844 shows Isabella MacLeod reaching for her Scottish heritage in order to describe his obsessions:

In Scotland when a man is a little cracked, we say that he has a bee in his bonnet; but it appears to me that Lord Vernon has a swarm in his . . . [then follows an account of his participation in a Swiss rifle-competition] The last new kick [i.e. fad] about his Dante, is that he rejects all modern assistance, nothing is to be admitted except copies from ancient art . . . So Lady Dalmeny & Kirkup are, I presume, to be thrown overboard. I should be but too thankful to pick up the crumbs from the rich man's table. I wish that Kirkup would give me the reversion of his Beatrice & of the Buondelmonte. Apropos of that, A[nna] M[aria] & I have just completed the [16]th Canto of Paradiso—38 shields of arms—Views of Campi—Luni—Val di Gr[]eve—Monte Buono, Monte Murlo &c and portraits. I have been forced to lend a hand to the landscape part, which I consider a great hardship imposed on me, but Anna is all uplifted, & there is no end of her crowing, for we have given her a superexcellent master in watercolour portrait painting . . . [133]

---

[129] HCA D 63/E/2a, f. 102 (letter posted 9 Jan. 1846) and 105 (22 Jan. 1846).

[130] Brooke's work on this topic seems to be taking shape in vol. 9 of his 'Travel Journals', BL Add. MS 6150, ff. 21ʳ–24ᵛ, with extensive notes on Fonte Branda, the counts of Romena, and existing Dante scholarship on the subject.

[131] Dante 1858–65 (Vernon's illustrated edition of the *Inferno*). Kirkup printed Brooke's material relating to Fonte Branda and referred to it in his letters (now Oxford, Bodley MS Eng. misc. d. 639, ff. 19ʳ, 20ʳ, and 26ᵛ–27ʳ), but neither Brooke nor Kirkup receive credit in Vernon's edition; see Dante 1858–65: 3. 205 and 215, and below, p. 240.

[132] HCA D 63/E/2a, f. 27 (4 Oct. 1844, including a poem about Kirkup accompanying a Macleod family painting excursion) and f. 145 (15 Mar. 1846).

[133] HCA D 63/E/2a, ff. 15–16 (17 Aug. 1844). Lady Dalmeny (Catherine Stanhope) had married the eldest son of the earl of Rosebery in 1843.

Vernon's fad for 'ancient art' may have derived from his interest in archaeology and is evident in some of the antiquities illustrated in his *Inferno*, but Kirkup's illustrations were certainly not 'thrown overboard': most of those in Vernon's eventual 'album' are his. The character and extent of Isabella MacLeod's own project are also evident in this letter, alongside glimpses of at least one other member of the family's participation.[134] Here, as in the letter of September 1843, she is referring to her work on one of the most Florentine of the cantos in the *Commedia* (*Paradiso* 16), and the one which, in the final collection, is the most fully illustrated.[135]

Also noticeable here is the rather apprehensive way in which Isabella Macleod measures her project against the illustrious Vernon venture. The possibility of collaboration with 'his lordship' is more assertively raised in a letter of a month later, and Kirkup once again is involved:

he [Kirkup] went all over the Battlefield of Montaperti [near Siena] & brought home two views & much curious information. I don't know whether it is from your [Francis Brooke's] puffing or Latouche[']s, but Kirkup wants our aid about the Dante Arms,—I think that if granted[,] I must condition that the Dante is to be 'Illustrated by Mrs Macleod & Edited by Lord Vernon.'—Why should not I claim as much immortal fame as his lordship?[136]

During one of Vernon's visits (in May 1845) she records a singular manifestation of the Dante cult in which he has become involved: 'Lord Vernon is here, the present kick [fad] is a Dante Club, the rule of which is, that the Members assemble and sit round a table, & each pulls from his pocket a Dante night cap, & wears it during the evening...'[137] Tantalizingly, she wrote nothing further about this club, its members, or any discussions they might have had, but its rituals reflect the kind of Dantemania that saw tourists and artists (such as John Everett Millais) impersonating the poet.[138]

During Vernon's next winter residence in Florence it seems that negotiations about possible collaboration with the Macleods are still under way. In December 1845 Isabella announces tersely that 'Lord V. lately sent an embassy to us, respecting our Dante arms. I said that I would be glad to give him any information we could.'[139] A few months later the polite rivalry seems to have grown more intense on both sides:

---

[134] On Anna MacLeod's contributions, see below, p. 223.

[135] In NLS MS 2171 the illustrations for *Paradiso* 16 occupy twenty-nine pages (ff. 82–110), including the landscape views and portraits mentioned, together with six pages of 'shields of arms' of Florentine families.

[136] HCA D 63/E/2a, f. 22 (10 Sept. [?] 1844). Montaperti was the scene of the defeat of the Florentines at the hands of the Sienese, the Imperial forces, and the Florentine Ghibellines in 1260; the battle is referred to in *Inf.* 10. 85–93 and 32. 79–111.

[137] HCA D 63/E/2a, f. 49 (14 May 1845).

[138] On Dante tourism in Florence (and Vernon's contribution), see Smith 2000: 20–1, and 2012: 90 and 92; also below, pp. 224–5. For a photograph of Millais dressed up as Dante, see Bindman *et al.* 2007: fig. 7 (p. 21).

[139] HCA D 63/E/2a, ff. 95–6 (14 Dec. 1845).

Lord Vernon and Kirkup are just now puzzling their brains over a little common place book of Arms of Bessie's; they disagree in some cases with us, but we stick to our text, for Lord V. knows little about the matter, & I suspect Cricky [Kirkup] not much more [. . .] This new idea of Lord V. to add the arms to his Dante, is entirely [due] to his conversations w[i]t[h] Bessie. He had never thought of doing it before, & his face was admirable, as he anxiously asked 'Do you mean to publish?'—A number of petites gallanteries [*sic*] Dantesques, pass between us,—enough to make the illiterate smile.[140]

In a later tribute to Vernon's scholarship, Isabella MacLeod would mischievously compare the progress of his scholarly work to that of the Tuscan railway system:

The Vernons are absent; on their return they will have the pleasing surprize of finding the Railway terminus close behind their house, in the garden of the Dominicans. The squeaks & creaking, fizzing & blowing of the Engines will help on amazingly Lord Vernon in his Dante, & give him a vivid idea of L'Inferno.[141]

Vernon's own collection of illustrations would not be published until near the end of his life, under the editorship of an Italian émigré (and friend of Gladstone), Giacomo Lacaita; but at the time when he was 'anxiously' asking about Isabella Macleod's publishing plans, Vernon had already been involved in producing several important works of Dante scholarship. Four years earlier he had published an edition of the *Inferno* designed 'for the use of foreigners', which acknowledged the distinguished precedents of Foscolo and Rossetti in bringing Dante to the British public and refers to commentaries such as Biagioli and 'above all (*sopratutto*) that of Zotti'.[142] The previous year he had sponsored publication of a major *trecento* commentary on the *Commedia*: that of Dante's son Pietro, a copy of which Roderick MacLeod had sent to Brooke;[143] and he would also publish editions of other commentaries later in the 1840s. Like Kirkup, he was a collector of manuscripts: for example, his 1848 edition of the early commentary by Graziolo de' Bambaglioli is based on a *codice Vernon*, and a mid-fifteenth-century copy of the *Commedia* now owned by the University of Chicago was acquired by Vernon some time before 1846.[144]

Doubtless aware of Vernon's standing as a *dantista*, Isabella Macleod is concerned to stress both her own intellectual credentials and those of her family. Writing to another scholarly expatriate (Brooke) in her letter of 15 March

---

[140] HCA D 63/E/2a, f. 145 (15 Mar. 1846).

[141] HCA D 63/E/2a, f. 173 (2 July 1847). She adds helpfully (for the benefit of railway historians) that 'That railroad to Prato opens in Sep[tember]. The Leghorn [Livorno] road was opened as far as Empoli on the 21st [June]' (ibid.). For grimmer examples of 'infernal' industrialization (in Carlyle, Melville, *et al.*), see Havely 2007*a*: 246–7.

[142] Dante 1842*b*: iv–v. On Foscolo, see the previous chapter; on Rossetti, Biagioli, and Zotti, see above, pp. 149 (with n. 142) and 137–40.

[143] *Petri Allegherii super Dantis . . . comoediam Commentarium . . . consilio et sumptibus G.J. Bar. Vernon, curante Vicentio Nannucci* (Florence, 1845). Roderick MacLeod notes that '[i]t is a handsome volume, crown octavo of 740 pages text and 150 more of various readings, indexes &c. &c.' (HCA D 63/E/2a, f. 86).

[144] The Bambaglioli commentary was published as *Comento alla cantica di Dante Alleghieri di autore anonimo* (Florence: Baracchi, 1848); Vernon's copy of the *Commedia* at Chicago, is MS 544 in the Joseph Regenstein Library; see Roddewig 1984: 33–4 (no. 72).

1846,[145] she refers to another of her daughters, 'Bessie'. Elizabeth Macleod (1815–1913) was the eldest of Isabella's three girls. Most of the information about her comes from her mother's letters of the 1840s and from a small, equally vivid group of her own, written much later, from a villa at Careggi, north of Florence, between 1871 and 1904.[146] She thus lived to a great age, although in the mid-1840s her mother describes her—then about 30—as fragile in health.[147] She also features on several occasions as the family's expert on Italian Renaissance art and on heraldry.[148] However, her brother Robert's later claim, when donating the Dante collection to the Society of Antiquaries at Edinburgh, that it was 'Collected and arranged by "Miss Elizabeth Macleod" of Cadboll in the years 1842–1848' is almost certainly inaccurate, not least (as we shall see) in its dating.[149] But it is quite possible that, although her mother was clearly the prime mover of the project, 'Bessie' may have been its primary researcher. She may well also, during her later years in Italy, have become the guardian of the collection, passing it on to her brother perhaps some time in the early 1880s.

Another Macleod who contributed substantially to the collection was, as we have seen, Elizabeth's younger sister, Anna (1816–1903). Her initials ('A.M.M.') appear alongside those of her mother in a copy of an illustration from an early fourteenth-century *Commedia* manuscript.[150] The 'beautiful drawings of the Casentino, Fonte Branda, & the Castle of Romena', which Mrs MacLeod reports that 'Anna has made' would all feature as illustrations for *Inferno* 30 in the Dante collection.[151] Her slightly fuzzy style of draughtsmanship is also evident in some other landscape drawings in the collection, such as a view of Monte Pisano, the mountain between Pisa and Lucca, depicting the setting for Ugolino's ominous dream (*Inf.* 33. 29–30), and one from the Porta del Sole at Perugia, illustrating Dante's story of St Francis (*Par.* 11. 46–7; see Fig. 15). Another Macleod sibling, Robert Bruce Aeneas—the eventual head of the family and donor of the volumes now in the National Library of Scotland—made one significant landscape contribution to the Dante collection. His sketch of Camaldoli, illustrating *Purgatorio* 5. 94–6, was copied for the collection by his sister Elizabeth (Fig. 16).[152] Perhaps it was inter-actions and collaborations of this kind that caused Robert's later attribution of the whole enterprise to his sister, although the sketch's date (1852) contradicts his own later claim that the collection was assembled between 1842 and 1848.[153]

Sketches of landscapes and engravings of monuments in the collection suggest affinities with contemporaneous travel journals and topographical albums—such as

[145] See above, p. 222 and n. 140.
[146] HCA D 63/E/2d, ff. 1–98 (1871–1904).   [147] HCA D 63/E/2d, ff. 55 and 116.
[148] HCA D 63/E/2d, ff. 100, 118, 142, 146.   [149] See above, p. 214 and n. 103.
[150] See below, pp. 228–9 and Fig. 20.
[151] HCA D 63/E/2d, f. 105 (22 Jan. 1846). The sketches are in NLS MS 2169, ff. 61–3. Another of her mother's letters, on 2 July 1847 (HCA D 63/E/2a, f. 172), reports that during her residence in Rome (newly married to a Yorkshire landowner), Anna took lessons from Rudolf Müller, a Swiss landscape painter.
[152] NLS MS 2170, f. 21.
[153] For Robert's 1885 description of the collection, see above, p. 214, and for further evidence about material later than the 1840s, see below, p. 231.

Fig. 15. Edinburgh, NLS MS 2171, f. 68, courtesy of the Society of Antiquaries of Scotland

the ten large volumes compiled and updated by Isabella's main correspondent, Francis Brooke.[154] Along with their meticulous notes on sites, artefacts, and texts, Brooke's journals include a number of sketches, engravings, and heraldic images which recall the material in the Macleod collection. Both collections reflect the vogue for Dante sightseeing, which had recently been given impetus by a number of works encouraging travellers to follow in Dante's 'footsteps', reading the Italian landscape through the *Commedia* and vice versa. Jean-Jacques Ampère's *Le Voyage dantesque* of 1839 (which was soon translated into German and Italian) had affirmed that 'Dante is an admirable *cicerone* throughout Italy, and Italy furnishes an excellent commentary on Dante'.[155] In the summer of 1845 Isabella MacLeod writes scathingly about the credulity of some British residents in Florence: 'all the literary English who are here have been making pilgrimages to the "Villa Dante" [at Fiesole]—quite convinced that it was the abode of the Poet!!!'[156] On the other hand, some of the locations and landscapes in her own collection imply similar 'pilgrimages'. Among the preliminary images is one of 'Dante's Bridge', captioned: 'By the Contadini [country people] about Fiesole, this Bridge is Il Ponte di Dante, there being a tradition that Dante was in habit of standing upon it in

[154] Brooke's 'Travel Journals' are in London, BL Add. MSS 62142–51.
[155] Friederich 1950: 161–2 and 431. Brooke refers to the Italian version of this guide in vol. 9 of his 'Travel Journals': '"Viaggio in Italia sulle orme di Dante" Venezia. 1841. This work is but superficial and occasionally incorrect' (BL Add. MS 62150, f. 4ʳ).
[156] HCA D 63/E/2a, f. 75 (23 July 1845).

Fig. 16. Edinburgh, NLS MS 2170, f. 21, courtesy of the Society of Antiquaries of Scotland

meditation.'[157] Moreover, some of the items in the body of the Macleod collection seem more like haphazard souvenirs or postcards. For example, the Lorelei rock on the Rhine (illustrating *Paradiso* 6) and Trajan's Tafel on the Danube (for *Paradiso* 19) reflect the world of early Victorian tourism but have very little connection with the landscape of the *Commedia*.[158]

'Our Dante collection' did, however, have aspirations to be rather more than a family scrapbook, and it is quite possible that its main compiler indeed meant to

---

[157] NLS MS 2168, f. 10. [158] NLS MS 2171, f. 26 and 2172, f. 31.

publish it in some form. Claims to scholarly and antiquarian credentials are not only articulated in Isabella Macleod's letters; they are also reflected in two of her collection's most vivid and frequently recurrent features. As we have seen, she took some pride in her own and her daughter's expertise in heraldry, and at one point in the letters, when referring to Dante's patrons the Conti Guidi of the Casentino, she speaks of painting 'pages of all the arms of all the branches of the honourable family'.[159] Lord Vernon's interest in what she had called 'our Dante arms' could have been sparked by her collection of heraldic material, such as the arms of the Alighieri themselves (as part of an illustration for *Paradiso* 15), or by the six pages of Florentine 'shields of arms' that illustrate Cacciaguida's account of his and Dante's native city in the following canto.[160] Pages of carefully copied emblems frequently occur in all five volumes of the collection, and—whatever their heraldic authenticity—they reflect the *Commedia*'s attention to the origins of Florentine families and its wider concerns about nobility, family, and ancestry. For example, a page of family arms illustrating *Inferno* 10 (Fig. 17) aptly reinforces the question posed by the canto's central figure, Farinata degli Uberti: 'Chi fuor li maggior tui?' ('Who were your ancestors?')[161]

The Macleods' own aristocratic background helped ensure access to major collections in Florence and elsewhere in Italy—thus providing resources for another scholarly feature of the collection: designs and illustrations copied from medieval manuscripts and early printed books. For this purpose they made use of at least four of Florence's major libraries. A letter of 1845 describes a visit to one of these (the Riccardiana)—a visit that began unpromisingly but would eventually provide important material: 'Yesterday we were at the Riccardi Library, the custode when he saw us, & when we asked for the Botticelli Dante looked towards the door, then at us. "Dov'è il Signor Capitano?" Alas! Echo answered "Where?" Was not this enough to move even a heart of iron . . . ?'[162] 'The Botticelli Dante' does not, of course, refer to the artist's original illustrations (which were by then in the Hamilton collection) but to the engravings—between two and twenty in number—attributed to Baccio Baldini and found in various copies of the edition with Landino's commentary first published at Florence in 1481.[163] The first two of these illustrations (produced between 1481 and 1484, and present in most of the surviving copies) are all that remain of Botticelli's designs for parts of *Inferno* 1 and 2. The copies in the Macleod collection give a fair impression of them and carefully note their source as the library where the encounter with the puzzled *custode* took place—as in the illustration for *Inferno* 3 (Fig. 18).[164] It seems likely that this visit to the Riccardiana was prompted by a conversation with the recipient of Isabella's letters, Francis Brooke, since Brooke's own journal for 1842 had already included some precise comments on the library's treasures:

XI. <u>Dante</u>, with Landini's [*sic*] commentary, published at Florence by Nichola della Magna on the 30th of August 1481. This is the edition which has the engravings by Baldini from the

[159] HCA D 63/E/2a, f. 105 (letter posted 9 Jan. 1845).
[160] NLS MS 2171, ff. 81, 104–8 and 110.   [161] *Inf.* 10. 42; NLS MS 2168, f. 61.
[162] HCA D 63/E/2a, f. 52 (14 May 1845).
[163] See Hind 1938–48: 1. 106 (on the Riccardiana copy), and Altcappenberg 2000: 326–34.
[164] NLS MS 2168, ff. 14, 20, and 22.

Fig. 17. Edinburgh, NLS MS 2168, f. 61, courtesy of the Society of Antiquaries of Scotland

designs of Sandro Botticelli, only two of which were printed on the leaves of the Book, these being the frontispieces of the first and second Cantos, and being, therefore found in all editions of this work. The frontispieces of the eighteen following cantos of the Inferno are of exactly the same dimensions, but were printed upon detached leaves which were pasted into the Book subsequently to publication . . . [165]

Several other Florentine libraries provided the family with further manuscript sources for page designs and illustrations. Illuminated title-pages usually introduce the illustrations for each canto, and the one for *Inferno* 5 is based on and attributed to a source in the 'Magliabecchiana'.[166] Five vivid illuminated capitals—for *Purgatorio* 31 and *Paradiso* 20, 24, 28, and 30—derive from a 'Choral Book [in] San Marco' said to be 'drawn by Fra Angelico' (Fig.19).[167] A caption beneath Isabella's

[165] Brooke, 'Travel Journals', vol. 7, BL Add. MS 62148, f. 86ᵛ. Brooke subsequently compares the copy (with 20 engravings) owned by Lord Spencer and notes also that 'Lord Vernon had once in his possession a copy with nineteen plates. It was sold about the year 1840 for 45 Pounds Sterling'; ibid. f. 87ᵛ.

[166] Brooke, 'Travel Journals', vol. 7, BL Add. MS 62148, f. 28.

[167] NLS MS 2170, f. 129, and 2172, ff. 33, 39, 47 and 48.

Fig. 18. Edinburgh, NLS MS 2168, f. 22, courtesy of the Society of Antiquaries of Scotland

and Anna's illustration (Fig. 20) of Dante facing Ugolino among the traitors in the ice at the opening of *Inferno* 33 indicates that it derived 'Dal codice il pi[ù] antico nella Laurentiana' ('From the oldest manuscript [of the *Commedia*] in the Laurentiana Library').[168] This manuscript—Florence, Laurenziana MS Strozz. 152 (of *c.*1335–45)—represents a significant early stage in the tradition of illustrating the *Commedia*.[169] Few of the illustrations in the Macleod collection are signed, but in this case the identities and tasks of mother and daughter as copyists are noted in ink, alongside the reference to the manuscript, at the foot of the page ('IM _ A.M.M.

---

[168] NLS MS 2169, f. 93.
[169] BMS 1. 49 and 234–8. The illustration copied is in Laurenziana MS Strozz. 152, f. 28ᵛ.

Fig. 19. Edinburgh, NLS MS 2172, f. 47, courtesy of the Society of Antiquaries of Scotland

del./IM pinxit'), thus recording their joint association with this important early copy of the poem. The title-pages for *Inferno* 33 and for the last canto of the whole poem are also attributed to manuscripts in the 'Laurentiana'.[170]

There are some signs in the Macleod collection of the special meanings the *Commedia* might have had for nineteenth-century readers. Although during the later 1840s—as the 'year of revolutions' approached—much of her attention was seized by events in the Grand Duchy of Tuscany and the Papal States, the Dante of the Risorgimento does not seem to figure significantly on Isabella Macleod's

A bocha ſileuo dal fiero paſto
quel peccatoz forben d'ola acapelli
ʒl capo ch'lh hauea diret° quaſto
Poi cerfiuo tutol oho nuouelli
Delpato dolor ch'l cure maſme
o'a purpenſando piu chome ſiuolli.

Dal codice il piu antico nella Laurentiana

Fig. 20. Edinburgh, NLS MS 2169, f. 94, courtesy of the Society of Antiquaries of Scotland

horizon.[171] By autumn of 1847 Francis Brooke and his family were back in England, and her letters to him convey the increasing turbulence of Italian politics—offering astute and detailed accounts of events in Florence and Rome and assessments of their implications for other players (Piedmont and Austria) on the Italian scene.[172] They reflect the family's Whig liberalism and a critical awareness of other British (particularly Tory) political views on the 'Italian question'.[173] Isabella MacLeod's own attitude towards the Risorgimento—like that of many in the British press and governing class—favoured the Italian 'moderates', and she was a reader of D'Azeglio and Gioberti rather than of radicals such as Mazzini.[174] Unlike Elizabeth Barrett—who was writing about the upheavals and demonstrations in Florence at exactly

[171] On the Risorgimento Dante, see Ciccarelli 2001*a*–*b*, and Jossa 2012.

[172] HCA D 63/E/2a, ff. 174–93 (11 Aug. and 8 Sept. 1847). These were discussed in my paper on 'Mrs MacLeod and an Italian Revolution' at the conference on *British Risorgimento* at the University of Bologna on 22 June 2011 and are the subject of a forthcoming essay.

[173] HCA D 63/E/2a, f. 191: 'The Tories are a strange set—After raving against the Jesuits for years out of number, they are now raving against those who wish to put them down' (8 Sept. 1847).

[174] HCA D 63/E/2a, f. 116 (16 Apr. 1846), and 189 (8 Sept. 1847); both are specific references to recent political writing by D'Azeglio and Gioberti.

the same time and would evoke the Risorgimento Dante in the first part of *Casa Guidi Windows*—Isabella Macleod emerges here as a detached and sceptical observer of the processes that would lead in the later 1840s from reform to revolution and reaction.[175]

One of the few occasions, however, when the drama of the Risorgimento evidently impinges upon her Dante collection is at a relatively late stage of its compilation. One of the *Commedia*'s references to the Angevin Kingdom of Naples (*Purg.* 20. 67) is illustrated through a contemporary engraving of the north coast of Sicily during the autumn of 1860.[176] The view had been published in one of several articles on Garibaldi's campaign in southern Italy in the *Illustrated London News* for October 1860, and the artist, Frank Vizetelly, was a war correspondent who had also reported on the Battle of Solferino in 1859.[177] Its inclusion here (along with another Vizetelly illustration from the same Italian campaign) reflects an interest in the later and more successful phase of the Italian Risorgimento. It also provides a very clear indication that the Macleods' Dante collection continued to accumulate well beyond the 1840s.

Only a few cantos are omitted from the collection's illustrative programme— mainly those which are hard to link with particular places in Italy and Europe or with prominent characters or known families. It is also quite even in its coverage— although it perhaps reflects something of the compiler's Protestant sensibility by giving more attention to the *Inferno* and the *Paradiso* (each in two volumes) than to the *Purgatorio* (which has only one). By comparison with other Dante illustration projects it, of course, has its eccentricities and irrelevancies. The illustrations in the third volume (the 'Album') of the Vernon *Inferno* published in 1858–65, for example, followed a somewhat more methodical and consistent design, as Isabella Macleod herself recognized in her references to 'his lordship's' rival enterprise.[178]

On the other hand, she perhaps deliberately avoided several of the more well-worn visual subjects in the *Commedia*. Unusually—for a resident in early nineteenth-century Italy—Isabella Macleod showed little interest in the much-illustrated *sventurati amanti*, Francesca and Paolo, whose tragic story was still attracting Italian painters in the 1840s and had lately provided a famous subject for her Scots contemporary William Dyce in 1837.[179] Only three folios illustrate *Inferno* 5, and none of these draws upon the Romantic or Victorian iconography of the lovers' story.[180] Also noticeable is the almost complete absence from this gallery of the

---

[175] For Elizabeth Barrett's letters of 13 Sept. and 1 Oct. 1847, describing the procession of the Tuscan National Guard, see Markus 1977: 65–70 and Kenyon 1897: 1. 345–6. For invocation of Dante as part of an appeal to Italian nationalism in Part 1 of *Casa Guidi Windows* (published 1851), see Markus 1977: 258–9 (ll. 601–61).

[176] NLS MS 2170, f. 109.

[177] The illustration is from the *Illustrated London News*, 1055 (20 Oct. 1860), 376; see also the illustrations for the article on 'Garibaldi's March through Calabria' a week earlier (1054, p. 331). On Vizetelly's career, see the article on his brother in *ODNB*, s.v. 'Vizetelly, Henry Richard (1820–1894), journalist and publisher'.

[178] For her views of Vernon and his project, see above, pp. 220–2.

[179] On Dyce's *Francesca*, see above, pp. 166–74.

[180] NLS MS 2168, ff. 28–30 (out of sequence).

figure whom a recent study has called 'A Victorian Muse': Dante's Beatrice.[181] The portrayals of Dante and Beatrice by Dyce and Scott, the developing British interest in the *Vita nuova*, and the proliferation of Rossettian Beatrices from around 1849 onwards all coincide with the decades when the Macleod collection was in progress.[182] The 1840s are admittedly an early stage in the British 'cult of the *Vita nuova*', but Charles Lyell had published translations of its poems in 1835, and Joseph Garrow's version (*The Early Life of Dante Alighieri: together with the original in parallel pages*) was published (by Le Monnier) in Florence while the Macleods were in residence there, in 1846.[183]

It may be significant that the Dantean women whom the Macleod collection does choose to portray are relatively minor figures in the *Commedia*'s cast-list. For example, there are two female figures who are mentioned by male characters within a few lines of each other at the opening of *Purgatorio* 24 (ll. 10 and 37). The first of these is Piccarda Donati, related to Dante by marriage and sister of his friend Forese, with whom the pilgrim is keeping company during this stage of the ascent through the circles of Purgatory. Piccarda, whose life as a Franciscan nun was interrupted by her abduction from the convent, will appear in person in *Paradiso* 3, completing what has been called 'an exemplary *itinerarium*'.[184] Isabella's choice of Piccarda for illustration in the guise of a nun (Fig. 21) anticipates that process. Another 'minor' female figure, 'Gentucca', is mentioned a few lines later in *Purgatorio* 24 (l. 37), and her portrait appears on the following page of the MacLeod collection.[185] The juxtaposition of the two women's portraits with, in each case, the words of the men describing them below, thus strikingly highlights the text's brief representations of women amidst all the male bonding of poets in *Purgatorio* 24.

Another notable female Tuscan is portrayed amongst the collection's large number of illustrations for *Paradiso* 16, but in this case she is a figure who does not actually appear in the poem. Umiliana de' Cerchi (1219–46) was, like Piccarda, a Franciscan religious.[186] Her life is commemorated in various forms at the Franciscan church of Santa Croce in Florence, and her portrait, which Isabella

---

[181] Straub 2009 (title). The only appearance of Beatrice in the Macleod collection is, as far as I am aware, in the copy of the Botticellian engraving illustrating *Inferno* 2 (NLS MS 2168, f. 20).

[182] On Dyce's and Scott's versions of the subject, see above, pp. 175–7, and on the Rossetti Beatrices, see Surtees 1971: e.g. cat. nos. 42, 50, 81.

[183] Dante 1842*a*. Joseph Garrow and his family had arrived in Florence in 1844, and his daughter would marry Thomas Adolphus Trollope; see *ODNB*, s.v. 'Trollope [*née* Garrow], Theodosia (1816–1865), author'. On Garrow's translation of the *Vita nuova* (mistakenly identifying him as 'American') see Friederich 1950: 529–31.

[184] Thus participating in a sequence that leads from Francesca in the *Inferno* through La Pia in the *Purgatorio*; see Boitani 2007: 29.

[185] NLS MS 2170, ff. 116–17. Gentucca (possibly a noblewoman who gave the exiled poet support during his time in Lucca) is mentioned at the start of Dante's encounter with the Lucchese poet Bonagiunta, whose words are quoted under the illustration.

[186] See *DBI*, s.v. 'Cerchi, Umiliana'; also Papi 1980: 87–117; and Schuchman 1997.

Ma dimmi, se tu sai, dov'è Piccarda:
Dimmi, s'io veggio da notar persona
Fra questa gente, che sì mi riguarda.
La mia sorella, che tra bella e buona
Non so qual fosse più, trionfa lieta
Nell'alto Olimpo già di sua corona.
*Purg:*XXIV 10

Fig. 21. Edinburgh, NLS MS 2170, f. 116, courtesy of the Society of Antiquaries of Scotland

Macleod described as 'just finished' in a letter of July 1844, is based on a seventeenth-century copy of a lost original attributed to the school of Giotto (Fig. 22).[187] Umiliana belonged to the great mercantile family of the Cerchi, who were leaders of the White Guelph faction in Dante's Florence and who, according to Dante's ancestor Cacciaguida, would have done better to have remained in their original parish, out in the Val di Sieve.[188] The reminder in the Macleod collection that the Cerchi, as well as being a cause of Florentine conflict, were also—through their most famous female member—a source of urban piety

[187] HCA D 63/E/2a, f. 10 (10 July 1844).   [188] *Par.* 16. 65.

Fig. 22. Edinburgh, NLS MS 2171, f. 92, courtesy of the Society of Antiquaries of Scotland

offers a way of reading this political canto against the grain—and one that is not inappropriate to the spirit of the *Paradiso*.

The *Paradiso* is of course a notoriously difficult *cantica* to render visually, as greater illustrators than Isabella Macleod have found; yet her interest in and emphasis on Dante's female figures helps to give the collection's programme some coherence, especially in its treatment of the poem's closing stages. Prompted by the Marian invocation at the opening of *Paradiso* 33, the eleven illustrations for this final canto include several portrayals of the Virgin, notably in the reproduction of a 'Deposition' scene which stresses her closeness to the body of Christ.[189] The folio on which this monochrome reproduction appears does not cite a source, but the image—giving prominence to the Virgin and to other female figures—is clearly that of Perugino's *Mourning of the Dead Christ* (1495), which in the 1840s formed part of the Grand Ducal collection in the Pitti Palace.

[189] NLS MS 2172, f. 59.

ARCO FELICE.

Near Naples, supposed to be one of the entrances to the ancient City of Cuma

Fig. 23. Edinburgh, NLS MS 2172, f. 66, courtesy of the Society of Antiquaries of Scotland

A less prominent, but powerfully suggestive, female presence in the final canto of the *Commedia* is that of Virgil's Sibyl—whose prophetic signs and verses scattered into disorder by the wind are a key simile for the dispersal of Dante's ultimate vision, and who here seems to have inspired the last group of illlustrations.[190] Beginning with a suitably antique print of the temple of the Tiburtine Sibyl in the Campagna, the Macleod collection concludes with six engravings of locations associated with the sibylline prophecies, leading up to the final gateway of the Arco Felice at Cumae (Fig. 23).[191] The last three, including the Arco Felice, are by the landscape artist Elizabeth Frances Batty, active around 1809–19. Batty's drawings of landscapes and monuments had been published as engravings in *Italian Scenery* in 1820.[192] It seems appropriate, then, that a collection which has been the project of a mother and several of her daughters should close with work by a female artist.

---

[190] See Virgil 1986, *Aeneid* 3. 448–51 and Dante, *Par.* 33. 58–66.

[191] NLS MS 2172, ff. 61–6.

[192] Characteristically, Isabella MacLeod seems to have had access to prints made earlier in 1818 and 1819 and has used these on a considerable number of occasions as images of classical and medieval sites (and occasionally landscape views) in Italy throughout her Dante collection; see NLS MS 2168, f. 125; 2170, ff. 6, 68, 86, 114; 2171, ff. 33, 38, 55, 83; 2172, f. 34.

KIRKUP'S CAPER: ANGLO-FLORENTINE
CONVERSATIONS, 1840–1875

> Kirkup caper'd, Anna danced
> Round about the room they pranced . . .[193]

The leaves of the five Macleod volumes remained sibylline. Unlike the widely circulated Gustave Doré illustrations of the *Inferno*—or even the limited edition of Vernon's 'Album'—the *Disegni ad Illustrazione della Divina Commedia* remained in their five velvet volumes with the Society of Antiquaries of Scotland.[194] Mrs Macleod's fellow Anglo-Florentine Lord Vernon did, on the other hand, 'mean to publish': his three-volume *Inferno* did eventually appear in print—although in a very limited edition of 1858–65. Many items in its 'Album' had the advantage of Seymour Kirkup's skill as an illustrator.

In his work for Vernon's edition of the *Inferno* Kirkup, unlike Isabella Macleod, focused quite frequently on an obvious and important feature of the *Inferno*: the grotesque. Among the most striking figures in the 'Album' are the image of the hybrid monster Geryon appearing out of the abyss of Malebolge and, a little later, the bizarre expedition of the 'Malebranche' devils, accompanying Dante and Virgil around the circle of pitch in the fifth pouch of Malebolge itself.[195] Kirkup's engraving of 'Lucifero' for *Inferno* 34 (Fig. 24) conveys several key features of Dante's text: the appearance of Lucifer like a windmill seen in the mist (*Inf.* 34. 4–6), and Dante's hesitation to follow Virgil and confront this final infernal vision (*Inf.* 34. 10, 22–7). By including the giant's foot (upper right corner) on the edge of the rock surrounding the frozen lake of Cocytus, Kirkup may also be paying homage to two major Dantean illustrators: Fuseli and Botticelli.[196]

An Anglo-Florentine conversation about Kirkup's 'Lucifero' and his other Dante illustrations took place long before Vernon's 'Album' was published. About twenty years earlier—in the letter that includes the account of Kirkup's 'capering' with Anna—Mrs MacLeod informed Francis Brooke of the latest developments in the two projects:

I have tamed Kirkup.

You cannot think how quietly he walked into our Gallery, with his book of Dante illustrations under his arm. Of course you have seen most of them, so I need say nothing of them—but a recent one of Lucifer appearing to Dante rising in clouds is really very fine & very infernal, the expression of the eyes is terrific. I hope that the Engraver won't spoil it.

---

[193] HCA D 63/E/2a, f. 28 (Isabella Macleod to Francis Brooke, postmarked 4 Oct. 1844).

[194] On the circulation of the Doré illustrations, which began to accompany editions of the Cary translation in 1866, see Milbank 1998: 196–200.

[195] Oxford Bodleian MS Eng. misc. d. 639, ff. 150ʳ and 163ʳ.

[196] For Fuseli's 1774 watercolour of *Dante and Virgil on the Ice of Cocytus* (Kunsthaus Zürich), see *Henry Fuseli 1741–1825* (London: Tate Gallery 1975), 23 and 101–2 (cat. 117); and for Botticelli's comparable depiction of the truncated giants' feet (at the top of the illustration for *Inferno* 32), see Altcappenberg 2000: p. 123.

Lucifero

Fig. 24. Oxford, Bodleian Eng. misc. d. 639, f. 193ʳ, Seymour Kirkup, 'Lucifero', by permission of the Bodleian Library, Oxford

Truly did I say, & modestly did K[irkup] disclaim when I said it, that his designs would make the value of the [Vernon's] book, but it is very true.

He came to look at all our Dante Collections—but as we have not yet so much of the first 7 cantos of L'Inferno, as we have of Purgatorio & Paradiso, I don't know that we can assist much; as he has already all the Tuscan Arms, & we are as much at a loss as he is for the Forestieri [foreigners].[197]

[197] HCA D 63/E/2a, ff. 25–6 (postmarked 4 Oct. 1844).

In a letter of January 1846, when her own Dante collection was yet further advanced, Isabella MacLeod would also acknowledge to Francis Brooke that 'Kirkup quite eclipses me in literary and artistical information'.[198]

Beyond 1847 there is (so far) no further evidence in Isabella MacLeod's letters about Kirkup's and Vernon's Dantean activities, nor about her own project. The codicils to her husband Roderick's will locate him still in Florence at the end of 1847, but then in London and Invergordon Castle (the family estate) in late 1848 and early 1850; so it is likely that the upheavals around the 'year of revolutions' caused the laird and his wife to return home at some point in 1848.[199] Other members of the family were in Italy for considerable periods in the later nineteenth century. In the 1860s there is correspondence from one of them, Isabella's eldest daughter Margaret (1814–1904), who had nothing to do with the Dante collection but gives a terrifying account of her mother's conduct during a vicious and protracted family squabble over her father's estate.[200] Margaret's letters are addressed to her brother, the political economist Henry Dunning MacLeod (who likewise plays no Dantean role); and they are chiefly of interest here in locating her sister Elizabeth ('Bessie') still in Florence, and in showing her to match her mother for energy and aggression.[201] It was Elizabeth who would also, during the 1870s, provide some further evidence about Kirkup's later Dantean activities.

Kirkup remained almost to the end of his long life a prominent figure among British expatriates in Florence. He was on good terms with, for example, the Brownings, Landor, the Trollopes, and Swinburne. Edmund Gosse remarked that he 'saw everyone worth seeing who came to Florence'.[202] He continued to correspond with Francis Brooke on personal, political, and Dantean topics, and a group of his letters (and some from other correspondents) is bound together with engravings for the Vernon 'Album' in a volume which must have been in Brooke's library.[203] The letters date from 1870 to 1871, when Kirkup was in his early eighties, but they show a strong and vigorously expressed interest in contemporary political events, as well as a continuing concern with issues of Dante scholarship.[204]

Kirkup's letters to Brooke refer to visits (probably around 1869–70) from two major American Dante scholars—Charles Eliot Norton and Henry Wadsworth

---

[198] HCA D 63/E/2a, f. 104 (22 Jan. 1846).

[199] The holograph of Roderick's will (registered after his death in 1853) and the codicils are in HCA D 63/E/1.

[200] Margaret converted to Catholicism and briefly became a nun, before marrying an Alsatian baron (Jean de Virte de Rathsamhausen de Ehenweyer) and living with him at Ripafratta near Pisa; see Morrison 1976: 103–4. Her letters are in HCA D63/E/2b and one of them (dated 7 Feb. 1865) gives a grim impression of Isabella in later life, as Macleod matriarch: 'Such hatred of a mother against her own children I cannot conceive.'

[201] 'Her letters are feared and she has the talent of convincing them'; HCA D63/E/2b, letters of 20 May, 14 Aug., and 26 Dec. 1864. Henry Dunning MacLeod is the only member of this generation of the family to receive an *ODNB* entry, s.v. 'Macleod, Henry Dunning (1821–1902), economist'.

[202] Gosse, 'Swinburne and Kirkup', in *London Mercury*, 3 (1920–1), 157–8, quoted by Lindon 2000*b*: 123 and n. 12.

[203] This is now Oxford, Bodley MS Eng. misc. d. 639. Some of the engravings are accompanied by Brooke's own annotations.

[204] Bodley MS Eng. misc. d. 639, esp. letters of 13 Mar., 8 Aug., and 13 Sept. 1870.

Longfellow—but he had long before that been in touch with leading British, French, German, and Italian *dantisti*.[205] From the late 1830s he had been an admirer and patron of Gabriele Rossetti, and, more than thirty years on, his letters to Brooke reaffirm his belief that 'Rossetti was the greatest genius . . . He was generous and learned, far beyond Foscolo'.[206] Even when he sold his library in 1871, he reports having 'saved Rossetti's works', which presumably included the commentary on the *Inferno* (1826–7) and the controversial *Sullo spirito antipapale* (1832).[207] It was to Rossetti in September 1841 that Kirkup had reported and sent tracings of the recently uncovered 'Bargello Dante';[208] and in a letter of 1870 to Francis Brooke he recalls the effect of 'my lucky preservation of Dante's portrait before it was spoiled by an ignorant dauber 29 years ago—& its publication by the A[rundel] Society who have sold two editions of many hundreds, a number of which are gone to America'.[209] In between the discovery and this reminiscence, Kirkup's contribution to Dante studies had been recognized by the award of the Order of SS Maurizio e Lazzaro from the king of Italy at the festival of 1865 in Florence marking the 600th anniversary of Dante's birth.[210] The other British recipients of this honour were Lord Vernon (whose three-volume *Inferno* was then in process of appearing) and another British Dante scholar and associate of Kirkup: Henry Clark Barlow.

Barlow, after training as an artist and physician, had begun, like Isabella MacLeod, to turn to Dante studies whilst in Italy during the 1840s. Like her, he was drawn into Kirkup's circle initially by an interest in illustrating the topography of the *Commedia*.[211] He and Kirkup continued to be in close contact on questions regarding Dante—for example, the progress of Karl Witte's critical edition of the *Commedia* (1862)—until the 1865 Florentine festival for the poet, on which Barlow reported as Britain's 'Representative'.[212] The hostile view of Barlow's scholarship which characterizes Kirkup's subsequent letters to Francis Brooke in 1870–1 may have been due to a combination of pique at Barlow's and Vernon's reception of equal honours at the festival, disapproval of the former's recent collection of Dante studies, and resentment at Barlow's favourable review of

---

[205] Bodley MS Eng. misc. d. 639, f. 10ᵛ. On Kirkup's contacts with Karl Witte (from 1831 on), Colomb de Batines (1844–5), and Gabriele Rossetti (from 1838 till Rossetti's death in 1854), see Lindon 2000*b*: 125–34. On Witte's editorial work and his founding of the first Dante Society, the Deutsche Dante-Gesellschaft (1865), see Friederich 1950: 408–13; Caesar 1989: 471–2; and *DE* 268, 300–1, and 886–7.

[206] Bodley MS Eng. misc. d. 639, f. 14ʳ (letter of 13 Mar. 1870). On Rossetti, see above, p. 149.

[207] Bodley MS Eng. misc. d. 639, 50ᵛ (letter of 12 Aug. 1871).

[208] See above, p. 218 and Fig. 14.

[209] Bodley MS Eng. misc. d. 639, f. 10ᵛ. The 'ignorant dauber' was Antonio Marini, who restored the damaged eye visible in Kirkup's early tracing and retouched other parts of the fresco (Holbrook 1921: 81).

[210] On the 1865 Florentine celebrations and their Tuscan and Italian resonances, see O'Connor 2008: 65–81, and the monograph by Yousefzadeh 2011.

[211] On Barlow's initial correspondence with Kirkup in 1847 and his presentation of sketches of the landscape referred to in *Inferno* 12. 4–9, see Lindon 2000*b*: 124–5. See also *ODNB*, s.v. 'Barlow, Henry Clark (1806–1876), literary scholar'.

[212] Lindon 2000*b*: 129–34. For Barlow's account of the 1865 events, see Barlow 1866.

Vernon's illustrated Dante (from which Kirkup had withdrawn).[213] Barlow, on the other hand, continued to take a not unfriendly interest in Kirkup's scholarly reputation, and to respect Brooke's judgement on questions about Dante—as his letter to Brooke in May 1870 shows:

In a letter from our old friend Kirkup received some weeks since[,] he says that 'William' [Vernon's second son] had called upon him and offered him a copy [of the 1858–65 illustrated *Inferno*]—I suppose requested his acceptance of one[.] It was hard that poor Kirkup (Baron! Kirkup) who had been once the living soul of the Album should have been overlooked—he took it very unkind—as well he might. Do you know that I have come round to your opinion of who was the <u>Grand Lombardo</u>—and have found the hard evidence of Cangrande being he.[214]

The distribution of the limited copies of Vernon's weighty three volumes seems to have been a vexed question at the time, and it is one that relates to the material production of Dante for an elite and for a wider public. Vernon's heir (Augustus Henry) was chiefly concerned to distribute the work to a 'very restricted' range of prestigious recipients, such as fellow aristocrats and major Italian libraries.[215] It is still difficult to find copies in public collections in Britain, and the presence of a copy in the library at Holkham Hall is explained by a note that it contains, from a baron to an earl:

My dear Leicester
        I shall be much gratified by your finding a place in the Holkham Library for a copy of the Inferno of Dante literally paraphrased with Documenti and Album privately printed in 3 vols: fol. by my Father.—
        Yours sincerely
        Vernon[216]

Holkham, with its Dante manuscripts (which Barlow had written about three years earlier), was obviously a suitably prestigious destination for the rare three folio volumes.[217] On the other hand, the Suffolk squire Francis Brooke does not seem to have been considered eligible for a copy, despite his contribution to the project and the representations on his behalf from Barlow.[218] Kirkup did eventually accept the copy that was (as Barlow had noted) offered him by Vernon's younger son, 'William' (who was himself an important Dante scholar),[219] but writing to Brooke a year later the elderly collector points out certain ironies attaching to the limited circulation of the edition: 'It was strange of the new editor [of William Vernon's

---

[213] These possible motives are suggested by Lindon 2000*b*: 134–5.

[214] Bodley MS Eng. misc. d. 639, f. 22ʳ⁻ᵛ.

[215] Augustus Vernon's intentions concerning copies of his father's edition are explained in a letter to Brooke in Bodley MS Eng. misc. d. 639, ff. 3ʳ–4ᵛ (16 May 1869).

[216] Note found in the Holkham Hall copy and dated 29 May 1870. The only copy of Vernon's edition listed (on the COPAC database) as being in a British public collection is in the Sir Duncan Rice Library at Aberdeen.

[217] For Barlow's account of the Holkham Dante manuscripts, see Barlow 1867.

[218] Letters in Bodley MS Eng. misc. d. 639, ff. 3ʳ–4v (Vernon to Brooke, 16 May 1869), 5ʳ⁻ᵛ and 23ʳ–24ᵛ (Barlow to Brooke, 5 June 1869 and 14 May 1870).

[219] On William Vernon, see below, p. 257 and n. 316.

Dante studies] Sir James Lacaita to advise me to sell my books, Lord V's *Inferno* being one of them[,] when the present Lord V. [Augustus] was so enraged at the Italians [i.e. Italian libraries] selling their copies which he gave them . . . '[220] Kirkup's reference to the sale of his books—which would take place at Sotheby's in December of that year—reflects a further feature of the circulation and ownership of Dante among the British abroad. Like Elphinstone and Grey, he had acquired manuscripts of Dante's work—although in much greater quantity and with a higher degree of expertise.[221] Unlike those two servants of Empire, who were in a position to perpetuate their memories through donation, Kirkup felt obliged to dispose of his manuscripts differently, and for reasons which he explained to Brooke in a postscript to a letter of September 1870: 'I think I shall sell my books. I am 82—& if I die they will be stolen & thrown away. I don't want money, but they will help provide for my daughter. They are worth 2000£.' Kirkup's books and manuscripts in fact fetched £2,555 at the Sotheby's sale a year later.[222] Most of his *Commedia* manuscripts subsequently passed into the collection of the fourth earl of Ashburnham; soon after (in 1884) they were purchased by the Italian government, returning to Florence as part of the Biblioteca Laurenziana's collection.[223]

The daughter whose dowry was being thus funded was Imogen ('Bibi'), through whose mediumship, for the previous fourteen years, Kirkup claimed to have been communicating with Dante. Belief in spiritualism was not uncommon among the educated and literary classes of the period, but Kirkup's unquestioning faith was a subject of some concern and comment in the Anglo-Florentine community. There seems to be no record of Francis Brooke's views on the subject, but he may well have been surprised by the frequency with which, in the letters of 1870–1, Kirkup describes communications coming through 'my daughter who is a medium and a favourite of Dante's'.[224] Brooke's attitude to this kind of dialogue may perhaps be inferred from his keeping, together with Kirkup's correspondence, a letter from another member of the Anglo-Florentine community a few years later. This letter of 1875 encloses (in Italian) a story told by a Florentine friend about visiting Kirkup in the company of the history-painter William Frederick Yeames, who had come to

---

[220] Bodley MS Eng. misc. d. 639, f. 39ᵛ (Kirkup to Brooke, 10 Jan. 1871).
[221] On Kirkup's ownership of *Commedia* manuscripts (and one of the *Convivio*), see Lindon 2000*b*: 124 and n. 21.
[222] December 1871; see *ODNB*, s.v. 'Kirkup, Seymour Stocker (1788–1880)'. Preparations for (and British interest in) the sale of 'old Kirkup's books' are mentioned by Dante Gabriel Rossetti in a letter of March 1871 to his brother William Michael; see Rossetti 2005: 35 (no. 71.34 and n. 1).
[223] On Ashburnham and his collection, see De Ricci 1930: 131–6. For details of the seven Ashburnham manuscripts of the *Commedia* previously owned by Kirkup, see Roddewig 1984: 77–82 (nos. 181–190). Three others from his collection are now at Harvard (MSS Ital. 54–6) and one at Manchester (John Rylands Library MS Ital. 2); see Roddewig 1984: 28–30 (nos. 60–2) and 197–8 (no. 466).
[224] Bodley MS Eng. misc. d. 639, ff. 10ᵛ (12 Feb. 1870), 35ᵛ (30 Oct. 1870) and 37ʳ (4 Dec. 1870). In the latter, Kirkup also describes the occasion on which his grand piano was shifted into the next room by four spirits, so that his late wife could sing (accompanied by Rossini) 'in her magnetic sleep', adding that: 'These things have been going on for 15 years in this house wh[ich] is really haunted.'

Florence 'to research a subject dealing with the life of Dante'.[225] The report continues:

> Since Kirkup was indeed the greatest expert on the subject, I took him to visit. Polite as always, he received us in a very friendly manner. I then told him the purpose of our call and asked him if he could show my friend his Dante costume, but he replied: 'My dear S[ir] I burnt it through Dante's express order, and yesterday I had such an interesting conversation with him'. Mr Yeames, who was entirely unfamiliar with Kirkup's foibles, stared and took a step back as if to say 'I'm dealing with a madman here'. Fortunately Kirkup, being deaf, was unable to hear me saying in a low voice to my friend: 'I will explain all this afterwards'.
>
> The costume that had been burnt was of the finest red cloth . . . [226]

The correspondent reporting the story to Brooke is unnamed and has so far been unidentified, but since the letter is sent from the 'Villa del Pino di Careggi' and includes friendly enquiries about Brooke's family, it seems very likely that this sketch of Kirkup late in life is provided by an Anglo-Florentine known to have been living at that address: Isabella Macleod's daughter Elizabeth.[227]

Elizabeth Macleod may still at that time have been in possession of—or would at least have remembered—the Dante collection which her mother had initiated thirty years before and which her brother would deliver to the Edinburgh Antiquaries ten years later. Something of her mother's sprightly malice is evident in Elizabeth's portrayal of the decrepit 'Cricky' here, but her account of Kirkup's conversations with the dead poet, like other reports of his eccentricities, can also be placed in relation to some of the slightly more sober manifestations of the nineteenth-century and Anglo-Florentine Dante-possession. Such conversations could be seen as more extreme versions of earlier recuperative dialogues, such as those of Landor's *Pentameron* and *Imaginary Conversations* in the 1830s ('Petrarch and Boccaccio', 'Dante and Beatrice', 'Dante and Gemma Donati'), or Carlyle's protracted communing with the 'tragic, heart-affecting face' of the Tofanelli portrait in 'The Hero as Poet'.[228] They perhaps reflect the urge to recover the poet's image that had motivated Kirkup himself at the Bargello in 1840 and had impelled those Anglo-Florentines who (like Vernon) sported 'Dante nightcaps' or (like Kirkup and Millais) wore a 'Dante costume'. Kirkup's and Bibi's necromantic dialogues may also represent an extreme form of the desire to embody Dante within the Italian landscape and to possess that presence in visible shape—as in the Vernon 'Album', the Macleods' 'Dante Collection', or in Kirkup's own images, costumes, and manuscripts.

---

[225] On Yeames and his work, see *ODNB*, s.v. 'Yeames, Wiliam Frederick (1835–1918), painter'.

[226] Bodley MS Eng. misc. d. 639, f. v^r–v (letter of 15 July 1875; my trans. of the Italian passages). Yeames is chiefly famous for later history paintings such as *The Death of Amy Robsart* (1877) and *And When Did You Last See Your Father?* (1878).

[227] See above, p. 223 and nn. 146–7. Elizabeth refers to her residence at the villa and to herself as 'E. del Pino' in several of her letters of the 1870s, e.g. HCA D 63/E/2d, ff. 1, 12 and 13.

[228] On Landor, see *DEL* 2. 84–116, and Ellis 1983: 103–4. For Carlyle and the Toffanelli portrait, see *DEL* 2. 498.

'FROM NEGLIGENT TO REVERENTIAL GUARDIANS': THE HAMILTON COLLECTION IN BRITAIN AND BERLIN

The late nineteenth-century migration of the 700 or so manuscripts in the Hamilton collection from Britain to Germany also entailed the final journey of the 'wandering *Comedy*' with which this book began.[229] As its present trilingual title (Berlin Staatsbibliothek Hamilton 207, Dante *Commedia*) indicates, Hamilton 207 is a text that travelled a long way before reaching its present destination. Having presumably returned to Italy with its Tuscan mercantile owner at some point after August 1451, it then disappears from the record for about three centuries, to re-emerge as part of the great manuscript collection which was gathered together at Hamilton Palace in the early nineteenth century and was eventually sold to the German government in October 1882.[230]

Hamilton 207—an unprepossessing paper copy—was not of course the 'gem' of the collection. That title was reserved, as we shall see, for one of the other six manuscripts of the *Commedia* that were sold at the same time: the late fifteenth-century folio with illustrations by Sandro Botticelli (Hamilton 201). The transfer of a collection including such a significant item from Britain to the newly unified Germany, and from private to public ownership, prompted wider questions about national cultural possessions and 'heritage', as well as the issue of Dante's status. The story of the 1882 dispersal of the Hamilton *Commedia* manuscripts and many other texts is thus a landmark for this narrative about Dante's British public, which began with travellers around Chaucer's time and another London sale in 1451. The 1882 Hamilton sale—which according to one contemporary source 'excited the attention of amateurs all over the world'[231]—is, as might be expected, much more fully documented than the transaction between those fifteenth-century Italian traders. It involves a number of identifiable figures and sources: the twelfth duke of Hamilton; several sharp-eyed German art historians, museum administrators, and Prussian government officials; correspondence between Queen Victoria and her eldest daughter; articles in the British and German press; and a letter from William Gladstone.

The founder of the Hamilton collection—besides being tenth duke of Hamilton, seventh duke of Brandon, marquess of Douglas and Clydesdale, and Baron Dutton—was also an extravagant and much-travelled dilettante.[232] Before succeeding to the dukedom he served as ambassador to St Petersburg (in 1807), where he passionately pursued a wealthy Polish countess described as 'an old battered

---

[229] See the 'Prologue' above, pp. 1–7.

[230] The whole Hamilton collection is currently the subject of a research project led by Dr Godfrey Evans, Curator of the National Museum of Scotland, and I am very grateful to Dr Evans for detailed information about its formation.

[231] *Athenaeum*, 74 no. 2872 (11 Nov. 1882), p. 628, col. 1.

[232] He became a member of the Society of Dilettanti (see above, pp. 114–21) in 1803, and his son, the eleventh duke, was elected in 1833.

beauty'.[233] He was also much enamoured of old books, paintings, and other collectibles and had begun to accumulate his collection during his continental travels even earlier, over a long period of residence in Italy during the 1790s and early 1800s.[234]

Exactly when Alexander Douglas-Hamilton acquired the seven *Commedia* manuscripts in his collection is uncertain, but he compiled a list of 'manoscritti da me acquistati in Italia' around 1802, and this includes a 'fine Dante in folio' ('Dante bello in foglio', assigned to the fifteenth century) that may have been bought the year before.[235] The even finer folio of Botticelli illustrations (Hamilton 201) is known to have passed through the hands of the Florentine dealer Giovanni Claudio Molini at Paris in 1803, and was probably bought by the marquess then or soon after.[236] It is also possible that the *Commedia* manuscript imported to Britain in 1451 (Hamilton 207) may have been purchased around the same time, since an undated list in the Hamilton Archive records an item fitting its modest description: *Dante MS. Cart. Sec. XV. 4º.*[237]

In 1810 the marquess married the second daughter of William Beckford, author of *Vathek.* This was a shrewd alliance for a bibliophile, since Susan Euphemia Beckford not only brought a substantial income and investments with her, but would also inherit her father's great library.[238] The marquess's own collection complemented that of his father-in-law—for, whereas Beckford seems to have been interested mostly in fine old printed editions, his son-in-law mainly concentrated on manuscripts, including a large number (nearly a hundred) from Italy.[239]

When the bibliographer William Clarke compiled his *Repertorium Bibliographicum or Some Account of the Most Celebrated British Libraries* (published in 1819), he noted that the Hamilton collection included amongst its 'valuable manuscripts and printed books' some items that 'will be found superior to many in the best public or private collections in this country'.[240] He includes three items under 'DANTE' in his list for the collection.[241] There is a 'Dante *with miniatures*, fol. MS. Saec. xiv' which could be any one of the collection's four fourteenth-century illuminated *Commedia* manuscripts.[242] There is also, as in many British collections of the time,

---

[233] Evans 2012: 125 and n. 5; also *ODNB*, s.v. 'Hamilton, Alexander Douglas-, tenth duke of Hamilton and seventh duke of Brandon (1767–1852), aristocrat'.

[234] Evans 2003: 55–9.

[235] The list (Hamilton Archive M12/30/38) is undated, but its watermark is of 1802, and a 'Dante foglio' is also listed in a consignment of manuscripts sent from Mestre to London on 22 July 1801 (Hamilton Archive M12/30/unnumbered); information from Dr G. Evans (personal communication).

[236] Altcappenberg 2000: p. 20 and fig. 8. On the previous ownership of all the illustrations (including the eight now in the Vatican), see ibid. 21–2 and Roddewig 1984: 7.

[237] Along with 'Dante MS. Fol. sec. XV' in Hamilton Archive, M12/30/10, although 'it is not clear if these items were acquired' (Dr G. Evans, personal communication).

[238] Evans 2012: 125–6 and n. 7.

[239] See Fletcher 1902: 328–31; De Ricci 1930: 86–7; *ED*, s.v. 'Hamilton, Collezione'; and Altcappenberg 2000: 20. On the development of his manuscript collection in the second decade of the nineteenth century, see Evans 2003: 59.

[240] Clarke 1819: 257. For other Dante items in Clarke's list of British collections, see *DEL* 2.300.

[241] Clarke 1819: 260.

[242] MSS Hamilton 202–5; see Roddewig 1984: 8–10 (nos. 14–17).

a large folio *Commedia*, 'col commento di Christophoro Landino, *Firenze* 1481', which would have included some of the Botticellian engravings.[243] Clarke's fullest description, however, is reserved for an item that would figure prominently on the later nineteenth-century cultural scene:

DANTE Alighieri, La Commedia, MS. on vellum, oblong folio. SAEC. xv.
   This fine MS. written about the year 1450, contains the entire poem, with the exception of some Cantos of the '*Inferno*.' It is ornamented with eighty-eight original designs supposed to be executed by the hand of *Sandro Botticelli* or some other eminent Florentine artist.[244]

Clarke's visit to the Hamilton Palace library took place about three years before the publication of his *Repertorium*, and he actually saw even more Dante manuscripts on its shelves. The marquess's own annotated 'List of my MSS as made by Mr: Clerk—July 1816' mentions six 'Dante folios', and it is possible that all of these may have been manuscripts.[245]

   Soon after succeeding to the title in 1819, the tenth duke also embarked on a substantial rebuilding of the family seat a few miles south of Glasgow, with a view to housing his treasures suitably.[246] The main rebuilding and refurnishing took place between 1824 and 1832,[247] and a purpose-built library to match the imposing quality and quantity of the collection was part of the duke's plan; the conditions of lighting, temperature, and humidity for the books in the west wing seem to have been 'carefully regulated';[248] and an ambitious decorative programme for new rooms in the palace seems to have been under way when William Dyce visited the 'Magnus Apollo of the Scottish Peers' in 1836.[249] By the middle of the century some interest from abroad was also being focused on the collection. Early in the 1850s the German art historian Gustav Friedrich Waagen, director of the Royal Paintings Gallery in Berlin, visited the palace in the course of compiling a survey of the great British collections.[250] Waagen was much impressed by the library, which he describes as 'rich in curiosities of the most costly description, contain[ing] a collection of MSS with Byzantine, Italian, German, Netherlandish, and French miniatures, from the 9th to the 16th century'.[251] He seems to have been 'obliged to hurry through' his inspection of the Italian manuscripts, although he notes the 'the Duke appeared to be gratified with my admiration of his treasures in this

---

[243] Probably only two or three (?). The copy later obtained by the tenth duke for £53 at the Stowe sale in 1848 contained nineteen of the engravings and is now in the Pierpont Morgan Library in New York; see the bill for this in Hamilton archive, bundle 681 (information from Dr Godfrey Evans). On this copy, see also Hind 1938–48: 1. 107.

[244] Clarke 1819: 260.

[245] The list is among the Hamilton Papers deposited at the Hamilton Town House Library, Hamilton, S. Lanarkshire (information from Dr G. Evans).

[246] Most of what remains on the site of Hamilton Palace now is a swimming-pool complex with a retail park; see Evans 2003: 67 and 2009: 35–6. On the instructive reasons for its abandonment and demolition, see Harvie 2002: 170.

[247] Evans 2009: 58–9.

[248] See the description of the library in *The Times* for 18 July 1882.

[249] On Dyce's visit, see above, p. 176, and his letter in NLS MS 8887, f. 76r–v.

[250] Waagen 1854.   [251] Waagen 1854: 3. 295.

department'.[252] In his select list of these treasures, Waagen, as might be expected, reserves his fullest attention for Hamilton 201:

La Divina Commedia, large folio of the second half of the 15th century; containing indubitably the richest illustrations of this great poem, each page having a picture; all, however, with the exception of one coloured page, consisting of drawings with the pen. Various hands, of various artistic skill, are discernible; that of Sandro Botticelli is very obvious: he is known to have studied Dante with great zeal, and to have furnished the drawings for Baldini's engravings in the Landino edition. While many of the drawings at the early part of the work are very interesting and spirited, the larger figures in the latter part are the finest and most original with which this poem has ever been illustrated. The publication of fac-similes of a selection of them, in woodcuts or lithography, now so easily accomplished, would be highly welcome equally to the lovers of Dante and of Italian art.[253]

Waagen's reference to Botticelli's having 'studied Dante with great zeal' is based on Vasari's *Life* of the painter, although, as he recognizes, Vasari knew only the engravings that accompanied the 1481 Florence edition. His preference for the 'larger figures in the latter part' of the work probably refers to the figures of Beatrice and Dante in the *Paradiso*, the drawings which William Dyce may have seen and imitated in the previous decade.[254] Waagen's final comment touches on an important question for the culture of the period: whether and how the illustrations might become accessible to a wider public. The 'fac-simile' edition he suggested would eventually appear (under the editorship of his compatriot, Friedrich Lippmann), but not until the Botticelli illustrations, along with the rest of the Hamilton manuscripts, had been transferred to public ownership in Berlin.[255]

The chief British and German agents of this transfer were a strikingly contrasting couple, although (unlike Waagen and the tenth duke) they almost certainly never met or dealt with each other directly. The vendor was William Alexander, twelfth duke of Hamilton, who had succeeded to the title in 1863. In 1873, at the age of 28, he was said to be engaged in 'learning nothing, hunting 5 days a week . . . his betting book is usually a sorry sight on settling day'.[256] On his death at the age of 49 in 1895 he was described as 'unweighted by any sense of responsibility and beset by all the deadly sins in a far greater degree than perhaps any other young man of his standing'.[257] Unlike his elegant grandfather, who was referred to as *Il Magnifico* and praised for his 'knowledge and discrimination' by Waagen, the twelfth duke was described as 'full bodied, of a rudely ruddy complexion . . . [with] a frankness of speech bordering on rudeness', and it was said that as a student at Oxford he 'went

---

[252] Waagen 1854: 3. 307.

[253] Waagen 1854: 3. On Waagen (1797–1868) and his associations with Britain, see the online *Dictionary of Art Historians* at: <http://www.dictionaryofarthistorians.org/waageng.htm>.

[254] See above, pp. 175–7 and Figs. 11 and 12.

[255] *Zeichnungen von Sandro Botticelli zu Dantes Göttlicher Komödie: nach den Originalen im K. Kupferstichkabinett zu Berlin* (Berlin: G. Grotes'sche, 1887).

[256] Commentary accompanying the 'Spy' cartoon of him in *Vanity Fair*, 18 Oct. 1873, quoted in the online Hamilton Palace website at: <http://hamilton.rcahms.org.uk//family14.html>, accessed on 13 July 2012.

[257] *Truth*, 23 May 1895, quoted in Cokayne and Gibbs (1910–59): 6. 276, n. (a).

in for boxing, as he went in later for horse-racing, yachting, and other amusements'. This was the heir to the premier dukedom of Scotland who, in 1882, decided to dispose of his grandfather's entire collection in order to reduce his enormous debts.[258]

The purchase was conducted by an erudite and well-organized team of German experts led by Friedrich Lippmann (1838–1903), art historian, authority on Holbein, and, since 1876, director of the engravings collection (*Kupferstichkabinett*) at Berlin.[259] Lippmann had long experience of acquiring artefacts for public collections: in the 1860s he had bought Renaissance furniture, paintings, and books for the Austrian Museum für Kunst und Industrie; and in 1877 he purchased the most valuable single item for the Berlin collection: Dürer's 1514 drawing of his mother.[260] In the early summer of 1882 he was looking out for new acquisitions in Paris and London, whilst reporting to Richard Schöne, general director of the Royal Museums at Berlin, and taking note of some important items that were coming on to the market, such as the Ashburnham manuscript collection and paintings from Blenheim Palace.[261] The Hamilton manuscripts were then with the booksellers Ellis & White in New Bond Street (successors to the firm that had sold manuscripts to Sir George Grey in the 1850s), and Lippmann saw them for the first time on 9 June. The following day he wrote at length to Schöne, focusing on what is clearly for him its most exciting item:

Vorallem ist da der Dante mit den Zeichnungen von Botticelli. Denken Sie sich ein Pergamentmanuscript in grossen folioformat, jedes Blatt auf einer Seite Text und auf der andren immer die ganze Seite bedeckend Feder und Silberstiftzeichnungen von Botticelli.

Above all, there is the Dante with drawings by Botticelli. Imagine a parchment manuscript of large folio size, every folio having the text on one page, and on the other the whole page throughout covered with pen and silverpoint drawings by Botticelli.[262]

He notes (as Waagen had done) that these are 'the illustrations to the *Divine Comedy* of which Vasari spoke', and then goes on to raise the question of whether the whole collection might be purchased en bloc for about a million marks, declaring that *der Dante* would not be overvalued at a tenth of that sum.[263] He

---

[258] 'The [twelfth] Duke had debts of about £1.5m, and the sale of the fine and decorative art and the Hamilton manuscripts did not even bring in a third of this amount' (Dr G. Evans, personal communication).

[259] An outline of the 'scanty and uncertain' evidence about German arrangements for the purchase and documentation about the early years of the Hamilton collection in Berlin is provided by Boese 1966: xvii–xx. In constructing the following account, I am indebted to some of Boese's references to publications and documents, as well as to staff at the Staatsbibliothek, Berlin.

[260] On Lippmann's career and publications, see the online *Dictionary of Art Historians* at: <http://www.dictionaryofarthistorians.org/lippmannf.htm>.

[261] Letter of 8 June 1882, in Lippmann's correspondence with Schöne, Berlin, Staatsbibliothek Nachlaß 248 Kast. 6. Umschlag II ('Museum 1882').

[262] Staatsbibliothek Nachlaß 248 Kast. 6. Umschlag II, letter of 10 June.

[263] Lippmann's estimate (equivalent to £50,000) is significantly lower than the eventual price paid by the Prussian Government (about £80,000). The Botticelli illustrations alone were subsequently valued by the English dealer who sold the collection (Ellis) at £20,000 (Berlin, Staatsbibliothek, Acta betreffend die Hamilton-Sammlung III.C.48 (1883), pp. 33 and 63).

continued to negotiate through Ellis during the second half of the month, and on 24 June he telegraphed Schöne to confirm that the deal would be for an en-bloc purchase at £80,000.[264] As a letter from Ellis to Lippmann indicates, other buyers—such as the Barons Adolphe and Alphonse Rothschild—were showing an interest in parts of the collection, so there was a need, as Lippmann had already urged, 'to strike fast' (*rasch zu greifen*).[265] With that purpose in mind, Lippmann went on in July to prepare a memorandum on 'Great Foreign Collections' (*Grosse auswärtige Sammlungen*) for Schöne to use in his own communications with the Prussian royal family (Crown Prince Friedrich) and with the relevant government ministries. Along with the Hamilton manuscripts, Lippmann lists a number of British collections that were or recently had been on the market: the manuscripts and paintings of Lord Ashburnham; the books of Lord Spencer at Althorp; the Sunderland Library and Gallery at Blenheim; as well as collections in Paris and Florence.[266] By the beginning of August Lippmann was back in London with a supporting team of experts, engaged in a closer examination of the collection which was due for sale at Sotheby's that November.

Meanwhile, higher powers had become involved in Berlin. On the strength of Lippmann's arguments, Schöne (in July) had submitted a report that had been seen and annotated by the German Crown Prince Friedrich, and this, together with evidence from Lippmann and his colleagues, formed the basis of a lengthy secret memorandum submitted by the Prussian minister of Culture, Gustav von Gossler, to the Finance Ministry on 30 September.[267] Gossler's memorandum provides the most detailed extant account of the German government's reasons for investing in the purchase, and its wider cultural implications will be considered later.[268] In emphasizing the importance of the opportunity represented by the purchase, he, like Lippmann, uses as a key example the 'Dante, illustrated by Botticelli, which appears to be the most exquisite pearl (*vorzüglichste Perle*) of the entire collection'.[269] Later in the argument, he elaborates further on its significance:

Noch über die Bedeutung selbst der schönsten Miniaturenhandschriften geht die große Pergamenthandschrift des Dante in Groß folio mit 88 blattgroßen Zeichnungen von Sandro Botticelli hinaus. Sie enthält eine Sammlung von Zeichnungen eines der ersten Künstler der Frührenaissance, wie sie nicht wieder existiert, und eine Illustration des großartigsten Denkmals der italienischen Literatur, welche vollkommen einzig dasteht.

---

[264] Berlin, Staatsbibliothek, Nachlaß 248 Kast 6, Umschlag II, telegram dated 24 June.

[265] Berlin, Staatsbibliothek, Nachlaß 248 Kast 6, Umschlag II, Ellis's letter is enclosed in Lippmann's of 30 June. Lippmann's comment about the need for swift action is from p. 8 of his letter of 10 June.

[266] Berlin, Staatsbibliothek, Nachlaß 248 Kast 6, Umschlag II, letter and enclosure of 17 July.

[267] Berlin, Geheimes Staatsarchiv Preussischer Kulturbesitz, I HA Rep. 151 Finanzministerium, I C Nr 7156 (Juli 1880 bis ult. 1885), 30 Sept. 1882.

[268] See below, pp. 255–6. Other documents relating to the purchase were probably destroyed during the Second World War.

[269] Berlin, Geheimes Staatsarchiv Preussischer Kulturbesitz, I HA Rep. 151 Finanzministerium, I C Nr 7156 (Juli 1880 bis ult. 1885), p. 3 of the unpaginated document.

The great parchment manuscript of Dante in large folio with 88 full-page illustrations by Sandro Botticelli surpasses the significance of even the finest illuminated manuscripts. It contains a group of drawings by one of the leading artists of the early Renaissance such as would never be brought together again, and an illustration of the most magnificent monument of Italian literature, which itself remains wholly unique.[270]

With this degree of scholarly and governmental coordination, the process of acquisition progressed swiftly. Within a month of Gossler's memorandum funds had been voted to purchase the Hamilton manuscripts en bloc before the scheduled November auction, at a price of around £80,000 (equal to about £4.5–5 million in today's terms). On 21 October Lippmann wrote from London to Wilhelm Bode—a young colleague (and future director of Royal Museums) who had been on the team examining the collection in August—announcing that most of the 'Hamilton items' were now packed up, and adding once again a note about the prize item:

Der Dante ist doch über alle Maßen herrlich! Ich bin sehr sehr glücklich daß wir ihn haben. Hoffentlich kommt alles gut nach Hause.

The Dante is indeed beyond measure magnificent! I am very very happy that we have got it. Let's hope it all gets home all right.[271]

It did. Nearly 700 items—including the seven *Commedia* manuscripts—were then shipped in twenty-seven zinc-lined chests, travelling (for security) as four separate cargoes, the first of which arrived in Berlin on 30 October and the last on 1 November—slightly less than five months after their purchase had first been suggested.[272]

The dispersal of the entire Hamilton collection—paintings, furniture, and libraries—was one of the major events of the late nineteenth-century art world and extended over a number of years.[273] The transfer of the manuscripts in particular—and notably the 'Botticelli Dante'—into foreign hands generated considerable comment and debate in the British cultural and political establishment, perhaps because it represented a dramatic early stage in the process of the dispersal of major private collections. The current director of the Berlin Kupferstichkabinett and editor of the catalogue for the 2001 Royal Academy exhibition of the Botticelli illustrations detects elements of trauma and betrayal here:

News that the collection was to be sold to Berlin unleashed a storm of indignation in Britain. Not only was the plan an offence to national sensibilities and the country's tradition of

---

[270] Berlin, Geheimes Staatsarchiv Preussischer Kulturbesitz, I HA Rep. 151 Finanzministerium, I C Nr 7156 (Juli 1880 bis ult. 1885), p. 7.

[271] Zentralarchiv der Staatlichen Museen zu Berlin, Nachlaß Bode 3346, letter of 21 October 1882. I am grateful to Carolin Pilgermann (Dipl.-Archivarin) for help in locating and transcribing part of this letter. On Bode and his role in developing the Berlin museums later in the century, see also Taylor 1997: 173. On 20 October, the day before Lipmann wrote this letter to Bode, he had added a second leaf to the description inside the cover of the manuscript, confirming Molini's collation of the manuscript folios; see Bertelli 2007: 122.

[272] Theinert 1884: 450.

[273] The wider dispersal of the collection is the subject of research by Dr C. Maxwell, as part of the project led by Dr G. Evans; see above, p. 243, n. 230.

collecting; it also involved—and this was perhaps more painful—work by two men, Dante and Botticelli, who had been set up as artistic and moral paradigms in the last third of the 19th century, partly as a result of the writings of Walter Pater and John Ruskin.[274]

This diagnosis focuses on some important aspects of the cultural value of the collection and of Hamilton 201 especially. It does not, however, acknowledge the full complexity of the British attitudes to the prospect of the loss, nor does it take account of German views about the national and international significance of the acquisition. There is a considerable amount of further evidence for both these features of the sale's cultural impact.

In Britain, already at the beginning of 1882, the planned sale of the collection was public knowledge, and its implications were being discussed at some length in the press. Ideas and action concerning the preservation of national antiquities were being generated by figures such as Octavia Hill, John Ruskin, and John Lubbock, who would succeed in getting the first 'Ancient Monuments Protection Act' passed in July 1882, the month in which Lippmann was preparing his memorandum on 'Great Foreign Collections'. Amongst the many British comments on the Hamilton sale, an early and relatively even-handed article in *The Times* acknowledged the possible benefits of wider access to the manuscripts: 'No danger threatens the safety or comfort of Psalters, the spoil of German abbeys, or invaluable illustrated Dantes, or lovely Greek manuscripts. Each will only fulfil its destiny the better for its transfer from a negligent to a reverential guardian.'[275] On the other hand, it went on immediately to raise some wider concerns about cultural capital and national status that it considered relevant to this particular 'dispersion':

Englishmen cannot, however, but be somewhat uneasy for themselves at the contingency each fresh dispersion of a celebrated collection suggests, that half its wealth may find a home abroad... There are Frenchmen and Russians and Americans, and even Germans, who suffer no thought of rival uses for money to stay their hand when the hammer is stooping to its fall... For a nation commanding incomparable wealth like England to permit treasures of the first order to be transplanted and domiciled elsewhere argues either inability to distinguish degrees in artistic value, or to comprehend the uses of money... It is not to the credit of British taste and munificence to come last in such a race.[276]

The language of international competition becomes increasingly evident here, as does an awareness of the role that could be played by an emerging national power ('even Germans...'). 'Patriotic' considerations would certainly come into play as the feared German bid materialized later in the year. They were, however, by no means the only issues at stake. Also early in 1882 an article in a newly founded and more specialist journal, the *Bibliographer*, gave a detailed account of the contents of 'The Beckford and Hamilton Libraries', identifying the Botticelli illustrations once again as 'probably the gem of the collection'.[277] It then spelled out the question of ownership, responsibility, and access yet more explicitly than the *Times* article had

---

[274] Altcappenberg 2000: 20–1.   [275] 'Hamilton Palace Library', *The Times*, 5 Jan. 1882.
[276] 'Hamilton Palace Library', *The Times*, 5 Jan. 1882.
[277] 'The Beckford and Hamilton Libraries', *Bibliographer*, 1 (Feb. 1882), 86.

done: 'Some persons will lament that two such magnificent libraries should be dispersed; but surely it is better that the books should enrich a considerable number of other libraries than remain on the shelves at Hamilton Palace unused.'[278] Later in the year, however—as the sale drew nearer and the interest of foreign purchasers became more real—further notes of concern came to be registered in several quarters. In July the *Bibliographer* begins to change its tone, continuing to recognize the benefits of the 'dispersion' whilst also deploying a discourse of quasi-religious duty:

For nearly forty years Hamilton Palace has been known to contain two of the finest libraries of the kingdom, but henceforth its chief glories will have departed. We do not say it is a misfortune that such collections should be dispersed, for probably the world at large benefits by the sale . . . [but] if it were blasphemy [for one man] to possess what the whole world must covet, it was something like sacrilege to disperse them.[279]

In the month when this second article was published a far less ambivalent view was being expressed at a high level in British society. The Hamilton sale became one of the topics of correspondence between Crown Princess Victoria of Prussia and her mother, Queen Victoria, in July 1882, and letters between them continued to refer to it until October of that year. The first and longest of Princess Vicky's four letters on the subject was written from her summer retreat in the South Tyrol, and strikes an urgent note:

I always forget to mention the sale of the Duke of Hamilton's works of art which I think such a pity; but the best and most valuable part of his possessions is going to be sold soon; it is his library—he has some books that are quite unique—amongst or rather before all others—a manuscript copy of Dante all illustrated in 88 pages by Sandro Botticelli. This extraordinary treasure ought not to leave England. The Berlin Museum would like to buy the whole collection for £88,000 if the parliament will vote the money. I must say I think it a shame that England should be spoiled of such a treasure[,] and I do not understand the British Museum and the Bodleian Library at Oxford not making an arrangement with the Duke of Hamilton, and his not having the right patriotism to offer his treasures to our own national collections before foreigners treat with him for them . . . If our great English families are obliged to sell their unique collections[,] at least I think, if possible, the nation ought to secure them. Mr Gladstone[,] as a lover of art and learning, would I am sure—even from a financial point of view—think money well invested that is spent on increasing the art collections of the nation. The day will come when these things can no longer be had and all is readily snapped up by the new collections of America and the Continent.[280]

The crown princess had some knowledge of art and art history: she was a talented painter and sculptor, and had visited Italy and its galleries with her husband, Crown Prince Friedrich, on a number of occasions from the 1860s onwards.[281] There was also a political motive and context for her intervention in this case. As a result of the protracted power-struggle through which Bismarck had succeeded in depriving the

---

[278] *Bibliographer*, 1 (Feb. 1882), 87.
[279] 'The Beckford Library', *Bibliographer* 2 (July 1882), 25.
[280] Fulford 1981: 122–3 (letter of 23 July 1882, from Merano).
[281] Pakula 2006: 157, 180–1, 272, 345, 367, and 415.

crown prince of influence, his wife's loyalties in the early 1880s were increasingly turning back to 'dear England', and she was expressing strong disapproval of German colonial ambitions.[282] Vicky's decision thus to oppose both her adopted country and her husband on this occasion must have been prompted by seeing or hearing of the report about the Hamilton collection that, as we have seen, had been sent to and commented on by the crown prince only a few days earlier by the *Generaldirektor* of the Royal Museums, Richard Schöne.[283]

The crown princess's concerns and those of the queen were then passed on to William Gladstone (whose concern for 'art and learning' had been mentioned in the letter), and in mid-August the prime minister responded to the queen's secretary in highly circumspect terms:

I write to say that I paid due attention to your note about the Hamilton Library, but that I have heard nothing on the subject from the Trustees of the [British] Museum.

It is sometimes said that in this country the State is illiberal to purchases connected with art & libraries. My impression is that we spend far more upon them than any other country, and that there is no library in the world . . . which is endowed like that of the Museum.

The Botticelli Dante is I believe an affair of many thousand pounds. But it derives its value I imagine almost entirely from its being in fact a collection of paintings [*sic*] by Botticelli; a great artist without doubt; but I can conceive a question whether in this view it is altogether an appropriate purchase for a National Library. At the same time, I do not venture to form that opinion. In truth it is difficult for any one connected with the Treasury to touch the initiative of these questions, there being another Department, namely the Museum Trust, of which it is the business to bring them before us when occasion arises.[284]

It was not Gladstone's finest hour, nor his finest prose. The reference to the Botticelli illustrations as 'paintings' fails to display his usual attention to detail, or perhaps a disinclination to associate the drawings too closely with his admired *Commedia*. Moreover, despite his lifelong devotion to Dante (affirmed in his letter to Giuliani later that same year), Gladstone—as the reference to 'many thousand pounds' recalls—had also been a chancellor of the exchequer, and he was now, in the midst of his second premiership, under pressure to spend large amounts of public money to suppress an Egyptian nationalist revolt.[285]

Early in October Vicky wrote to her mother again, and yet more urgently, about 'that precious illustration of Dante by Botticelli', reporting on the telegrams being sent by the 'Berlin Museum authorities' and of how 'they boast here of having the finest collections of England over here in a few years!'[286] But by then the die had almost been cast—at least as far as the Hamilton manuscripts and the Botticelli Dante were concerned. By the end of the month the crown princess had once again been outmanoeuvred by the Prussian government and could only 'regret bitterly'

[282] Pakula 2006: 433–4 and 438–9.
[283] Schöne's report of 20 July and Friedrich's annotations of it are mentioned by Gustav von Gossler on p. 1 of his memorandum of 30 September; see above, p. 248 with n. 267.
[284] *GD* 10: 313–14 (16 Aug. 1882).
[285] On the Egyptian revolt, see Jenkins 1995: 501–8. On Gladstone's letter to Giuliani about Dante (Dec. 1882), see above, pp. 177–8.
[286] Fulford 1981: 126.

Britain's loss of 'the Hamilton library with the Botticelli manuscript', once more accusing the duke of having 'been most unpatriotic in offering these treasures to a foreign government without knowing whether the British nation wished to possess them or not'.[287]

That nation's press and parliament were even slower to react to the German coup. On 31 October, the day after the first consignments of manuscripts reached Berlin, *The Times*'s correspondent was still reporting the Prussian purchase as an intention which readers might be 'inclined to doubt' (given the high cost involved), and raising the question of whether, 'if it is not too late, it might not be possible to procure the transference of the Hamilton manuscripts into the archives of Blooms-bury [i.e. the British Museum] instead of seeing them triumphantly catalogued in the Royal Library at Berlin'. The following day (1 November) the same corres-pondent ruefully acknowledged that this 'warning' had 'come . . . too late'—citing the confirmation of the sale that had been reported that morning:

In making this announcement the *North German Gazette* naturally writes in a tone of satisfaction and enumerates the chief treasures of the acquisition, among which may be mentioned a psaltery [*sic*], dating from the 7th century, and a grand manuscript folio copy of Dante's great work, with illustrative drawings from the hand of Sandro Botticelli. The *literati* and archaeologists are rubbing their hands in high glee.[288]

It was probably this report, published in *The Times* on 2 November, that led to a question being raised in parliament on the same day:

MR COCHRANE-PATRICK asked the Financial Secretary to the Treasury whether there was any truth in the report that the Prussian Government had bought the Hamilton Collection of MSS; and if not, whether there was any ground to hope that the whole or any part of such an invaluable collection could be secured for the nation.

MR COURTNEY—Nothing is known at the Treasury about this rumoured sale, nor, so far as I am aware, at the British Museum. No communication from the trustees of that institution has been received on the subject of the Hamilton manuscripts; and I cannot learn that any offer of them was made to the trustees.[289]

The question was put by a Scottish Conservative MP whose constituency (North Ayrshire) was not far from Hamilton Palace.[290] The response on behalf of Glad-stone's government was delivered by the new financial secretary to the Treasury, Leonard Courtney, who had been a *Times* leader writer and professor of political economy, and now 'often irritated the Commons by his portentous and long-winded speeches'.[291] On this occasion his response combined brevity with obfus-cation. The prime minister (and first lord of the Treasury), Gladstone, had indeed

[287] Fulford 1981: 127–8.   [288] 'Germany', *The Times*, 2 Nov. 1882
[289] 'Parliamentary Intelligence', *The Times*, 3 Nov. 1882 (p. 5 col. A).
[290] During his brief period in the Commons (1880–5) Cochran-Patrick spoke frequently on educational matters He had been a member of the Scottish Society of Antiquaries, represented Britain at the International Congress of Archaeology in 1874, and published several studies of coinage; see *ODNB*, s.v. 'Patrick, Robert William Cochran- (1842–1897), politician'.
[291] *ODNB*, s.v. 'Courtney, Leonard Henry, Baron Courtney of Penwith (1832–1918), journalist and politician'.

known about the planned sale since early August of that year, and in his letter to the queen's secretary he had explicitly ducked the issue, declaring it to be the province of 'another Department, namely the Museum Trust'.[292] The government's later parliamentary response about 'this rumoured sale' seems, therefore, to have been at best evasive.

Meanwhile, the acquisition of 'the invaluable collection' continued to be hailed as a triumph in Berlin. Also in the first week of November, *The Times*'s correspondent would have augmented Princess Vicky's 'bitter regret' by revealing to English readers that her husband had 'used his personal influence to secure the purchase', and by recording that the German papers were 'full of exulting articles on the Hamilton collection of manuscripts lately acquired'.[293] Three articles written for the Berlin newspaper *Die Post* indeed reflect something of this mood. The first (perhaps significantly included in a 'Political Review of the Day') begins by declaring the purchase to be 'worthy of being ranked among the great acquisitions which during the past decade have raised our scholarly and artistic institutions to the highest level in the world'.[294] Assuming that its readers are interested in the details, *Die Post* then goes on to describe several categories of the manuscripts (English, Byzantine, Old French, and Italian), as well as claiming, with a touch of exaggeration, that one of the *Commedia* texts (dated 1347) is 'the oldest known manuscript' of the poem.[295]

Further detailed discussion of the manuscripts and the significance of the acquisition was provided for the Berlin readers in the form of two opinion pieces in a front-page column by the art historian Carl Adolf Rosenberg.[296] In the first of these Rosenberg begins with what would become a frequent parallel, between the purchase of the Hamilton manuscripts and another spectacular national project: the German archaeological excavations in Asia Minor (1878–86) that would eventually bring the Great Altar of Pergamon to Berlin.[297] He then dramatizes the manuscripts' transition from being 'hidden away in the library of a Scottish castle and more or less inaccessible to researchers', to emerge 'only now into the public sphere . . . as objects of scholarly study', with relevance especially to the early history of graphic art and illumination. This leads once again to the appreciation of the 'chief item in the collection', the Botticelli illustrations, to which a quarter of this

---

[292] See above, p. 252 and n. 284.

[293] *The Times*, 3 Nov. and 6 Nov. 1882 (reports from Berlin on 2 and 5 Nov.).

[294] 'Politische Tagesübersicht', in *Die Post*, 5 Nov. 1882 (my trans.). A comparable example of manuscript acquisition arousing public interest was the Hungarian response (some five years earlier) to the return of items that had been taken by the Ottomans from the library of Matthias Corvinus in the sixteenth century; these included a late fourteenth-century illustrated copy of the *Commedia* (now Budapest Univ. Library Ital. I). See Roddewig 1984: 25–6; BMS 1. 212–15; and Tanner 2008: 204–7. The 1884 purchase of some of the Ashburnham manuscripts (including a number of the *Commedia*) by the government of the newly unified Italy would also be worth comparing; see above, p. 241 and n. 223.

[295] *Die Post*, 5 Nov. 1882 (my trans.). The manuscript referred to is Hamilton 203; see Roddewig 1984: 9 (no. 15).

[296] *Die Post*, 5 Nov. 1882 (*Feuilleton*). On Rosenberg (1850–1906) and his wide interests, see the *Metzler-Kunsthistoriker-Lexikon* (Stuttgart: Metzler, 1999), 329–30.

[297] *Die Post*, 5 and 7 Nov. 1882 (*Feuilleton*).

first article is devoted and which, Rosenberg notes, amount to by far the largest and most coherent assembly of the artist's drawings in any European gallery. Over another five front-page columns, the second part of Rosenberg's article then surveys the resources for a wide range of cultural and art-historical scholarship that the collection now offered—from images of Arabic, Persian, and Indian costume, through the iconography of illuminated gospels, psalters, books of hours, and antiphonals, to copies of Greek and Roman classics and Old French and Provençal texts.[298] Amongst the works by the other two 'crowns of Florence' (Petrarch and Boccaccio), Rosenberg also draws attention at the end of his article to 'the valuable manuscript of Boccaccio's *Decameron* dating from the fourteenth century'.[299] At almost the same time, in Britain, the *Athenaeum*—as well as carrying Sothebys' announcement of the collection's sale as a fait accompli—was also identifying the same 'most valuable fourteenth century manuscript' (MS Hamilton 90) as one of the 'treasures' of the collection.[300] It would not be until the mid-twentieth century that this *Decameron* would be identified as Boccaccio's autograph, so neither the British writer nor the German knew at the time the full extent of what in this case had been lost and gained.[301]

German national issues were also involved, and had been for some time. In his second article on the Hamilton purchase Rosenberg had begun by acknowledging the role played by Gustav von Gossler as *Kultusminister* and celebrating the purchase as one of his ministry's 'highest achievements'. Gossler had indeed fought his corner hard. A few months earlier, in his secret memorandum to the Finance Ministry (30 September 1882), he had, like Rosenberg, emphasized the intrinsic value of the collection to the intellectual and artistic community, its relevance to 'the fields of fine and applied art and historical scholarship', and its provision of resources and 'examples' for a variety of related fields.[302] He had also spelled out rather more fully some of the broader cultural and political implications of the purchase, introducing his proposal in the context of Berlin's development as capital since unification in 1871, and drawing attention to the 'competition' of France, Austria, and England in funding galleries and museums.[303] In the conclusion to his argument he had declared his intention

mit Rücksicht auf die politische Bedeutung einer Ausgestaltung der Kunstsammlungen der Hauptstadt und der zu diesem Behufe erforderlichen Maßnahmen[,] Abschrift der Denkschrift vom 10 Juli d[ieses]. J[ahres]. dem Herrn Reichskanzler mitzutheilen.

---

[298] *Die Post*, 7 Nov. 1882 (*Feuilleton*). Another major Hamilton item highlighted by Rosenberg and several other commentators of the time is the works of Horace written and illustrated for Ferdinand I of Naples by the late fifteenth century Florentine miniaturist Marco Attavanti.

[299] *Die Post*, 7 Nov. 1882, col. 5 (my trans.).

[300] 'The Hamilton Manuscripts', in *Athenaeum*, 74 (11 Nov. 1882), p. 614, col. 3 and p. 628, col. 2.

[301] See Branca and Ricci 1962.

[302] Berlin, Geheimes Staatsarchiv Preussischer Kulturbesitz, I HA Rep. 151 Finanzministerium, I C Nr 7156 (Juli 1880 bis ult. 1885), 30 Sept. 1882, p. 7 (my trans.). On the circumstances of the Gossler memorandum, see above, pp. 248–9.

[303] Berlin, Geheimes Staatsarchiv Preussischer Kulturbesitz, I HA Rep. 151 Finanzministerium, I C Nr 7156 (Juli 1880 bis ult. 1885), 30 Sept. 1882, pp. 1, 11.

in view of the political significance of this project to develop the art collections of the capital city and the measures required for this purpose, to send a copy of the memorandum of 10 July of this year to His Excellency the Imperial Chancellor.[304]

The *Kultusminister*'s whole argument—involving Berlin's political prestige, the prospect of an appeal to Bismarck, and, in conclusion, a reminder of the Prussian crown prince's 'pronounced interest' in the matter—must (when his twelve-page *Denkschrift* landed on the finance minister's desk) have amounted to a compelling combination. Interestingly, however, neither he nor any of the German or English sources mentioned here seem to have considered whether another newly unified nation—Italy—might have been a bidder, or an appropriate home, for the Hamilton collection's Italian treasures.[305]

The national significance of the Prussian purchase was quickly recognized elsewhere in the new German empire. In January 1883 a newspaper in the far south of the country published a long article on 'Die Hamilton-Manuscripte' by a leading art historian, Wilhelm Lübke.[306] Lübke was closely acquainted with at least two of the museum experts (Lippmann and Bode) who were directly involved in the previous year's acquisition process, and the Berlin authorities had, as he here acknowledges, allowed him several weeks to sample the 'wealth and splendour of the Hamilton treasures'.[307] Like Lippmann, Gossler, and others, he gives prominence 'in the first place' to the Botticelli illustrations, describing in detail the 'brooding absorption' with which the artist enters into dialogue with and renders the images of the 'most sublime and original poet', and giving some close attention to such features as perspective in the *Inferno* and the rendering of figures in the *Paradiso*.[308]

Framing this detailed account of the Dante illustrations and the other illuminated manuscripts are assertions about the acquisition's significance for the newly unified nation, including the local readers of the *Münchner Allgemeine Zeitung*. At the beginning of his article Lübke exploits the phonetic and cultural connections between *Pergaminier* (the Pergamon antiquities then being excavated by Karl Humann) and *Pergament* (the parchment of the Hamilton manuscripts).[309] He goes on to emphasize Prussia's 'peaceful conquests' and the leading role of what his readers might regard as a 'military state' in developing the nation's 'higher cultural

---

[304] Berlin, Geheimes Staatsarchiv Preussischer Kulturbesitz, I HA Rep. 151 Finanzministerium, I C Nr 7156 (Juli 1880 bis ult. 1885), 30 Sept. 1882, p. 12 (my trans.). On the development of Berlin (which almost doubled its population between 1871 and 1890), and the expansion of its museums and galleries, see Taylor 1997: 153–6 and 172–3.

[305] On the Italian government's purchase of the Ashburnham Dante manuscripts shortly afterwards (1884), see above, p. 241 and n. 223.

[306] *Münchner Allgemeine Zeitung: Beilage* 24 (24 Jan. 1883), 337–9.

[307] *Münchner Allgemeine Zeitung: Beilage* 24 (24 Jan. 1883), 337 (my trans.). On Lübke (1826–93), see the online *Dictionary of Art Historians* at <http://www.dictionaryofarthistorians.org/lubkew.htm> (accessed 11 March 2014). In 1871 he had participated with Lippmann and Bode in the 'Holbein Convention' at Dresden (to determine which of two versions of the Meyer *Madonna* was the autograph).

[308] *Münchner Allgemeine Zeitung: Beilage* 24 (24 Jan. 1883), 337 (my trans.).

[309] On the Pergamon excavations, see above, p. 254 and n. 297.

life'.[310] In conclusion, he spells out, even more explicitly than Gossler had done, what such enterprises might mean for the German cultural identity: 'Daher hat denn auch die Nachricht von dieser grossartigen Erwerbung in ganz Deutschland das Gefühl patriotischen Stolzes erweckt' ('Hence also the news of this magnificent acquisition has aroused a sense of patriotic pride throughout Germany').[311] News that was thus cause for 'patriotic pride' in München was being described at almost the same time in London as 'com[ing] upon most patriotic Englishmen like a shock'.[312] In its December issue the *Bibliographer*—whose attitude towards the Hamilton sale had become progressively more apprehensive through the year— began to marshal public opinion in support of a rearguard action:

It was enough for most of us to know that a Dante illustrated by Botticelli, and a copy of the Gospels in Latin of the seventh century, were among the manuscripts [bought by the German Government], and that the others were worthy of such companions. The apathy of the English Government in respect to the purchase for the nation of artistic and literary treasures is well known, but one might have hoped that in the present instance it would have been aroused so as to have saved the country from the disgrace of parting with that which can never be replaced to a foreign state.[313]

The British government's 'apathy' on this matter had already been condemned from several quarters in the course of the year. In his letter to Lippmann, the London dealer responsible for the sale (F.S. Ellis, of Ellis & White) had earlier expressed the 'hope', for Lippmann's sake, that the German government would not be 'so dead to artistic matters in Manuscripts as ours is'.[314] The disingenuousness of the statement to parliament by Gladstone's minister had been exposed by *The Times*'s Berlin correspondent, and a brief letter to *The Times* at the end of November suggested who might be held to account and what might be learned from the lesson:

After the statement of your Berlin Correspondent that the trustees of the British Museum and the Government were both aware of the offer made by the Berlin authorities, it seems that we may fairly demand on what grounds the Government based its refusal to make the acquisition.
    Probably a question asked in the House of Commons may attain this result; at any rate, the expression of opinion in this instance may prevent such a calamity happening in the future.[315]

The letter is signed 'V.' and may thus perhaps represent an intervention by one of the Vernon family—possibly William Warren Vernon, whose interest in Dante scholarship continued well after the fifth baron's death.[316] Other belated measures

---

[310] *Münchner Allgemeine Zeitung: Beilage* 24 (24 Jan. 1883), pp. 337 and 339 (my trans.).
[311] *Münchner Allgemeine Zeitung: Beilage* 24 (24 Jan. 1883), p. 339 (my trans.).
[312] Anon, 'The Hamilton Manuscripts', *Bibliographer*, 3 (1882–3), 5.
[313] *Bibliographer*, 3 (1882–3), 5.
[314] Berlin, Staatsbibliothek Nachlaß 248 Kast. 6. Umschlag II ('Museum 1882'); Ellis's letter (27 June 1882) is enclosed with Lippmann's (to Schöne) on 30 June.
[315] 'The Hamilton Manuscripts: To the Editor', *The Times*, 27 Nov. 1882, p. 8, col. C.
[316] On Vernon senior (d. 1866), see above, pp. 217–18 and 220–2. His second son, William Warren Vernon (1834–1919), funded the publication of an edition of Benvenuto da Imola's *Comentum* on the *Commedia* by J. P. Lacaita (5 vols., Florence: Barbèra 1887) and himself published *Readings* on all

to remedy the 'calamity' were already under way. The December article in the *Bibliographer* went on mention the German authorities' willingness 'to sell back to England the English State papers 1532–85'; their readiness to consider repatriating some of the items of British interest had been reported by *The Times*'s correspondent in Berlin; and some repurchasing would indeed later take place, though it would not involve any of the Dante manuscripts.[317]

A wider perspective is opened up by the conclusion to the article in the *Bibliographer*, which refers to the concerns of a major figure on the late Victorian cultural scene: John Ruskin. A pamphlet by Ruskin, 'lately' published by the London book-dealer Bernard Quaritch, had mentioned visiting the Hamilton manuscript collection 'some thirty years ago', and he now proposed to establish a fund to retain such items on behalf of the 'English public'.[318] The article ends by once more castigating the 'apathy' of the established authorities: 'Had the Government of this country been of the same mind with Mr. Ruskin, these manuscripts would not have been lost to us.'[319] Questions about public responsibility for such artefacts were not, of course, new, nor had the government of the time been wholly inactive in this area. The National Art Collections Fund would not be established for another twenty years, but, as Gustav von Gossler's memorandum had pointed out, Britain's National Gallery had already received a grant of £35,000 to purchase some of the major paintings from the Hamilton collection.[320] And despite the alleged inertia of the British Museum trustees on this occasion, the late librarian, Antonio Panizzi, had hugely increased its purchase grant, and as early as 1842 secured the bequest of the Grenville collection, with amongst its rarer items early printed editions of the *Commedia* and other Dantean works.[321]

The migration of the Hamilton manuscripts and their Botticellian 'gem' thus seems to have had the effect of intensifying public concern about the nation's heritage, as the columns of *The Times* continued to make clear. On Saturday, 4 November 1882—two days after the Prussian government's purchase had been publicly confirmed, and a day after the question about it had been asked in the British parliament—a long *Times* leader focused upon the implications of 'the alienation of so much national property'.[322] From start to finish the leader displays some tendency to adopt an elegiac tone on the subject ('It will not be without a pang... we may be allowed a passing regret...') which had by now been rather overdone, not least by *Times* writers themselves. On the other hand, the article also expresses concern about cultural conditions in Britain beyond the metropolis: the

---

three parts of the *Commedia* (1889, 1894, 1900), which included a complete prose translation and which were recommended by T. S. Eliot, to show 'how far into medieval philosophy, theology, science and literature a thorough study of Dante must go' (Eliot 1929: 13). See also Cunningham 1965: 155–8; and Parker 1993: 8 and nn. 15 and 18.

[317] 'The Hamilton Manuscripts', *Bibliographer*, 3 (1882–3), 5, and 'The Hamilton Manuscripts', *The Times*, 20 Nov. 1882, p. 5, col. F.

[318] 'The Hamilton Manuscripts', *Bibliographer*, 3 (1882–3), 6.

[319] *Bibliographer*, 3 (1882–3), 6.

[320] Berlin, Geheimes Staatsarchiv Preussischer Kulturbesitz, I HA Rep. 151 Finanzministerium, I C Nr 7156 (Juli 1880 bis ult. 1885), 30 Sept. 1882, p. 11.

[321] *DEL* 2. 600.   [322] Leader, *The Times* (4 Nov. 1882), p. 9, col. E.

preservation of great collections 'in country seats rarely visited'; and the relative absence in 'our largest and wealthiest cities' of 'public collections like those which give a European dignity to some very small Continental towns'. Crucially, too, it points to the discrepancy between claims about the increasing availability of education and the actual lack of wider acquaintance with the contents of such collections:

Of the millions now supposed to have received an education sufficient to give them the key of all knowledge, it can only be a very small per cent. that have seen anything so rare and precious as a copy of the Gospels of the seventh century . . . or a Psalter of the ninth century, or a MS. copy of 'Dante' illustrated by the pencil of SANDRO BOTTICELLI . . . [323]

The loss of such a 'Dante' thus served to focus a larger debate about the ownership and use of Britain's cultural possessions. In its reference to the 'education' of 'millions', the *Times* article raises questions about whether and how the 'national property' about which it is so concerned might be made available to a wider public.

[323] Leader, *The Times* (4 Nov. 1882), p. 9, col. E.

8

Widening Circles, 1320–2013

> *M.L.*: It seems odd to talk about popularizing Dante, but you would—
> seriously—you would like people who think 'I couldn't possibly take that
> on—it's too much for me'—you are at that level trying to raise the audience?
>
> *C.J.*: I'm afraid that I have been guilty of hoping that a small proportion of
> Dan Brown's audience—he who translated—well he didn't translate the
> 'Inferno'; he used it in his latest thriller—I was hoping that a small proportion
> of that audience might want to check up on the poem. It's available—that's all
> I can say—it's in every good bookshop.[1]

'Author most beloved by the masses' (*vulgo gratissimus auctor*) is how a contemporary epitaph describes Dante.[2] This final chapter begins by reaching back beyond
the beginning of this book, to consider the poet's broader appeal to the public of his
own time, for whom the notion of 'popularizing' his work did not seem particularly
'odd', even if many of those whose opinions have survived did not approve. It then
reviews some of the evidence of access to and expanding interest in that author
among the British public over the centuries with which the preceding chapters have
been concerned. Finally, outlining some developments and examples up to the
present, it suggests some directions through which Dante's wider currency among
an increasingly internationalized anglophone audience could be further investigated.

THE COMMON *COMEDY*: DANTE TO CHAUCER

Only a 'few' readers are imagined following in Dante's wake at the beginning of the
Paradiso, but his work as a whole also has a larger audience in mind.[3] His political
writing, both in Latin and in the vernacular, was addressed to a wide public of
cities, secular and religious leaders, and Christian communities. His lyric poems
were widely circulated, and the *Commedia* was 'speech' and 'song' that would
not only be seen, read, and written about but also spoken and heard. For his

---

[1] Mark Lawson interviewing Clive James about his translation of the *Commedia* (2013) on BBC
Radio 4, 'Front Row', 17 July 2013. On James's translation, see below, pp. 283 (with n. 147) and 298.

[2] Del Virgilio 1902: 174; trans. from Armour 2007: 20.

[3] *Voi altri pochi* (*Par.* 2. 10). A modern Italian commentator notes that 'it is a fact we can all vouch
for today, after Dante's *Paradiso* has been in circulation for six centuries: that it has always been
understood and loved by a "few"' (Dante 1997: 3. 52–3, n. on l. 10, my trans.).

contemporary public the 'sacred poem'[4] was also, to a great extent, 'a "performed" text, immediate in its use of the vernacular and in the vividness of the oral expression that accompanies and even underlies it as its principal means of transmission in the first centuries'.[5]

Oral performance and common currency were, from the start, features of the *Commedia*'s own text and context. Its very title was, in part, a mark of humility, underlining its difference from the *Aeneid*, linking it with satire, and associating it with the middle and humble vernacular; and 'comedy' may also have been intended to convey the inclusiveness of the project.[6] The poem itself draws upon the traditions of early Italian vernacular performance, as well as on more illustrious sources, and it shows the influence of the dramatic *laude* and *contrasti*, as well as of civic spectacle.[7] It is also likely that whilst the poem was in the making Dante would have been called upon to recite episodes or cantos from the poem at the court of one or other of his patrons, and on those occasions 'the effect upon the audience must have been overwhelming: for the only time ever, the *io* ["I"] who visited the afterlife and the *io* who was then describing it to them were the same person'.[8]

The popularity of the *Commedia* proved a problem for some of Dante's contemporaries and successors. Already during the poet's lifetime a professor of classical poetry at Bologna, Giovanni del Virgilio—he who would also acknowledge Dante's mass appeal as *vulgo gratissimus auctor*[9]—raised the question in the first of his Latin verse epistles to the poet. Here he regrets that the poem's grave themes may be thrown away upon the 'illiterate masses' (*gens idiota, vulgo*)—anxiously foreseeing them 'croaked out at street corners by some shock-haired comic buffoon' (*comicomus nebulo*)—and pointing out that none of the group of poets with whom Dante associates in Limbo (*Inferno* 4) 'wrote in the language of the marketplace'.[10]

By the time Chaucer travelled to Florence in 1373 Dante's fame and the transmission of his poem in an oral as well as literary culture had become issues for further comment and debate. This was also the year in which the Florentine Commune decided to fund Boccaccio's lectures on Dante, which began in the autumn following Chaucer's visit.[11] The lectures did not get beyond the middle of the *Inferno*,[12] but they were an important civic and public occasion. The proposal to appoint 'a worthy and wise man, learned in the art of poetry . . . to read the book that is commonly called *El Dante* in the city of Florence to all who wish to hear' had

[4] *Sacrato poema/poema sacro* (*Par.* 23. 62 and 25. 1).   [5] Armour 2007: 21.
[6] Armour 1991: 25, n. 15, and *DE* 185B–186B. *Commedia* is used twice to describe the poem, and on both occasions in the *Inferno*: 16. 128 and 21. 2.
[7] Armour 1991: 9–12, and Ahern 1997: 219–20. For example, in 1304 (three or four years before the exiled poet began the *Inferno*) a 'lifelike pageant of Hell' was staged on a bridge in Florence, with grim consequences for the over-large audience (Villani 1990: 9. 70).
[8] Armour 2007: 20.   [9] In the epitaph quoted above, p. 260.
[10] Giovanni del Virgilio 1902: 146–9, esp. ll. 6–7, 12–13, 15–19, 21–2, and 33–4. For further discussion of *trecento* concerns about Dante as a poet 'popular in style', see Havely 1997: 74–6.
[11] The *Esposizioni sopra la Comedia di Dante*; see Boccaccio 1965, Padoan 1959, and Minnis and Scott with Wallace 1991: 456–8 and 503–19.
[12] They break off early in *Inf.* 17.

been put before the Priors and the Council of Twelve by a number of Florentine citizens, who wished 'to be instructed about the book of Dante on their own behalf and that of other citizens aspiring to virtue, as well as for the benefit of their followers and descendants'.[13]

Chaucer could not have attended Boccaccio's lectures, since they began a few months after he had left Italy, but he could well have heard something of the city's plans to present them; and the idea of Boccaccio interpreting Dante would have meant that during the time of the English poet's visit to Florence links between the city's great authors were being publicly recognized. The popularity and performance of the *Commedia* in the urban culture of late fourteenth-century Florence, may also have informed Chaucer's reception of the *Commedia* and his initial appropriation of it in *The House of Fame*.[14]

The reference to Dante (as one of several writers on Hell) in the first book of Chaucer's poem is the first known reference to the 'grete poete of Ytaille' by a writer in English.[15] *The House of Fame* was not widely circulated to begin with, yet Chaucer's own continuing fame in the fifteenth and sixteenth centuries would have ensured that his naming and appropriation of Dante here and in his more well-known works—such as the *Troilus* and the *Canterbury Tales*—reached a wider public onwards into the age of print. Some of Chaucer's imitations of Dante provide the earliest versions of lines from the *Commedia* in English,[16] and from the sixteenth century on the continuing translation and quotation of passages from the poem indicate a widening circle of knowledge.

'THE CONVERSATION OF THIS COUNTRY',
*c.*1500–1900

As late as 1821, however, the Whig politician and bibliophile Thomas Grenville would argue that: 'The names of Petrarch and of Dante are familiar enough in the conversation of this country, but I doubt whether that familiar use extends itself to their works.'[17] Grenville was writing over two centuries since Jonson's Lady Politick Would-be had unloaded all those weighty Italian authorial names at Volpone's bedside, and his lofty judgement on the British public's capacities might suggest that (as Lady Pol had claimed) few, even now, could understand Dante.[18] Yet 1821 was three years after Foscolo's influential articles on the *Commedia* in the *Edinburgh Review* and two after the second, enlarged edition of Cary's translation. It was the year of Shelley's portrayal of Dante (in *A Defence of Poetry*) as the 'awakener of entranced Europe' and the publication of Byron's

---

[13] Del Lungo 1881: 164–5 (my trans.).

[14] For a fuller account of this argument, see Havely 1997.

[15] *The House of Fame*, in Chaucer 1994: ll. 445–50. See also the discussion of Adam Easton's references to Dante's *Monarchia* in the 1370s, above pp. 24–6.

[16] See above, p. 8, with nn. 3, 4, and 6. Other examples include *The House of Fame*, ll. 523–8 and 1101–9; *Troilus and Criseyde*, book 3, ll. 1261–7.

[17] Letter of 24 May 1821, see above, p. 146.   [18] See above, p. 68.

Prophecy of Dante. It was the year, too, in which an English periodical, the *New Monthly Magazine*, would make numerous references to Dante and would remark upon Foscolo's admiration for the poet of the *Commedia* as evidence of his grounding 'in the best authors of antiquity'.[19] Grenville's caution about 'familiar use' was and is salutary, but the 'conversation of this country' about Dante, as previous chapters have shown, had long been increasing in volume and participation, and, during the following century, would do so even more rapidly. Cultural activities and productions that promoted—and were promoted by—that increase include translation, illustration, performance, and fiction.

Translation is the most obvious form of activity and production through which the currency of 'Dante in English' was extended.[20] Significant renderings of the *Commedia* especially—as the previous chapters have shown—include phrases and passages, as well as cantos, *cantiche*, and the whole work. The history of the poem's excerpting for British readers reaches back more than four centuries before the belated appearance of the first complete English version to be published in1802, and it includes in the medieval and early modern periods writers as various as Chaucer, Serravalle, Flacius, Birckbek, and Milton. From the mid-seventeenth century adventurous professionals like John Davies of Kidwelly and Thomas Salusbury experimented with Dante's poem by turning short passages they found in their originals into English verse.[21] Such experiments may have helped to encourage the more sustained attempts that began with Jonathan Richardson's 'Ugolino' early in the following century. The development of some of the early partial translations and the complete versions from Boyd and Cary onwards has been surveyed, but there is still scope for research on their contexts, circulation, and reception. The same goes for the later production of translations of Dante's other works, such as the *Vita nuova* and the *Convivio*.[22]

Illustrations also provided a means through which awareness of the *Commedia* and its author could reach a wider British public. Neither Serravalle's Latin translation nor the first known manuscript copy of the poem in the original to reach Britain in 1451 (Hamilton 207) were illustrated, but the first printed text that can be linked to an English owner in 1520 certainly was.[23] Manuscripts, editions, and commentaries with miniatures, woodcuts, diagrams, and engravings are, as we have seen, in British possession—from John Pennant, Thomas Hoby, and Thomas Seget in the sixteenth century, through the illustrated texts in collections such as the 'Biblioteca Digbeiana' (built up in the seventeenth century), to the codices collected by Coke and Hobart on their Grand Tour and the copies of the 1481 Florence

---

[19] *DEL* 2. 329–33.
[20] For this form of 'Dante in English', the key resource for primary material is Griffiths and Reynolds 2005.
[21] See above, pp. 76–8.
[22] On these versions, see Appendix 1 (Chronology) for 1846–62, 1887, and 1889; on early translations of these works, see Webb 1976: 291–7; Ellis 1983: 44, 103–4; Milbank 1998: 104–9 and 124; and Laurence 2011: 282–4.
[23] The Venice 1493 edition (with woodcuts), presented by John Pennant to Lord Morley; see above, pp. 41–2.

and 1757 Venice *Commedia*s that were so much desired by the 'Dilettanti'.[24] Such items—like the illuminated manuscripts of Holkham—were 'trophy' possessions, acquired by the elite, but that status itself could have made them likely to become objects for a certain amount of wider display. Such illustrations would have communicated a powerful visual impression of Dante's otherworlds, as well as, in many cases, embodying the presence of the 'Dante' persona himself.[25] The impact of the earlier images was substantial, and from the late eighteenth century onwards paintings, prints, and programmes of illustration—by Reynolds, Flaxman, the Pre-Raphaelites, Doré, and many modern and contemporary graphic artists—become yet more widely circulated and increasingly influential in shaping British perceptions of the *Commedia*.[26]

Performance, too, becomes a highly significant medium for presenting Dante in the early twentieth century and onwards, but there is some earlier evidence of such a presence. Dante's appearance as a 'hard' author in Act 3 of *Volpone* is his first outing on the British stage, and Lady Pol's reference to him here can be seen as parodying a learned opinion that would continue to be current through the seventeenth century.[27] The 1607 quarto edition of *Volpone* was dedicated to 'The Two Famous Universities', and the play's early performances were probably at Oxford and Cambridge—where allusions to the difficulty of an Italian author, along with other 'erudite comic elements', would have been appreciated.[28] Yet it was also one of Jonson's most successful comedies and had a London public too, who might have shown a broader, more Rabelaisian appreciation of Lady Pol's learned and Italianate folly.

Already in Jonson's time there were early hints of the *Commedia*'s theatrical potential in Italy. Early seventeenth-century examples of Dantean language and allusion in drama include a comedy (*La Tartarea, Commedia Infernale*, 1614), the libretto of Monteverdi's *Orfeo* (premiered in 1607), and the first of many Ugolino tragedies (though this was not published until 1724).[29] Such potential would be realized more fully in the eighteenth and nineteenth centuries, when Dante would make an increasingly strong impression on British theatregoing audiences. One of the more adventurous eighteenth-century travellers in Italy encountered a famous episode from the *Inferno* in this form: the Irish antiquary and academician Joseph Cooper Walker recorded a disastrous production of Andrea Rubbi's *Ugolino Conte de' Gherardeschi* at Bassano in 1779.[30] Ugolino's voice (and those of other characters

---

[24] See above, pp. 41 (with n. 55), 79, 89–90, 101 (with n. 192), 105 (with n. 221), 111, 117, 129 (with n. 4), and 141–2.

[25] On the 'image of Dante' in the early illustrations, see Owen 2007.

[26] See Braida and Calè 2007: chs. 7–9.

[27] It would gain reinforcement from translations of critics such as Emanuele Tesauro and Madeleine de Scudéry; see above, p. 73 (with nn. 36–7).

[28] Bednarz 2010: esp. 186 and 190–4.

[29] On Dante in early seventeenth-century Italian comedy and tragedy, see *DE* 319.

[30] An account of how the spectacle 'of a man dying of hunger through five long acts' became too much for both performers and audience is, along with a number of other references to Dante, recorded in Walker's *Historical memoir of Italian Tragedy* (1799), 275, cited in *DEL* 1. 545. He was a friend of Henry Boyd, translator of the *Commedia* (above, pp. 121–2 and 124), and encouraged his work

in the poem) was projected from the London stage in 1839 through an evening of recitations by the great Italian tragedian and Risorgimento exile Gustavo Modena, who had already (according to Mazzini) won applause in France for renditions of Dante's tragic count, and who seems to have repeated the show at least once in Britain.[31] Ugolino, along with a number of figures from the *Commedia*—notably Francesca and La Pia—would tread the boards of theatres in Italy and elsewhere in Europe and the United States throughout the nineteenth century, and would later feature on screen. Dantean characters' presence on the tragic and operatic stage and in the early cinema has been traced in a number of surveys, and the impact of such performances on their public (including their British public) deserves further exploration.[32]

In the later part of this period Dante also gained wider currency through allusion and appropriation in another popular genre: the novel. The 'sombrous grotesque' of the *Inferno* was recognized by a reviewer as an appealing element in the gothic orientalism of William Beckford's *Vathek*, when its English version appeared in 1786, and Beckford's own notes to that edition, and later in 1816, reinforce the association.[33] Dante's more extensive presence in nineteenth-century fiction could well be explored in more detail, as some recent studies have suggested. Mary Shelley's reading of Italian authors and its impact on such works as *Mathilda* and *Valperga* is one example.[34] Another is George Eliot's appropriation of the *Commedia* and the *Vita nuova* in her later novels (*Romola, Felix Holt, Middlemarch, Daniel Deronda*). Other best-selling novelists of the century might be included in that discussion too, as a recent essay on Dantean processes in Dickens has shown.[35]

'BARROWLOADS OF BROOCHES': PROMOTING THE POET, *c.*1900

The forms in which Dante was introduced and marketed to a wider public from the later nineteenth century onwards may also repay further attention, as part of the history of publishing, education, and popular culture. At the Florentine celebrations of the sixth centenary of the poet's birth (May 1865), the official British

---

(*DEL* 1. 544 and 548). He was also, as a member of the Royal Irish Academy, in the circle of Lord Charlemont (above, p. 114); see *ODNB*, s.v. 'Walker, Joseph Cooper (1761–1810), antiquary'.

[31] Caesar and Havely 2012: 115 and 117–27. Other episodes in Modena's London show were those involving Francesca, Farinata, Capaneus, the Malebranche devils (*Inf.* 21–2), and Manfred (*Purgatorio.* 3). A British witness to one of his later Dante performances in Italy was Frances Trollope at Bagni di Lucca in August 1841; ibid. 126–7.

[32] For recent surveys, see Cooper 2007 and Roglieri 2012. Significant directions are pointed to by Caesar in Caesar and Havely 2012: 112–13 and 124–7.

[33] Beckford 1980: xx (referring to the *New Review* (1786), 9: 410–12, and 10: 33–9); see also Beckford's notes on 119 and 160–1. In 1790 Anna Seward, writing to Humphrey Repton, compared *Vathek*'s 'Halls of Eblis' to 'the fiery Deserts of Dante' (*DEL* 1. 398).

[34] On Mary Shelley and Dante, see De Palacio 1969: 46–61, Keach 1998, Havely 1999, and Saglia 2012: 196–200. See also above, p. 151 and nn. 157–9.

[35] Tambling 2010. Among other popular authors of the period, Walter Scott should also be considered: see Jack 1972: 213–24, and esp. 218–19 (for allusions in *Rob Roy*). Scott was also an early reader of Leigh Hunt's *Story of Rimini* (Webb 2011*a*: 32).

representative on that occasion, Henry Clark Barlow, reported on the vast quantity and variety of merchandise on display:

Programmes of the festivities were published at all prices, from five centimes to a hundred. People who had anything to sell were proud to avail themselves of the Poet's patronage; placards bearing his name were stuck up everywhere; his medals and portraits filled the shop windows; and his sacred head was made to recommend barrowloads of brooches, pins, and buttons. Whatever was said, or sold, or done, had a reference to Dante.[36]

The festival had an international as well as popular appeal, and was widely reported in the press abroad, including in Britain.[37] It served a political purpose in the context of the ongoing process of Italian unification, seeking 'to promote a programme of education and legitimation and involve the masses in a communal Festival of national unity'.[38] In addition to the material souvenirs, lectures, readings, exhibitions, and performances were available to the public, and these drew upon the proliferation of Dantean texts and editions that had taken place during the preceding decades, to serve (as Barlow put it) 'the literary tastes of all readers'.[39] The precise degree to which the huge increase in production of texts such as the *Commedia*, the *Vita nuova*, and the lyric poems corresponded with expanding readership and knowledge of Dante in Italy and elsewhere remains uncertain, but the publishers seem to have had 'a new market in view, or two markets: a spreading middle-class and lower middle-class readership, and, especially, the schools'.[40]

Introductions designed for the general reader supplemented the continuing output of texts and translations. Two such guides appeared a few years after the 1865 festival: Maria Francesca Rossetti's *A Shadow of Dante* (1871), and Margaret Oliphant's *Dante* in Blackwood's series of 'Foreign Classics for English Readers' (1877). Both seem to have been highly successful, each going through six editions by the end of the century. Margaret Oliphant—a much more prominent figure in the late nineteenth-century literary world—had in 1870 become 'the sole breadwinner for two families', and, in order to extend her range of remunerative publishing, she had become general editor of the Blackwood's series in which her Dante introduction was published.[41] Oliphant's introduction solemnly invokes the

---

[36] Barlow 1866: 7. He also notes the variety of materials used for souvenir images of Dante: from marble and bronze to ostrich egg (p. 46). On Barlow, Dante, and the Anglo-Florentines, see above, pp. 239–40, and on his role in promoting the 1865 commemoration (through a letter to the *Athenaeum* on 25 Dec. 1858), see Smith 2000: 51.

[37] There were, for example, two articles in the *Illustrated London News* for 27 May and 3 June 1865, cited in Smith 2000: 50.

[38] O'Connor 2008: 171 and 178 (and, on the festival as a whole, 65–81). On the political and regional significances of the 1865 festivals, see Yousefzadeh 2011.

[39] Barlow 1866: 7.

[40] Caesar 1989: 67. Caesar's publishing statistics indicate four new editions of the *Commedia* each year between 1820 and 1870, with 52 new editions of the *Vita nuova*, and 38 of the *Rime* in the course of the century (ibid. 66 and nn. 124–6).

[41] *ODNB*, s.v. 'Oliphant, Margaret Oliphant Wilson (1828–1897), novelist and biographer'. She spent time in Italy in the late 1850s, and one of her later projects was 'a series of books which purveyed cultural history through biographical sketches', the first of which, *The Makers of Florence* (London: Macmillan, 1876), appeared the year before her Blackwood Dante guide and focused on Dante

great European tradition—with the 'twitterings of native song' beginning its dawn chorus against the gloom of 'awful Latin'—and she requires the reader to see Dante heading the succession of writers 'who furnish at once the clearest and surest revelation of the races in whose hands, for the last five hundred years, has lain all the progress of the world'.[42] Rossetti, on the other hand, begins her preface with some more basic questions:

> If in cultivated society we start him [Dante] as a topic of conversation, how far is our interlocutor likely to sympathize with our interest? How many young people could we name as having read Dante as a part of their education?
>
> Yet the Divina Commedia has been translated, especially of late years, again and again: copiously treated of by authors of European reputation. The few pore over such works; but what of the many?[43]

Maria Rossetti dedicated her work to her father, Gabriele, who had marked her out as *ingegnosa* ('clever'). She had a talent for languages, and by the time she published her guide to Dante she was an experienced teacher of Italian.[44] As an educator she keeps the capacities of the learner firmly in view, and the clear structure of her guide—like her earlier approach to teaching the language—reflects awareness of a new readership's needs.

'What of the many?' was a topical question, especially for the decade following Gladstone's Education Act of 1870.[45] It is also highly pertinent to the expansion of what both Lord Grenville and Maria Rossetti called the 'conversation' about Dante in nineteenth-century Britain. To trace the course of that wider conversation around the turn of the century would require yet more work on sources such as journals and correspondence, but several recent studies of texts and institutions aiming to promote it have opened up some significant lines of enquiry. As the activities of Rossetti and Oliphant in the 1870s suggest, the contribution of female writers in providing broader access to Dante's work in the late nineteenth century and beyond was considerable. It has been shown that in this period 'female popularizers' produced 'dozens of translations, versions and retellings of Dante', and that 'their work appeared in prose, verse and drama, from serious studies of aspects of his work and new translations, to a Dante calendar'.[46] Amongst their output were further introductory guides, following those of Rossetti and Oliphant, and translations not only of the *Commedia* and the *Vita nuova* but also the first two English versions of the *Convivio*.[47] As Maria Rossetti had envisaged, the intended audience for the introductions and paraphrases was often 'young people',

---

alongside Giotto and Savonarola. Some of the articles on Dante in *Blackwood's Edinburgh Magazine* in the 1880s may also be by her; see Laurence 2011: 286 and n. 31.

[42] Oliphant 1877: 3 and 5.   [43] Rossetti 1884: 2 (4th edn.).

[44] See *ODNB*, s.v. 'Rossetti, Maria Francesca (1827–1876), author and Anglican nun'. Her manual of *Exercises in Idiomatic Italian through Literal Translation from the English* (London: Williams & Norgate, 1867) was published a few years before her guide to Dante.

[45] For a brief account of the Act and its context, see e.g. Shannon 1974: 86–91.

[46] Laurence 2011: 281.   [47] Laurence 2011: 282–5.

including children, and 'the paramount aim was educational', sometimes with an explicitly religious end in view.[48]

In November 1882 the *Times* leader deploring the loss of the Hamilton collection placed that event firmly within the context of the nation's broader educational and cultural condition.[49] It dramatized the lack of access to such items as the 'MS. copy of "Dante" illustrated by the pencil of SANDRO BOTTICELLI' on the part of 'the millions now supposed to have received an education sufficient to give them the key of all knowledge', and it then asked: 'Are we never to see in our towns libraries, galleries and collections of art that shall carry to future ages the memories of our merchant princes?' The *Times* leader's question was particularly pertinent to the culture of one of the great northern industrial and commercial cities of the time: Manchester. One of the city's 'merchant princes' would within a few years be commemorated by his wife's foundation of the John Rylands Library there. A recent essay explores the cultural context for that foundation and portrays the ambitions of the city (which some early nineteenth-century visitors such as Foscolo, Engels, and Holyoake had seen as an industrial *Inferno*) to emulate 'the glorious example of Florence of old, under her Prince-merchants'.[50] It traces links between such civic aspirations and the acquisitions of early editions and manuscripts around the turn of the century that gave the John Rylands Library one of the major public Dante collections. It relates that development to the foundation in 1906 of the Manchester Dante Society, which brought together members from the arts, industry, and education, promoting activities that (its records show) 'permeated all aspects of social life in Manchester and the North' and would include public lectures and classes for a variety of groups, including the Workers' Educational Association.[51]

Dante had been proposed as material for a wider educational project much earlier, by John Ruskin's lectures on *The Political Economy of Art* which had been delivered at Manchester in 1857. Ruskin, like some of his contemporaries, anticipated Ezra Pound's concern with 'how the whole hell reeks with money' and with the usurers perched on the edge of Dante's Malebolge—and his comments on the latter may not have gone down particularly well with some of the Mancunian civic audience.[52] Ruskin's lectures of 1857 are not far distant in time and argument from his claims about Dante's cultural and historical centrality in *The Stones of Venice*

[48] Laurence 2011: 286–9 and 290–2. On Dante for children, within the context of popular instruction in the USA at around this same time, see also La Piana 1948: 148–9.

[49] See above, pp. 258–9.

[50] The *Art Treasures Examiner* publicizing the Art-Treasures Exhibition of 1857 at Old Trafford, as quoted by Milner 2013: 70. Milner also cites an earlier claim by the Chair of the Manchester Athenaeum in 1847: 'that it was in the manufacturing city of Florence that a rival was found in Dante to the genius of ancient poetry' (pp. 69; see also 63–5). For views of Manchester as Dantean underworld, see Milner 2013: 66–8; for Foscolo's visit to Manchester, see above, p. 143, n. 98; and on the infernality of the nineteenth-century industrial and urban scene, see Milbank 1998: 84–90 and Havely 2007*a*: 246–7.

[51] Milner 2013: 82 The Society's first president, Dr Louis Charles Casartelli, Roman Catholic bishop of Salford, was also a noted orientalist and admirer of the comparative studies on Dante and Persian vision-narratives produced by J. J. Modi; on the latter, see above, pp. 207–8.

[52] Milner 2013: 71; Yates 1951: 100–1; Pound 1954: 211.

(1851), and it has been shown that, in arguing for 'the primacy of cultural worth over exchange value', he significantly 'chooses Dante and Homer as the authors made available to the poor man as a result of the invention of mechanised printing and moveable type'.[53] Whether and to what degree Dante would ever become a 'popular' author remains uncertain, but, as we have seen, there was certainly an intention evident among writers, educators, and philanthropists of the later nineteenth century to extend his currency substantially as—in Maria Rossetti's words— a 'topic of conversation'.

What the 'popularity' of Dante might mean for his public varies immensely over the centuries up to 1900, and has remained so. In Italy, with the poet's developing cult and canonization in the nineteenth century, he is constructed as an icon of Italian nationalism, and as a brand marketed successfully to large numbers of visitors, as at the Florence festival of 1865. In Florence during July 2006—a century-and-a-half after that festival—a crowd of more than 4,000 spectators filled the piazza of Santa Croce where, on a stage beside the statue inscribed 'A Dante Alighieri L'Italia', the actor and comedian Roberto Benigni performed cantos from the *Commedia*—an event described by one newspaper as 'a gigantic celebration' (*tripudio gigantesco*), using a term which Dante himself had used to describe the circling and dancing lights of Paradise.[54]

In Britain celebration of Dante has been somewhat more restrained in scale and volume, but at several cultural levels, and over a variety of genres, the modern British reception of the foreign poet has, over the past century, become increasingly open to a diversity of international influences.[55] Most of the major modern and contemporary voices who have appropriated Dante in one way or another for writing in English have, in doing so, crossed significant borders—from Eliot, Joyce, Yeats, Beckett, and Pound to Walcott and Heaney.

One such porous border in the twentieth century was the north Atlantic. It was while, in Seamus Heaney's words, 'the intellectual mystery man from Missouri was mutating into the English vestryman' that T. S. Eliot wrote his most extensive account of what Dante might mean in Western culture between the wars.[56] In his essay of 1929 (for Faber's 'Poets on the Poets' series), Eliot's definition of Dante's role as 'the most *universal* of poets in the modern languages' is, as Heaney recognized, controversial in some of its implications for language, nationality, and locality, but one of his most significant and intriguing assertions in the course of that argument is the avowedly 'surprising' claim that 'the poetry of Dante is...in one sense, extremely easy to read'.[57] This 'ease' certainly does not, as Eliot explains, confer instant comprehensibility, but is associated with 'lucidity', 'directness of speech', and even—and perhaps more disputably—capacity for translation.[58] That which is accessible, 'clear', and 'simple' in, for example,

---

[53] Milner 2013: 71. [54] *Par.* 12. 22 and 28. 124.
[55] On the readings of Dante as part of 'a global process of extension, elaboration, and randomization', and for the argument that the *Commedia* 'has always been...as global as a fourteenth-century poem can be', see Dimock 2001: 178 and 181.
[56] Eliot 1929: 17; Heaney 1985: 9. [57] Eliot 1929: 16.
[58] Eliot 1929: 18, 19, and 21.

Francesca's lines about love and passion or the description of Brunetto's departure across the burning sand is also, for Eliot, what 'hits' the reader and makes Dante's otherworld characters, whether from history or myth, 'of the same reality and contemporary'.[59] One such 'contemporary' for whom such a claim is clearly designed is Dante's Ulysses, whose narrative Eliot characterizes as 'particularly "readable"' and 'straightforward': 'a well-told seaman's yarn'.[60] It may be significant that Eliot himself had a few years earlier retold this yarn, in a draft of the 'Death by Water' section of *The Waste Land*.[61] On Pound's advice the passage was omitted from the published text, but it is still a highly 'readable' narrative, and one which represents one of Eliot's closest approaches to sustained translation from the *Commedia*.[62]

It is beyond the scope of this chapter to engage with all the complex 'envies' of or 'identifications' with Dante among writers and artists of the past century, or to consider how, for example, the major modernists' appropriation of the versatile medieval poet might relate to their sense of a modern 'public' or 'the audience of the artist'.[63] Yet Eliot's remarks on Dante's 'lucidity', 'readability', and translatability may serve to introduce some final suggestions about how the wider access to and reception of Dante in the twentieth and twenty-first centuries might be further investigated. Here we turn to four areas of cultural production, including three that were identified in the previous section: translation, illustration, fiction, and performance.

BEYOND BORDERS: TRANSLATION AND ILLUSTRATION, *c.*1900–*c.*2000

Ezra Pound's encounter with Dante began with a translation, and he later recorded how he was 'thankful in 1906 to Dent for the Temple bilingual edition, it saved one from consulting Witte, Toynbee, God knows whom'.[64] The Temple Classics parallel-text edition of the *Commedia* with prose translations had appeared around the turn of the century, beginning with Philip Wicksteed's *Paradiso* (1899), continuing with John Carlyle's 1849 version of the *Inferno* (revised by Hermann Oelsner, 1900), and concluding with Thomas Okey's *Purgatorio* (1901).[65] This major popularizing project was undertaken, as Wicksteed explained in its first

---

[59] Eliot 1929: 22–30.　　　[60] Eliot 1929: 30–2.　　　[61] Eliot 1971: 62–9.

[62] Manganiello 1989: 28–31.

[63] Stead 1967: 109 (for remarks by Eliot, Pound, and Yeats). For more provocative statements from a major modernist about the artist and the 'multitude', see the early essay by Joyce on 'The Day of the Rabblement' (published in 1901; repr. in Joyce 2000: 50–2). I owe the Joyce reference to Dr James Robinson of the University of Durham.

[64] Pound 1954: 208 (review of Laurence Binyon's *Inferno*, originally in *The Criterion* (Apr. 1934), and reprinted in his *Polite Essays* of 1937). '1906', when he was in graduate school at the University of Pennsylvania, is when Pound dates the beginning of his 'twenty-eight' years of 'struggle with early Italian verse' (Pound 1954: 202), although he was already reading Dante's prose and poetry even earlier, during his first year at Hamilton College in 1903–4 (Moody 2007: 22).

[65] The project (itself part of a series edited by Sir Israel Gollancz) was completed by translations of *Convivio* (Dante 1903), *Latin Works* (Dante 1904*a*), and *Vita nuova* (along with *Early Italian Poets* in D. G. Rossetti's 1861 version, edited by Edmund Gardner, Dante 1904*b*).

volume, 'for the sole purpose of enabling the publisher to bring out a cheap edition of the text, accompanied with an English version'.[66] Its prime movers, Wicksteed and Okey, were scholars with diverse backgrounds, careers, and talents, and both were strongly committed to extending what Okey called 'the ever-growing interest in Dante studies in England'.[67] Their promotion of the *Commedia* in this form made its Italian accessible to the thankful young Pound. It helped Eliot to 'puzzle out the *Divine Comedy*' at around the same time, as he would acknowledge both early and late in his career; and he would use it, with only a little modernizing, as the framework for the translations throughout his 1929 *Dante* essay.[68] It would be the version that would accompany Dorothy Sayers to an air-raid shelter in 1943 and thus inspire her best-selling post-war version of the poem.[69] Despite the advent of more lucid and scholarly parallel-text editions (from Sinclair onwards), the portable Temple Classics volumes continued to provide an initial point of entry into the *Commedia*'s Italian for many new readers and writers. Over a century after its first publication the Northern Irish poet Ciaran Carson mentions it as his 'primary source' when he 'began reading the *Inferno*', and acknowledges that his translation 'owes much to it'.[70]

For a mainland British public, Carson's own translation of the *Inferno* moves beyond borders in several ways. Its publishers announced it as 'the first ever version of Dante by an Irish poet'. Carson himself, in explaining his use of '*terza rima* crossed with ballad', describes how he came to think that a 'model for the translation' might be provided by 'the measures and assonances of the Hiberno-English ballad'—thus responding to what he hears in the original's 'relentless, peripatetic, ballad-like energy, going to a music which is by turns mellifluous and rough, taking in both formal discourse and the language of the street'.[71] The result is some fiercely articulate rendering of the *Inferno*'s imagined squalor, violence, and partisan hostility—as voiced, for instance, through Ciacco (Carson's 'Jacko'), Brunetto bad-mouthing Florence, or Dante going head to head with Bocca degli Abati (*Inf.* 32. 94–111).[72] At the start of his introduction Carson stresses the

---

[66] Wicksteed in Dante 1899: 416.

[67] Okey in Dante 1901: 440. On Wicksteed, see: Cunningham 1965: 167–9; *ODNB*, s.v. 'Wicksteed, Philip Henry (1844–1927), Unitarian minister and economist'; Armstrong 2011: 211–13; Pearce 2011: 234–5; Laurence 2011: 282 and 284. On Okey, see Cunningham 1966: 29–30; Limentani 2000: 158–62; and *ODNB*, s.v. 'Okey, Thomas (1852–1935), basket-maker and Italian scholar'. In later life, as first Serena Professor of Italian at Cambridge, Okey also gave a public lecture during the exhibition of the Holkham manuscripts at Norwich in October 1921 (see above, p. 107, n. 230, and James 1921: 3).

[68] Eliot refers to 'Messrs. Dent's invaluable *Temple Classics* edition' and its price ('3 volumes at 2s. each') in the original preface to *Dante* (Eliot 1929: 13). His more striking departures from it are in the translations of passages that fed his own poetry: the end of Ulysses's 'yarn' (*Inf.* 26. 133–42); and Arnaut Daniel's speech before re-entering the refining fire (*Purg.* 26. 142–8).

[69] On Sayers's version for Penguin Classics (Dante 1949–62; *Paradiso* completed by Barbara Reynolds), see Cunningham 1966: 211–20, and Bray 2001: 169 and 171.

[70] Carson in Dante 2002: ix. J. D. Sinclair's parallel text *Commedia* (Dante 1939–46) was reissued by Oxford University Press (New York) in 1948 and subsequently much used by students in Britain and the USA; see Cunningham 1966: 162–7.

[71] Dante 2002: xxi. On the *Commedia* and the streets, see above, p. 261 and n. 10.

[72] Dante 2002: 39–40, 102, and 226–7.

connection between engaging with the *Inferno*, walking the streets of Belfast and identifying one of its 'sectarian fault lines'.[73] The translation itself often gives a local accent to a poem whose fear of civic division and *discordia* it conveys forcefully in the question: 'are they all sectarians?'[74] There may be some broad affinity between Carson's ways of localizing the *Inferno* here and Heaney's earlier insistence (against Eliot) on 'the untamed and thoroughly *parochial* elements' of Dante's language.[75] An important precedent for this approach can be found (and compared) in a version that appeared a few years before Carson's *Inferno*: Steve Ellis's *Hell*.[76] The concise, unrhymed verse of this translation and its rendering of the *Inferno*'s voices draw at many points upon a regional or (to use Heaney's term) 'parochial' vernacular—which in Ellis's case is a language deriving from his own 'native Yorkshire background'.[77] Several of the more perceptive reviewers in Britain and Italy saw Ellis's version as a significant innovation, and one which could point the way towards a plurality of locally spoken Dantes.[78]

A further form of translation, illustration, has taken an enormous range of popular—if not particularly regional—forms over the past century. Illustrations, of course, accompanied Dante's text from a very early stage in its circulation, and as previous chapters have shown, they also featured in a number of editions acquired by the *Commedia*'s early British public. In a number of cases, too, they have accompanied widely circulated translations of the poem. The perennially popular Doré engravings—still the default Dante for hard-pressed picture editors—were marketed in Britain at an early stage and converged with one of the most successful verse translations (Cary's) in 1866.[79] Of the more recent illustrated English versions, one that is likely to have reached a sizeable readership is the edition of *The Divine Comedy* published in Britain by Everyman's Library. Together with Allen Mandelbaum's translation (previously published in the United States) and the late Peter Armour's notes, the Everyman volume also reinforced its wider appeal by including a generous selection of the Botticelli drawings.[80]

Some modern illustrated editions and translations have also become collectors' items. An example limited to 180 copies was what one present-day dealer describes (with some appropriateness) as: 'One of the great 20th-century livres d'artiste, and certainly the great 20th-century edition of Dante, far surpassing Dali and Rauschenberg in quality and rarity.'[81] This was the original Talfourd Press edition

---

[73] Dante 2002: xi.   [74] Carson's rendering of *Inf.* 6. 63 (Dante 2002: 40).

[75] Heaney 1985: 12 (my emphasis).   [76] Dante 1993.

[77] Dante 1993: x. On 17 March 1994, a local paper, the *Yorkshire Evening Post*, gleefully greeted Ellis's version with the headline: *WELCOME TO HELL, IT'S YORKSHIRE!*

[78] Especially Mark Balfour in *Medium Aevum*, 65 (1996), 148, Robert Gordon, in *RES* 47 (1996), 230–1, and Eduardo Crisafulli in *Culturiana*, 29 (June 1996), 10–11.

[79] See Milbank 1998: 196–200 and Audeh 2010.   [80] Dante 1995*b*.

[81] AbeBooks online catalogue of 'divine comedy, dante, Signed', which prices this copy at a mere $9,500. On Salvador Dalí's 102 watercolour illustrations (exhibited in Rome, Venice, and Milan in 1954), see Schiaffini 2007. For Robert Rauschenberg's 34 ink, watercolour, and pencil drawings for the *Inferno* (exhibited in New York in 1960 and published in an edition of 300 boxed sets by Abrams in 1964), see Francini 2011. For a brief survey of twentieth-century illustrators, see Nassar 1994: 22–5. A *de luxe* edition of Robert and Jean Hollander's verse translation of the *Commedia* (Verona:

in two volumes of Tom Phillips's *Inferno. A Verse Translation with Images and Commentary*.[82] Its 138 colour etchings and silkscreens have occasionally been exhibited, and they were subsequently republished by Thames & Hudson in a cheaper, 'democratised' edition, still including Phillips's own lucid and straightforward translation.[83] Phillips's sustained dialogue with Dante had begun with his first experience of the 'scary' Doré illustrations as a child during the Second World War; and its earliest product was the painting called *Beginning to think about Dante* (1976–8).[84] It also extended (as we shall see) into yet other genres, such as the novel and video.

As 'intellectual pop-art', Phillips's 1983 illustrations to the *Inferno* also pose questions about how Dante's creatures might appear in visual imaginations over the centuries, through what Phillips calls his 'iconographic Odyssey', and how they might circulate among the few and the many.[85] A striking example is the sole occasion when—amongst a multitude of graphic allusions to Doré *et al.*—Phillips makes use of one of 'Blake's fine and eccentric visions': that of the two devils converging in flight at the end of *Inferno* 22.[86] Here Phillips draws out the 'comic-book aspect' of the Blake watercolour drawing (and of the scene in the text itself) by placing the two figures in a scenario that explicitly recalls mid-air combat as depicted by the comic-books of the 1940s.[87] He elsewhere shows and acknowledges the influence of such commercial graphic work,[88] and in his Blakeian/comic image of Dante's devils Alichino and Calcabrina 'swooping towards a collision', he also drew upon the skills of a 'professional illustrator' to produce the desired effect.[89] What he does not acknowledge—and may not have been aware of—is that well before he published this image such 'commercial' artists were already appropriating Dante and representing monsters and aerial battles in the *Inferno*.

The graphic violence and grotesquerie of the *Commedia*'s underworld does not seem to have featured in the famous 'Classics Illustrated' series from the 1940s onwards;[90] but three years before Phillips's illustrated *Inferno*, an *X-Men Annual* announced a tale of how 'BEYOND DANTE'S DARKSOME DOORWAY LIES . . . NIGHT-CRAWLER'S *INFERNO!*'[91] In this version even the SHOOOOM of Phillips's diabolic collision is anticipated and outdone by the SKRRRRRRRROOM! of the

---

Valdonega, 2007; 500 copies) has 100 illustrations by the German artist Monika Beisner (originally published in 2001–2). On Beisner's work, see Hawkins 2006: 149 and pls. 1–4.

[82] Dante 1983; see also Phillips 1992: 227–32.   [83] Dante 1985; see Phillips 1992: 232.

[84] Phillips 1992: 219–23.

[85] Phillips 1992: 283. For a concise account of the issues, see Calè 2007: 179–85.

[86] Dante 1985: 183; see also Calè 2007: 184–5.

[87] These he had 'devoured eagerly when they arrived in parcels from my American aunts towards the end of the war'; Dante 1985: 299.

[88] Another of the illustrations for *Inferno* 22 reproduces a selection of 'crude commercial drawings' from *Combat* magazine to convey Dante's and Virgil's precarious position 'Behind Enemy Lines'; Dante 1985: 179 and 299 (XXII.2).

[89] Dante 1985: 299 (XXII.4).

[90] Although that of, for example, *Dr Jekyll and Mr Hyde*, *Frankenstein*, and even *Faust* did: *Classics Illustrated*, issues 13, 26, and 167.

[91] *Marvel Comics Group, King-Size Annual 4* (1980) [unpaginated]. I am grateful to Kenneth Kwok for drawing my attention to this version.

X-Men's battle with an army of demons in Dis. The X-Men's rampage through their *Inferno* follows the broad outlines of Dante's underworld, frequently cites his text, and presents episodes of 'cultural translation'. Their Virgil is the lantern-jawed, kiss-curled 'Doctor Strange, Master of the Mystic Arts, Sorcerer Supreme of Earth', who has read his Dante and is even capable of quoting the right lines (in Italian and translation) to Minos, who is here metamorphosed into a *Cabaret*-style nightclub host.[92] As their journey progresses, however, doubts emerge about whether this is 'the *true* hell', and the rescue mission becomes one of recognition and redemption.

Versions of the *Inferno* in this medium vary widely in scope and implied intention. Cultural translation of the text can be taken in a broadly educative direction, as in John Agard's and Satoshi Kitamura's *Young Inferno*, where the hooded child goes 'Off 2 Hell with teacher Aesop'.[93] On the other hand, the *Devil May Cry* manga series—portraying its 'Dante' as 'demon slayer and bounty hunter with a demon heritage of his own that haunts his past'—looks like a more limited exploitation of the name and brand.[94]

'HELL'S CARTOGRAPHER': FICTION *c.*1900–*c.*2000

In a work that claims to deal with the interests of the British reading public, a few more questions may justifiably be raised about a major genre that continues to reach a large proportion of that public. An important—and recently revised—concise introduction to 'Dante in English' makes some pertinent suggestions about the modern novel:

> One temptation for novelists is to let a Dantean work supply their narrative structure; the novelist then concentrates on working out local details. William Golding's *Free Fall* (1959), in which the painter Sammy Mountjoy sights Beatrice in an art class, tries to rework the pattern of the *Vita nuova*; the pulp-novel *Inferno* (1976) by Larry Niven and Jerry Pournelle, which features Benito Mussolini as guide through the underworld, is the worst of many attempts to repeople or relocate the first canticle. The best remains Joseph Conrad's *Heart of Darkness* (1899).[95]

A number of complex issues about novelistic appropriation, adaptation, and popularization are involved here, but a few simpler questions may serve to promote discussion. For example: is there scope for an extended project (or forum) on Dante and the novel, and how has recent fiction represented Dante and his work? The first of these questions suggests another: about the scope and stages of an enquiry about

---

[92] *Marvel Comics Group, King-Size Annual* 4 (1980). As the X-Men's Minos explains: 'Times change, *compadre*. Alighieri saw me in terms of his world. You see me in terms of yours. Considerate, hm?'

[93] Agard and Kitamura 2008: canto 2, line 3. On earlier versions of Dante for children, see Laurence 2011: 290–2.

[94] Suguro Chayamachi, *Devil May Cry*, 3.1 (Los Angeles: Tokyopop, 2005), the back cover. For further discussion of 'graphic' and 'comic' Dantes, see e.g. Hölter and Hölter 2012.

[95] Wallace 2007: 300–1. On *Heart of Darkness* and the *Inferno*, see also Bowers 2004.

novelists' appropriations of Dante over the last century, and the extent to which (in some cases) these have already been addressed.

'Dantellising peaches' in major modernist prose fiction—as in modernist poetry—have been sampled in a fair range of critical writing. The many directions and indirections of James Joyce's recourse to Dante, in texts from *Stephen Hero* to *Finnegans Wake* (where those peaches grow) have been and continue to be traced.[96] So have Samuel Beckett's Dantean characters and scenes, from Belacqua's first appearance in *More Pricks than Kicks* to a number of his subsequent novels and plays, including the late 'dramaticules'.[97] Obviously enough, though, Beckett and Joyce are Irish and European (in Beckett's case also francophone) writers, and they reflect the fact that many of the more adventurous appropriations of Dante in English-language fiction seem to take place in writing which—although it has a British public—originates beyond the borders of Britain.

Even a superficial account of Dante's presence in the English-language novel would have to move well beyond those borders. American fiction of the nineteenth century was already experimenting with the 'sombrous grotesque of Dante'—from Herman Melville and Nathaniel Hawthorne to Rebecca Harding Davis and William Wells Brown.[98] A recent account of the African-American reception of Dante not only considers Brown's novel (*Miralda/Clotelle*) in the context of late nineteenth-century Abolitionist politics, but also goes on to explore the presence of the *Inferno* in some significant twentieth-century 'Negro Dante' and 'Black Dante' narratives, notably Ralph Ellison's *Invisible Man* (1952), Amiri Baraka's *The System of Dante's Hell* (1965), and Gloria Naylor's *Linden Hills* (1985).[99]

Some other, and very different, appropriations of Dante's work in the late twentieth and early twenty-first centuries might be compared across the English-speaking world, among novelists from Australia, Canada, Guyana, Nigeria, and South Africa, as well as the United States. A brief selection of the more interesting examples here would include: David Malouf's reworking of a Dantean 'new life' in his debut novel *Johnno* (1975);[100] J. M. Coetzee's evocations of the 'doorway' into 'Hades' in *Age of Iron* (1990);[101] and reinventions of the *Paradiso* in Wilson

---

[96] In e.g. Reynolds 1981, Wallace 2007: 297–8, Boldrini 2001, Robinson 2011, 2012*a*, and 2012*b*.

[97] See Appendix 1 (Chronology), under 1934 and 1972–83. On Beckett and Dante, see Fowlie 1985, Elam 1994, Haughton 1998, and Caselli 2005.

[98] Major examples are: Hawthorne's 'Young Goodman Brown' (1835) and *The Marble Faun* (1865); Melville's *Moby Dick* (1851), *Pierre* (1852), and 'The Paradise of Bachelors and the Tartarus of Maids' (1855); Harding Davis's 'Life in the Iron Mills' (1861); and Brown's *Miralda* (1861), renamed *Clotelle* (1864, 1867). On Melville and Hawthorne, see Cambon 1969: 120–6; on Harding Davis, see Bigsby 1995: 155; on Brown, see Fabi 2001:21–6, and Looney 2011: 51–4.

[99] Looney 2011: 87–183. See also Wallace 2007: 300 and Havely 1998*b*.

[100] The narrator is given the nickname 'Dante' by Johnno, after he has written a poem 'To Beatrice' for the school magazine (p. 49). Is Malouf's 'big country town' Brisbane of the 1940s and 1950s more like Dante's 'city of pain', his circle of neutral souls, or the 'twilight city' of the *Vita nuova* (or Joyce's 'Araby')? On other allusions, see Malouf 1976: 51–2, Slarke 2005: 94, and Duckworth 2006. On Dante in Australia, see Pesman Cooper 1989; Rando 1990; Baker and Glenn 2000; Slarke 2005; and Duckworth 2009: 80–2, 245–7, 288–92, and 296.

[101] Virgilian and Dantean underworlds perhaps converge at points here (e.g. pp. 69–70). On Dante in South Africa, see also above, p. 213 and n. 97.

Harris's *Carnival* (1985) and Ben Okri's *Astonishing the Gods* (1996);[102] *In the Hand of Dante* (2002), Nick Tosches's ambitious combination of Mafia thriller (discovery and pursuit of a *Commedia* autograph) with quaintly archaic quest (featuring Dante and other medievals);[103] and a ripping gothic yarn, Andrew Davidson's *The Gargoyle* (2008), which begins with a road accident on Good Friday between a 'mountain's slope' and 'a dark wood'.[104]

Elements of crime fiction and mystery are evident in the novels of Tosches and Davidson. The *Inferno* itself contains crime and involves the investigation of crime, so it is not surprising that novelists exploring various patterns of violence, detection, and retribution—from Hawthorne to Naylor—should have been drawn to its imagery, nor that various novels in this sub-genre should have exploited its procedures in portraying those who leave the straight path or seek to uncover an unwelcome truth. On the first page of *The Zebra-Striped Hearse* (1962), Ross Macdonald's Lew Archer, a private investigator of the mean streets and suburbs of California, greets a client 'in an exploratory way' by misquoting the famous inscription over the gate of *Inferno*'s 'city of pain'; and more significant resonances have been detected later in the novel.[105] Reading the *Commedia* itself—checking and interpreting references—has proved a useful procedure in some crime novels and movies—from Jane Langdon's unpretentious whodunit *The Dante Game* (1991) and David Fincher's movie *Se7en* (1995), to Matthew Pearl's *The Dante Club* (2003) and David Hewson's *Dante's Numbers* (2008).[106] In several of these works it might perhaps be asked whether (as one critic said of the *Gargoyle*) the novel may be 'straining to feel like something more substantial', or whether (as suggested in another case) Dante is merely being brought on as 'prestigious prop'.[107] In some cases the appropriation is effective when less explicit, as in David Lynch's darkly brilliant film *Blue Velvet* (1986), which imagines an infernal crime-scene beneath and around the lawns and picket-fences of American suburbia.[108]

Crime fiction has also portrayed Dante himself as detective. Giulio Leoni's atmospheric series of *gialli* (thrillers) is premised on the idea that around the sweltering summer months of Dante's term as one of the Priors in Florence (June–August 1300), the city experienced repeated outbreaks of serial murder. English readers can now encounter Dante (with some of the characters who will 'later' inhabit his *Commedia*) in Leoni's Florentine Priorate procedurals.[109] 'Dante

[102] On Harris, see <http://postcolonialstudies.emory.edu/wilson-harris/>. On Okri's *Astonishing the Gods*, see Havely 2007a: 263.

[103] Described by a British reviewer as 'a high tightrope spin of a novel . . . a threefold meditation on the written "I", the writer's life, and writing's holy lie' (Ian Penman, *Guardian*, 25 Jan. 2003).

[104] 'An entertaining novel straining to feel like something more substantial' (Sophia Gee, *New York Times*, 17 Aug. 2008).

[105] See Ó Cuilleanáin 2003: 115–20 and n. 11.

[106] On the significance of the murders in the nineteenth-century-Boston setting of Pearl's *The Dante Club* being investigated by 'the first colored member of the police', see Looney 2011: 205–6.

[107] Looney 2011: 109, referring to N. J. Crisp's *The Ninth Circle* (1988).

[108] On the movie's subversive features, see esp. Preston 1990; also Iannucci 1998: 27–9.

[109] *The Mosaic Crimes* (also published as *The Third Heaven Conspiracy*, 2007), *The Kingdom of Light* (2010), and (set in Rome) *The Crusade of Darkness* (2011). The first novel in the series, *I delitti della Medusa* (2000) has not yet been translated.

Alighieri indaga' ('Dante Alighieri Investigates') announces the cover of the second in this series—thus offering one way, perhaps, of seeing the procedure of the *Inferno*, in which Dante and his partner Virgil go underground, collaborating to make their suspects talk.[110]

Within the first decade of the present century more ambitious post-modern descents into underworlds have continued to invoke the *Inferno* in various ways. Two novels that have made some impact on the British (and international) reading public might be compared from this point of view. Direct references to Dante (including one character's distinctive 'Dante' typeface) appear in Mark Z. Danielewski's labyrinthine *House of Leaves* (2000). Quotations (in Italian) from 'hell's most famous tourist' occur at the beginning of chapters 1 and 3, and one of the novel's main characters, the photographer Navidson, moves into the house, goes 'deep' into its terrors, and 'br[ings] that vision back'. Reluctance to engage in that journey evokes the pilgrim's fears at the opening of *Inferno* 2:

Why Navidson? Why not someone else?

When the great Florentine howls, 'Ma io perché venirvi? o chi 'l concede?/ Io non Enëa, io non Paulo sono'[111] Homer's rival calls him a coward and orders him to get moving because the powers above have taken a personal interest in his salvation.

For hell's cartographer, the answer is mildly satisfying. For Navidson, however, there is no answer at all. During 'Exploration # 4' he even asks aloud, 'How the fuck did I end up here?' The house responds with resounding silence. No divine attention. Not even an amaurotic guide.[112]

A similarly unpromising structure of infernal journeys develops in Marcel Möring's *In a Dark Wood* (2006, translated 2009), whose English title perhaps draws upon a passage in the middle of the urban 'limbo' of the novel's first part: 'The heart of the heart. The midst of the battle. Midway through our lives, when we find ourselves in a dark wood. In the shit. That's where we are now.'[113] The original Dutch title of Möring's novel (*Dis*) located it deeper in Dante's underworld, and its approach to the *Commedia*'s catabasis gives it some affinities to Danielewski's representation of 'hell's cartographer', both in its profanity and its sense of 'where we are now'.

Dante has also been addressed seriously and subversively in recent British fiction. Tom Phillips—as translator, illustrator, and collaborator on the *TV Dante*—is featured several times in the 'widening circles' of reception that are being traced in this book's last chapter.[114] Before and during the time of those projects, Phillips continued to produce editions (five to date) of a 'work in progress': *A Humument:*

---

[110] An encounter such as that with Guido da Montefeltro, for example (*Inferno* 28), provides an object lesson in interviewing someone with something to hide.

[111] 'But I, why should I venture there, and who permits it? I am not Aeneas, I am not St Paul' (*Inf.* 2. 31–3).

[112] See Danielewski 2000: 4, 19–21 (quoted here) and 23. Comparisons between *House of Leaves*, Borges, and Conrad's *Heart of Darkness* might themselves suggest Dantean resonances; see Dawson 2012.

[113] Möring 2009: 77. On *In a Dark Wood* and its borrowings from 'Homer, Dante, Joyce, Greek myth, Arthurian romance', see the review by Jem Poster (*Guardian* 14 Feb. 2009).

[114] See above, pp. 272–4 and below, pp. 280–1.

A Treated Victorian Novel—a graphic reworking of *A Human Document* (1892) by the conservative social critic W. H. Mallock.[115] *A Humument* reflects some Dantean features—for example, in dwelling visually and verbally on what it is 'to rise on wings—in Paradise. the dawn of love'.[116] The main way in which it can be said to address Dante, however, is through its interaction with another of Phillips's extended projects: the illustrations for the *Inferno*, where Mallock's novel is 'plundered and "treated" anew, mined and undermined for possible insights into Dante's thought'.[117]

A more direct engagement with Dante by another diversely talented writer and performer furnishes some final novelistic notes and queries. Described (on the basis of his career in the 1980s and 1990s) as 'the Godfather of alternative comedy', Alexei Sayle turned to fiction over the subsequent decade, producing two collections of short stories in 2000 and 2001, followed by several novels. The second of the collections, *The Dog Catcher*, concludes with an ambitious novella, 'The Mau Mau Hat'.[118] A quest for the eponymous hat is one of the trials endured by an aging and unproductive poet 'Hilary Wheat', who, in attempting a 'last great original task', finds himself considering various metrical models, yet 'inevitably drawn to the rhymes and rhythms of the "Divine Comedy"'.[119] The hat itself is lost by the self-proclaimed 'Million Pound Poet', Emmanuel Porlock (perhaps not his real name), during his first visit to the older artist. A desperate search for its replacement leads the would-be reinventor of the *Commedia* into a complex relationship with a much younger woman, with the name of 'Mercy Rush'—a name and surname that might perhaps recall the pilgrim's intrepid female rescuers (the *donne benedette*) in *Inferno* 2.[120] Wheat's poem, however—described by a publisher as a potential masterpiece—remains (following his involvement with Mercy) 'inert upon [his] desk', even when, towards the end, the Million Pound Poet calls to reclaim his hat and urge the flagging writer to 'be ruthless, be focused' in pursuit of his poetic goal.[121] Might Sayle's Mercy Rush then be a kind of anti-Muse, a bogus Beatrice? Or could she be the Beatrice of a (non-literary) new life?

'CULTURE AND REFINEMENT': SCREENING HELL

Concern has long been expressed about the wider exploitation of the classics, especially through a perennial source of cultural anxiety: performance. Over the

---

[115] Phillips's 'Notes' to the most recent edition (2012) give the beginning of the work's 'life' as 'around noon on 5th November 1966'.

[116] Phillips 2012: 34. The phrase (omitting 'in Paradise') also forms part of Phillips's third illustration for *Inferno* 5 (the souls of the lustful as birds in flight); Dante 1985: 45.

[117] Dante 1985: 283. See also Phillips's comments in *A Humument* on 'the long suite of illustrations to Dante's *Inferno* in which Mallock provided an excellent foil to the all-knowing Virgil' (Phillips 2012: 'Notes' [unpaginated]).

[118] Sayle 2001: 201–312.   [119] Sayle 2001: 226–7.

[120] *Inf.* 2. 124.   [121] Sayle 2001: 298, 306.

past century such anxiety has often been aroused by adaptations on screen, for example, as advertised thus:

> *Dante's Inferno Part One*
> 'Culture and Refinement'
> (*Kensington cinema billboard*, A.D. 1915).[122]

Ezra Pound's memory of an advertisement in a London street some twenty years earlier thus interrupts his initial broodings upon 'the devil of translating medieval poetry into English', and it is a memory that continues to haunt him as he moves closer to the main subject of the essay in progress:

> *Dante's Inferno Part Two*
> 'Not a Dull Moment'
> (*Kensington billboard*).[123]

These imagistic flashbacks, punctuating Pound's 1935 review of Laurence Binyon's *Inferno*, are probably recollections of the publicity for one of the most successful products of early twentieth-century Italian cinema: the Milano-Films' *Inferno*. This version had been released in Italian cities during March 1911, and was screened in the United States (as Pound may have heard) during the summer; it reached Paris in early March 1912, and was being shown at a number of venues in England by the late autumn of that year.[124] Its production, content, and circulation have been the subject of a number of studies,[125] but it is worth mentioning here, not only because of Pound's concern and his disparaging remark that, 'Heaven knows critical sense has not abounded in Italy', which presumably refers to the event announced by the 'cinema billboard'.[126]

Others with an eye to the market had expressed a much higher opinion of the Milano *Inferno*'s cultural value for a wider public. A full-page review article in *The Bioscope* at the time of the film's British release begins by promoting the 'extraordinary educational influence' of the cinema, and especially that of 'animated masterpieces'. It then takes up a similar argument to that of the *Times* leader discussing the Botticelli Dante back in 1882, but turns it in a rather different direction:

It is a lamentable fact that the average 'man in the street' has no acquaintance at all with the classics of his own or any other land, save for the cursory study of them he was compelled to make at school, when unable to appreciate or understand their greatness. How many people

---

[122] Pound 1954: 203. On Pound's review of Binyon's translation of the *Inferno*, see also Cunningham 1966: 117–18 and Fitzgerald 1985: 156–64.

[123] Pound 1954: 207.

[124] See Havely 2012: 353 n. 1, for the film's circulation in the USA, Paris, and London; also below, n. 130.

[125] See Havely 2012 for references to these.

[126] Pound 1954: 203 (immediately before the first reference to the 'Kensington cinema billboard'). Pound was, however, by no means averse to the medium of film itself, and 'is said to have told a friend in the 1930s that he went to the movies in Rapallo on average twice or more per week, finding that the only way to come to a stop after a hard day's work' (Prof. A. D. Moody, personal communication; forthcoming in *Ezra Pound: Poet*, vol. 2 (Oxford: Oxford University Press, 2014)).

read Homer or Shakespeare or Dante or Cervantes, or any of the ancient, mighty writers, at the present day, except as a purely artificial 'educational' exercise? It is safe to say that only the merest handful of students and artists ever grow to realise the true beauty and joy of the great literary works of the world . . . It is here that the cinematograph steps in.[127]

The same issue also carried a report that, following a decision by Sheffield Education Committee, 'the possibility of utilizing the cinematograph for educational purposes has aroused considerable interest in the North of England'.[128] As the full-page advertisements for the Milano-Films *Inferno* in this and other issues of *The Bioscope* show, it was very much in such journals' interest to promote these 'educational purposes'; indeed, an earlier advertisement had urged potential purchasers to attend the current showing at the Theatre de Luxe in the Strand 'and hear the opinion of the London Public, including many of the Clergy'.[129]

Precise details about the circulation of such early films are hard to obtain, but views about this cinematic best-seller—from Pound to *The Bioscope*'s advertisers—highlight the debate about the adaptation of 'mighty writers' and the 'educational influence' of 'animated masterpieces'.[130] So too does the reception of the various later *Infernos* on the large and small screen: from the reviews of the moralizing Hollywood makeovers in 1924 and 1935,[131] to the responses to the small-screen *A TV Dante* mounted by Tom Phillips and Peter Greenaway in the late 1980s and shown on Channel 4 in 1990.[132]

A TV Dante made an ambitious but incomplete attempt to bring the *Commedia* to a larger audience. It was envisaged by Phillips as a translation into a modern 'vernacular' medium and an attempt 'to match Dante's claim in visual terms, to have the richness of an illuminated manuscript combine with the directness and impact of a newspaper's front page'.[133] Problems, as Greenaway later acknowledged, derived from that very 'richness' of material: 'Sometimes it works, sometimes it doesn't work at all and is appalling . . . Dante's *Inferno* has so many ideas, so many metaphors, so many games to play, so many references to make, you could put anything into it really, which of course we did . . . '[134] The debate about *A TV Dante*—whether seen as 'a thinking person's pop video', 'a genuinely post-modern examination of Dante's *Inferno*',[135] or as 'trite video wallpaper' fronted by 'silly

[127] *The Bioscope*, 7 Nov. 1912, p. 385.

[128] *The Bioscope*, 7 Nov. 1912, p. 391, col. A. The mayor of Blackpool was reported in the same article as saying that, 'although some sensational pictures of the cowboy type might be harmful, he considered that as an educational factor the cinematograph has great possibilities'.

[129] *The Bioscope*, 31 Oct. 1912, p. 320. A brisker 'GO . . . TO . . . HELL' advertisement appeared in the 7 Nov. issue, p. 396.

[130] It was also screened at the Free Trade Hall, Manchester in April 1913; see Milner 2013: 83, fig. 14.

[131] For reviews of the Fox Studios versions of *Dante's Inferno*, see Havely 2011c: 272 and 275–6.

[132] On the Phillips and Greenaway TV Dante, see Phillips 1992: 240–6; Vickers 1995; Taylor 2004; and Calè 2007: 185–92.

[133] Phillips 1992: 246; see also Vickers 1995: 266–7, with pertinent comments on the project as 'translation'.

[134] Interview with Greenaway in *Transcript*, 1.1 (Dec. 1994), 6–7.

[135] Robert Koehler, *Los Angeles Times* (31 Oct. 1990), F12, as quoted in Vickers 1995: 265.

pundits whose explanations were more obscure than the poem'[136]—has been vigorous and wide-ranging, and has raised questions about the intentions and reception of more recent translations and appropriations in popular media.

In the twenty-first century it remains to be seen whether such cultural translations of the text—for example, into 'California-inflected youth-speak' in Sean Meredith's puppet movie *Inferno* (2007), witty as it is—will significantly widen access to and interest in Dante.[137] Such adaptations rarely venture beyond the safe confines of the *Inferno*. The successful Electronic Arts video-game and 'animated epic' of 2010–11 portrayed 'Dante' as a disturbed, demon-bashing crusader with a mission to get Beatrice out of Hell.[138] This project's own mission and vision were aptly summed up when (at the launch in 2008) it was presented as 'the perfect opportunity to fuse great gameplay with great story'.[139]

BEYOND MORE BORDERS: 2009–2013

April 2009 in London was a busy month for performances of Dante on stage and screen. On the 19th the Milano *Inferno*—like other films of the time, never a 'silent' performance—was shown with an introduction and live piano-and-percussion accompaniment to a large audience at the Barbican.[140] At the beginning of the month, and also at the Barbican, the avant-garde Italian theatre-group Societas Raffaello Sanzio (director Romeo Castellucci) staged an often spectacular but progressively more bemusing *Commedia* trilogy. This began with an *Inferno* featuring an initial attack by guard-dogs, a combustible piano, a blood-drenched white horse, and a crashed car. It continued on a smaller scale with a tense, domestic *Purgatorio* in which a child endures and survives abuse from a father whose portrait forms the programme image for the whole trilogy. It concluded in a *Paradiso* described by one reviewer as 'a womb-like walk through an installation where water drips in the darkness and a figure glimpsed above in the dim light seems to be trying to free himself from eternal entrapment'.[141]

---

[136] Jarman 1991: 309 (journal for 1 Aug. 1990). Jarman's hostility can perhaps be seen in the context of the complex engagement with Dante in his own ongoing project, the film of *Edward II* (1991); on this, see Miller 2011.

[137] On Sandow Birk's and Marcus Sanders's three-volume illustrated 'paraphrase' of *The Divine Comedy* (2003–5), see Hawkins 2006: 154–9 and figs 9 and 11; on the Meredith movie, see De Rooy 2011. An unsystematic survey among students of the 'Dante's Inferno' and 'Dante in English' modules (and their housemates) at the University of York in 2009–10 revealed that the movie version may be great fun if you already know some Dante, but rather mystifying if you don't.

[138] *Dante's Inferno: An Animated Epic*, Starz Media and Electronic Arts (2011), based on the Electronic Arts video-game. On this version, see Appendix 1 (Chronology), under 2008, 2010, and 2011).

[139] Electronic Arts executive producer Jonathan Knight, quoted on the *Eurogamer* website, 15 Dec. 2008, at: <http://www.eurogamer.net/articles/ea-confirms-dantes-inferno-game>, accessed 21 January 09.

[140] See above, pp. 279–80.

[141] Lyn Gardner, review of 'Inferno/Paradiso', *Guardian*, 4 Apr. 2009.

The Barbican audience for Castellucci's *Commedia* were (as befitted readers of *Guardian* reviews) serious and subdued, whilst for Roberto Benigni's one-night *TuttoDante* in the same week the crowd at the Theatre Royal Drury Lane seemed touched by the 'football fever' (*tifo di stadio*) that had been reported at his earlier performances in the Florentine piazza. Apart from his restrained and focused rendering of the Francesca canto at the end of the show, Benigni's performance London was avowedly in a carnivalesque mode: 'Dante language is sublime; mine revolting—like Mr Bean in Rome, talking about John Milton in Italian . . .' His sense of the 'preposterous' project of 'talking about Dante in English in London' was matched by an obvious delight in the coincidence of being in the British capital at the same time as Silvio Berlusconi.[142] Scabrous political allusions thus recurred—for example, in the introduction to *Inferno* 5, where the audience were invited to imagine Francesca's disappointment in being married to Gianciotto rather than his handsome brother: 'As if George Clooney gives you marriage contract; you find in your bed—Ignazio La Russa' (the latter being one of the less glamorous members of the Berlusconi administration).[143]

Fig. 25. Steve Bell, cartoon, *Guardian*, 9 April 2013, courtesy of Belltoons

[142] Berlusconi was attending the G20 summit in London and a few days earlier (1 April) at a reception in Buckingham Palace had been reprimanded by the Queen for unruly behaviour.
[143] Benigni, London, Theatre Royal, Drury Lane, 5 April 2009. Ignazio La Russa was then Minister of Defence in the Berlusconi government. Contemporary political commentary is intrinsic to Benigni's *TuttoDante* performances, including the recent ones at Florence in 2012 and 2013.

A few years later, in 2013—as this chapter and this book are coming to their conclusion—three other appropriations have appeared, all with significant (if markedly different) implications for the British public's awareness of Dante. One, like Benigni's performance, was political: Steve Bell's *Guardian* cartoon marking the death of Margaret Thatcher in April of this year. This is based on the Gustave Doré illustration of Dante's resolute and divisive 'noble sinner' Farinata 'scorning Hell', and it shows the late Baroness demanding to know 'WHY IS THIS PIT STILL OPEN?' (Fig. 25).[144]

Another is the publication of Dan Brown's *Inferno*, described recently as an 'astonishingly bad novel'—and one that is set to achieve an astonishingly large readership in Britain and elsewhere.[145] Hoping to tap into 'a small proportion of [Brown's] audience' is a new complete translation of the *Commedia* that itself reaches beyond borders: a version in quatrains by an Australian poet and critic who is resident in Britain and published by an American press.[146] The wider impact of Clive James's translation remains to be felt, and initial responses have been mixed.[147] But like Bell's cartoon and Brown's *Inferno*, it argues that Dante's pit—and the rest of his poetry—are still wide open for British and global business. This 'comedy' is thus by no means finished with its wanderings through time, genre, and space.

[144] Steve Bell, *Guardian*, 9 Apr. 2013 (referring to the coalpit closures of the 1980s).

[145] Robert Pogue Harrison, *New York Review of Books*, 24 Oct. 2013, currently online at: <http://www.nybooks.com/articles/archives/2013/oct/24/dante-most-vivid-version/>. I am grateful to Alvin Pang for drawing my attention to this article. For further discussion of how Brown 'repurposes' the *Inferno*, see Parker 2013*a* and *b*.

[146] The translation by Clive James: Dante 2013. See the quotation above, p. 260.

[147] Varying responses can be found in the reviews by Joseph Luzzi in the *New York Times* (19 April 2013, currently online at: <http://www.nytimes.com>); by Sean O'Brien in the *Independent* (13 July 2013, 'Independent Radar/Books', p. 25); and by Ian Thomson in the *Financial Times* (30 Aug. 2013, currently online at: <http://www.ft.com>). James discussed his translation during interviews in the *Guardian* (6 July 2013, 'Review', pp. 12–13) and on BBC Radio 4's 'Front Row' (17 July 2013), quoted at the beginning of this chapter.

APPENDIX 1

Chronology, *c*.1320–2013

The book's account of Dante's British public has been broadly thematic in its treatment of material over six centuries and more. Without implying that the subject should be tied to a narrow timeline, this chronology provides a further context for the main examples and case-studies, for example, by enabling comparisons to be drawn between various contemporaneous responses. It also makes selective references to continental European and global sources for those responses. For more detailed information on those wider contexts, see Friederich 1950, Branca and Caccia 1965, Caesar 1989, and Esposito 1992.

c.1320	A Bologna professor, Giovanni del Virgilio urges Dante to stop writing in the vernacular and avoid having his work 'sounded tritely on the lips of women' or 'croaked forth at street corners by some buffoon'.
c.1322–5	Summaries of the *Commedia* and commentary on *Inferno* by Iacopo di Dante (Dante's third son).
c.1323–33	First complete commentary on the *Commedia*, by Iacopo della Lana in Italian.
1327/34	The *Monarchia* censured by a Dominican friar, Guido Vernani.
1328/9	The pope's legate condemns the *Monarchia* to be burnt, along with Dante's remains; official condemnation of the work was revoked in 1881.
1328–33	Guido da Pisa's commentary on the *Inferno* in Latin.
1335?	Boccaccio's romance, *Il Filostrato*, shows influence of Dante.
c.1340–58	Commentary on the *Commedia* by Pietro di Dante (Dante's second son) in Latin; three recensions.
1351–2	Friar Rogerius de Cicilia—possibly identifiable with a Franciscan scholar who quoted Dante in his sermons—is listed as lecturing at Cambridge.
1351–60	Boccaccio's 'Life of Dante' (*Trattatello in laude di Dante*), first two versions.
1370s	An English Benedictine, Adam Easton, cites and argues with Dante's *Monarchia* in *Defensorium ecclesiastice potestatis*, composed at Avignon and probably presented to Urban VI at Rome *c*.1378–81.
1373–4	Boccaccio's public lectures in Italian on the *Commedia* (*Esposizioni*), at Florence (Oct.–Jan.); text finishes at the start of *Inferno* 17.
1375–80	Benvenuto da Imola's commentary on the *Commedia* in Latin.
c.1380	Chaucer mentions and appropriates Dante in *The House of Fame*.
1385–95	Francesco da Buti's commentary on the *Commedia* in Italian.
c.1392	Matteo Ronto translates the *Commedia* into Latin hexameters.
1416–17	Giovanni da Serravalle produces translation of and commentary on the *Commedia* in Latin at the Council of Constance, partly at the instigation of two English bishops.

1423–4	John Whethamstede, abbot of St Albans (d. 1465), travels to Italy for the Council of Pavia. He later refers to Dante in three works: *Palearium poetarum*, *Manipularium doctorum*, and *Vitarum poetarum compendium*.
1428	Enrique de Villena completes translation of the *Commedia* into Castilian prose.
1429	Andreu Febrer completes translation of the *Commedia* into Catalan verse.
1436	Leonardo Bruni's *Life of Dante*.
1444	Copy of Serravalle's translation of and commentary on the *Commedia* donated to Oxford University by Humfrey, duke of Gloucester.
*c.*1445–50	Giovanni di Paolo illustrates the *Paradiso*.
1451	Copy of the *Commedia* in Italian (Berlin Hamilton MS 207) bought by a Tuscan merchant in London, probably from a Venetian galley captain.
1467–8	Marsilio Ficino translates the *Monarchia* into Italian.
1472	First printed editions of the *Commedia* (Foligno, Mantua, and Venice).
1477	William Caxton prints Chaucer's *Canterbury Tales* (later editions 1483–1526), containing references to Dante and allusions to the *Commedia* (Boswell 1999: 1–2).
*c.*1480–95	Botticelli produces 92 drawings for presentation manuscript of the *Commedia*; now in Berlin (MS Hamilton 201) and the Vatican (MS Reg. lat. 1896). Images in Altcappenberg 2000 and Columbia Digital Dante online.
1481	Edition of *Commedia* (Florence: della Magna), with commentary by Cristoforo Landino, Florentine humanist.
*c.*1483	William Caxton prints *The House of Fame*, containing Chaucer's first reference to Dante and allusions to the *Commedia*.
1490	First printed edition of the *Convivio* (Florence).
1502	Plain text octavo edition of the *Commedia* printed by Aldo Manuzio (Venice).
1515	Giovanni Trissino's tragedy *Sofonisba* alludes to *Purg.* 1.117 in final chorus.
1519	William Horman (Eton schoolmaster) names Dante (along with Petrarch, Boccaccio, Chaucer, Gower, and Lydgate) among 'goodly makers of feyned narrations' in *Vulgaria uiri doctissimi*.
1520	John Pennant (English cleric) presents a copy of the 1493 Venice edition of the *Commedia* (with Landino's commentary) to Henry Parker, tenth Baron Morley.
1528	Possible allusion to *Paradiso* 29 in ll. 1750–61 of William Roy's and Jerome Barlowe's verse satire *Rede Me and Be Not Wrothe* (*DEL* 1. 25–6).
1529	Italian translation of *De vulgari eloquentia* by Giovanni Trissino, published in Vicenza.
1532	William Thynne publishes *The workes of Geffray Chaucer* (later editions 1542–1602), containing references to Dante and allusions to the *Commedia* (Boswell 1999: 11–12).
1533–42	John Leland ('King's antiquary') searches British libraries and notes the presence of Serravalle's Latin translation of the *Commedia* in libraries at Wells and Oxford.
1536	Richard Morison (Henrician propagandist) cites Dante as a 'good Italian poet' in his *Remedy for Sedition*.

1543	Henry Parker, tenth Baron Morley, refers to the 'maternal eloquens' of the 'dyvyne Dante' in the preface to his translation of forty-six lives from Boccaccio's *De mulieribus claris* presented to Henry VIII.
*c.*1545	John Bale in Part 3 of *The Image of Bothe Churches* (publ. London, 1548) names Dante and Petrarch among fifty-one 'notabile doctours' who have 'called upon the churches reformacion'.
1550	Thomas Hoby buys a copy of the 1544 edition of the *Commedia* (now at St John's College, Cambridge) in Venice during his continental travels.
	William Thomas's *Principal Rules of the Italian Grammer, with a Dictionarie for the better understanding of Boccace, Petrarca, and Dante* published in London.
1554	The *Monarchia* placed on Catholic Index of prohibited books.
1556–62	Matthaus Flacius (Vlachich), Protestant historian, mentions and translates from Dante in *Catalogus testium veritatis* (publ. Oporinus, Basel).
1559	Johannes Oporinus (Herbst) publishes first printed edition of the *Monarchia* at Basel; also a translation into German by Johann Herold.
1566–70	Dante cited by Elizabethan Protestant polemicists (Horne, Jewel, Foxe).
1576	First printed edition of *Vita nuova* and fifteen *canzoni*, published at Florence.
1577	First printed edition of *De vulgari eloquentia* in original (Paris: Jacopo Corbinelli).
1587–8	Galileo, in lectures to the Florentine Academy, speculates on the dimensions of Dante's Hell (Caesar 1989: 301–3).
1591	Sir John Harington cites 'that excellent Italian poet *Dant*' in the preface to his translation of *Orlando Furioso in English heroical verse*, and translates *Inferno* 1. 1–3.
1595	Sir Philip Sidney's *An apologie for poetrie* shows knowledge of Landino's 1481 commentary on the *Commedia*.
1596	First published translation of the *Commedia* in French (verse), by Balthasar Grangier.
*c.*1598–1601	Scottish scholar Thomas Seget owns an important manuscript of the *Commedia* (now Milan Ambrosiana MS C 198 inf) during residence in Padua.
1602–3	Two copies of the *Commedia* and one of the *Monarchia* listed in the catalogue of the Bodleian Library at Oxford.
1603	Robert Persons [Parsons] (Jesuit) attacks Protestant conscription of Dante in his *Treatise of Three Conversions of England*.
1605	Thomas James's catalogue of books in the Bodleian Library lists three more copies of the *Commedia* (with commentaries of Landino and Velutello).
1606–7	Composition and early performances of Ben Jonson's *Volpone*, in which a character claims that '*Dante* is hard, and fewe can understand him'.
1610	William Drummond of Hawthornden buys a copy of Lodovico Dolce's edition of the *Commedia* (Venice: Giolito, 1555) in London.
1621–3(?)	The young Kenelm Digby quotes from the *Paradiso* in the first of his orations to the Accademia dei Filomati at Siena.
*c.*1628–30	Sir Henry Wotton's list of Italian authors describes the *Commedia* with Landino's commentary as 'Worthy the studying'.

1633–40	Three of the catalogues published by the London bookseller Robert Martin advertise editions of the *Commedia*.
1637	Sir Henry Wotton's will bequeaths manuscripts to Eton College, probably including copies of the *Commedia* (MS 112) and Lana's commentary on it (MS 115).
*c.*1637	John Milton refers and alludes to Dante in his Commonplace Book and *Lycidas* (publ. 1638).
1641	Milton translates *Inf.* 19. 115–17 into blank verse in *Of Reformation*.
1650	Catalogue of the library at the Presbyterian Sion College in London includes a copy of Dante's *Monarchia*.
1653–9	James Howell (translator and lexicographer) cites Dante as bearer of fame and refiner of the Italian language.
1660	Thomas Salusbury provides verse renderings of three passages from the *Commedia* in his translation of Bartoli's *The Learned Man Defended and Reform'd*.
1669	René Rapin criticises the *Commedia*'s failure to observe proper 'unity of action' in *Observations sur les poèmes d'Homère et de Virgile*, translation by John Davies of Kidwelly, published in 1672.
1674	Rapin's further critique of Dante in *Réflexions sur la poètique d'Aristote*, translated by Thomas Rhymer the same year (*DEL* 1. 161–3).
1680	Catalogue for auction of books owned by Sir Kenelm Digby and his kinsman George Digby includes editions of the *Commedia* and *Convivio*, critical works on Dante, and a manuscript of Ficino's translation of the *Monarchia*.
1684	John Dryden's lines prefaced to the Earl of Roscommon's *Essay on Translated Verse* refer to 'Dante's polished page'.
1692	Bishop Gilbert Burnet's *The Life of William Bedell, D.D.* cites Dante among victims of Catholic censorship.
1695	English translation of the Abbé Claude Fleury's *Traité du choix et de la méthode des études* (1686) lists Dante among '*Florentines* who Studied to Write well in their Vulgar Tongue'.
1700	Dryden's preface to his *Fables* reiterates the view 'that Dante had begun to file [the Italian] language, at least in verse, before the time of Boccace'.
*c.*1714–18	Thomas Coke of Holkham purchases six manuscripts of the *Commedia* in Italy.
1715	1,800 manuscripts formerly owned by John Moore, bishop of Ely (d. 1714), presented to Cambridge University. They include three of the *Commedia* (MSS Gg. 3.6 and Mm. 2.3a–b).
1719	Jonathan Richardson's verse translation of the Ugolino episode (*Inf.* 33. 1–77) in *A Discourse on the Dignity . . . of the Science of a Connoisseur*.
1726–76	Voltaire's various writings and attacks on Dante (*DEL* 1. 204–13).
1731	*An Argument for the Authority of Holy Scripture: from the Latin of Socinus* published in London quotes and paraphrases *Par.* 24. 88–111.

*c.*1737–40	Thomas Gray's verse translation of the Ugolino episode (*Inf.* 33. 1– 77).
1746	Joseph Spence, Professor of Poetry at Oxford (1728–38), publishes verse translation of *Inf.* 24. 1–18 anonymously in *The Museum: Or the Literary and Historical Register* (reprinted under his name in 1782).
1753–77	Giuseppe Baretti (Italian resident in England) publishes critical work on Dante, including responses to Voltaire's criticisms (*DEL* 1. 256–74).
1754	James Caulfeild, first earl of Charlemont, present at a debate about Dante during his travels in northern Italy; he later composes a *History of Italian Poetry from Dante to Metastasio* (ed. Talbot 2000).
*c.*1755–60	William Huggins's complete verse translation of the *Commedia* (lost).
1757–8	Antonio Zatta's collected edition of Dante's works published at Venice in five quarto volumes, accompanied by the commentaries of G. A. Volpi (1726–7) and P. Venturi (1732), and illustrated with 106 engravings.
1766–8	Charles James Fox 'devouring Dante and Ariosto' during his tour of Italian cities.
1767–9	First complete translation of the *Commedia* into German prose, by Leberecht Bachenschwanz, a Dresden lawyer, 'condemned by modern critics in no equivocal terms' (Friederich 1950: 365).
1771	Arthur Masson's *Rudiments of the Italian Language*, published at Edinburgh, cites Dante as author suitable for students of modern Italian.
1773	Joshua Reynolds's painting of *Ugolino and his Sons* exhibited.
1774–81	Detailed references to Dante and his influence in Thomas Warton's *The History of English Poetry* (*DEL* 1. 279–97).
1778	Philip Yorke (subsequently third earl of Hardwicke) reads the *Inferno* with an Italian tutor while on tour in Florence ('rather a bold undertaking').
1780–2	First German verse translation of the *Inferno* by Christian Joseph Jagemann, a former monk; a version described as 'iambic water-gruel' (Friederich 1950: 373).
1782	Charles Rogers (art collector) publishes first complete English translation of the *Inferno* in blank verse (*DEL* 1. 382–6).
1784	Three-volume edition of the *Commedia* by Andrea Rubbi (Venetian Jesuit), in the *Parnaso italiano* series.
1785	William Parsons's version of 'The Story of Francesca' (*Inferno* 5) appears in *The Florence Miscellany*.
1785–1802	Henry Boyd (clergyman) publishes the *Inferno* and then (1802) the first complete English translation of the *Commedia* (in six-line stanzas).
1788	The Revd John Seally describes the *Commedia* as 'an epic poem, replete with every characteristic of genuine poetry' in *The Lady's Encyclopedia*. Antonio Curioni's *Istoria dei Poeti italiani ad uso dei Principanti nella Lingua Italiana* (London, 1788) gives extensive attention to Dante.
1792–3	John Flaxman produces 109 drawings to illustrate the *Commedia* (engraved and printed at Rome in 1793).

1798	*I fiori del Parnasso italiano* (anthology published in London) includes five passages from the *Inferno* among excerpts and lyrics from popular Italian poets in the original with following translations. Vol. 6 of *Saggi di prose e poesie de' più celebri scrittori d'ogni secolo* published in London by the poet, printer, and editor Leonardo Nardini includes substantial excerpts from the *Commedia* and Dante's other poetry.
1800	Lorenzo Da Ponte's London 'Catalogue of Italian Books' for sale lists at least ten editions of the *Commedia*.
1800–5	Pencil and ink designs for the *Inferno* and *Purgatorio* by Josef Anton Koch, Austrian artist resident in Rome; also watercolours of Paolo and Francesca, 1805–10 and 1823.
1802–3	August Wilhelm Schlegel discusses structure and number-symbolism of the *Commedia* in lectures on literature and art at Berlin (excerpt translated in Caesar 1989: 421–6); he also translated episodes from the *Commedia* and several of Dante's lyrics (Friederich 1950: 376–81).
1802–30	Thomas Mathias publishes lyrics by Dante in a number of anthologies of Italian poetry published in London, Florence, and Naples (*DEL* 1. 556–64).
1805–6	Henry F. Cary publishes translation of *The Inferno of Dante Alighieri* (blank verse).
1806	Henry Fuseli's painting of *Ugolino and his Sons* exhibited.
1806–7	Maria Dundas (later Graham and Callcott) studies Dante 'with great care' as part of her reading programme during convalescence.
1807	Flaxman's illustrations for the *Commedia* (produced at Rome in 1792–3) published in London by Longman, as *Compositions . . . from the Divine Poem of Dante Alighieri*.
1808	First Italian editions of the *Commedia* published in England (by G. Boschini and R. Zotti).
1813	Mountstuart Elphinstone, British Resident at Poona, reads the *Inferno* in the original with Lady Hood (Mary Elizabeth Frederica Stuart-Mackenzie).
1814	Henry F. Cary publishes his complete translation of *The Vision; or Hell, Purgatory, and Paradise, of Dante Alighieri* (begun 16 January 1797, completed 8 May 1812) (blank verse). Translation of Ugo Foscolo's *Ultime lettere di Jacopo Ortis* (*The Letters of Ortis to Lorenzo*) published in London; numerous allusions to Dante (*DEL* 2. 160).
1815	William Hazlitt's discussion of Dante and other Italian poets in the *Edinburgh Review*; Silvio Pellico's tragedy *Francesca da Rimini* staged at La Scala, Milan.
1816	Leigh Hunt, *The Story of Rimini* (story of Francesca in four cantos).
1817	The Bodleian Library, Oxford, acquires fifteen manuscripts of the *Commedia* as part of the collection owned by Matteo Luigi Canonici (d. 1805/6) (*DEL* 2. 242).
1818	Coleridge lectures on Dante (27 Feb.); Foscolo's articles on Dante for the *Edinburgh Review*.

1818–19	G. Biagioli's three-volume edition of the *Commedia* published in Paris, with a number of British subscribers listed.
1819	Second, expanded edition of Cary's translation of the *Commedia* published by Taylor & Hessey. J. A. D. Ingres's *Paolo and Francesca* painted at Rome and exhibited at the Paris Salon (one of eighteen paintings and drawings of the subject). Composition of John Keats's sonnet on *Inferno* 5 ('As Hermes once . . .'). William Clarke publishes his *Repertorium Bibliographicum*, listing early editions of Dante in British libraries and the Botticelli illustrations of the *Commedia* in the Hamilton Palace Collection.
1819/20	Byron's translation of *Inf.* 5. 97–142 ('Fanny of Rimini') and *The Prophecy of Dante* (1820, published 1821).
1820	Mountstuart Elphinstone, Governor of the Bombay Presidency, donates a manuscript of the *Commedia* (now Mumbai Town Hall MS 19) to the Literary Society of Bombay, along with other books.
1820–2	Shelley, translation of *Purg.* 28. 1–51 (1820), *Epipsychidion* and *Defence of Poetry* (1821), *The Triumph of Life* (1822).
1821–4	Frances Kemble, future Shakespearean actor, studies Dante in Paris with Biagioli.
1822	John Taaffe, friend of Byron and the Shelleys, publishes *Comment on the Divine Comedy of Dante Alighieri*, the first free-standing English commentary, but covers only the first twelve cantos of the poem.
1823	'A Parallel between Dante and Petrarch' published in English as one of Foscolo's *Essays on Petrarch*. Foscolo also discusses Dante in one of his public 'Lectures on Italian Literature'. Mary Shelley's historical novel *Valperga* presents Dante as poet of 'liberty' and of 'that clash and struggle which awaken the energies of our nature'.
1824	Wiliam Pickering contracts with Foscolo to produce the *Poemi maggiori italiani*, beginning with Dante. Of the Dante edition, only the *Discorso sul testo* (1825) appears in Foscolo's lifetime.
1824–7	William Blake's illustrations for the *Commedia* (102 watercolours, seven engravings) commissioned by John Linnell (Paley 2003: ch. 3).
1826	Antonio Panizzi (Italian exile and future Librarian of the British Museum) provides Foscolo with material about the Oxford *Commedia* manuscripts (in the Canonici collection).
1826–7	Gabriele Rossetti's *Comento analitico* on the *Commedia* published in London.
1832	Gabriele Rossetti's *Spirito antipapale*, on Dante as radical reformer (translated in 1834 as *Disquisitions on the Antipapal Spirit*).
1833–50	Tennyson's *In Memoriam*, 'a sort of *Divine Comedy*', and *Ulysses* (published 1842).
1834–6	W. E. Gladstone's initial readings of Dante's *Commedia* (his diaries record subsequent readings in 1841, 1846, 1866–7, 1879, and 1887–8).
1835	Ary Scheffer exhibits painting of *Paolo and Francesca* (now in the Wallace Collection, London) at the Paris Salon. This is one of a number of versions produced between the 1820s and 1850s.

1835–7	Gladstone translates passages from the *Commedia*, including the Ugolino story (*Inf.* 33. 1– 78), into *terza rima*.
1837	William Dyce's painting of *Francesca da Rimini* exhibited at the Royal Scottish Academy in Edinburgh.
1838–40	Thomas Carlyle's discussions of Dante in *Lectures on the History of Literature* (1838) and *On Heroes, Hero Worship and the Heroic in History* (1840).
1839	A. F. Ozanam, *Dante et la philosophie catholique au treizième siècle*, a scholarly approach to the intellectual context. Gladstone views and comments on Koch's Dantean frescos and drawings during a visit to Rome.
early 1840s (?)	Gladstone's annotations of the *Commedia* in his copy now at Eton College.
1842	Margaret Fuller, translator and friend of R. W. Emerson, undertakes a translation of *Vita nuova* but does not complete it; Emerson publishes his version in 1843.
1842–3	Mazzini completes an edition of the *Commedia di Dante Allighieri illustrata da Ugo Foscolo*, published in London by Pietro Rolandi (4 vols.).
*c.*1842–8	Isabella Macleod in Florence, collecting material for her *Disegni ad Illustrazione della Divina Commedia* (now Edinburgh, NLS MSS 2168–72; see also 1885).
1843	First published American translation of the *Inferno*, cantos 1–10, by Thomas William Parsons (in quatrains; Cunningham 1965: 77–82).
1844	Gladstone reviews Lord John Russell's translation of *Inf.* 5. 73–142 (Francesca) in the *English Review or Quarterly Journal of Ecclesiastical and General Literature* (excerpt in *DEL* 2. 686–9).
1846–62	Earliest translations of the *Vita nuova* into English: J. Garrow (1846), D. G. Rossetti (1861), T. Martin (1862).
1848–52	Dante Gabriel Rossetti's poem 'Dante at Verona'.
1849	J. A. Carlyle's prose translation of the *Inferno*; subsequently revised (by H. Oelsner) for the Temple Classics parallel-text edition (1899–1901).
1851	John Ruskin's discussion of Dante as the 'central man of all the world' in *The Stones of Venice*.
1852	Alexander Munro's sculpture of *Paolo and Francesca*, completed to a commission from Gladstone.
1854	George Eliot views 'that unforgettable Francesca di [*sic*] Rimini of Ary Scheffer's' at the Pall Mall Gallery in London. Gustav Friedrich Waagen, director of the Royal Paintings Gallery in Berlin, publishes *Treasures of Art of Great Britain*, which includes a description of the Botticelli drawings at Hamilton Palace ('indubitably the richest illustrations of this great poem').
1855	Dante Gabriel Rossetti's watercolour triptych of Paolo and Francesca (one of a number of versions produced *c.*1846–*c.*1867), commissioned and much admired by Ruskin. G. H. Boker's play *Francesca da Rimini* premiered in New York (revived in 1882 and 1901); see Iannucci 2002.
1857	Sir George Grey, Governor of Cape Colony, South Africa, purchases a manuscript of Dante's *Commedia* (now MS Grey 4 b 11), donated to the

	Cape Town Library in 1861 along with many other manuscripts, including a late fifteenth-century *Commedia* (now MS Grey 3 c 25).
1858–65	Lord Vernon's edition of the *Inferno* with a volume of illustrations published as *L'Inferno di Dante Alighieri disposto in ordine grammaticale e corredato di brevi dichiarazioni* (3 vols., London: Boone).
1859	Frances Kemble's poem 'On a Picture of Paolo and Francesca by Ary Scheffer' published in Boston; reprinted in *Poems by Frances Anne Kemble* (London, 1866). William Dyce's *Beatrice*, subtitled 'Lady with the Coronet of Jasmine', painted for Gladstone, with the former prostitute Marian Summerhayes as model.
1861–6	Gustave Doré's wood-block engravings for the *Commedia*. Matthew Arnold's essay on 'Dante and Beatrice' (1863); see Caesar 1989: 606–14.
1863–76	George Eliot's novels allude to and quote from Dante: *Romola* (1863); *Felix Holt* (1866; prologue); *Middlemarch* (1871–2; epigraphs to chs. 19 and 54); *Daniel Deronda* (1876; epigraphs to chs. 55 and 64).
1864	Frederic Leighton's *Dante in Exile* exhibited (Ellis 1983: 55–6 and pl. 4).
1865	(May) Celebrations in Florence of the sixth centenary of Dante's birth; reported for English readers by H. C. Barlow (Caesar 1989: 620–4); also in two Italian journals of 1864–5, *Giornale del Centenario* and *Festa di Dante*; foundation of the Deutsche Dante-Gesellschaft, first of the Dante Societies. William Rossetti's blank-verse translation of the *Inferno* as *The Comedy of Dante Allighieri. Part I—The Hell*; completed seven or eight years earlier.
1867	H. W. Longfellow's translation of the *Commedia* published in Boston and London; begun in 1845, with first draft completed in 1863.
1870–1	Francesco de Sanctis's discussion of Dante in *Storia della letteratura italiana*.
1871	Maria Francesca Rossetti, *A Shadow of Dante: being an essay towards studying himself, his world and his pilgrimage*, six editions up to 1894. Seymour Kirkup's books, including manuscripts of the *Commedia*, fetch £2,555 at a Sotheby sale (December).
1874	James Thomson, *The City of Dreadful Night*, poetic version of *Inferno* and 'a reverse image of Ruskin's utopian stones of Venice' (Milbank 1998: 112).
1876	Tchaikovsky, *Francesca da Rimini*, op. 32, symphonic poem; foundation of the Oxford Dante Society.
1877	Margaret Oliphant, *Dante* (introduction with passages of translation from *Inferno*, *Purgatorio*, and *Paradiso*), six editions up to 1898.
1880	Auguste Rodin's sculpture *The Gates of Hell* commissioned.
1881	Foundation of the Dante Society of America (Longfellow as president).
1882	Sale of the Hamilton collection of *c.*700 manuscripts, including the Botticelli illustrations of the *Commedia* and six other *Commedia* manuscripts (now Berlin MSS Ham. 201–7), to the German Government.
1884	Christina Rossetti, 'Dante: the poet illustrated out of the poem', in the *Century* (Feb.), 566–73.
1885	Five volumes of 'drawings, engravings &c. Archaeological, Topographical and Heraldic' illustrating the *Commedia* presented to the National Library Edinburgh by R. B. A. Macleod of Cadboll (now NLS MSS 2168–72).

1887	First English translation of the *Convivio* by Elizabeth Price Sayer published in Morley's Universal Library as *The Banquet of Dante Englished*; see Laurence 2011: 282–3.
1888	Società dantesca italiana (Italian Dante Society) founded in Florence.
1889	Stephen Phillips's verse drama *Paolo and Francesca: A Tragedy in Four Acts*, published; it subsequently receives a much-delayed but highly successful production at the St James's Theatre (1902). Katharine Hillard's translation of the *Convivio* published as *The Banquet (Il Convito) of Dante Alighieri*.
1891	William Robert Macdonell delivers a paper to the Bombay Branch of the Royal Asiatic Society about the text of the manuscript of the *Commedia* donated by Elphinstone in 1820.
1893	Selection of Blake's illustrations of the *Commedia* exhibited at the Royal Academy (further exhibition in 1913).
1896	W. B. Yeats's three-part essay on 'William Blake and his Illustrations' in the *Savoy*: part 2 on Blake's 'Opinions on Dante' (Aug.) and part 3 on 'The Illustrators of Dante' (Sept.).
1899–1901	Temple Classics (parallel-text) edition of the *Commedia*, ed. P. Wicksteed and H. Oelsner; widely circulated and later used by, among others, Pound, Eliot, Auden, MacNeice, Sayers, and Carson.
1901	Gabriele D'Annunzio's play *Francesca da Rimini* staged at Rome, subsequently in New York (1902) and Milan (1927).
1903	Daniel Rees of Carnarvon (journalist, linguist, and statistician) publishes translation of the *Divina Commedia* into Welsh: *Dwyfol Gân Dante*, with an introduction by T. Gwynn Jones, 'the first Welsh poet in whose verse the influence of Dante is discernible' (Griffith 1966: 297). In the same year Rees and Jones collaborate on a drama, *Dante and Beatrice*.
1906	Foundation of the Manchester Dante Society; first president Dr Louis Charles Casartelli, Roman Catholic bishop of Salford (Milner 2013: 76–8). Publication of *The Dante calendar, representing incidents in the life of Dante Alighieri*, with quotations from Dante in English for each month.
1907–8	Dante on film: *Francesca da Rimini*, dir. William V. Ranous (Vitagraph Company of America); see Uricchio and Pearson 1993: 99–103.
1908–9	Early short films on Francesca, Ugolino, and La Pia (*Purg.* 5. 130–6); see Casadio 1996: 123.
1910	Ezra Pound's *The Spirit of Romance*, with chapter on Dante stressing the importance of *De vulgari eloquentia*. William Rossetti publishes his translation of the *Convivio*: *Dante and his 'Convito': A Study with Translations*.
1911	Milano Films fifty-four-scene *Inferno* (Padovan/Bertolini), internationally successful, including in London, Los Angeles, and New York.
1914	R. Zandonai's opera *Francesca da Rimini*, with libretto by T. Ricordi, based on D'Annunzio's play (1901). James Joyce's *Dubliners*, with a number of allusions to Dante (e.g. in 'Araby' and 'Grace') published in London, whilst in Trieste Joyce is writing *A Portrait of the Artist*, which appropriates the *Vita nuova* and the *Purgatorio*, and beginning *Ulysses*, which extends his dialogue with Dante.

1917–60	Ezra Pound's 116 *Cantos*, taking Dante's journey as model (but see also Ellis 1983: 203–5 and Milbank 1998: 233–8, for influence of the *Convivio*).
1917–22	T. S. Eliot's collections of poems, *Prufrock and other Observations* (1917), *Ara vus prec* (1920), *The Waste Land* (1922), with epigraphs, quotations, and allusions from Dante, and the essay on 'Dante' in *The Sacred Wood* (1920). Publication of Joyce's *Ulysses* (1922).
1918	Blake's 102 illustrations of the *Commedia* auctioned at Christie's (15 March) and distributed initially between the National Gallery of Victoria, Melbourne; the Tate Gallery; the British Museum; the City Museum, Birmingham; the Ashmolean, Oxford; and two private collectors.
1923–39	Joyce's *Finnegans Wake* ranges through the poem of 'the divine comic Denti Alligator'.
1924	Henry Otto's silent movie *Dante's Inferno* (Fox studios): ruthless capitalist converted by reading Dante.
1925	Yeats's *A Vision*, setting out 'phases' of history, presenting Dante as 'poet [who] saw all things set in order' and opposing him to Pound.
1927	Samuel Beckett takes his student edition of the *Commedia* on holiday to Italy (it will also be his holiday reading in 1971 and 1975).
1929–30	Eliot's *Dante* (1929), his most extended critical essay on the subject, and *Ash Wednesday* (1930), appropriating *Purgatorio* and the *Vita nuova* and quoting *Purg.* 26. 147; Beckett's essay 'Dante . . . Bruno . . . Vico . . . Joyce' (1929), on parallels between Dante and Joyce.
1932	W. H. Auden begins epic modelled on the *Commedia* (abandoned in 1933; see Spears 1985: 84).
1933	Laurence Binyon, *Dante's Inferno translated into English Triple Rhyme* (versions of *Purgatorio* and *Paradiso* followed in 1938 and 1943). Osip Mandelstam's 'Conversation about Dante' (published in 1960s).
1934	Beckett's story collection *More Pricks than Kicks* introduces the character of Belacqua (cf. *Purg.* 4. 103–35), who is to reappear in his later novels *Murphy* (1938), *Watt* (1945), and *Molloy* (1951), and at the end of *Company* (1980). Pound reviews Binyon's translation of *Inferno* (*Criterion*, Apr.).
1935	Harry Lachman's *Dante's Inferno* (Fox studios), with spectacular ten-minute Hell sequence (see also 1924); see Havely 2011c.
1938	Giuseppe Ungaretti's essay *Dante e Virgilio* on *Inf.* 3 and *Aen,* 6, publ. as 'Dante et Virgile' in *Innocence et mémoire* (Paris, 1969); Pound corresponds with Laurence Binyon about the latter's *terza rima* translation of the *Commedia* (published 1933–43; see Fitzgerald 1985).
1942	Eliot composes 'Little Gidding', the last of *Four Quartets* (published 1943–4).
1943–5	Vittorio Sereni's poems about his POW experiences in *Diario d'Algeria* (published 1947) evoke the *Purgatorio* (Robinson 1998).
1944	Spencer Williams, African-American filmmaker, uses material from the Milano Films *Inferno* in his fable of 'the Battle of GOOD AGAINST EVIL', *Go Down Death* (Looney 2011: 72–86).

*c.*1948	Jorge Luis Borges completes *Nueve ensayos dantescas*, essays on Dante (published in 1982).
1949	Derek Walcott's early poem, *Epitaph for the Young*, published in Barbados. In 1977 Walcott acknowledges Dante among the 'visible, deliberately quoted influences here' (Balfour 1998: 224).
1949–62	Dorothy L. Sayers's *terza rima* version of the *Commedia* for Penguin Classics (3 vols., Harmondsworth); *Paradiso* completed by Barbara Reynolds.
1950	Eliot gives a talk called 'What Dante Means to Me' to the Italian Institute (later published in *To Criticize the Critic* (1965)); Walcott's radio play, *Senza Alcun Sospetto*, based on latter half of *Inf.* 5 (Balfour 1998: 227).
1951–2	Salvador Dalí issues 100 lithograph illustrations, one for each canto of the *Commedia* (*DE* 244A–245A; and Columbia Digital Dante online).
1954	Louis MacNeice publishes *Autumn Sequel*, twenty-six cantos appropriating form and structure of the *Commedia* (Ellis in Havely 1998*a*). John Ciardi publishes *The Inferno: A New Translation* (New York), a best-selling version in partial *terza rima*, followed by his *Purgatorio* (1961) and *Paradiso* (1970).
1956	Andrzej Wajda's film *Kanal* traces an infernal journey by resistance fighters through the Warsaw sewers at the end of the 1944 rising; part of the director's *Ashes and Diamonds* trilogy.
1959–75	The *Commedia* provides 'a structuring informing model' for much of Pier Paolo Pasolini's work in film, fiction, and poetry, from 'La mortaccia' (story, 1959) and *La divina mimesis* (novel, 1961) to *Salò* (film, 1975) (Rumble 2004: 153).
1960	Pound concludes the *Cantos* with quotation from Dante's *sestina*, 'Al poco giorno ed al gran cerchio d'ombra' (Canto 116).
1962	Giorgio Bassani's novel *Il giardino dei Finzi Contini* quotes the *Commedia*, but uses *Vita nuova* as its 'key text' (Woolf 1998).
1964	Antonioni's *Deserto Rosso* ('Red Desert') alludes to Dante's Ravenna (Kirkham 2004).
1965	LeRoi Jones (Amiri Baraka), prose fiction, *The System of Dante's Hell* (Looney 2011: 106–36).
1972	Wole Soyinka's collection of poems *A Shuttle in the Crypt* includes prison-poem, 'Purgatory'.
1972–83	Beckett's late 'dramaticules' (especially *Not I* (1972)), where the *Inferno* 'comes to dominate [his] later theatrical imagination' (Elam 1994: 145).
1976–83	Tom Phillips translates, designs, and illustrates the *Inferno* (four prints per canto), published by Talfourd Press in 1983.
1979–2010	Seamus Heaney's collection *Fieldwork* (1979) begins a dialogue with Dante that continues through translation of the first three cantos of the *Inferno* (early 1980s), to *Station Island* (1984), 'Envies and Identifications' (1985), *Seeing Things* (1991), *The Spirit Level* (1996), *Electric Light* (2001), *District and Circle* (2006), and *Human Chain* (2010).
1982	Sidney Nolan produces two sets of thirty illustrations for Dante's *Inferno* (Duckworth 2006).
1982–93	Canadian filmmaker Bruce Elder directs two versions of the *Inferno*: *Illuminated Texts* (1982) and *Lamentations: Monument to a Dead World*

(1985); with *Consolations* (1988) and *Exultations* (1993), these form a screen version of the *Commedia* running to over forty hours.

1985   Gloria Naylor's novel *Linden Hills* reconstructs the *Inferno* in a prosperous African-American suburb; see Havely 1998*b* and Looney 2011: 156–83.

1986   David Lynch's film *Blue Velvet*: the *Inferno* in American suburbia (see Preston 1990).

1988   Hundred-part *lectura Dantis* on the *Commedia* produced by the Dipartimento Scuola Educazione of RAI, Italian TV ('bookish television', Iannucci 1989: 9).

1989–91   Federico Tiezzi directs theatrical versions of the *Commedia* by three Italian poets at Prato and Bari. These are: *Commedia dell'Inferno: un Travestimento dantesco* (Edoardo Sanguineti); *Il Purgatorio: La notte lava la mente* (Mario Luzi); and *Il Paradiso: Perché mi vinse il lume d'esta stella* (Giovanni Giudici).

1990   Walcott's *Omeros*, 'a poem full of ghostly encounters', includes a *Malebolge*-like sequence in Book 7 (Balfour 1998: 234–6); (July) *A TV Dante* (Peter Greenaway and Tom Phillips) broadcast on Channel 4: video version of the first eight cantos of the *Inferno*. 'A good old text is always a blank for new things' (Phillips's opening comment).

1993   Douglas Dunn uses *terza rima* ('Dante's drum-kit') for an extended poem about forms of afterlife: 'Disenchantments' in *Dante's Drum-kit* (pp. 31–46); Ecco Press in the United States publishes a translation of the *Inferno* by twenty poets (cantos 1–3 by Heaney), ed. Daniel Halpern.

1994   Translations of the *Inferno* by Steve Ellis (blank verse) and Robert Pinsky (partial *terza rima*).

1995   David Fincher's film *Se7en* cites and alludes to Dante (Iannucci 2004: 15–16).

1997   Issue on *Dante, Ezra Pound and the Contemporary Poet*, published by the poetry magazine *Agenda*, ed. W. Cookson (vol. 34, nos. 3–4).

2000   Heaney's poem 'A Dream of Solstice' published on the front page of the *Irish Times* (18 Jan.) begins with a translation of *Par.* 33. 58–61. Philippe Sollers publishes *La Divine Comédie: Entretiens avec Benoit Chantre* (Paris: Gallimard), a 700-page conversation about the *Commedia*, raising such questions as 'Why does no-one read the *Paradiso*?' (answer on p. 548). Programme of contemporary poets' renderings of cantos from the *Inferno* at the South Bank Centre, London (Oct.).

2000–7   Giulio Leoni's four crime novels in which 'Dante Alighieri investigates': *I delitti della Medusa* (2000) *I delitti del mosaico* (2004), *I delitti della luce* (2005), and *La crociata delle tenebre* (2007) (English translations 2007, 2010, 2011).

2001   Conference and film festival, *Dante and Cinema*, organized by the University of Toronto Humanities Centre (30 Mar.–7 Apr.) (Iannucci 2004: vii); publication of *The Poets' Dante*, including essays and excerpts from Pound, Yeats, Eliot, Mandelstam, Borges, Auden, Robert Duncan, James Merrill, Seamus Heaney, W. S. Merwin, and Robert Pinsky (Hawkins and Jacoff 2001).

2002	Translations of the *Inferno* by Ciaran Carson and Michael Palma (both in forms of *terza rima*). *Divina Commedia* dance-mime show by Russian Derevo company (at Edinburgh and London, Aug.–Sept.). *In the Hand of Dante* by Nick Tosches involves the New York mob, Dante, Nick Tosches, and an autograph manuscript of the *Commedia*.
2003	*The Dante Club* by Matthew Pearl, a nineteenth-century murder mystery set in Boston, featuring H. W. Longfellow and a cast of Boston brahmins.
2003–5	Sandow Birk and Marcus Sanders, *The Divine Comedy* (San Francisco), a three-volume 'paraphrase' using 'California-inflected youth-speak' (Hawkins 2006: 154–9 and figs. 9 and 11).
2004–5	20 December–2 January: *Dante's Inferno by Arthur Smith* at the Comedy Theatre London; 'inspired by his worrying passion for medieval Italians and his own battle with the demon drink'.
2005	Jean-Luc Godard's *Notre Musique*, version of Hell, Purgatory, and Paradise, using newsreel footage and clips from westerns; Cristi Puiu's *The Death of Mr Lazarescu*, the infernal journey through the Bucharest health-system by the dying Dante Lazarescu (released in UK in 2006; 'one of the best films of the year': *Independent, Information* 19 Aug. 06).
2006	Promenade production of *Inferno* at the Arches, Glasgow (Mar.). July: a crowd of more than 4,000 people fills the Piazza Santa Croce in Florence to hear Roberto Benigni perform cantos from the *Commedia*.
2006–7	Translation of the *Commedia* in blank verse by Robin Kirkpatrick (3 vols., London: Penguin Classics).
2007	Californian puppet-movie, *Dante's Inferno*, directed by Sean Meredith, produced by Paul Zaloom and Sandow Birk (see 2003–5); Dante voiced by Dermot Mulroney, Virgil by James Cromwell.
2008	John Kinsella's *Divine Comedy: Journeys through a Regional Geography* (New York: Norton and St Lucia: University of Queensland Press); sequence of poetic 'distractions' set in the wheatbelt of Western Australia. Andrew Davidson's *The Gargoyle* (New York: Doubleday and Edinburgh: Canongate), a novel in which a modern burns victim meets a sculptor/nurse who claims to have been born in 1300 and to have translated the *Inferno* into German. Electronic Arts (California) announces project on *Inferno* video-game.
2009	2–9 April: staging of *Inferno, Purgatorio, Paradiso* by the Societas Rafaello Sanzio, directed by Romeo Castellucci at the Barbican Theatre, London; 5 April: Roberto Benigni, *TuttoDante* at the Theatre Royal, Drury Lane (with reading of *Inferno* 5); 19 April: showing of the 1911 Milano Films and Helios Studio versions of the *Inferno* at the Barbican Cinema, London.
2010	*Inferno* video-game released by Electronic Arts, Redwood Shores, California, following an extended publicity campaign including faked 'Christian' protests and slogans ('Just say inferNO'; 'Hell is not a Game').
2011	DVD spin-off from the *Inferno* video-game: *Dante's Inferno: An Animated Epic* (Starz Media and Electronic Arts); animation by studios in Japan, South Korea, and the United States.

2012   Roberto Benigni returns to the Piazza Santa Croce, Florence, with
                            TuttoDante performances of *Inf.* 11–22 (20 July–6 Aug.); total audience
                            estimated at 70,000. Fifth edition of Tom Phillips's *A Humument:*
                            A Treated Victorian Novel, whose text also appears in his *Inferno*
                            illustrations. US poet Mary Jo Bang publishes a new translation of the
                            Inferno: 'Bang mines American pop and high culture. Yes, traditionalists
                            and scholars may shriek upon seeing Eric Cartman (of *South Park* fame),
                            sculptures by Rodin, John Wayne Gacy, and many others make
                            anachronistic cameos in Bang's version of Hell, but this is still very much
                            Dante's underworld, updated' (*Publishers Weekly*).

2013   January: Dan Brown's *Inferno* novel announced (published in May). Steve
                            Bell's cartoon of Baroness Thatcher based on Gustave Doré's illustration
                            for *Inf.* 10 (*Guardian*, 9 Apr.). May: Clive James's verse translation of the
                            Commedia published (New York: Norton/Liveright).

                            Benigni returns to the Piazza Santa Croce, Florence, with *TuttoDante*
                            performances of *Inf.* 23–34 (20 July–6 Aug.), linked, as before, to 'an
                            analysis in satirical terms of recent Italian history'.

Finally, for the moment, the whirligig of reception turns full circle in 2013, and a Bologna
academic (perhaps following in the footsteps of Giovanni del Virgilio, *c.*1320) seeks to cut
the poet down to size. On 29 August an article by Giuseppe Plazzi, of the Dipartimento di
Scienze biomediche e neuromotorie at the University of Bologna, appeared in *La Repubblica*
under the title of *Il sonno di Dante: Perché La Divina Commedia è scritto da un Narcolettico*
('Dante's Sleep: Why the *Divine Comedy* was Written by a Narcoleptic'), arguing that 'the
symptoms of illness [are] concealed in the poetry'.

    As a recent example of an Anglo-Italian conversation about Dante, see the measured
response by Sarah Bakewell (biographer of Montaigne) to such '*retrospective* diagnos[e]s of
pathological conditions in famous people' and their basis in 'historical triumphalism'
(*Guardian*, 28 Sept. 2013). 'To speak to the past in this way', Bakewell argues, 'is to take
a liberty with it', although, as she acknowledges—and as many of the readings by Dante's
British public show—that is what continues to happen.

    And later still—in the spring of 2014—BBC Radio 4's Sunday afternoon 'Classic Serial'
presents a 'dramatisation of Dante's epic poem—the story of one man's incredible journey
through Hell, Purgatory and Paradise' (30 March, 6 April, 13 April).

New/Old Dantes, *c*.1600–*c*.1700

Drawing upon resources in the 'Early English Books Online' database, this appendix includes some thirty-three printed books making references to Dante (occasionally multiple ones) which do not appear in previous accounts of reception in the period (*DEL*; Wilson 1946; Boswell 1999). Of these the largest proportion are from English translations of foreign (mostly French and Italian) works, and the vast majority (twenty-nine out of thirty-three) date from 1650 onwards. However, there is substantial evidence of Dantean texts in British private and public collections and catalogues well before this (see above, pp. 79–99); and—as with the other material covered by this volume—it is likely that further references to Dante in seventeenth-century manuscript sources remain to be found.

1580 Humfrey Gifford, *A Posie of Gilloflowers, eche differing from the other* (London: John Perin).
p. 16: 'ambition and cloudes of couetousnesse . . . are the two beasts, compared by the Poet Dante, to a Lion and a shee wolfe, which let & hinder us from leaping to the mount of felicity' [*Inferno* 1. 45–54].

1611 Anon., *A Brief Chronicle of the Successe of Times, from the Creation of the World, to this instant* (London: Jaggard).
p. 59: '[1347] *Charles* the fourth, Author of the golden Bull, raigned 32 yeares; *Dante* then lived [*sic*]'. Conversely, Petrarch and Boccaccio are listed as living in 1314.

1615 Pierre d'Avity (tr. Edward Grimstone), *The Estates, Empires & Principalities of the World* (London: Adam Islip for Matthew Lownes and John Bill).
p. 1223, in chapter on 'the beginning of all religious orders': 'Saint *Lodolfe*', founder of 'the order of Font-Auellana' on mountains 'called Mont Latria and Mont Coruo, both celebrated by the Poet *Dante*', who is also here said to have 'remained some time' at Camaldoli, 'where he composed part of his verses'.

1625 M[atthew] S[utcliffe], *The Blessings on Movnt Gerizzim and the Cvrses on Mount Ebal. Or, The Happie Estate of Protestants, compared with the miserable Estate of Papists vnder the Popes Tyrannie* (London: Andrew Hebb) [repr. with different title, 1629];
p. 105: 'Dante sheweth, that the friers of his time wrested scriptures, and little regarded them. *Quand e posposta la diuina scrittura, & quando e torta* [*Par.* 29. 89–90, followed by quotation of 94–6 and 103–7 in the same canto]'.

1653 James Howell, *A German Diet: or The Balance of Europe . . . Made fit for the Meridian of ENGLAND By* James Howell *Esq.* (London: Humphrey Moseley).
p. 25, in part of 'The Oration of the Lord Laurence Vorwensin for Italy' and examples of 'the great Captaines of Italy': 'Who hath not heard of *Farinata Uberti*, celebrated by *Dante*?'

1654 Scipio Mazzella (tr. Samson Lennard and James Howell), *Parthenopoeia, or the History of Naples* (London: Humphrey Moseley).

p. 15, on Pier della Vigna: 'Of this *Pietro, Dante* maketh mention in the first part of the 13 *Cant[o]* [of the *Inferno*], saying I am he which holdeth both the Keys' [*Inf.* 13. 58–61].

1655 Hugo Grotius (tr. Clement Barksdale), *The Illustrious Hugo Grotius of the Law of Warre and Peace with Annotations in III. Parts* [Part 2] (London: T. Warren for William Lee).

p. 416, in chapter 110, 'Of the Title of universal Emperour': 'Nor ought any one be mov'd with *Dante's* arguments [in *Monarchia* 1]whereby he endeavours to prove the Emperour hath such a right, because it is expedient for mankind. For the commodities hereof are equalld with incommodities'.

1656 Thomas Stanley, *History of Philosophy, in Eight Parts* [Part 2] (London: Humphrey Moseley and Thomas Dring).

p. 97, translating 3rd Book of Pico della Mirandola's 'Platonick discourse' on love (1486) and its account of 'the Idea or Exemplar': 'to this *Dante* alludes' [in *Conv.* 4, canzone, 52–3, which Stanley translates but does not attribute].

1657 Gabriel Naudé (tr. John Davies of Kidwelly) *The History of Magick* (London: John Streater).

p. 233: '*Dante the Florentine*' is cited as one of those who have cast discredit upon Michael Scot [*Inferno* 20. 115–17, here quoted in original and in verse translation], who was 'one of the most excellent Philosophers, Mathematicians, and Astrologers of his time';

pp. 233–4: the account of Michael Scot's death is taken from '*de Granger* in his Commentary upon *Dante* [Balthasar Grangier, 1596, second French translation of the *Commedia*, as used by Naudé]'.

1659 Henry Stubbe(s), *A Light Shining out of Darknes: or Occasional Queries submitted To the Judgment of such as would enquire into the true state of things in our Times* (London: n.p.).

pp. 174–5: '*Christianity* it self in the primitive times did neither want able *pastours*, nor was so disquieted with *politically complying* opinions, curiosities, &c, untill *Constantine* began to enrich the Churches, at what time a voice was heard from Heaven, *This day poyson hath been shed in the Church*, and of which act of his *Dantes* the famous *Italian* poet in his 19. *Canto* of *Inferno* singeth thus, as the excellent Mr. *J. Milton* [shouldernote: 'I.M of refutn. p. 30] doth render it in English blank verse.

> *Ah Constantine, of how much ill was cause*
> *Not thy conversion, but those rich demeans*
> *That the first wealthy Pope received of thee.'*

[Stubbe(s) then goes on to quote the pseudo-Chaucerian *Plowmans Tale* on the same subject and then the 'May' eclogue in the *Shepheardes Calendar* by 'the famous *Spencer*', on the worldliness of 'our *Presbyeriall Ministers*'].

1660 Tommaso Campanella (tr. Edmund Chilmead), *Thomas Campanella An Italian Friar and Second Machiavel. His advice to the* King of Spain *for attaining the universal* Monarchy *of the World* (London: Philemon Stephens).

p. 11, in chapter 4 the account of 'the end of the four Monarchies' includes 'the death of Antichrist, who shall continue for the space of three Weeks and a half, according to the opinion of *Lactantius, Irenaeus, Tertullian, Origen* [. . .] *Joachimus Abbas, Dante, Petrarch,* and some others, both Divines, Philosophers, Prophets, and Poets';

p. 21, in chapter 5: the Pope is here claimed to have been 'constituted a *Regal Priest* [. . .] as I have proved in my Treatise Touching *Monarchy*, against *Dante*, who, looking only upon the Priesthood of *Aaron* [*Mon.* 3. 14. 5], allowes to the *Pope* nothing but *Spiritualities* and *Tithes* only [*Mon.* 3. 10. 17]';

pp. 211–12, in chapter 31, on ideas about 'That *Other Hemisphere*': 'some others believed, (among whom was *Dante*) that those Countries were Inhabited, and were a certain kind of Earthly Paradise'.

1660 Daniello Bartoli (tr. Thomas Salusbury), *The Learned Man Defended and Reform'd* (London: R. and W. Leyburn for Thomas Dring).

pp. 149–50, on 'Plagianisme': translation into couplets of what '*Dante* very finely [says] of the fearful Sheep that follow their Leader' [*Purgatorio* 3. 79–84];

p. 184, on 'Lasciviousnesse': those defending the hidden meaning of 'Lascivious Composures . . . may write in the frontispiece of their Poems that *Terzet* of *Dante*,

> *Ye soules indue'd with sound intelligence,*
> *Observe the hidden lessons that do lye*
> *Veil'd up in their mysterious Poetry:*
> [*Inferno* 9. 61–3]';

p. 314, on 'Ambition': 'Vale your too venturous plumes, that would sooner make you fall than flie, and do

> *Like to the un-flegg'd Stork, that strives to fly,*
> *And being untimely hasty, fluttering leaves*
> *Its lothed nest, and so a fall receives.*
> [*Purgatorio* 25. 10–12, misread]'

1664 Giovan Francesco Loredano ('Englished By J.B.'), *Accademical Discourses Vpon several Choice and Pleasant Subjects. Written Originally in* Italian, *by the Learned and Famous Loredano* (London: Thomas Mabb for John Playfere and Margaret Shears).

p. 2, to support the claim that 'love will not cast away his shafts upon ignoble breasts' (p. 1), Loredano and 'J.B.' cite Dante's Francesca on *Amor* and the *cor gentil* [*Inferno* 5. 100].

1671 David Blondel (tr. John Davies of Kidwelly), *A Treatise of the Sibyls* (London: T.R., for the Authour).

p. 45, in chapter 15, on Virgil: 'it happened (about three hundred years since) that the Poet *Dante*, mov'd by an Admiration of that incomparable Wit, would needs deliver him out of his Hell';

pp. 151–2, in chapter 28, on the 'new opinion of *Purgatory*' and visions of the afterlife: 'And as we finde the *Poet Dante* (by a Liberty truly *Poetical*) confined to the *Hell* where the *Damned* were, all his *enemies*; advanced into *Paradise* the best of his *Friends*, and reduced the rest to be content with the *Purgatory*: so were there about the midst of the *sixth Age*, a sort of People, that had the boldness to affirm (upon the *Authority* of their own *pretended Visions*) the damnation of the Greatest men';

p. 154, at the end of the same chapter, a further reference to Dante's and Ariosto's representations of Purgatory.

1672 René Rapin (tr. John Davies of Kidwelly), *Observations on the Poems of Homer and Virgil [. . .] Out of the* French, *By John Davies of Kidwelly* (London: S.G. and B.G. for Dorman Newman and Jonathan Edwin).

pp. 89–90: a claim by an Italian 'Apologist of *Dante . . .* that his Poem is more perfect in regard it is the action of one single person' is quoted and translated.

1673 Barten Holyday, *Decimus Junius Juvenalis and Aulus Persius Flaccus Translated and Illustrated, As well with Sculpture as Notes. By Barten Holyday* (Oxford: William Downing for Francis Oxlad Senior *et al.*).

p. 121 (col. 2), Holyday compares a Roman critic of Cicero with 'another Hypercritick, [Lodovico] *Nogarola*, a learned Italian, who . . . does . . . censure at once the whole Italian tongue, even the *Tuscan* puritie', naming 'the three most famous of the ancient poetical wits in that language: *Dante, Petrarch* and *Boccace*'.

1678 Madeleine de Scudéry [here attributed to George de Scudéry] (anon. tr.), *Clelia, an Excellent New Romance: the Whole Work in Five Parts* (London: H. Herringman, D. Newman *et al.*).

p. 508 (col. 1), in Part 4, Book 2 a review of Italian culture presents Dante as 'a man, who shall choose a very difficult Subject to treat of in Verse, and express himself . . . obscurely'.

1680 (April) *Bibliotheca Digbeiana, sive Catalogus Librorum In variis Linguis Editorum, Quos post Kenelmum Digbeium eruditiss[imum]. Virum possedit Illustrissimus Georgius Comes Bristol. nuper defunctus. Accedit & alia Bibliotheca non minus Copiosa & Elegans* (auction catalogue; London: H. Brome and B. Tooke).

The 'Libri italici' in the catalogue include two editions of the *Commedia* (1544 and 1564), one of *Convivio* (1521), and a manuscript of Ficino's translation of the *Monarchia* (1467–8): pp. 69 (no. 21), 73 (130–1), 77 (116–17), 133 (26).

1680 (November) *A Catalogue Of two Choice and Considerable Libraries of Books, Latin and English of Two Eminent and Learned Men Deceased* (auction catalogue; London: Bridges and Crouch).

p. 15 (no. 8), among 'Italici, Gallici, Hisp[anici]. in Folio', the Venice 1596 edition of the *Commedia* with the commentaries of Landino and Vellutello.

1681 James Craufurd, *The History of the House of Este, from the time of Forrestus until the Death of Alphonsus the last Duke of Ferrara* (London: J.M. for Richard Chiswell).

p. 52: '*Dante*' mentioned as one of a number of writers who 'spoke of' the Este family (cp. *Inferno* 12. 110–12 and *Purgatorio* 5. 77–8).

1683 François Eudes de Mézeray (tr. John Bulteel), *A General Chronological History of France, Beginning before the Reign of King Pharamond, And ending with the Reign of King Henry the Fourth: Concerning both the Civil and the Ecclesiastical Transactions of that Kingdom* (London: T.N. for Thomas Basset *et al.*).

p. 330, in chapter 45 on Philip the Fair: '*Dante Alighieri*, one of the rarest wits of his time, who was of the faction of the *White* [Guelfs] . . . was put into the number of the banished and could never obtain to be recalled. He lays the fault upon the Earl of *Valois*, for not having provided against those injurious proceedings, and tried to place his revenge upon all the House of *France*, by the cruel bitings of his Pen'.

1683 Jean Claude (tr. 'T.B.'), *An Historical Defence of the Reformation: In Answer to a Book Intituled, Just Prejudices Against the Calvinists* (London: G.L. for John Hancock and Benjamin Alsop).

p. 133: '*Dante*' named, among 'I know not how many others, who cried out as loudly against the abuses of the Court of *Rome*, as those of the rest of the Prelats'.

1684 Lionardo di Capua (tr. 'J[ohn] .L[ancaster].', with dedication to Robert Boyle FRS), *The Uncertainty of the Art of Physick, Together With an Account of the innumerable Abuses practised by the Professors of that Art* (London:).

sig. B3r, the preface 'to the Reader': '. . . how many there formerly have been, and at present are, who both in Medicine and other Arts melt their Brains in pursuit of that, which either is not, or not to be found; and as our *Dante* has it,

> Trattando l'ombre, come cosa salda.
> Treating of shadows, as substantial things.
> [Statius to Virgil in *Purgatorio* 21. 136]'

1690 *Bishop OVERALLs Convocation Book* [composed 1609] (London: Walter Kettilby).

pp. 331–2: 'Dant Aligerius' is listed in shouldernote [p. 332] as, in the time of Ludwig of Bavaria, one of 'many learned Men, both Divines and Civil Lawyers [who] did justify the Emerour's Proceedings, and condemn the Popes'.

1692 Gilbert Burnet, *The Life of William Bedell, D.D. Lord Bishop of Killmore in Ireland* (London: Richard Chiswell).

p. 396: Dante and Petrarch are listed among 'Authors of six or seven hundred years old [who] are set to School to learn the *Roman* language, and agree with the *Trent* faith'.

1695 René Le Bossu (tr. 'W.J.'), *Monsieur Bossu's Treatise of the Epick Poem* (London for Thomas Bennet).

sig. a 1ᵛ–a 2ʳ, in 'The [translator's] Preface': Le Bossu is here said to be taking 'notice of several among the *Italians*, namely *Dante, Petrarch, Boccace . . . Ariosto, Tasso, Sannazarius . . .* but he thinks the three first deserve not the very name of *Heroick* Poets'.

1695 Charles–Alphonse Dufresnoy (tr. John Dryden), *The Art of Painting* (London: John Heptinstall for William Rogers).

p. 254, in an account 'by another Hand [than Dryden's]' of 'Modern Masters', it is said that Giotto 'flourish'd in the time of the famous *Dante* and *Petrarch*, and was in great esteem with them'.

1695 Claude Fleury (tr. D. Poplar [?]), *The History, Choice and Method of Studies by Monsieur Fleury* (London: Samuel Keble *et al.*).

p. 35, in the account of 'the Thirteenth Age': 'about the end of the same Age, there were some *Florentines* who Studied to Write well in their Vulgar Tongue; as *Brunetto Latini, John Villani*, and the Poet *Dante*'.

1696 Anon, *Some Considerations about the Raising of Coin. In a Second Letter to Mr.* [John] Locke (London: A. and J. Churchill).

pp. 26–7: 'The excellent *Italian* Poet *Dante*, whose Works will live, has fixt a lasting Epithite of reproach upon the Memory of *Philip le Bel*, King of *France*, calling him *Falsificatore di Moneta*; The false Coiner [cp. *Paradiso* 19. 119]; Because he was the first that debased the Coin of *France*'.

1697 *A Catalogue of the Library Of the Reverend and Learned Dr Scattergood, Deceased. Containing A Curious Collection of* Greek *and* Latin *Fathers, Councils, Historians, Philosophers, Poets, Orators, Lexicographers, &c. Also an Excellent Collection of* English, French, Italian, *and* Spanish Books in all Faculties (auction catalogue; London: Hinchman *et al.*).

p. 56 (no. 2 of '*Libri Italici*, Folio): 'Comedia dell' Inferno, del Purgatorio & del Paradiso di Dante Alighieri con l'Isposizone [*sic*] di Christophero La[n]dino—*Venet.* 1529'.

p. 57 (no. 32 of '*Libri Italici*, Quarto): 'Dante con Nuove Ispositioni—1551' [probably the 16° edition published by Guillaume Rouillé at Lyon].

1699 Pierre Monier (anon. tr.), *The History of Painting, Sculpture, Architecture, Graving; And Of those who have Excell'd in them: In Three Books* (London: T. Bennet *et al.*).

p. 119, in chapter 9, 'Of the Perfection of Painting in the last Age': the work of '*Franco de Bologna* Painter, contemporary of Giotto' is said to have been 'very much praised by *Dante*' [cp. *Purgatorio* 11. 82–4].

1699 Arthur Duck (anon. tr.), *The Life of Henry Chichele, Archbishop of* Canterbury, *Who lived in the Times of Henry the V and VI. Kings of England* [Latin version 1617; see Boswell 1999: 163] (London: Richard Chiswell).

p. 8: '*Dante Alighieri* and *Francis Petrarch*, two *Italian* poets who liv'd in those Times in the Court of *Rome* at *Avignon*, do very severely reprehend the Rapine, the debauchery, Luxury and Excess of those Popes, and particularly of *Clement* the Fifth, and *John* the Twenty-second; which they did either out of their Hatred to the *French* in general; or because being Men of Integrity themselves, they could not bear the debauch'd and profligate Lives of the Popes'.

1700 Michel de Montaigne (tr. Charles Cotton), *Essays of Michael Seigneur de Montaigne. In Three Books* (London: M. Gillyflower *et al.*).

p. 225, in Book 1, Chapter 25, 'Of the Education of Children': 'only let this Diversity of Opinions be propounded to, and laid before him, he will himself choose, if he be able; if not he will remain in doubt.

        Che non menche saper dubiar m'aggrade

I love sometimes to doubt, as well as know.'

    [The quotation is attributed to '*Dante inferno, Canto 12*' in the shouldernote here, but is in fact from *Inferno* 11. 93. This edition thus repeats a mistake made in the 1603 Florio translation; for that, and two other references, see Boswell 1999: 121–2.]

Bibliography

MANUSCRIPT AND ARCHIVAL SOURCES CONSULTED

Berlin

Geheimes Staatsarchiv Preussischer Kulturbesitz
I HA Rep. 151 Finanzministerium, I C Nr 7156 (Juli 1880 bis ult. 1885) (Von Gossler, memorandum about purchase of the Hamilton manuscripts).

Staatsbibliothek
'Acta betreffend die Hamilton-Sammlung' III.C.48 [1883].
MS Hamilton 207 (*Commedia* sold in London, 1451).
MS Magdeb. Domkirche 231 (Rogerius de Eraclea/Platea, sermons).
Nachlaß 248, Kast. 6., Umschlag II ['Museum 1882'] (Friedrich Lippmann's correspondence with Richard Schöne).

Zentralarchiv der Staatlichen Museen zu Berlin
Nachlaß Bode 3346, (Lippmann's letter of 21 October 1882 about dispatch of the Hamilton mss. from London).

Cambridge

Gonville and Caius College
MS 230/116 (Whethamstede's commonplace book).

St John's College
MS S.10 (Seget, letter to James I, 1622).

Cape Town

National Library of South Africa
MS C 57. 23 [1] (inventory of the Grey Collection).
MS Grey 3 c 25 (late 15th-c. paper *Commedia*).
MS Grey 4 b 11 (15th-c. vellum and paper *Commedia* with miniatures).

Western Cape State Archives
GH 30/11 (letter from Grey to his London book-dealer).

Edinburgh

National Gallery of Scotland
Reports and correspondence relating to Dyce's *Francesca da Rimini*.

National Library of Scotland
MS 15879 (John Purves, notes on Thomas Seget).
MSS 2168-72 (*DISEGNI AD ILLUSTRAZIONE DELLA DIVINA COMMEDIA*).
MS 2212 (Society of Antiquaries of Scotland papers).
MS 8887 (letter from William Dyce, *c*.1836).

National Archives of Scotland
MS GD 46/17/42 (Elphinstone, letters to Lady Hood).

Royal Scottish Academy MS collection
'Letters, Exhibition, Scottish Academy 1837'.
'Council Minutes, January 1862–October 1867'.
'Council Minutes, July 1876–December 1887'.

Eton

Eton College Library
Loo. I. 14. *La Divina Commedia di Dante Alighieri*, ed. L. Pezzana (Venice: Gaspari, 1827); 'Mr Gladstone's Pocket Dante'.
MS 112 (mid 14th-c. copy of *Commedia*).
MS 115 (15th-c. copy of commentary on the *Inferno* and *Purgatorio* by Iacopo della Lana).

Holkham

Holkham Hall Library
MSS 513, and 515–18 (*Commedia* texts, from 2nd half of the 14th c. to late 15th c., purchased by Thomas Coke *c.*1717).
MS 530 (*Convivio* of early 15th c., purchased by Thomas Coke).
Archives F/G2/2 (letters from Thomas Coke).
Archives F/TWC 5 (letters from William Roscoe to Thomas William Coke).

Inverness

Highland Council Archive
D 63/E/1/1 (Macleod of Cadboll family documents).
D 63/E/2a (Isabella Macleod letters to F. C. Brooke, 1843–7).
D63/E/2b (Margaret De Virte (*née* Macleod), letters to H. D. Macleod).
D 63/E/2d (Elizabeth Macleod letters, 1871–1904).

London

British Library
Add. MS 26764 (Whethamstede's *Palearium poetarum*).
Add. MS 35378 (Hardwicke Papers, vol. 30).
Add MS 38597 (Thomas Reid's *Letterbook*).
Add. MS 40676 (Sir Richard Morison's library list).
Add. MS 41846 (Kenelm Digby papers).
Add. MS 44683 (Gladstone, draft of review of Russell's translation, 1844).
Add. MS 44731 (Gladstone's essay on the *Commedia*).
Add. MSS 47235, 56540, and 56538 (Hobhouse Diaries).
Add. MSS 62142–51 (Francis Brooke's 'Travel Journals').
Cotton Titus MS D XX (Whethamstede's compendium on poets).
MS Egerton 2629 (Serravalle's translation of and commentary on the *Commedia*).
MSS Eur F88/254–5, 282, 359, 363–4, 368, 370 (Elphinstone, letters and journals).
MS L/AG/34/27/19 ('Bengal Inventories').

London Metropolitan Archive
MS 9171/5/(Carlo Gigli's will, registered 12 July 1465).

National Archive (Kew)
E122/209/1 (Venetian galley visits to Southampton, 1437–8).
SP 80/3 (Seget, letter to James I and VI, 1613).

Tate Gallery, Archive and Special Collections
Dyce papers (microfiche of typescript at Aberdeen Art Gallery).

Milan

Biblioteca Ambrosiana
MS C 198 inf. (Seget's and Pinelli's copy of the *Commedia*).
MS C 225 inf. (Seget's copy of the *Decameron*).
MS I 69 sup. (Seget's copy of the Italian *Heroides* in Italian).

Mumbai

Asiatic Society
Town Hall MS 19 (Dante, *Commedia*, donated by Elphinstone).
'Minute Book 1804–20', 'Minute Book 1865–98'.

New York

Pierpont Morgan Library
MS M 676 (Thomas Hobart's illustrated *Commedia*).

Oxford

Bodleian Library
University of Oxford Archives, MS Registrum F (Duke Humfrey's donation of books).
MS. Eng. C. 2731 (Maria Callcott, 'Reminscences', early 1840s).
MS Eng. misc. d. 639 (Seymour Kirkup and others, letters and engravings).
Holkham misc. 48 (illustrated *Commedia*, 2nd half of the 14th c., from Holkham Hall (purchased by Thomas Coke *c.*1717)).

Vatican

Biblioteca Apostolica Vaticana
MS Cappon. 1 (Serravalle, *Liber Dantis*; photocopies).
MS Vat. lat. 4116 (Easton's *Defensorium*; microfilm).

Venice

Archivio di Stato
Senato Deliberazioni Mar, registro 4 (voyage of Venetian Flanders galleys, 1451).

PRINTED SOURCES

Agard, J. and Kitamura, S. (2008), *The Young Inferno* (London: Frances Lincoln).
Ahern, J. (1997), 'Singing the Book: Orality in the Reception of Dante's *Comedy*', in *Dante: Contemporary Perspectives*, ed. A. Iannucci (Toronto and London: University of Toronto Press), 214–39.
Alakas, B. C. (2009), '"Partners in the Same": Monastic Devotional Culture in Late Medieval Literature', Ph.D thesis, Queen's University, Kingston, Ontario (available online).
Albertini, S. (1996), 'Dante in camicia nera: uso e abuso del divino poeta nell'Italia fascista', *The Italianist*, 16: 117–42.

Altcappenberg, H.-T. S. (2000) (ed.), *Sandro Botticelli: The Drawings for Dante's 'Divine Comedy'* (London: Royal Academy of Arts).

Ampère, J.-J. (1839) *Voyage dantesque* (Paris).

Anceschi, G. (2002) (ed.), *Un professore a Londra: studi su Antonio Panizzi* (Novara: Interlinea).

Andrews, K. (1964), *The Nazarenes: A Brotherhood of German Painters in Rome* (Oxford: Clarendon Press).

Anon. (1798) (ed.), *I fiori del Parnasso italiano ovvero una raccolta di rime estratta dall'opere de' più celebri Poeti Italiani* (London: Rivington & Hatchard).

Aquilecchia, G. *et al.* (1971) (eds.), *Collected Essays on Italian Language and Literature Presented to Kathleen Speight* (Manchester: Manchester University Press).

Armour, P. (1991), 'Comedy and the Origins of Italian Theatre around the Time of Dante', in *Writers and Performers in Italian Drama from the Time of Dante to Pirandello*, ed. J. R. Dashwood and J. E. Everson (Lewiston, Queenston, and Lampeter: Edwin Mellen Press), 1–31.

Armour, P. (2007), 'The *Comedy* as a Text for Performance', in Braida and Calè (2007) (eds.), 17–22.

Armstrong, G. (2011), 'Nineteenth-Century Translations and the Invention of Boccaccio-*dantista*', in Havely (2011*a*) (ed.), 201–20.

Arnold, J. (2008), *What is Medieval History?* (Cambridge: Polity).

Arthos, J. (1968), *Milton and the Italian Cities* (London: Bowes & Bowes).

Artom Treves, G. (1953), *Anglo-fiorentini di cento anni fa* (Florence: Sansoni).

Audeh, A. (2010), 'Gustave Doré's Illustrations for Dante's *Divine Comedy*: Innovation, Influence and Reception', *Studies in Medievalism*, 18: 125–64.

Audeh, A. and Havely, N. R. (2012) (eds.), *Dante in the Long Nineteenth Century: Nationality, Identity, and Appropriation* (Oxford: Oxford University Press).

Aveling, J. C. H. (1976), *The Handle and the Axe: The Catholic Recusants in England from Reformation to Emancipation* (London: Blond & Briggs).

Axton, M. and Carley, J. P. (2000) (eds.), *'The Triumphs of English': Henry Parker, Lord Morley, Translator to the Tudor Court. New Essays in Interpretation* (London: The British Library).

Baker, M. and Glenn, D. (2000) (eds.), *Dante Colloquia in Australia, 1982–1999* (Adelaide: Australian Humanities Press).

Baker, P. R. (1964), *The Fortunate Pilgrims: Americans in Italy, 1800–1860* (Cambridge, Mass.: Harvard University Press).

Bale, J. (1548?), *The Image of Bothe Churches after the most wonderfull and heauenly Reuelacion of Sainct John the Euangelist* (enlarged edn., Antwerp: Stephen Mierdeman for Ruchard Jugge).

Bale, J. (1549), *The Laboryouse Iourney [and] serche of Iohan Leylande, for Englandes Antiquitees: geuen of hym as a newe yeares gyfte to Kynge Henry VIIJ in the XXVIJ yeare of his Reyne, with declaracyons enlarged: by Iohhan Bale* (London: Mierdeman).

Bale, J. (1557–9), *Scriptorum Illustrium Maioris Brytannie quam nunc Angliam & Scotiam uocant: Catalogus* (2nd edn., Basel: Oporinus).

Bale, J. (1990), *Index Britanniae Scriptorum: John Bale's Index of British and Other Writers*, ed. R. L. Poole and M. Bateson (Cambridge: Brewer).

Balfour, M. (1998), 'The Place of the Poet: Dante in Walcott's Poetry', in Havely (1998*a*) (ed.), 223–41.

Ballhatchet, K. (1957), *Social Policy and Social Change in Western India 1817–1830* (London: Oxford University Press).

Banfi, F. (1938), 'Marino Ghetaldi da Ragusa e Tommaso Segeth da Edimburgo', *Archivio storico per la Dalmatia*, 26: 323–45.

Barbi, M. (1934) 'La lettura di Benvenuto da Imola e i suoi rapporti con altri commenti', *Studi danteschi* 18: 79–98.

Barlow, H. C. (1864), *Critical, Historical, and Philosophical Contributions to the Study of the Divina Commedia* (London and Edinburgh: Williams & Norgate).

Barlow, H. C. (1866), *The Sixth Centenary Festivals of Dante Alleghieri in Florence and Ravenna by A Representative* (London, Edinburgh, Florence, and Turin: Williams & Norgate and Hermann Loescher).

Barlow, H. C. (1867), 'The Codici of the *Divina Commedia* at Holkham', *Athenaeum*, 2056: 388a–c.

Beard, T. (1625), *Antichrist the Pope of Rome: or, The Pope of Rome is Antichrist, proued in Two Treatises* (London: I. Jaggard for J. Bellamie).

Beaty, F. L. (1960), 'Byron and the Story of Francesca da Rimini', *PMLA* 75: 395–401.

Bec, C. (1983), 'I mercanti scrittori, lettori e giudici di Dante', *Letture classensi*, 12: 99–111.

Beckford, W. (1980), *Vathek*, ed. R. Lonsdale (Oxford: Oxford University Press).

Bednarz, J. P. (2010), 'Was *Volpone* Acted at Cambridge in 1606?', *Ben Jonson Journal*, 17.2: 183–96.

Berkowitz, D. S. (1984) (ed.), *Humanist Scholarship and Public Order: Two Tracts against the Pilgrimage of Grace by Sir Richard Morison* (Washington, DC, London, and Toronto: Folger Shakespeare Library and Associated University Presses).

Bernard, E. (1697), *Catalogi Manuscriptorum Hiberniae et Angliae*, 2 vols. (Oxford: *E Theatro Sheldoniano*).

Bernard, G. W. (2005), *The King's Reformation: Henry VIII and the Remaking of the English Church* (New Haven, Conn. and London: Yale University Press).

Bertelli, S. (2007), *La 'Commedia' all'antica* (Florence: Mandragora).

Berton, C. (1857), *Dictionnaire des Cardinaux, contenant des notions generals sur le cardinalat*. Paris: Migne.

Biadene, L. (1887), 'I manoscritti italiani della collezione Hamilton', *GSLI* 10: 313–55.

Biagini, E. (2000), *Gladstone* (Basingstoke: Macmillan).

Bianchi, R. (1988), *Intorno a Pio II: un mercatante e tre poeti* (Messina: Sicania).

Bigsby, C. (1995) (ed.), *Nineteenth-Century American Short Stories* (London and Rutland, Vt.: Dent and Tuttle).

Billanovich, G. (1947), *Petrarca letterato: I. Lo scrittoio del Petrarca* (Rome: Edizioni di storia e letteratura).

Bindman, D. (1979) (ed.), *John Flaxman, R.A.* (London: Royal Academy of Arts).

Bindman, D. *et al.* (2007) (eds.), *Dante Rediscovered: From Blake to Rodin* (Grasmere: The Wordsworth Trust).

Birckbek, S. (1634), *The protestants evidence, taken out of good records* (London: for R. Milbourne).

Birley, R. (1970), *The Eton College Collections: The History of the College Library* (Eton: Provost and Fellows).

Birrell, T. A. (1994), 'Some Rare Scottish Books on the Old Royal Library', in *The Renaissance in Scotland: Studies in Literature, Religion, History and Culture Offered to John Durkin*, ed. A. A. MacDonald *et al.* (Leiden, New York, and Cologne: Brill), 404–16.

Bishop, M. C. (1894), *A Memoir of Mrs Augustus Craven* (London: Bentley).

Black, J. (2003), *Italy and the Grand Tour* (New Haven, Conn. and London: Yale University Press).

Blank, P. (2006), 'The Babel of Renaissance English', in *The Oxford History of English*, ed. L. Mugglestone (Oxford: Oxford University Press), 212–39.

Boccaccio, G. (1965), *Tutte le opere di Giovanni Boccaccio* (gen. ed. V. Branca) *VI: Esposizioni sopra la Comedia di Dante*, ed. G. Padoan (Milan: Mondadori).

Boccaccio, G. (1972), *Opere minori in volgare IV*, ed. M. Marti (Milan: Rizzoli).

Boccaccio, G. (1974), *Tutte le opere di Giovanni Boccaccio* (gen. ed. V. Branca) *III: Trattatello in laude di Dante*, ed. P. G. Ricci (Milan: Mondadori).

Boese, H. (1966), *Die lateinischen Handschriften der Sammlung Hamilton zu Berlin* (Wiesbaden: Harrassowitz).

Boitani, P. (1983) (ed.), *Chaucer and the Italian Trecento* (Cambridge: Cambridge University Press).

Boitani, P. (2007), *Dante's Poetry of the Donati: The Barlow Lectures on Dante . . . 2005* (Leeds: Maney).

Boldrini, L. (2001), *Joyce, Dante, and the Poetics of Literary Relations: Language and Meaning in 'Finnegans Wake'* (New York: Cambridge University Press).

Boschi Rotiroti, M. (2004), *Codicologia trecentesca della Commedia: entro e oltre l'antica vulgata* (Rome: Viella).

Bossy, J. (1976), *The English Catholic Community, 1570–1850* (New York: Oxford University Press).

Boswell, J. B. (1999), *Dante's Fame in England: References in Printed British Books 1477–1640* (Newark, N.J. and London: University of Delaware Press and Associated University Presses).

Boswell, J. C. (1975), *Milton's Library* (New York and London: Garland).

Bosworth, R. J. B. (2002), *Mussolini* (London: Arnold).

Bosworth, R. J. B. (2005), *Mussolini's Italy: Life Under the Dictatorship, 1915–1945* (London: Allen Lane).

Bowers, T. N. (2004), 'Conrad's *Heart of Darkness* and Dante's *Inferno*', *The Explicator*, 62.2: 91–4.

Bradley, H. (1992), 'Italian Merchants in London, *c.* 1350–*c.* 1450', D.Phil. thesis, RHBNC, University of London.

Braggion, G. (1980/81), 'Ricerche attorno al carteggio tra Gianvincenzo Pinelli e Alvise Mocenigo', Laurea thesis, Facoltà di Lettere e Filosofia, Università del Sacro Cuore di Milano.

Braida, A. (2004), *Dante and the Romantics* (Houndmills: Palgrave Macmillan).

Braida, A. and Calè, L. (2007) (eds.), *Dante on View: The Reception of Dante in the Visual and Performing Arts* (Aldershot and Burlington, Vt.: Ashgate).

Branca, V. (1965), 'Un biadaiolo lettore di Dante nei primi decenni del '300', *Rivista di cultura classica e medievale*, 8: 200–15.

Branca, V. and Caccia, E. (1965) (eds.), *Dante nel mondo: Raccolta di studi promossa dall' Associazione internazionale per gli studi di lingua e di letteratura italiana* (Florence: Olschki).

Branca, V. and Ricci, P. G. (1962), *Un autografo del Decameron (Codice hamiltoniano 90)* (Padua: CEDAM).

Brand, C. P. (1957), *Italy and the English Romantics: The Italianate Fashion in Early Nineteenth-century England* (Cambridge: Cambridge University Press).

Brand, C. P. (1971), 'The Italian Exiles in Britain in the Early Nineteenth Century: A Survey of their Writings', in Aquilecchia *et al.* (1971) (eds.), 257–75.

Bratchel, M. E. (1978), 'Italian Merchant Organization and Business Relationships in Early Tudor London', *Journal of European Economic History*, 7: 5–32.

Bratchel, M. E. (1980), 'Regulation and Group-Consciousness in the Later History of London's Italian Merchant Colonies', *Journal of European Economic History*, 9: 585–610.

Bratchel, M. E. (1995), *Lucca 1434–1494: The Reconstruction of an Italian City-Republic* (Oxford: Clarendon Press).

Bray, S. (2001), 'Dante et la littérature anglaise du XXe siècle', in *Dante et ses lecteurs (du moyen âge au xxe siècle)*, ed. H. Levillain (Poitiers: La Licorne).

Brewer, D. S. (1978), *Chaucer: The Critical Heritage*, 2 vols. (London: Routledge & Kegan Paul).

Brooks, C. (1931), *Antonio Panizzi, Scholar and Patriot* (Manchester: Manchester University Press).

Brown, H. F. (1900) (ed.), *Calendar of State Papers and Manuscripts (Venice)*, 10 (London: Stationery Office).

Brown, K. D. (1986), 'The Franciscan Observants in England, 1482–1559', D.Phil. thesis, University of Oxford.

Bruni, F. (1980), 'La cultura e la prosa volgare nel '300 e nel '400', in *Storia della Sicilia* 4, ed. R. Romeo (Palermo: Società editrice Storia di Napoli e della Sicilia), 180–237.

Burke, W. J. (1933), 'Leigh Hunt's Marginalia', *Bulletin of the New York Public Library*, 37: 87–107.

Burwick, F. and Douglass P (2011) (eds.), *Dante and Italy in British Romanticism* (Basingstoke: Palgrave Macmillan).

Cachey, T. J. (1995) (ed.), *Dante Now: Current Trends in Dante Studies* (Notre Dame, Ind. and London: University of Notre Dame Press).

Caesar, M. P. (1989), *Dante: The Critical Heritage 1314(?)–1870* (London and New York: Routledge).

Caesar, M. P. and Havely, N. R. (2012), 'Politics and Performance: Gustavo Modena's *dantate*', in Audeh and Havely (2012) (eds.), 111–37.

Calè, L. (2007), 'From Dante's *Inferno* to *A TV Dante*: Phillips and Greenaway Remediating Dante's Polysemy', in Braida and Calè (2007) (eds.), 177–92.

Cambon, G. (1969), *Dante's Craft: Studies in Language and Style* (Minneapolis, Minn.: University of Minnesota Press).

Cambon, G. (1980), *Ugo Foscolo: Poet of Exile* (Princeton, N.J.: Princeton University Press).

Camilletti, F. (2005), *Beatrice nell'Inferno di Londra: saggio su Dante Gabriel Rossetti* (Trento: la Finestra).

Camilletti, F. (2011), '*Ninfa fiorentina*: The Falling of Beatrice from Florence to Modern Metropolis', in Havely (2011*a*) (ed.), 117–35.

Campana, A. (2014), 'Foscolo dantista e il possibile influsso della cultura protestante', in *Atti del XV convegno internazionale di letteratura italiana 'Gennaro Barbarisi' su 'Foscolo critico'*, ed. P. Borsa (Milan: Università degli studi [forthcoming]).

Campbell, I. (2000), 'Carlyle and Italy', in McLaughlin (2000) (ed.), 107–20.

Capaci, B. (2008), *Dante oscuro e barbaro: Commenti e dispute (secoli XVII e XVIII)* (Rome: Carocci).

Caputo, R. (2004), 'Dante by Heart and Dante Declaimed: The "Realization" of the *Comedy* on Italian Radio and Television', in Iannucci (2004) (ed.), 213–23.

Carley, J. P. (2000*a*) (ed.), *The Libraries of King Henry VIII* (London: The British Library/British Academy).

Carley, J. P. (2000*b*), 'The Writings of Henry Parker, Lord Morley: A Bibliographical Survey', in Axton and Carley (2000), 27–68.

Carley, J. P. (2004), *The Books of Henry VIII and his Wives* (London: The British Library).

Carlson, D. P. (1988), 'Politicizing Tudor Court Literature: Gaguin's Embassy and Henry VII's Humanists' Response', *Studies in Philology*, 85: 279–304.

Carlson, D. P. (1999), 'The Civic Poetry of Abbot John Whethamstede of St Albans (d. 1465)', *Mediaeval Studies*, 61: 205–42.

Casadio, G. (1996) (ed.), *Dante nel cinema* (Ravenna: Longo).

Casciani, S. (2006), 'Bernardino, Reader of Dante', in *Dante and the Franciscans*, ed. S. Casciani (Leiden and Boston, Mass.: Brill), 85–111.

Caselli, D. (2005), *Beckett's Dantes: Intertextuality in the Fiction and Criticism* (Manchester: Manchester University Press).

Caspar, M. (1954) (ed.), *Johannes Kepler: Gesammelte Werke*, 16 (Munich: Beck).

Cassell, A. K. (2004), *The Monarchia Controversy* (Washington, DC: Catholic University of America Press).

Casson, L. F. (1959), 'The Medieval Manuscripts of the Grey Collection in Saleroom and Bookshop', *QBSAL* 14.1: 3–33.

Cecchetti, D. (1996), 'Un umanista tra Italia e Francia. La poetica di Giovanni Moccia', in *Studi di storia della civiltà letteraria francese*, ed. D. Cecchetti (Paris: Champion), 55–128.

Cenci, C. (1995), 'Il *Quaresimale delle scuole* di Fr. Ruggero da Eraclea', *Archivum Franciscanum Historicum*, 88: 269–318.

Chacón, A. (1630), *Vitæ, et res gestæ Pontificvm Romanorum et S. R. E. Cardinalivm ab initio nascentis Ecclesiæ vsque ad Vrbanvm VIII. Pont. Max.* (Rome).

Chadwick, O. (1979), 'Young Gladstone and Italy', *JEH* 30: 243–59.

Chaucer, G. (1994), *The House of Fame*, ed. N. R. Havely (Durham: Durham Medieval Texts; 2nd edn., Toronto: PIMS, 2013).

Chaucer, G. (2008), *The Riverside Chaucer*, gen. ed. L. D. Benson (3rd edn., Oxford: Oxford University Press).

Chiari, A. (1970) (ed.), *Galileo Galilei: scritti letterari* (Florence: Le Monnier).

Childs, W. (1983), 'Anglo-Italian Contacts in the Fourteenth Century', in Boitani 1983 (ed.), 65–87.

Chojnacki, S. (1973), 'In Search of the Venetian Patriciate: Families and Factions in the Fourteenth Century', in *Renaissance Venice*, ed. J. R. Hale (London: Faber), 47–90.

Choksey, R. D. (1971), *Mountstuart Elphinstone: The Indian Years* (Bombay: Popular Prakashan).

Ciccarelli, A. (2001*a*), 'Dante and the Culture of Risorgimento: Literary, Political or Ideological Icon?', in *Making and Remaking Italy: The Cultivation of National Identity around the Risorgimento* (Oxford and New York: Berg), 77–102.

Ciccarelli, A. (2001*b*), 'Dante and Italian Culture from the Risorgimento to World War I', *Dante Studies*, 119: 125–54.

'Clare, J.' (1630), *The Converted Jew or certaine dialogues betweene Micheas a learned jew, and others, touching divers points of religion controuerted betweene the Catholicks and Protestants* (S. I. [printed by English secret press] Permissu superiorum).

Clark, J. G. (2004), *A Monastic renaissance at St Albans: Thomas Walsingham and his Circle c.1350–1440* (Oxford: Clarendon Press).

Clarke, K. P. (2007), '"I shal fynde it in a maner glose": Commentary and Hermeneutics: Chaucer and his Italian Sources', D.Phil. thesis, University of Oxford.

Clarke, K. P. (2011a), *Chaucer and Italian Textuality* (Oxford: Oxford University Press).

Clarke, K. P. (2011b), 'Chaucer and Italy: Context and/of Sources', *Literature Compass* 8: 526–33.

Clarke, W. (1819), *Repertorium Bibliographicum or Some Account of the most Celebrated Libraries* (London: William Clarke).

Clebsch, W. A. (1964), *England's Earliest Protestants, 1520–1535* (New Haven, Conn. and London: Yale University Press).

Cline, C. L. (1952), *Byron, Shelley and their Pisan Circle* (London: Murray).

Clough, C. H. (2003), 'Three Gigli of Lucca during the Fifteenth and Early Sixteenth Centuries: Diversification in a Family of Mercery Merchants', *The Ricardian*, 13: 121–47.

Cobban, A. B. (1975) *The Medieval Universities: Their Development and Organization* (London: Methuen).

Cobban, A. B. (1988) *The Medieval English Universities: Oxford and Cambridge to 1500* (Aldershot: Scolar).

Cochrane, E. (1988), *Italy 1530–1630*, ed. J. Kirshner (Harlow: Longman).

Cokayne, G. E. and Gibbs, V. (1910–59), *The Complete Peerage of England, Scotland, Ireland, Great Britain, and the United Kingdom, extant, extinct, or dormant*, 13 vols. in 14 (London: St Catherine's Press).

Colebrooke, T. E. (1884), *Life of the Honourable Mountstuart Elphinstone*, 2 vols. (London: Murray).

Collinson, P. (1989) 'Shepherds, Sheepdogs and Hirelings: The Pastoral Ministry in Post-Reformation England', *Studies in Church History*, 26: 185–220.

Comparato, V. I. (1970), *Giuseppe Valletta: Un intellettuale napolitano della fine del seicento* (Naples: Istituto italiano per gli studi storici).

Concolato, M. P. (1993), 'Di alcuni aspetti del Baretti inglese', in *Giuseppe Baretti letterato e viaggiatore (atti del Convegno Napoli, 15 dicembre 1989)*, ed. A. Martorelli (Naples, 1993), 9–29.

Condon, P. with Cohn, M. (1983), *Ingres: In Pursuit of Perfection*, ed. D. Edelstein (Bloomington, Ind.: Speed Art Museum/Indiana University Press).

Connor Bulman, L. M. (2003), 'Moral Education on the Grand Tour: Thomas Coke and his Contemporaries in Rome and Florence', *Apollo*, 157: 27–34.

Cooper, R. (2007), 'Dante on the Nineteenth-century Stage', in Braida and Calè (2007) (eds.), 21–37.

Cope, C. H. (1891), *Reminiscences of Charles West Cope R.A.* (London: Bentley).

Corrigan, B. (1971), 'Foscolo's Articles on Dante in the *Edinburgh Review*: A Study in Collaboration', in Aquilecchia *et al.* (1971) (eds.), 212–25.

Cotton, J. S. (1892), *Mountsuart Elphinstone and the Making of South-Western India* (Oxford: Clarendon Press).

Coville, A. (1934), *Gontier et Pierre Col et l'humanisme en France au temps de Charles VI* (Paris: Droz).

Craster, E. (1952), *History of the Bodleian Library 1845–1945* (Oxford: Clarendon Press).

Cressy, D. and Ferrell, L. A. (1996) (eds.), *Religion and Society in Early Modern England: A Sourcebook* (London and New York: Routledge).

Crisafulli, E. (2003), *The Vision of Dante* (Market Harborough: Troubadour Press).

Crisafulli, L. M. (2002), ' "An infernal triangle": Foscolo, Hobhouse, Di Breme and the Italian Context of the *Essay on the Present Literature of Italy*', in *Immaginando l'Italia: Itinerari letterari del Romanticismo inglese*, ed. L. M. Crisafulli (Bologna: CLUEB), 251–85.

Crombie, A. C. (1969), *Augustine to Galileo*, Volume 2: *Science in the Later Middle Ages and Early Modern Times, 13th to 17th centuries* (Harmondsworth: Penguin).

Cross, C. (1999), *Church and People: England 1450–1660* (2nd edn., Oxford: Blackwell).

Crow, M. M. and Olson C. C. (1966), *Chaucer Life-Records* (Oxford: Clarendon Press).

Cullinan, P. and Watson, S. (2005) (eds.), *Dante in South Africa* (Cape Town: Centre for Creative Writing, University of Cape Town).

Cunningham, G. F. (1965), *The Divine Comedy in English: A Critical Bibliography, 1782–1900* (Edinburgh and London: Oliver & Boyd).

Cunningham, G. F. (1966), *The Divine Comedy in English: A Critical Bibliography, 1901–1966* (Edinburgh and London: Oliver & Boyd).

Curioni, A. (1788), *Istoria dei Poeti italiani ad uso dei Principianti nella Lingua Italiana* (London: Curioni).

Cust, L. H. and Colvin, S. (1898), *History of the Society of Dilettanti* (London: Macmillan).

Dalrymple, W. (2003) (ed.), *Begums, Thugs and Englishmen: The Journals of Fanny Parkes* (New Delhi: Penguin).

Danielewski, M. Z. (2000), *House of Leaves* (London: Transworld, Anchor).

Dante Alighieri (1493), *Commedia*, ed. Pietro da Figino, comm. Cristoforo Landino (Venice: Matteo di Codecà).

Dante Alighieri (1757–8) *Opere di Dante Alighieri*, ed. A. Zatta, 5 vols. (Venice: Zatta).

Dante Alighieri (1785), *A Translation of the 'Inferno' of Dante Alighieri in English Verse, with historical notes and the Life of Dante, to which is added a specimen of the 'Orlando Furioso' of Ariosto, By Henry Boyd A.M.*, 2 vols. (London: Dilly).

Dante Alighieri (1802), *The Divina Commedia of Dante Alighieri: Consisting of the Inferno—Purgatorio—and Paradiso. Translated into English Verse, with Preliminary Essays, Notes and Illustrations, By the Rev. Henry Boyd, A.M.*, 3 vols. (London: Cadell & Davies).

Dante Alighieri (1808*a*), *La Divina Commedia . . . illustrate di note da varj comentatori scelte*, ed. R. Zotti (London: Zotti).

Dante Alighieri (1808*b*), *La Divina Commedia di Dante, Passo passo riscontrata, con lunga e scrupolosa diligenza, sui Testi delle più approvate Edizioni antiche e moderne . . . da G.B. Boschini* (London: P. Ponte).

Dante Alighieri (1809), *Canzoni e Sonetti di Dante Alighieri*, ed. R. Zotti (London: Zotti).

Dante Alighieri (1818–19), *La Divina Commedia di Dante Alighieri con comento di G. Biagioli*, ed. G. Biagioli, 3 vols. (Paris: Dondey–Dupré).

Dante Alighieri (1819), *La Divina Commedia . . . seconda edizione, di nuove osservazioni accresciuta e migliorata*, ed. R. Zotti, 3 vols. (London: Zotti).

Dante Alighieri (1822–3), *La Divina Commedia di Dante*, ed. W. Pickering, 2 vols. (London: Pickering).

Dante Alighieri (1842*a*), *The Early Life of Dante Alighieri [Vita nuova]: together with the original in parallel pages*, tr. J. Garrow (Florence: Le Monnier).

Dante Alighieri (1842*b*), *L'Inferno secondo l testo di B. Lombardi . . . corredato di brevi dichiarazioni per uso degli stranieri*, ed. G. J. Warren Vernon (Florence: Piatti).

Dante Alighieri (1842–3), *Commedia di Dante Allighieri illustrata da Ugo Foscolo*, ed. G. Mazzini, 4 vols. (London: Pietro Rolandi).

Dante Alighieri (1858–65), *L'Inferno di Dante Alighieri disposto in ordine grammaticale e corredato di brevi dichiarazioni da G. G. Warren Lord Vernon*, 3 vols. (London: Boone).

Dante Alighieri (1899), *The Paradiso of Dante Alighieri*, ed. and tr. P. H. Wicksteed (London: Dent [Temple Classics]).

Dante Alighieri (1900), *The Inferno of Dante Alighieri*, tr. J. A. Carlyle, rev. H. Oelsner, notes by P. H. Wicksteed (London: Dent [Temple Classics]).

Dante Alighieri (1901), *The Purgatorio of Dante Alighieri*, ed. and tr. T. Okey (London: Dent [Temple Classics]).

Dante Alighieri (1903), *The 'Convivio' of Dante Alighieri*, ed. and tr. P. H. Wicksteed (London: Dent).

Dante Alighieri (1904*a*), *A Translation of the Latin Works of Dante Alighieri*, ed. and tr. P. H. Wicksteed and A. G. Ferrers Howell (London: Dent).

Dante Alighieri (1904*b*), *The Early Italian Poets Together with Dante's 'Vita Nuova' Translated by D. G. Rossetti*, ed. E. G. Gardner (London: Dent).

Dante Alighieri (1939–46), *The Divine Comedy of Dante Alighieri with translation and comment by John D. Sinclair*, 3 vols. (London: Bodley Head).

Dante Alighieri (1949–62), *The Comedy of Dante Alighieri the Florentine*, tr. D. L. Sayers [*Paradiso* completed by B. Reynolds], 3 vols. (Harmondsworth: Penguin).

Dante Alighieri (1983), *Inferno. A Verse Translation with Images and Commentary*, tr. and illustrated by Tom Phillips (London: Talfourd Press).

Dante Alighieri (1985), *Dante's Inferno: The First Part of the Divine Comedy of Dante Alighieri. Translated and Illustrated by Tom Phillips* (London: Thames & Hudson).

Dante Alighieri (1993), *Dante Alighieri: Hell. Translated, annotated, and introduced by Steve Ellis* (London: Chatto & Windus).

Dante Alighieri (1994), *Dante, The Divine Comedy: The Vision of Dante, Translated by Henry Cary*, ed. R. Pite (London and Rutland, Vt.: Dent and Tuttle).

Dante Alighieri (1995*a*), *Dante Alighieri: Opere minori*, Volume II, tomo I: *Convivio*, ed. C. Vasoli and D. De Robertis (Milan and Naples: Ricciardi).

Dante Alighieri (1995*b*), *Dante Alighieri: The Divine Comedy*, tr. Allen Mandelbaum (London: Everyman's Library/David Campbell).

Dante Alighieri (1995*c*), *Monarchia*, ed. and tr. P. Shaw (Cambridge: Cambridge University Press).

Dante Alighieri (1996), *The Divine Comedy of Dante Alighieri*, Volume 1: *Inferno*, ed. and tr. R. M. Durling (New York and Oxford: Oxford University Press).

Dante Alighieri (1997), *Dante Alighieri: Commedia con il commento di Anna Maria Chiavacci Leonardi*, 3 vols. (Milan: Mondadori).

Dante Alighieri (2002), *The Inferno of Dante Alighieri: A new translation by Ciaran Carson* (London and New York: Granta).

Dante Alighieri (2013), *The Divine Comedy by Dante. Translated by Clive James* (New York: Liveright Publishing).

Da Ponte, L. (1918), *Memorie*, ed. G. Gambarin and F. Nicolini, 2 vols. (Bari: Laterza).

Da Ponte, L. (1929), *Memoirs of Lorenzo Da Ponte, Mozart's Librettist*, tr. L. A. Sheppard (London: Routledge).

Davie, M. (1994), '"Not an after-dinner relaxation": Gladstone on Translating Dante', *Journal of European Studies*, 24: 385–401.

Davis, N. (2004) (ed.), *The Paston Letters and Papers of the Fifteenth Century*, part II (Oxford: Early English Text Society and Oxford University Press).

Dawson, C. M. (2012), '"The Horror! The Horror!": Traumatic Repetition in Joseph Conrad's *Heart of Darkness* and Mark Z. Danielewski's *House of Leaves*', *Postgraduate English*, 25: 1–31.

De la Mare, A. C. (1982), 'Further Manuscripts from Holkham Hall', *Bodleian Library Record*, 10: 327–34.

De la Mare, A. C. (1985), 'Further Illuminated Manuscripts in the Bodleian Library', in *La Miniatura italiana tra gotico e Rinascimento*, ed. E. Sesti, 2 vols. (Florence: Olschki) 127–54.

Del Lungo, I. (1881), *Dell'esilio di Dante, discorso commemorativo* (Florence: Successori Le Monnier).

Del Virgilio, G. (1902), *Dante and Giovanni del Virgilio: Including a Critical Edition of the text of Dante's "Eclogae Latinae" and of the poetic remains of Giovanni del Virgilio*, ed. P. H. Wicksteed and E. G. Gardner (Westminster, Colo.: Constable).

De Mornay, P. (1612), *The mysterie of iniquitie: that is to say, the historie of the papacie*, tr. Samson Lennard (London: Adam Islip).

De Palacio, J. (1969), *Mary Shelley dans son oeuvre* (Paris: Klincksieck).

De Ricci, S. (1930), *English Collectors of Books and Manuscripts (1530–1930) and their Marks of Ownership* (Cambridge: Cambridge University Press).

De Ricci, S. (1932) (ed.), *A Handlist of the Manuscripts in the Library of the Earl of Leicester at Holkham Hall* (Oxford: Bibliographical Society).

De Rooy, R. (2011), 'A Cardboard Dante: Hell's Metropolis Revisited', in Gragnolati *et al.* (2011) (eds.), 355–65.

De Sua, W. (1964), *Dante into English* (Chapel Hill, N.C.: University of North Carolina Press).

Dibdin, T. F. (1814–15), *Bibliotheca Spenceriana or a Descriptive Catalogue of the books printed in the Fifteenth Century and of many valuable first editions in the library of George John Earl Spencer K.G.*, 4 vols. (London: Longman Hurst *et al.*).

Di Cesare, M. A. (1991) (ed.), *Milton in Italy: Contexts, Images, Contradictions* (Binghamton, N.Y.: MARTS).

Digby, Sir K. (1827), *Private Memoirs of Sir Kenelm Digby*, ed. N. H. Nicolas (London: Saunders & Otley).

Dimock, W. C. (2001), 'Literature for the Planet', *PMLA* 116.1: 173–88.

Duckworth, M. R. (2006), 'Everyday Infernos: *The Divine Comedy* in Australian Literature and Art', paper given at the International Medieval Conference, Leeds, 10 July 2006 (unpublished).

Duckworth, M. R. (2009), 'Medievalism and the Language of Belonging in Selected Works of Les Murray, Randolph Stow, Francis Webb and Kevin Hart', Ph.D thesis, University of Leeds.

Dupont, C. Y. (2012), 'Charles Eliot Norton and the Rationale for American Dante Studies', in Audeh and Havely (2012) (eds.), 248–65.

Eberle-Sinatra, M. (2005), *Leigh Hunt and the London Literary Scene: A Reception History of his Works, 1805–1828* (London: Routledge).

Edgecombe, R. S. (1994), *Leigh Hunt and the Poetry of Fancy* (London and Toronto: Associated University Presses).

Edwards, R. R. (2002), *Chaucer and Boccaccio: Antiquity and Modernity* (Basingstoke: Palgrave).

Elam, K. D. (1994), 'Dead Heads: Damnation Narrative in the "Dramaticules"', in *The Cambridge Companion to Beckett*, ed. J. Pilling (Cambridge: Cambridge University Press), 145–66.

Eliot, T. S. (1929), *Dante* (London: Faber & Faber).

Eliot, T. S. (1971), *The Waste Land: A Facsimile and Transcript of the Original Drafts, including the Annotations by Ezra Pound*, ed. V. Eliot (London: Faber & Faber).

Ellis, S. (1983), *Dante and English Poetry: Shelley to T. S. Eliot* (Cambridge: Cambridge University Press).

Ellis, S. (1988), 'Chaucer, Dante and Damnation', *Chaucer Review*, 22: 282–94.

Elton, G. R. (1972), *Policy and Police: The Enforcement of the Reformation in the Age of Thomas Cromwell* (Cambridge: Cambridge University Press).

Esposito, E. (1982), 'Panizzi dantologo', in *Atti del convegno di studi su Antonio Panizzi (Roma, 21–22 aprile 1980)*, ed. E. Esposito (Galatina: Salentina), 67–106.

Esposito, E. (1992) (ed.), *L'opera di Dante nel mondo: edizioni e traduzioni nel Novecento* (Ravenna: Longo).

Eubel, K. (1897), 'Vom Zaubereiunwesen anfangs des 14. Jahrhunderts', *Historisches Jahrbuch* 18: 608-31.

Evans, G. (2003), 'The Hamilton Collection and the 10th Duke of Hamilton', *Journal of the Scottish Society for Art History*, 8: 53–72.

Evans, G. (2009), 'The Restoration and Enlargement of Hamilton Palace by the 10th Duke of Hamilton, 1806–32', *Review of Scottish Culture*, 21: 35–66.

Evans, G. (2012), 'In the Shadow of Jacques-Louis David's *Napoleon*: The 10th Duke of Hamilton and Raeburn', in *Henry Raeburn: Context, Reception and Reputation*, ed. V. Coltman and S. Lloyd (Edinburgh: Edinburgh University Press), 122–52.

Ewals, L. (1980), 'La Carrière d'Ary Scheffer', in *Ary Scheffer, 1795–1858: dessins, aquarelles, esquisses à l'huile: [exposition], 16 octobre–30 novembre 1980* (Paris: Institut néerlandais), [introduction].

Fabi, M. G. (2001), *Passing and the Rise of the African American Novel* (Urbana, Ill.: University of Illinois Press).

Fagan, L. (1880*a*), *The Life of Sir Anthony Panizzi K.C.B.*, 2 vols. (London: Remington).

Fagan, L. (1880*b*) (ed.), *Lettere ad Antonio Panizzi di uomini illustri e di amici* (Florence: Barbèra).

Faithfull, R. G. (1953), 'The Concept of "Living Language" in Cinquecento Vernacular Philology', *Modern Language Review*, 48: 278–92.

Falconieri, T. (2002), *Cola di Rienzo* (Rome: Salerno).

Farinelli, A. (1908), *Dante e la Francia dall'età media al secolo di Voltaire*, 2 vols. (Milan: Hoepli).

Farrell, J. (1999), 'The Afterlife of Francesca da Rimini', *Italia and Italy*, 1: 3–6.

Faucon, M. (1886), *La Librarie des papes d'Avignon* (Paris: Thorin).

Favaro, A. (1900) (ed.), *Le opere di Galileo Galilei*, 10 (Florence: Barbèra).

Favaro, A. (1901), *Le opere di Galileo Galilei*, 11 (Florence: Barbèra).

Favaro, A. (1911), *Amici e corrispondente di Galileo Galilei: XXV.—Tommaso Segeth* (Venice: Ferrari).

Fetherstone/Featherstone, H. (1628), *Catalogus librorum in diversis locis Italiae Emptorum, Anno 1628* (London: Typis Iohannis Legati).

Figueredo, C. (2004), 'Illuminating the *Divine Comedy*: A Reading of the Illustrations of Bodleian MS Holkham misc. 48', MA dissertation, University of York.

Firpo, L. (1969), 'Dante e Campanella', *L'Alighieri*, 10: 31–46.

Fitzgerald, R. (1985), 'Mirroring the *Commedia*: An Appreciation of Laurence Binyon's version', in McDougal (1985) (ed.), 153–75.

Flacius, M. (1556), *Catalogus testium veritatis qui ante nostram aetatem reclamarunt Papae* (Basel: Oporinus [Johann Herbst]).

Flacius, M. (1562), *Catalogus testium veritatis qui ante nostram aetatem reclamarunt Papae* (enlarged edn., Strasbourg: Machaeropeus).

Fletcher, W. Y. (1902), *English Book Collectors* (London: Kegan Paul, Trench, Trübner).

Foscolo, U. (1818*a*), 'Art[icle]. IX. *Dante: with a new Italian Commentary*. By G. Biagioli . . . *The Vision of Dante*. Translated by the Reverend H.F. Cary', *Edinburgh Review*, 29: 453–74.

Foscolo, U. (1818*b*), 'Art[icle]. II. *Osservazioni Intorno alla Questione sopra la Originalita del Poema di Dante. Di* F. Cancellieri', *Edinburgh Review*, 30: 317–51.

Foscolo, U. (1825), *Discorso sul testo e su le opinioni diverse prevalenti intorno alla storia e alla emendazione critica della Commedia di Dante* (London: Pickering).

Foscolo, U. (1850–), *Opere edite e postume*, ed. F. S. Orlandi and E. Mayer (Florence: Le Monnier).

Foscolo, U. (1991), *Ultime lettere di Jacopo Ortis*, ed. W. Binni and L. Felici (Milan: Garzanti).

Fowlie, W. (1985), 'Dante and Beckett', in McDougal (1985) (ed.), 128–52.

Foxe, J. (1570), *The Ecclesiasticall history contaynyng the Actes and Monumentes of thynges passed in euery kynges tyme in this Realme especially in the Church of England. Newly recognised and inlarged* (London: John Day).

Francini, A. (2011), 'Transferring Dante: Robert Rauschenberg's Thirty-Four Illustrations for the *Inferno*', in Gragnolati *et al.* (2011) (eds.), 323–37.

Frank, C. B. M. (1990), 'Untersuchungungen zum *Catalogus testium veritatis* des Matthias Flacius Illyricus', Ph.D thesis, Tübingen; self-published.

Friederich, W. P. (1950), *Dante's Fame Abroad, 1350–1850: The Influence of Dante Alighieri on the Poets and Scholars of Spain, France, England, Germany, Switzerland and the United States* (Chapel Hill, N.C.: University of North Carolina Press).

Frontain, R. J. (2003), 'Donne's Protestant *Paradiso*: The Johannine Vision of the *Second Anniversary*', in *John Donne and the Protestant Reformation: New Perspectives*, ed. M. A. Papazian (Detroit, Mich.: Wayne State University Press), 113–42.

Frova, A. and Marenzana, M. (2011) (eds., tr. J. McManus), *Thus Spoke Galileo: The Great Scientist's Ideas and their Relevance to the Present Day* (Oxford: Oxford University Press).

Fryde, E. B. (1983), *Studies in Medieval Trade and Finance* (London: Hambledon Press).

Fulford, R. (1981) (ed.), *Beloved Mama: Private Correspondence of Queen Victoria and the German Crown Princess, 1878–1885* (London: Evans Brothers).

Furnas, J. C. (1982), *Fanny Kemble: Leading Lady of the Nineteenth-Century Stage* (New York: The Dial Press).

Gabrieli, V. (1957), *Sir Kenelm Digby: un inglese italianato nell'età della Controriforma* (Rome: Edizioni di storia e letteratura).

Galloway, A. (2011), 'The Account Book and the Treasure: Gilbert Maghfeld's Textual Economy and the Poetics of Mercantile Accounting in Ricardian Literature', *Studies in the Age of Chaucer*, 33: 65–124.

Gialluca, B. and Reynolds, S. (2009), 'Il manoscritto Holkham Hall MS 809 e la genesi del *De Etruria regali*: novità e conferme', *Symbolae antiquariae*, 2: 9–60.

Giamatti, A. B. (1983) (ed.), *Dante in America: The First Two Centuries* (Binghamton, N.Y.: Medieval & Renaissance Texts and Studies).

Giambullari, P. F. (1544), *Pierfrancesco Giambullari accademico Fior[entino]. Del Sito, Forma, & Misure dello Inferno di Dante* (Florence: Neri Dortelata).

Giffin, M. (1956), *Studies on Chaucer and his Audience* (Hull, Québec: L'Éclair).

Gilson, S. A. (2005), *Dante and Renaissance Florence* (Cambridge: Cambridge University Press).

Ginsberg, W. (2002), *Chaucer's Italian Tradition* (Ann Arbor, Mich.: University of Michigan Press).

Girardi, E. N. (2003), 'Dante in the Poetic Theory and Practice of Tommaso Campanella', in Haywood (2003*a*) (ed.), 105–25.

Gizzi, C. (1985) (ed.), *Füssli e Dante* (Milan: Mazzotta).

Gladstone, W. E. (1838), *The State in its Relations with the Church*, 2 vols. (London: Murray).

Gladstone, W. E. (1844), 'Art[icle]. V.—Lord John Russell's Translation of the "Francesca da Rimini," from the *Inferno* of Dante, Canto V. 73–142. In the "*Literary Souvenir*" for 1844', *English Review or Quarterly Journal of Ecclesiastical and General Literature*, 1: 164–80.

Gladstone, W. E. (1892), 'Did Dante Study at Oxford', *Nineteenth Century*, 31: 1032–42.

Gordon, B. (1996) (ed.), *Protestant History and Identity in Sixteenth-Century Europe*, 2 vols. (Aldershot: Scolar Press).

Gotch, R. B. (1937) *Maria Lady Callcott* (London: John Murray).

Grabmann, M. (1931), 'Das *Defensorium ecclesiae* des Magister Adam, eine Streitschrift gegen Marsilius von Padua und Wilhelm von Ockham', in *Festschrift Albert Brackmann*, ed. L. Santifaller (Weimar: Böhlau), 569–81.

Gragnolati, M. *et al.* (2011) (eds.), *Metamorphosing Dante: Appropriations, Manipulations, and Rewritings in the Twentieth and Twenty-First Centuries* (Berlin and Vienna: Turia and Kant).

Gransden, A. (1974–82) *Historical Writing in England*, 2 vols. (London: Routledge & Kegan Paul).

Graver, B. (2011), 'Sitting in Dante's Throne: Wordsworth and Italian Nationalism', in Burwick and Douglass (2011) (eds.), 29–37.

Grieben, H. (1869), 'Ein Dante Codex in der Capstadt', *Jahrbuch der Deutschen Dante-Gesellschaft*, 2: 239–44.

Griffith, T. G. (1966), 'Italy and Wales', *Transactions of the Honourable Society of Cymmrodorion*, 75. 2: 281–98.

Griffith, T. G. (1971), 'The Yeast of Mazzini', in Aquilecchia *et al.* (1971) (eds.), 277–302.

Griffith, T. G. (2000), 'Italian Nationalism, Welsh Liberalism, and the Welsh Translation of the Divina Commedia', in McLaughlin (2000) (ed.), 32–44.

Griffiths, E. and Reynolds, M. (2005) (eds.), *Dante in English* (London: Penguin).

Grimm, H. J. (1973), *The Reformation Era* (New York: Macmillan).

Gualdo, P. (1607), *Vita Joannis Vincentii Pinelli* (Augsburg: Christophorus Mangus).

Guidi-Bruscoli, F. (2014) 'Creating Networks through Languages: Italian Merchants in Late Medieval and Early Modern Europe', in *Commercial Networks and European Cities, 1400–1800*, ed. A. Caracausi and C. Jeggle (London: Pickering and Chatto).

Haight, G. S. (1954), *George Eliot Letters* (London: Oxford University Press).

Halpern, D. (1993) (ed.), *Dante's 'Inferno': Translations by 20 Contemporary Poets* (New York: Ecco Press).

Harrison, C. and Newall, C. (2010) (eds.), *The Pre-Raphaelites and Italy* (Oxford: Ashmolean Museum).

Harvey, M. (1985), 'John Whethamstede, the Pope and the General Council', in *The Church in Pre-Reformation Society: Essays in Honour of F. R. H. Du Boulay*, ed. C. M. Barron and C. Harper-Bill (Woodbridge and Dover, N.H.: Boydell Press), 108–22.

Harvey, M. (1999), *The English in Rome, 1362–1420: Portrait of an Expatriate Community* (Cambridge: Cambridge University Press).

Harvie, C. (2002), *Scotland: A Short History* (Oxford: Oxford University Press).

Hassall, W. O. (1950*a*), *The Books of Sir Christopher Hatton at Holkham* (London: Bibliographical Society).

Hassall, W. O. (1950*b*) (ed.), *A Catalogue of the Library of Sir Edward Coke* (New Haven, Conn. and London: Yale University Press and Oxford University Press).

Hassall, W. O. (1959), 'Portrait of a Bibliophile II: Thomas Coke, Earl of Leicester, 1697–1759', *The Book Collector*, 8: 249–61.

Hassall, W. O. (1970) (ed.), *The Holkham Library: Illuminations and Illustrations in the Manuscript Library of the Earl of Leicester* (Oxford: Roxburghe Club).

Hassall, W. O. (1983), 'Holkham Manuscripts Acquired for the Nation', *Apollo*, 117: 83–6.

Haughton, H. (1998), 'Purgatory Regained? Dante and Late Beckett', in Havely (1998*a*) (ed.), 140–64.

Havely, N. R. (1995), 'Francesca Frustrated: New Evidence about Hobhouse's and Byron's Translation of Pellico's *Francesca da Rimini*', *Romanticism* 1.1: 106–20.

Havely, N. R. (1997), 'Muses and Blacksmiths: Italian Trecento Poetics and the Reception of Dante in *The House of Fame*', in *Essays on Ricardian Literature in Honour of J. A. Burrow*, ed. A. J. Minnis *et al.* (Oxford: Clarendon Press), 61–81.

Havely, N. R. (1998*a*) (ed.), *Dante's Modern Afterlife: Reception and Response from Blake to Heaney* (Houndmills: Macmillan).

Havely, N. R. (1998*b*), '"Prosperous People" and "The Real Hell" in Gloria Naylor's *Linden Hills*', in Havely (1998*a*) (ed.), 211–22.

Havely, N. R. (1999), 'Losing Paradise: Dante, Boccaccio and Mary Shelley's *Valperga*', *La questione romantica*, 7/8: 29–39.

Havely, N. R. (2002), '"This Infernal Essay": English Contexts for Foscolo's *Essay on the Present Literature of Italy*', in *Immaginando l'Italia: Itinerari letterari del Romanticismo inglese*, ed. L. M. Crisafulli (Bologna: CLUEB), 233–50.

Havely, N. R. (2003), '"An Italian Writer Against the Pope"? Dante in Reformation England, *c.* 1560–*c.* 1640', in Haywood (2003*a*) (ed.), 127–49.

Havely, N. R. (2004*a*), *Dante and the Franciscans: Poverty and the Papacy in the 'Commedia'* (Cambridge: Cambridge University Press).

Havely, N. R. (2004*b*), 'Feeding the Flock with Wind: Protestant Uses of a Dantean Trope, from Foxe to Milton', in *John Foxe at Home and Abroad*, ed. D. Loades (Aldershot and Burlington, Vt.: Ashgate), 91–103.

Havely, N. R. (2005), 'The Italian Background', in *Chaucer: An Oxford Guide*, ed. S. Ellis (Oxford: Oxford University Press), 313–31.

Havely, N. R. (2007*a*), *Dante* (Oxford: Blackwell).

Havely, N. R. (2007*b*), 'Francesca Observed: Painting and Illustration, *c*.1790–1840', in Braida and Calè (2007) (eds.), 95–107.

Havely, N. R. (2009) (tr. J.-M. Fournier), '"Un présent d'un si grand prix et d'une telle beauté": le manuscrit de Dante d'Elphinstone et la Literary Society de Bombay', *Synergies Inde*, 4:127–44.

Havely, N. R. (2010), 'From "Goodly Maker" to Witness Against the Pope: Conscripting Dante in Henrician England', *Textual Cultures*, 5: 76–98.

Havely, N. R. (20011*a*) (ed.), *Dante in the Nineteenth Century: Reception, Canonicity, Popularization* (Oxford and Bern: Lang).

Havely, N. R. (2011*b*), '*Francesca Franciosa*: Exile, Language and History in Foscolo's Articles on Dante', in Havely (20011*a*) (ed.), 55–74.

Havely, N. R. (2011*c*), '"Hell on a Paying Basis": Morality, the Market and the Movies in Harry Lachman's *Dante's Inferno*', in Gragnolati *et al.* (2011) (eds.), 269–84.

Havely, N. R. (2012), 'Dante and Early Italian Cinema: The 1911 Milano-Films *Inferno* and Italian Nationalism', in Audeh and Havely (2012) (eds.), 353–71.

Hawkins, P. S. (1999), *Dante's Testaments: Essays in Scriptural Imagination* (Stanford, Calif.: Stanford University Press).

Hawkins, P. S. (2006), *Dante: A Brief History* (Malden, Mass. and Oxford: Blackwell).

Hawkins, P. S. and Jacoff, R. (2001) (eds.), *The Poets' Dante: Twentieth-Century Responses* (New York: Farrar, Strauss & Giroux).

Haywood, E. G. (2003*a*) (ed.), *Dante Metamorphoses: Episodes in a Literary Afterlife* (Dublin: Four Courts Press).

Haywood, E. G. (2003*b*), 'Ariosto on Dante: Too Divine and Florentine', in Haywood (2003*a*) (ed.), 71–104.

Heal, F. (2006), 'Appropriating History: Catholic and Protestant Polemics and the National Past', in *The Uses of History in Early Modern England*, ed. P. Kewes (San Marino, Calif.: Huntington Library), 105–28.

Heaney, S. (1985), 'Envies and Identifications: Dante and the Modern Poet', *Irish University Review*, 15: 5–19.

Heddle, D. (2008), *John Stewart of Baldynneis' 'Roland Furious': A Scots Poem in its European Context* (Leiden: Brill).

Hellinga, L. and Trapp, J. B. (1999) (eds.), *The Cambridge History of the Book in Britain*, III: *1400–1557* (Cambridge: Cambridge University Press).

Hind, A. M. (1938–48), *Early Italian Engraving: A Critical Catalogue*, 7 vols. (London: Quaritch).

Hirsh, J. C. (1977), 'The Politics of Spirituality: the Second Nun and the Manciple', *Chaucer Review*, 12: 129–46.

Hobbins, D. (2009), *Authorship and Publicity Before Print: Jean Gerson and the Transformation of Late Medieval Learning* (Philadelphia, Pa.: University of Pennsylvania Press).

Hobson, A. (1971), 'A Sale by Candle in 1608', *The Library*, 5th ser. 26: 215–33.

Holbrook, R. T. (1921), *Portraits of Dante, from Giotto to Raffael* (London and Boston, Mass.: Medici Society).

Holloway, J. B. (1987), 'Brunetto Latini and England', *Manuscripta*, 31: 11–21.

Holmes, G. A. (1960–1), 'Florentine Merchants in England, 1346–1436', *Economic History Review*, 13: 193–208.

Holmes, G. A. (1996), 'The Medici London Branch', in *Progress and Problems in Medieval England*, ed. R. Britnell and J. Hatcher (Cambridge: Cambridge University Press), 273–85.

Hölter, A and Hölter, E. (2012), 'Dante im Comic', in *Comic und Literatur: Konstellationen*, ed. M. Schmitz-Emans (Berlin and Boston, Mass.: De Gruyter), 17–49.

Horman, W. (1519), *Vulgaria uiri doctissimi* (London: Richard Pynson).

Horne, R. (1566), *An answeare made by Rob. bishoppe of Wynchester, to a booke entituled, The declaration of suche scruples, touchinge the othe of supemacy, as Iohn Fekenham by writing did deliuer unto the L. Bishop of Winchester, with his Resolutions made thereunto* (London: Wykes).

Howlett, D. (1975), 'Studies in the Works of John Whethamstede', D.Phil. thesis, University of Oxford.

Hughes, J. (1992), 'Stephen Scrope and the Circle of Sir John Fastolf: Moral and Intellectual Outlooks', in *Medieval Knighthood IV*, ed. C. Harper-Bill and R. E. Harvey (Woodbridge: Boydell), 109–46.

Humphrey, L. (1584), *Jesuitismi pars secunda: Puritanopapismi* (London: George Byshop).

Hunt, A. (1996), '*Bibliotheca Heberiana*', in *Antiquaries, Book Collectors and the Circles of Learning*, ed. R. Myers and M. Harris (Winchester and New Castle, Del.: St Pauls Bibliographies and Oak Knoll Press), 83–112.

Iannucci, A. A. (1989), 'Dante, Television and Education', *Quaderni d'Italianistica*, 10: 1–33.

Iannucci, A. A. (1998), 'From Dante's Inferno to Dante's Peak: The Influence of Dante on Film', *Forum Italicum*, 32: 5–35.

Iannucci, A. A. (2002), 'The Americanization of Francesca: Dante on Broadway in the Nineteenth Century', *Dante Studies*, 120: 53–82.

Iannucci, A. A. (2004) (ed.), *Dante, Cinema, and Television* (Toronto, Buffalo, N.Y., and London: University of Toronto Press).

Irving, D. (1804), *Lives of the Scotish Poets* (Edinburgh: Lawrie).

Isabella, M. (2006), 'Exile and Nationalism: the Case of the Risorgimento', *European History Quarterly*, 36: 493–520.

Isabella, M. (2009), *Risorgimento in Exile: Italian Émigrés and the Liberal International in the Post-Napoleonic Era* (Oxford: Oxford University Press)

Isba, A. (2006), *Gladstone and Dante* (Woodbridge: Royal Historical Society and the Boydell Press).

Iser, W. (1980), *The Act of Reading: A Theory of Aesthetic Response* (Baltimore, Md. and London: Johns Hopkins University Press).

Jack, R. D. S. (1972), *The Italian Influence on Scottish Literature* (Edinburgh: Edinburgh University Press).

Jack, R. D. S. (1986), *Scottish Literature's Debt to Italy* (Edinburgh: Edinburgh University Press)

James, C. W. (1921) 'Dante Sexcentenary Exhibition at the Norwich Public Library of Dante Manuscripts and Books lent by the Rt Hon. the Earl of Leicester from the Holkham Library' (Norwich: Norwich Public Library Committee).

James, C. W. (1922), 'Some Notes upon the Manuscript Library at Holkham Hall', *The Library*, 4th ser. 2: 213–37.

James, C. W. (1929), *Chief Justice Coke, his Family and Descendants at Holkham* (London: Country Life).

Jarman, D. (1991), *Modern Nature: The Journals of Derek Jarman* (London: Century).

Jarry, L. (1873), 'La Libraire de l'Université d'Orléans', *Mémoires de la Société Archéologique de l'Orléanais*, 12: 422–70.

Jauss, H. R. (1982), *Towards an Aesthetic of Reception*, tr. T. Bahti (Minneapolis, Minn.: University of Minnesota Press).

Jenkins, R. (1995), *Gladstone* (London: Macmillan).

Jenkins, R. (2005), *Fanny Kemble: The Reluctant Celebrity* (London and Sydney: Simon & Schuster).

Jewel, J. (1567), *A defence of the Apologie of the Churche of Englande, an answeare to a certaine booke by M. Hardinge* (London: Wykes).

Johnston, A. (1637) (ed.), *Delitiae Poetarum Scotorum huius aevi Illustrium*, 2 vols. (Amsterdam: Blaeu).

Jones, M. R. (2011), *Radical Pastoral 1381–1594: Appropriation and the Writing of Religious Controversy* (Farnham and Burlington, Vt.: Ashgate).

Jones, R. F. (1953), *The Triumph of the English Language: A Survey of Opinions Concerning the Vernacular from the Introduction of Printing to the Restoration* (Stanford, Calif. and London: Stanford University Press and Oxford University Press).

Jonson, B. (1607), *Volpone or the Foxe* (London: Thomas Thorppe).

Jossa, S. (2012), 'Politics vs. Literature: The Myth of Dante and the Italian National Identity', in Audeh and Havely (2012) (eds.), 30–50.

Joyce, J. (2000), *James Joyce: Occasional, Critical and Political Writing*, ed. K. Barry (Oxford: Oxford University Press).

Jullien de Pommerol, M.-H. and Monfrin, J. (1991), *La Bibliothèque pontificale à Avignon et à Peñiscola pendant le grand schisme d'occident et sa dispersion*, 2 vols. (Rome: École française).

Kay, R. (1998) (ed.), *'Monarchia', Translated with a Commentary* (Toronto: PIMS).

Keach, W. (1998), 'The Shelleys and Dante's Matilda', in Havely (1998*a*) (ed.), 60–70.

Kellas Johnstone, J. F. (1924), *The Alba Amicorum of George Strachan, George Craig, Thomas Cumming* (Aberdeen: University of Aberdeen).

Keller, P. (2000), 'The Engravings in the 1481 Edition of the *Divine Comedy*', in *Sandro Botticelli: The Drawings for Dante's Divine Comedy*, ed. H.-Th. Schulze Altcappenberg (London: Royal Academy), 326–33.

Kelly, H. A. (1989), *Tragedy and Comedy from Dante to Pseudo-Dante* (Stanford, Calif.: Stanford University Press).

Kelly, J. M. (2009), *The Society of Dilettanti: Archaeology and Identity in the British Enlightenment* (New Haven, Conn. and London: Yale University Press).

Kemble, F. (1832), *Francis the First: An Historical Drama* (London: John Murray).

Kemble, F. (1878), *Record of a Girlhood*, 3 vols. (London: Richard Bentley).

Kenyon, F. G. (1897) (ed.), *The Letters of Elizabeth Barrett Browning*, 2 vols. (London: Smith, Elder).

Ker, N. R. (1977), *Medieval Manuscripts in British Libraries*, II: *Abbotsford–Keele* (Oxford: Clarendon Press).

Kerr, D. (2000), 'Sir George Grey and the English Antiquarian Book Trade', in *Libraries and the Book Trade: The Formation of Collections from the Sixteenth to the Twentieth Century*, ed. R. Myers *et al.* (New Castle, Del.: Oak Knoll Press), 85–123.

Keynes, G. (1969), *William Pickering, Publisher: A Memoir and a Check-list of his Publications* (London: Galahad Press).

King, J. N. (1982), *English Reformation Literature: The Tudor Origins of the Protestant Tradition* (Princeton, N.J.: Princeton University Press).

King, J. N. (1993), 'John Bale (21 November 1495–1563)', in *The Dictionary of Literary Biography vol. 132: Sixteenth-Century British Nondramatic Writers*, ed. D. A. Richardson (Detroit, Mich., Washington DC, and London: Gale Research), 27–35.

Kirkham, V. (2004), 'The Off-Screen Landscape: Dante's Ravenna and Antonioni's *Red Desert*', in Iannucci (2004) (ed.), 106–28.

Kirkpatrick, R. (1995), *English and Italian Literature from Dante to Shakespeare: A Study of Source, Analogue and Divergence* (London and New York: Longman).

Koebner, R. (1953), '"The Imperial Crown of This Realm": Henry VIII, Constantine the Great and Polydore Vergil', *Bulletin of the Institute for Historical Research*, 26: 29–52.

Köhler, H. O. (1867), 'Flacius und Dante', *Zeitschrift für die gesammte lutherische Theologie und Kirche*, 28: 684–704.

Kolb, J. (1981) (ed.), *The Letters of Arthur Henry Hallam* (Columbus, Ohio: Ohio State University Press).

Landino, C. (1974), *Cristoforo Landino: scritti critici e teorici*, ed. R. Cardini, 2 vols. (Rome: Bulzoni).

Lane, F. C. (1973), *Venice: A Maritime Republic* (Baltimore, Md.: Johns Hopkins University Press).

Lane Ford, M. (1999), 'Importation of Printed Books into England and Scotland', in Hellinga and Trapp (1999) (eds.), 179–202.

La Piana, A. (1948), *Dante's American Pilgrimage: A Historical Survey of Dante Studies in the United States 1800–1944* (New Haven, Conn. and London: Yale University Press and Oxford University Press).

Laurence, E. A. (2011), 'Exploiting Dante: Dante and his Women Popularizers, 1850–1910', in Havely (2011*a*) (ed.), 281–301.

Lawler, J. (1898), *Book Auctions in England in the Seventeenth Century (1676–1700)* (London: Elliot Stock).

Lawrence, J. (2005), *'Who the Devil Taught Thee so Much Italian?': Italian Language Learning and Literary Imitation in Early Modern England* (Manchester: Manchester University Press).

Leask, N. (1992), *British Romantic Writers and the East: Anxieties of Empire* (Cambridge: Cambridge University Press).

Lehmann, P. (1959), *Erforschung des Mittelalters: Ausgewählte Abhandlungen und Aufsätze von Paul Lehmann*, Band 1 (Stuttgart: Hiersemann).

Leland, J. (1542), *Naeniae in mortem Thomae Viati equitis incomparabilis* (London: R. Wolfe).

Leland, J. (1715), *Joannis Lelandi antiquarii De Rebus Britannicis Collectanea, ex autographis descripsit ediditque Tho. Hearnius*, ed. T. Hearne (Oxford: E Theatro Sheldoniano).

Lerer, S. (1999), 'William Caxton', in *The Cambridge History of Medieval Literature*, ed. D. Wallace (Cambridge: Cambridge University Press), 720–38.

Lewalski, B. K. (1998), 'How Radical was the Young Milton?', in *Milton and Heresy*, ed. S. B. Dobranski and J. P. Rumrich (Cambridge: Cambridge University Press), 49–72.

Lewalski, B. K. (2000), *The Life of John Milton: A Critical Biography* (Oxford and Maiden: Wiley-Blackwell).

Lievsay, J. L. (1969), *The Englishman's Italian Books, 1550–1700* (Philadelphia, Pa.: University of Pennsylvania Press).

Limentani, U. (2000), 'Leone and Arthur Serena and the Cambridge Chair of Italian 1919–1934', in McLaughlin (2000) (ed.), 154–77.

Lindon, J. (1987), *Studi sul Foscolo 'inglese'* (Pisa: Giardini).

Lindon, J. (2000*a*), 'Foscolo as a Literary Critic', in *Reflexivity: Critical Themes in the Italian Cultural Tradition*, ed. P. Shaw and J. Took (Ravenna: Longo), 145–59.

Lindon, J. (2000*b*), 'Dante "intra Tamisi ed Arno" (and Halle-am-Saale): The Letters of Seymour Kirkup to H. C. Barlow', in McLaughlin (2000) (ed.), 121–41.

Lister, A. (1989), 'The Althorp Library of Second Earl Spencer, now in the John Rylands University Library of Manchester: Its Formation and Growth', *Bulletin of the John Rylands Library*, 71.2: 67–86.

Little, A. G. (1938) 'Oxford and the Ordinations of Benedict XII', *Archivum Franciscanum Historicum*, 31: 205–9.

Little, A. G. (1951) (ed.), *Fratris Thomae vulgo dicti de Eccleston: Tractatus De Adventu Fratrum Minorum in Angliam* (Manchester).

Lockwood, S. (1991), 'Marsilius of Padua and the Case for Royal Ecclesiastical Supremacy', *Transactions of the Royal Historical Society*, 6th ser. 1: 89–119.

Loewenstein, D. and Stevens, P. (2008) (eds.), *Early Modern Nationalism and Milton's England* (Toronto: University of Toronto Press).

Lombardi, T. (1987), 'Giovanni Bertoldi da Serravalle tra i grandi cultori di Dante', in *Lectura Dantis Metelliana: Dante e il francescanesimo*, ed. A Mellone (Cava dei Tirreni: Avagliano), 97–124.

Looney, D. (2011), *Freedom Readers: The African American Reception of Dante Alighieri and the* Divine Comedy (Notre Dame, Ind.: University of Notre Dame Press).

Looney, D. (2012), 'Dante Abolitionist and Nationalist in the Nineteenth Century: The Case of Cordelia Ray', in Audeh and Havely (2012) (eds.), 284–301.

Luzzi, J. (2008), *Romantic Europe and the Ghost of Italy* (New Haven, Conn. and London: Yale University Press).

Luzzi, J. (2012), '"Founders of Italian Literature": Dante, Petrarch, and National Identity in Ugo Foscolo', in Audeh and Havely (2012) (eds.), 13–29.

Lyttelton, A. (1993), 'The National Question in Italy', in *The National Question in Europe in Historical Context*, ed. M. Teich and R. Porter (Cambridge: Cambridge University Press), 63–105.

McCall, J. P. (1965) 'Chaucer and John of Legnano', *Speculum*, 40: 484–9.

MacCulloch, D. (2004), *Reformation: Europe's House Divided, 1490–1700* (London: Penguin Books).

McDiarmid, M. P. (1950), 'John Stewart of Baldynneis', *Scottish Historical Review* 29 no. 107: 52–63.

McDiarmid, M. P. and Stewart, J. (1948), 'Notes on the Poems of John Stewart of Baldynneis', *RES* 24 (1948): 12–18.

Macdonell, W. R. (1891), 'The Manuscript of Dante's *Divina Commedia* in the Library of the B.B.R.A.S.', pamphlet (Bombay: Education Society).

McDougal, S. Y. (1985) (ed.), *Dante Among the Moderns* (Chapel Hill, N.C. and London: University of North Carolina Press).

MacFarlane, L. J. (1955), 'The Life and Writings of Adam Easton O.S.B.', Ph.D thesis, 2 vols. University of London.

McGann, J. J. (1996), *The Poetics of Sensibility: A Revolution in Literary Style* (Oxford: Clarendon Press).

McGrath, A. E. (1999), *Reformation Thought: An Introduction* (3rd edn., Oxford: Blackwell).

McInally, T. (2012), *The Sixth Scottish University: The Scots Colleges Abroad, 1575–1799* (Leiden and Boston, Mass.: Brill).

McKay, W. D. and Rinder, F. (1917), *The Royal Scottish Academy 1826–1916* (Glasgow: Maclehose).

MacKenzie, A. (1889) *History of the MacLeods* (Inverness).

Mackintosh, R. J. (1836) (ed.), *Memoirs of the Life of the Right Honourable Sir James Mackintosh*, 2 vols. (London: Moxon).

McLaughlin, M. (2000) (ed.), *Britain and Italy from Romanticism to Modernism* (Oxford: Legenda).

MacMillan, A. (2005), '*L'effetto voluto*: Dantesque Allusion in the Romantic Period', *The Italianist*, 25: 5–34.

McMullan, G. and Matthews D. (2007) (eds.), *Reading the Medieval in Early Modern England* (Cambridge: Cambridge University Press).

Macray, G. D. (1883), *Codices a viro clarissimo Kenelm Digby, Eq. Aur., anno 1634 donatos, complectens, adiecto indice nominum et rerum* (Oxford: Clarendon Press).

Mallett, M. E. and Hale, J. R. (1984), *The Military Organization of a Renaissance State: Venice c. 1400 to 1617* (Cambridge: Cambridge University Press).

Malouf, D. (1976), *Johnno* (Ringwood, Victoria: Penguin Books Australia).

Mandelstam, O. (1991), 'Conversation about Dante', in *Osip Mandelstam: The Collected Critical Prose and Letters*, ed. J. G. Harris, tr. J. G. Harris and C. Link (London: Collins Harvill), 397–451.

Manganiello, D. (1989), *T. S. Eliot and Dante* (Basingstoke: Macmillan).

Markus, J. (1977) (ed.), *Elizabeth Barrett Browning: 'Casa Guidi Windows'* (New York: The Browning Institute).

Martin, R. (1639), *Catalogus librorum, ex praecipuis Italiae Emporiis selectorum per Robertum Martinum* (London: Thomas Harper).

Martin, R. (1650), *Catalogus librorum, ex praecipuis Italiae Emporiis selectorum per Robertum Martinum* (London: Thomas Harper).

Marzot, G. (1969), 'La critica letteraria fra Settecento e Ottocento: Linee, motivi, figure', in *I critici: per la storia della filologia e della critica moderna in Italia*, ed. G. Grana (Milan: Marzorati), 3–176.

Matteini, N. (1958), *Il più antico oppositore politico di Dante: Guido Vernani da Rimini: testo critico del 'De reprobatione monarchiae'* (Padua: CEDAM).

Matthew, H. C. G. (1988), *Gladstone 1809–1874* (Oxford: Oxford University Press).

Mazzocco, A. (1993), *Linguistic Theories in Dante and the Humanists: Studies of Language and Intellectual History in Late Medieval and Early Renaissance Italy* (Leiden, New York, and Cologne: Brill).

Mazzoni, F. (1996), 'William E. Gladstone a Giambattista Giuliani', in *Operosa parva per Gianni Antonini*, ed. D. De Robertis and F. Gavazzeni (Verona: Valdonega), 311–14.

Meek, C. (1978), *Lucca 1369–1400: Politics and Society in an Early Renaissance City-state* (Oxford: Oxford University Press).

Melville, J. (2006) (ed.), *William Dyce and the Pre-Raphaelite Vision* (Aberdeen: Aberdeen City Council).

Mentzel-Reuters, A. and Hartmann, M. (2008) (eds.), *Catalogus und Centurien: Interdiszi-plinäre Studien zu Matthias Flacius und den Magdeburger Centurien* (Tübingen: Mohr Siebeck).

Metcalfe, T. (1995), *Ideologies of the Raj* (Cambridge: Cambridge University Press).

Michel, M. R. (1909), 'Le Process de Matteo et de Galeazzo Visconti', *Mélanges d'archéologie et d'histoire de l'École française de Rome*, 29: 269–327.

Miglio, L. (2001), 'Lettori della *Commedia:* i manoscritti', in *Per correr miglior acque: bilanci e prospettive degli studi danteschi sulle soglie del nuovo millennio*, ed. L. Battaglia Ricci, 2 vols. (Rome: Salerno), 1. 295–323.

Milbank, A. (1998), *Dante and the Victorians* (Manchester and New York: Manchester University Press).

Milbank, A. (2011), 'Dante, Ruskin and Rossetti: Grotesque Realism', in Havely (2011) (ed.), 139–58.

Miller, E. (1967), *Prince of Librarians: Antonio Panizzi of the Britsh Museum* (London: Deutsch).

Miller, J. (2011), 'Man with Snake: Dante in Derek Jarman's *Edward II*', in Gragnolati *et al.* (2011) (eds.), 213–34.

Milner, S. J. (2013), 'Manufacturing the Renaissance: Modern Merchant Princes and the Origins of the Manchester Dante Society', in *Culture in Manchester: Institutions and Urban Change since 1850*, ed. J. Wolff and M. Savage (Manchester and New York: Manchester University Press), 61–94.

Milton, J. (1953–73), *Complete Prose Works of John Milton*, ed. D. M. Wolfe, 6 vols. (New Haven, Conn.: Yale University Press).

Milton, J. (1968), *Complete Shorter Poems*, ed. J. Carey (London: Longman).

Milton, J. (1979), *John Milton: Paradise Lost*, ed. A. Fowler (London: Longman).

Milward, P. (1977), *Religious Controversies of the Elizabethan Age: A Survey of Printed Sources* (London: Scolar).

Milward, P. (1978), *Religious Controversies of the Jacobean Age: A Survey of Printed Sources* (London: Scolar).

Minnis, A. J. (2005), '"Dante in Inglissh": What *Il Convivio* Really Did for Chaucer', *Essays in Criticism*, 55: 97–116.

Minnis, A. J. and Scott, A. B., with Wallace, D. (1991), *Medieval Literary Theory and Criticism c.1100–c.1375: The Commentary Tradition* (rev. edn., Oxford: Clarendon Press).

Modi, J. J. (1892), 'The *Divine Comedy* of Dante and the *Virâf-nâmeh* of Ardâi Virâf', *JBBRAS* 18: 192–205.

Modi, J. J. (1911–12), 'An Iranian Precursor of Dante and an Irish Precursor of Dante', *JBBRAS* 23: 189–216.

Modi, J. J. (1914), *Dante Papers: Virâf, Adamnan and Dante, and Other Papers* (Bombay: privately printed).

Mombello, G. (1971), 'I manoscritti delle opere di Dante, Petrarca e Boccaccio nelle principali librerie francesi del secolo XV', in *Il Boccaccio nelle cultura francese*, ed. C. Pellegrini (Florence: Olschki), 81–209.

Monfrin, J. (1961), 'La Bibliothèque de Matteo della Porta', *Italia medioevale e umanistica*, 4: 223–51.

Moody, A. D. (2007), *Ezra Pound: A Portrait of the Man and His Work*, I: *The Young Genius 1885–1920* (Oxford: Oxford University Press).

Moore, E. (1889), *Contributions to the Textual Criticism of the 'Divina Commedia'* (Cambridge: Cambridge University Press).

Moorman, J. R. H. (1947), 'The Foreign Element among the English Franciscans', *English Historical Review*, 62: 289–303.

Moorman, J. R. H. (1952), *The Grey Friars in Cambridge 1225–1538* (Cambridge: Cambridge University Press).

Moorman, J. R. H. (1968), *A History of the Franciscan Order from its Origins to the Year 1517* (Oxford: Clarendon Press).

More, T. (1981), *A Dialogue concerning Heresies*, ed. T. M. C. Lawler, G. Marc'hadour and R. C. Marius, vol. 6 of *The Complete Works of Saint Thomas More* (New Haven, Conn.: Yale University Press).

Morét, U. (2000), 'An Early Scottish National Biography: Thomas Dempster's *Historia ecclesiastica gentis Scotorum* (1627)', in *A Palace in the Wild: Essays on Vernacular Culture and Humanism in Late-Medieval and Renaissance Scotland*, ed. L. A. J. R. Houwen *et al.* (Leuven: Peeters), 249–69.

Möring, M. (2009), *In a Dark Wood* (London: Fourth Estate).

Morison, R. (1536), *A Remedy for Sedition, wherein are conteyned many thynges, concernyng the true and loyall obeysance, that comme[n]s owe vnto their prince and soueraygne lorde the Kynge* (London: Thomas Berthelet).

Morison, R. (1537) *Apomaxis calumniarum, convitiorumque, quibus Ioannes Cocleus . . . epistola studuit. Authore Ricardo Morisino Anglo* (London: Thomas Berthelet).

Morley, H. P., Lord (1539), *Exposition and declaration of the Psalme, 'Deus ultionum Dominus'* (London: Thomas Berthelet).

Morrison, A. (1976), *The MacLeods—Genealogy of a Clan: Section Five* (Edinburgh: Associated Clan MacLeod Societies).

Mortlock, D. P. (2006), *Holkham Library: A History and Description* (London: Roxburghe Club).

Mortlock, D. P. (2007), *Aristocratic Splendour: Money and the World of Thomas Coke Earl of Leicester* (Stroud: Sutton).

Mottram, S. (2005), 'Reading the Rhetoric of Nationhood in Two Reformation Pamphlets by Richard Morison and Nicholas Bodrugan', *Renaissance Studies*, 19: 523–40.

Mottram, S. (2008), *Empire and Nation in Early Renaissance Literature* (Cambridge: Brewer).

Mumford, I. L. (1971), 'Petrarchism and Italian Music at the Court of Henry VIII', *Italian Studies*, 26: 49–67.

Munby, A. N. L. (1954), *The Formation of the Phillipps Library up to the Year 1840 (Phillipps Studies No. 3)* (Cambridge: Cambridge University Press).

Nardini, L. (1796–8) (ed.), *Saggi di prose e poesie de' più celebri scrittori d'ogni secolo*, 6 vols. (London: Cooper & Graham)

Nassar, E. P. (1994), *Illustrations to Dante's* Inferno (Rutherford, N.J., etc.: Fairleigh Dickinson University Press and Associated University Presses).

Nicholson, R. A. (1943), 'A Persian Forerunner of Dante', *JBBRAS* 19: 1–5.

Nicoletti, G. (2006), *Foscolo* (Rome: Salerno).

Nicoloso, P. (2008), *Mussolini architetto: Propaganda e paesaggio urbano nell' Italia fascista* (Turin: Einaudi).

Nightingale, P. (1995), *A London Mercantile Community: The Grocers' Company and the Politics and Trade of London, 1000–1485* (New Haven, Conn. and London: Yale University Press).

Nolhac, P. de, (1887), *La Bibliothèque de Fulvio Orsini: contributions à l'histoire des collections d'Italie et à l'étude de la renaissance* (Paris: Bouillon et Vieweg).

Nuovo, A. (2007), 'The Creation and Dispersal of the Library of Gian Vincenzo Pinelli', in *Books on the Move: Tracking Copies through Collections and the Book Trade*, ed. R. Myers *et al.* (New Castle, Del. and London: Oak Knoll Press and The British Library), 39–67.

O'Connell, M. R. (1964), *Thomas Stapleton and the Counter-Reformation* (New Haven, Conn. and London: Yale University Press).

O'Connor, A. (2008), *Florence: City and Memory in the Nineteenth Century* (Florence: Città di Vita).

O'Connor, M. (1998), *The Romance of Italy and the English Imagination* (Basingstoke and London: Macmillan).

Ó Cuilleanáin, C. (1984), *Religion and the Clergy in Boccaccio's 'Decameron'* (Rome: Edizioni di storia e letteratura).

Ó Cuilleanáin, C. (2003), 'Dante in *The Zebra-Striped Hearse*', *Quaderni di cultura italiana*, 3: 107–24.

Odložilík, O. (1966), 'Thomas Seget: A Scottish Friend of Szymon Szymonowicz', *Polish Review*, 11: 3–39.

O'Grady, D. (2003), 'Francesca da Rimini from Romanticism to Decadence', in Haywood (2003*a*) (ed.), 221–39.

Okay, C. (2012), 'The Reception of Dante in Turkey through the Long Nineteenth Century', in Audeh and Havely (2012) (eds.), 339–52.

Oliphant, M. (1877), *Dante* (Edinburgh and London: Blackwood).

Olson, O. K. (2002), 'Mathias Flacius (1520–1575)', in *The Reformation Theologians: An Introduction to Theology in the Early Modern Period*, ed. C. Lindberg (Oxford: Blackwell), 83–93.

O'Neill, M. (2011), '"My Vision Quickening": Dante and Romantic Poetry', in Bindman *et al.* (2011) (eds.), 45–66.

O'Neill, T. (1985), 'Foscolo and Dante', in *Dante Comparisons*, ed. E. Haywood and B. Jones (Dublin: Irish Academic Press), 109–35.

Ormond, L. (1975), *Lord Leighton* (New Haven, Conn. and London: Yale University Press).

Ornato, E. (1967), 'Il *De contemptu mortis* di Jean Muret', in *Miscellanea di studi e ricerche sul quattrocento francese*, ed. F. Simone (Turin: Giappichelli), 243–353.

Ornato, E. (1969), *Jean Muret et ses amis* (Geneva: Droz).

Owen, R. (2007), 'The Image of Dante, Poet and Pilgrim', in Braida and Calè (2007) (eds.), 83–94.

Padoan, G. (1959), *L'ultima opera di Giovanni Boccaccio. Le 'Esposizioni sopra il Dante'* (Padua: CEDAM).

Pakula, H. (2006), *An Uncommon Woman: The Empress Frederick* (London: Orion).

Paley, M. D. (2003), *The Traveller in the Evening: The Last Works of William Blake* (Oxford: Oxford University Press).

Palumbo, G. (1966), 'Il codice 492 della Biblioteca di S. Francesco nella Comunale di Assisi', in *Dante e l'Italia meridionale: Atti del congresso nazionale di studi danteschi . . . 1965*, ed. A. and E. Borraro (Florence: Olschki), 463–78.

Palumbo, M. (2004), 'Foscolo lettore di Dante', *Rivista di studi danteschi*, 4: 396–413.

Panaino, A. (2008), 'L'aldilà zoroastriano e quello dantesco', in *Dante e la fabbrica della Commedia*, ed. A. Cottignoli *et al.* (Ravenna: Longo), 171–87.

Pantin, W. A. (1936), 'The *Defensorium* of Adam Easton', *English Historical Review*, 51: 675–80.

Pantin, W. A. (1955), *The English Church in the Fourteenth Century* (Cambridge: Cambridge University Press).

Paolazzi, C. (1989), *Dante e la 'Commedia' nel trecento* (Milan: Vita e Pensiero).

Papi, A. B. (1980) 'Umiliana dei Cerchi: nascita di un culto nella Firenze del Dugento', *Studi francescani*, 77: 87–117.

Parker, D. (1993), *Commentary and Ideology: Dante in the Renaissance* (Durham, N.C. and London: Duke University Press).

Parker, D. and Parker, M. (2013*a*), *Interpreting Dan Brown's 'Inferno': Reading between the Lines* (New York and London: Palgrave Macmillan).

Parker, D. and Parker, M. (2013b), *Inferno Revealed: From Dante to Dan Brown* (New York and London: Palgrave Macmillan).

Parks, G. B. (1954), *The English Traveller to Italy*, 1: *The Middle Ages* (Rome: Edizioni di storia e letteratura).

Parmegiani, S. (2011), *Ugo Foscolo and English Culture* (London: Legenda, MHRA and Maney).

Payton, R. (1995), 'Paradiso XXIX', *Lectura Dantis Virginiana*, 3. 16–17 (Spring–Fall 1995), 435.

Pearce, S. (2011), 'Dante and Psychology in the Late Nineteenth Century', in Havely (2011) (ed.), 221–39.

Persons [Parsons], R. (1603), *A Treatise of the Three Conversions of England from Paganisme to Christian Religion* (Saint-Omer: Bellet).

Persons [Parsons], R. (1612) (completed by Thomas FitzHerbert), *A Discussion of the answere of M. William Barlow D. of Diunity to the booke intituled: The judgment of a new catholike Englishman* (Saint-Omer: English College).

Pesman Cooper, R. (1989), 'Sir Samuel Griffith, Dante, and the Italian Presence in Nineteenth-Century Australian Literary Culture', *Australian Literary Studies*, 14.2: 199–215.

Petrarca, F. (1955), *Prose*, ed. G. Martellotti (Milan: Ricciardi).

Petrarca, F. (1966), *Letters from Petrarch*, ed. M. Bishop (Bloomington, Ind.: Indiana University Press).

Petrarca, F. (1974), *Sine nomine lettere polemiche e politiche*, ed. U. Dotti (Bari: Laterza).

Petrarca, F. (1996), *Francesco Petrarca: Trionfi, Rime estravaganti, Codice degli Abbozzi*, ed. V. Pacca and L. Paolino (Milan: Mondadori).

Petrina, A. (2004), *Cultural Politics in Fifteenth-century England: The Case of Humphrey Duke of Gloucester* (Leiden: Brill).

Petrina, A. (2009), *Machiavelli in the British Isles: Two Early Modern Translations of The Prince* (Farnham and Burlington, Vt.: Ashgate).

Phillips, T. (1973–2012), *A Humument: A Treated Victorian Novel* (5 edns., London: Thames & Hudson).

Phillips, T. (1992), *Works & Texts* (London and Stuttgart: Royal Academy of Arts and Hansjörg Mayer).

Piccard, G. (1980), *Wasserzeichen: Fabeltiere: Greif. Drache. Einhorn* (Stuttgart: Kohlhammer).

Pieri, G. (2007), 'Dante and the Pre-Raphaelites: British and Italian Responses', in Braida and Calè (2007) (eds.), 109–22.

Pite, R. (1994), *The Circle of Our Vision: Dante's Presence in English Romantic Poetry* (Oxford: Clarendon Press).

Pizzoli, L. (2004), *Le Grammatiche di italiano per inglesi (1550–1776): un' analisi linguistica* (Florence: Accademia della Crusca).

Pointon, M. (1979), *William Dyce, 1804–1864: A Critical Biography* (Oxford: Clarendon Press).

Poppi, C. (1994) (ed.), *Sventurati amanti: Il mito di Paolo e Francesca nel l'800* (Milan: Mazzotta).

Postle, M. (1995), *Sir Joshua Reynolds: The Subject Pictures* (Cambridge: Cambridge University Press).

Pound, E. (1954), 'Hell', in *Literary Essays*, ed. T. S. Eliot (London: Faber & Faber), 201–13.

Powell, E. (1902) (ed.), *The Travels and Life of Sir Thomas Hoby… Written by Himself. 1547–1564* (London: Camden Society).

Preger, W. (1859–61), *Matthias Flacius Illyricus und seiner Zeit*, 2 vols. (Erlangen: Theodor Bläsing).

Preston, J. L. (1990), 'Dantean Imagery in *Blue Velvet*', *Literature Film Quarterly*, 18: 167–72.

Pulsoni, C. (1993), 'Il Dante di Francesco Petrarca: Vaticano Latino 3199', *Studi petrarcheschi*, 10: 155–208.

Purves, J. (1940), 'Fowler and Scoto-Italian Cultural Relations in the Sixteenth Century', in *The Works of William Fowler*, vol. III, ed. H. W. Meikle *et al.* (Edinburgh and London: Blackwood), pp. lxxx–cliv.

Putter, A. (1996), *An Introduction to the 'Gawain'-Poet* (London and New York: Longman).

Quaglioni, D. (2011) 'Un nuovo testimone per l'edizione della "Monarchia" di Dante: il Ms. Add. 6891 della British Library', *Laboratoire italien*, 11: 231–79.

Queller, D. E. (1986), *The Venetian Patriciate: Reality versus Myth* (Urbana and Chicago, Ill.: University of Illinois Press).

Randall, D. (2008), 'Ethos, Poetics, and the Literary Public Sphere', *Modern Language Quarterly*, 69: 221–43.

Rando, G. (1990) (ed.), *Language and Cultural Identity* (Wollongong, NSW: Dante Alighieri Society).

Ransome, E. (1978), *The Terrific Kemble: A Victorian Self-Portrait from the Writings of Fanny Kemble* (London: Hamish Hamilton).

Raymond, J. (2008), 'Look Homeward Angel: Guardian Angels and Nationhood in Seventeenth-Century England', in Loewenstein and Stevens (2008) (eds.), 139–72.

Reeves, M. (1969), *The Influence of Prophecy in the Later Middle Ages: A Study in Joachimism* (Oxford: Clarendon Press).

Resta, G. (1967), 'La conoscenza di Dante in Sicilia nel tre e quattrocento', in *Atti del convegno di studi su Dante e la Magna Curia… 7–11 novembre 1965*, ed. F. Restivo (Palermo: Centro di studi filologici e linguistici siciliani), 413–24.

Reynolds, M. T. (1981), *Joyce and Dante: The Shaping Imagination* (Princeton N.J.: Princeton University Press).

Reynolds, S. (1982) 'Medieval urban history and the history of political thought', *Urban History Yearbook*, 9: 14–23.

Rhodes, D. E. (1966), 'Some Notes on the Import of Books from Italy into England, 1628–1650', *Studi secenteschi*, 7: 131–8.

Rhodes, D. E. (1987), 'Some Neglected Aspects of the Career of Giovanni Battista Ciotti', *The Library*, 6th ser. 9: 225–39.

Ricci, P. G. (1965), 'Il commento di Cola di Rienzo alla *Monarchia* di Dante', *Studi medievali* (3a serie), 6.2: 665–708.

Richardson, B. (1995), 'Editing Dante's *Commedia*, 1472–1629', in Cachey (1995) (ed.), 237–62.

Riley, H. T. (1870–1), *Annales Monasterii S. Albani a Johanne Amundesham, ut videtur, conscripti*, 2 vols. (London: Longmans Green).

Ringrose, J. (1998), 'The Royal Library: John Moore and his Books', in *Cambridge University Library: The Great Collections*, ed. P. Fox (Cambridge: Cambridge University Press), 78–89.

Rivolta, A. (1933), *Catalogo dei codici Pinelliani dell' Ambrosiana* (Milan: Tipografia Pontificia Arcivescovile).

Robinson, J. C. (2011), '*Purgatorio* in the *Portrait*: Dante, Heterodoxy and the Education of James Joyce', in Havely (2011*a*) (ed.), 261–79.

Robinson, J. C. (2012*a*), 'Nuvoletta and the "Dantellising Peaches": Dante, Femininity, and the Poetic Intertexts of Issy in *Finnegans Wake*', *Joyce Studies Annual 2012*: 208–41.

Robinson, J. C. (2012*b*), 'Uneasy Orthodoxy: The Jesuits, the Risorgimento and the Contexts of Joyce's First Readings of Dante', *Anglia*, 130.1: 34–53.

Robinson, P. (1998), '"Una Fitta di Rimorso": Dante in Sereni', in Havely (1998*a*) (ed.), 185–208.

Roccaro, C. (1987), 'I *sermones* di Ruggero da Piazza', *Schede medievali*, 12–13: 273–94.

Roccaro, C. (1992) (ed.), *Rogerii de Platea, O. Min.: Sermones I* (Palermo: Officina di studi medievali).

Roddewig, M. (1984), *Dante Alighieri, die göttliche Komödie: vergleichende Bestandsaufnahme der Commedia-Handschriften* (Stuttgart: Hiersemann).

Roe, J. A. (1998), 'Foreseeing and Foreknowing: Dante's "Ugolino" and the Eton College Ode of Thomas Gray', in Havely (1998*a*) (ed.), 17–30.

Roglieri, M. A. (2012), 'Dante and Nineteenth-Century Music: Listing and Selective Bibliography', in Audeh and Havely (2012) (eds.), 372–90.

Romano, M. M. (2008), 'Il *Quadrageisimale* di frate Ruggero: *status quaestionis* e proposte di lavoro', *Schede medievali*, 46: 169–77.

Rook, A. (1969), 'Medicine at Cambridge 1660–1760', *Medical History* 13.2: 107–22.

Roscoe, H. (1833), *The Life of William Roscoe*, 2 vols. (London: Cadell and Edinburgh: Blackwood).

Rosen, E. (1949*a*), 'Thomas Seget of Seton', *Scottish Historical Review* 28: 91–5.

Rosen, E. (1949*b*), 'The Correspondence between Justus Lipsius and Thomas Seget', *Latomus: Revue d'études latines*, 8: 63–7.

Rosenblum, R. (1967), *Ingres* (London: Thames & Hudson).

Ross, T. (1991), 'Dissolution and the Making of the English Literary Canon: The Catalogues of Leland and Bale', *Renaissance and Reformation/Renaissance et Réforme*, 26.1: 57–80.

Rossetti, D. G. (2005), *The Correspondence of Dante Gabriel Rossetti: The Chelsea Years, 1863–1872*, III: *1871–1872*, ed. W. E. Fredeman (Cambridge: Brewer).

Rossetti, M. F. (1884), *A Shadow of Dante. Being an Essay towards Understanding Himself, his World and his Pilgrimage* (4th edn., London: Rivingtons).

Rossi, L. (1990), *Le chiose ambrosiane alla 'Commedia'* (Pisa: Scuola Normale Superiore).

Rossiter, W. T. (2010), *Chaucer and Petrarch* (Cambridge: Brewer).

Rotolo, F. (1981), 'Fra Nicolo' Ginco da Agrigento, O. Min.', *Miscellanea francescana*, 81: 516–43.

Roy, W. and Barlow, J. (1528), *Rede me and be nott wrothe for I saye no thynge but trothe* (Strasbourg: Johan Schott).

Roy, W. and Barlow, J. (1546), *The Boke Reade me frynde and Be Not Wrothe* (Wesel and London: Henry Nycolson and Richard Jugge).

Roy, W. and Barlow, J. (1992), *Jerome Barlowe and William Roye: 'Rede Me and be Nott Wrothe'*, ed. D. Parker (Toronto, Buffalo, N.Y., and London: University of Toronto Press).

Ruddock, A. (1951), *Italian Merchants and Shipping in Southampton 1270–1600* (Southampton: University College).

Rumble, P. (2004), '*Dopo Tanto Veder*: Pasolini's Dante after the Disappearance of the Fireflies', in Iannucci (2004) (ed.), 166–75.

Rundle, D. (1995), 'A New Golden Age? More, Skelton, and the Accession Verses of 1509', *Renaissance Studies*, 9.1: 58–76.

Rundle, D. (2004), 'Habits of Manuscript-Collecting: The Dispersals of the Library of Humfrey, Duke of Gloucester', in *Lost Libraries: The Destruction of Great Book Collections since Antiquity*, ed. J. Raven (Basingstoke: Palgrave), 104–24.

Rundle, D. (2013), 'Beyond the Classroom: International Interest in the *studia humanitatis* in the University Towns of *Quattrocento* Italy', *Renaissance Studies*, 27: 534–48.

Ruskin, J. (1851), *The Stones of Venice*, 3 vols. (London: Smith, Elder).

Rutherford, J. (1961), *Sir George Grey KCB . . . A Study in Colonial Government* (London: Cassell).

Ryrie, A. (1996), 'The Problems of Legitimacy and Precedent in English Protestantism, 1539–47', in Gordon (1996), 1. 78–92.

Sager, P. (2002), *East Anglia: Essex, Suffolk and Norfolk* (4th edn., rev., London: Pallas Athene).

Saglia, D. (2007), 'Liberali, libertari e libertini. Dante e la dissidenza romantica', in *Dante e la cultura anglosassone*, ed. D. Saglia *et al.* (Milan: Unicopli), 9–47.

Saglia, D. (2012), 'Dante and British Romantic Women Writers: Writing the Nation, Defining Culture', in Audeh and Havely (2012) (eds.), 184–203.

Salvadori, F. (2005), *The Illustrations for Dante's 'Divine Comedy'* (London: Royal Academy of Arts).

Salvadori, F. (2004) (ed.), *La Divina Commedia commentata da Flaxman* (Milan: Electa).

Sammut, A. (1980), *Unfredo, duca di Gloucester e gli umanisti italiani*, (Padova: Antenore).

Samuel, I. (1966), *Dante and Milton: The Commedia and Paradise Lost* (Ithaca, N.Y.: Cornell University Press).

Sánchez-Jáuregui, M. D. and Wilcox, S. (2012) (eds.), *The English Prize: The Capture of the 'Westmoreland', an Episode of the Grand Tour* (New Haven, Conn. and London: Yale University Press).

Sanders, L. (1908), *The Holland House Circle* (London: Methuen).

Sayle, A. (2001), *The Dog Catcher* (London: Sceptre).

Scarisbrick, J. J. (1997), *Henry VIII* (New Haven, Conn. and London: Yale University Press).

Scarpati, C. (1977), 'Nota sulla fortuna editoriale del Boccaccio. I volgarizzzamenti cinque-centeschi delle opere latine', in *Boccaccio in Europe: Proceedings of the Boccaccio Conference, Louvain, December 1975*, ed. G. Tournoy (Leuven: Leuven University Press).

Scattergood, J. (1983) (ed.), *John Skelton: The Complete English Poems* (Harmondsworth: Penguin Books).

Schiaffini, I. (2007), 'From Hell to Paradise or the Other Way Round? Salvador Dalí's *Divina Commedia*', in Braida and Calè (2011) (eds.), 141–50.

Schildgen, B. D. (2002), 'Dante in India: Sri Aurobindo and *Savitri*', *Dante Studies*, 120: 83–98.

Schildgen, B. D. (2012), 'Dante and the Bengali Renaissance', in Audeh and Havely (2012) (eds.), 323–38.

Schless, H. (1984), *Chaucer and Dante: A Revaluation* (Norman, Okla.: Pilgrim Books).

Schlueter, J. (2011), *The Album Amicorum and the London of Shakespeare's Time* (London: British Library).

Schuchman, A. M. (1997), 'The Cult of Umiliana de' Cerchi (1219–1246)', *Essays in Medieval Studies*, 14, online at <http://www.illinoismedieval.org/ems/V14.html>, accessed 11 March 2014.

Schulckenius, A. (1613), *Apologia Adolphi Schulckenii Geldiensis* [. . .] *Pro Illustrio Domino D. Roberto Bellarmino* [. . .] *Adversus librum falsò inscriptum, Apologia Card. Bellarmini Pro iure Principum, &c. Auctore Rogero Widdringtono Catholico Anglo* (Cologne: Hemmerden).

Schumacher, T. L. (1993), *The Danteum: Architecture, Poetics, and Politics under Italian Fascism* (London: Triangle Architectural Publishing).

Schuster, L. A. (1973) (ed.), *The Confutation of Tyndale's Answer*, in Vol. 8 of *The Complete Works of Saint Thomas More*, 3 vols. (New Haven, Conn. and London: Yale University Press).

Scorrano, L. (2001), *Il Dante 'fascista': saggi, letture, note dantesche* (Ravenna: Longo).

Scott, W. B. (1850), *A Memoir of David Scott RSA* (Edinburgh: A & C Black).

Scotti, M. (1972), 'I primi cinque anni del Foscolo inglese, attraverso l'epistolario', *Atti e memorie dell' Arcadia* (ser.3^A), 5.4: 93–118.

Seally, J. (1788), *The Lady's Encyclopedia or a Concise Analysis of the Belles Lettres the Fine Arts and the Sciences in Three Volumes, Illustrated with Fifty Engraved Heads and Thirty-Four Maps*, 3 vols. (London and Edinburgh: J. Murray and W. Creech).

Seget, T. (1607), *Thomae Segheti Britanni Meletemata Ypogeia* (Hanau: Marnius).

Seget, T. (1611), *Thomae Segheti Britanni Idyllia duo* (Cracow: Andreas Petricovius).

Seget, T. (1622), *Thomas Segethus a gravi calumnia vindicatus* (Magdeburg: Mauritius Voigt).

Seget, T. (completed by Jan de Laet) (1628), *De principatibus Italiae: Tractatus varij* (Leiden: Elzevir).

Serravalle, G. B. da (1891), *Fratris Iohannis de Serravalle . . . Translatio et comentum totius libri Dantis Aldigherii*, ed. M. Da Civezza and T. Domenichelli (Prato: Giacchetti).

Shannon, R. (1974), *The Crisis of Imperialism 1865–1915* (London: Hart Davis, MacGibbon).

Shannon, R. (1984), *Gladstone 1809–1865* (London: Methuen).

Sharpe, R. *et al.* (1996), *Corpus of British Medieval Library Catalogues*, 4: *English Benedictine Libraries: The Shorter Catalogues* (London: British Library and British Academy).

Shaw, G. (2009), 'The British Book in India', in *The Cambridge History of the Book in Britain*, Vol. V: *1695–1830*, ed. M. F. Suarez and M. L. Turner (Cambridge: Cambridge University Press), 560–75.

Shaw, P. (1974–5), 'La versione ficiniana della "Monarchia', *Studi danteschi*, 51: 289–408.

Shaw, P. (2011), 'Un secondo manoscritto londinese della *Monarchia*', *Studi danteschi*, 76: 223–64.

Shell, A. (1999), *Catholicism, Controversy and the English Literary Imagination, 1558–1660* (Cambridge: Cambridge University Press).

Shelley, M. (1987), *The Journals of Mary Shelley 1814–1844*, ed. P. R. Feldman and D. Scott-Kilvert, 2 vols. (Oxford: Clarendon Press).

Shelley, M. (1996), *Valperga or, The Life and Adventures of Castruccio, Prince of Lucca*, ed. N. Crook (London: Pickering &Chatto).

Shelley, M. (1997), *Valperga or, The Life and Adventures of Castruccio, Prince of Lucca*, ed. S. Curran (Oxford: Oxford University Press).

Shoaf, R. A. (1995), '"Noon English Digne": Dante in Late Medieval England', in Cachey (1995) (ed.), 189–203.

Simone, F. (1961), *Il rinascimento francese: studi e ricerche* (Turin: Società editrice internazionale).

Simonini, R. C. (1952), *Italian Scholarship in Renaissance England* (Chapel Hill, N.C.: University of North Carolina Press).

Simpson, J. (2002), *The Oxford English Literary History*, Vol. 2. *1350–1547: Reform and Cultural Revolution* (Oxford: Oxford University Press).

Sismondi, J. C. L. (1819), *Histoire des républiques italiennes du moyen âge* (Paris: Nicolle).

Slarke E. (2005), 'Dante in Australian Cultural History', in *History in Words and Images: Proceedings of the Conference on Historical Representation . . . 26–28 September 2002*, ed. H. Salmi (Turku, Finland: Dept of History), 94–108.

Smith, G. (2000), *The Stone of Dante and Later Florentine Celebrations of the Poet* (Florence: Olschki).

Smith, G. (2012), 'The Holy Stone where Dante Sat: Memory and Oblivion', in Audeh and Havely (2012) (eds.), 89–110.

Smith, L. P. (1907), *The Life and Letters of Sir Henry Wotton*, 2 vols. (Oxford: Clarendon Press).

Sottili, A. (1966), 'Tracce petrarchesche a Colonia', in *Köln und Italien* (Cologne: Italienische Institut), 109–20.

Sowerby, T. A. (2006), 'A Brave Knight and Learned Gentleman: The Careers of Sir Richard Morison (*c*.1513–1556)', D.Phil. thesis, University of Oxford.

Sowerby, T. A. (2010), *Renaissance and Reform in Tudor England: The Careers of Sir Richard Morison* (Oxford: Oxford University Press).

Spaggiari, W. (2005), 'The Canon of the Classics: Italian Writers and Romantic-period Anthologies of Italian Literature in Britain', in *British Romanticism and Italian Literature: Translating, Reviewing, Re-writing*, ed. L. Bandiera and D. Saglia (Amsterdam and New York: Rodopi).

Spaggiari, W. (2006), 'Panizzi, Rolandi e gli esuli italiani a Londra', in *I fratelli Rolandi di Quarona . . . editori e librai a Londra: Atti del convegno, Quarona 15 dicembre 2001*, ed. F. Tonella Regis (Borgosesia: Società valsesiana di cultura), 35–49

Spear, P. (1963), *The Nabobs: A Study of the Social Life of the English in Eighteenth Century India* (London: Curzon).

Spear, P. (1965), *A History of India*, Vol. 2 (Harmondsworth: Penguin).

Spears, M. K. (1985), 'The Divine Comedy of W. H. Auden', in McDougal (1985) (ed.), 82–101.

Speight, K. (1961–2), 'The John Rylands Library Dante Collection', *Bulletin of the John Rylands Library*, 44: 175–212.

Spohr, H. O. (1962), 'The Grey Collection a Century Ago', *QBSAL* 17.1: 5–16.

Spufford, P. (2002), *Power and Profit: The Merchant in Medieval Europe* (London: Thames & Hudson).

Stanford, W. B. and Finopoulos, E. J. (1984) (eds.), *The Travels of Lord Charlemont in Greece and Turkey, 1749* (London: A. G. Leventis Foundation).

Stanhope, P. H. (1888), *Notes of Conversations with the Duke of Wellington, 1831–1851* (London: Murray).

Stapleton, T. (1567), *A Counterblast to M. Hornes vayne blast against M. Fekenham [. . .] touching, the Othe of the Supremacy* (Louvain: Foulerus).

Stapleton, T. (1600), *Vere Admiranda, seu De Magnitudine Romanae Ecclesiae Libri Duo: editio secunda correctior* (Rome: Mutius).

Starkey, D. (2000), 'An Attendant Lord? Henry Parker, Lord Morley', in Axton and Carley (2000) (eds.), 1–25.

St Clair, W. (2004), *The Reading Nation in the Romantic Period* (Cambridge: Cambridge University Press).

Stead, C. K. (1967), *The New Poetic: Yeats to Eliot* (Harmondsworth: Penguin).

Steyn, C. (2002), *The Medieval and Renaissance Manuscripts in the Grey Collection of the National Library of South Africa, Cape Town*, 2 vols. (Salzburg: Institut für Anglistik und Amerikanistik).

Stoye, J. (1989), *English Travellers Abroad, 1604–1667: Their Influence in English Society and Politics* (rev. edn., New Haven, Conn. and London: Yale University Press).

Straub, J. (2009), *A Victorian Muse: The Afterlife of Dante's Beatrice in Nineteenth-Century Literature* (London and New York: Continuum).

Straub, J. (2012), 'Dante's Beatrice and Victorian Gender Ideology', in Audeh and Havely (2012) (eds.), 204–22.

Stretch, L. M. (1798), *Beauties of History or, Pictures of Virtue and Vice drawn from Real Life; Designed for the Instruction and Entertainment of Youth* (10th edn., London: Dilly, Longman, *et al.*).

Sunstein, E. W. (1989), *Mary Shelley: Romance and Reality* (Boston, Mass.: Little, Brown).

Surtees, V. (1971), *The Paintings and Drawings of Dante Gabriel Rossetti (1828–1882)*, 2 vols. (Oxford: Clarendon Press).

Sushma, V. (1981), *Mountstuart Elphinstone in Maharashtra, 1801–1827* (Calcutta and New Delhi: Bagchi).

Sutcliffe, M. (1592), *Mattei Sutliuii de Catholica, Orthodoxa et Vera ChristiEcclesia Libri Duo* (London: Reg. Typog. [deputies of C. Barker]).

Sutcliffe, M. (1599*a*), *De Pontifice Romano eiusque iniustissimo in Ecclesia dominatione, aduersus R. Bellarminum libri quinque* (London: George Bishop, Ralph Newbery and Robert Barker).

Sutcliffe, M. (1599*b*), *De turcopapismo* (London: George Bishop, Ralph Newbery and Robert Barker).

Sutcliffe, M. (1600), *A briefe replie to . . . N.D.* and *A new Challenge made to N.D.*, 2 parts (London: Arn. Hatfield, 1600).

Sutton, A. (2005), *The Mercery of London: Trade, Goods and People, 1130–1578* (Aldershot and Burlington, Vt.: Ashgate).

Sweet, R. (2007), 'British Perceptions of Florence in the Long Eighteenth Century', *Historical Journal*, 50: 837–59.

Talbot, G. R. S. (2000) (ed.), *Lord Charlemont's History of Italian Poetry from Dante to Metastasio: A Critical Edition from the Autograph Manuscript* (Lewiston, N.Y. and Lampeter: Edwin Mellen Press).

Talbot, G. R. S. (2012), 'Lord Charlemont's Dante and Irish Culture: A Whig Interpretation of Dante at the Turn of the Nineteenth Century', in Audeh and Havely (2012) (eds.), 305–22.

Tambling, J. (2010), 'Recalled to Life: Survival in Dickens and Dante', in *Imagining Italy: Victorian Writers and Travellers*, ed. C. Waters *et al.* (Newcastle: Cambridge Scholars), 115–37.

Tanner, M. (2008), *The Raven King: Matthias Corvinus and the Fate of his Lost Library* (New Haven, Conn. and London: Yale University Press).

Tasso, T. (1968), *La Gerusalemme Liberata*, ed. P. Nardi (Milan: Mondadori).

Taylor, A. (2004), 'Television, Translation, and Vulgarisation: Reflections on Phillips' and Greenaway's *A TV Dante*', in Iannucci (2004) (ed.), 145–52.

Taylor, K. (1989), *Chaucer Reads the 'Divine Comedy'* (Stanford, Calif.: Stanford University Press).

Taylor, R. (1997), *Berlin and its Culture: A Historical Portrait* (New Haven, Conn. and London: Yale University Press).

Terzoli, M. A. (2000), *Foscolo* (Rome: Laterza).

Theinert, H. (1884), 'Die Hamilton'sche Handschriften-Sammlung im Berliner Museum und ihre Beziehungen zur Geschichte des Nachrichten- und Verkehrswesens', *Archiv für Post und Telegraphie*, 15: 449–76.

Thompson, A. (1991), 'George Eliot, Dante, and Moral Choice in *Felix Holt, the Radical*', *MLR* 86: 553–66.

Thompson, A. (2003), 'Dante and George Eliot', in Haywood (2003*a*) (ed.), 199–220.

Thompson, D. and Nagel, A. F. (1972) (eds.), *The Three Crowns of Florence: Humanist Assesssements of Dante, Petrarca and Boccaccio* (New York and London: Harper & Row)

Thorne, R. G. (1986), *The History of Parliament: The House of Commons 1790–1820*. Vol. IV (*Members G–P*) (London: Secker & Warburg).

Thynne, W. (1532), *Workes of Geffray Chaucer* (London).

Tinkler-Villani, V. (1989), *Visions of Dante in English Poetry: Translations of the Commedia from Jonathan Richardson to William Blake* (Amsterdam: Rodopi).

Tissoni, R. (1993), *Il commento ai classici italiani nel sette e nel ottocento (Dante e Petrarca)* (Padua: Antenore).

Tivarekar, K. (1886), *Index to the Transactions of the Literary Society of Bombay and to the JBBRAS* (Bombay: Education Society).

Toynbee, P. J. (1921), *Dante Studies* (Oxford: Clarendon Press).

Trapp, J. B. (1999), 'The Humanist Book', in Hellinga and Trapp (1999) (eds.), 283–315.

Ullmann, W. (1979), 'This Realm of England is an Empire', *JEH* 30.2: 175–203.

Uricchio, W. and Pearson, R. E. (1993), *Reframing Culture: The Case of the Vitagraph Quality Films* (Princeton, N.J.: Princeton University Press).

Usher, J. (2005), 'Petrarca per stillicidio', *Cuadernos de Filogia Italiana*, número extraordinario: 187–96.

Vaisz, I. (1883), 'Un codice dantesco in Ungheria', *GSLI* 2: 358–65.

Varma, S. (1981), *Mountstuart Elphinstone in Maharashtra, 1801–1827* (Calcutta and New Delhi: K. P. Bagchi).

Vasina, A. (1982), 'Dante di fronte ad Avignone', *Letture classensi*, 9/10: 173–89.

Venn, J. and Venn, J. A. (1924), *Alumni Cantabrigienses*, Part 1, vol. 3 (Cambridge: Cambridge University Press).

Verdecchia, E. (2010), *Londra dei cospiratori: l'esilio londinese dei padri del Risorgimento* (Milan: Tropea).

Verduin, K. (1996), 'Dante in America: The First 100 Years', in *Reading Books: Essays on the Material Text and Literature in America*, ed. M. Moylan and I. Stiles (Amherst, Mass.: University of Massachusetts Press), 16–51.

Vergerius, P. P. (1560), *Postremus Catalogus Haereticorum Romae conflatus, 1559 [. . .] Cum Annotationibus Vergerii MDLX* (Pforzheim: Corvinus).

Vickers, K. H. (1907), *Humphrey Duke of Gloucester: A Biography* (London: Constable).

Vickers, N. J. (1995), 'Dante in the Video Decade', in Cachey (1995) (ed.), 263–76.

Viglione, F. (1910), *Ugo Foscolo in Inghilterra (saggi)* (Catania: Muglia).

Vinay, V. (1965), 'Domenico Antonio Ferrari, bibliofilo napoletano in Inghilterra nella prima metà del XVII secolo', in *Studi di letteratura, storia e filosofia in onore di Bruno Revel*, ed. B. Revel (Florence: Olschki), 597–615.

Vincent, E. R. (1938), 'Foscoliana in Hudson Gurney's Diaries', *Italian Studies*, 1.3: 101–7.

Vincent, E. R. (1949), *Byron, Hobhouse and Foscolo: New Documents in the History of a Collaboration* (Cambridge: Cambridge University Press).

Vincent, E. R. (1953), *Ugo Foscolo: An Italian in Regency England* (Cambridge: Cambridge University Press).

Vincent, E. R. (1961), 'Pietro Rolandi', *Italian Studies*, 16: 84–95.

Virgil (1986), *Virgil with an English Translation I: Eclogues, Georgics, Aeneid I–VI*, ed. H. R. Fairclough (Cambridge, Mass. and London: Harvard University Press and Heinemann).

von Dyck, W. and Caspar, M. (1941) (eds.), *Johannes Kepler: Gesammelte Werke*, 4 (Münich: Beck).

von Maltzahn, N. (2008), 'Milton: Nation and Reception', in Loewenstein and Stevens (2008) (eds.), 401–42.

Waagen, G. F. (1854), *Treasures of Art of Great Britain: Being an Account of the Chief Collections of Paintings, Drawings, Sculptures, Illuminated MSS. &c. &c.*, tr. Lady Eastlake; 3 vols. (London: Murray).

Wade Martins, S. (2009), *Coke of Norfolk (1754–1842): A Biography* (Woodbridge: Boydell Press).

Wakelin, D. (2007), *Humanism, Reading, and English Literature 1430–1530* (Oxford: Oxford University Press).

Walker, G. (2005), *Writing Under Tyranny: English Literature and the Henrician Reformation* (Oxford: Oxford University Press).

Wallace, D. (1985), *Chaucer and the Early Writings of Boccaccio* (Cambridge: Brewer).

Wallace, D. (1997), *Chaucerian Polity: Absolutist Lineages and Associational Forms in England and Italy* (Stanford, Calif.: Stanford University Press).

Wallace, D. (1999), 'Dante in Somerset: Ghosts, Historiography, Periodization', *New Medieval Literatures*, 3: 9–38.

Wallace, D. (2007), 'Dante in English', in *The Cambridge Companion to Dante*, ed. R. Jacoff (2nd edn., Cambridge: Cambridge University Press), 281–304.

Warner, G. F. (1893) (ed.), *The Library of James VI. 1573–1583, from a Manuscript in the Hand of Peter Young, his Tutor* (Edinburgh: Scottish History Society).

Watt, D. (1999), 'Literary Genealogy, Virile Rhetoric, and John Gower's *Confessio Amantis*', *Philological Quarterly*, 78: 389–415.

Webb, E. T. (1976), *The Violet in the Crucible: Shelley and Translation* (Oxford: Clarendon Press).

Webb, E. T. (2011*a*), 'Stories of Rimini: Leigh Hunt, Byron and the Fate of Francesca', in *Dante in the Nineteenth Century: Reception, Canonicity, Popularization*, ed. N. Havely (Oxford and Bern: Peter Lang), 31–53.

Webb, E. T. (2011*b*), ' "Syllables of the Sweet South": The Sound of Italian in the Romantic Period', in Burwick and Douglass (2011), 205–24.

Weiss, R. (1936), 'Per la conoscenza di Dante in Inghilterra nel Quattrocento', *Giornale storico della letteratura italiana*, 108: 357–9.

Weiss, R. (1947), 'Lineamenti di una biografia di Giovanni Gigli, collettore papale in Inghilterra e vescovo di Worcester (1434–1498)', *Rivista di storia della Chiesa in Italia*, 1: 379–91

Weiss, R. (1967), *Humanism in England during the 15th Century* (Oxford: Blackwell).

Wheeler, G. W. (1927) (ed.), *Letters of Sir Thomas Bodley to the University of Oxford, 1598–1611* (Oxford: Oxford University Press).

White, J. (1610), *The Way to the True Church* (2nd edn., London: Bill and Barret).

Wicks, M. C. W. (1937), *The Italian Exiles in London, 1816–1848* (Manchester: Manchester University Press).

Wiese, B. (1929), 'Die in Deutschland vorhandenen Handschriften der *Göttlichen Komödie*', *DDJb* 11: 44–52.

Williman, D. (1980), *Bibliothèques ecclésiastiques au temps de la Papauté d'Avignon I* (Paris: Centre national de la recherche scientifique).

Wilson, F. P. (1946), 'A Supplement to Toynbee's *Dante in English Literature*', *Italian Studies*, 3: 50–64.

Windscheffel, R. C. (2008), *Reading Gladstone* (Basingstoke: Palgrave Macmillan).

Woolf, J. (1998), 'Micòl and Beatrice: Echoes of the *Vita Nuova* in Giorgio Bassani's *Garden of the Finzi-Contini*', in Havely (1998*a*) (ed.), 167–84.

Woolfson, J. (1998), *Padua and the Tudors: English Students in Italy, 1485–1603* (Cambridge: James Clarke).

Woolfson, J. (2009), 'Thomas Hoby, William Thomas, and Mid-Tudor Travel to Italy', in *The Oxford Handbook of Tudor Literature 1485–1603*, ed. M. Pincombe and C. Shrank (Oxford: Oxford University Press), 404–17.

Wright, H. G. (1943), *Forty-six Lives translated from Boccaccio's 'De Claris Mulieribus' by Henry Parker, Lord Morley* (London: Early English Text Society and Oxford University Press).

Wyatt, M. (2005), *The Italian Encounter with England: A Cultural Politics of Translation* (Cambridge: Cambridge University Press).

Yates, F. A. (1951), 'Transformations of Dante's Ugolino', *Journal of the Warburg and Courtauld Institutes*, 14: 92–117.

Yousefzadeh, M. (2011), *The City and the Nation in the Italian Unification: The National Festivals of Dante Alighieri* (Basingstoke: Palgrave Macmillan).

Zagonel, G. (1995), *Lorenzo Da Ponte: Lettere, epistole in versi, dedicatorie e lettere dei fratelli* (Vittorio Veneto: De Bastiani).

Zeitlin, J. (1959), 'Thomas Salusbury Discovered', *Isis*, 50: 455–8.

Zeltner, G. G. (1729), *Historia Crypto-Socinismi* (Leipzig: Gleditsch).

Zoppio, G. (1602), *Riprove delle Particelle poetiche sopra Dante disputate dal Sig. I. Zoppio, bolognese/per B. Bulgarini scritte nell'idioma toscano di Siena* (Siena: Bonetti).

Zuccato, E. (1996), *Coleridge in Italy* (Cork: Cork University Press).

ELECTRONIC SOURCES

As the footnotes acknowledge, a large number of websites have been occasionally accessed, and addresses have been provided there. The list below includes only databases which have been frequently consulted.

Dante Society of America, at:
http://www.dantesociety.org

Dartmouth Dante Project, at:
http://dante.dartmouth.edu/

Dictionary of Art Historians ed. Lee Sorensen, at:
http://www.dictionaryofarthistorians.org/

Early English Books Online, at:
http://eebo.chadwyck.com/home

Eighteenth Century Collections Online, Part I and Part II, at:
http://gdc.gale.com/products/eighteenth-century-collections-online/

Oxford Dictionary of National Biography, at:
http://www.oxforddnb.com/

Princeton Dante Project (2.0), at:
http://etcweb.princeton.edu/dante/index.html

The Times Archive, at:
http://www.thetimes.co.uk/tto/archive/

Index

Abbot, George, archbishop of Canterbury, 57
Accarisi, Alberto, 70 n. 16
Adrian V, Pope. *See* Papacy: popes
Agard, John, 274
Aglietti, Francesco, 131
Alfieri, Vittorio, 131, 132 n. 25, 139, 216, 217 n. 113
Alighieri. *See* Dante; Iacopo di Dante; Pietro di Dante
Allen, John, 131, 134
Allen, Thomas, 100
Ambrosiana Library. *See* Milan
Ampère, Jean-Jacques, 189 n. 198, 224
Angiolieri, Cecco, 125
Antaldi, Antaldo, Marchese, 212–13
Anticlericalism, 42–4, 49–50, 55–6 and n. 39, 59–60, 79, 130, 147–8, 187–9
Antipapalism. *See* Papacy: antipapalism
Antonioni, Michelangelo, 295
Aragon, Catherine of, 35, 39–40, 45
Aragon, Juana de, 35
Ariosto, Ludovico, 68, 74, 123, 136
  in book collections and catalogues, 96–7, 100, 103 n. 206, 104, 111, 138
  preferred to Dante, 90, 125, 303
  read with Dante, 67, 76, 98, 115, 147, 197, 288, 301
  references to works:
    Orlando Furioso, 76 and n. 55, 96, 100, 145, 152, 198–9, 204
Aristotle, 73, 183
Armour, Peter, 260 n. 2, 261 nn.6–8, 272
Arnold, Matthew, 168 n. 81
Ashburnham manuscript collection, 241, 248, 254 n. 294
Ashby, George, 36
Asiatic Society of Mumbai. *See* Bombay
Auden, Wystan Hugh, 293, 294, 296
Augustus, Emperor, 38, 40, 42
Avignon, 24–32
  as seat of Papacy, 26–7, 31, 50, 189
  clerics at, 9, 14, 24, 26, 28–30, 32, 284
  Dante's view of Papacy at, 26–7, 189, 304
  Papal library, 29, 31
  Petrarch's criticisms of, 28, 54, 57, 304
  writers at, 24, 26–8, 284

Bacon, Francis, Sir, 94
Baldini, Baccio, 226, 246
Bale, John, 33 n. 5, 46–9, 51, 53–4, 286
Bang, Mary Jo, 298
Baraka, Amiri (LeRoi Jones), 275, 295
Baretti, Giuseppe, 124 n. 342, 196 n. 10, 199, 288

Barker, William, 78
Barksdale, Clement, 300
Barlow, Henry Clark
  and Kirkup, Seymour Stocker, 239–40
  as British representative at Dante Festival, Florence (1865), 266, 292
Barlowe, Jerome, 43–6, 59, 108, 285
Barrett, Elizabeth, 155, 160, 161, 162 n. 49, 217, 230–31, 238
Bartholomew of Pisa, 45
Bartoli, Daniello, 77, 287, 301
Baruffaldi, Girolamo, 111
Bassani, Giorgio, 295
Batty, Elizabeth Frances, 235
Beaufort, Margaret, 39
Beckett, Samuel, 269, 275, 294–5
Beckford, Susan Euphemia, 244
Beckford, William, 244, 265
Beisner, Monika, 273
Bell, Steve, xiv, 282–3 and Fig. 25, 298
Bellarmine, Robert, Cardinal, 56, 63, 88, 93
Bembo, Pietro, Cardinal, 74 n. 44, 100 n. 189, 113, 116
Benedict XII, Pope. *See* Papacy: popes
Benedict XIII, Pope. *See* Papacy: popes
Benedictines. *See* Religious orders
Benigni, Roberto, 269, 282–3, 297–8
Benivieni, Girolamo, 78
Benvenuto da Imola, 16–17, 104 n. 216, 257 n. 316, 284
Berkeley, Henry, 159
Berlin, 246–9, 254–8
  as national capital, 247–8, 255–6
  Kupferstichkabinett, 176, 247, 249
  museums, 245, 247, 249, 251–2
  Royal Library/Staatsbibliothek, 1–2, 7, 11, 243, 247–8, 253, 257
Berlusconi, Silvio, 210, 282
Bernard of Clairvaux, Saint, 47
Bernard, Edward, 95, 104, 113
Bernardino of Siena, Saint, 45
Bertoldi. *See* Serravalle
Bettinelli, Saverio, 125
Biagioli, Niccolò Giosafatte, 139–40, 141 n. 84, 147, 156–7, 222, 290
  See also Foscolo, Ugo; Kemble, Frances ('Fanny')
Binyon, Laurence, 270 n. 64, 279, 294
Birckbek, Simon, 64–5, 105, 263
Birdwood, George, Sir, 206–208, 212
Birk, Sandow, 281 n. 137, 297
Bismarck, Otto von, Count, 251, 256
Blake, William, 125, 155, 217, 273, 290, 293–4
Bleek, W. H. I., 212 n. 89

Index

Blondel, David, 73 n. 41, 75, 301
Boccaccio, Giovanni, 8, 20, 38, 41–2, 56 n. 39,
  57 n. 44, 96 n. 155, 97, 100–1, 103–4,
  107–8, 137, 167–8, 284–6
  as biographer of Dante, 11, 27–8, 52,
    116, 284
  as commentator on the *Commedia*, 28, 74,
    137, 167–8, 261–2, 284
  as one of the 'Three Crowns of Florence',
    21–22, 36, 40, 42, 70–1, 74, 255, 302–3
  at Avignon, 27–8
  manuscripts of his work, 18 n. 54, 38, 88,
    110, 112, 143 n. 97, 212, 255
  references to works:
    De casibus virorum illustrium, 5, 22, 41, 104
    De Genealogiis Deorum, 20, 22, 41, 97, 108
    De mulieribus claris, 40–2, 108 n. 236,
      112, 286
    Decameron, 4, 18 n. 54, 41, 57 n. 44, 88,
      96–7, 98 n. 168, 100, 104, 108 n. 236,
      110, 255
    Fiammetta, 100, 212
    Filocolo, 100, 103 n. 206
    Filostrato, 284
    Teseida, 108 n. 236
    Trattatello in laude di Dante, 27–8, 101, 284
Bode, Wilhelm, 249, 256
Bodley, Thomas, Sir, 98–100
Boiardo, Matteo Maria, 136, 152, 204
Boitani, Piero, xviii, 8 n. 8, 232 n. 184
Boker, G.H., 291
Boleyn, Anne, 39–40
Bologna: British visitors to, 9, 85
  University of, 9, 149, 230, 261, 284, 298
Bombay: British visitors to, 196–7
  Literary Society of, 194–5, 203–4, 211, 290
  Royal Asiatic Society (Bombay branch)/Asiatic
    Society of Mumbai 194–5, 203–10,
    212, 293; *see also* Elphinstone,
    Mountstuart
Bonaparte, Napoleon, 140, 203 n. 44
Boniface VIII. *See* Papacy: popes
Boniface IX. *See* Papacy: popes
Book collectors, 5–7, 17–18, 34–5, 67, 69, 75,
  79, 82, 87–8, 90–96, 99–105, 107,
  109–16, 119–20, 129, 135–6, 141–2
  and n. 89, 286; *see also* Coke, Thomas,
  Baron Lovel, earl of Leicester; Coke,
  Thomas William, earl of Leicester
  (second creation); Digby, Kenelm, Sir;
  Easton, Adam; Elphinstone,
  Mountstuart; Grenville, Thomas, Hon.;
  Grey, George, Sir; Hamilton collection;
  Harley, Edward, second earl of Oxford;
  Heber, Richard; Humfrey of Lancaster,
  duke of Gloucester; Kirkup, Seymour
  Stocker; Mead, Richard; Moore, John,
  bishop of Ely; Pinelli, Gian Vincenzo;
  Scattergood, Anthony; Seget, Thomas;

Spencer, Charles, third earl of
  Sunderland; Spencer, George John,
  second earl; Storer, Anthony; Wotton,
  Henry, Sir
Book-trade, 1–5, 34, 79, 88–9, 95–100, 120,
  126–7, 133, 203–5, 212; *see also*
  Hamilton collection; Florence; London;
  Venice
Borges, Jorge Luis, 277, 295–6
Borromeo, Federico, 87–8
Boschini, G. B., 139, 289
Boswell, Jackson C., 56 n. 36, 63 n. 73, 71 n. 19,
  99 n. 175, *et passim*
Botticelli, Sandro
  illustrations of the *Commedia*, drawings, xiv,
    xvi, 176 and Fig. 12, 177, 194, 226, 227,
    243–8, 250–9, 268, 272, 279, 285,
    290–2; *see also* Hamilton collection
  illustrations of the *Commedia*, engravings, 129
    n. 4, 142, 146, 226–7, 232 n. 181,
    245, 246
Boyd, Henry, 77, 121–2, 124–5, 127, 137–8,
  146, 149, 263–4, 288
Braida, Antonella, 116 n. 298, 117 n. 300, 121 n.
  322, 130 n. 10, n. 14, 135 n. 49, 137 n.
  57, 147 n. 127, 150 n. 147, 264 n. 26
Brand, C. P., 124 n. 340, 128 n. 3, 136 n. 56,
  142 n. 94, 203 n. 44
Bridget, St (of Sweden), 30
Brooke, Francis Capper, Captain, xvi, 215,
  218–24, 226, 230, 236, 238–41; *see also*
  Kirkup, Seymour Stocker; Macleod,
  Isabella
Brown, Dan, xiv, 260, 283, 298
Brown, William Wells, 275
Browne, Thomas, Sir, 101, 102 n. 202
Browning, Robert, 154, 160, 162, 216–17, 238
Brucioli, Antonio, 98
Bruges, 4–6
Bruni, Leonardo, 20, 36 n. 22, 285
Bubwith, Nicholas, bishop of Bath and Wells,
  15–18, 32
Bucer, Martin, 43
Bulgarini, Bellisario, 101 n. 190
Bulteel, John, 302
Buonmattei, Benedetto, 67
Burnet, Gilbert, Bishop, 72, 110, 287, 303
Burney, Charles, 115
Burns, Robert, 196 n. 9
Butler, Joseph, Bishop, 183 n. 156
Butler, Pierce, 159, 160
Byron, George Gordon, Lord, 116, 128–30,
  132, 137, 138 n. 64, 147, 149–51, 158,
  161–2, 183, 185, 196, 262, 290
  references to works
    Childe Harold's Pilgrimage, 129, 196 n. 9
    'Fanny of Rimini' (*Inferno* 5), 150, 290
    Parisina, 158, 196 n. 9
    Prophecy of Dante, 132, 150, 263, 290

Caesar, Michael, xvi, xvii, 23 n. 91, 69–70, 117, 120–1, 265 n. 32 *et passim*
Calabria, 11, 231 n. 17
Calcagnini, Teofilo, 110
Calcutta, 195–7, 201, 203, 210,
Cambridge
  colleges and college libraries, 22, 79, 85–6, 103, 109, 286
  Italians at, 9, 13–14, 284
  study of Italian and Dante at, 79, 158, 264, 271 n. 67
  University Library, 104, 105, 106, 287
Campanella, Tommaso, 69, 72 n. 29, 300
Campion, Edmund, 62
Canonici, Matteo Luigi, 144, 203 n. 44, 289–90
Canonicity. *See* Dante: as canonical author; *Commedia* as canonical text
Cape Town, 194, 212, 213, 292
Capuchins. *See* Religious orders
Carleton, Dudley, 87 n. 112
Carlyle, John, 270, 291
Carlyle, Thomas, 137 n. 58, 154, 157, 164, 191–2, 222 n. 141, 242, 291
Carmelites. *See* Religious orders
Carson, Ciaran, 271–2, 293, 297
Cary, Henry Francis, 135, 137–8, 146, 149, 150 n. 146, 182, 184–5, 236 n. 194, 262–3, 272, 289–90
Casartelli, Charles Louis, Bishop, 208 n. 67, 268 n. 51, 293
Cassell, Anthony, 10 n. 16, 29 n. 117
Castellucci, Romeo, 281–2, 297
Castelvetro, Giacomo, 89 n. 124, 90 n. 133, 94
Castiglione, Baldassare, 37, 71, 79, 96, 100 n. 187, 104
Catalogues
  of auction sales, 99–101, 103, 105, 120, 212, 287, 302
  of booksellers, 96–7, 104, 126, 213, 287, 289
  of collections and libraries, 17–18, 29, 31, 34–5, 38, 80, 87, 94–5, 98–9, 105, 107, 126, 142–3 and n. 97, 194, 212, 244–5, 286–7, 303
Caulfeild, James, earl of Charlemont, 114, 117, 120, 264 n. 30, 288
Cavalcanti, Guido, 116 n. 296, 125
Caxton, William, 35–6, 285
Celestine V, Pope. *See* Papacy: popes
Celotti, Luigi, 203 n. 44
Cervantes, Miguel de, 166 n. 73, 280
Charles I (of England), 85, 87, 94
Chaucer, Geoffrey, 1, 8–10, 13, 15, 18, 26, 29–32, 36–40, 42, 47, 57, 63 n. 72, 71, 74, 263, 284–5
  access to *Commedia*, 4, 18, 34, 262
  as canonical author, 36–9, 53, 74, 108, 262
  early editions as source of references to Dante, 32, 35, 285
  journeys to Italy, 30, 261–2

references to works:
  Canterbury Tales (generally), 4, 8, 16, 24, 262, 285
  Clerk's Tale, 30, 38
  Friar's Tale, 8, 35
  General Prologue, 8
  Monk's Tale, 8, 35
  Plowman's Tale (apocryphal), 42, 300
  Prologue of the Clerk's Tale, 8, 30
  Prologue of the Prioress's Tale, 8
  Prologue of the Second Nun's Tale, 8
  Second Nun's Tale, 30, 31
  Wife of Bath's Tale, 8, 35
  House of Fame, 9, 13, 15, 29, 35, 262, 284–5
  Troilus and Criseyde, 4, 35, 262
Chayamachi, Suguro, 274 n. 94
Childs, Wendy, 7 n. 36, 9 n. 12
Chilmead, Edmund, 300
Ciardi, John, 295
Cicero, Marcus Tullius, 40, 94, 141, 302
Cino da Pistoia, 116 n. 296
Ciotti, Giovanni Battista, 89 n. 124, 94
Clare, John (Jesuit), 57
Clarke, Kenneth P., 8 n. 8, 9 n. 9
Clarke, William, 244–5, 290
Claude, Jean, 302
Claudian, 15
Clement V, Pope. *See* Papacy: popes
Clement VI, Pope. *See* Papacy: popes
Clerke, Bartholomew, 37
Clooney, George, 282
Cocchi, Antonio, 122
Cochran-Patrick, Robert William, 253
Coetzee, J. M., 275
Cohen, Francis, 129
Coke, Edward, Sir, 103 n. 207, 106 n. 227, 107–8
Coke, Thomas, Baron Lovel, earl of Leicester, 105–14, 142, 263, 287
Coke, Thomas William, earl of Leicester (second creation), 143
Cola di Rienzo, 28
Coleridge, Samuel Taylor, 135, 137, 144, 289
Commedia. *See* Dante: references to works: *Inferno*; *Purgatorio*; *Paradiso*
Commentaries. *See* Dante: commentaries on the *Commedia*.
Conrad, Joseph, 274, 277 n. 112
Convivio. *See* Dante: references to works: *Convivio*.
Cope, Charles West, 177 n. 118
Cornelius, Peter, 165
Cotton, Charles, 304
Courtney, Leonard Henry, Baron, 253
Cracow, 84
Craufurd, James, 302
Craven, Augustus, 159
Crisp, N. J., 276 n. 107
Cromwell, James, 297

Cromwell, Thomas, 37, 39, 43, 46
Cunninghame, William (of Lainshaw), 216
Curioni, Antonio, 124–5, 288

D'Annunzio, Gabriele, 293
d'Arezzo, Guittone, 116 n. 296
D'Avity, Pierre, 75, 299
D'Azeglio, Massimo, 230
D'Este, Borso, 110
Da Ponte, Lorenzo, 126, 137, 139, 142, 289
Da Ponte, Paolo, 139
Dacre, Lord, 144–5
Dacres, Thomas, 76 n. 57
Dalí, Salvador, 272 n. 81, 295
Damian, Peter, St, 44, 47, 71, 189
Danielewski, Mark Z., 277
Dante
    and Beatrice, 71, 96, 131, 165, 175–7, 191,
        232, 242, 246, 274–5, 281, 292–3
    and Protestantism, xv, 33, 37, 42, 46–50,
        50–67, 70, 72, 93, 108, 114, 122–3,
        147, 189, 231, 286; *see also* Papacy:
        antipapalism, and Polemic
    and Virgil, 101–2, 121, 131, 155, 200, 236,
        273 n. 88, 277, 294, 301
    as canonical author, 10, 30, 35, 38, 42, 71, 74,
        78, 94, 103, 108, 114, 122, 136, 143,
        194, 243, 263, 268–9, 285, 291
    as one of the 'three crowns of Florence', xv, 22,
        36–7, 40, 42, 71, 74, 302
    as popular author, 260–1, 265, 267, 269, 280
    as prophet of Italian nationalism, 132, 159,
        188, 209, 269
    comic books, allusions to and versions of the
        Commedia in, 273–4
    Commedia as canonical text, 41, 78, 126,
        212, 261
    commentaries on the *Commedia*, 1, 4, 10,
        15–17, 20, 31, 34, 41, 57–9, 71, 79, 80,
        88, 94, 95–8, 100, 103–5, 116–17,
        137–8, 140, 146, 156, 181, 222, 226,
        257, 284–7, 290, 302, 304
    early printed texts of: the *Commedia*, 33–5,
        41–2, 68–9, 71, 79, 90, 95, 97, 99–100,
        103–5, 113, 116, 120, 129, 141, 146,
        226, 258, 263, 285–7, 302
        the *Convivio*, 34, 38, 78, 100, 116, 120,
            129, 146, 285, 287, 302
        the *De vulgari eloquentia*, 286, 120, 129
        the *Monarchia*, 29, 48, 53, 61, 98–9, 286
        the *Vita nuova*, 116, 120, 286
    editions of the *Commedia*: nineteenth-century,
        127, 137–41,147, 152, 157, 181, 202,
        217, 220, 222, 231, 236, 239, 266, 289,
        290, 292; twentieth-century, 270–2,
        291–3
    exhibitions, 207, 249, 266, 293
    films, allusions to the *Commedia* in, 276, 281,
        294–7

illustrations of the *Commedia*, 41, 80, 89–90,
    101, 105–7, 111, 115–7, 120, 137, 142,
    146, 155 , 162, 164, 165, 166, 167, 169,
    171, 174, 176, 177, 206, 214–15, 220,
    221, 222, 223, 226–8, 231–5, 236,
    244–6, 252, 263–4, 268, 272–3, 278,
    283, 285, 288–90, 292–5; *see also*
    Botticelli, Sandro; Dyce, William
    Hamilton collection
illustrations of the *Vita nuova*, 177, 232
introductions to, xiv, 147, 266–7, 292
lectures on, 89, 101, 116, 133–5, 144, 261–2,
    266, 268, 284, 289, 296
manuscripts of: the *Commedia*, xiv–xv, 1–5, 7,
    18, 24, 27, 29, 31, 34–5, 79–81, 87–93,
    95, 98, 104–7, 110–15, 120, 129, 143–4,
    155, 176–7, 194–5, 203, 205–7, 209–10,
    212–13, 223, 228, 240–1, 243–4, 249,
    252, 254, 263, 268, 285–7, 289–93
    the *Convivio*, 106, 241 n. 221
    the *Monarchia*, 23, 28–9, 51
    the *Vita nuova*, 88
merchandise, 266–7, 293
novels, allusions to the *Commedia* in, 73, 151,
    163–4, 265, 269, 274–8, 292–4
passages from the *Commedia* in anthologies,
    121–2, 124–6, 137, 142, 146, 289
performance of the *Commedia*: dance, 297
    film, 279–81, 293–5, 297
    opera, 289, 293 oral performance, 260–1,
        265–6, 269, 296–8
    television, 269, 277, 280
    theatrical, 164, 264–5, 281–2, 291,
        293, 296
portraits and miniatures of, 123, 137, 139,
    160, 175, 206, 212, 214, 218, 239,
    264, 266
references to works:
    Convivio, 8, 28, 34, 38, 76, 78, 100–1, 106,
        113, 116, 120, 129, 146, 241, 263, 267,
        287, 293–4, 302
    De vulgari eloquentia, 120, 129, 181,
        285–6, 293
    Inferno (generally), 13, 29, 58, 89, 120,
        157, 221
    Inferno (canto numbers in bold), **1**, 18, 76,
        138, 148, 182, 226, 286, 299; **2**, 182,
        226, 232, 277; **3**, 151, 182, 187, 226,
        294; **4**, xvi n. 14, 36, 182, 261; **5**, 115,
        125, 129–30, 140, 150, 154–8, 161–8,
        171, 174, 182–5, 202, 227, 231, 265,
        270, 278, 282, 288, 290–1, 295, 297,
        301; **6**, 182, 271; **7**, 71, 187; **9**, 77, 185,
        301; **10**, xiv, 71, 74, 130, 187, 221, 226,
        265, 283, 298–9; **11**, 187, 304; **12**, 187,
        239, 302; **13**, 57, 71, 163, 300; **14**, 265;
        15, 129, 187, 270–1; **16**, 97, 143,
        200–1, 236, 261; **17**, 117, 131, 200,
        261, 284; **19**, 43, 55, 58, 67, 187–8,

287, 300; **20**, 16, 72, 76, 300; **21**, 71,
159, 236, 261, 265; **22**, 159, 236, 265,
273; **23**, 71, 187, 265, 298; **24**, 121,
125, 288; **26**, 102, 270, 271; **27**, 10, 58,
187–8; **29**, 179, 187, 277; **30**, 220, 223;
32, 125, 157, 163, 202, 236, 271; **33**,
116–7, 179, 182, 187, 197, 218, 223,
228–9, 265, 287–8, 291; **34**, 236
Monarchia, xiii, 10, 23–9, 32, 38, 47–53, 55,
57, 59, 61–2, 70, 72, 76, 98–9, 101, 108,
112, 148, 181, 209, 262, 284–7, 300–1
Paradiso (generally), 58, 90
Paradiso (canto numbers in bold), **1**, 12; **2**,
9, 176, 260; **3**, 179, 232; **5**, 182; **6**, 20,
225; **8**, 90, 97, 183, 187; **9**, 55, 59, 64,
107, 179, 187–8, 191; **10**, 179; **11**, 90,
179, 187, 223; **12**, 269; **13**, 187, 190;
15, 182, 226; **16**, 130, 179, 219–21,
232; **17**, 130, 137, 187, 191; **18**, 59,
187; **19**, 21, 72, 187, 225, 303; **20**, 21,
187, 227; **21**, 44, 71, 90, 187, 189; **22**,
187, 189; **24**, 58, 122, 187, 227, 287;
25, 187; **26**, 71; **27**, 10, 11, 43, 187; **28**,
102, 191, 227, 269; **29**, 44, 50, 58–64,
66–7, 72, 187, 285, 299; **30**, 10, 227;
33, 8, 31, 131, 234–5, 296
Purgatorio (generally), 79, 90
Purgatorio (canto numbers in bold), **1**, 187,
285; **2**, 131; **3**, 77, 265, 301; **4**, 90, 294;
5, 183, 218, 223, 265, 302; **6**, 182; **7**, 8,
76; **8**, 72, 130; **10**, 187; **11**, 179, 187,
304; **19**, 182, 188; **20**, 72, 187, 231; **21**,
78, 187, 303; **24**, 71, 187, 232; **25**, 77,
107, 301; **26**, 271, 294; **27**, 174; **28**,
290; **31**, 227; **32**, 55, 59, 187–8
Rime, 96, 110, 116, 142, 260, 266, 289
Vita nuova, 88, 120, 150, 159, 177, 180–1,
232, 263, 265–7, 274–5, 286, 293–5
sculpture, 179, 209, 217, 269, 291–2, 298
textual scholarship on, 152, 203, 207, 212
translations of and from the *Commedia*:
  Afrikaans, xv n. 9
  English, 8, 58, 64–7, 69, 72, 76–9,
  115–16, 121–5, 135, 137–8, 146, 150,
  160 n. 37, 162, 168, 179, 182–5, 260,
  262–3, 267, 269–72, 279, 283, 286–8,
  290–2, 295–7, 300–1, 303
  French, 286
  German, 288–9
  Latin, 4, 6–7, 15–17, 20, 22, 24, 31–2, 34,
  49, 58–9, 62, 263, 284–6
  Spanish, 35, 285
  Welsh, 293
translations of and from: the *Convivio* 76, 78,
  263 267, 270, 293, 300
  the *De vulgari eloquentia*, 285
  the *Monarchia*, 51, 72, 101, 270, 285,
  287, 302
  the *Vita nuova*, 159, 232 263, 267, 270, 291

video-games, allusions to the *Commedia* in,
  281, 297
Dante da Maiano, 116 n. 296
Dante Societies, 208 n. 67, 221, 239 n. 205,
  268, 292, 293
Danvers, Henry, 98
Davidson, Andrew, 276, 297
Davies, John (of Kidwelly), 73–4, 76, 263, 287,
  300–1
Davis, Rebecca Harding, 275
Davy, Humphrey, 129
Dawkins, James, 114
De Mornay, Philippe, 54–5, 64, 103, 108
De Sanctis, Francesco, 77, 292
De vulgari eloquentia. See Dante: **references to
  works**: *De vulgari eloquentia*
De Worde, Wynkyn, 35
Decamp, Adelaide, 159
degli Uberti, Farinata. *See* Dante: **references to
  works**: *Inferno* 10
Delacroix, Eugène, 171
Delfino, Giovanni, Cardinal, 95
della Rena, Andrea (Ammonio), 38
Dempster, Thomas, 85–6, 112
di Capua, Lionardo, 78 n. 66, 303
di Maria Francisci Nini, Antonio, 106 n. 225
di Tuccio Manetti, Marbettino, 106
Dibdin, Thomas Frognall, 120
Dickens, Charles, 265
Digby, George, second earl of Bristol 99,
  101, 287
Digby, Kenelm, Sir, 67, 93, 99–103, 105,
  286–7
Dilettanti, Society of, 114–5, 117, 119, 136,
  122, 243, 264
Dolce, Lodovico, 42 n. 61, 90, 286
Döllinger, Johann Joseph Ignaz von, 179
Dominicans. *See* Religious orders
Donne, John, 78–9, 94, 100
Doré, Gustave, xiv, 162, 164, 200, 236, 264,
  272–3, 283, 292, 298
Drummond, William (of Hawthornden), 68, 90,
  286
Dryden, John, 75, 196, 287, 303
du Poujet, Bertrand, Cardinal, 27–9
Duck, Arthur, 304
Dufresnoy, Charles-Alphonse, 75 n. 50, 303
Dunbar, William, 36
Duncan, Robert, 296
Dunn, Douglas, 296
Dyce, William, xvi, 165–77
  and German artists in Rome, 165–6, 169
  and Gladstone, William Ewart, 165, 177, 179
  and Newman, John Henry, 165
  and Pre-Raphaelites, 165, 168
  and Ruskin, John, 165
  references to works:
    Arthurian frescos for Palace of Westminster,
    165–6

Dyce, William, (*cont.*)
    Beatrice (Lady with the Coronet of Jasmine), 177, 292
    Dante and Beatrice, 175–7 and Fig. 11, 179, 231–2, 246
    similarity to Botticelli *Paradiso* illustration, 176–7
    Design for Royal Academy's Turner Medal, 174
    Francesca da Rimini, composition, 166–71 and Figs. 7, 9, and 10, 291
    damage to, 171–4
    influences upon, 169–72
    Pegwell Bay, 166
    sources for the story of Francesca, 167–8
    visit to Hamilton Palace, 176–7, 245–6
    visits to Italy, 165–6, 177

East India Company, 195, 197–8, 206–7
Easton, Adam, xiii, 24–32, 34, 48, 51, 262, 284
Edinburgh
    National Gallery of Scotland, 167–8, 170
    National Library of Scotland, 90, 214, 292
    Royal Scottish Academy, 166, 172, 177 n. 117, 291
    Society of Antiquaries, 214, 223, 242
    University of, 80, 195
Edinburgh Review, 123, 129–37, 139–40, 142, 145, 147, 150, 262, 289; *see also* Foscolo, Ugo.
Editions. *See* Printed texts.
Edward III (of England), 40
Edward VI (of England), 63
Elder, Bruce, 295–6
Eliot, George, xiii, 154, 162–4, 265, 291–2
Eliot, Thomas Stearns, xiii, 258 n. 316, 269–72, 294
    references to works:
    Ash Wednesday, 294
    Dante (1929), 257 n. 316, 269–72
    Four Quartets, 294
    Prufrock and other Observations, 294
    The Waste Land, 270, 294
Elizabeth I (of England), 52, 55, 107
Ellis, F.S., 247–8, 257
Ellis, Steve, xvi, 13 n. 25, 150 n. 146, 161–2, *et passim*
    references to works:
    Dante Alighieri: Hell, 272, 296
Ellison, Ralph, 275
Elphinstone, Mountstuart, xv–xvi, 194–211, 213, 241
    and Adam, John, 203
    and British 'dominion' in India, 195, 198–201
    and Heber, Reginald, bishop of Calcutta, 196
    and Literary Society of Bombay, 194–5, 212
    and Mackenzie, Mary Elizabeth Frederica, Lady Hood, 201–2, 289
    and Mackintosh, James, 204
    and Strachey, Edward, 197
    diplomatic career prior to Bombay, 195
    education, 195–6
    educational policy, 211
    his MS of the *Commedia*: acquisition, 203, 205–6
    cultural status, 205, 208, 210–11
    donation, 194–5, 197, 203–5, 208, 211
    textual status, 203, 207, 210, 293
    learning Italian, 195, 197, 198, 199
    purchasing of books, 196, 203–4
    reading: attitudes to, 197
    of Ariosto, 198
    of Tasso, 197–8, 204
    of the *Inferno*, 201–3
    range of, 196
    shared reading, 201–3, 289
    references to Dante: in his journals, 198, 200–1
    in his letters, 202–3
    references to works:
    Account of the Kingdom of Caubul, 195
Emerson, Ralph Waldo, 160 n. 37, 291
Empire: British, 33, 38–9, 42, 194–5, 19–201, 208
    Holy Roman, 5–2, 57, 72
    Roman, 39–40
English College in Rome, 56–7
Erskine, William, 207 n. 66
Eton College, 33, 36, 94–5, 115–6, 180–1, 183–91, 285, 287, 291; *see also* Gladstone, William Ewart
Evans, Godfrey, 243 n. 230, 244 n. 233, n. 234, n. 238, 245 n. 243, n. 245, n. 247, 247 n. 258, 249 n. 273
Evelyn, John, 67
Exile, 43, 46, 48, 123, 128, 140, 156; *see also* Foscolo, Ugo; Italians in Britain; London: Italian exiles in

Fairfax, Edward, 77
Fane, Augusta, Countess Lonsdale, 138 n. 65
Farinata degli Uberti. *See* Dante: **references to works:** *Inferno* **10**
Febrer, Andreu, 285
Fekenham, John, abbot of Westminster, 48, 55–6
Ferdinand I, (of Naples), 255
Ferdinand I, Holy Roman Emperor, 52
Ferrara, 7, 16–7, 110–12
Ferrari, Domenico Antonio, 110 n. 259, 112
Fetherstone, Henry, 96–7
Feuerbach, Ludwig, 162
Ficino, Marsilio, 51 n. 6, 101, 285, 287, 302
Film. *See* Dante: films, allusions to the *Commedia* in; performance of the *Commedia*
Finch, Robert, 136, 139
Fincher, David, 276, 296
Fiocchi, Andrea, 20
Fitzralph, Richard, archbishop of Armagh, 14

Flacius, Matthias (Matija Vlačić), 48–55, 59– 62, 64, 66, 263, 286
references to works:
  Catalogus testium veritatis, 48–9, 51, 59, 61, 286
Flaxman, John, 115, 137, 150 n. 146, 155, 168–71 and Fig. 8, 174, 179, 264, 288–9
Fleury, Claude, Abbé, 75, 287, 303
Florence
  Anglo-Florentines, xvi, 194, 213–14, 216–20, 224, 236, 238, 241–2, 266, 291
  British visitors to and tourists in, 7, 94, 109, 111–13, 115, 119, 216, 221, 224, 288
  British writers in, 94, 122, 216–17
  Chaucer's visit to (1373), 30, 261–2
  Dante festival in (1865), 239, 265, 269, 292
  performances of the *Commedia* in, 262, 269, 282, 297–8
  production of Dante manuscripts in, 1, 106
  publication of Dante texts in, 59, 105 n. 221. 116, 146, 226, 232, 246, 263, 285–6, 289
Florentine libraries: Gabinetto Vieusseux, 216; Laurenziana, 4 n. 20, 11 n. 22, 214, 228–9, 241
  Magliabechiana, 214, 227
  Riccardiana, 155 n. 6, 226–7
  San Marco, 227
Florio, John, 68–71, 73, 79, 90, 108, 304
Foscolo, Ugo, xv, 128–53
  and Biagioli, Niccolò Giosafatte, 139–40
  and Byron, George Gordon, Lord, 150
  and Gladstone, William Ewart, 190
  and Graham, Maria, 147, 204
  and Grenville, Thomas, 146
  and Gurney, Hudson, 144
  and Hallam, Henry, 145
  and Hobhouse, John Cam, 128–9, 132–3
  and Holland House circle, 129–34, 145
  and Knight, Payne, 145
  and Longman, 133–4
  and Mazzini, Giuseppe, 132, 151–2, 291
  and Murray, John, 134, 136, 140, 145, 150
  and Panizzi, Antonio, 142–3, 151–2
  and Pickering, William, 136, 141, 148–9, 152
  and Roscoe, William, 142–3
  and Rose, William Stewart, 133, 138, 144–5
  and Santa Rosa, Santorre, Count, 143
  and Shelley, Mary, 150–1
  and Spencer, George John, second earl, 142
  and Taaffe, John, 149–50
  and Taylor, Edgar, 148–9
  and Wilbraham, Roger, 129, 135, 144–5
  and Wilmot, Barbarina, Lady Dacre, 147
  and Zotti, Romualdo, 139
  as political exile, 128–31, 133, 140, 143, 145, 150
  early allusions to Dante, 130, 150

editorial practice, 143–9
identification with Dante, 128, 130–4
lectures on Italian literature (1823), 133, 144–6, 290
project for edition of Dante and Italian classics, 131, 133–6, 139–41, 143–5, 148–9, 151, 290
'Protestantizing' Dante, 147–8
references to works:
  Dei Sepolcri, 130–2, 150
  Discorso sul testo . . . della Commedia di Dante, 141, 143–8, 150–3, 181, 290
  Edinburgh Review articles on Dante, 129, 131–3, 135–7, 139–40, 145, 147, 150, 262, 289
  Essays on Petrarch, 133, 146–7, 153, 290
  Ultime lettere di Jacopo Ortis, 129–32, 139, 146, 150, 153, 289
visits to Liverpool and Manchester, 143, 268 n. 50
Fowler, William, 89–90, 95–6
Fox, Charles James, 115
Fox, Henry Richard Vassal, Baron Holland, 131
Foxe, John, 45, 47–8, 50 n. 3, 52–7, 59–62, 66–7, 148, 286
Fra Angelico, 227
Francesca da Rimini. *See* Dante: **references to works**: *Inferno* 5
Francesco da Buti, 284
Francis, Saint, 10–11, 45, 187, 223; *see also* Dante: **references to works**: *Paradiso* 11
Franciscans. *See* Religious orders
Frederick II, Holy Roman Emperor, 51, 57
Friederich, W. P., 32 n. 135, 52 n. 11, n. 13, 56 n. 40, 120 n. 319, 148 n. 136, 224 n. 155, 232 n. 185, 239 n. 205, 284, 288–9
Friedrich, Crown Prince of Prussia, 248, 251, 252, 254, 256
Fuller, Margaret, 291
Fuseli, John Henry, 137, 155, 171, 174, 236, 289

Galileo (Galilei, Galileo), 77 n. 59, 82–6, 88–90, 93, 96 n. 155, 286
Gardner, Edmund, 270 n. 65
Gardner, Lyn, 281 n. 141
Garibaldi, Giuseppe, 231
Garrow, Joseph, 216, 232, 291
Gawain-poet, 8–9
Gelli, Giovanni Battista, 78, 116
Gentile, Giovanni, 209
Ghirlandaio, Domenico, 166
Giacomo della Marca, 45
Giambullari, Pier Francesco, 101, 104 n. 211
Gifford, George, 66
Gifford, Humfrey, 299
Gigli, Carlo, 4–6
Gigli, Giovanni, 6
Gioberti, Vincenzo, 230

Giotto di Bondone, 75 n. 50, 233, 267 n. 41,
    303–4
Giovanni della Marca, 14
Giovanni di Paolo, 285
Giovanni, Fra' (of Florence), 10
Giudici, Giovanni, 296
Giuliani, Giambattista, 177–8, 252
Giunta, Filippo, 116
Gladstone, William Ewart, xiii, xvi, 152–3,
    177–93, 251–2
  and Carlyle, Thomas, 191–2
  and Döllinger, Johann Joseph Ignaz von, 179
  and Dyce, William, 165, 177, 179, 292
  and Giuliani, Giambattista, 177–8, 252
  and Gladstone, Catherine (*née* Glynne),
    180, 186
  and Gladstone, Herbert, 181
  and Gladstone, John Neilson, 180
  and Gladstone, Mary, 180
  and Hallam, Arthur, 178–80, 190
  and Hallam, Henry, 180
  and Lacaita, Giacomo, 179, 222
  and Mazzini, Giuseppe, 152, 192
  and Munro, Alexander, 179, 291
  and Newman, John Henry, Cardinal, 190
  and Panizzi, Antonio, 179
  and Phillimore, Robert Joseph, 186
  and Rio, Apollonia, 180
  and Russell, John, 291
  and Summerhayes, Marian, 177, 292
  annotation practices, 181–6, 188–9
  correspondence regarding the Hamilton
    collection, 243, 252–4
  'Mr Gladstone's Pocket Dante' (at Eton),
    181–3, 185–91
  ownership of Foscolo's *Discorso sul testo*,
    152–3, 181, 190
  reading of the *Commedia*: relation to other
    reading, 179–81
    shared reading, 180
    stages, 152, 178–81, 186, 190–1, 290–1
  reading of other works by Dante, 181
  references to works:
    'Did Dante study at Oxford' (article), 179
    'Lord John Russell's Translation of the
      Francesca da Rimini' (review), 178–9,
      183, 192
    Manuscript essay on Dante (BL Add.
      44731), 179, 191
  translation of *Commedia*: practice of, 179,
    182–3, 291
    views on, 178, 182, 184
  'tutorship' under Dante, 178–9, 193
  views on Italian nationalism, 152, 192
  views on Roman Catholicism, 187–8, 190–1
  visits to Italy, 179, 186, 190, 291
Globalization, xv n. 9, 260, 269, 275–7
Godard, Jean–Luc, 297
Godwin, William, 150

Golding, William, 274
Goldoni, Carlo, 119 n. 310, 136
Gollancz, Israel, 270 n. 65
Gosse, Edmund, 238
Gossler, Gustav von, 248–9, 252, 255–8
Gower, John, 8, 9 n. 8, 36, 71, 285
Gozzoli, Benozzo, 166
Graham, Maria (*née* Dundas), 147, 204, 289
Grand Tour, 109, 112–15, 117, 119, 197, 263
Grangier, Balthasar, 120 n. 319, 286, 300
Grant, Charles, Captain, 181
Gray, Thomas, 116 n. 298, 288
Gray, William, 7
Greenaway, Peter, 280, 296
Grenville, Thomas, Hon., xiv, 146–7, 258,
    262–3, 267
Greville, Charles, 161
Grey, George, Sir, xv–xvi, 211–13, 241, 247
  and Boone, Thomas and William (book
    dealers), 212, 247
  and Elphinstone, Mountstuart, 212, 241
  collections of his books and manuscripts:
    Auckland Public Library, 212
    National Library of South Africa, 211–13,
      291–2
  donations of books, motives for, 211–213
  his MSS of the *Commedia*: acquisition,
    212–13, 291–2
    cultural status, 212
    donation, 211–13, 291–2
    textual status, 212
  purchasing of books, objectives, 213
Griffiths, Eric, 125 n. 347, 142 n. 95, 183 n.
    158, 263 n. 20
Grigoletti, Michelangelo, 171
Grimstone, Edward, 299
Grotius, Hugo, 300
Guarini, Giovanni Battista, 77, 96–7, 100, 104,
    125, 139
Guarino, Francesco, 70, 73
Guazzo, Stefano, 96–7, 103 n. 206, 108
Guicciardini, Francesco, 97 n. 161, 198
Guido da Pisa, 10, 284
Guido da Polenta, 88, 167
Guido delle Colonne, 125
Guinizzelli, Guido, 125
Gurney, Hudson, 144

Hallam, Arthur, 155, 158, 161, 178–80, 190
Hallam, Henry, 145, 180
Hallum, Robert, bishop of Salisbury, 16–18
Hamilton collection, 177, 226, 243–59
  Commedia **manuscripts**
    Hamilton 201, *Commedia* manuscript with
      Botticelli illustrations, xiv, xvi, 176–7,
      205, 243–6, 249–50, 253–4, 256, 285,
      290–1
    Hamilton 207, *Commedia* manuscript, xv,
      1–7, 243–4, 263, 285

early history, 243–6
sale of the manuscripts, xvi, 243, 246–51,
    255–7, 292
views of the sale, xiv, 243, 249–57, 268
Harding, Thomas, 53
Harington, John, Sir, 76–7, 100, 286
Harley, Edward, second earl of Oxford 113, 120
'Harley', Nick, Professor, 210–11
Harley, Robert, first earl of Oxford, 120
Harris, Wilson, 275–6
Harvey, William, 67
Hatfield, Jonathan, 143
Hatton, Christopher, 107–8
Haultin, Jean-Baptiste, 104
Hawes, Stephen, 36
Hawkins, Peter S., 10 n. 14, 273 n. 81, 281
    n. 137, 296–7
Hawkwood, John, 30
Hawthorne, Nathaniel, 275–6
Hayley, William, 125
Hazlitt, William, 289
Heaney, Seamus, xiii, 269, 272, 295, 296
Heber, Reginald, bishop of Calcutta, 196
Heber, Richard, 129
Henry IV (of France), 85
Henry VI (of England), 17, 19
Henry VII (of England), 6, 39
Henry VII (of Luxemburg, Holy Roman
    Emperor), 51
Henry VIII (of England), 33–8, 42, 45–7, 286
Hewson, David, 276
Hill, Octavia, 250
Hillard, Katharine, 293
Hobart, Thomas, 109–12, 113 n. 277, 263
Hobbes, Thomas, 67
Hobhouse, John Cam, 128–9, 131–2, 134–5, 145
Hoby, Thomas, 37, 71, 79, 90, 95–6, 263, 286
Holkham Hall and Library, 105–14, 142–3,
    240, 287; *see also* Coke, Edward, Sir;
    Coke, Thomas, Baron Lovel, earl of
    Leicester; Coke, Thomas William, earl of
    Leicester (second creation)
Holland House, 115, 129, 130–1, 134, 147
Hollander, Jean, 272 n. 81
Hollander, Robert, 272 n. 81
Holyday, Barten, 73, 302
Homer, 108, 143, 146, 179, 269, 277, 280
Hope, James, 190
Hope, Thomas, 115
Horace, 141, 255 n. 298
Horman, William, 33, 36–7, 38 n. 38, 285
Horne, Robert, bishop of Winchester, 48, 52,
    55–6, 60, 286
Horner, Francis, 142 n. 91
Howard, Frederick, fifth earl of Carlisle, 116
Howell, James, 74, 287, 299
Huggins, William, 288
Humfrey of Lancaster, duke of Gloucester, 6,
    17–19, 21, 23, 34, 285

Humphrey, Laurence, 62
Hunt, Holman, 165
Hunt, Leigh, 126 n. 350
    references to works:
    The Story of Rimini, 137, 151, 168, 174
        n. 109, 265, 289
Hus, John, 47

Iacopo della Lana, 94, 104 n. 216, 116, 284, 287
Iacopo di Dante, 104 n. 216, 106, 284
Iannucci, Amilcare, 276 n. 108, 291, 296
Illustration. *See* Dante: illustrations of the
    Commedia/Vita nuova
Index, Papal. *See* Papacy
Inferno. *See* Dante: **references to works**: *Inferno*
Ingres, Jean Auguste Dominique, 155, 164,
    168–9, 290
Innocent VI, Pope. *See* Papacy: popes
Irving, David, 80 n. 78, 87
Isabella, Maurizio, 128 n. 3, 130
Isba, Anne, 180 n. 136, 181 *et passim*
Italian language, learning and teaching, 49, 62–3,
    66, 70–1, 74, 77, 93–4, 98, 100, 105, 108,
    114, 119–20, 123–6, 136, 138, 140, 143–4,
    156, 178, 195, 197–9, 267, 286, 288
Italians in Britain
    as writers and teachers, 13–16, 137–9, 288
    exiles, political, 128–53, 179, 290
    exiles, religious, 63, 112
    mercantile activity, xv, 3, 5–6, 32, 34, 126,
        243, 285
    mercantile communities, 1, 4, 6, 8–9, 34 n. 10
    printers and publishers, 126–7, 137, 139,
        142, 289

Jagemann, Christian Joseph, 288
James I (of England)/James VI (of Scotland), 82,
    84–6, 90, 94
James, Clive, xiv, 260, 283, 298
James, Henry, 161
James, M.R., 95, 104 n. 216
James, Thomas, 98, 99
Jameson, Anna, 155
Jarman, Derek, 281
Jauss, Hans Robert, xiv n. 8
Jeffrey, Francis, 136
Jerome, Saint, 47
Jesuits. *See* Religious orders
Jewel, John, bishop of Salisbury, 52–3, 55
Joachim of Fiore, 10, 47, 53, 300
John of Rupescissa, 53
John XXII, Pope. *See* Papacy: popes
Johnson, Samuel, 124, 196
Jones, Inigo, 68
Jones, T. Gwynne, 293
Jonson, Ben, 68–70, 94, 264, 286
    references to works:
    Volpone, 68–9, 94, 262, 264, 286
Joyce, James, xiii, 269–70, 275, 277, 293–4

Keats, John, 155, 217, 290
Kemble, Adelaide (Mrs Sartoris), 157, 160
Kemble, Charles, 155, 159
Kemble, Frances ('Fanny'), xvi, 140, 154–62
  and Barrett, Elizabeth, 155, 160–1
  and Biagioli, Niccolò Giosafatte, 140 n. 82,
    156, 157, 290
  and Butler, Pierce, 159–60
  and Craven, Augustus, 159
  and Hallam, Arthur, 155, 158, 161
  and Kemble, Adelaide (Mrs Sartoris), 157, 160
  and Kemble, Charles, 155, 159
  and Kemble, John Mitchell, 158
  and Kemble, John Philip, 155, 157
  and Leighton, Frederic, 160–1
  and Scheffer's *Paolo and Francesca*, 154–5, 162
  career as actor, 155, 157, 159–60
  description of Italian language, 156–7
  reading of Byron, 158, 161
  reading of Dante, 155–8, 160
  references to works:
    Francis I, 161
    Journal of Residence on a Georgia Plantation,
      155–6
    'On a Picture of Paolo and Francesca', 154,
      155, 162, 292
    Record of a Girlhood, 156–7, 159
  sharing interests in the *Commedia*, 155, 158–9
Kemble, John Mitchell, 158
Kemble, John Philip, 155, 157
Kent, William, 109
Kepler, Johannes, 83–4, 86, 90
Kinsella, John, 297
Kirkup, Seymour Stocker xvi, 236–42 and
    Fig. 24
  and American visitors to Florence, 238
  and Barlow, Henry Clark, 239–40
  and Barrett, Elizabeth, 238
  and British expatriates in Florence, 217, 238
  and Brooke, Francis Capper, Captain, 218,
    220, 236, 238–9, 241
  and Browning, Robert, 238
  and Macleod, Elizabeth, 238, 242
  and Macleod, Isabella, 217–18, 220–2, 236,
    238
  and other Dante scholars, 238–9
  and Rossetti, Gabriele, 239
  and Trollope, Frances, 238
  and Trollope, Thomas Adolphus, 238
  and Vernon, William Warren, 240
  and Warren, George, fifth Baron Vernon, 218,
    220–2, 236, 239–40
  and Yeames, William Frederick, 241–2
  as illustrator of Vernon's *Inferno*, 221,
    236–7, 240
  belief in spiritualism, 241
  Dante costume, 242
  discovery of the 'Bargello Dante' portrait, 218
    and Fig. 14, 239

  honoured at the 1865 Dante festival, 239
  ownership and sale of *Commedia* and *Convivio*
    manuscripts, 241, 292
  references to works:
    Letters in Bodley MS (Eng. misc. d. 69),
      220, 236, 238–42
Kitamura, Satoshi, 274
Knight, Payne, 129, 145
Knowles, Sheridan, 155 n. 11
Koch, Joseph Anton, 155, 169–70, 174, 179,
    289, 291
Konstanz, Council of, 9, 15, 17, 31, 32, 34

La Russa, Ignazio, 282
Labensky, Xavier de, 143
Lacaita, Giacomo/James Philip, Sir, 179, 222,
    241, 257 n. 316
Lachman, Harry, 294
Landino, Cristoforo, 33 n. 2, 41, 57–8, 59 n. 54,
    71, 95–8, 100, 103–4, 105, 108 n. 238,
    141, 226, 245–6, 285–6, 302, 304
Landor, Walter Savage, 217, 238, 242
Langdon, Jane, 276
Langham, Simon, 24
Langland, William, 53, 63 n. 72
Latini, Brunetto, 4 n. 23, 75, 125, 303; *see also*
    Dante: **references to works**: *Inferno* 15
Lazarescu, Dante, 297
Le Bossu, René, 74, 303
Legnano, Giovanni da, 30
Leighton, Frederic, 160–1, 164–5, 292
Leland, John, 17, 34–5, 47, 71, 285
Lennard, Sampson, 54 n. 27, 55 n. 33, 64, 299
Leoni, Giulio, 276–7, 296
Lesieur, Stephen, 84
Lewes, George Henry, 163
Libraries
  ecclesiastical (monastic and cathedral), 17, 19,
    24, 32, 34–5, 45, 110, 285
  national, 1–2, 7, 11, 8 n. 55, 25 n. 98, 35, 69
    n. 5, 90, 100, 113 n. 280, 146, 209, 212,
    214, 223, 227–8, 243, 247–8, 252–3,
    255–7, 292, 294
  of learned societies, 194–5, 203–4, 206–7
  papal, 29
  private, 7, 24, 32, 41, 75, 79, 88, 93–6,
    99–100, 103–4, 106–14, 116–17, 120,
    141–2, 146, 153 n. 169, 176–7,
    183–91, 196, 204, 212, 214, 238,
    240–1, 243–5, 250, 259, 286, 303
  public, 4 n. 20, 11 n. 22, 80, 98, 153 n. 169,
    181, 186–9, 190–1, 205, 212, 214,
    226–7, 228–9, 241, 250, 259
  royal, 104, 253
  university and college, 17 n. 51, 33, 41–2, 63
    n. 70, 78 n. 64, 79, 98–101, 106–7, 115,
    129, 142, 144, 183–91, 236, 241, 251,
    285–7, 289 *See also* Berlin, Cambridge,
    Florentine libraries, London, Oxford etc.

Lindon, John, 147 n. 132, 24 n. 213 *et passim*
Linnell, John, 290
Lippmann, Friedrich, 246–50, 256–7
Lipsius, Justus, 80, 82, 86, 88
Liverpool, 142–3
Livy (Titus Livius Patavinus), 38
Locke, John, 148, 303
Lombard, Peter, 14
Lombardi, Baldassare, 139–40, 181
London,
    book-trade in, 1–7, 126–7, 137, 139, 142,
        212–13, 243, 247, 285–7, 289
    British Library, 18 n. 55, 35, 69 n. 5, 100, 113
        n. 280, 146, 294
    British Museum, 28, 113, 144, 146, 251–3,
        257, 258, 290, 294
    Italian editions of the *Commedia* published in,
        137–9, 147, 202–3, 289–90
    Italian exiles in, 63, 112, 128–53, 179, 290
    Italian merchants in, xv, 1–6, 8–9, 32, 34
        n. 10, 126, 243, 285
    Italian visitors to, 1–7, 32, 126–7, 137–9, 285
    performances of the *Commedia* in, 264–5,
        281–2, 296–7
    Royal Academy, 116, 164, 174, 249, 293
Longfellow, Henry Wadsworth, 160 n. 37, 239,
    292, 297
Longman (publishers), 128–9, 132–3, 141, 145,
    204, 289
Longman, Thomas Norton, 133
Loredano, Giovan Francesco, 301
Lowther, William, 138 n. 65
Lubbock, John, 250
Lübke, Wilhelm, 256
Lucan (Marcus Annaeus Lucanus), 29
Lucca, 4–5, 119, 223, 232 n. 185, 265 n. 31
Ludwig of Bavaria, Holy Roman Emperor, 50–3,
    56, 60, 303
Luther, Martin, 38–9, 48, 148
Luzi, Mario, 296
Lydgate, John, 19, 22 n. 77, 35 n. 21,
    36–7, 285
Lyell, Charles, 232
Lynch, David, 276, 296

Macaulay, James, 211
Macdonald, Ross, 276
Macdonell, William Robert, 207–8, 293
Machiavelli, Niccolò, 38–9, 43, 76, 90, 100,
    196–8, 204
Mackenzie, Mary Elizabeth Frederica, Lady
    Hood, 196, 201–2, 289
Mackintosh, James, 131, 197, 204
Macleod, Anna Maria, 220–1, 223, 228
Macleod, Elizabeth, 214–15, 223, 238, 242
Macleod, Henry Dunning, 238
Macleod, Isabella, xvi, 214–35, 238, and
    Figs. 13–23
    and Americans in Florence, 217

    and Barrett, Elizabeth, 217, 230
    and Batty, Elizabeth Frances, 235
    and British expatriates in Florence, 216–8
    and Brooke, Francis Capper, Captain, 215,
        218–20, 222, 224, 226
    and collaboration with family, Macleod, Anna,
        220–1, 223, 228
        Macleod, Elizabeth, 214, 216, 222–3, 238
        Macleod, Robert Bruce Aeneas, 223
    and Florentine galleries, 234
    and Florentine libraries, 226–7, 229, 291
    and Florentine society, 216, 226
    and Gabinetto Vieusseux, Florence, 216
    and Kirkup, Seymour Stocker, 217–18,
        220–2, 238
    and Trollope, Thomas Adolphus, 217
    and Warren, George, fifth Baron Vernon,
        217–18, 220–2, 226
    'Dante Collection': architecture in, 214, 218,
        223–4, 235
        first reference to, 218
        heraldry in, 214, 218–23, 226
        illustrative programme, 214, 218, 220–1,
            225, 231
        landscapes in, 214, 220, 223–4, 231, 235
        portraits in, 214, 218, 232
        present location, 214, 236, 292
        women in, 232–3
    letters in Highland Council Archive, Inverness
        (HCA D 63/E/2a), 215, 217–24, 226,
        230, 233, 236–8
    views on cult of Dante and Dante tourism,
        220–1, 224–5
    views on Italian nationalism and
        Risorgimento, 216–17, 229–31
Macleod, Robert Bruce Aeneas, 214, 223
Macleod, Roderick IV of Cadboll, 216, 222, 238
MacNeice, Louis, 293, 295
Madden, Frederic, 107 n. 230, 109 n. 153, 143
Magagnati, Girolamo, 82
Maggiotti, Quirina Mocenni, 134–5, 146
Magliabechi, Antonio, 111
Malcolm, John, 195
Mallock, W.H., 278
Malory, Thomas, Sir, 165–6
Malouf, David, 275
Manchester: Dante Society, 208 n. 67, 268, 293
    John Rylands Library, 33 n. 2, 41, 42 n. 58,
        101 n. 190, 129 n. 4, 142 n. 89, 241 n.
        223, 268
    performances of the *Commedia* in, 280 n. 130
    Ugo Foscolo visits, 143 n. 98
Mandelbaum, Allen, 182 n. 155, 272
Mandelstam, Osip, xiv, 294, 296
Manning, Henry, Cardinal, 190
Manuscripts
    acquisition, xv, 1–7, 9, 17–18, 29, 31–2,
        79–80, 87–90, 95, 100, 104–5, 107,
        109, 110, 111, 112–13, 115, 143–4,

194, 203, 209, 212–13, 222, 243–4,
    247–9, 285–7, 289
dispersal, 17 n. 52, 18, 21, 35, 88, 106, 110,
    203 n. 44, 241, 248, 249–51, 254, 257–9
dissemination, xv, 4–7, 18 n. 55, 34–5, 51,
    79, 88, 95, 104, 195, 206, 243, 249, 258
donation, 17–18, 21, 24, 32, 94–5, 100
    n. 182, 104–6, 194–5, 197, 203–6,
    211–12, 241, 285, 287
monastic, 24
production of, 1, 29, 80, 89, 106, 110
Manuzio, Aldo, 285
Manzoni, Alessandro, 179
Marini, Antonio, 239 n. 209
Marino, Giambattista, 77, 96, 104
Marmi, Anton Francesco, 111
Marshall, William, 39
Marsilius of Padua, 22–25, 39, 47, 53, 54, 61, 72
Marston, John, 68
Martin, Robert, 97, 104
Martin, Thomas, 291
Marvell, Andrew, 67
Mary I (of England), 39, 52
Mason, Arthur, 124
Mathias, Thomas, 125, 126 n. 350, 138–9,
    153, 289
Mazzella, Scipio, 299
Mazzini, Giuseppe, 130, 132, 141 n. 85, 148 n.
    135, 151–3, 192, 230, 265, 291
Mead, Richard, 112–13
Medici Bank, 4
Medici, Giuliano de', 83–4
Medici, Lorenzo de', 138, 179
Melville, Herman, 222 n. 141, 275
Meredith, Sean, 281, 297
Mérian, J.B., 139 n. 68
Merrill, James, 296
Merwin, William Stanley, 296
Metastasio, Pietro, 125, 136, 138
Mézeray, François Eudes de, 302
Milan: Ambrosiana Library, 80–1, 87–93, 205,
    207, 210, 286
    Chaucer's visit to (1378), 30
Milano-Films, 279–81, 293–4, 297
Milbank, Alison, xvi, 140 n. 82, 154, 164, 174
    n. 108, 292 *et passim*
Mill, John Stuart, 211
Millais, John, 165, 221, 242
Milton, John, 50, 65–7, 72, 78–9, 89, 93–6,
    124, 156, 182, 196, 200, 263, 282,
    287, 300
    references to works:
    Commonplace Book, 78
    'Lycidas', 65–7, 287
    Paradise Lost, 66–7, 156, 181–2, 200
Minnis, Alistair, 8 n. 6, 10 n. 13, 261 n. 11
Mocenigo, Alvise, 88
Mocenigo, Leonardo, 86
Modena, Gustavo, 265

Modi, Jivanji Jamshedji, Sir, 207–8, 268
Molini, Giovanni Claudio, 205, 244, 249 n. 271
Monier, Pierre, 304
Montaigne, Michel de, 298, 304
Monteverdi, Claudio, 264
Moore, Edward, 106, 207
Moore, John, bishop of Ely, 104–6, 287
Moore, Thomas, 133, 150 n. 151
More, Thomas, Saint, 45
Möring, Marcel, 277
Morison, Richard, Sir, 33, 37–9, 42–3, 46, 76, 285
Morley, Lord. *See* Parker, Henry, Baron Morley
Morsius, Joachim, 84 n. 95
Mulroney, Dermot, 297
Mumbai. *See* Bombay
Munro, Alexander, 179, 291
Munro, Thomas, 195, 198 n. 19
Murray, John, 129 n. 6, 133–4, 136, 140,
    143–5, 149–51, 161
Mussolini, Benito, 208–10, 274

Napoleon Bonaparte. *See* Bonaparte, Napoleon
Nardini, Leonardo, 124–7, 142, 289
Nationalism: German, 194, 243, 254–7;
    Italian, 124, 130, 132, 152, 192, 209,
    229–30, 256, 266, 269
Naudé, Gabriel, 73, 75–6, 300
Naylor, Gloria, 275–6, 296
Neville, Henry, 76
Newman, Dorman, 301–2
Newman, John Henry, Cardinal, 165, 190
Nicholas III, Pope. *See* Papacy: popes
Niven, Larry, 274
Nolan, Sidney, 295
Norton, Charles Eliot, 238
Novel. *See* Dante: novels, allusions to the
    Commedia in

Ocheda, Tommaso de, 126
Oelsner, Hermann, 270, 291, 293
Okey, Thomas, 270–1
Okri, Ben, 276
Olgiati, Antonio, 87–8
Oliphant, Margaret, 266–7, 292
Oporinus, Johannes (Johann Herbst), 48,
    53, 286
Orality. *See* Dante: performance of the
    Commedia
Orcagna (Andrea di Cione Arcangelo), 166
Orsini, Fulvio, 88
Otto, Henry, 294
Overbeck, Friedrich, 165, 170
Ovid, 20, 29, 88, 94
Oxford, 7, 17–19, 62, 95, 99, 246–7, 294
    Bodleian Library, 63, 78, 98–100, 105–7,
        120, 144, 251, 285–6 289
    colleges and college libraries, 5 n. 26, 19, 118,
        207 n. 61, 285
    Italians at, 6, 9, 13

study of Italian and Dante at, 71 n. 21, 73, 99, 264, 292
Ozanam, A.F., 291

Padua: British visitors to, 7–9, 82, 86–90, 109–10, 113 n. 276, 286
  University of, 34, 37–8,
Palma, Michael, 297
Panizzi, Antonio/Anthony, Sir, 142–4, 146, 151–2, 179, 258, 290
Papacy, 22, 26–7, 29, 37–8, 50, 188–91
  antipapalism, Protestant and reformist, xv, 29, 38, 43–6, 49–50, 52–9, 72, 99, 103, 105, 108, 122, 18–9, 290, 304
  condemnation of Dante's *Monarchia*, 27–9, 50–1, 284–6
  Dante's views of, 22–9, 32, 48, 50–1, 54–7, 59 n. 57, 61–2 72, 79, 103, 122, 147–8, 187–9, 290, 302
  Foscolo and, 148
  Gladstone and, 187–8
  Papal Indexes, 52, 70, 98, 286
  Petrarch and, 27–8, 31, 62
  Popes: Adrian V, 187–8
    Benedict XII, 13–14
    Benedict XIII, 31
    Boniface VIII, 188
    Boniface IX, 24
    Celestine V, 47, 187
    Clement V, 26, 72, 304
    Clement VI, 28, 29 n. 119
    Innocent VI, 27
    John XXII, 26–7, 50–2, 60, 72, 304
    Nicholas III, 55, 187–8
    Paul IV, 52
    Pius II, 6, 106, 110
    Pius V, 52
    Pius IX, 160
    Urban VI, 24, 30, 284
Paradiso. *See* Dante: **references to works**: *Paradiso*
Parini, Giuseppe, 131–2
Parker, Henry, Baron Morley, 33, 39–3, 45, 79, 177, 183, 263, 285–6
Parkes, Frances (Fanny), 197
Parsons, Thomas William, 291
Parsons, William, 115, 288
Pasolini, Pier Paolo, 295
Paston, John, 5
Pater, Walter, 250
Paton, Joseph Noël, 172–4
Paul IV, Pope. *See* Papacy: popes
Paul, Saint, 11–12, 41, 45, 277
Payne, John Thomas, 212
Pearl, Matthew, 276, 297
Peel, Robert, 183
Pellegrini, Pietro, 82, 86
Pelli, Giuseppe, 117
Pellico, Silvio, 289

Pennant, John, 33, 41, 90, 96, 263, 285
Peranzone, Niccolo, 105
Performance. *See* Dante: performance of the *Commedia*
Persons, Robert, 56–7, 72, 93, 108, 286
Perugino, Pietro, 166, 234
Petrarch, Francesco, 8, 18 n. 54, 20–22, 30–1, 38, 40–2, 64, 67–8, 70, 90, 96–101, 107–8, 110, 116 n. 297, 123, 125, 136, 138, 140–1, 146–7, 242; *see also* Avignon: Petrarch's criticisms of; Foscolo, Ugo: **references to works**: *Essays on Petrarch*; Papacy: Petrarch and
  as one of the 'three Crowns of Florence', 21–2, 36, 71, 74, 255, 302
  as reader of Dante, 27–8
  compared with Dante, 22, 40, 47, 53–7, 62, 72, 74–5, 103, 133, 262, 285–6, 290, 304
Pettie, George, 97
Phillimore, Robert Joseph, 186
Phillips, Stephen, 164, 293
Phillips, Tom, 273, 277–80, 295–6, 298
  references to works:
    Beginning to think about Dante, 273
    A Humument: A Treated Victorian Novel, 277–8, 298
    Inferno: A Verse Translation with Images and Commentary, 273, 278, 295
    A TV Dante, 277, 280, 296
Phiston, William, 62
Piccolomini, Aeneas Sylvius. *See* Papacy: Pius II
Pickering, William, 134 n. 41, 136–7, 141, 143, 148, 149, 152, 290
Pico della Mirandola, 78, 300
Pier delle Vigne, 57; *see also* Dante: **references to works**: *Inferno* 13
Pietro di Dante, 104 n. 216, 222, 284
Pigou, G., 147
Pinelli, Gian Vincenzo, 82, 87–9, 93
Pinsky, Robert, 296
Pinturicchio (Bernardino di Betto), 166
Pius II, Pope. *See* Papacy: popes
Pius V, Pope. *See* Papacy: popes
Pius IX, Pope. *See* Papacy: popes
Plato, 68, 77, 78
Plazzi, Giuseppe, 298
Polemic: Catholic, 10, 24, 50, 55–7, 60, 64, 93, 286
  Protestant, 33, 43–8, 50–5, 59–60, 62–4, 67, 72, 79, 93, 98–9, 108, 286; *see also* Papacy: antipapalism
Ponsonby, Frederick, Viscount Duncannon, 117, 119–20
Pope, Alexander, 146
Porta, Matteo, archbishop of Palermo, 13, 29, 223
Pound, Ezra Loomis, 268–71, 279–80, 293–6
Pournelle, Jerry, 274
Powers, Hiram, 217

Pre-Raphaelite Brotherhood, 154, 165, 174, 264
Primrose, Archibald, Lord Rosebery, 181
Printed texts. *See* Dante: early printed texts of the *Commedia/Convivio/Monarchia/Vita nuova*; editions of the *Commedia*, nineteenth-century/twentieth-century
Printers, 34–5, 45, 53, 71, 116
Prynne, William, 99
Publishers, 42, 48, 116–17, 133–7, 139, 141, 149; *see also* Dante: early printed texts, editions
Puiu, Cristi, 297
Pulci, Luigi, 136, 204
Purgatorio. See Dante: references to works: *Purgatorio*
Pusey, Edward, 165
Pynson, Richard, 35

Quaritch, Bernard, 258
Quarterly Review, 123, 134, 136

Ranous, William V., 293
Raphael (Raffaello Sanzio da Urbino), 139, 166
Rapin, René, 73–5, 287, 301
Rauschenberg, Robert, 272
Reading practices, xiii–xiv, 19, 23, 55–8, 62, 66, 76, 79, 95–6, 119, 120, 157–9, 179–81, 186, 190–1, 195–6, 197–8, 201–2
Rees, Daniel, 293
Rees, Owen, 128–9, 133–4, 136
Reid, Thomas, 85
Religious orders
    Benedictines, xiii, xv, 9, 18–19, 24, 28–32, 37, 48, 187, 189, 284
    Capuchins, 203
    Carmelites, 10, 46, 203
    Dominicans, 10, 13, 27, 69, 187, 222, 284
    Franciscans, xv, 9–16, 29, 32, 58, 96, 110, 232, 284
        Observant Franciscans, 43–6, 110
    Jesuits, 54, 56–7, 62–3, 77, 93, 98, 108, 117, 120 n. 319, 147, 208, 230, 286, 288
Repton, Humphrey, 265
Reynolds, Joshua, Sir, 116–17, 176, 264, 288
Rhymer, Thomas, 287
Richardson, Jonathan, 263, 287
Richardson, Jonathan (the Elder), 121
Riches, David, 84
Ricordi, Tito, 293
Rime. See Dante: references to works: *Rime*
Rimini, 9–10, 15
Rimini, Francesca da. *See* Dante: references to works: *Inferno* 5
Rio, Apollonia, 180
Risorgimento, Italian, 132, 153, 192, 229–31, 265–6
Robinson, James C., xviii, 270 n. 63, 275 n. 96
Roddewig, Marcella, xvi, 80 n. 72, *et passim*
Rodin, Auguste, 292, 298

Rogerius de Platea (or de Heraclea), 11–14, 16, 284
Rogers, Charles, 288
Rogers, Samuel, 131, 135, 137, 147–8
Romanticism, xv, 121, 128, 136–7, 149–51, 155, 157–8, 168–71, 198, 201, 217, 231, 262–3, 265, 288–90
Rome, 7, 16, 24, 31, 57, 73, 79, 82 n. 85, 101 n. 193, 102 n. 199, 122, 209, 230, 272 n. 81, 276 n. 109, 282, 293
    as seat of Papacy, 6, 8, 24, 26, 37–9, 43, 48, 50, 52–6, 62–3, 72–3, 79, 98, 148, 188–91, 284, 302
    British and other foreign artists in, 115, 160, 165–6, 169, 171, 177 n. 117, 179, 288–90
    British residents in, 29–30, 41 n. 56, 67, 109, 111, 113 n. 276, 136, 159–61, 179, 180, 186, 223 n. 151
    Dante's idea of, 26–8
Ronto, Matteo, 284
Roscoe, William, 107 n. 230, 109 n. 253, 138–9, 142–3, 179
Rose, William Stewart, 133, 144–5
Rosenberg, Carl Adolf, 254
Rossetti, Christina, 292
Rossetti, Dante Gabriel, 165, 174 n. 109, 232, 241 n. 222, 270 n. 65, 291
Rossetti, Gabriele, 149, 180, 190, 222, 239, 267, 290
Rossetti, Maria Francesca, xiv, 266–7, 269, 292
Rossetti, William Michael, 241 n. 222, 292–3
Rossini, Gioachino, 164, 241
Rouillé, Guillaume, 104, 304
Roy, William, 43–5, 59, 285
Rubbi, Andrea, 126, 137, 264, 288
Rubens, Peter Paul, 176
Ruggiero, Renato, 210
Ruskin, John, xiv, 136, 154, 165, 194, 216, 250, 258, 268, 291–2
Russell, John, Lord, 183–5, 190
Rymer, Thomas, 73–4

Sackville, Charles, 122
Saglia, Diego, 115 n. 292, 151 n. 158, 183 n. 158, 265 n. 34
Salusbury, Thomas, 74, 77, 105, 263, 287, 301
Salutati, Coluccio, 20
Saluzzo, Amedeo di, Cardinal, 15, 16, 31
Samuel, Irene, 67 n. 96, n. 100, 79 n. 68
Sanders, Marcus, 281 n. 137, 297
Sanford, John, 71
Sanguineti, Edoardo, 296
Sannazzaro, Jacopo, 104, 303
Santa Rosa, Santorre, Count, 143
Sarpi, Paolo, 88, 99 n. 177, 103 n. 207, 104
Sartoris, Edward John, 160
Sastres, Francesco, 124
Savonarola, Girolamo, 47, 267 n. 41
Sayer, Elizabeth Price, 293
Sayers, Dorothy, 271, 293, 295

Sayle, Alexei, 278
Scattergood, Anthony, 36, 103–4, 303
Scheffer, Ary, 154–5 and Fig. 6, 162–4, 166, 290–2
Schlegel, August Wilhelm, 289
Schöne, Richard, 247–8, 252
Scott, David, 177
Scott, Walter, Sir, 138 n. 64, 151, 158, 196, 198, 265 n. 35
Scudéry, Madeleine de, 73, 264, 302
Seally, John, 123–4, 288
Seget, Thomas, 79–95, 105, 263
  'album of friends' (*album amicorum*), 80 and n. 79, 82, 86, 89
  arrest and imprisonment in Venice, 82, 86, 89
  astronomical work, 83, 90, 93
  connections with humanists and scientists, 80, 82–4, 86, 88–9
  education, 80, 82, 84–5
  knowledge of Dante's text, 93
  ownership of early manuscript of *Commedia*, 80, 87–9, 93, 286
  political connections, 84–85
  travels in: Eastern Europe, 83–84
    Germany, 82, 83–5
    Holland, 85
    Italy 82–89, 286
  work as poet, 82–3, 86
Sereni, Vittorio, 294
Serravalle, Giovanni Bertoldi da, 4, 15–18, 20–22, 24, 31–2, 34–5, 58–9, 263, 284–5
Seward, Anna, 265
Shakespeare, William, 116, 142, 159–60, 166, 196, 280
Shelley, Mary, 136, 147, 149–51, 265, 290
Shelley, Percy Bysshe, xiii, 136, 147, 149–51, 217, 262, 290
Siddons, Sarah, 155
Sidney, Philip, Sir, 71, 74, 98, 286
Simpson, James, 33 n. 6, 36 n. 23, 37 n. 30, 42 n. 62
Sinclair, John D., 271
Sion College (London), 99, 103, 287
Sismondi, Jean Charles Léonard, 151
Skelton, John, 36
Sloane, Francis, 217
Smith, Arthur, 297
Smith, James Edward, Dr, 142 n. 96
Smollett, Tobias, 198
Socino, Fausto, 122
Sollers, Phillipe, 296
Soyinka, Wole, 295
Spelman, Edward, 113
Spence, Joseph, 122, 288
Spencer, Charles, third earl of Sunderland, 120
Spencer, George John, second earl, 126, 129, 141–2 and n. 89, 146

Spencer, John, 99
Spenser, Edmund, 60, 146
Stanhope, Catherine, Lady Dalmeny, 220
Stanley, Thomas, 77–8, 105, 120, 300
Stapleton, Thomas, 56–7, 60
Statius, 20
St Clair, William, 121 n. 321, 128, 133 n. 34, n. 35, 135 n. 48, 138 n. 64, 144 n. 108
Stead, William Thomas, 186
Sterling, John, 155, 227
Sterne, Laurence, 130
Stewart, John (of Baldynneis), 90
Storer, Anthony, 115, 116, 117
Strachey, Edward, 197
Straub, Julia, 140 n. 82, 154 n. 1, n. 3, 158 n. 26, 180 n. 135, 232 n. 181
Stretch, L. M., 123
Stubbes, Henry, 300
Summerhayes, Marian, 177, 292
Sutcliffe, Matthew, 54, 63–4, 72, 99, 105, 108, 299
Swinburne, Algernon Charles, 238
Szymonowicz, Szymon, 84

Taaffe, John, 149–50, 290
Tarhan, Abdülhak Hamid, 179
Tasso, Torquato, 68, 77, 88, 90, 96–100, 103, 123, 125, 136, 138–9, 141, 197–9, 204, 303
  references to works:
    Gerusalemme liberata, 100, 199, 204
Taylor, Edgar, 148–9
Tchaikovsky, Pyotr Illyich, 292
Television. *See* Dante: performance of the *Commedia*
Tennyson, Alfred, Lord, 140 n. 82, 155, 158, 290
Terence (Publius Terentius Afer), 141
Tesauro, Emanuele, 73, 264 n. 27
Thackeray, Annie, 161 n. 42
Thatcher, Margaret, Baroness, xiv, Fig. 25, 283, 298
Theatre. *See* Dante: performance of the *Commedia*
Thomas of Eccleston, 13
Thomas, William, 70, 108
Thomason, George, 97
Thomson, James, 292
'Three Crowns of Florence'. *See* Boccaccio; Dante; Petrarch
Thynne, William, 35, 38–9, 42, 71, 285
Tiezzi, Federico, 296
Tinkler-Villani, Valeria, 125 n. 347, 137 n. 57
Tiptoft, John, earl of Worcester, 7
Toit, Delamaine du, 213
Tosches, Nick, 276, 297
Toynbee, Paget Jackson, x, 18 n. 53, 53 n. 19, 71 n. 26, 99 n. 175, 106 n. 226, 149, 184, 270
Trissino, Giovanni, 285

Trollope, Frances, 217, 238, 265
Trollope, Thomas Adolphus, 217, 238
Tuke, Brian, 39–40
Turin, 106, 109, 113 n. 276
Turner, Joseph Mallord William, 217
Tyndale, William, 43, 47

Ubertino of Casale, 47
Ugolino della Gherardesca. *See* Dante: **references to works**: *Inferno* **32** and **33**
Ungaretti, Giuseppe, 294
Unitarians, 123, 133, 148, 271
Urban VI, Pope. *See* Papacy: popes
Usher, Jonathan, 54 n. 29, n. 30, 55 n. 34, 64 n. 79, 214 n. 102

Valla, Lorenzo, 47, 98
Valletta, Giuseppe, 110–11
van Dyck, Anthony, 176
Vasari, Giorgio, 246, 247
Vellutello, Alessandro, 57, 79, 98, 100–1, 103, 105, 108, 286, 302
Venice, 49, 51 n. 7, 95, 209 n. 76, 272 n. 81
  book-trade in, 34 n. 11, 67, 79, 88–9, 96–8, 119, 285
  British visitors to, 67–8, 79, 82–3, 86, 87 n. 112, 89, 94, 109, 119, 122, 150 n. 151, 285
  Dante texts published at, 33 n. 2, 34, 38, 41 n. 55, 42 n. 61, 79, 90, 96–8, 100, 103–5, 108 n. 238, 116–18, 120, 126 n. 350, 181, 263 n. 23, 264, 285–6, 288, 302
  mercantile activity at, 3–4
Venturi, P., 117, 137, 139, 288
Vergerio, Pier Paolo, 52, 112
Vernani, Guido, 10, 27, 284
Vernon, Augustus Henry Warren, sixth Baron Vernon, 240
Vernon, George John Warren, fifth Baron Vernon, xvi, 217–18, 220–2, 226, 227 n. 165, 236, 239, 292
Vernon, William Warren, 240, 257
Victoria ('Vicky'), Crown Princess of Prussia, 243, 251–4
Victoria, Queen (of England), 243, 251
Vieusseux, Giovan Pietro, 216; *see also* Florentine libraries
Villani, Giovanni, 75, 303
Villegas, Pedro Fernández de, 35
Villena, Enrique de, 35, 285
Villiers, Anna, 124
Villiers, Carlotta, 124
Viràf, Ardài, 207
Virgil, 15, 20–1, 29, 40, 42, 73–4, 101, 108, 141, 143, 182, 187, 198, 201 n. 34, 235, 278, 303
  references to works:
    Aeneid, 21, 198, 235, 261, 294
Virgilio, Giovanni del, 260–1, 284, 298

Visconti, Bernabò, 30
Visual arts. *See* Dante: comic books; films; illustrations; sculpture
Vita nuova. *See* Dante: **references to works**: *Vita nuova*
Vituri, Benedetto, 2–3
Vizetelly, Frank, 231
Volpi, G. A., 117, 288
Voltaire, 287, 288
Voyon, Simon de, 62

Waagen, Gustav Friedrich, 245–7, 291
Wajda, Andrzej, 295
Walker, Joseph Cooper, 264
Wallace, David, 8 n. 8, 10 n. 13, 15 n. 39, 16 n. 42, 67 n. 100, 79 n. 68, 274 n. 95, 275 n. 96, n. 99
Walcott, Derek, 269, 295–6
Wanley, Humphrey, 113
Warren, George John, fifth Baron Vernon. *See* Vernon, George John Warren
Warton, Thomas, 288
Watermeyer, E. B., 213
Webb, Timothy, 86 n. 109, 137 n. 59, 147 n. 127, 157 n. 19, 263 n. 22, 265 n. 35
Wellesley, Richard, first earl of Mornington, 197
Wells, 16–18, 21, 32, 34–5, 285
Wendelin of Speier, 116
Whethamstede, John, abbot of St Albans, 18–4, 26, 30, 32, 36, 51, 285
White, John, 54
Whitgift, John, 63
Wicksteed, Philip, 270–1, 293
Wilbraham, Roger, 129 and n. 4, 135, 144–5
William of Ockham, 53–4
William of Saint-Amour, 47, 53
Williams, Spencer, 294
Wilmot, Barbarina, Lady Dacre, 147
Windscheffel, Ruth, 178 n. 123, 179 n. 127, 180 n. 142, 182 n. 149, n. 150, 184 n. 165, 186 n. 180, n. 181
Windsor, Henry, 5
Wiseman, Nicholas Patrick, Cardinal 165
Witte, Karl, 239, 270
Wolsey, Thomas, Cardinal, 43–5
Worcester, William, 5, 6
Wordsworth, William, 138, 152
Wotton, Henry, Sir, 79, 82, 84, 94–6, 99, 105, 286–7
Wright, I. C., 168
Wyatt, Michael, 74, *et passim*
Wyatt, Thomas, 36 n. 24, 47
Wycliffe, John, 25, 47, 53–4, 57, 98

Xenophon, 113, 201
X-Men (Comics), 273–4

Yeames, William Frederick, 241–2
Yeats, William Butler, 269, 270 n. 63, 293–4, 296

Yorke, Philip, 119–20, 288
Young, Edward, 124

Zaloom, Paul, 297
Zandonai, Riccardo, 293

Zatta, Antonio, 117–20, 137, 288
Zell, Matthias, 43
Zoppio, Girolamo, 101
Zotti, Romualdo, 127, 137–9, 140, 145, 146–7, 222, 289